DATE DUE

JA 27 '92			
OC 30 '92			
DE 22 '95			
NO 3 '98			

DEMCO 38-296

COMPETENCY
IN COSMETOLOGY

SECOND EDITION

A Professional Text

Anthony B. Colletti

© Copyright 1984, 1985
1st Printing January 1984
2nd Printing March 1984
3rd Printing January 1985
4th Printing February 1985
5th Printing July 1985
6th Printing November 1985
7th Printing January 1986
8th Printing July 1986
Keystone Publications, Inc.
250 West 57th Street
New York, New York 10107-0109
800-223-0935
In NY State 212-582-2254

ISBN # 0-912126-70-1 (Hard Cover)
ISBN # 0-912126-71-X (Soft Cover)

MEET THE AUTHOR
ANTHONY B. COLLETTI

Probably, there is no person in the entire beauty industry who possesses the unique combination of talent, knowledge and ability of Anthony B. Colletti.

A leading member of the committees that developed the New York State Competency Based, Performance Oriented Curriculum, the National Examination, endorsed by the Interstate Council of State Boards of Cosmetology and the New York State Board Examinations, Mr. Colletti is known as an outstanding seminar leader and as the teacher's teacher.

Mr. Colletti is a business executive and a recognized authority consulted by the largest cosmetic companies. He has a creative talent and is able to write with simplicity and clarity. Mr. Colletti is a school director and an outstanding educator who has developed outstanding beauty training curricula for both large and small schools. He has also developed criteria for a cosmetology student admissions examination that predicts, with a high degree of accuracy, whether or not an applicant has the potential of becoming a practicing cosmetologist.

Mr. Colletti is a subject of biographical record in The Marquis *Who's Who in the World* and is clearly a man who has dedicated his life to the improvement and advancement of the beauty industry by sharing his knowledge with those who are without limited goals. He has gained worldwide recognition and acceptance for his accomplishments.

The publisher is delighted that he was able to take advantage of Mr. Colletti's knowledge and skills when publishing this book.

Books and educational materials written by Mr. Colletti include:
COMPETENCY IN COSMETOLOGY: A Professional Text
*****STUDENT'S THEORY AND PRACTICE WORKBOOK** for COMPETENCY IN COSMETOLOGY: A Professional Text
CURRICULUM FOR COSMETOLOGY
*****DICTIONARY OF COSMETOLOGY & RELATED SCIENCES**
*****COSMETOLOGY:** The Keystone Guide to Beauty Culture
TEACHER'S REFERENCE MANUAL FOR COSMETOLOGY
*****STATE BOARD REVIEW EXAMINATIONS IN COSMETOLOGY**
*****24 PRACTICE HAIRSTYLES**
THE STANDARD SCORE GUIDE FOR PRACTICAL EXAMINATIONS
*****COSMETOLOGY STUDENT ADMISSIONS EVALUATION**
*****COSMETOLOGY REVIEW BOOK**
TEACHING TIPS FOR COSMETOLOGY
A COMPLETE QUESTION & ANSWER GUIDE TO HAIRDRESSING AND COSMETOLOGY
TRICHOLOGY: The Keystone Guide to Hair Analysis
LESSON PLANS AND THE TEACHER

*Also available in Spanish

TABLE OF CONTENTS

Introduction

COMPETENCY IN COSMETOLOGY: A Professional Text was written and designed to develop students with entry level skills, knowledge and attitudes so that they can enter a successful and profitable career in the world of cosmetology. Cosmetology is one of the most exciting, rewarding and diversified fields of employment in the world today. Many forces have combined to ensure that there is continued growth within the practice of the art and science of cosmetology and that it is a most enjoyable and profitable occupation for everyone in it.

As the field of cosmetology advances with changes and improvements, we change with it. The years since I wrote **COSMETOLOGY: The Keystone Guide to Beauty Culture** have witnessed many changes in the practice of cosmetology. This text was written and designed so that it reflects the effects of these changes. It conforms to the overall current requirements of competency-based education. This textbook contains many new features: anatomy and chemistry charts, chapter objectives, student goals, the metric system and many more.

The practice of cosmetology is performance oriented, and so is the text of this book. The introduction to each chapter is written in behavioral terms. The title page of each chapter contains a brief overview of the subject matter and a behavioral objective which ensures the performance of the skills set out in the chapter.

Each chapter contains many units of learning. Each unit contains the general objectives and student goals for the assigned learning material. By conducting a task analysis, each unit was developed to meet the requirements of most State Boards of Cosmetology. Each task was evaluated for its level of importance and its frequency. One or more units may be used for a lesson depending on the complexity of the subject matter. The theory and procedures are studied together with systematic step-by-step directions that lead to specific results and accomplishments. All units of work were developed in a logical sequence for building on the skills and knowledge previously gained.

The behavioral objectives and student goals are set out at the beginning of each unit so that the students know the completeness of what they are to learn and demonstrate. Every performance objective represents observable behavior, and can be measured clearly and accurately with the aid of tests which determine whether the student has met the minimum requirements of a task.

Designed as a competency-based educational text, each chapter is a self-contained unit of study. This concept of education requires that each chapter in the book be so complete that it include every aspect of a particular subject. The unavoidable result of this, however, is the creation of a certain amount of duplication throughout the text. For example, the subject of straightening hair appears in both the chapter on Hair Straightening and the chapter on Super Curly Hair. It is also the case with the subjects of chemistry, histology and anatomy. Each of these subjects are covered in individual chapters exclusively devoted to them, but some information from each chapter is repeated in the other chapters. The subsequent effects of this are chapters which may be read as complete units of study, but also the overlapping of information between chapters of related subject matter.

The chapters may be covered in any order. This allows it to correspond to the widest range of an individual school's course and curriculum without any loss of continuity. In some chapters and/or in portions of some chapters, learning will be provided by information lessons, and the student will demonstrate understanding by writing and/or giving a brief overview of the subject.

The chapters on the basic sciences of cosmetology (anatomy, chemistry, cosmetic dermatology, histology, trichology, bacteriology and sanitizing) contain some material beyond the actual needs of our study. Everyone who intends to be a competent and accomplished cosmetologist should know as much as possible about these sciences as well as about the skin, hair and nails.

The chapter on anatomy will be found to be more comprehensive, not because cosmetologists need to know more anatomy, but because what knowledge of anatomy they need to know, they should learn thoroughly. The structures to be studied in detail are limited to those actually affected by cosmetic treatments, e.g., nerves, motor points and venous circulation.

Certain theories, methods and techniques that are not in common use today have been retained for reference purposes.

Teaching is the cosmetology school's business. Students should set aside all previous knowledge of hair, skin and nails which they may have acquired and do things the way they are taught in school. Friends and/or relatives who are cosmetologists may want to show the cosmetology student a shorter or different way of making pin curls, wrapping perms, placing rollers or cutting hair. Our advice is that the student not accept this outside advice during the early part of training. *We know that there may be easier and better methods, techniques and procedures for making pin curls or any other operation detailed in this book, but the methods, techniques and procedures in this book contain exercises that are designed to develop skills, coordination of movement, and the hand, finger and fingertip dexterity that is needed in order to attain the highest degree of competence in the practice of cosmetology. Once these skills are acquired, the students may practice any other professional method, technique or procedure.*

Always follow the manufacturer's instructions and State Board regulations.

All instructions and step-by-step procedures in this book are based on the assumption that the right hand is the preferred hand. If your left hand is the preferred hand, use your left hand when following the instructions and procedures.

This is not a book to be discarded after school days and the start of your career. This book offers answers to almost all technical questions which may arise during your practice of cosmetology. It should be one of the most important reference books in your library.

The author would like to thank Gary Chiranky, Ph.D. for his outstanding editorial work and efforts which greatly contributed to this work's high quality of perfection.

A.B.C.
January 1984

Student guide

As your teacher will explain, there is no single, accepted right way to perform all of the techniques used in the various phases of cosmetology. Different procedures can be used to accomplish the same end results, and techniques and terms often vary in different sections of the country. This book represents simplified, step-by-step methods that have been developed, refined and tested in actual practice. Your teacher will explain the desired modifications for state and school regulations.

The first part of the book deals with actual beauty operations. It is followed by the related theory. In your school, the related theory of cosmetology may be taught either before or in conjunction with the practical operations. This is a choice based on the school's curriculum, state regulations and the administrator's experience. It should help you accomplish the most during the time you spend in school. Throughout the book, the why as well as the how of the various practical operations is explained.

Your school may or may not follow the exact sequence of the chapters as they appear in this book. As explained above, there are too many variables for any one book to follow the precise order in which subjects are taught in states with varying license requirements. Therefore, the first chapters deal with the basic hairdressing procedures: shampooing, hairstyling and haircutting. The book goes on to describe procedures for cold waving, hair coloring, hair straightening, scalp treatments and other techniques. The nonhairdressing chapters on manicuring, facials, make-up and other subjects follow.

The text has been prepared with attention to the newest developments in cosmetology and the latest teaching techniques. Students will use it in its entirety in order to increase their knowledge and acquire new skills. Experienced hairdressers will use it as a tool for developing a better understanding of a specific subject or to check a point. Knowledge, understanding and determination to give real and dependable service to a customer are the cornerstones upon which success in cosmetology depends.

Cosmetologists have a unique opportunity to develop and express their own personalities. Changing hairstyles, new cosmetic products, and the development of new methods and processes create a constant demand for skilled cosmetologists. Many female cosmetologists work for a while, stop to marry, start raising a family and then return to work. Still others find it convenient to work only part-time in order to supplement family income. Cosmetology is one of the few businesses in which how much money you earn is really entirely up to you. Many successful cosmetologists have launched their own businesses with a small investment. In addition, cosmetology offers exposure to a wide variety of people with interesting and varied backgrounds. Use this book to help you make the most of the time you spend in school to better prepare yourself for success after graduation.

Careers in
hairdressing and cosmetology

Careers in hairdressing and cosmetology: The industry has a rich past and a bright future.

Overview: This chapter provides an introduction to the beauty culture industry and gives a thumbnail description of what is expected when you start your career in the wonderful world of beauty.

Behavioral objectives-student goals: After completion of this chapter, and after instruction and study, you will be able to demonstrate competency, knowledge and understanding of the beauty industry by identifying, describing and/or listing a brief description of the past and future of the art and science of beautification and the various job opportunities available to the licensed cosmetologist.

Congratulations! You are about to become involved in the wonderful and exciting world of beauty. The beauty industry, already one of the largest in the world, is growing at an astounding pace. It is a huge, dynamic, varied field full of personal challenge.

Cosmetology is the art and science of beautifying and improving the complexion, skin, hair and nails. It is the branch of applied science that deals with the external beautification of a person through the use of cosmetic products and treatments.

It is difficult to imagine any other industry that offers such interesting, highly paid and rewarding career opportunities. Today, a cosmetologist ranks with professional people in all walks of life. The profession has never enjoyed the prestige and earning power that it does today.

People are not born with the talents required for hairdressing and cosmetology. Hairdressing is an art that can be developed through proper training.

Modern systematic teaching techniques have been developed in order to keep pace with the growth and changing needs of the field. The techniques and principles outlined in this book have made it possible for individuals with widely different backgrounds to become successful in the beauty field. There is no reason why anyone with a sincere desire to succeed cannot do so, often in far less time than you might imagine.

The three main factors that will determine your success are your school, your teacher, and most important, you and your attitude toward yourself, others and your chosen career.

Unit 1
The past

Unit 1
The past

General objectives-student goals:
After study, instruction and completion of this unit, you will be able to demonstrate understanding of the history of hairdressing and cosmetology by writing and/or giving a brief overview of the subject.

200 B.C.

500 A.D.

Careers in
hairdressing and cosmetology

Beautification has a history that is thousands of years old. Cosmetology, sometimes referred to as beauty culture, is a term that comes from the Greek word kosmetikos, which means skilled in adornment. Some people misuse the term. They think that the word refers only to the application of cosmetics. It does not. The term has a wide meaning. It refers to the entire field of beautification including hairdressing, esthetics (facial work) and skin, hair and scalp treatments.

Long before the Greeks, the Egyptians were well-versed in the arts of make-up and hairdressing. In order to vary the appearance of their naturally black hair, the Egyptians mixed henna with mud. Then, they wet their hair with the mud and wound small strands of hair around thin sticks. The hair was allowed to dry in the sun. The first such recorded use of henna as a hair dye was in approximately 1500 B.C. The celebrated Egyptian Queen Cleopatra was skilled not only in the art of applying make-up, but also in the science of compounding cosmetics and perfumes.

With the advent of Greek experts, the hairdressing arts flourished and came to Rome. Roman ladies had their hair both dyed and bleached in admiration and envy of the golden-haired natives of the northern countries who were brought to Rome as slaves.

Cosmetology continued to grow and eventually became identified with medicine. However, during the Middle Ages cosmetology was separated from medicine. It resumed its development as a separate profession at the beginning of the 14th century.

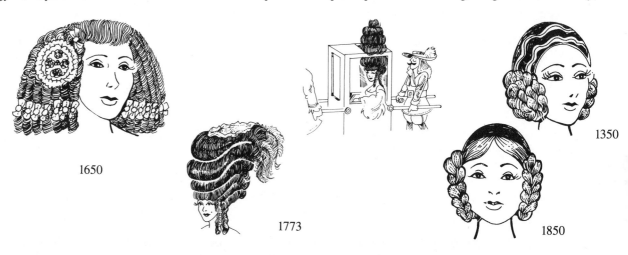

1650

1773

1350

1850

The first man to serve as a ladies' hairdresser was Champagne. He had a very successful hairdressing practice in Paris during the first half of the 17th century.

After centuries of neglect, the study of physical therapy was revived, and great advances were made. Systematic massage was introduced in England about 1800, and a Manual of Swedish Movements was developed by Peter H. Ling of Stockholm in 1813.

2

The 19th century was a remarkable period of research and innovation. In 1872, Marcel Grateau devised the famous method of waving hair that still bears his first name. Hydrogen peroxide was adopted as a bleaching agent in 1867. Synthetic organic dyes started a new era of hair coloring in 1883. The first schools for cosmetologists and cosmetology teachers started in the 1890s.

1862

1893

1916

1921

1935

In the early 1900s, developments started to accumulate one on the other: machine waving with heat (spiral method) in 1905, amino dyes in 1919, the croquignole method of heat permanent waving in 1922, machineless permanents (chemical heat) in 1927, cold waving (with chemicals) in 1934, acid balanced shampoos in 1940, acid balanced hair conditioners in 1966, acid balanced perms in 1975, and many others.

These developments were matched by better products and the need for increased skill on the part of cosmetologists. All these factors are part of the long history and tradition of cosmetology.

1950

1959

1962

1964

1977

1945

1945

1947

1948

1980

Careers in hairdressing and cosmetology

Unit 2
You and your training

Unit 2
You and your training

General objectives-student goals:
After study, instruction and completion of this unit, you will be able to demonstrate understanding of the qualities that you must exhibit in order to ensure a successful career in cosmetology by writing and/or giving a brief overview of the subject.

Your future is in your hands. If you apply yourself, the road to success is clearly ahead of you. The techniques in this book and the assistance of your teacher will enable you to progress rapidly.

What qualities must you have? They are a desire to learn, willingness to cooperate with your teacher, a positive attitude and some plain old-fashioned persistence. If you bring these qualities to your training, there is no limit to the professional future that awaits you.

You will not get a second chance to make a first impression. First impressions are lasting ones. The image that you project will definitely influence the degree of success you attain. Now is the time for you to begin developing the proper habits and attitude that will make your work pleasant and more enjoyable. In addition to these responsibilities to yourself, you also have a responsibility to the profession, your teachers, classmates and the public. The practice of hairdressing and cosmetology, like any other professional field, will reward you in direct proportion to the effort you put into it.

In addition to your personal appearance and proficiency in your work, you must learn to do little things that will make your teacher, classmates and patrons like you. They will help you reach your highest level of success. Remember, hairdressing and cosmetology is a business as well as an art and a science. A wide variety of exciting and challenging business opportunities will be available to you as an experienced cosmetologist.

Unit 3
The future

Unit 3
The future

General objectives-student goals:
After study, instruction and completion of this unit, you will be able to demonstrate understanding of the projected bright future of the beauty industry by writing and/or giving a brief overview of the subject.

The future of the beauty industry is boundless. New products, processes and techniques appear every day. Today, the research facilities of hundreds of large corporations are constantly engaged in exploring new areas. The field of biochemistry alone shows promise of offering a tremendous number of new products to the future cosmetologist. More women and men of all ages visit more unisex salons, contemporary salons and conventional beauty salons, and spend more dollars for services than ever before. There is no limit as far as your future is concerned. There is probably no other field that has such a constant growing demand for qualified professionals as does cosmetology. The number of new, individually owned beauty salons is growing at a staggering rate.

How fast and how far you go depend on the effort that you put into your training. It is equally important for you to develop a professional attitude and appearance. While you are in school, you should be conscious of improving your personal habits, grooming, poise, personality and your ability to get along pleasantly with other people.

The ethics and ethical standards of practicing hairdressers and cosmetologists contribute greatly to the successful future and advancement of the beauty industry. The field of hairdressing and cosmetology requires ethical standards from everyone in the

Careers in hairdressing and cosmetology

beauty business. Although the rules used to guide the conduct of a cosmetologist's everyday life are many, you can start developing some of your own ethics by being loyal to your school, teachers, classmates, models and patrons. Observe the school rules and state regulations. Maintain a pleasant personality, a good image and reputation by being honest and by keeping your personal life out of your work atmosphere.

The beauty industry has grown, and continues to grow, at a rapid rate. With over a quarter million beauty salons and well over a million licensed cosmetologists, it is now one of the largest service industries in our country. Expansion and replacement create a constant demand in a field that is without seasonal recessions.

Cosmetology is a challenging and rewarding profession that offers the opportunity for artistic expression as well as financial security. The training period is short and emphasizes performance of the procedures and techniques while you are learning.

Unit 4
Job opportunities

1. A beauty salon owner is usually a cosmetologist who has developed administrative skills and has maintained his or her practice in cosmetology by developing a large following of patrons. A successful salon owner also has the personal qualities that are necessary for dealing with a wide variety of problems. The salon owner takes all of the financial risk but a successful owner makes much more money than his or her employees.

2. A beauty salon manager is responsible for the overall salon operation when the owner is not present. At all other times, he or she assists the owner in managing the salon. To be an effective manager, he or she must have several years work experience as well as the personality and temperament for dealing with employees' and patrons' problems. The beauty salon manager, like most salon owners, is usually a manager-operator who works as a cosmetologist while managing the salon. The beauty salon manager usually receives the same type of compensation as an operator but with one or more of the following additions:

   1. A higher weekly commission

   2. 2.5% of the gross salon receipts paid monthly

   3. 5% of the net profits over the net profits of the previous year

After several years of practice, the manager-operator is qualified for salon ownership. A good incentive program, however, can make manager-operator a profitable lifetime career.

3. The make-up artist is an expert on cosmetics for the skin. The make-up artist is required to have product knowledge and expertise in the application of facial cosmetics. He or she must be able to give expert advice to patrons who purchase cosmetics or pay for the application of them. The make-up artist is one of the most glamorous of the job opportunities in the field of cosmetology. The specialized areas of make-up include: daytime, evening, high fashion, theatrical, television, character and balmasque (fantasy)

Unit 4
Job opportunities

General objectives-student goals: After study, instruction and completion of this unit, you will be able to demonstrate understanding of the job opportunities that are available to licensed cosmetologists by writing and/or giving a brief overview of the following 13 job opportunities:

1. Beauty salon owner
2. Beauty salon manager
3. Make-up artist
4. Specialist in any particular branch of cosmetology, i.e., hair colorist, hair and scalp specialist, permanent wave specialist, esthetician, unisex haircutter, hairstylist, trichologist

Careers in
hairdressing and cosmetology

5

5. Beauty school owner
6. Cosmetology teacher
7. School supervisor; school director
8. Beauty salon operator
9. Manufacturer's representative
10. Member of a research staff that tests new products for manufacturers of beauty products
11. Platform artist
12. Technical writer; beauty editor
13. Cosmortologist (desairologist)

4. The specialist in any particular area of cosmetology devotes or limits his or her practice to one of the following areas: hair coloring, hairstyling, unisex haircutting, skin care, permanent waving or hair and scalp care (trichology). The specialist's position can be a lucrative one but there are only a limited number of them available.

5. Beauty school owners are licensed and certified by their state's Department of Education. The school owner is required to provide training that will develop students with marketable skills in the field of cosmetology. The school owner, like the salon owner, must also have the personal qualities necessary for dealing with a wide variety of problems, as well as the personalities of employees, students and patrons. Above all, he must be a good business administrator in order to be successful.

6. The cosmetology teacher is licensed, registered and/or certified by the state to teach hairdressing and cosmetology. Teachers are required to take Teacher Training Courses, and some states require instructors to take yearly courses that provide ongoing training. The teacher is usually knowledgeable in all aspects of hairdressing and cosmetology.

The successful teacher will have the personal qualities necessary for dealing with a wide variety of problems, as well as the personalities of students and clinic patrons. At times, the teacher must be like a guidance counselor, parent or friend to the students.

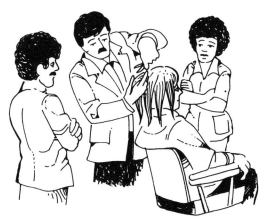

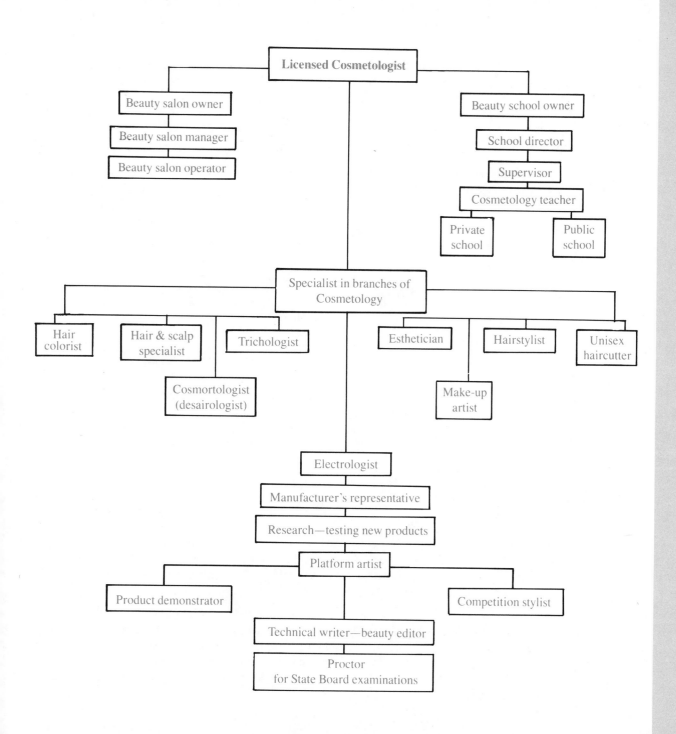

Licensed Cosmetologist

Beauty salon owner
Beauty salon manager
Beauty salon operator

Beauty school owner
School director
Supervisor
Cosmetology teacher
Private school
Public school

Specialist in branches of Cosmetology

Hair colorist
Hair & scalp specialist
Trichologist
Cosmortologist (desairologist)
Esthetician
Hairstylist
Unisex haircutter
Make-up artist

Electrologist
Manufacturer's representative
Research—testing new products
Platform artist
Product demonstrator
Competition stylist
Technical writer—beauty editor
Proctor for State Board examinations

The cosmetology teacher is above average because he or she has both a trade and teaching skills. A good teacher is a professional and a dynamic educator, a planner, questioner, demonstrator, leader, evaluator, and a fair and impartial judge.

7. The supervisor is a licensed cosmetologist who has been appointed to assist the manager or director of a school or salon. The supervisor needs many of the special skills required for a manager, director or owner. The knowledge and experience that a person gains as a supervisor can prepare him or her for the position of manager, director or owner.

8. The beauty salon operator is licensed or registered by the state after successfully completing written and practical examinations that are given by the state. The licensed beauty operator is also known as a cosmetologist, hairdresser, hairstylist and cosmetician

The successful operator will develop a large following of patrons, work with or without appointments, practice all aspects of cosmetology, including wig work, and sell extra services and/or hair care and skin care products. The successful operator who develops a large volume of loyal patrons has reached the first important stage for starting his or her own business.

9. The manufacturer's representative is a field technician who travels throughout a given area and demonstrates a manufacturer's product in beauty salons, cosmetology schools and at beauty conventions. This type of work requires the cosmetologist to be an expert on the use of the product which he or she demonstrates. The representative must be mature, poised, a good listener, observant and able to speak effectively before any size group. Some states require special licenses for demonstrators. The base wages are good, and the company pays all expenses.

10. The research technician works in a manufacturer's laboratory and then tests the new and/or improved products in actual salon practice. The products are tested in order to determine their quality, safety and marketability. The research technician works on patrons who generally pay a small fee for service. In some cases, the patrons receive their services at no charge. The research technician is not required to travel like the manufacturer's representative. The technician's traveling is limited to special problem assignments only.

Careers in hairdressing and cosmetology

11. The platform artist is a cosmetologist who is featured as an attraction. He or she usually demonstrates and explains the latest fashions, techniques and methods in all aspects of hairdressing and cosmetology.

The platform artist may conduct classes in a salon, school or at educational seminars and conventions. In order to be effective, the platform artist must have a good speaking voice, be able to explain clearly how and why things are presented as they are, keep current with the latest techniques, methods and fashions and have a sense of humor.

A platform artist is paid exceptionally well and receives travel expenses. The frequency of a platform artist's performances is, however, limited. It is not a full time job opportunity.

12. The technical writer is a cosmetologist who is able to write in a manner that can be clearly understood. The technical writer must be extremely knowledgeable of all subjects related to cosmetology. He or she must be able to explain clearly how and why things are done, keep current with the latest hairstyles, methods, techniques, fashions in hair color and maintain up-to-date product knowledge.

The technical writer has many job opportunities. He or she may be a columnist or a contributing editor for a trade publication, or a beauty editor for a newspaper. He or she can write curricula, textbooks and educational material, and can serve as a cosmetologist for one of the many publishers of educational materials for the beauty industry.

13. The cosmortologist, also known as a desairologist, is a cosmetologist who is skilled in the arts of hair care, make-up and fingernail services for the deceased. The techniques and procedures for servicing the decedent's hair, make-up and fingernails are just about the same as those practiced in the beauty salon with the exception of the decedent's position. In the beauty salon, a patron is serviced in a straight-up or tilted back sitting position. A deceased person, however, is laid out on an adjustable work table with the head placed on a head block. The cosmortologist's work includes such services as hair coloring, the application of artificial eyelashes and fingernails, wig work and hairpieces. The cosmortologist's work on a deceased person in a casket is limited to facial make-up and styling the hair without wetting it.

Review questions

1. Is the beauty industry rated as a large industry?

2. Is the field of cosmetology limited to special individuals?

3. Do you need a natural flair for hair in order to become a successful hairdresser?

4. Does the term cosmetology refer only to the application of cosmetics?

Careers in
hairdressing and cosmetology

5. Is there a limit to your future in the field of cosmetology?

6. Name two characteristics that a successful cosmetologist must develop during his or her training.

7. Are beauty services seasonal?

8. Why is there a constant demand for cosmetologists?

9. Explain why the length of the cosmetology training program is short.

10. Is it possible to start your own beauty salon with a small investment?

11. Name three personal accomplishments which a successful career in cosmetology can bring about.

12. Name some job opportunities available to the licensed cosmetologist.

13. What is required of you in order to develop self-confidence along with skill?

14. Which field shows the greatest promise of offering new products to the cosmetologist?

15. Why does the future of the beauty industry appear boundless?

Personal development

Personal development: Improving habits, developing a good attitude and increasing knowledge are a cosmetology student's areas of personal development.

Overview: This chapter discusses numerous aspects of personal development as they relate to a successful career in the world of beauty.

Behavioral objectives-student goals: After completion of this chapter, and after instruction, study and practice, you will be able to show understanding and competency in personal development by demonstrating the correct standing, sitting, and stooping postures. You will also be able to demonstrate competency by identifying, describing and/or listing six characteristics of personal hygiene, three components of personality and three character traits.

Hygiene is a branch of applied science that deals with health and healthful living. Good health is a well-balanced condition of body and mind which enables one to perform all functions normally.

Your appearance reflects your true image, and your image should complement the image of a cosmetologist. Although people should not be judged by appearances, these play a big part when making first impressions. Remember: you do not get a second chance to make a first impression.

Hygienic practices are very important in the practice of cosmetology. The rules of hygiene vary with the requirements of each individual, and each person adapts what is needed from the general rules in order to formulate a code of rules for personal hygiene. The rules cover all considerations of personal characteristics, including, but not limited to:

1. Cleanliness
2. Oral hygiene
3. Diet including weight control
4. Posture
5. Clothing
6. Relaxation

Unit 1
Cleanliness

General objectives-student goals:
After study, instruction and completion of this unit, you will be able to demonstrate understanding of cleanliness as it relates to personal development by writing and/or giving a brief overview of the subject.

Unit 2
Oral hygiene

General objectives-student goals:
After study, instruction and completion of this unit, you will be able to demonstrate understanding of oral hygiene as it relates to personal development by writing and/or giving a brief overview of the subject.

Personal development

12

Unit 1
Cleanliness

The first and simplest means of assuring cleanliness of the body are daily baths or showers. The principal objective of bathing is the removal of perspiration and its odor, oiliness and superficial dirt.

Use a daily application of an antiperspirant or deodorant that is effective for you and meets your needs. Antiperspirants control wetness and prevent perspiration stains on your clothing. Deodorants mask body odor. Clothing must be kept clean and free from perspiration odor, and undergarments should be changed daily. Underarm hair collects perspiration which causes an offensive odor.

The hands should always be washed before and after each meal, after using the toilet, smoking and handling solid objects such as trash containers.

Unit 2
Oral hygiene

Oral hygiene is the care of the mouth and teeth. Neglected oral hygiene is especially objectionable both socially and at business. Proper daily care of the mouth, nose, teeth and throat will help to guard against bad breath (halitosis).

Your teeth should be cleaned with dental floss at least once a day and brushed a minimum of twice a day with a thick paste mixture of USP, 3% hydrogen peroxide solution and baking soda. The mouth houses millions of germs and, if neglected, becomes the breeding place for countless more. These microbes cannot survive with oxygen in their environment. The baking soda shrivels the germs by depriving them of water. All contaminated objects such as hair pins, curl clips, coins and your germ-laden fingers should be kept away from the mouth.

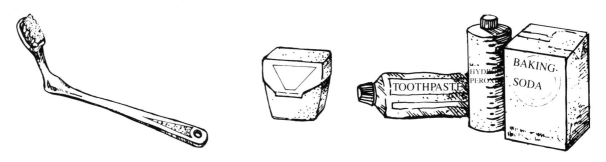

Scented mouthwashes or mints used to counter bad breath are effective for a very limited period. The cause of persistent bad breath is usually beyond the mouth and it must always be sought out and corrected if a permanent cure is to be attained.

Unit 3
Weight control

For the sake of health, appearance and efficiency, cosmetologists should keep their weight at the proper average for their height and age. Any person more than 25% overweight is considered obese. Excessive obesity is usually because of carelessness in diet. Those who are afflicted through their own self-indulgence usually know it.

Weight control requires good nutrition, and good nutrition is the balance between the kind of food and the amount of food you eat. If you are uncertain about your diet, consult a competent medical authority. To prevent obesity and to help maintain your proper weight, follow this simple plan:

1. Limit the amount of food consumed at mealtime. Avoid sugar, salt and fats.

2. Avoid cake, candy and bread.

3. Avoid eating between meals.

4. Exercise daily.

Those who are underweight should consult a competent medical authority in order to determine what their normal weight should be.

Unit 4
Posture in a standing position

Correct posture will help you feel your best and make your work less tiring. The four types of posture most commonly seen are:

Unit 3
Weight control

General objectives-student goals: After study, instruction and completion of this unit, you will be able to demonstrate understanding of weight control as it relates to personal development by writing and/or giving a brief overview of the subject.

Unit 4
Posture in a standing position

General objectives-student goals: After study, instruction and comple-

Personal development

tion of this unit, you will be able to demonstrate understanding of posture in a standing position as it relates to personal development by demonstrating the correct posture when standing.

1. Poor   3. Correct

2. Good   4. Careless

While the ideal, correct posture, is all too rarely seen, an approximation of it is satisfactory for the average person and not too difficult to acquire. Good posture — the military stand calling for chin in, chest out, elbows in, waist flat, hips back and toes out — often looks unnatural and uncomfortable. The modern stance is one of ease and naturalness. Good posture provides you with an uplifted feeling of height, muscular control, good body alignment and graceful balance.

Standing, sitting and walking all involve correct posture which can improve your personal appearance considerably. Good posture is a habit that should be developed. Standing and walking about are the cosmetologist's daily routine, and continued practice of the following exercise will develop the muscles that aid good posture.

Stand correctly with ease and naturalness by developing this basic stance:

1. Distribute your weight in order to attain body balance.

2. Hold your feet about 2 inches (5.08 cm.) apart. Point them straight ahead.

3. Keep the abdomen pulled in flat and your shoulders back and dropped in a relaxed position.

4. Let your arms hang freely at the sides, palms turned in toward the body. Your thumbs should touch the side seams with the elbows out a little.

5. Your head should be erect with the chin parallel to the floor so that the ceiling may be seen by raising the eyes.

6. Hold your head as if suspended from above. Pull the top of your head up.

7. Keep the chest high and the knees relaxed.

Note: For long periods of standing, support your weight on the forward foot with the other foot resting a little behind it. To test your posture and body alignment, stand with your back about 3 inches (7.62 cm.) from a wall. Keep your feet slightly apart and lean back. Your body alignment is good if your back, shoulders and head touch the wall. If you fail this test or find it uncomfortable, you have defective body posture. Practice the above seven point exercise until you strengthen and straighten your back.

Unit 5
Posture during a shampoo

Avoid back strain and look professional. Maintain good posture during a shampoo by keeping your feet approximately 6 inches (15.24 cm.) apart and the back straight. You should bend from the waist. Avoid curving your back and bending closely over

Unit 5

Posture during a shampoo

General objectives-student goals:
After study, instruction and comple-

Personal development

14

your patron. Keeping your arms high while massaging the scalp will help you maintain your proper posture and correct distance from the shampoo basin.

bend
slightly at waist
for
comfort...

POSTURE DURING

A SHAMPOO

Unit 6
Posture at the styling station

Comfort for both the patron and the cosmetologist at the styling station is easily controlled by raising or lowering the styling chair to a comfortable working height. This will vary with each patron, depending on the height of the patron, the height of the operator and the hairstyle. A styling chair set at an incorrect height will force the cosmetologist into a poor posture that will lead to fatigue.

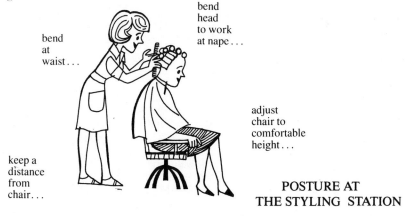

bend
at
waist...

bend
head
to work
at nape...

adjust
chair to
comfortable
height...

keep a
distance
from
chair...

POSTURE AT
THE STYLING STATION

Do not bend your knees when working at the nape area. Tilt the patron's head forward and down. Bend from your waist. Increase the distance between you and the styling chair in order to maintain your proper posture while working the nape area on a short, low seated patron.

tion of this unit, you will be able to demonstrating this posture. You must have the proper equipment in order to complete this unit successfully.

Unit 6
Posture at the styling station

General objectives-student goals: After study, instruction and completion of this unit, you will be able to demonstrate understanding of the correct posture for working at the styling station by giving a visual demonstration of this posture. You must have the proper equipment in order to complete this unit successfully.

Personal development

Unit 7
Posture in a sitting position

General objectives-student goals:
After study, instruction and completion of this unit, you will be able to demonstrate understanding of the correct posture for working in a sitting position by demonstrating the posture. You must have the proper equipment in order to complete this unit successfully.

Unit 8
Posture for a stooping position

General objectives-student goals:
After study, instruction and completion of this unit, you will be able to demonstrate understanding of the correct posture for a stooping position by demonstrating it.

Personal development

Unit 7
Posture in a sitting position

Sitting properly on the operator's stool during a facial or manicure helps prevent back strain and general fatigue. Sit squarely on the stool. Lean slightly forward from the waist while giving the service. Keep the chest up and the body weight over the thighs. Do not slouch. Place the soles of your shoes flat on the floor. Keep your feet and knees close together and place the feet out slightly farther than the knees. Never place them under your seat. Adjust the operator's stool in order to maintain proper posture throughout the entire service.

adjust operator's stool for proper posture...

POSTURE IN A
SITTING POSITION

Unit 8
Posture for a stooping position

Stooping to pick up or lift an article from the floor can be done gracefully if these basic rules are followed:

1. Place your feet 2 inches (5.08 cm.) apart. Stand directly beside the object which you want to pick up.

2. Bend at the knees. Place one foot slightly in front of the other for balance.

3. Keep the back straight and the buttocks under.

4. Pick up the article and come straight up, slowly. When lifting, lift with the muscles of your legs not with your arms and/or back.

bend at your knees...

lift with your legs—not with your back...

POSTURE IN A STOOPING POSITION

When you stoop incorrectly, you place yourself in an unbecoming and unflattering position. You can hurt yourself lifting a light object incorrectly just as much as you can lifting a heavy object.

Unit 9
Clothing

In today's modern buildings, clothing for indoor wear can be the same in weight and quantity all year round. Outdoor clothing will vary and should be selected by the thermometer not the calendar.

The female cosmetologist should wear a neat simple uniform dress. The male cosmetologist should wear a uniform coat. Both should be of a good quality which can be kept fresh and crisp by frequent laundering. Avoid the use of dangling jewelry. Wear low heeled and well-fitted shoes. Your clothes should complement your figure as well as your personality and life-style. Vertical lines create the illusion of height and make you look slimmer. Horizontal lines should be considered when you want to create a shorter and heavier illusion. Color is important too. If you wish to appear slimmer, wear black, navy blue or brown clothes.

Unit 10
Relaxation

Regardless of how interesting you find your work, the practice of hairdressing and cosmetology calls for both mental and physical exertion. Allowing sufficient time for rest and relaxation will keep you at your best.

Relaxation can be in the form of recreation such as exercise, dancing or sports. These activities, like all other recreation, keep the body fit. The body, however, calls for rest when fatigued. Fatigue can be caused by exercise, worry and mental effort as well

General objectives-student goals:
After study, instruction and completion of this unit, you will be able to demonstrate understanding of clothing as it relates to personal development by writing and/or giving a brief overview of the subject.

General objectives-student goals:
After study, instruction and comple-

Personal development

17

tion of this unit, you will be able to demonstrate understanding of relaxation and how it relates to personal development by writing and/or giving a brief overview of the subject.

Unit 11

Cosmetologist's personal hygiene check list

General objectives-student goals:
After study, instruction and completion of this unit, you will be able to demonstrate understanding of the cosmetologist's personal hygiene check list and how it relates to personal development by writing and/or giving a brief overview of the subject.

as by work. Fatigue is caused by overexertion and lack of rest. Complete rest with mental relaxation can only occur with sleep. Six to eight hours are considered an adequate amount of sleep. Sleep allows the body to recover the energy which was used for the day's activities. Oversleeping can be exhausting and is one of the worst foes of true relaxation. More than eight hours sleep can begin to cancel out sleep's benefits and make you feel very listless and cranky for part of the day. Excessive sleep (more than ten hours) puts a tremendous strain on the heart.

To put only the mind at rest requires a means of occupying yourself with something that is not part of your everyday life. Supreme relaxation involves both the mind and body.

Unit 11
Cosmetologist's personal hygiene check list

The rules of hygiene vary with the requirements of each individual, and each person adapts what is needed from the general rules in order to formulate a code of rules for personal hygiene. The rules cover all considerations of personal characteristics including but not limited to those outlined in this check list:

1. Daily bath and deodorant.

2. Oral hygiene: Brushing teeth, use of dental floss and scented mouthwash.

3. Diet and weight control.

4. Hairstyle: Keep the hair clean and attractive in a contemporary style.

5. Clothes: Uniform and shoes should be fitted properly and kept clean.

6. Facial make-up: Wear appropriate cosmetics and keep the eyebrows shaped. Males should be clean shaven or have trimmed beard.

7. Posture: Sit, walk and stand correctly.

8. The hands must be clean and the fingernails manicured.

9. Avoid dangling jewelry.

10. Be relaxed.

Unit 12
Personality and character

An individual's personality is a reflection of habits, attitudes and values. Character refers to those socially relevant behavior patterns which have particular moral and ethical implications.

Components of personality

1. Personality places emphasis on the qualities which set one individual apart from another.

2. Personality reflects one's socially relevant physical and behavioral characteristics.

3. Personality is the impression one makes on other people.

Character traits

1. Honesty   2. Sincerity   3. Good manners

A pleasing personality and a good character are as important to a cosmetologist as expert workmanship or an attractive appearance. Your personality and character will affect your success as a cosmetologist greatly. Your personality and character may be developed by adopting:

1. Good thinking: Positive thoughts keep you alert and aggressive.

2. Good manners: These reflect your thoughtfulness toward others.

3. Behavior: Temperamental is a word too often associated with cosmetologists. Control your temper.

4. Humor: Develop a sense of humor and strive to look at the bright side of things.

5. Attitude: This measures your responsiveness to people and reflects your emotional stability. Develop a pleasant and professional attitude.

6. Voice control: Your voice conveys the real you. The things you say and how you say them label you.

General objectives-student goals: After study, instruction and completion of this unit, you will be able to demonstrate understanding of the components of personality and character traits and how they relate to personal development by writing and/or giving a brief overview of the subject.

Personal development

19

1. With what does hygiene deal?

2. Does every individual require the same rules of hygiene?

3. What is the first and simplest method of assuring cleanliness of the body?

4. What is oral hygiene?

5. List five characteristics of personal hygiene.

6. When is a person considered obese?

7. Why should a cosmetologist avoid wearing dangling jewelry?

8. Why is correct posture important to the cosmetologist?

9. Why is voice control important?

10. How can you develop your personality and character?

11. How can you achieve supreme relaxation?

12. How can you put your mind at rest?

13. What is one of the worst foes of true relaxation?

14. How many hours of sleep are considered an adequate amount?

15. How many hours of sleep constitute excessive sleep?

16. Name three forms of relaxation.

Shampooing

Shampooing: A hair cleansing process designed to remove all foreign matter from the hair.

Overview: This chapter provides you with everything you need to know about shampooing hair. You will learn about the different types of shampoo and methods of shampooing, preliminary preparation, procedures and after-shampoo products.

Behavioral objectives-student goals: After completion of this chapter, and after instruction, study and practice, you will be able to demonstrate competency in shampooing by: demonstrating the techniques and procedures for draping a patron, brushing the hair, shampooing with soap, scalp manipulations, both liquid and powder dry shampoos and the brush applicator shampoo method for cleansing the hair and scalp. You will be able to demonstrate competency by identifying, describing and/or listing six different kinds of shampoo, seven implements and supplies required for shampooing and the two types of after-shampoo rinses. You must have the proper supplies and equipment in order to complete this chapter successfully.

Shampooing the hair is the most important preliminary service which the cosmetologist offers. A good shampoo is the basis of all good hairdressing and a business builder. A careless shampoo may lose a good patron. Unsatisfactory results in other work done on the hair can often be traced to a poor shampoo.

Shampooing **cleanses** the hair and scalp of **sebum** (natural scalp oil), **hair spray** and all other **foreign matter** and **residue**. You will learn to master the task of shampooing early in your training program since it is the most important preliminary service for most hair services. Your patrons get their first impression of your level of ability when you shampoo their hair. Although the shampoo procedure is the easiest to learn when compared to all the other procedures used in the practice of hairdressing and cosmetology, you should emphasize and practice your shampoo techniques until they are of the highest standard.

Hair should be shampooed as often as necessary depending on how quickly the hair and scalp accumulate dust, dirt, oils, hair cosmetics and natural skin scales. **Frequency** varies from one individual to another. Most individuals shampoo their hair once a week. Anyone with overactive sebaceous glands, however, may need to shampoo daily or several times a week.

In **hard water** areas, some shampoos will not lather and rinse out of the hair thoroughly because the water contains certain **minerals.** There are specially prepared products which may be used in conjunction with the shampoo so that perfect results can be obtained in hard water areas. Hard water can be **softened** by using chemicals or zeolite tanks. These are available in various sizes. The water passes through a mineral ion-exchange material which exchanges the calcium and magnesium ions for sodium ions.

Shampooing

Unit 1
Physical and chemical actions

General objectives-student goals:
After study, instruction and completion of this unit, you will be able to demonstrate understanding of the physical and chemical actions of shampooing by describing and/or writing a detailed explanation of both actions.

Unit 2
Shampoo chemistry

General objectives-student goals:
After study, instruction and completion of this unit, you will be able to demonstrate understanding of shampoo chemistry by describing and/or writing a brief overview of the subject.

Shampooing

Sanitary and safety precautions for shampooing

1. Wash your hands before beginning the shampoo procedure.

2. Use sanitized implements and supplies.

3. Check the water temperature before wetting the hair. Always keep the little finger of the hand, which is holding the shampoo hose, in the water spray in order to notice any sudden change in water temperature.

4. Do not permit shampoo to get in the patron's eyes or ears. Protect the patron's ears with clean cotton pledgets.

5. Shampoo with the cushion of your fingertips. Avoid scratching the patron's scalp with your fingernails.

6. Follow the manufacturer's instructions when using medicated shampoos and medicated hair rinses.

7. Clean and sanitize the shampoo bowl after each use.

Unit 1
Physical and chemical actions

The physical action of a shampoo takes place when the shampoo is applied over the entire surface of the hair and scalp. Shampoo tends to soften and loosen foreign matter (sebum, hair spray, natural skin scales) from the hair and scalp. The chemical action takes place after the foreign matter has been softened and loosened. The shampoo molecules attract the foreign matter away from the hair and scalp during the entire shampoo manipulation procedure. The particles of foreign matter are then attracted to the molecules of the rinse water and washed away. The rinse water provides both chemical and physical action because the foreign matter is attracted to the water molecules and removed from the hair and scalp.

Unit 2
Shampoo chemistry

A shampoo is not just an agent for cleansing the hair and scalp. A shampoo must leave the hair soft, manageable and lustrous. A good shampoo should not strip the hair clean since this will leave the hair dry, harsh feeling, lacking luster, in an uncontrollable fly away condition and could possibly promote scalp disorders. Stripping the hair removes sebum normally present on the scalp. Sebum inhibits the growth of pathogenic organisms.

There are three basic types of shampoos:

1. Soap shampoos   2. Soapless shampoos (detergents)   3. Dry shampoos

Soap shampoos

Soap shampoos are made by mixing an alkali (usually sodium hydroxide or potassium hydroxide) with an oil or fat. The oil or fat may be a vegetable oil like olive oil or coconut oil or an animal fat like tallow or lanolin. Soap has been made by this process for centuries. The very first patent signed by George Washington as President was for a process to make potassium hydroxide for soap.

Shampoos made with olive oil are better for the hair and skin but produce little lather and are often wasted by inexperienced operators. Olive oil shampoos are called castile shampoos, although some manufacturers now use the term castile for blended shampoos. Coconut oil shampoos lather profusely but may be harsh to the scalp and hair. Therefore, the shampoos recommended for use are: blends of olive oil and coconut oil, hydrogenated coconut oil or olive oil with an added lathering agent.

It is important to know the pH of a shampoo. The pH should be available upon request. For cosmetologists who prefer to make their own quick and easy pH test, sets of pH papers are available at many supply houses. Soaps with a higher pH may clean better but may be too harsh and drying. Soaps with a pH from 8.5 to 9.5 are generally satisfactory. Soaps whose pH is above 9.5 may be too strong.

Soap shampoos are usually purchased in concentrated form: jellies, granules or liquid. Prior to using them, add just enough hot water to dilute the shampoo. Retain the liquid solution when it cools. The shampoo solution should be diluted again with warm water when it is used. Do not boil the solution because this will hydrolyze the soap and release alkali.

Soapless shampoos (detergents)

In order to overcome some of the disadvantages of soap shampoos, particularly the lack of lather and/or the residue formed in hard water, chemists have developed products commonly called soapless shampoos. Although they do not contain soap, these shampoos are able to lather. Soapless shampoos are made by a process similar to that used for soap shampoos except that the oils are first treated with sulfuric acid. These substances are known as wetting agents. The resulting soapless detergent is known as a surfactant. The term detergent is commonly used to refer to shampoos made from sodium lauryl sulfonate or triethanolamine lauryl sulfate with the addition of foaming agents.

An anionic detergent is the main ingredient found in most synthetic detergent shampoos. This detergent ion carries a negative electrical charge. A monionic detergent is used as a neutral additive and does not carry a positive or negative charge. Its main function is to make the shampoo lather freely and leave the hair in better condition.

Amphoteric detergents are neutral because their molecules contain an equal number of positive and negative charges. Shampoos with amphoteric detergents will not irritate or sting if they accidently drip into the eyes during the shampoo procedure. This type of shampoo is excellent for shampooing children's hair.

Synthetic detergent shampoos do not form an insoluble curd when used with hard water. They lather well and rinse easily and freely. They do not dull the hair. Synthetic shampoos have a greater cleansing efficiency than soap shampoos but they leave the

Shampooing

23

hair feeling harsher, more unmanageable and with a considerable amount of static electricity (the fly away look). Because they are powerful detergents, repeated applications may cause extreme dryness, extra absorption of dyes or cold wave solutions and possible stripping of color from dyed hair.

Cream shampoos are usually emulsions containing sulfonated products. Therefore, they have the same advantages and disadvantages as soapless shampoos. Cream shampoos aid uniform distribution and are sometimes easier to apply, particularly if they contain an antiseptic ingredient or other additive that may be irritating to the eyes. These shampoos are often more expensive to use. The emulsifier used to thicken the shampoo adds cost but does not increase the cleaning power.

The term oil shampoo may refer to a treatment with hot oil followed by a shampoo or to a shampoo containing some extra oil or lanolin which is supposed to penetrate and remain on the hair after the shampoo.

Dry shampoos

If a cosmetologist or barber wishes to clean a patron's hair without using water (for example, in cases of illness), dry shampoos are available. These are not shampoos in the strict sense but rather cleansing or absorption products. For example:

1. Liquid dry shampoos are liquid solvents similar to the dry cleaning agents that are used on clothes. The solvent, such as benzine or carbon tetrachloride, dissolves the greasy hair coating which is holding tiny particles of dirt. They should not be used regularly since they extract natural oil from the hair. Some of these products are highly flammable and must be used with caution.

2. Powdered dry shampoos are mixtures of such products as orris root, talc, chalk and starch. They absorb the greasy material that holds the dirt. Thorough brushing removes the resulting substance.

Unit 3
The effects of shampoo on hair

The pH (potential of hydrogen) rating of a shampoo can be acid, alkaline or neutral. The pH liquid mantle of hair (about 4.5) is acid. Alkaline shampoos cause the cuticle imbrications (flat scale-like cells) to soften, swell and lift. This causes the hair to tangle, become more porous and dull and reduces its tensile strength and elasticity.

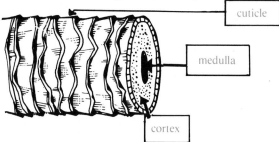

THE HAIR
FOLLICLE

cuticle

medulla

cortex

Unit 3
The effects of shampoo on hair

General objectives-student goals:
After study, instruction and completion of this unit, you will be able to demonstrate understanding of the effects of shampoo on hair by describing and/or writing a brief overview of how hair reacts to shampoos.

Shampooing

Acid balanced hair products, including shampoos, tighten the cuticle imbrications and reduce hair porosity. The tight hardened cuticle gives the hair its natural luster. Always use an acid (low pH) after-shampoo rinse or hair conditioner after any shampoo, especially after an alkaline shampoo. Natural acids like household vinegar (acetic acid) and lemon juice (citric acid) are just as effective for use as after-shampoo rinses as formulated products.

Wet hair dries by moisture evaporation. The moisture evaporates from the cortex. The use of a hot air hair dryer accelerates this process.

Unit 4
Selecting shampoos

The first consideration should be the type of water. If soft water is available in your area, your first choice of shampoo should be a plain soap shampoo. It is relatively inexpensive, cleanses most hair satisfactorily and leaves the hair in good condition. However, you must also have soapless shampoos available for situations requiring extra cleansing power (for oily hair, scalp conditions, oil or coarse residues left on the hair after a salon service). In addition, specialty shampoos are desirable for certain tinted, bleached, damaged hair or dandruff conditions.

Hard water is caused by the presence of certain salts of calcium, magnesium and other metals in the water. Such water can be softened by means of chemicals or zeolite tanks. The water passes through a mineral ion-exchange material that exchanges the calcium and magnesium ions for sodium ions.

Use the right shampoo: Know your shampoos and select the proper shampoo for each hair and scalp condition. The list and illustration below will serve to acquaint you with the various shampoos available for specific hair and scalp conditions.

Hair and/or scalp condition	Shampoo
1. Normal	Alkaline or acid balanced
2. Dandruff	Medicated
3. Oily	Soapless or detergent
4. Tinted	Nonstripping
5. Dry; abused; damaged	Conditioning
6. Bleached	Protein-conditioning

normal

tinted

Unit 4
Selecting shampoos

General objectives-student goals: After study, instruction and completion of this unit, you will be able to demonstrate understanding of the requirements for selecting shampoos by identifying six kinds of shampoos and giving and/or writing a brief overview of the subject.

dandruff

oily

dry-abused & damaged

bleached

Shampooing

25

Normal hair conditions: A shampoo for normal hair conditions is considered a plain shampoo and may be used on all hair in good condition.

1. An **alkaline shampoo** has a pH of about 7.5 to 8.5 and contains a soap or detergent base. An acid (low pH) after-shampoo rinse and/or hair conditioner should be part of the shampoo procedure. They will restore the acid balance of the hair and scalp.

2. An **acid balanced shampoo** has about the same pH as the hair (about 4.5). It does not cause the hair to swell or change the pH of the hair. An after-shampoo rinse is not required because the cuticles remain flat.

Dandruff: Antidandruff shampoos are also called **medicated shampoos.** There are two formulations. One is for oily hair and scalp conditions. The other is for dry hair and scalp conditions. Always follow the manufacturer's instructions when using an antidandruff shampoo. Products of this type usually must remain on the hair for a minimum of five minutes. A vigorous massage of the scalp is required before water rinsing the shampoo and loose dandruff from the hair.

Oily hair and/or scalp: Shampoo for oily hair and/or scalp is of a **soapless** and/or **synthetic detergent** type. A detergent molecule is composed of two functional groups: the **polar** or **hydrophilic group** and the **nonpolar** or **hydrophobic group.** The polar group is the part of the molecule which has a strong action attraction for the water molecules. The nonpolar is the part of the molecule which has a strong attraction for oil molecules.

The polar group attracts the oil away from the hair shaft and scalp while the nonpolar group aids in removing the emulsifier and hair oil during the final water rinse.

Shampoos for oily hair conditions do not eliminate the condition. They are designed to clean oily hair better than soap shampoos. The hair remains free from oil for a longer period of time.

Tinted hair: Shampoo for tinted hair is marketed as a nonstripping shampoo designed for use on hair that has had a permanent color change. A shampoo for tinted hair is usually acid (low pH) and is also mild on the hair.

All shampoos strip some color from tinted hair. The pH value and the concentration of the active ingredients in the shampoo control the degree of stripping. Shampoos that are slightly acidic (lower pH) will strip less color than alkaline shampoos (higher pH). An acid shampoo can also strip color if the ingredients include large amounts of suds-creating agents (alkaline).

Dry, abused and damaged hair: Shampoo for this type of hair is also known as a **conditioning shampoo.** It usually contains animal, vegetable or protein additives. Some additives penetrate into the cortex while others coat the outer cuticle of the hair. Both types are effective and although they only last from shampoo to shampoo, the effects of the penetrating protein additive last many days longer.

Bleached hair: Shampoo for hair which has been treated with a hair lightener or which has been sun bleached has a low pH (acid balanced) and contains animal, vegetable or protein additives as well as a hair conditioning ingredient.

Shampooing

Unit 5
Shampooing implements, supplies and materials

The following are important shampooing implements, supplies and materials:

1. **Firm bristle hair brush:** Used to stimulate the scalp, loosen and remove foreign matter from the hair and remove tangles.

2. **Comb:** Used to section and subsection hair for the brushing procedure. The comb is also used to untangle hair.

3. **Neck strip:** This implement is placed around the neck in order to keep the shampoo cape from coming in contact with the patron's skin.

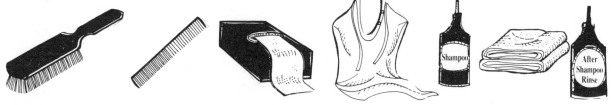

SHAMPOOING IMPLEMENTS & MATERIALS

4. **Shampoo cape:** This is placed around the neck on top of the neck strip in order to protect the skin and clothing from damage.

5. **Shampoo:** Shampoo is applied to the hair and scalp for the purpose of cleaning the hair and scalp.

6. **Towels:** Clean towels are used as a protective covering and for removing excess water and moisture from the hair.

7. **After-shampoo rinse:** This is used to tighten the cuticle layer of the hair and to restore pH balance and luster.

Unit 6
Draping

All hairdressing and cosmetology services require the protection of the patron's skin and clothing. Proper draping of the patron is extremely important. It is the first step in the sanitary procedure for all services practiced by the cosmetologist.

Check the services a patron is to receive and drape accordingly.

1. If the services to be performed are hair coloring, permanent waving or hair relaxing, place a towel underneath the shampoo cape. This will help protect the patron's clothing.

General objectives-student goals: After study, instruction and completion of this unit, you will be able to demonstrate understanding of the implements, supplies and materials needed for shampooing hair by identifying, describing and listing the seven items presented in this unit.

Unit 6
Draping

General objectives-student goals: After study, instruction, practice and completion of this unit, you will be able to demonstrate understanding of draping a patron by demon-

Shampooing

27

strating the procedure for draping a patron for shampooing and most nonchemical services as well as the proper draping procedure for all types of chemical services. You must have the proper supplies in order to complete this unit successfully.

Unit 7
Hair brushing

General objectives-student goals:
After study, instruction, practice and completion of this unit, you will be able to demonstrate knowledge of hair brushing by demonstrating the technique and procedure for brushing hair as part of a shampoo. You must have the proper implements in order to complete this unit successfully.

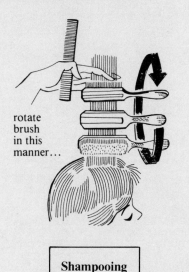

rotate brush in this manner...

Shampooing

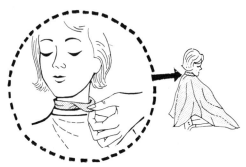

keep neck strip high enough to fold over cape

2. When draping a patron for a haircut or a shampoo and set, a neck strip alone may be used in place of a towel. The neck strip is used for sanitary as well as protective reasons. Regardless of whether a towel or a neck strip is used, the shampoo cape should never come in direct contact with the patron's neck skin.

Unit 7
Hair brushing

Healthy hair needs frequent brushing, scalp manipulations and shampooing. Brushing the hair with a good natural bristle hair brush will stimulate the scalp. It will also clean and polish the hair. Remember, the purpose of a hair brush is indicated by its name. Use it to brush the hair not the scalp. When the scalp area needs brushing, use a special scalp brush not a hair brush.

A natural bristle hair brush is recommended for hair hygiene and professional hair and scalp treatments. Natural bristle has many tiny imbrications which clean and polish hair whereas a nylon bristle is shiny, smooth and is recommended only for hairdressing and blow-dry styling.

Hair should always be brushed before a shampoo unless the scalp is irritated or the shampoo is to be followed by a permanent wave, hair color or hair relaxer treatment. Hair brushing is good exercise for the scalp and helps remove foreign matter from the hair.

Authorities agree that the best manner of brushing is always up, starting with the hair close to the scalp. This gives mild massage by gently pulling on the various muscles. It is also advisable to brush the hair forward, parting off small sections with a finger or a comb and forcing the bristles well down on the hair close to the scalp. The brush should be held firmly, and the wrist moved with each stroke so that the brush itself goes through a semicircular motion.

Subsection the hair and hold the hair brush near the scalp with the bristles facing your body. Have the bristles along the outside part of the side of the hair brush touch the hair close to the scalp first. With a circular motion, have the entire area of bristles press through the lower area of the hair strand. Then, pass the brush through the entire strand of hair.

Unit 8
Preshampoo procedure

1. Drape the patron for a shampoo.

2. Remove all hairpieces, bobbie pins, hair pins, ornaments and combs from the hair.

3. Examine the hair and scalp for any abnormal conditions.

4. Determine the type of shampoo to be used.

5. Brush the hair in order to free it from snarls and tangles. Avoid catching unwanted hair in the brush.

Unit 9
Shampoo procedure and manipulations

1. Seat the patron comfortably at the shampoo bowl. Place one hand behind the patron's head and gently lower it into the shampoo bowl. Adjust the cape over the back of the chair and place a towel between the patron's neck and the shampoo bowl.

support
head and
place
cape
over
back
of
chair

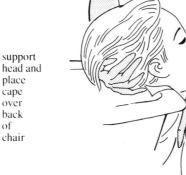

2. With one hand, hold the spray nozzle so that it faces the bottom of the bowl. With the other hand, first turn on the cold water to a medium force. Then, add hot water slowly until the temperature is comfortable. Since the temperature of the water should be fairly warm for best results in shampooing, test the temperature on the wrist of the free hand or on the under part of the forearm. Allow some water to touch the patron's head. Then, remove the spray and ask if the temperature is comfortable. If so, proceed with the shampoo. Trail one finger of the hand holding the spray in the flow of water. This will enable you to detect any sudden change in water temperature before the patron is made uncomfortable.

Unit 8
Preshampoo procedure

General objectives-student goals: After study, instruction and completion of this unit, you will be able to demonstrate understanding of the preshampoo procedure by describing and listing the five step preshampoo procedure.

Unit 9
Shampoo procedure and manipulations

General objectives-student goals: After study, instruction, practice and completion of this unit, you will be able to demonstrate understanding of the shampoo procedure and manipulations by giving a complete shampoo. You must have the proper supplies in order to complete this unit successfully.

Shampooing

keep a check
on water
temperature
with little
finger...

3. Saturate the hair and scalp with water. Cover all areas of the head. Protect the face and ears with the left hand while applying the water with the right hand. When spraying water around the ears, cup the left hand over the ear and allow the spray to run off the fingers. When applying the spray at the hairline, hold the left hand firmly against the skin just beyond the hairline so that it forms a barrier against the spray. Lift the patron's head up slightly with your left hand so that you expose the nape area to the spray but keep the patron's neck in firm contact with the neckrest of the bowl. When the hair is completely saturated, hold the spray down into the bowl. Turn off the hot water first and then turn off the cold. Do not release the spray until the flow of water has stopped completely.

protect
face
area...

4. Before applying shampoo, loosen the hair all over the head. Apply shampoo in small quantities to the various areas of the head. Work each application into a lather until the entire head is lathered. Start the application of shampoo at the front hairline and work down. Lift the patron's head with your left hand while keeping the neck in firm contact with the shampoo bowl. Apply shampoo across the nape area. Work from front to back. Use the fingertips of both your hands. Massage the shampoo into a lather over the entire head. You should apply pressure firm enough to cause the scalp to move with each stroke. This will help ensure that the scalp is clean. It will also have a relaxing effect on the patron. Avoid getting shampoo or water on penciled eyebrows or facial make-up.

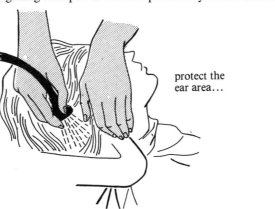

protect the
ear area...

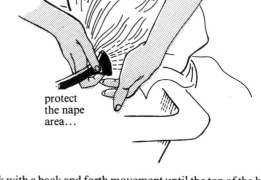

protect
the nape
area...

5. Start the manipulations at the hairline in front of the ears. Work with a back and forth movement until the top of the head is reached. Always use both hands and the tips of your fingers.

Shampooing

6. Move your fingers a little at a time toward the back of the head. Continue the back and forth movement until you cover the entire back of the head.

7. While the patron braces the neck against the shampoo bowl, lift the patron's head and use the same back and forth movement behind both ears. Start at the right ear and slowly work your way across the head to the left ear. While the patron is in this position, use a circular movement at the back hairline.

8. With the patron's head resting on the shampoo bowl, work around the front hairline.

9. Repeat all these motions several times until the scalp and hair have been massaged and cleansed thoroughly.

10. Squeeze excess foam and shampoo from the hair.

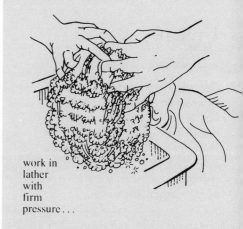

work in lather with firm pressure...

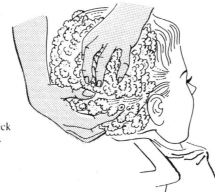

lift patron's head while patron braces neck firmly against bowl...

11. Rinse the hair thoroughly. Follow the same procedure used when wetting the hair at the start of the shampoo.

12. Loosen the hair before starting the second shampoo application. The shampoo will lather more easily and there will be more suds on the second application. Therefore, apply the shampoo sparingly. The application of too much shampoo is useless, wasteful and expensive. Repeat the same procedure used for the first soaping.

13. Rinse thoroughly. Check all the areas of the patron's head in order to be certain that all the shampoo is removed, especially in the nape area. When lifting the patron's head to rinse the nape area, the neck remains firmly against the neckrest of the shampoo bowl.

14. After the rinse, wring out the excess water from the patron's hair (see step 10). Assist the patron to a sitting position and wrap a towel turban-style around the hair to prevent drippage.

15. Use the towel to damp-dry the hair. Be certain that all excess water is removed from the patron's hair before proceeding. Begin to comb the patron's hair with the wide teeth of the comb. Start at the nape area. Comb through small sections until all the hair is free of tangles and ready to dress.

Note: Always use very light movements when a permanent wave, tint, bleach or hair relaxing will follow the shampoo.

Shampooing

31

Unit 10
After-shampoo rinses

General objectives-student goals:
After study, instruction and completion of this unit, you will be able to demonstrate understanding of after-shampoo rinses by identifying and describing the effects of after-shampoo rinses and by listing three types of after-shampoo rinses.

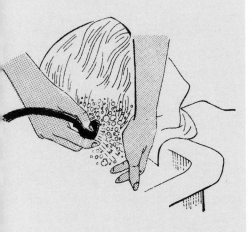

Shampooing

32

Unit 10
After-shampoo rinses

After-shampoo rinses are used after a shampoo to remove soap, soap scum and soap curds from the hair. Rinses will untangle the hair, give it a lustrous appearance and medicate scalps with a dandruff condition. There are three types of after-shampoo rinses. Each serves a specific purpose.

Types of after-shampoo rinses

1. Creme rinses   2. Acid rinses   3. Medicated rinses

A creme rinse is used to soften the hair, untangle it and add luster. Creme rinses stick to the hair. Ordinary water rinsing does not remove it. A creme rinse is only slightly acid and is not effective as a soap curd remover.

The acid after-shampoo rinse usually has a very low pH (between pH 2 and pH 3). It is designed to remove soap scum and soap curds, untangle the hair and add brilliance. It will not soften the hair like a creme rinse.

Soap scum is the filmy residue that remains on the surface of hair after a shampoo. The minerals in the water and the fatty acids of soap combine to form soap scum which leaves the hair dull and difficult to untangle and comb smooth.

Soap curds are the substances formed and separated from soap when large amounts of minerals are present in the water (hard water). It is almost impossible for water alone to remove all the soap curds from the hair. Acid rinses remove all soap curds and soap scum from the hair.

The active ingredients of prepared acid hair rinses include either acetic acid (vinegar) or citric acid (lime or lemon juice) or both these substances.

Most creme and acid rinses are diluted in water before use.

Medicated rinses contain ingredients with medicinal properties so that they control minor dandruff and scalp conditions. Medicated rinses can be applied with cotton or be poured through the hair and over the scalp. They are made effective with a one minute scalp massage. This after-shampoo rinse also leaves the hair lustrous, tangle-free and manageable. The active ingredients are one or more of the following: benzalkonium chloride, lauryl isoquinolinium bromide and polysorbate. These ingredients are usually mixed with isopropyl alcohol, water and artificial coloring.

All after-shampoo rinses should be applied to the hair at the end of the shampoo, after step 13 of the shampoo procedure. They should be combed through and rinsed off.

Unit 11
Dry shampoos

Dry shampoos are cosmetic products used for cleansing the scalp and hair without soap and water. They are available as a liquid or powder. The advantage of a dry shampoo is the fact that it can be used to clean the scalp and hair of superficial dirt and grease when it would be considered unwise to wet the head.

Liquid dry shampoo procedure

1. Drape the patron.

2. Brush the hair thoroughly and comb it lightly.

3. The application is made in 1½ inch sections (3.81 cm.) from the forehead to the crown and horizontally across the back of the head.

4. Saturate a piece of cotton with the liquid. Squeeze the cotton out lightly, and then apply the liquid along each part. Remove soil by lightly rubbing with a towel swiftly along the part. Repeat this procedure on the entire head. Next, apply liquid with a cotton pledget along the length of the hair strands.

5. Rub the hair strands with the towel to complete the cleansing action.

6. Remoisten the hair lightly with the liquid. Set, dry and comb or pin into the desired hairstyle.

Powder dry shampoo procedure

1. Drape the patron.

2. Divide the hair into four sections. Use long partings as in the illustration. Knot three of these out of the way and leave one loose.

3. Start at the top of the head and raise the hair. Shake a little powder at a time onto the hair so that it sifts through to the scalp. Add powder until the scalp of the whole section holds a thick covering.

> **Note:** When using powder from an aerosol can:
> 1. Shake can well.
> 2. Hold can 6 to 8 inches from hair.
> 3. Lift sections of hair and spray top and underside of each section.

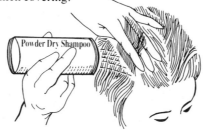

General objectives-student goals: After study, instruction, practice and completion of this unit, you will be able to show understanding of dry shampoos by demonstrating the technique and procedure for giving a liquid dry shampoo and a powder dry shampoo. You must have the proper supplies and implements in order to complete this unit successfully.

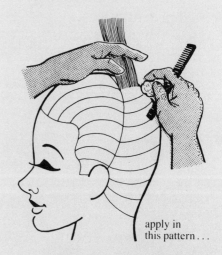

apply in this pattern...

LIQUID DRY SHAMPOO PROCEDURE

Shampooing

cover bristles completely
and change frequently...

Unit 12
Brush applicator shampoo

General objectives-student goals:
After study, instruction, practice and completion of this unit, you will be able to demonstrate understanding of the brush applicator method of shampooing by demonstrating the technique and procedure for giving a brush applicator shampoo. You must have the proper supplies and implements in order to complete this unit successfully.

SHAMPOO APPLICATOR
BRUSH

Shampooing

34

4. Loosen the other three sections of hair one at a time and repeat the procedure.

5. When the entire scalp has been covered with powder, allow it to remain undisturbed for about five minutes.

6. Prepare two brushes by forcing the bristles of each through the mesh of a piece of gauze.

7. Use one brush at a time and brush the hair thoroughly. Go systematically over the head in all directions and be sure to do both the top and the bottom of each strand. Change to the other brush as soon as the piece of gauze becomes soiled. Change the gauze on both brushes as soon as they show any trace of soil or they will no longer remove powder from the hair. This will leave the hair with a dusty appearance.

8. Repeat steps 6 and 7 if the first application has not cleansed the hair properly.

9. Arrange the hair in the desired style. Comb and pin it in place.

Unit 12
Brush applicator shampoo

Applying shampoo with a brush is a specialized method of shampooing hair. The procedure involves the unusual technique of applying shampoo to the hair and scalp using a uniquely designed shampoo brush while the patron is in a straight upright position.

The cleansing action of this procedure on the hair and scalp is superior to all other methods, and the refreshing and stimulating effect is equal to that of a scalp massage.

The brush applicator shampoo technique is also the most thorough cleansing method for shampooing a scaly scalp as well as for keeping it in good hygienic condition. This procedure will not aggravate a scaly scalp condition.

The brush application may require five minutes more than a conventional shampoo. As a specialized service, however, a higher fee is usually charged for a brush applicator method shampoo.

The preparation, scientific preshampoo brushing and draping procedure are the same as for a conventional shampoo. The only extra equipment is a shampoo cup (a 6-8 ounce [177.44–236.59 ml.] plastic cup with a handle) and a shampoo applicator brush (7 inches [17.78 cm.] long and 5/8 inch [1.59 cm.] wide). This implement has three rows of natural bristle and a pointed handle.

Technique for handling the shampoo cup

Hold the shampoo cup in your left hand with your thumb through the handle and your small finger against the bottom. The fourth finger supports the cup as illustrated and the other two fingers are left free.

technique
for
holding
cup

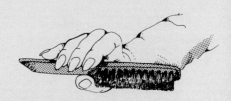

place thumb against the
handle near the bristle

Technique for holding the brush

Hold the shampoo applicator brush in your right hand with your thumb against the inside side of the handle near the bristles and the other four fingers against the outside of the handle away from the pointed end.

Technique for application

Dip the brush into the shampoo cup. Remove excess shampoo and avoid unnecessary dripping by pressing the bristles against the upper inside part of the cup as the brush is lifted from the cup.

Place the bristles firmly against the parting of subsections at a 90 degree angle. Apply shampoo by brushing the scalp thoroughly with three strokes in a back and forth motion from left to right. Go along the full length of the parting. Spread the shampoo on the hair shaft and smooth the hair strands on both sides of the part with two strokes of the brush on each side.

Seven strokes are used on each parting. From left to right, it is 1–2–3 along the parting and 1–2 along the hair shaft on each side of the part.

The shampoo application along the front hairline section requires nine backward sweeping strokes. The back hairline from ear to ear requires eight upward sweeping strokes.

use tip of brush
for subsectioning . . .

Procedure

1. Comb the hair back from the forehead with a conventional styling comb and section it into four quadrants.

2. Pour the appropriate shampoo (approximately 3 ounces [88.72 ml.]) into a shampoo cup.

3. Hold the cup in your left hand as directed.

4. Start at the top back right with a pie-shaped subsection. All other subsections will be made of parallel partings less than 1 inch (2.54 cm.) apart according to the density of the hair and the condition of the scalp.

Shampooing

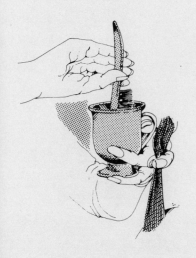

5. Hold the subsectioned hairs between the middle and index fingers of your left hand. This hand holds the shampoo cup.

6. Dip the applicator brush into the cup and begin the application of shampoo by spreading it along the parting and smoothing the hair strands on both sides of the part.

7. Continue the application with parallel horizontal subsections down to the nape.

8. Repeat the same procedure on the left back quadrant as outlined in step 7.

9. Continue the application on the left front section with parallel partings to within 1 inch (2.54 cm.) of the front hairline.

10. Repeat the same procedure on the right front section as outlined in step 9.

11. Apply shampoo along the front hairline. Start at the ear level of the right side and brush the entire front hairline section with nine backward sweeping strokes. Dip the brush into the shampoo cup as needed.

12. Complete the hairline brushing with eight sweeping strokes for the back hairline, from the left to the right ear, without applying extra shampoo.

13. Finish applying shampoo around the head using sweeping strokes away from hairline.

14. Seat the patron at the shampoo bowl. Use a gentle spray to moisten the hair and to bring up suds.

15. Complete the shampoo procedure with the conventional scientific shampoo manipulations and finishing steps.

Review questions

1. What is the most important preliminary service which a cosmetologist offers?

2. How frequently should hair be shampooed?

3. Is it difficult to shampoo hair when only hard water is available?

4. List six hair and/or scalp conditions for which special shampoos are available.

Shampooing

5. What determines the manner in which a cosmetologist drapes a patron?

6. Why must the shampoo cape never come in direct contact with the skin on the patron's neck?

7. Why is it advisable to brush the hair before shampooing?

8. Is there ever a time when the hair should not be brushed before a shampoo?

9. How can you detect changes in water temperature while shampooing?

10. What is the best water temperature to use in order to obtain the best results when shampooing?

11. How much finger pressure should be used when giving shampoo manipulations?

12. What is the best way to test water temperature before beginning the shampoo?

13. Should the hair brush be used at the scalp?

14. Does the standard shampoo procedure require more than one application?

15. Do you apply more or less shampoo for the second shampoo application?

16. Do you use the wide or narrow side of the comb to comb and disentangle the hair after a shampoo?

17. When is it not advisable to use firm movements during a shampoo?

18. What is a dry shampoo?

19. How many types of dry shampoos exist?

20. Why are after-shampoo rinses necessary?

21. How often should you change the gauze on the brushes during a powder dry shampoo?

22. In which area of the head do you begin shampoo manipulations?

23. Describe the correct method of applying shampoo to the hair.

24. In which area of the head do you start applying shampoo?

Shampooing

Shampooing

NOTES

38

Hair care, hair and scalp treatments, scalp massage

Hair care, hair and scalp treatments, scalp massage: A hair hygiene program designed to preserve the health and beauty of both the hair and scalp.

Overview: This chapter provides you with the necessary information for a complete hair care program. It includes a method of hair treatment as well as scalp treatment and scalp manipulations.

Behavioral objectives–student goals: After completion of this chapter, and after study, instruction and practice, you will be able to perform and demonstrate competency in hair and scalp treatments and scalp massage by demonstrating: a scalp treatment, a hair treatment and scalp manipulations. You will also demonstrate competency by identifying, explaining and/or listing: the anatomy related to scalp treatments, the accessories required for hair and scalp treatments and the application and effects of hair conditioners.

Care of the hair and scalp constitutes one of the most important services that the cosmetologist offers. Many men and women neglect **hair and scalp hygiene** because they are not educated about the seriousness of this need. Today, however, people are more conscious of their hair and scalp. The cosmetologist, therefore, should be prepared to recognize individual needs and provide whatever service may be necessary.

Product knowledge is an important part of hair and scalp care. One must know the correct product, the method of application and the type of service to perform in order to treat a specific condition. As a successful hairdresser and cosmetologist, you will be required to make product knowledge an important part of your practice.

Scalp treatments are recommended for the normal healthy person in order to preserve the natural health and beauty of the hair. Avoid scalp treatments immediately before:

1. A permanent wave

2. A hair coloring application

3. A hair straightening treatment

Hair care, hair and scalp
treatments, scalp massage

Sanitary and safety precautions for hair care, hair and scalp treatments, scalp massage

1. Read and follow the product manufacturer's directions.

2. Omit scalp treatments before cold waving, hair coloring and chemical straightening.

3. Do not use metal items together with a heating cap.

4. When using a heating cap, use a low setting on sensitive heads.

5. Always wrap the hair with wax paper before using a heating cap.

6. Sanitize implements before each use.

7. Check all electrical appliances for safe wiring.

Unit 1
Hair brushes and brushing

The health and beauty of the hair reflect the condition of the scalp. Hair cannot look healthy unless the scalp is also in a healthy condition.

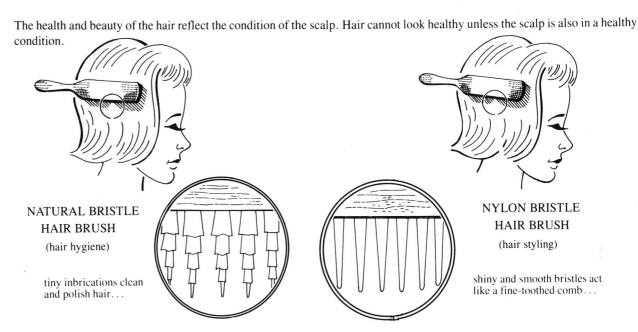

NATURAL BRISTLE HAIR BRUSH

(hair hygiene)

tiny inbrications clean and polish hair...

NYLON BRISTLE HAIR BRUSH

(hair styling)

shiny and smooth bristles act like a fine-toothed comb...

Unit 1
Hair brushes and brushing

General objectives-student goals:
After study, instruction and completion of this unit, you will be able to demonstrate understanding of hair brushes by writing and/or giving a brief overview of the subject.

> **Hair care, hair and scalp treatments, scalp massage**

40

Scalp treatments help preserve the health and beauty of both the hair and scalp. Healthy hair needs frequent brushing, scalp manipulations and shampooing. Brushing the hair with a good natural bristle hair brush will stimulate the scalp and clean and polish the hair. Remember that the purpose of a hair brush is indicated by its name: use it to brush the hair, not the scalp.

A natural bristle hair brush is recommended for hair hygiene and for professional hair and scalp treatments. Natural bristle has many tiny imbrications which clean and polish hair. A nylon bristle is shiny and smooth and recommended only for hairdressing and blow-dry styling.

Brushing the hair and scalp prior to a hair or scalp treatment is very important. It removes tangles, loose dandruff, oil and dust particles from the hair. It also provides stimulation of the nerves, muscles and glands of the scalp. It increases the circulation of the blood which, in turn, nourishes the scalp tissues.

Unit 2
Scalp manipulations

The scalp, like other exterior muscular tissues, needs exercise in order to remain healthy. However, since the muscles of the scalp are involuntary, a person cannot exercise his scalp in the same manner as he would his arms or legs. Therefore, we must exercise the scalp with scientific massage. Periodic scalp massage brings the same benefits as if the scalp were exercised.

A scientific scalp massage consists of a program of scalp manipulations. Scalp manipulations stimulate:

1. The circulation of blood to the scalp

2. The muscles

3. The scalp glands

Correct manipulations stimulate the flow of blood through the capillaries. The additional nutriment secreted by the papilla contributes to a healthier hair and scalp condition. It also relieves itching, a very common scalp complaint.

Pulling the hair at the scalp helps to stimulate the scalp and prevents shedding. The correct hair pulling technique is to grasp a small amount of hair between the thumb and forefinger about 1 inch (2.54 cm.) above the scalp, hold tightly and pull firmly. Repeat over the entire head area. The hair pulling technique to stimulate the scalp is an excellent substitute for the scalp exercise usually obtained from hair brushing and should be used daily if the hair is not brushed.

When manipulations are given in the hair area, the hands are placed under the hair. This permits the cushion side of the fingers to have direct contact with the scalp. A basic knowledge of anatomy and the locations of the muscles, nerves and blood vessels of the scalp, face and neck area are necessary in order to achieve the best results.

Unit 2
Scalp manipulations

General objectives-student goals: After study, instruction and completion of this unit, you will be able to demonstrate understanding of scalp manipulations by writing and/or giving a brief overview of the subject.

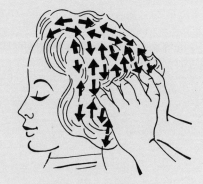

work fingers under
hair with cushions
in contact with scalp...

Hair care, hair and scalp
treatments, scalp massage

41

ANATOMY FOR SCALP TREATMENT

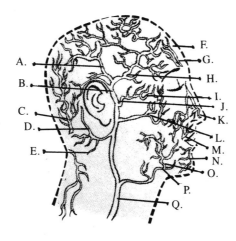

Arteries

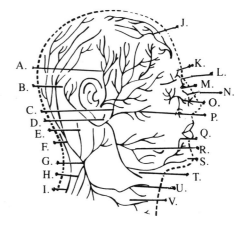

Nerves

A. parietal branch
B. anterior auricular
C. occipital
D. posterior auricular
E. sternocleidomastoid
F. supraorbital
G. frontal
H. frontal branch (anterior temporal)
I. orbital
J. superficial temporal
K. lateral nasal
L. transverse facial branch
M. septal
N. inferior labial
O. external maxillary
P. submental
Q. external carotid artery

A. auricular
B. posterior auricular
C. temporal
D. great auricular
E. lesser occipital
F. third occipital
G. great occipital
H. accessory
I. spinal
J. supraorbital
K. supratrochlear
L. lacrimal
M. infratrochlear
N. nasal
O. infraorbital
P. zygomatic
Q. buccal
R. inferior alveolar
S. mental
T. mandibular
U. cutaneous colli
V. cervical cutaneous

Hair care, hair and scalp
treatments, scalp massage

42

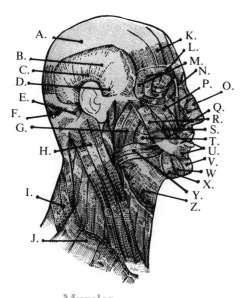

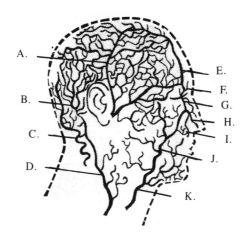

Muscles

Veins

A. galea aponeurotica
B. temporal fascia
C. auricularis superior
D. auricularis anterior
E. auricularis posterior
F. occipitalis
G. masseter
H. sternocleidomastoid
I. trapezius
J. platysma
K. frontalis
L. corrugator
M. orbicularis oculi
N. procerus
O. nasalis
P. quadratus labii superioris
Q. depressor septi
R. zygomaticus
S. caninus
T. buccinator
U. orbicularis oris
V. mentalis
W. quadratus labii inferioris
X. triangularis
Y. risorius
Z. platysma

A. superficial temporal
B. posterior auricular
C. occipital
D. external jugular
E. supraorbital
F. frontal
G. angular
H. nasal
I. supra labial
J. anterior facial
K. common facial

Hair care, hair and scalp
treatments, scalp massage

Unit 3
Basic scalp movements

Unit 3
Basic scalp movements

General objectives-student goals:
After study, instruction, practice and completion of this unit, you will be able to display understanding of two basic scalp movements by identifying stroking and compression as the two basic scalp movements for scalp massage and by demonstrating both techniques.

Scalp manipulations utilize modifications of two basic movements:

1. Stroking

2. Compression

Stroking: A smooth light gliding stroke (effleurage), without pressure, over the surface of the skin in linear or circular motion.

Compression:

1. **Friction** is pressure applied to the tissues with your fingers or hand along the nerve tracts.

2. **Kneading** is grasping the skin and flesh with your hand and fingers, lifting the tissues and squeezing them.

All manipulations should be performed very slowly and with continuous, firm and even motion and pressure. Once the manipulations begin, maintain contact with the patron by sliding your fingers into position for each movement. Do not remove your hands from the scalp between movements.

A **motor point** is the region where **motor nerves** are close enough to the skin surface so that they can be stimulated by massage. Motor nerves relay impulses to the muscles during certain movements. A **stopping point** is the place where the manipulation in a particular massage movement ends or stops before continuing with the next movement.

Unit 4
Program of movements

Unit 4
Program of movements

General objectives-student goals:
After study, instruction, practice and completion of this unit, you will be able to display understanding of the program of nine scalp massage

> Hair care, hair and scalp treatments, scalp massage

Movement 1: Used to stimulate the nerves of the neck, activate the occipital muscle and increase circulation to the scalp. Place your left hand on the forehead and the fingertips of your right hand firmly between the two lowest cervical vertebrae. Rotate three times in an upward counterclockwise motion. Without losing contact with the skin, slide to the two next higher vertebrae and repeat. Continue up the neck to the base of the skull. At the base of the skull, slide along the hairline on both sides as you apply pressure. With your left hand on the forehead and your right hand at the base of the skull, complete the movement by applying a slow but firm upward pull on the whole head. Then, let it relax gently. Slide your fingers down the neck to the starting position and repeat the entire movement three times.

MOVEMENT ONE

when
movement is
completed
slide back
to original
starting point...

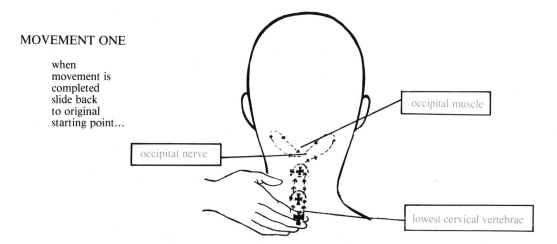

occipital muscle

occipital nerve

lowest cervical vertebrae

Movement 2: Used to stimulate all the nerves leading to the scalp. The left hand holds the head steady. The fingers of your right hand are moved over to the auricular nerve, and three upward rotations are made at the base of the neck. Continue upward from this point. Switch to a clockwise motion, behind, above and in front of the ear. Finally, slide to the motor point of the temporal nerve and press for three seconds. Repeat this movement five times. Reverse the position of your hands for the opposite side of the head.

MOVEMENT TWO

switch to
a clockwise
motion where
indicated...

anterior nerve

superior nerve

temporal nerve

posterior nerve

auricular muscles

auricular nerve

sternocleidomastoid muscle

Movement 3: Used to loosen the skin of the scalp. Hold one hand at the back of the head and press the fingers of the other hand firmly against the scalp near the front hairline. Move the scalp back and forth over the skull with slight pressure. Slide the fingers up a little with each full movement up. Repeat the movement by working the scalp up the back and up both sides of the head. Change the position of the hands as required. This movement affects the epicranius, temporalis, frontalis and occipital muscles as well as the occipital nerve.

**Hair care, hair and scalp
treatments, scalp massage**

MOVEMENT THREE

use firm pressure while loosening skin area of the scalp...

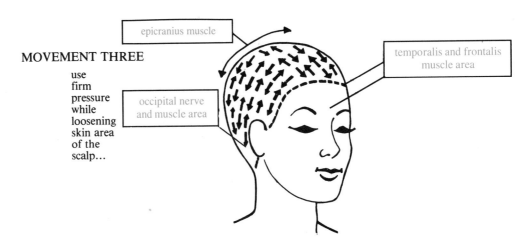

epicranius muscle

temporalis and frontalis muscle area

occipital nerve and muscle area

Movement 4: Movements 4, 5, 6 and 7 are designed to stimulate all the nerves leading to the scalp. In addition, they loosen the scalp. Hold both thumbs on the occipital nerve at the base of the skull. Hold your fingers on the temporal nerve at each side of the forehead. Press firmly and rotate three times. Continue moving all your fingers up the head, rotating and pressing, until your hands meet at the top of the head. Reverse the movement of your hands. Work downward to the mastoid bone using pressure and rotations.

MOVEMENT FOUR

movements 4, 5, 6 and 7 are designed to stimulate scalp nerves...

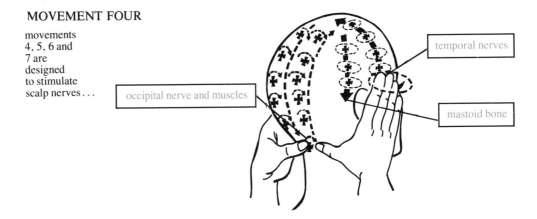

temporal nerves

occipital nerve and muscles

mastoid bone

Movement 5: Hold your thumbs against the right side of the head with the fingers of your left hand on the occipital nerve and those of your other hand at the forehead. Gradually work the hands toward each other, sliding and rotating until they meet over the ear. Repeat the movement on the opposite side of the head. Start with your thumbs behind each ear and repeat the movement working the fingers directly up the head from the forehead to the crown. The frontalis, auricular and occipital muscles as well as the auricular and occipital nerves are affected by this movement.

MOVEMENT FIVE

working
thumbs in
one area
slide and
rotate fingers
until both
hands meet
over the ear...

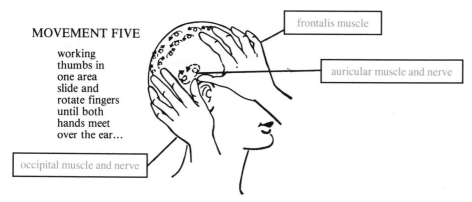

frontalis muscle

auricular muscle and nerve

occipital muscle and nerve

Movement 6: Start on the right side and knead the entire scalp by pressing the open palms firmly against the skull and quickly contracting the hand. This movement affects the epicranius, occipital, frontalis, temporalis and auricular muscles as well as the occipital and auricular nerves.

MOVEMENT SIX

kneading
involves
squeezing by
contracting
the hand...

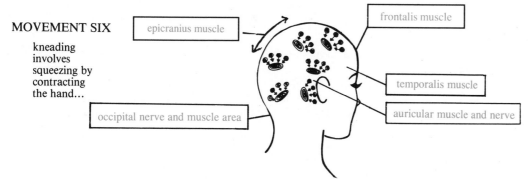

epicranius muscle

frontalis muscle

temporalis muscle

occipital nerve and muscle area

auricular muscle and nerve

Movement 7: Repeat a kneading action by spreading the hands out to cover as large an area as possible and by pressing and rotating the scalp over the skull. Shift the position of your hands and repeat the movement until the whole scalp has been kneaded. This movement affects the epicranius, occipital, frontalis, temporalis and auricular muscles as well as the occipital and auricular nerves.

MOVEMENT SEVEN

knead
with
wide
spread
hands...

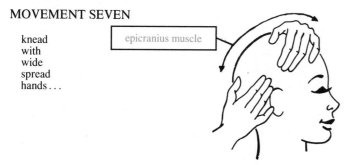

epicranius muscle

Hair care, hair and scalp treatments, scalp massage

Movement 8: Used to stimulate the frontalis muscle area and relax the patron. Place the patron's head against the head rest. Place the palm of your right hand against the left side of the forehead and, in a broad stroking movement, gradually draw it toward the right. Trail your fingers without applying pressure. When the fingertips reach the right temporal nerve, press and rotate. Repeat this movement with your left hand on the left side. Repeat five times.

MOVEMENT EIGHT

the palm is
used in this
movement . . .

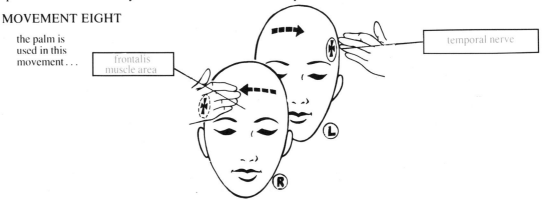

frontalis
muscle area

temporal nerve

Movement 9: Used to coordinate all movements and to stimulate circulation. At the end of the eighth movement, slide both your hands down the neck and out on the shoulders. Hold your fingers toward the front and your thumbs toward the back. Start to work the thumbs toward the spine with a continuous circular effleurage. When your thumbs meet, draw the closed fingers up to enclose the side of the neck and make a firm stroke down the neck and out on the shoulders to the starting position. Repeat the entire movement three times. The anatomy affected includes the occipital and mastoid nerves, the deltoid and trapezius muscles, the auricular artery and the jugular vein.

MOVEMENT NINE

at the end of
the 8th movement,
slide both hands
down the neck
and out on the
shoulders . . .

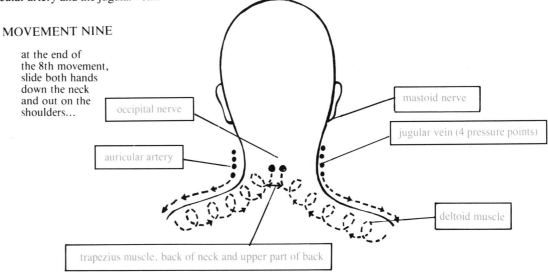

occipital nerve

mastoid nerve

jugular vein (4 pressure points)

auricular artery

deltoid muscle

trapezius muscle, back of neck and upper part of back

**Hair care, hair and scalp
treatments, scalp massage**

Unit 5
Accessories for scalp treatments

All scalp treatments and some hair treatments include the employment of various appliances. Their use supplements the beneficial effects of massage and products used for these treatments. Here is a brief description of the seven most widely used accessories.

1. Infrared lamp: A device that furnishes evenly reflected active heat without pressure. The heat warms the skin and relaxes the tissues. It makes them more receptive to the beneficial effects of the manipulations. Infrared rays are radiant heat energy. When used during a scalp treatment, they help hair preparations to penetrate better, stimulate circulation and permit the patron to relax. The source of heat should be kept at a distance of 15–20 inches (38.10–50.80 cm.) for scalp treatments; 20–30 inches (50.80–76.20 cm.) for facials. Infrared radiation should remain on as long as necessary because the rays do not cause a burn or increase body temperature.

2. Steamers: Equipment that generates steam at 180–190°. This relaxes the skin and tissues.

3. Heating cap: A thermostatically controlled device which supplies an even heat at a low-medium or high range. It produces a mild heat which is either thermostatically controlled or worked with a high-medium-low control switch. The heating cap is especially designed for use on the head during scalp and hair treatments.

   The main function of a heating cap is to produce heat. It does not increase body temperature. The heating cap is very effective for both hair and scalp treatments. It assists in activating hair and scalp preparations, liquifies creams and makes the penetration of hair preparations such as protein and cholesterol more effective.

   Bobby pins, hair pins, curl clips or any metal clip absolutely should not be used to secure the hair in place when using the heating cap. They can puncture the lining of the cap and thereby make electrical contact. This might cause serious injury to the patron.

   The proper application of the heating cap requires several steps. First, a fine plastic cap or wax paper must be used to cover the treated hair. Next, a heavier protective cap is placed on top of the first cover. This will keep the heating cap clean and free from lotions and creams. Finally, the preheated heating cap is placed on the head.

4. Hot towels: These generate a mild form of heat which softens the skin and relaxes the tissues.

5. Accelerating machines: A device that utilizes photon units of energy in a range which is effective and harmless. Penetration time of hair and scalp preparations is shortened by 80%.

6. High frequency, high voltage and low amperage violet ray: This produces a deep stimulation with oscillations so rapid that they do not affect the nerves. Use the direct method when treating oily conditions and the indirect method or vibrator for dry conditions. The indirect method dries the skin less. The vibrator does not help check an oily condition.

Unit 5
Accessories for scalp treatments

General objectives-student goals: After study, instruction and completion of this unit, you will be able to demonstrate understanding of the accessories used for scalp treatments by identifying and describing the use of seven different accessories. You must have the proper supplies and equipment in order to complete this unit successfully.

...use infrared lamp during manipulations...

Hair care, hair and scalp treatments, scalp massage

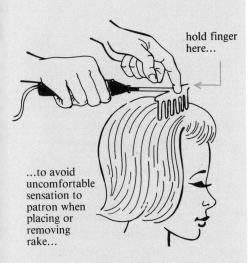

hold finger here...

...to avoid uncomfortable sensation to patron when placing or removing rake...

indirect application involves both patron and operator...

Hair care, hair and scalp treatments, scalp massage

With the indirect application, the patron holds the electrode, and the cosmetologist directs the sparks to a specific point with the fingertips. This creates good stimulation without a drying effect. If deeper stimulation than the direct method is necessary for facial or scalp treatments, this can be done by placing a piece of gauze, silk or linen over the electrode.

High frequency currents must never be used with a flammable hair preparation because the friction of the rays may cause combustion. To determine whether the lotion, oil or tonic you use is flammable, apply the glass applicator (with the current on) close to a small piece of absorbent cotton saturated with the preparation. If the lotion is flammable, the cotton will burst into flames almost upon contact.

The germicidal action of the violet ray results from the breakup of tiny air particles and the release of pure ozone.

A. **Direct high frequency current:** Also known as violet ray. It can be used for scalp treatments in a direct application with a glass rake attachment. It stimulates the scalp as the long rounded teeth are passed through the hair. When the rake is reversed, it may be used as a bar for the back of the neck and shoulders. The violet ray is most effective when used immediately after the shampoo on dry hair, before the application of either lotion or pomade. You can, however, apply scalp pomades, creams or ointments before using high frequency current. Scalp lotions and tonics containing alcohol are applied to the scalp only after the use of high frequency equipment.

Note: Place a finger of your left hand on the violet ray attachment when placing it on or removing it from the patron's scalp in order to avoid an uncomfortable sensation.

B. **Indirect high frequency current:** Consists of manipulating the scalp with the fingers while the patron holds an electrode in her hand. All electricity passes to the ground through the patron's body and through the hands and body of the operator.

Note: With indirect application, the operator's hands must be in contact with the patron's scalp before the patron turns on current. This will prevent an uncomfortable sensation.

7. **Vibrators:** These intensify the stimulating effects of hand massage. There are two types:

A. Motor driven devices with hard rubber attachments

B. A complete motor attachment that fits on the operator's hand

Unit 6
Procedure and technique for the application of liquids and creams for scalp treatments

1. Drape the patron and brush the hair.

2. Section the hair into four quadrants. Fasten three of these out of the way. Leave one loose.

3. Hold the comb between your middle and index fingers. Hold a cotton pledget between your thumb and index finger. Subsection each quadrant with partings $1/4$–$1/2$ inch (.64–1.27 cm.) apart. Apply tonic or lotion. Rub it on the scalp along the lines of the partings.

apply in
this pattern . . .

4. If a pomade or cream is to be applied, place a small dab on the back of your left hand. Hold the comb between the index and middle fingers of your right hand, and apply the pomade with the tips of these two fingers.

5. Adjust the infrared lamp or other heating device over the patron's head.

6. Give scalp manipulations 1–9.

7. Shampoo the hair and dry under a hair dryer until it is thoroughly dry.

8. Use high frequency equipment. Use either the direct or indirect method.

9. Apply an appropriate scalp tonic or pomade.

10. Set, dry and comb the hair into the desired style.

Unit 6
Procedure and technique for the application of liquids and creams for scalp treatments

General objectives-student goals: After study, instruction, practice and completion of this unit, you will be able to demonstrate understanding of the procedure and technique for the application of liquids and creams for scalp treatments by giving a brief overview of the subject and by demonstrating the procedure. You must have the proper implements and supplies in order to complete this unit successfully.

this technique of application
saves time and motion . . .

Hair care, hair and scalp
treatments, scalp massage

51

General objectives-student goals:
After study, instruction, practice and completion of this unit, you will be able to demonstrate understanding of hair treatments by writing and/or giving a brief overview of the subject and by demonstrating the procedure. You must have the proper implements and supplies in order to complete this unit successfully.

heating cap
accelerates
the action
of the
conditioner

Hair care, hair and scalp
treatments, scalp massage

52

Unit 7
Hair treatments and procedure

Hair treatments are intended to treat the hair shaft not the scalp. Corrective hair treatments are recommended for dry, abused and damaged hair. They are also recommended for before and/or after a permanent wave, hair tinting, bleaching or straightening treatment.

There are many different types of hair conditioning treatments. Select the one for the specific condition which needs to be treated. Most of the preparations have penetrating value and show excellent results after the first treatment.

The natural laws of nature do not permit instant healing of broken bones or cuts. The same is true with hair. It is not possible to repair damaged hair instantly. When hair is damaged, it is damaged both on the inside and on the outside. All repairs are temporary.

The cationic substance of hair conditioning products makes a very strong bind to the hair but the bond is not permanent. Most hair conditioning products are composed of substances which have positive charges (cationic). When applied to the hair they neutralize the negative charges (anionic) in the hair. A cationic substance resists removal by hair brushing but it cannot resist removal by shampooing because most shampoos and hair are anionic

Hair that has had continuous exposure to alkaline products or mixtures lacks the important disulfide bonds. When large amounts of these bonds are missing, the results of a cold wave or a set and the general appearance of the hair will be unsatisfactory.

The ultimate objective is to tighten the cuticle (outer layer of the hair) and restore the hair's proper moisture content. Hair conditioning products are not effective conditioners unless they provide the hair with moisture and improve the hair's ability to absorb moisture from the atmosphere.

Procedure for hair treatments

1. Drape the patron.

2. Brush the hair.

3. Shampoo the hair and blot it dry. If the preparation is not water soluble, eliminate shampooing as the third step and shampoo instead of water rinsing as the eighth step.

4. Apply hair conditioner to the scalp area. Use the same technique as for a scalp treatment. When the application to the scalp is complete, apply the conditioner to the entire hair shaft.

5. Apply movements 3–7 of the scalp treatment procedure.

6. Use the heating cap or accelerating machine.

7. Remove the heating cap or accelerating machine and section the hair into four quadrants. Subsection each quadrant with ¼ to ½ inch (.64–1.27 cm.) partings. Hold a comb in your right hand. Slide the thumb, index and middle fingers of both hands over the entire length of each hair strand. Begin with the hair nearest the scalp and slide towards the ends. This is achieved with a circular motion. Start with your left hand and pull and slide upward towards yourself. As your left hand reaches the ends of the strand, your right hand starts again at the scalp area. This is repeated three times on each strand over the entire head.

8. Rinse the hair, blot it dry and set.

The scalp treatment procedure is the same for all scalp conditions including baldness (alopecia areata), premature baldness, unnatural fall of the hair, dry dandruff and oily dandruff. It is important to select and use the hair preparations, tonic, lotion or cream manufactured for the condition that you want to treat.

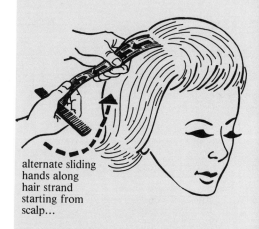

alternate sliding hands along hair strand starting from scalp…

Unit 8
Hair conditioners

Reconditioning hair through the use of hair conditioners is a service practiced by cosmetologists for restoring and improving the texture, appearance and manageability of normal, damaged or chemically processed hair. The improved hair condition which results from the use of hair conditioners is, however, only temporary.

The reconditioning process consists of the application of an acid balanced hair conditioner or an after-shampoo rinse. These products restore cuticle strength and sheen to the hair. The ingredients of hair conditioners do not become a permanent part of the cuticle's surface.

The cortex constitutes the major portion of the hair fiber. Conditioners are absorbed into the cortex but the results cannot last because the hair components are dead and cannot function biologically. Shampooing the hair, therefore, will remove any and all deposits made through the conditioner's processes of absorption and adsorption. Therefore, the results of hair conditioners are always temporary.

Hair conditioners have an acid pH and are used after shampooing the hair. The functions of a good hair conditioner are to:

1. Help prevent damage to the hair

2. Help protect damaged hair from further damage

3. Help restore damaged hair to normal or a less damaged condition

4. Leave the hair untangled, easy to comb, supple and glossy

5. Add more body to limp or fine hair

Unit 8
Hair conditioners

General objectives-student goals: After study, instruction and completion of this unit, you will be able to demonstrate understanding of hair conditioners by writing and/or giving a brief overview of the types of hair conditioners and their effects.

Hair care, hair and scalp treatments, scalp massage

53

Many hair conditioners contain the organic, water soluble substance called protein. Protein hair conditioners are compatible with hair and protect it from chemical and environmental influences. It will also provide normal hair with a thin, protective film and fill the voids and damaged sections of the hair. Water alone can remove protein conditioners from the hair.

There are five types of hair conditioners:

1. Time measured conditioners are those that are applied to the hair at the shampoo basin and remain on the hair from three to five minutes before they are water rinsed from the hair. They are coating conditioners which do not penetrate the hair shaft because the size of their molecules is too large for penetration. They leave the hair soft, tighten the cuticle, add luster and seal in natural moisture.

2. Instant conditioners are applied to the hair after the shampoo at the styling station. These conditioners have a very small molecule size. They penetrate the hair shaft and do not have to be water rinsed from the hair. These conditioners also leave the hair soft, tighten the cuticle, add luster and seal in normal moisture.

3. Conditioners combined with styling lotion are applied on wet hair after the shampoo. These conditioners coat the hair and give it extra body. They tighten the cuticle, seal in normal moisture and add some luster to the hair.

4. Neutralizing conditioners are used at the shampoo bowl after the shampoo when the hair has been exposed to strong alkaline hair products. They have a low acid pH with both a penetrating and coating action. They are left on the hair from three to five minutes and are then water rinsed.

5. Heat activated conditioners are those which require a mild application of heat from an infrared lamp, hair dryer or heating cap in order to effect some penetration. They also coat the hair. After five minutes, the hair is water rinsed. The hair is left soft with added luster. The cuticle is tightened and has a higher moisture content.

Review questions

1. Do the health and beauty of the hair reflect the condition of the scalp?

2. What type of hair care does healthy hair need?

3. What does brushing the hair with a good natural bristle hair brush do for the hair and scalp?

4. Why is the natural bristle hair brush recommended for hair hygiene and professional scalp treatments?

5. How effective are scalp manipulations?

6. What is one of the most common scalp complaints?

7. Can pulling the hair at the scalp area help stimulate the scalp and prevent shedding?

8. Why are scalp treatments recommended for individuals with normal hair and scalp conditions?

9. When should you avoid scalp treatments?

10. Why is an infrared lamp used during a scalp treatment?

11. Why is a steamer used during a scalp treatment?

12. Why is a heating cap used during a scalp treatment?

13. Are high frequency scalp treatment equipment and violet ray the same?

14. How is the high frequency equipment used for a direct application during a scalp treatment?

15. How can you avoid an uncomfortable violet ray sensation during the direct application of high frequency current?

16. What is the indirect method of applying high frequency current as a scalp treatment?

17. Are hair treatments very effective on the scalp?

18. Can hair treatments be sold as preliminary protective conditioning treatments?

19. Is the basic scalp treatment procedure the same for all scalp conditions?

20. Should a hair conditioner be applied to the scalp area when giving a hair treatment?

Hair care, hair and scalp
treatments, scalp massage

NOTES

Hair care, hair and scalp
treatments, scalp massage

Hair shaping

Hair shaping: The basic skill that is the foundation for all hairstyling. The durability of any hairstyle is influenced by the shape of the hair.

Overview: This chapter provides three individual methods and procedures for cutting hair. Your school may teach one or all three.

Behavioral objectives-student goals: You must use the proper supplies and equipment in order to complete this chapter. After completion of this chapter, and after instruction, study and practice, you will be able to perform and demonstrate competency in hair shaping by: demonstrating the technique for removing hair bulk, giving a complete haircut with a scissors, giving a complete haircut with a razor, giving a neckline cut, stacking hair, cutting bangs and clipping split ends. You also will be able to demonstrate competency by identifying, explaining and/or listing hair shaping implements, the procedure for children's haircutting, the importance of child patronage, techniques for coping with child behavior, the requirements for teenage haircuts, the multi-level haircut and mini-scissors precision haircutting.

Hair shaping is an important basic hairdressing skill because it is the foundation of all hairstyling. A haircut aims at the creation of the correct hair length for the desired hairstyle. The results depend entirely on your skill as a haircutter. The term haircut does not always mean that the hair is shortened. Haircutting removes excess hair bulk as well as hair length. Hair can be shaped by thinning excess hair bulk without shortening it. The haircut establishes the foundation for the hair design and it assists in maximizing good head and facial features and minimizing poor ones. It influences the durability of the hairstyle.

Hair shaping has an effect on several other services such as permanent waving, thermal curling, pin curling, air waving, blow dry styling and permanent hair coloring. It is the bulk, length and the cut at the hair ends which affect the application and procedure for these services as well as the results.

In this chapter, you will find instructions for a basic circular haircut, a basic five section haircut and the multi-level cut. Your school may teach one or all three. The important thing is that hair bulk and length, properly shaped to the contour of the head or into a definite style pattern, help you achieve professional results in the final hairstyle.

The circular haircut is almost foolproof. It is a blunt cut method of shaping hair and can be used for shaping any hairstyle except the cap-shaped neckline cut. A razor can be used for the circular haircut instead of scissors. However, it is suggested that the scissors be your first choice until you have confidence in your ability to control your hands and the hair at the same time. The only difference between a scissors haircut and a razor haircut is the implement used to cut the hair. If you use the implements correctly, there will be no difference in the results.

Hair shaping

57

The basic five section haircut is another time-tested method of cutting hair. The procedure and technique may be modified to agree with your teacher's instructions. A razor can also be used with this technique. Again, it is suggested that the scissors be your first choice until you have confidence and the ability to control your hands and the hair at the same time.

Note:

1. Hair may be cut either wet or dry when using conventional haircutting scissors.

2. Hair must be thoroughly wet when cutting with a razor.

3. For best results, it is advisable to use thinning scissors on hair that is not wet.

You must give special consideration to:

1. The direction in which the hair grows.

2. The growth direction of cowlicks.

3. The bone structure and head shape. The occipital bone is an important factor in determining hair length.

4. The amount of split hair ends.

5. The desired hairstyle. This must be kept in mind throughout the entire haircut in order to arrive at the correct hair length for the selected hairstyle.

6. The angle at which the hair is held from the head (elevation).

7. Hair texture as it relates to hair shaping.

8. Not removing too much hair.

Sanitary and safety precautions for hair shaping

1. Always use the razor with the protective guard over the cutting edge.

2. When using scissors, always protect the patron from the points of the scissors. Use caution around the eyes and ears.

3. Sanitize haircutting implements with 70% alcohol.

4. Store implements in a protective sanitary container when they are not in use.

5. Always use sanitized materials, equipment and supplies for each patron.

Hair shaping

6. Wash your hands before and after working on a patron.

7. Sweep up the hair clippings after completing each haircut.

Unit 1
Implements and supplies for haircutting

1. Standard size conventional haircutting scissors

2. Mini-scissors (conventional haircutting scissors)

3. Notched single-edge thinning scissors

4. Notched double-edge thinning scissors

5. Razor with safety guard

6. Scissors-razor combination

7. Neck strip

8. Haircutting cloth or cape

9. Water applicator

10. Haircutting combs

Conventional haircutting scissors (items 1 and 2): Scissors are available in a variety of sizes, from as long as $7\frac{1}{2}$ inches (19.05 cm.) to as short as 4 inches (10.16 cm.). The size of the scissors is important.

Standard size: These scissors range from $6\frac{1}{2}$ inches (16.51 cm.) to $7\frac{1}{2}$ inches (19.05 cm.). They are used for shingling, slithering, effilating, club cutting and conventional blunt cutting.

Mini-scissors: These scissors range from 4 inches (10.16 cm.) to $5\frac{1}{2}$ inches (13.97 cm.). They are used for precision blunt cutting. They provide full control by limiting the amount of hair cut with each cutting action. Mini-scissors are designed primarily to cut and layer the hair in such small gradations that the line of demarcation between layers is eliminated. The hair will have a naturally blended appearance regardless of the style in which the hair is cut.

Each part of the scissors has a name. You must be familiar with these parts in order to use the scissors properly.

1. The point is the front tip of both the moving and the still blades. The point of the scissors is used to cut superfluous hairs on the skin and to cut a sharp line around hairline areas.

2. Cutting edges are the inside edges of the movable and still blades. The tips and the cutting edges are the only parts of the blades that touch as the scissors are closed.

3. The action blade is the blade which the thumb controls. The action of the thumb while cutting moves the blade.

4. The still blade is the blade which the fingers control. This blade remains stationary while cutting.

Unit 1
Implements and supplies for haircutting

General objectives-student goals: After study, instruction and completion of this unit, you will be able to demonstrate understanding of the implements required for haircutting by identifying and describing the parts and uses of ten implements and supplies used for haircutting. You must have the proper implements and supplies to complete this unit successfully.

Hair shaping

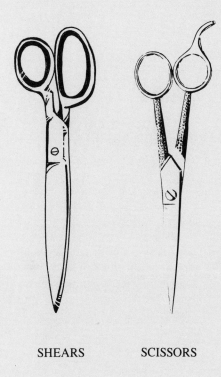

SHEARS   SCISSORS

Hair shaping

5. The pivot screw holds the scissors together and is used to increase or decrease the tension on the cutting blades.

6. The shank is the area between the finger grips and the pivot screw. The middle and index fingers rest on the shank while cutting. This gives you control of the still blade.

7. The fourth finger grip is the circular hole at the end of the still blade in which the tip of the ring finger is placed.

8. The scissors' control tang extends from the fourth finger grip at the end of the still blade. The tang is a finger rest for the little finger. Some mini-scissors do not have a tang.

9. The thumb grip is the circular hole in the action blade. Insertion of the thumb should take place just a little beyond the nail matrix and the mantle of the thumb nail.

   Note: Scissors are not shears. Shears are cutting implements similar to scissors but larger and heavier.

Thinning scissors (items 3 and 4) are also known as texturizing scissors. They are designed to remove excess hair bulk by thinning the bulky areas. They are not for removing hair length.

Notched single-edge scissors remove more hair with each cutting action than a notched double-edge scissors..

Notched double-edge scissors are similar to notched single-edge scissors. The two notched sides, however, provide twice the amount of space for hair which you do not want to cut. Only the hair that comes in direct contact with the toothlike cutting edges is cut.

Razor with safety guard (item 5): This cutting implement is also known as a shaper. The razor comes with a disposable blade and has a protective blade guard over the cutting edge. The disposable blades can be removed safely and are easy to replace. The terms used to describe the parts of a razor are as follows:

1. The blade is designed to be replaced when it becomes dull.

2. The cutting edge is the sharp part of the blade. It is used to cut the hair.

3. The removable guard fits over the back of the razor slot which holds the disposable blade.

4. The back of the razor has the blade slot into which the blade fits.

5. The pivot is a rivet type connection used to attach the handle to the part that holds the blade and blade guard.

6. The shank is the area between the end of the tang and the back end of the blade slot. The middle and index fingers rest on top of the shank, and the thumb is placed underneath. The underneath area is usually curved so that it forms a better thumb grip.

7. The tang is the curved extension of the shank just beyond the pivot rivet. When holding the razor in certain positions, the tang is used as a finger rest for the little finger.

8. The handle is used to help balance and hold the razor in a cutting position.

Scissors-razor combination (item 6): This scissors is made of quality steel. It is a well-balanced scissors about 7 inches long (17.78 cm.). It has a disposable razor blade attachment and a removable guard attached to the still blade of the scissors.

Neck strips (item 7) are a crepe type tissue paper strip. They are placed around the neck as a protective measure. They keep the haircutting cloth or shampoo cape from coming in contact with the skin.

Haircutting cloths and capes (item 8): These protective coverings are designed to protect the patron's clothing. The haircutting cloth is usually made of easy to wash nylon which is cool and comfortable. It is cut full so that it gives overall protection. Haircutting cloths are used when cutting hair while it is dry. The haircutting cape is usually made of durable vinyl cloth or plastic. It is waterproof, easy to keep clean and used when cutting hair that is wet.

The water applicator bottle (item 9) is usually a 16 ounce (473.18 ml.) plastic bottle with a pistol grip adjustable spray nozzle.

Haircutting combs (item 10): There are two types of haircutting combs. The all-purpose haircutting comb is designed for use with most haircutting techniques except neckline and hairline cutting. It is usually 7 inches long (17.78 cm.) with both coarse and fine teeth of the same size. The neckline haircutting comb is much thinner and more flexible than the all-purpose comb. It is usually 7 inches long (17.78 cm.) and is tapered toward the fine tooth part of the comb. It is designed for close cutting along the hairline areas.

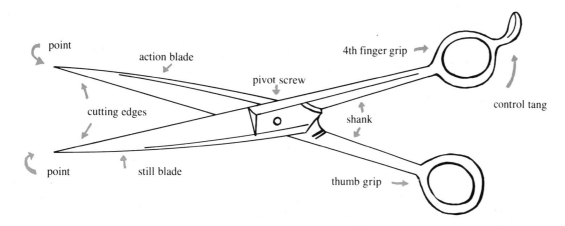

CONVENTIONAL HAIRCUTTING SCISSORS

Hair shaping

61

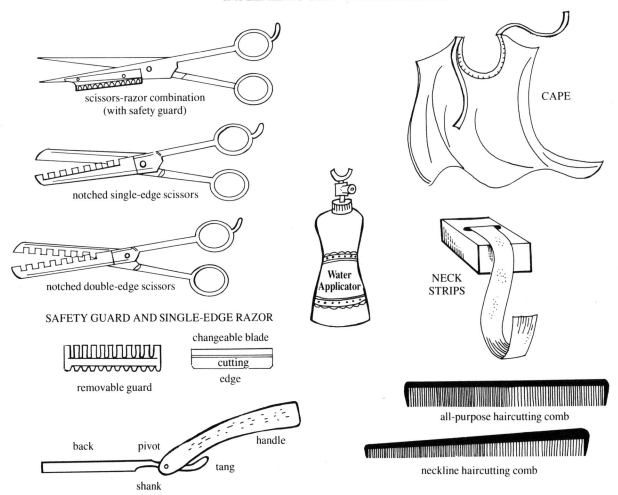

scissors-razor combination
(with safety guard)

notched single-edge scissors

notched double-edge scissors

CAPE

Water
Applicator

NECK
STRIPS

SAFETY GUARD AND SINGLE-EDGE RAZOR

changeable blade

cutting
edge

removable guard

back   pivot   handle

tang

shank

all-purpose haircutting comb

neckline haircutting comb

Unit 2
Handling haircutting implements

General objectives-student goals:
After study, instruction, practice and completion of this unit, you will be able to demonstrate understand-

Hair shaping

62

Unit 2
Handling haircutting implements

1. **Conventional haircutting scissors:** Grip the scissors with the right hand. Insert the fourth finger (up to the first joint) into the finger grip of the still blade and rest the little finger on the control tang. Insert the end of your thumb into the ring of the action blade. This grip ensures complete control of the scissors at all times. When you are not using the scissors during the haircut, close the blades, remove only your thumb from the ring and rest the scissors in the palm of your right hand secured by your fourth finger. Your thumb and index fingers are now free to hold and use the comb. Practice this technique. Also

practice transferring the comb between the thumb and index fingers of your left hand so that you can open and use the scissors.

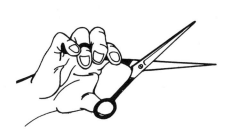

ing of handling haircutting implements by demonstrating the technique for holding and handling conventional scissors, thinning scissors and the scissors-razor combination as well as scissors-comb positions. You must have the proper implements in order to complete this unit successfully.

Note: There are many correct ways to hold haircutting scissors while giving a haircut. The scissors-comb positions shown here are the most widely accepted of them all.

2. Thinning scissors: Hold in the same manner as conventional haircutting scissors. The notched single-edge thinning scissors removes more hair with each cut than the double-edge scissors does.

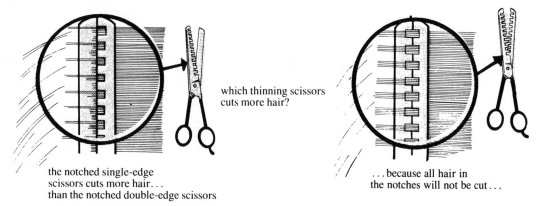

which thinning scissors cuts more hair?

the notched single-edge scissors cuts more hair... than the notched double-edge scissors

...because all hair in the notches will not be cut...

3. Razor: Hold the handle straight and grip the razor by placing the ball of the thumb of your right hand in the groove of the shank between the blade and the hinge. The index finger is placed on top of the shank and above the thumb. The other three fingers are folded over the handle. The handle rests near the crease between the fingers and the palm of your hand. The thumb and index fingers control the razor while the other three fingers maintain balance. Your hand should be turned so that the guard is toward you and so that the blade is on the underside. This is necessary for the slithering technique.

4. Scissors-razor combination: When used as a scissors, it is held and used in the same manner as conventional haircutting scissors. When it is used as a razor:

Hair shaping

63

A. Hold as a scissors.

B. Close the blades.

C. Remove your thumb from the ring and leave the fourth finger in the finger grip of the still blade.

D. Rest the scissors in the palm of your right hand.

E. Place your thumb on one side of the hinge and your index finger on the other side. The thumb and index fingers resting on the hinge allow full control of the instrument.

Unit 3
Haircutting techniques

In this chapter, several haircutting techniques are shown. They include the use of both scissors and razors. The techniques shown may be used with any haircut.

1. **Blunt cutting wet or dry hair with a scissors:** Blunt cutting is a technique used when you want a **minimum** amount of **taper** in a layered haircut with the hair as bulky as possible. The angle at which the hair is held from the head is an important factor for achieving the desired results. Hair strands held and cut at an **even (medium) elevation** (perpendicular 90° angle) produce results in which the hair at the crown and upper areas is longer than the rest of the hair. **High elevation** (hair strands held higher than a perpendicular angle) creates a layered effect over the entire head. **Low elevation** (hair strands held lower than a perpendicular angle) creates a stacked one length look by leaving the upper hairs longer than the lower hair strands.

BLUNT CUTTING (SCISSORS)

Pick up a strand of hair according to the instructions for the haircut. Hold the still blade of the open scissors parallel to the fingers just touching the strand of hair. Hold the fingers, the still blade and the hair strand without moving. Close the action blade in order to blunt cut the hair.

General objectives-student goals:
After study, instruction, practice and completion of this unit, you will be able to demonstrate understanding of haircutting techniques by describing and demonstrating the technique for:
1. Blunt cutting with a scissors
2. Blunt cutting with a razor
3. Slithering with a scissors
4. Slithering with a razor
5. Effilating
6. Club cutting
7. Precision haircutting
You must have the proper implements in order to complete this unit successfully.

Hair shaping

2. **Blunt cutting wet hair with a razor:** Blunt cutting with a razor confines the cutting action entirely to the ends of each strand of hair.

Hold a strand of hair horizontally between the middle and index fingers of your left hand with the back of your hand toward the patron's head. Hold the razor in your right hand and place it underneath the strand of hair with the cutting edge up and flat against the middle finger of the left hand. Without moving your hands or fingers, raise your arms upward, and the hair is automatically cut. The motions involved make use of the arms which move up while the razor and fingers remain firmly together at all times.

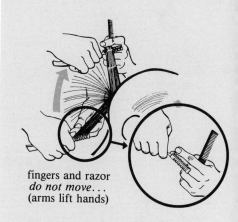

fingers and razor
do not move...
(arms lift hands)

3. **Slithering technique with a scissors for wet or dry hair:** Slithering with a scissors is a haircutting technique that tapers the hair ends. Pick up a strand of hair according to the instructions for the haircut. Slide the scissors up and down the underside of the strand. Unevenly remove a few hairs with each stroke toward the head. The scissors is closed very slightly on each stroke toward the head and is opened as it is brought back.

SLITHERING

4. **Slithering technique with a razor for wet hair:** This technique is a scraping action on the hair strand. It employs short, quick strokes of the razor and develops smooth, graduated hair ends. The angle of the razor determines the amount of hair cut with each stroke. The flatter the razor is held to the hair and the greater the pressure on the back edge of the razor, the less hair will be cut. Pick up a strand of hair according to the instructions for the haircut. Slide your fingers along the hair strand to approximately 1/2 inch (1.27 cm.) beyond where it is to be cut. Place the razor on the hair strand between your fingers and the patron's head with the cutting edge close to the fingers. Move the razor toward the fingers in short jagged strokes and cut the hair.

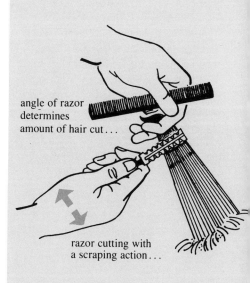

angle of razor determines amount of hair cut...

razor cutting with a scraping action...

5. **Effilating:** The technique of effilating the hair is similar to slithering with a scissors. During the effilating action, the scissors is always in an opened position with each sliding movement. Results: With each stroke, effilating removes less hair than the slithering action.

6. **Club cutting:** This is the technique of cutting the hair in order to develop a hairstyle which does not require tapered ends or layers. The hair is held straight down as close to the contour of the head as possible and cut blunt with scissors. All the cutting action takes place below the natural hairline at the back and sides of the head. The same principle applies to the front hairline when cutting a hairstyle with bangs.

Hair shaping

make at
least seven
cuts on
each strand . . .

Unit 4
Removing hair bulk

General objectives-student goals:
After study, instruction and completion of this unit, you will be able to demonstrate understanding of all the factors that influence the amount of hair bulk to be removed in order to shape hair properly by writing and/or giving a brief overview of the subject.

Hair shaping

7. **Precision haircutting:** This haircutting technique is designed to produce a precision haircut cut so carefully that it will fall and drape into its natural line and eliminate all lines of demarcation between the layers of hair. The graduated lengths will be so perfect that the hair will have a smooth and even appearance.

A. Limit your subsection to a narrow $\frac{1}{4}$-$\frac{1}{2}$ inch (0.64–1.27 cm.).

B. Use a mini-scissors with the blunt cut method and start cutting across the strand of hair. Use only the very tips of the scissors. If this procedure is followed, a minimum of seven cutting actions will be required to cut across one strand completely. Do not try to save time by cutting larger amounts of hair. If less than seven cutting actions are used to cut across one strand, there will be lines of demarcation between the layers of hair.

C. Use the same technique throughout until the haircut is completed.

Unit 4
Removing hair bulk

Removing hair bulk is also known as **thinning the hair**. The purpose of this technique is to give shape to the hair by removing excess bulk without shortening its length. It helps to distribute the bulk and weight of the hair so that there is support for the completed hairstyle.

Removing hair bulk precedes cutting the hair. Hair texture, hair length, hair density and the hairstyle to be designed are all factors that influence the amount of bulk to be removed.

1. **Hair texture: Fine hair** may be thinned closer to the scalp than coarse hair. Coarse stubby ends will protrude from the top layer, while fine hair, being softer, will lie closer to the head. Fine hair may be cut as close as $\frac{1}{2}$ inch (1.27 cm.) from the scalp. **Coarse hair** should be cut no closer than $1\frac{1}{2}$ inches (3.81 cm.) from the scalp.

thinning
removes
excess bulk . . .

BEFORE   AFTER

2. **Hair length:** Hair cut with a wide variance in the lengths of the strands will require less thinning than hair cut with strands essentially the same length over the entire head.

3. **Density of hair growth:** The average hair thickness varies from 150 to 400 hairs per square inch. Hair with greater density usually requires more bulk removal.

4. **Hairstyle:** If the finished hairstyle is one shaped to the contour of the head, the amount of bulk removed will be greater than in a bouffant style.

Unit 5
Techniques for removing hair bulk

There are three implements which may be employed to remove bulk:

1. Thinning scissors:

    A. Notched single-edge thinning scissors

    B. Notched double-edge thinning scissors

2. Conventional scissors

3. Razor

1. **Thinning scissors:** Hold an oblong subsection strand of hair ½ inch (1.27 cm.) by 2½ inches (6.35 cm.) straight out from the head between the fingers of your left hand. Place the thinning scissors at the correct distance from the scalp and cut once into the hair. Move out another 1 or 1½ inches (2.54 or 3.81 cm.) on the same strand and cut again. Repeat a third time if the hair is long enough. Remove the cut hairs by combing through the strand of hair.

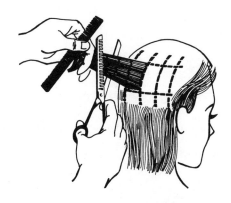

THINNING SCISSORS

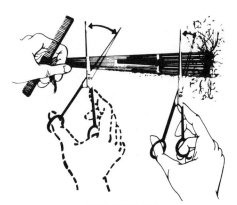

SLITHERING

2. **Conventional haircutting scissors:**

    A. **Slithering:** Hold a strand of hair and slide the scissors up and down the underside of the hair strand. Unevenly remove a few hairs with each stroke toward the head. The scissors is closed very slightly on each stroke toward the head and is opened as it is brought back.

General objectives-student goals: After study, instruction, practice and completion of this unit, you will be able to show understanding of removing hair bulk by demonstrating the techniques using:
1. Thinning scissors
2. Conventional scissors
    A. Slithering
    B. Back combing
3. A razor

You must have the proper supplies and implements in order to complete this unit successfully.

Hair shaping

keep pressure on
back edge...

Unit 6
Procedure for removing hair bulk

General objectives-student goals:
After study, instruction and completion of this unit, you will be able to demonstrate understanding of the procedure for removing hair bulk by describing and/or listing the procedure.

Unit 7
Procedure for a basic circular haircut with a scissors using the blunt cutting technique

General objectives-student goals:
After study, instruction, practice

> **Hair shaping**

68

B. **Back combing:** Hold the same size strand of hair as for slithering. Back comb most of the hair up to the amount you wish to remove. Blunt cut the remaining hairs level with the matted hair.

BACK COMBING

3. **Razor:** A scraping action is used with short quick strokes of the razor. Develop smooth graduated ends in the area where thinning is required by using very light pressure on the cutting edge and concentrating pressure on the back edge of the razor. The angle of the razor determines the amount of hair cut with each stroke. The flatter the razor is held, the less hair is cut. Pick up vertical subsections of about $\frac{1}{2}$ inch (1.27 cm.) by $2\frac{1}{2}$ inches (6.35 cm.). Use the front end of the razor and start about 1-1$\frac{1}{2}$ inches (2.54–3.81 cm.) from the scalp. Move the razor toward you with short jagged strokes at several points on each hair strand selected for thinning.

Unit 6
Procedure for removing hair bulk

1. Check the head to see where it will be necessary to thin the hair.

2. Section off the areas that require thinning. Pin the remaining hair securely out of the way.

3. Remove bulk from the hair one section at a time.

4. Regardless of implement used, the hair should not be thinned near the ends of a strand, since this will destroy the shape of the haircut.

Unit 7
Procedure for a basic circular haircut with a scissors using the blunt cutting technique

1. Wet the hair and blot it.

2. Comb the hair straight out from the crown in a circular fashion. Allow it to fall in an umbrella shape around the entire head.

3. Cut to establish the hair length by placing the comb in your right hand and picking up a 1 inch (2.54 cm.) wide strand of hair at the center of the nape of the neck.

4. With the palm of your hand toward you, close the middle and index fingers of your left hand in a scissors position on the strand of hair at the point you would like to cut. Hold the hair straight down.

5. Transfer the comb to the palm of your left hand and blunt cut the hair immediately above the fingers of your left hand.

6. Pick up the next 1 inch (2.54 cm.) strand of hair to the left of the hair that has been cut along with $1/_2$ inch (1.27 cm.) of the cut hair. Repeat steps 4 and 5. Use the cut hair as a guide.

7. Work to the left and repeat step 6 until you reach the center of the forehead.

8. Return to the nape area and repeat step 6. Work to the right until the entire right side is cut.

9. After completing the full circle, check for evenness and trim any uneven ends.

10. Section the hair into five sections. Start by drawing a part all around the head 2 inches (5.08 cm.) inside the hairline. Then, divide the hair within the circle into four equal sections using two parts: one from the center front to center rear; the other from side to side. Twist the hair within each of the four sections and fasten it out of the way.

and completion of this unit, you will be able to demonstrate understanding of the procedure for a basic circular haircut with a scissors, using the blunt cutting technique by demonstrating the entire 21 step procedure. You must have the proper supplies and implements in order to complete this unit successfully.

Hair shaping

69

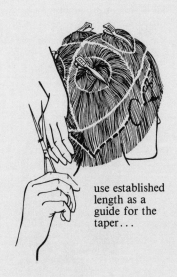

use established
length as a
guide for the
taper...

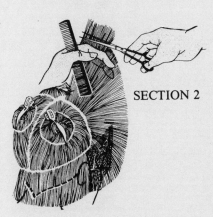

SECTION 2

Hair shaping

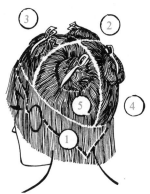

FIVE SECTIONS

11. Section 1 is the hair within the 2 inch (5.08 cm.) circle around the hairline. Section 2 is the patron's top front right section, and 3 is the top front left section. The back right section is 4, and the remaining back left section is 5.

12. Comb the hair in section 1 into its original umbrella shape and again starting at the nape, subsection a $1/2$ inch (1.27 cm.) strand of hair vertically from the parting down to the hairline.

13. Grasp this strand firmly between the index and middle fingers of your left hand with the palm toward the head and the fingers pointing down.

14. Cut the hair according to the guideline which was cut for the established hair length by:

    A. Holding the hair directly outward

    B. Sliding your fingers along the strand until the hairs cut for the established hair length are just visible

    C. Blunt cutting the rest of the strands protruding through your fingers

15. Work around the left side of the head to the front. Repeat steps 12, 13 and 14, each time picking up some of the cut hair from the preceding vertical cut to serve as a guide.

16. Complete the left side. Return to the nape and shape the right side in the same way.

17. Unfasten section 2 and subsection a slender triangle which is $1/2$ inch (1.27 cm.) wide at the circular parting. It should narrow down as it reaches the crown.

18. Secure the slender triangle of hair between the middle and index fingers of your left hand, along with a few strands of hair from section 1. These will serve as a guide. Keep the palm turned towards the head with the fingers pointing towards the forehead. Cut the hair according to the guideline established in section 1.

19. Repeat this procedure until the entire section has been shaped. Always pick up part of the previously cut triangle as a guide.

20. Follow the same procedure for sections 3, 4 and 5. Always keep the fingers of your left hand pointing toward section 1.

21. Complete by checking the accuracy of the haircut by parting at random and taking up some hair on the comb on each side of this parting. Hold the hair directly out from the head at a right angle. Slide the comb through the hair to the ends and observe how the lengths of the cut ends blend together. Any uneven ends should be cut so that they conform to the overall length of the hair. There should never be more than a $\frac{1}{4}$ inch (0.64 cm.) variation between any two neighboring strands of hair.

Unit 8
Procedure for a basic circular haircut with a razor using the blunt cutting technique

Follow the same procedure used for the basic circular haircut with a scissors but work with smaller subsections when necessary. Picking up smaller subsections makes the hair held between the middle and index fingers easier to control.

1. Wet the hair and blot it.

2. Comb the hair straight out from the crown in a circular fashion and allow it to fall in an umbrella shape around the entire head. The cutting action is entirely at the ends of each strand of hair. This procedure does not use the conventional scraping action along the length of a hair strand.

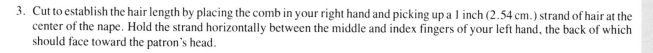

3. Cut to establish the hair length by placing the comb in your right hand and picking up a 1 inch (2.54 cm.) strand of hair at the center of the nape. Hold the strand horizontally between the middle and index fingers of your left hand, the back of which should face toward the patron's head.

4. Hold the razor in your right hand and place it underneath the strand of hair between your fingers and the patron's scalp. The cutting edge must face up and be flat against the middle finger of your left hand.

5. Without moving your hands or fingers, raise your arms upward, and the hair is automatically cut.

Note: The motions involved make use of the arms. They move up while the razor and fingers remain firmly together at all times.

Unit 8
Procedure for a basic circular haircut with a razor using the blunt cutting technique

General objectives-student goals: After study, instruction, practice and completion of this unit, you will be able to demonstrate understanding of the procedure for a basic circular haircut with a razor, using the blunt cutting technique by demonstrating the entire procedure. You must have the proper supplies and implements in order to complete this unit successfully.

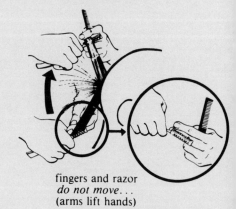

fingers and razor
do not move...
(arms lift hands)

Hair shaping

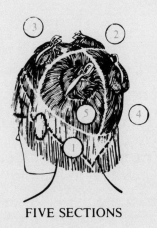

FIVE SECTIONS

Hair shaping

6. Pick up the next 1 inch (2.54 cm.) strand of hair to the left of the hair that has been cut along with $\frac{1}{2}$ inch (1.27 cm.) of the cut hair. This will serve as a guide. Repeat steps 4 and 5.

7. Work to the left. Repeat step 6 until you reach the center of the forehead.

8. Return to nape area and repeat step 6. Work to the right until the entire right side is cut.

9. After completing the full circle, check for evenness and trim any uneven ends.

10. Section the hair into five sections. Start by drawing a part all around the head 2 inches (5.08 cm.) inside the hairline. Then, divide the hair within the circle into four equal sections. Use two parts: one from the center front to center rear; the other from side to side. Twist the hair within each of the four sections and fasten it out of the way.

11. Section 1 is the hair within the 2 inch (5.08 cm.) circle around the hairline. Section 2 is the patron's top front right section, and 3 is the top front left section. The back right section is 4, and the remaining back left section is 5.

12. Comb the hair in section 1 into its original umbrella shape. Start at the nape and subsection a $\frac{1}{2}$ inch (1.27 cm.) strand of hair horizontally from below the parting.

13. Grasp this strand firmly between the index and middle fingers of your left hand and cut it according to the guideline which was cut for the established hair length by:

   A. Holding the hair directly outward

   B. Sliding the fingers along the strand until the hairs cut for the established hair length are just visible

   C. Blunt cutting the rest of the strands protruding through the fingers

14. Work around the left side of the head to the front. Repeat steps 13 and 14, each time picking up some of the cut hair from the preceding vertical cut to serve as a guide.

15. Complete the left side. Return to the nape and shape the right side in the same way.

16. Unfasten section 2 and cut the hair according to the guide established in section 1.

17. Repeat this procedure until the entire section has been shaped. Always pick up part of the previously cut triangle as a guide.

18. Follow the same procedure for sections 3, 4 and 5.

19. Complete by checking the accuracy of the haircut by parting at random and taking up some hair on the comb on each side of the parting. Hold it directly out from the head at a right angle. Slide the comb through the hair to the ends and observe how

the lengths of the cut ends blend together. Any uneven ends should be cut so that they conform to the overall length of the hair. At no time should there be more than a $\frac{1}{4}$ inch (0.64 cm.) variation between any two neighboring strands of hair.

Unit 9
Procedure for the basic five section haircut with a scissors using the slithering technique

The following procedure is another one of the several ways to cut a head of hair. The procedure and technique may be modified to agree with your teachers' instructions.

1. Divide the hair into five sections. Make the first parting across the crown from the back of the right ear to the back of the left ear.

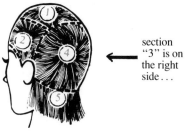

section "3" is on the right side...

2. Part the hair from each temple to the crown and secure the three front sections.

3. Divide the back into two sections by making a part across the back of the head from ear to ear. Start at about ear level.

4. Use $\frac{1}{2}$ inch (1.27 cm.) subsections and cut the hair in the nape section (section 5) to the desired length. Use a slithering action. Confine the slithering to the ends of the hair strand in the area of the desired length.

5. Cut the hair in section 4 (above the nape). Make subsections across the back of the head. Use the hair from the nape section as a guide.

6. Continue with the slithering action and cut both side sections 2 and 3. Use subsections. Use the hair from the nape area as a guide.

7. The front top section (section 1) is cut to blend with sections 2 and 3. Alternatively, it is cut into a definite style pattern such as bangs.

Unit 9
Procedure for the basic five section haircut with a scissors using the slithering technique

General objectives-student goals: After study, instruction, practice and completion of this unit, you will be able to demonstrate understanding of the procedure for a basic five section haircut with a scissors, using the slithering technique by demonstrating the entire procedure for a basic five section haircut. You must have the proper supplies and implements in order to complete this unit successfully.

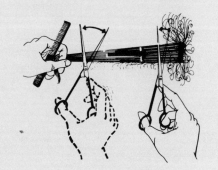

SLITHERING

Hair shaping

Unit 10

Procedure for the basic five section haircut with a razor using the slithering technique

Unit 10

Procedure for the basic five section haircut with a razor using the slithering technique

General objectives-student goals:
After study, instruction, practice and completion of this unit, you will be able to demonstrate understanding of the procedure for the basic five section haircut with a razor, using the slithering technique by demonstrating the entire procedure for the basic five section haircut with a razor. You must have the proper supplies and implements in order to complete this unit successfully.

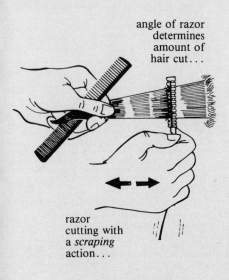

angle of razor determines amount of hair cut...

razor cutting with a *scraping* action...

Hair shaping

This is a method of cutting hair to a high taper with a razor. Use the same fundamental procedure outlined for the basic five section haircut with a scissors but use vertical subsections of 2½ inches (6.35 cm.) by ½ inch (1.27 cm.).

1. The hair must be thoroughly wet. Partially wet hair will cause pulling and create discomfort.

2. For best results, always use several short strokes in a jagged motion on each strand.

section "3" is on the right side . . .

3. With the middle and index fingers of your left hand, hold a vertical strand about ¼ inch (0.64 cm.) below the point where the length is to be removed.

4. The cutting edge of the blade is placed on the right side of the strand with pressure on the back of the blade.

5. Use a scraping action of short jagged strokes. Start cutting about ¼ inch (0.64 cm.) above the fingers which are holding the hair strand.

6. As the cutting action is performed, the strand of hair is directed to conform with the desired contour.

Procedure

1. Divide the hair into five sections. Make the first parting across the crown, from the back of the right ear to the back of the left ear.

2. Part the hair from each temple to the crown and secure the three front sections.

3. Divide the back into two sections by making a part across the back of the head from ear to ear. Start at about ear level.

4. Cut the hair in the nape section (section 5) to the desired length. Use a slithering action. Confine the slithering to the ends of the hair strand in the area of the desired length.

5. Cut the hair in section 4 (above the nape). Make subsections across the back of the head. Use the hair from the nape section as a starting guide.

6. Continue with the slithering action. Cut both side sections 2 and 3. Use subsections. Use the hair from the nape area as a starting guide.

7. The front top section (section 1) is cut to blend with sections 2 and 3. Alternatively, it is cut into a definite style pattern such as bangs.

Unit 11
Neckline shaping

The tailored neckline haircut will always be in demand regardless of the prevailing hair fashion. Many women prefer its smart tailored lines. When napeline shaping is the "in" fashion, it is worn almost universally. Neckline shaping should not have a hard, masculine look. It should always be very soft and very feminine.

The nape area is usually the starting point for all hair shaping routines. The length of a completed haircut is established by the nape strands.

The natural head contours and growth tendencies at the napeline influence napeline shapings. Napeline shaping should be designed while keeping both the hair length and hairstyle in mind. If the patron has a long neck, the napeline design should have a wide natural hairline effect. The short fat neck requires an oval finish at the nape. Avoid mannish, straight, square and sharp pointed effects. Emphasis should be placed on rounded and curved lines. The sectioning and procedure are essentially the same as any basic haircut. The action and technique at the napeline are changed as outlined below.

The hair at the nape is cut to the desired length first. Then, the napeline shaping is a graduated haircut. You use a combination of scissors and comb. You up-angle cut the hair into layers which are progressively longer from the innermost layer to the outermost layer.

1. Start at the right side of the neckline.

2. Hold the comb in your right hand with teeth upward and pressing against your index finger. The back of the comb presses against your thumb.

3. Insert the comb with the teeth upward through the nape section. Use the large tooth section. The comb should be held close to the scalp at the neckline and gradually moved away from it as the action progresses.

4. Using a rolling motion and describing a semicircle, draw the comb slowly upward through the hair.

General objectives-student goals: After study, instruction, practice and completion of this unit, you will be able to demonstrate understanding of neckline shaping by demonstrating the technique and procedure for neckline shaping. You must have the proper supplies and implements in order to complete this unit successfully.

long neck
appears
shorter and . . .

short fat neck
appears
longer and thinner. . .

Hair shaping

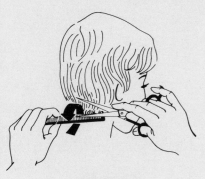

**NECKLINE
SHAPING**

5. The still blade of the scissors is held parallel to the comb. Only the action blade moves and cuts the hair. Practice opening and closing the scissors so that you will develop speed and control. Only the thumb and the action blade should move. As the hairs slip through the teeth of the comb, they are snipped off. The action continues across the entire napeline until the desired taper is obtained. Avoid cutting the hair too closely behind the ears.

6. Comb the upper sections of the back hair down and, using the scissors with a slithering action, shape it to blend with the nape section.

7. From this point on, continue whatever basic haircut technique you are using.

Many necklines have an untidy growth of hair extending far down the neck. The removal of these hairs is part of the napeline haircut. This **superfluous hair** may be removed by:

1. Snipping with a scissors

2. Using a hand or electric hair clipper

3. Careful use of a straight razor

Snipping with the scissors is preferred because it has the most natural looking finish and regrowth. Use the back of the comb as a rest for the still blade of the scissors. Cut one or two hairs at a time while holding the point of the still blade against the skin. The scissors and comb move simultaneously in the same direction. They have a sliding motion. Use a fast cutting action with the points of the scissors.

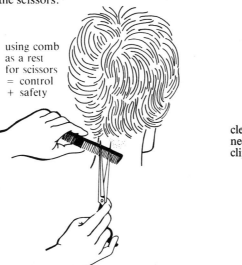

using comb
as a rest
for scissors
= control
+ safety

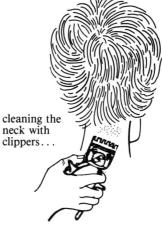

cleaning the
neck with
clippers...

Hair shaping

76

The **hair clipper** gives a closer cut in a shorter period of time. The hair clipper is held in the right hand with the thumb along the still handle which is attached to the lower blade. Hold the movable handle in the first joint of your fingers and place your index finger in front of the projecting guide. Cutting is done using the movable handle.

The **razor** requires that the hair be softened first. Because the hairs are removed closer to the skin, the cleaned area stays clean looking longer. There is a belief that the use of a razor or hair clipper will make the hair grow thicker, coarser or darker. This is not true. The use of any cutting implement at the neck or in any area does not influence the number of hair follicles, texture or pigment.

Unit 12
Mini-scissors, precision haircutting

Mini-scissors are available in several sizes. Their lengths vary from 4 inches to 5½ inches (10.16 to 13.97 cm.). They provide full control by limiting the amount of hair cut with each cutting action. The mini-scissors are designed primarily to cut and layer the hair in such small gradations that the line of demarcation between layers is eliminated. The hair will have a naturally blended appearance regardless of the style in which it is cut.

Mini-scissors technique

The objective of the step-by-step procedure which follows is to produce a precision haircut that is cut so carefully that it will fall and drape into its natural line. It will eliminate all lines of demarcation between the layers of hair. The graduated lengths will be so perfect that the hair will have a smooth and even appearance.

1. Limit your vertical subsection to a narrow ¼ to ½ inch (0.64 to 1.27 cm.).

2. Use a mini-scissors with the blunt cut method. Start cutting across the strand of hair. Use only the very tips of the scissors. If this procedure is followed, a minimum of seven cutting actions will be required to cut completely across one strand. Do not try to save time by cutting larger amounts of hair. If less than seven cutting actions are used to cut across one strand, there will be lines of demarcation between the layers of hair.

make at
least seven
cuts on
each strand . . .

mini-scissors
vary in size
between
4″-5½″
(10.16-13.97 cm.)

hairs must
be wet and
softened
before
removing . . .

Unit 12

Mini-scissors, precision haircutting

General objectives-student goals: After study, instruction, practice and completion of this unit, you will be able to demonstrate understanding of mini-scissors by describing and/or listing a brief overview of mini-scissors and by demonstrating the technique for cutting hair with mini-scissors. You must have the proper supplies and implements in order to complete this unit successfully.

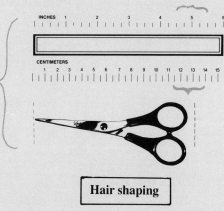

Hair shaping

Unit 13

The multi-level haircut

General objectives-student goals:
After study, instruction, practice and completion of this unit, you will be able to demonstrate understanding of the multi-level haircut by demonstrating the around the head procedure using mini-scissors. You must have the proper supplies and implements in order to complete this unit successfully.

MULTI-LEVEL CUT

Hair shaping

3. Use the same technique throughout until the haircut is complete.

Unit 13

The multi-level haircut

The multi-level cut is a procedure for cutting hair by cutting one subsection of hair from each section. You work around the head instead of completing one entire section on one part of the head.

The objective is to cut all sections continuously as you go around the head in a semioval pattern in order to achieve total perfection in hair shaping. This method and procedure eliminate the possibility of having a separation or sharp contrast in lengths between the hair on the side of the head above the ear and the hair from behind the ear to the nape.

Any subsectioning procedure, pattern or method may be used for the multi-level cut with two limitations:

1. Section 1 is at least a continuous $\frac{1}{2}$ inch (1.27 cm.) panel around the head from temple to temple.

2. Panel 1 is cut first and used as a guide for the rest of the haircut.

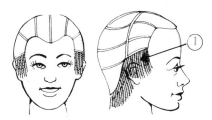

SECTION

PANEL

The hair may be wet or dry for the multi-level cut, and you can use either razor or scissors. Any haircutting technique, i.e., blunt cutting, slithering, tapering or effilating, can be applied to this cutting procedure.

Procedure for the multi-level cut with a $4\frac{1}{2}$ inch (11.43 cm.) mini-scissors using the blunt cutting technique

1. Drape the patron.

2. Shampoo the hair. A low 6.5 pH acid balanced shampoo is recommended.

3. Blot the hair in order to remove excess water.

4. Comb the hair smoothly.

5. Divide the hair into sections as illustrated.

6. Start the haircut at the center of the nape (section 1) and cut to establish a guideline length. Use very narrow subsections.

7. Cut all the hair in panel 1 according to guideline which was cut in step 6. Cut across the strand of hair using only the very tips of the scissors and a minimum of seven cutting actions.

8. Continue by cutting one subsection from each of the above sections. Work around the head, one level at a time.

9. The top and crown sections are cut in lengths according to the style.

10. Complete by blow drying or setting the hair.

Unit 14
The stacking technique

When hair is to be cut into a hairstyle which requires the maximum amount of fullness with anywhere from the smallest amount of taper to absolutely no taper, the hair should be undercut at a lower than perpendicular angle (low elevation) and stacked. With low elevation shapings, the outermost layers (upper strands) are progressively longer than the innermost layers (lower strands). This leaves the hair as bulky as possible in order to build body and achieve fullness.

The stacking technique requires the use of very narrow horizontal subsections. The hair must be blunt or club cut while wet.

1. Start by cutting the strand from the first very narrow horizontal subsection of the lowest part of a section in order to establish the length for that section.

2. The strand of the next narrow horizontal subsection from above is held in a relaxed, flat, close to the head position directly over the previously cut strand.

3. Position your fingers so that the hair will be cut in a direct line with the established length.

4. Continue by using the same technique for each strand of each narrow subsection until the entire section is cut.

It is the relaxed, flat, close to the head position of stacking hair which will give you fullness where you need it. If the strand to be cut is not held in a relaxed position, it will result in a tapered effect because of the natural lifting of the hair after it dries.

for fullness
like this...use the
"stacking" technique
of haircutting...

Unit 14
The stacking technique

General objectives-student goals:
After study, instruction, practice and completion of this unit, you will be able to demonstrate understanding of the stacking technique of cutting by demonstrating the technique and procedure for stacking a haircut. You must have the proper supplies and implements in order to complete this unit successfully.

Hair shaping

Unit 15
Children's haircutting

Unit 15
Children's haircutting

General objectives-student goals:
After study, instruction and completion of this unit, you will be able to demonstrate understanding of the differences between cutting hair for children and for adults by describing and/or listing a brief overview of child patronage and child behavior.

The procedures and methods for cutting children's hair are exactly the same as those for cutting the hair of teenagers and adults. There are some areas of differences, and cosmetologists, especially those who specialize in haircutting, should be aware of the following:

1. Children's hair texture
2. Cutting techniques related to child behavior
3. Hair care for children
4. Style lines for boys, girls and toddlers
5. Special consideration for teenagers

CHILDREN'S HAIRCUTTING

Hair shaping

Child patronage

Special care must be used when cutting children's hair. If their patronage is desired, everything should be made comfortable for them. Convertible chairs, high chairs and small hair brushes are important items for children's haircutting. Teenagers require more adult treatment.

The hair brush used on young children's hair should have long soft bristles, so that it does not irritate or scratch the scalp. For older children, however, a somewhat stiffer bristle hair brush will be necessary. Toddlers are treated most gently.

Child behavior

Cutting children's hair is a problem because of their inability to hold still. Improper methods of holding a child's head while you are cutting their hair can result in a very bad experience for both the child and the haircutter.

Small children move their heads suddenly. They are constantly moving and want to see everything that is going on. Make the child comfortable before attempting to hold his or her head and start cutting. Keeping the child still can be more time consuming than the actual haircut. It can become a serious problem unless you follow some basic rules.

1. The child should be carefully introduced to the haircut. Be friendly toward the child before seating him or her in the chair.

2. Be certain that your uniform is not similar to something which children do not like.

3. After placing the child in the chair, give the child something with which he or she can be entertained.

4. When a child's seat is used over the arms of a chair, be certain that you provide a backrest so that the child can relax.

5. Free the child's hands by taking them from under the cloth. This will make the child feel free and less confined.

6. Massage the child's scalp so that the child becomes familiar with your gentle touch and accepts your actions.

7. Comb and gently brush the child's hair to help build confidence.

8. Show the child the scissors' action and allow him to hear the cutting sound of the scissors before you start cutting.

9. If you are giving a wet cut, show the child the spraying action of the bottle before wetting the hair.

Unit 16
Children's hair texture

There are three stages in the development of the hair covering of the human head. The first covering is wool-like hair. This is called baby hair.

Baby hair usually lasts from one to three years. On occasion, it can last up to five years. This type of baby hair requires a very sharp scissors for cutting because it is very fine and soft and contains considerable moisture.

The secondary stage of hair covering lasts until about the age of twelve. As the child grows older, the outer cells of the hair shaft begin to lose their moisture and become hardened. The hair becomes coarser. The change in texture makes it possible to obtain better haircutting results.

The third stage is the permanent hair covering. The texture, elasticity, porosity and density of the hair will vary according to the sex, race and the individual. Best haircutting results are obtained when cutting hair which is in its third stage.

Unit 17
Head holding techniques

To keep a child's head relatively still and to avoid an unpleasant experience, follow this guide:

Do hold the child by the chin from below when cutting the front area. Hold the chin gently with the left hand. Avoid a firm hold.

the first hair covering is "wool-like"...

Unit 16
Children's hair texture

General objectives-student goals: After study, instruction and completion of this unit, you will be able to demonstrate understanding of children's hair texture by describing and/or listing a brief overview of the three stages of children's hair covering.

Unit 17
Head holding techniques

General objectives-student goals: After study, instruction and completion of this unit, you will be able to demonstrate understanding of head holding techniques for children's

Hair shaping

81

haircutting by describing and/or listing the do's and don'ts of children's head holding techniques.

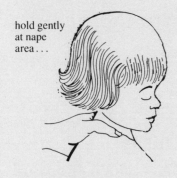

hold gently at nape area . . .

Unit 18
Hair care and style lines for children

General objectives-student goals: After study, instruction and completion of this unit, you will be able to demonstrate understanding of hair care and style lines for children by describing and/or listing a brief overview of the hair care and style lines for children and the technique for cutting children's bangs.

Hair shaping

82

Do hold gently at the nape area when cutting the sides. The left hand is at the nape with the thumb on the right side and the fingers on the left.

Don't spread your hand across the child's eyes. The child cannot see what is going on and will want to leave.

Don't hold the child's head from the back with your fingers around his neck. This type of pressure will make the child uncomfortable.

Don't spread your hand across the child's mouth while holding the chin. This action may cause difficulty in breathing.

Don't spread your hand over the top of a child's head in order to hold it still. This action can frighten any child.

Children's haircutting requires the haircutter to:

1. Handle the child properly
2. Make friends with the child
3. Make the child comfortable
4. Avoid any action which can frighten the child

Unit 18
Hair care and style lines for children

Use only a **low pH shampoo** (acid balanced) when shampooing children's hair. This type of shampoo is not only best for children's hair but it is also nonirritating and will not leave a burning sensation if it should accidently get into the child's eyes.

Avoid setting children's hair. Children's hair should be styled by using either a blow dryer, thermal irons, hot air comb or heat lamps. It is not necessary to use hair spray. If flyaway ends are a problem, apply some hair wax dressing to control them.

the most popular hairstyle for a little girl is one with bangs . . .

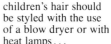

children's hair should be styled with the use of a blow dryer or with heat lamps . . .

STYLE LINES

The most popular hairstyle for a little girl is one with **bangs**. When deciding hairstyles for young girls, the type and texture of the hair are the most important factors. Plan a style that will not need frequent combing or attention.

Children's hair should be cut so that the hair will always look combed regardless of whatever movements the child might make. The haircut should be checked for forward, backward and side movements.

The back should be cut short whenever possible. Although the top is cut in straight bangs, allow enough length above the eyebrows so that they may be combed to one side if necessary. Bangs should always be cut with sharp scissors while the hair is wet. Razor cutting is not recommended for children unless the blunt method of razor cutting is used.

Cutting bangs

When cutting children's bangs, start on the left side. Place the still blade of the scissors at the hairline against the head. The cutting blade is on the outside. The middle fingers of your left hand are used for balancing and guiding the scissors. Use the club cutting action across the entire bang.

Cut a curved line from the ends to the center. Avoid cutting the side hair. Cut only the hair that comes forward into the bang area.

If a child has extreme hair density and the bangs are too thick, either cut the hair into slight layers or texturize the ends with a thinning scissors.

Always use caution when cutting around the ears and be alert for sudden movements of the head. A blunt cut on children's fine hair will add body to the hair ends. Boys' hair is usually cut without sideburns and in layers.

Unit 19
Teenagers and longer hair

Teenagers require adult treatment. Unlike young children, teenager requirements and services are no different than adult ones. They need perms, hair treatments, conditioners, color treatments and contemporary styling.

teenagers require
adult treatment . . .

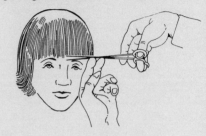

the middle fingers
of the left hand are
used for balancing and
guiding the scissors . . .

boys' hair
is usually
cut without
sideburns
and in layers . . .

Unit 19
Teenagers and longer hair

General objectives-student goals: After study, instruction, practice and completion of this unit, you will be able to demonstrate understanding of haircutting for teenagers by

Hair shaping

describing and/or listing a brief overview of the subject and by demonstrating the technique for clipping split ends. You must have the proper supplies and implements in order to complete this unit successfully.

Just trimming the teenager's long straight hair usually requires more time and greater skill than a conventional hair shaping. Long hair usually has split ends (trichoptilosis). Every haircutter should be a master of the technique for cutting split ends without shortening the hair.

Clipping split ends

In order to remove split ends effectively, follow this procedure:

1. Comb the hair thoroughly.

2. Section the hair into four quadrants.

3. Divide the hair into 1 inch square (6.45 cm^2.) subsections as you proceed.

4. Twist the strand of each subsection from the scalp to the hair ends.

5. With the twisted strand in your left hand, ruff the strand upward toward the scalp with the thumb and index finger of your right hand. This action allows the hair ends to protrude away from the twisted strand.

6. Remove the protruding split ends with the points of the scissors.

7. Begin near the scalp and cut all protruding hair ends alongside the strand. Work your way toward the end of the strand.

8. Untwist the strand and comb through. When the cut is complete, brush the hair in order to remove all the hair end clippings.

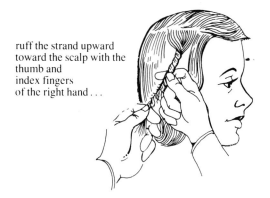

ruff the strand upward toward the scalp with the thumb and index fingers of the right hand . . .

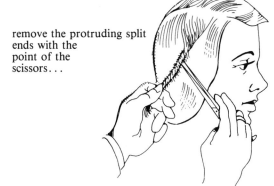

remove the protruding split ends with the point of the scissors . . .

1. Can a razor be used for the blunt cutting technique?

2. Must hair be cut wet or dry when using scissors?

3. Should hair be cut wet or dry with a razor?

4. Must you use a special technique for holding thinning scissors or can you use the technique used for conventional scissors?

5. Which thinning scissors removes more hair with each cut: the notched single-edge or the notched double-edge?

6. How does pressure on the back edge of the razor affect the cutting action of the slithering technique?

7. What is the difference in technique between slithering and effilating with a scissors?

8. Which removes more hair with each stroke: the effilating or slithering technique?

9. What is club cutting and how does it differ from blunt cutting?

10. What is another term for "removing hair bulk?"

11. When is it best to remove hair bulk: before or after the hair is cut into style?

12. Which can be thinned closer to the scalp: coarse or fine textured hair?

13. Does hair cut with a wide variance in the length of the strands require more or less thinning than hair cut with the strands essentially the same length over the entire head?

14. When cutting hair into layers, how much variation can there be between two neighboring strands of hair?

15. What are the results when hair is not thoroughly wet during a razor haircut?

16. Which area of the head is the usual starting point for all haircuts?

17. Is the scissors, hair clipper or straight razor the preferred implement for removing superfluous hair below the neckline after a napeline haircut?

Hair shaping

18. Are both handles of a hand held hair clipper movable?

19. Should the superfluous hair at the nape area be removed with a razor if the hair is not wet?

20. What is the advantage of giving a haircut with layers of small graduations?

21. Should you limit the size of the subsections when using the mini-scissors technique of haircutting?

22. What is the technique for blunt cutting a strand of hair with a mini-scissors?

23. Is it possible to develop lines of demarcation when cutting hair with a mini-scissors?

24. What is the stacking technique of haircutting?

25. Does the stacking technique for cutting hair require horizontal or vertical subsections?

26. Can the stacking technique be used successfully for cutting dry hair as well as wet hair?

Hair shaping

Hairstyling

Hairstyling: The art and skill of arranging hair in line with the current trend, styled for the individual and designed so that it will accentuate good facial features while minimizing the poor ones.

Overview: This chapter will provide you with everything from the basic fundamentals of hairstyling to hairstyling for the individual. Quick service salon techniques such as blow dry styling, lamp sets and thermal curling are also included.

Behavioral objectives-student goals: After completion of this chapter, and after instruction, study and practice, you will be able to perform and demonstrate competency in hairstyling by: demonstrating the techniques and procedures for fingerwaving, pin curl setting, roller setting with cylindrical and conoid hair rollers, lamp dry styling, blow drying, styling hair for the individual, thermal roller curling, teasing and combing hair into style. You will also be able to demonstrate competency by identifying, explaining and/or listing what fingerwave lotion is and what it is used for, the procedure for fingerwaving, the components of a pin curl, shapings, carved curls, ridge curls, stand-up curls, hair partings, the "C" shaping, skip waving, instant hair rollers, air waving and curvature hairstyling.

Modern hairstyling is the result of art and skill in designing and arranging the hair into a style. A well-trained hairstylist will adapt coiffures to accentuate a patron's good features and minimize poor ones. Naturally, the style should also be in line with the current trends.

hair style minimizes bad features   hair style accentuates bad features

OPTICAL ILLUSION

A well-trained hairstylist must understand **fingerwaving, pin curling** and **roller curling.** He or she must know whether these should be used individually or in combination. He or she must also know how **hair shaping** and **permanent waving** influence the final results.

SYMMETRICAL　　**ASYMMETRICAL**

TOP MASS　　**BACK MASS**
ARRANGEMENT　　**ARRANGEMENT**

FINGER –
WAVING
(shaping)

PIN
CURLS

HAIR
ROLLERS

(applied individually
or in combinations)'

Hairstyling

88

Hairstyles run in **cycles** and **echo the modes of previous ages**. The cycle is influenced by the fads, fashions and the political and social events of the day. Yet, there are only four possible arrangements for a hairstyle. These are:

1. Symmetrical arrangements
2. Asymmetrical arrangements
3. Top mass arrangements
4. Back mass arrangements

These arrangements, in various combinations, have been repeated continuously from 2500 B.C. to the present time. They will continue to appear in future hairstyles. The ambitious hairdresser must learn to anticipate future styling trends by studying the styles of the past.

There are **two methods** of setting and styling hair. One involves working with **wet hair**, and the other is known as **thermal styling**.

Wet settings involve:

1. **Fingerwaving**

   A. Molding　　B. Shapings　　C. Ridges

2. **Pin curling**

   A. Flat (stem directed) curls
   B. Flat (carved) curls
   C. Stand-up curls (volume and indentation)
   D. Ridge curls (overlapping)
   E. Lift curls (semistand-up curls)

3. **Roller curling**

   A. Cylindrical　　B. Conoid

4. **Lamp sets:** Placing the hair into style without hair rollers or curl clips

5. **Blow dry styling**

   A. Setting and combing hair in a single process with a hand held hair dryer, comb and brush
   B. Air waving with a comb, brush and curling iron attachments

Thermal styling involves:

1. Thermal irons

    A. Various sizes in diameter

    B. Electric (thermostatically controlled)

    C. Nonelectric (electric heater or gas flame required)

2. Instant rollers: Preheated hair rollers

Although there are many factors that affect the results of a hairstyle, the following are the most important:

1. Hair length   4. Direction of hair growth

2. Hair density   5. Condition of the hair

3. Hair texture   6. Head shape

The most complementary hairstyle is obtained when it is styled according to the patron's head size, shoulder line and body type and when it achieves an illusion of balance with symmetrical or asymmetrical styling lines.

Sanitary and safety precautions for hairstyling

1. Protect the patron's eyes by shielding them with your left hand when using spray applicators.

2. Avoid having curl clips come in contact with the patron's skin.

3. Do not leave thermal irons and heaters plugged into an electric outlet unattended with switch in the on position.

4. Do not allow the hair brush to scrape against the scalp when doing a combout.

5. Test thermal implements prior to each use.

6. Sanitize combs and brushes after each use.

7. Keep hair rollers and curl clips free from loose hair.

8. Use only hard rubber combs with all thermal implements and equipment.

Hairstyling

9. Protect the patron's ears when placing him or her under the hair dryer.

10. Protect the back of the patron's neck when placing him or her under the hair dryer.

Unit 1

Hair partings

The parting of a patron's hair is determined by head shape, the grain of the hair, hairstyle, facial structure and any natural partings. The grain of the hair, unless it is the exception to the rule, grows from right to left. A proper part can provide better balance to facial structure, minimize unbecoming facial features, correct a faulty hairline and emphasize a widow's peak.

A center part is not suited for a round or square facial structure. It tends to accentuate the roundness by equalizing the distribution of the hair. A long thin facial structure should not wear a center part because the line will emphasize the face's length. Center parts are especially appropriate for an oval face, the ideal facial shape. The center part can also be used to emphasize a widow's peak. For round and square facial structures, the aim is to create an illusion of ovalness and less width. This is accomplished by starting the part off center on the right side and slanting it down and away from the center of the head.

The long thin facial structure requires the illusion of width in the upper part of the face. This is accomplished by placing the part very low on the right side and by combing the hair across the head.

perfect oval face

center part goes best with oval face...

round or square face

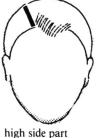

high side part creates an illusion of length on round or square faces...

long thin face

a low side part creates the appearance of width on long thin faces....

where cowlicks exist comb hair

in the direction of the natural partings

Natural parts at the back of the head, sometimes called cowlicks, are often annoying because they prevent the crown hair from lying flat and smooth. A correctly placed back part may overcome this problem. In order to determine the correct position for the natural hair part, you should:

1. Comb the hair smoothly away from the face, over the crown and down the back of the head

---

Unit 1

Hair partings

General objectives-student goals:
After study, instruction, practice and completion of this unit, you will be able to show understanding of hair partings by demonstrating the hair parts required for the oval, round, square and long thin faces and for natural cowlick partings. You must have the proper implements and supplies in order to complete this unit successfully.

Hairstyling

2. Relax or blouse the hair on the back of the head by pushing up with your hand

3. Observe where the cowlick occurs and how the hair around the cowlick parts naturally

4. Continue the front part over the crown and down the back in a direct line to the back cowlick

5. Stop the part at the cowlick not through the cowlick and comb the hair in the direction of the natural partings

Under **normal conditions,** all **side parts** should be on the **right side** of the head in order to follow the natural hair growth pattern and to avoid having the hair "pop up" at the crown.

Unless it is the exception to the rule, the **natural growth pattern** over the entire head is as follows:

1. The **hair on top of the head** (from a little above the temple line on both sides of the head and from the front hairline back to the crown) grows straight up and out from the scalp. This makes it possible to comb the hair in this area in any direction without going against the natural growth pattern.

2. The **hair on the left side of the head** (from a little above the temple line down to the ear and from the front hairline back to about 1 inch [2.54 cm.] behind the ear) grows back away from the face.

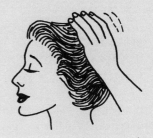
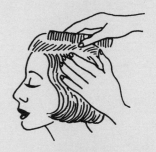

determining position
for natural hair part

1. 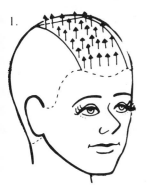   2. 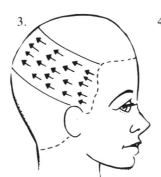   3. 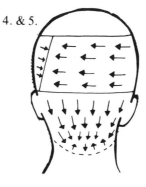   4. & 5.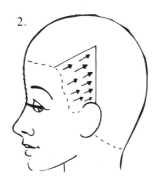

3. The **hair on the right side of the head** (from a little above the temple line down to the ear and from the front hairline back completely across the back of the head to about 1 inch [2.54 cm.] behind the left ear) grows from right to left. This region of growth includes the back of the head from the crown to about 1 inch (2.54 cm.) below the top of the ears.

4. The **hair across the back of the head** (from about 1 inch [2.54 cm.] below the top of the ears to the nape) grows downward toward the nape.

5. **At the nape,** the hair may grow in various directions.

Hairstyling

Unit 2
Introduction to fingerwaving

General objectives-student goals: After study, instruction and completion of this unit, you will be able to demonstrate understanding of the importance of fingerwaving by describing and/or listing a brief overview of the subject.

Fingerwaving provides an excellent introduction to hairstyling because it is the art of directing the hair into waves with the fingers and comb. Waving lotion, hair pins and clips are aids, but good fingerwavers rely mainly on their ability to manipulate the hair into waves with comb and fingers rather than with aids. Fingerwaving helps develop a good understanding of head contour and head shape. It helps to develop the techniques of molding, shaping and ridge work. These are important for good hairstyling.

Fingerwaves are molded into basic wave shapings with elongated crests (ridges) between two alternating semicircles. By mastering fingerwaving techniques, you will develop hand, finger and fingertip dexterity. You will gain the coordination necessary for all the required hairstyling techniques.

Unit 3
Fingerwaving lotion

General objectives-student goals: After study, instruction, practice and completion of this unit, you will be able to show understanding of the types of fingerwaving lotion and the application procedure by giving a brief overview of the two types of lotion and by demonstrating the procedure for applying fingerwave lotion. You must have the proper implements and supplies in order to complete this unit successfully.

Modern wave setting lotions vary in chemical content and consistency. Some are more effective than others for specific types of hair. The texture and condition of the hair influence the choice of lotion.

There are two types of lotion. One contains wetting agents as the prime ingredient; the other functions primarily because of its viscosity.

1. Wetting agents: A good setting lotion containing wetting agents makes the hair wetter than water does. It clings to the hair when applied and makes the hair more pliable.

2. Viscosity: This is the measure of how thick a fingerwaving lotion is and how quickly or slowly it pours. The greater the viscosity of a lotion, the better it will hold the hair. It dries to a hard finish while holding the hair in place. It combs into a soft natural look.

A good fingerwaving lotion is harmless to the hair and scalp. It should not flake or powder when dry. It should be applied to wet hair so that it is distributed smoothly and evenly.

Application of fingerwaving lotion

After the hair has been shampooed or made wet with water, apply a liberal but not excessive amount of lotion. Applying the lotion to one side of the head at a time and only to the hair that is to be fingerwaved will keep the lotion from drying. You will not have to make additional applications.

To apply the lotion to the hair:

1. Hold the bottle in your right hand.

2. Loosen the hair with the fingers of your left hand in order to create air spaces and to guard against dripping.

3. Cup your left hand against the patron's head along the front side hairline. This will prevent excess lotion from flowing down the hair.

4. Apply the lotion slowly to the hair on top of the head.

5. Comb the lotion into the hair with even strokes. Begin with the hair nearest the scalp. Then, work along the entire strand of hair to its end. Start the stroke with the comb at a right angle to the scalp and gradually turn your wrist upward as you comb down.

6. As you near the end of the strand, flick your wrist so that the palm of your hand is upward. This will hold excess lotion on the comb and prevent dripping and waste.

7. Turn the comb flat against the top of the head so that the excess lotion on it may be reapplied to the hair.

8. Repeat this procedure until the hair is completely saturated.

Unit 4
The "C" shaping

1. A shaping has a closed end and an open end. The closed end of the shaping is convex. The open end is concave. When the direction of the hair growth permits, start a "C" shaping at the closed end. Always start a ridge at the open end of the shaping.

2. The hair is molded into a "C" shaping using a clockwise or counterclockwise movement of the comb. Start at the closed end and work toward the open end where you start making the ridge.

Open End

Closed End

Unit 4
The "C" shaping

General objectives-student goals: After study, instruction, practice and completion of this unit, you will be able to show understanding of the "C" shaping by demonstrating the technique and procedure for making a "C" shaping. You must have the proper implements and supplies in order to complete this unit successfully.

Hairstyling

Unit 5
Semiwave

General objectives-student goals:
After study, instruction, practice and completion of this unit, you will be able to show understanding of the semiwave by demonstrating the technique and procedure for making a semiwave. You must have the proper implements and supplies in order to complete this unit successfully.

Unit 5
Semiwave

When fingerwaving with a side part, start the wave on the side with the larger area.

1. Make a $2\frac{1}{2}$ – 3 inch (6.35 – 7.62 cm.) part on the right side of the head.

2. Stand behind the patron as you make the part. As you look into the mirror, catch the hairline hairs with the front teeth of the comb. Hold the comb at a slight angle with the teeth toward you, and draw it straight back for the length of the part.

3. Comb the hair on both sides away from the part until it is smooth.

4. Stand behind the patron's left shoulder.

5. Shape the hair on the left side back from the hairline at an angle.

shape hair smoothly
in this direction . . .

Procedure for the first ridge

1. Place the index finger of your left hand directly above the position for the first ridge. The first ridge will be from the front hairline above the center of the left eyebrow to the end of the part. It will follow the contour of the head.

2. Press your left index finger firmly against the head. The palm of your hand is held away from the head. Only your index finger touches the hair.

3. Insert the teeth of the comb through the hair to the scalp directly under and angle toward the index finger.

4. In order to form a forward ridge, direct the comb and hair about 1 inch (2.54 cm.) along your finger toward the hairline.

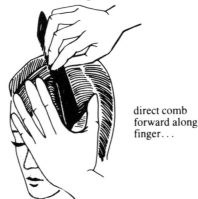

direct comb
forward along
finger . . .

Hairstyling

5. With the teeth still inserted in the ridge, flatten the comb against the head in order to hold the ridge in place. Remove (peel) your left index finger from the head. Place your middle finger above the ridge and your index finger on the tips of the teeth of the comb beneath the ridge.

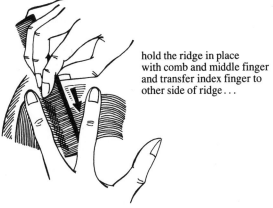

hold the ridge in place
with comb and middle finger
and transfer index finger to
other side of ridge...

6. Emphasize the ridge by closing the two fingers and applying slight pressure to the hair between them.

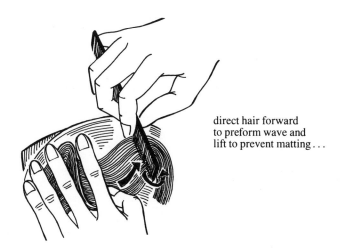

direct hair forward
to preform wave and
lift to prevent matting...

semicircular effect
preforms wave...

7. Without removing the comb, and while holding the ridge firmly with your fingers, draw the comb down through the hair. Turn the teeth downward toward the scalp and direct the hair in the opposite direction.

8. In order to lengthen the ridge by joining new extensions to the original length in an even unbroken line, repeat steps 1 to 7.

Hairstyling

repeat procedure
completing first ridge
at part . . .

9. This procedure is repeated approximately 1 inch (2.54 cm.) at a time until the full length of the part has been reached or until the ridge has faded at the crown.

Procedure for the second ridge

The second ridge starts at the crown. The direction of the movements is the opposite of that used when forming the first ridge. The ridge begins at the crown and ends at the front hairline. In order to form the second ridge, you draw the comb back from the hairline.

1. Place your left middle finger immediately above and your left index finger below the first ridge and hold it firmly.

2. Insert the teeth of the comb into the hair directly below your left index finger.

3. In order to form the second ridge, comb downward in a semicircular counterclockwise motion and direct the hair approximately 1 inch (2.54 cm.).

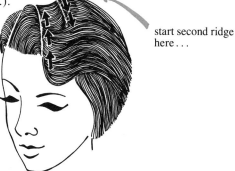

start second ridge
here . . .

4. Continue by following steps 5, 6 and 7 of the procedure for the first ridge. Direct the hair in the opposite way until the front hairline is reached. This completes the second ridge.

The third and subsequent ridges: Movements for the third ridge are the same as those used for the first ridge. The third ridge is formed from the hairline to the back of the head. Continue the ridges by alternating the direction until the left side of the head has been completed. Follow the same procedure when fingerwaving the right side of the head.

the style
determines
the shaping . . .

Unit 6
Joining the fingerwaves

Waves are blended and joined at the crown and in the back area of the head. In order to match and join the two semiwaves from opposite sides of the head, use this procedure:

1. Fade out the first ridge on the left side of the head at the crown. Fading out consists of flattening the crown of the ridge by shaping the hair toward the ridge but not raising it.

2. The first ridge on the right side of the head will join the second ridge on the left side of the head.

3. Lengthen the first ridge on the right side of the head. Match and join it to the second ridge on the left side of the head.

4. Continue until all the waves are blended and all the ridges are connected at the back of the head.

When there are more waves on one side of the head than on the other, it is called an asymmetrical line. It is created by discontinuing or dropping a wave instead of carrying it all around the head.

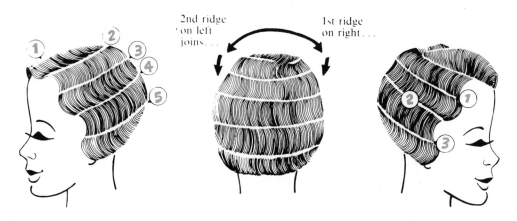

2nd ridge on left joins... 1st ridge on right...

Unit 6
Joining the fingerwaves

General objectives-student goals: After study, instruction, practice and completion of this unit, you will be able to show understanding of joining the fingerwaves by demonstrating the technique and procedure for joining waves at the back area of the head. You must have the proper implements and supplies in order to complete this unit successfully.

Hairstyling

Completing the fingerwave

General objectives-student goals:

After study, instruction, practice and completion of this unit, you will be able to show understanding of the procedure and technique for completing a fingerwave by demonstrating the technique for completing a fingerwave on medium length hair and by writing or giving a brief description of the procedure for long and short hair and the procedure to follow after completing the fingerwave. You must have the proper implements and supplies in order to complete this unit successfully.

Unit 8

Pin curls

General objectives-student goals:

After study, instruction and completion of this unit, you will be able to demonstrate understanding of pin curls by writing and/or giving a brief overview of the components to be considered when making pin curls and by listing six types of pin curls.

Hairstyling

Unit 7

Completing the fingerwave

1. **Long hair:** The entire head is fingerwaved, and the long ends are combed into a **chignon** at the back of the head.

2. **Medium length hair:** The completed fingerwave is finished with **pin curls** at the nape. These are combed into a soft casu effect when the hair dries.

3. **Short hair:** The entire head is fingerwaved. The short hair over the ears and at the nape is **pin curled** in the same directi as the wave would be if the hair were long enough.

Procedure after completing the fingerwave

1. Place a hair net over the hair.

2. Protect the patron's ears from the heat and air blowing from the hair dryer.

3. Place the patron under the dryer and allow the hair to dry.

4. Remove the hair net and any pins from the hair.

5. Comb through the hair and retrace the waves.

Unit 8

Pin curls

A pin curl, also known as a **sculpture curl** or **ringlet**, is a strand of hair wound into a series of circles so that it forms a coil. Pins or clips hold the coil in place. When carefully executed in exact patterns, pin curls will open into smart lines of waves and/o curls. There are six kinds of pin curls:

1. Flat pin curls
2. Lift curls
3. Stand-up curls
4. Overlapping curls
5. Carved curls
6. Ridge curls

There are many correct ways to make a pin curl. The methods and techniques in this chapter were developed so that students in basic training will obtain the best results. They have a built-in exercise which helps develop the hand, finger and fingertip dexterity required for expertise in setting hair. Once the student has developed this skill, he or she is free to use any other professional method. It should be noted, however, that most cosmetologists continue to use the methods and techniques in this chapter after they have become accomplished hairstylists.

Pin curl components

The components to be considered when making a pin curl include the:

1. Panel
2. Shaping
3. Base
4. Stem
5. Circle

 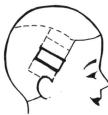 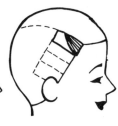  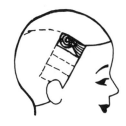

PANEL   BASE   STEM   CIRCLE   COMPLETE TOP PANEL

The average panel is a section of hair about 1 – 1½ inches (2.54 – 3.81 cm.) wide. It is made vertically or horizontally in the area where the pin curls are to be made. The base is made in the panel, and the finished curl is fastened in the base. The size of the panel determines the size of both the base and the curl. Hairstyle, hair texture and length of hair are also factors that determine the size of the base and curl. A casual hairstyle, long hair and thick texture dictate a larger base area per curl whereas fine short hair, styled tight and curly, requires a smaller base area.

The shaping is an area of hair, the size of which will vary depending upon where on the head it is being made and how the hair it contains will be used in the finished hairstyle. It may be formed vertically, diagonally, horizontally, smooth or with a ridge. When curls are made in a shaping, special care must be taken not to disturb the hair in the shaping. Curls made in a shaping are carved out usually on a "C" or arc base.

The curl itself consists of three parts:

The base is the foundation of the curl. It is the area at the scalp where the pin curl is secured.

The stem is approximately the first ¼ inch (0.64 cm.) of hair nearest the base. The direction of the stem indicates the direction in which the hair will be combed.

The circle is the wound part of the strand. The size of the circle controls the width of the wave and the tightness of the curl.

the style determines the shaping . . .

Hairstyling

Unit 9

Pin curl bases

General objectives-student goals:
After study, instruction and completion of this unit, you will be able to demonstrate understanding of pin curl bases by identifying, writing and/or giving a brief description of the four pin curl foundation bases outlined in this unit.

Unit 9
Pin curl bases

There are four pin curl foundations:

1. The square base is used over the entire head except when any of the other three bases are substituted because of the specific purposes which they serve. Square bases are to be of equal size and may or may not be staggered in a formation similar to that of a staggered brick pattern.

2. The triangle or pyramid base is used along the top front hairline to minimize breaks or splits in the finished hairstyle. The triangle allows part of the base hair from each curl to overlap the next curl and comb into a uniform line without splits. The apex of the bases are in alternating directions.

3. The slanted oblong base is used along the front sides of the hairline. Its purpose is to minimize breaks or splits in this area. Here, too, the overlapping action assures a uniform line.

4. The "C" or arc base is used at the top, back or side of the head and is generally made with a shaping. This base places the curl in line with the direction in which the hair is to be styled and helps the hair comb into place with the least effort.

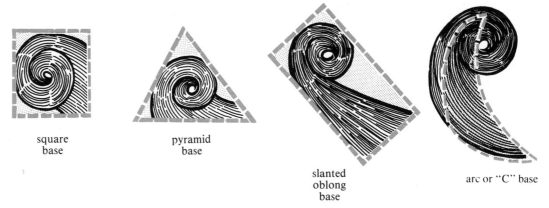

square base

pyramid base

slanted oblong base

arc or "C" base

Unit 10

Curl stem directions

General objectives-student goals:
After study, instruction and completion of this unit, you will be able

Unit 10
Curl stem directions

The number of ways in which stem direction changes the effect of a curl is infinite. The stem direction may be toward the front or back, up, down or outward. The lines of the finished hairstyle determine the stem direction. For example, if the finished hairstyle is to be combed toward the face, the stem direction should be toward the face.

Three basic stems that determine the degree of mobility of a curl are:

1. **Full stem curl:** This does not lie on its base and serves only to give direction and body to the hair. This curl has the greatest mobility.

2. **Half stem curl:** This lies half on and half off its base but retains reasonable strength and mobility.

3. **No stem:** This is the firmest and longest lasting curl. It has the least mobility.

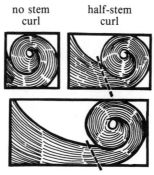

no stem curl   half-stem curl

full stem curl

Unit 11
Pin curl directions

There are basically only two pin curl directions:

1. **Counterclockwise curls**

2. **Clockwise curls**

 OR

CLOCKWISE CURL   COUNTERCLOCKWISE CURL

Pin curls are best described by referring to specific combinations of stem and winding directions. They may be combed into waves, curls, sleek smooth hairstyles or fluffy full-bodied effects.

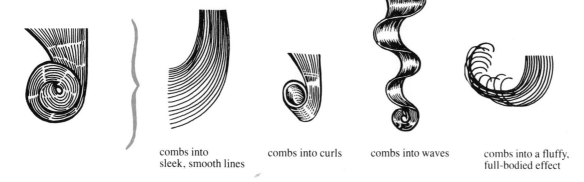

combs into sleek, smooth lines   combs into curls   combs into waves   combs into a fluffy, full-bodied effect

There are two ways of making pin curls: those that are made in a panel and those made in a shaping.

Curls are described as curling toward the face, away from the face, forward, backward, reverse, upward or downward. These terms can be interpreted differently by students, cosmetologists and educators. Unless there is uniform interpretation of these words, any curl can be interpreted as forward, backward, reverse, toward the face, away from the face, upward or downward.

to demonstrate understanding of stem directions and curl mobility by identifying, writing and/or giving a brief description of stem directions and the three basic stems which determine the degree of mobility of a curl as outlined in this unit.

Unit 11
Pin curl directions

General objectives-student goals: After study, instruction, and completion of this unit, you will be able to demonstrate further understanding of stem directions and clockwise and counterclockwise pin curls by writing and/or giving a brief overview of the two directions of pin curls outlined in this unit.

Hairstyling

In order to avoid confusion and to understand what is expected, it is best to describe the construction of a pin curl in an exact manner. Refer to the hourly numbers on the face of a clock for the direction of the stem and to the words clockwise and counterclockwise for the direction of the curl.

The principle of making a pin curl is always the same but the technique will vary.

Unit 12
Securing pin curls

The technique for securing a pin curl is important. Professional methods secure pin curls firmly in a single motion. The technique must be practiced before it can be mastered. There are many professional methods of securing pin curls. All of them, however, have one thing in common: the curl clips are inserted so that, with the one motion, they secure each pin curl for the entire setting and drying period.

Although all curl clips should be inserted in one continuous direction, it is essential that common sense be used so that the direction and position of a curl clip does not interfere with the surrounding work areas and with the formation of other pin curls.

Procedure

1. Hold the curl clip between your thumb and index finger with the top of the clip under your thumb.

2. Press down on the top of the clip. This will open the clip.

3. Insert the lower prongs at the base of the pin curl with the upper prongs over the pin curl.

4. Release your thumb.

one continuous direction wherever possible . . .

there are many professional methods for securing pin curls . . .

avoid touching the skin . .

The size of the curl clips should be determined by the size of the pin curl. Do not permit the curl clips to touch the patron's ears, face or skin. Failure to take this precaution may cause the patron to experience discomfort during the drying process because the curl clip will absorb heat. If the style line setting requires one or more curl clips to come in contact with the ears, face or neck, place absorbent cotton under the part of the curl clip that comes into contact with the skin. This is an important protective measure. It must be observed in order to prevent skin burns caused by heated curl clip metal.

General objectives-student goals:
After study, instruction, practice and completion of this unit, you will be able to show understanding of securing pin curls by describing and demonstrating the technique. You must have the proper implements and supplies in order to complete this unit successfully.

Hairstyling

Unit 13
Shapings for pin curl settings

Combing and molding wet hair flat and close to the head and in the direction you want it to go is known as shaping. Shapings can be molded and combed in either a clockwise or counterclockwise direction and in a vertical or horizontal position. A shaping has an open end and a closed end. The open end of the shaping is concave; the closed end is convex. The direction of a shaping can start at either end of the shaping depending on the natural growth pattern of the hair. Start with the direction of the hair growth. If the position of the shaping is in the same direction as the hair growth, begin with the open end. If the position of the shaping is contrary to the growth pattern of the hair, begin the shaping at the closed end.

Shapings combined with overlapped carved curls develop smooth, beautiful, curved lines and waves. You can use a combination of shapings and carved curls on the top, sides and back of the head in an effective manner. Combinations are developed by directing the hair into a style line and inserting a carved curl pattern into the shaping. It is important, however, not to disturb the shaping while placing curls into it or when securing the curl with the curl clip.

The technique used to make this pin curl varies according to:

1. The type of shaping which precedes the pin curl

   A. Smooth

   B. With a ridge

2. The side of the head on which you are working

3. The direction and movement of the shaping and the curl, i.e., clockwise or counterclockwise

The technique for making a shaping is as follows:

1. Wet the hair thoroughly.

2. Use the fine teeth of the comb to mold the hair flat, close to the head and into the desired curved or swirled shaping or into a shaping with a ridge.

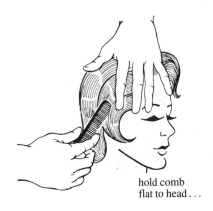
hold comb
flat to head . . .

Unit 14
Carved curls

Carved curls are formed in a shaping. Each hair strand is sliced out from the open end of a shaping in a "C" formation. You must not disturb the shaping. The technique for making a carved curl is as follows:

Unit 13
Shapings for pin curl settings

General objectives-student goals: After study, instruction, practice and completion of this unit, you will be able to show understanding of shapings for pin curl settings by writing or giving a brief description of shapings for pin curl settings and by demonstrating the technique for making a shaping. You must have the proper implements and supplies in order to complete this unit successfully.

Unit 14
Carved curls

General objectives-student goals: After study, instruction, practice and completion of this unit, you will

Hairstyling

103

be able to show understanding of carved curls by giving a brief description of carved curls and by demonstrating the technique. You must have the proper implements and supplies in order to complete this unit successfully.

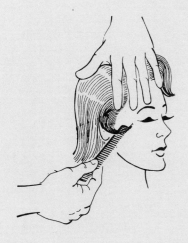

slice strand
in a "C" shape...

1. To make a counterclockwise curl in a shaping on the right side of the head, first make a shaping to conform with the style. With the back of your left hand facing you, place the tip of your index finger in the shaping.

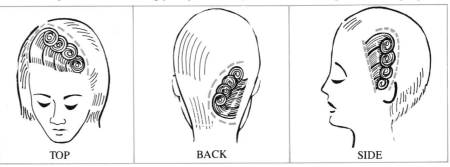

TOP   BACK   SIDE

SHAPING

2. Hold the comb flat to the head with the tips of the first two teeth of the comb at the point where you want to start the curl. This will vary depending on the size of the curl to be made. Use the utmost care and slice a strand of hair carefully. Do not disturb the shaping.

3. Slice the strand by inserting the teeth of the comb to the scalp. Then, carefully draw the comb to the end of the hair strand. Separate it from the rest of the shaping.

4. Lift the strand from the top of the comb with the index finger and thumb of your left hand. Carefully reinsert the comb into the hair from underneath the strand.

use this technique
when forming additional curls...

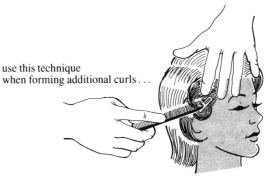

5. Place your thumb on top of the strand on the comb so that the hair is held between the comb and your thumb. This permits complete control over the strand.

6. As you hold the position of the comb and the thumb of your right hand, place the index finger of your left hand — with the palm toward the head — flat in the shaping with the tip of the finger holding the stem of the curl firmly to the head while ribboning.

ribbon the hair
in a circular
motion...

7. To ribbon, draw the comb through the hair in a circular motion in the same direction as the shaping until you reach the end of the strand. Do not let the hair ends slip out of the comb. Ribboning causes the hair to comb smoothly and wind flatly. More than one ribboning action may be necessary on each strand.

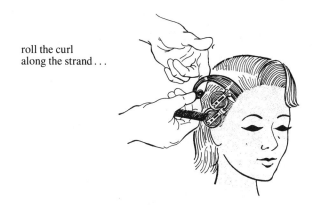

roll the curl
along the strand...

8. Move your index finger from the scalp and grasp the strand of hair approximately 1 inch (2.54 cm.) from the hair ends with your index finger and thumb.

9. Let the ends of the hair off the comb. Comb them smooth. Make a small loop at the end of the strand with the thumb and index finger of your right hand.

10. Form the proper starting diameter for the curl. Keep the hair ends in the inner side of the curl. Roll the curl along the strand toward the scalp.

11. Pin or clip the curl securely.

12. Supporting rows of curls, i.e., those not in the shaping, are formed with any appropriate base.

Hairstyling

13. All carved curls overlap each other. It does not matter if they are in the shaping or are supporting curls. Overlapping curls are pin curls in which a small portion of each curl is placed on top of a small portion of the curl before it.

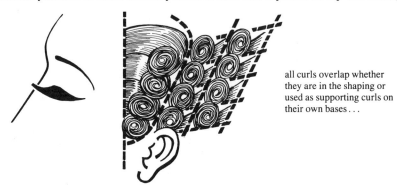

all curls overlap whether they are in the shaping or used as supporting curls on their own bases . . .

When shaping without a ridge for a waved line either at the sides or the top of the head, the first row of carved curls closest to the face is made using a forward curl direction. Start the first curl at the front hairline at the bottom of the shaping.

Successive curls are made by working toward the top of the shaping and overlapping each curl. The second row, which is composed of directional carved curls, is curled in the opposite direction and started behind the last curl made in the shaping.

When shaping for a swirl effect at either the sides or the back, the next row of carved curls is made immediately after the molded line. These carved curls will have the same direction as the first row. All supporting rows of forward curls are carved with a "C" base.

Unit 15
Pin curls in a panel

Pin curls in a panel are construction curls. They are not carved from a shaping. They are made with a greater degree of tension within a panel and curl base in order to provide a foundation for making a tighter and longer lasting curl. Pin curls within a shaping, however, result in softer style lines. The skills necessary for making pin curls in a panel are also excellent exercises for developing the hand, finger and fingertip dexterity required for all techniques practiced in the field of cosmetology.

The counterclockwise curl (left side of the head)

1. Use the tip of the comb to make a panel about 1 inch (2.54 cm.) wide.

2. Subsection the panel and make a square base.

3. Place the teeth of the comb in the hair strand and draw it straight out until the hair is perfectly smooth, evenly distributed and slightly stretched. Ribbon in line with the stem direction.

Unit 15

Pin curls in a panel

General objectives-student goals:
After study, instruction, practice and completion of this unit, you will be able to show understanding of pin curls in a panel by giving a brief description of pin curls in a panel and by demonstrating the technique. You must have the proper implements and supplies in order to complete this unit successfully.

Hairstyling

4. Shift the comb to the palm of your hand and secure the hair between the thumb and index finger of your right hand.

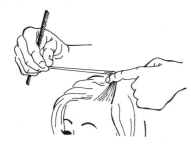

5. Curve the index finger of your left hand and place it on top of the hair strand, pointing downward toward the head. Wind the strand around your index finger and press the thumb of the same hand against the index finger in order to hold the hair in place.

6. Continue to wrap the hair around your index finger in a spiral motion toward the nail.

7. As each turn of the curl is made, place your thumb against your index finger until the entire strand is wound.

8. Using the index finger and thumb of your other hand, slide the curl from your finger and roll it to the patron's head.

9. The curl is now within the curve of its own stem. Hold it in place with the index finger and thumb of your left hand.

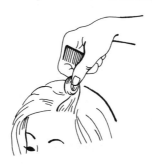

The Counterclockwise Curl
(left side of head)

Hairstyling

10. In order to tighten the curl to a circumference even smaller than the size of your finger, place the index finger of your right hand firmly into the curl's center and turn in the direction it was wound. Use a screwdriver action.

11. Secure the curl with a curl clip.

The clockwise curl (left side of the head)

1. When the panel, curl base and stem direction are completed, secure the hair between the thumb and index finger of your right hand.

2. Point the index finger of your left hand downward and hold it underneath the hair strand. Wind the strand around your finger and hold it in place by pressing your thumb against the hair on your index finger.

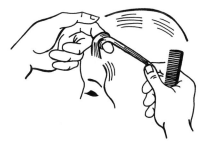

3. Continue to wind the hair around your index finger in a spiral motion toward the nail.

4. As each turn of the curl is made, place your thumb against the index finger until the entire strand is wound.

5. Slide the curl from your finger and roll it to the patron's head using the index finger and thumb of your other hand.

6. The curl is now within the curve of its own stem. Hold it in place with the index finger and thumb of your left hand.

7. In order to tighten the curl to a circumference even smaller than the size of your finger, place the index finger of your right hand firmly into the curl's center and turn in the direction it was wound. Use a screwdriver action.

8. Secure the curl with a curl clip.

The Clockwise Curl
(left side of head)

Unit 16
Stand-up curls

Stand-up curls are known as volume curls because they cause the hair to lift away from the head. The stem of each curl is raised away from the scalp. They are used with flat pin curls or hair rollers. They can also be used by themselves.

A stand-up curl is also called a cascade curl and a barrel curl. It is a pin curl secured in a standing position. It has a large center opening. The stand-up curl is usually recommended for the top section of the head. In a stand-up curl, the stem is directed straight out from the scalp. It may be wound either clockwise or counterclockwise depending on whether the top of the hairstyle will be combed toward or away from the face.

The stand-up curl is wound from the hair ends to the scalp. It gives height to the finished hairstyle through the use of pin curls instead of rollers.

Procedure for stand-up curls

1. Section the top of a head whose hair has been made wet with setting lotion or water.

2. Start at the back of the section furthest away from the front hairline and make a 1 inch (2.54 cm.) panel.

3. Start from a square base. Hold the strand with a straight up stem direction and comb it smooth.

4. Direct the strand clockwise or counterclockwise.

5. Use the conventional pin curl technique to wind the curl to the base.

6. Place the curl in a standing position on its base and secure it firmly.

Unit 17
Ridge curls

Stand-up Curls

Pin curls placed behind the ridge of a fingerwave are called ridge curls. They are formed following the same procedure used to make carved pin curls or curls in a shaping. They are wound in the direction of the shaping on the side of the ridge where they are being placed.

Ridge curls will add greater depth and softness to a fingerwave. The width of the wave is determined by the distance between a ridge and the row of pin curls following it. For a narrow wave, ridge curls should be placed as close to the ridge as possible.

Start to make ridge curls by following the same procedure used to make the first ridge of a fingerwave.

Unit 16
Stand-up curls

General objectives-student goals: After study, instruction, practice and completion of this unit, you will be able to show understanding of stand-up curls by giving a brief description of stand-up curls and by demonstrating the technique. You must have the proper implements and supplies in order to complete this unit successfully.

Note: The lift curls are in the same family of stand-up curls. They are secured at the base and stem of the inner side of the curl while the back and outer curved portion of the curl is free standing and slightly lifted away from its base. The lift curl is used to achieve added width and flair to a style. Unlike stand-up curls they can be overlapped within a ridge to provide flair and added width to a wave.

Unit 17
Ridge curls

General objectives-student goals: After study, instruction, practice and completion of this unit, you will

Hairstyling

be able to show understanding of ridge curls by giving a brief description of ridge curls and by demonstrating the technique for making ridge curls. You must have the proper implements and supplies in order to complete this unit successfully.

1. After completing the ridge, hold the middle finger of your left hand above the ridge and your index finger below the ridge.

2. Start at the end of the ridge and slide the tip of the comb slightly under the index finger close to the scalp. Lift a strand of hair up in the same direction as the shaping.

3. Peel your fingers away from ridge and the patron's head.

4. Make a pin curl following the procedure outlined earlier for making pin curls. Always be certain that the strand has ribbon-like smoothness.

5. Place the completed pin curl in position according to the width of the desired wave. Secure it with a curl clip.

6. Continue working your way along the ridge. Allow each curl to overlap the previously completed curl slightly.

start
pin curls
where you
finished ridge...

Unit 18
Skip waving

Unit 18
Skip waving

Skip waving is a combination of alternating fingerwaves and ridge curls. This technique is used to develop strong deep waves. Although it may be used anywhere on the head, it is generally used when wide, smooth, vertical waves are desired at the sides. The hair should not be longer than 4 inches (10.16 cm.).

The technique used to make a skip wave is the same as the technique for ridge curls with one exception. A row of pin curls may be set either below or behind the first ridge. Immediately behind this row of curls, form another fingerwave and behind its ridge, set another row of curls. The pin curls for skip waving are always started where the ridge was ended. They are always wound in the direction of the shaping on the side of the ridge where they are being placed.

skip wave

General objectives-student goals:
After study, instruction, practice and completion of this unit, you will be able to show understanding of skip waving by giving a brief description of skip waving and by demonstrating the technique and procedure for skip waving. You must have the proper implements and supplies in order to complete this unit successfully.

Hairstyling

110

The space base is an area of smooth shaping. It is used immediately behind a row of pin curls in order to develop a wider wave pattern. The space base allows the pin curls to open more fully into place. This permits the hair to drape rather than cramp into the wave line. The length of the space base is one and a half times the diameter of the pin curl set into the space base. It leaves an exposed base area of half the curl diameter after the curls are secured.

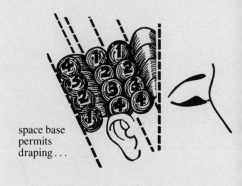

space base permits draping...

Unit 19
Roller curls

Unit 19
Roller curls

Setting hair with hair rollers is the most popular method of setting hair. Setting hair with hair rollers is less time-consuming than setting with pin curls. Hair rollers can be used to create volume (height and fullness) and indentation (closeness, valleys and hollowness).

General objectives-student goals: After study, instruction, practice and completion of this unit, you will be able to show understanding of roller curls by describing and/or listing a brief overview of the subject and by demonstrating the technique and procedure for roller setting. You must have the proper implements and supplies in order to complete this unit successfully.

It is important to place the roller on the appropriate side of the hair strand. Volume is created by rolling the hair around the roller so that the hair at the scalp area of the roller base rolls over what is considered the front part of the roller after it has been secured. With indentation, the hair is rolled so that the hair at the scalp area of the roller base is under what is considered the front part of the roller after it has been secured.

The roller base is a subsection parted off at the scalp. The size of the base is determined by the width and length of the hair roller. A hair roller which is rolled and secured entirely on its base will give maximum fullness and lift to the hair. A hair roller that is secured half off its base will create less fullness and lift than one which is secured entirely on its base. A roller that is secured entirely off the roller base gives the least amount of fullness and lift.

A roller curl is a broad curl formed by winding a wet strand of hair around a cylindrical object and securing it in position until dry.

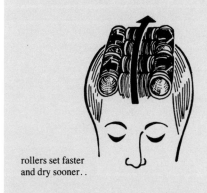

rollers set faster and dry sooner..

Rollers come in many shapes, sizes and compositions. There are several factors to consider when choosing a roller with the proper circumference. Remember the following guidelines:

1. For long hair, use a roller with a large circumference.

2. For a casual hairstyle, use a roller with a large circumference.

3. When a style is detailed with waves or ridges, use a roller with a smaller circumference.

4. When the hairstyle needs body, use a roller with a smaller circumference.

for long hair or casual hairstyles...

large

for average use...

medium

for waves, ridges, or when style needs body...

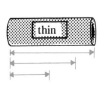

thin

Hairstyling

111

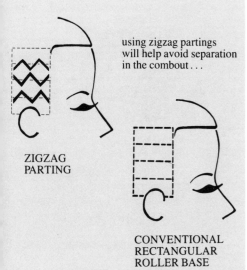

using zigzag partings will help avoid separation in the combout...

ZIGZAG PARTING

CONVENTIONAL RECTANGULAR ROLLER BASE

Complete control over the hair ends can be attained best by using end papers when winding hair around a roller. After practice, the use of end papers can be discontinued. A **rectangular curl base** is used with roller settings. The use of zigzag partings for the curl bases along the front hairline will help prevent separations during the combout. The size of the base is determined by the size of the roller. The larger the roller, the larger the base required. When the hair is wound, the roller is placed on its base and secured with a roller clip, curl clip, roller pin or bobby pin.

Roller setting technique: Depending on the hairstyle, roller curls may be placed anywhere on the head and at almost any angle.

1. Section a rectangular base wherever rollers are required for the style.

2. Hold the comb with your right hand and the hair with your left. Comb the strand upward.

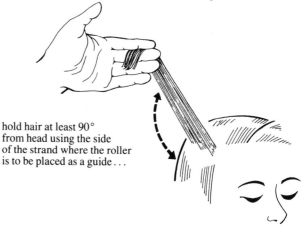

hold hair at least 90° from head using the side of the strand where the roller is to be placed as a guide...

3. Secure the strand between the index and middle fingers of your left hand. Use your right hand to fold the end paper over and under the strand. Slide the paper so that it extends at least $^1/_2$ inch (1.27 cm.) beyond the hair ends.

4. Hold the hair strand and the paper with your left hand and place the roller even with the end of the paper.

5. Place the index and middle fingers of your right hand behind the roller in order to hold the hair in place. Place your right thumb in front of the roller.

finger action helps control short hairs...

Hairstyling

112

6. Repeat step 5 with your left hand. Turn the roller alternately with the fingers of both your hands until the roller is placed on the base.

7. Fasten the roller securely on its base. Use a roller clip.

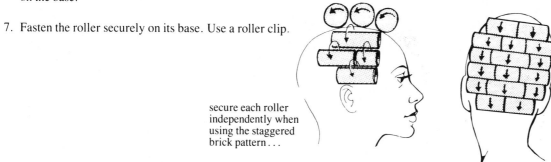

secure each roller independently when using the staggered brick pattern . . .

8. Repeat steps 1-7. Secure each additional roller to the previously secured roller in order to limit the degree of separation during the combout. This will minimize breaks or splits.

Unit 20
Curvature hairstyling

Curvature hairstyling is a method of hairstyling and design that creates an exciting look with an added dimension which is based on the fact that the hairstylist always works with a rounded object. All partings and sectioning should be in a curved form in order to blend better with the curvature of the head and the flow of the style.

INDENTATION

VOLUME

MOLD

MOVEMENT

3-DIMENSIONAL

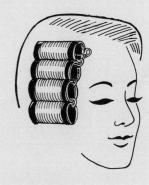

Unit 20
Curvature hairstyling

General objectives-student goals: After study, instruction and completion of this unit, you will be able to demonstrate understanding of curvature hairstyling by writing and/or giving a brief overview of the subject.

Hairstyling

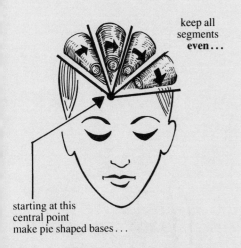

keep all segments **even...**

starting at this central point make pie shaped bases...

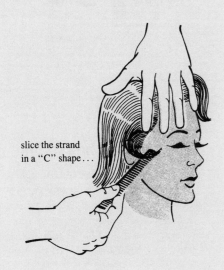

slice the strand in a "C" shape...

Hairstyling

114

In curvature hairstyling, partings usually start from a central point of the hair design in the area of the head involved (i.e., front, back or sides). This starting point is sometimes called the pivot point.

The styling may consist of a series of straight lines coming from the central point, curved lines from the central point blending into a half or full circle or curved lines of unequal length blending into an oval design. In addition, these straight or curved lines may also be designed into raised or depressed areas like hills and valleys in order to give an effect of fullness or depth.

curved lines from this central point blending into a half or full circle

unequal length curved lines starting from central point...

The stylist has a choice of implements and techniques for creating these curved or straight lines and for developing fullness or depth. Pin curls, rollers, thermal irons or a hot air curling comb may be used.

In curvature hairstyling, pin curls are usually formed from a shaping. Therefore, the base is usually "C" shaped. Its direction or flow of motion blends into the direction and motion of the finished style. Rollers may be placed on oblong or triangular (pie-shaped) bases according to the direction or flow of the motion of the finished style.

The stylist first molds the general shape or pattern of the desired style from the central point and sections off curved areas according to the particular effects desired and the implements which are used.

Maximum fullness with an airy volume may be obtained by using stand-up curls or rollers placed directly on their bases with the hair starting over the roller and rolling under. The degree of fullness can be varied by over or underdirecting the rollers and curls in relation to their base area. In order to achieve depth to a style line (depressed area), roll the hair up and over.

The general direction of the lines radiating from the starting point is usually designated by referring to a clock. The angles from the central point can be visualized by comparing them to the hands of a clock. The flow of the motion of the style is either clockwise or counterclockwise.

Since much of the subsectioning in roller curvature hairstyling is pie-shaped, a tapered roller, sometimes called a conoid or cone-shaped roller, is often used. This type of roller is smaller at one end than at the other.

Curvature styling is designed to accommodate defined hairstyles with a defined curve and controlled volume.

Unit 21
Conoid hair rollers

Conoid hair rollers are also known as cone-shaped or tapered rollers. They are available in assorted sizes. The size of the roller used is determined by the desired effect of the hairstyle and by the texture of the hair. Fine hair requires a thinner roller. The hair is set with curved (arched) panels and pie-shaped bases. The pivot point is always in the midsection of a semicircle. The curved panels have concave and convex sides. The concave side is always shorter than the convex side. Always secure the rollers on the concave side of the curved panel.

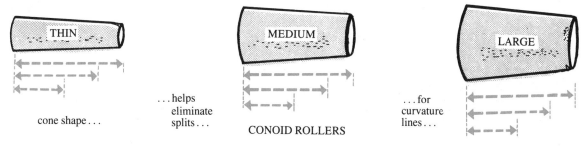

cone shape...   ...helps eliminate splits...   ...for curvature lines...

CONOID ROLLERS

Conoid rollers are placed in position with the narrow end towards the point of the pie-shaped bases and the concave side of a curved panel. Conoid rollers enable the stylist to use rollers closer to the central point and to develop stronger curved forces than is possible with cylindrical rollers.

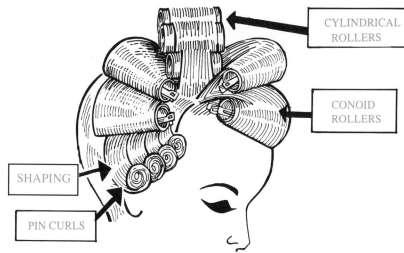

CYLINDRICAL ROLLERS

CONOID ROLLERS

SHAPING

PIN CURLS

Their cone-shaped design also helps to minimize splits and to make the curvature lines of the styles more fluid and smooth. They can be used in combination with conventional cylindrical rollers when necessary. You should maintain a controlled look with freedom and direction. The use of conoid rollers on hair that is too short will result in an uncontrolled look with a wild restless volume. Extra long hair may need to be accessorized in order to compensate for the extra length.

General objectives-student goals: After study, instruction and completion of this unit, you will be able to show understanding of conoid hair rollers by giving a brief description of conoid hair rollers and their use and by identifying the various sizes. You must have the proper implements and supplies in order to complete this unit successfully.

Hairstyling

Unit 22

Procedures for curvature styling with pin curls and hair rollers

Unit 22

Procedures for curvature styling with pin curls and hair rollers

General objectives-student goals:
After study, instruction, practice and completion of this unit, you will be able to show understanding of the procedures for curvature styling with pin curls and hair rollers by demonstrating both procedures. You must have the proper implements and supplies in order to complete this unit successfully.

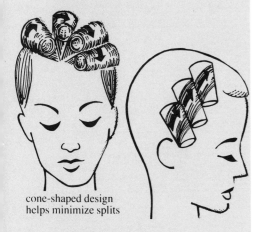

cone-shaped design helps minimize splits

Procedure for setting with pin curls

1. Mold or make a curved shaping in the area to be set.

2. Carve and lift a few strands of hair from within the shaping with the tip of your comb. Do not disturb the shaping.

3. Curl the strands into a pin curl and pin securely. All pin curls are carved overlapping curls within a shaping.

Procedure for setting with rollers

1. Section the area to be set using the necessary curved lines.

2. Shape or mold the section.

3. Determine the type of base to be used according to whether you are using a pie-shaped or oblong roller.

4. Place the roller on the appropriate side of the hair strand.

5. Turn the roller as you direct the hair strand slightly in the same direction as the point of the conoid roller and the concave side of the curved panel.

6. Roll the hair in the usual manner over or under for a raised or depressed effect, depending on the style.

7. Secure the roller firmly in position on the concave side of the curved panel.

When designing hairstyles with conventional lines, longer lasting styles may be obtained by alternating the position of the narrow ends of the conoid rollers. The hair may then be rolled in whatever direction the style requires.

When conditions call for it (depending on the hairstyle and the length of the hair), it is correct to combine cylindrical rollers, conoid rollers and pin curls in order to develop a desired hairstyle.

Unit 23

Combout

Unit 23

Combout

General objectives-student goals:
After study, instruction, practice and completion of this unit, you will

Hairstyling

The combout is an art in itself. The creative skills of a hairstylist are always demonstrated during the combout procedure. The art of hairdressing was originally practiced long before anyone knew how to set hair. The art of hairdressing was in the act of combing hair into a hairstyle. Continuous practice will develop this art.

116

Teasing the hair: Teasing, ratting, French lacing, back combing and ruffing are terms for matting hair. The resulting base or cushion creates a solid foundation for a lasting hairstyle. It also may be used to give exaggerated height to a hairstyle.

Teasing, ratting and **French lacing** are the same. The technique involves placing the fine teeth of the comb at the tips of a strand of hair and gently pushing down toward the scalp. This causes the hair to mat at the scalp. This method, however, is not very practical because it becomes difficult to remove the matting without breaking the hair.

teasing
pushing hair all the
way from the ends to
the scalp…

Back combing is the technique recommended for most hair. When hair is back combed, it is easy to unmat and recomb without damage. The hair remains undamaged because the matting action is directed from the scalp to the hair ends and not from the hair ends to the scalp.

Back combing and **ruffing** are basically the same. In ruffing, the hair brush is used instead of the comb to mat the hair. Ruffing is a great timesaver for matting long hair.

Procedure for back combing and ruffing

1. Section a strand of hair 2 inches by ¹/₂ inch (5.08 by 1.27 cm.).

2. Hold the strand of hair firmly between the middle and index fingers of your left hand. Keep it away from the rest of the hair.

3. Place the fine teeth of the comb in the strand of hair, a short distance from the scalp.

4. Push the hair firmly down toward the scalp. Work up the strands until they are matted against one another.

5. Repeat steps 3 and 4 on each strand until all the hair not needed for the final combing is matted.

6. The final combing is performed with a light raking action. Use either a comb, hair brush, cushion brush or a combination of comb and brush.

be able to demonstrate understanding of how to comb out hair into a style by demonstrating some of the techniques and the combout procedure. You must have the proper implements and supplies in order to complete this unit successfully.

back combing
pushing hair
from the scalp to
the hair ends…

pushing hair in short
sections working from
the scalp toward hair
ends using a
hair brush…

ruffing (back-brushing)

Hairstyling

117

starting here will
make hair comb
smoother and avoids
packing...

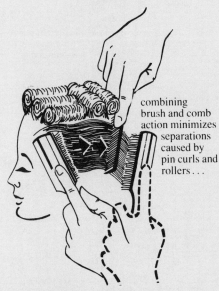

combining
brush and comb
action minimizes
separations
caused by
pin curls and
rollers...

Unit 24

Instant hair rollers
(hot rollers)

General objectives-student goals:

After study, instruction and comple-

Hairstyling

118

The brush and comb are the implements used for completing a hairstyle. The combout procedure is very important for achieving a smooth well-dressed hairstyle. Most hairstylists are judged or evaluated by their combouts. A good hairstylist will comb and brush a setting thoroughly before the final dressing in order to ensure a smooth and long lasting hairstyle.

Procedure for the combout. Let the hair dry after it is set. Remove rollers, clips and pins. Proceed as follows:

1. Start at the lower back of the head. Loosen all the curls row by row by combing through them.

2. Use a hand-over-hand motion and employ both the comb and brush in the direction in which the style is to be combed.

3. Hold the comb in your right hand. Relax or drape the hair into the desired style with the fingers of your left hand.

relaxing hair into
desired style before combing
makes sets last longer...

as a final touch,
smooth only the
wispy ends...

4. For a smooth finish at the ends, leave the hair fluffy. Smooth only the wispy ends.

Note: If the hair is to be teased or back combed, it should be done between steps 2 and 3.

Unit 24
Instant hair rollers (hot rollers)

Instant hair rollers are made from a hard plastic composite. They are designed to hold heat and put a curl into straight hair within a few minutes.

Instant rollers are recommended for setting wigs, wiglets, falls and all types of hairpieces as well as any human head of hair. They are used on hair that has not been wet. Instant rollers employ a dry process that leaves the hair soft and bouncy with a set that holds. They are extremely effective and gentle on hairpieces.

There is a little red dot on the top of each roller. Place the rollers on the heating posts for preheating. The red dot turns black when the roller is warm enough to use. There are three different roller sizes in a unit: small, medium and large. The pins that hold the rollers are in sizes too. It is important to use the correct size pin. The small foam pads are used if the roller or pin rests on the skin or scalp where it might cause the patron discomfort.

Procedure

1. Prepare the hair for setting. For best results, it should be thoroughly dry.

2. Open the lid of the preheat unit.

3. Plug the unit into an electric outlet.

small foam pad

4. When the little red dots turn black, the rollers are preheated and ready for use.

5. As a safety precaution, turn off or unplug the unit until it is needed again.

6. Set the hair with the preheated rollers in the same manner as you would with conventional hair rollers.

7. Secure the roller by placing the proper size pin lengthwise.

8. Use a small foam pad where the roller rests on the skin or scalp since this might cause the patron discomfort.

9. By the time the last roller is in, the first roller is usually ready for removal. For maximum curl strength, the hair should be left on the roller until the dot turns red again. Do not pull the rollers out. Unwind them.

10. Let the hair cool. Then, comb it into style.

Unit 25
Thermal roller curling

Thermal roller curling irons come in many different types and with different circumferences. Some roller curling irons may have adapters which change their circumference. Others have perforations for steaming oils back into the hair with vapors. Some irons are designed for heating by means of gas flames or small electric heaters. On these irons, it is possible to maintain pressure between the shell and the rod. Others have a built-in heating element and operate from an electric outlet. On these irons, the hair fits freely between the blade and the barrel. Pressure cannot be applied to the hair. The roller iron with the built-in heating element is lightweight and thermostatically controlled to maintain constant heat throughout the setting process. Some irons have a low, medium and high heat control. The heat control becomes important when setting bleached, dry or abused hair because they require mild heat.

The roller iron saves time for both the stylist and patron. Once the entire head is set, the hair is ready for combing into style. Controlled mild heat makes the hair more supple, gives it body and allows it to be shaped into any hairstyle.

Procedure

1. Shampoo the hair.

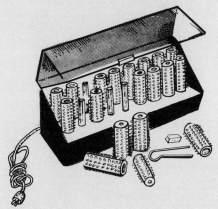

tion of this unit, you will demonstrate understanding of instant hair rollers by writing and/or giving a brief overview of the subject.

Unit 25
Thermal roller curling

General objectives-student goals: After study, instruction, practice and completion of this unit, you will be able to show understanding of thermal roller curling by giving a brief description of thermal roller curling and by demonstrating the technique and procedure. You must have the proper implements and supplies in order to complete this unit successfully.

Hairstyling

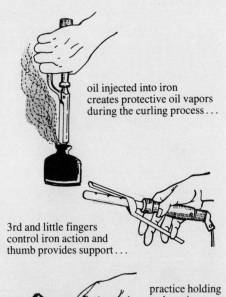

oil injected into iron creates protective oil vapors during the curling process...

3rd and little fingers control iron action and thumb provides support...

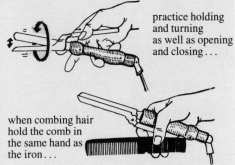

practice holding and turning as well as opening and closing...

when combing hair hold the comb in the same hand as the iron...

2. Apply cream or styling lotion in order to eliminate static electricity. All hair has a natural negative charge. This can be eliminated with a styling cream or lotion containing neutralizing positive molecules.

3. Dry the patron's hair. While the hair is drying, heat the roller curling iron.

4. Use the same type of sectioning and subsectioning as in roller setting.

5. Subsection one strand of hair and comb smoothly. Hold the strand of hair at an angle of at least 90 degrees from the head.

6. Hold the strand and the comb in your left hand. Place the barrel of the thermal iron $1^{1}/_{2}$ inches (3.81 cm.) from the scalp so that the strand of hair is between the barrel and the curved blade.

7. Hold the strand of hair in your left hand and rotate the iron a half turn.

8. Open the curved blade and wind the strand one complete turn around the barrel of the iron.

9. Close the iron.

10. Rotate the iron half a turn until the curved blade is close to the scalp. Direct the strand being held in the same direction as the rotation of the iron.

11. Open the curved blade.

12. Wind one more turn of the strand around the barrel.

all hair must be wound on barrel

13. Close the curved blade.

14. Rotate a fraction of a turn in order to bring the curl closer to the scalp.

15. Hold this position for a few seconds.

...only the barrel has heat with which to form curl...

16. Rotate back to the position with the curved blade down.

17. Open the curved blade and repeat steps 12—16 until the strand is completely wound. Rotate while opening and closing the curved blade until the hair ends are between the curved blade and the barrel.

18. Roll the curl to the scalp. Protect the scalp from the hot iron by placing a comb on the scalp underneath the iron and curl. Hold this position long enough to develop a firm curl.

19. Slide the comb through beneath the iron. Open the curved blade and direct the curl off the barrel with the large teeth of the comb. Withdraw the hot iron at the same time.

20. Continue the same procedure (steps 12—19) on all strands until the entire head is curled.

21. After the last curl has cooled, comb and brush the hair.

place comb
under iron to
protect scalp…

Unit 26
Thermal croquignole curling

Thermal curling is a popular method of setting hair that has been pressed. It is also used as a foundation setting for all types of hair. It eliminates working with wet hair, the use of hair rollers and drying hair after it is set.

When thermal curling is done properly, the foundation can be used for brushing and combing the hair into any hairstyle. There are two methods of thermal curling:

1. Thermal roller curling

2. Thermal croquignole curling

Thermal croquignole curling makes a stronger foundation than thermal roller curling. It also requires more skill. Croquignole curling is recommended for hairstyles with a soft, casual or draped effect.

Thermal curling irons come in many thicknesses. They are made of either blue or white steel. They hold heat evenly. Irons are available with revolving handles or insulated stationary handles. The thickness of the prongs varies from very thin to large, bouffant and extra large. The extra large iron has a $1\frac{1}{4}$ inch (3.18 cm.) diameter and is called a directional iron.

Procedure for thermal croquignole curling

1. Shampoo the hair and dry it under a dryer.

2. Press the hair if required.

3. Apply a small amount of cream or oil to the hair.

4. Heat the irons to the correct temperature.

5. Comb the hair smooth and part it on the right side.

NOTE: Bob curling is a technique for setting short hair with a thermal curling iron. The bob curl requires only that you slide the iron down the hair strand to the ends, guide the ends of the strand into the center of the thermal iron, and form the curl by rotating the curl toward the scalp.

Unit 26
Thermal croquignole curling

General objectives-student goals: After study, instruction, practice and completion of this unit, you will be able to show understanding of thermal croquignole curling by giving a brief description of croquignole curling and by demonstrating the technique and procedure. You must have the proper implements and supplies in order to complete this unit successfully.

Hairstyling

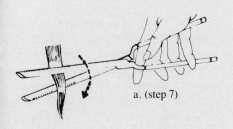

a. (step 7)

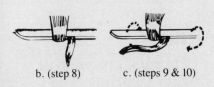

b. (step 8)   c. (steps 9 & 10)

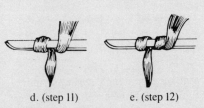

d. (step 11)   e. (step 12)

THERMAL CROQUIGNOLE CURLING

Unit 27
Blow dry styling

General objectives-student goals:
After study, instruction, practice and completion of this unit, you will be able to show understanding of blow dry styling by giving a brief description of blow dry styling and by demonstrating the technique and procedure. You must have the proper implements and supplies in order to complete this unit successfully.

Hairstyling

6. Start at the front hairline below the part on the patron's right side. Part off an oblong hair strand 3/4 inch (1.90 cm.) wide by 1½ inches (3.81 cm.) long.

7. Hold the hair strand with the thumb and index finger of your left hand. When the iron is heated to the correct temperature, insert it with the shell on the top about 1 inch (2.54 cm.) from the scalp. The points should face away from the patron's face.

8. Hold the iron firmly and roll it under one complete turn. The technique of clicking the iron constantly during the operation permits the hair to glide easily over the iron.

9. Draw the end of the hair strand toward the points of the iron with your left hand.

10. Loop the strand underneath the tip of the iron. Hold the iron tightly and direct it slightly forward toward the face.

11. By directing the iron forward and pulling the hair with your left hand, two loops are formed around the iron with the ends of the strand between the loops.

12. Roll and click the iron under until the hair ends disappear and the iron rolls freely within the hair.

13. Roll the curl to the scalp. Protect the scalp from the hot iron by placing a comb on the scalp below the iron and curl. Hold the curl on the iron and allow heat to penetrate into it.

14. Slide the comb from beneath the iron and direct the curl off the iron using the large teeth of a comb. At the same time, draw the hot iron out.

15. Perform the same procedure on all strands until the entire head is curled.

16. Comb and brush the hair into the desired style.

Unit 27
Blow dry styling

There are various hairstyling techniques which eliminate having to set the hair. These methods are often called quick service salon techniques. Quick service techniques include blow styling, lamp cutting and styling, air waving, thermal roller curling and instant roller curling. These salon techniques result in a carefree natural look and create a total look, such as is achieved when the hair is set with rollers and pin curls.

Blow dry styling is a technique of styling and drying wet hair in a single process. This technique was used by barbers when cutting women's hair during the late 1920s and early 1930s. During that period, it was known as physiognomical haircutting: the art of cutting and styling hair to the individual in a single process. Today, an identical technique is used for men and women. It is often called unisex styling or blow dry styling.

Blow drying is a skill that every cosmetologist should know and use. Once the basic techniques for creating waves and curls, and molding and shaping the hair with combs, brushes, blowers or any other type of hand dryer have been mastered, the cosmetologist will have the expertise needed for the quick service patrons.

The use of cushion-backed, heat resistant nylon bristle, thermo and natural bristle, plastic bristle and air flow brushes as well as metal combs is very effective for blow dry styling. Metal instruments and implements hold heat longer and concentrate the heat where you want it. The technique is the same for both male and female hairstyling.

The length of the hair and the desired hairstyle are the factors which determine the type and size of the hair brushes and combs used during the blow dry styling process.

Blow dry styling, when combined with a good haircut, will result in a natural, carefree, fluid style line. It is easy for the patron to care for and manage until the next visit to the professional stylist. For the male, it eliminates the flat, close to the head hair comb. Blow drying has given men a natural looking hairstyle. For the female, blow drying does away with the stiff overteased hairdo.

Blow dry styling is skillfully contoured to the shape of the head and does not rely on the conventional hair set to give the hairstyle shape and form. Use the variable temperatures of the blow dryer. Hot air is for forced drying: to remove excess water and moisture from the hair. Warm air dries and styles. Cool air finishes and adds lasting power to the hairstyle.

Methodology

1. Use a large diameter round bristle brush to force dry the hair. Remove the excess moisture using hot air before you begin to form the style.

apply hot air to remove excess moisture…

2. Use the same small partings and subsections used when you cut the hair.

3. Determine the final hair direction of the finished style.

4. Use a large, medium or small round bristle brush to blow dry the hair into a style. The style and length of the hair determine the size of the brush. As a rule, short hair is styled with a small diameter brush. For long hair, best results are obtained with a large diameter brush.

styled without being set

Hairstyling

123

you can hold it
by the barrel . . .

5. Place the round bristle brush in the same position you would use if you were setting the style with hair rollers.

6. Fine limp hair should be given additional cooling time with the brush in position. Alternatively, each section should be allowed to remain in its roller form until the hair is cool. Then, comb and brush it into the finished style.

The blow dryer uses electrically heated air to dry the hair. Most professional hand model hair dryers have from two to four heat settings. Some have two speeds. The high setting is between 900 and 2000 watts. The higher watt rated appliances will produce hotter air. The styling dryer may be held by the handle or the barrel. Both techniques are professional. As a rule, the dryer is held in the left hand, and the brush or comb is held in the right hand unless the cosmetologist is left-handed. Some cosmetologists have the skill to use either hand to operate the blow dryer while others transfer their tools to opposite hands when they move from one side of the head to the other.

Round hair brushes are used in conjunction with or in place of a conventional professional styling comb. The hair is brushed and directed at the same time it is being blown dry. When used in this way, the round brush creates volume and provides complete control of the hair while it is blow styled. Round brushes are available in many different circumferences. A round styling brush with a large diameter will increase the volume of the style. Round brushes with small diameters are used when less volume is desired.

The art of blow dry styling

The procedure and technique for using the blow styling dryer is very basic.

1. Drape the patron.

2. Shampoo the hair. Use a low pH, acid balanced shampoo.

3. Remove excess wetness by blotting with a towel.

4. Apply blow dry lotion and/or conditioner to the hair.

5. Comb the hair in the general direction of the desired hairstyle.

6. Connect the blower to an outlet.

7. Select the speed and/or desired heat control.

8. Begin by blow drying most of the excess water and moisture out of the hair. Use the high speed for forced drying. This is done by holding sections of hair out and away from the scalp with your comb or a large diameter hair brush so that the hair near the scalp may be dried by the hot air flow. Do not apply the flow directly to the scalp. This will create discomfort. Use the same small partings and subsections as when you cut the hair.

9. Next, apply the air flow to the mid-lengths and at the ends of the hair in order to remove excess moisture from the complete strand.

Hairstyling

124

10. Reduce the heat to medium. Determine the hair direction of the finished style.

11. Continue by brushing the damp hair into the style arrangement. Coordinate the use of the dryer and brush. The dryer always follows the movement and direction of the brush. Use a large, medium or small round bristle brush when blow drying the hair into style. The style and length of the hair determine the size of the brush. As a rule, short hair is styled with a small diameter brush. For long hair styling, the best results are obtained with a large diameter brush.

12. Place the round bristle brush in the same position you would use if you were setting the style with hair rollers.

13. The finishing steps of the style should be done with cool air. This will make it last longer. Fine limp hair should be given additional cooling time with the brush in position. Alternatively, each section should be allowed to remain in its roller form until the hair is cool. Then, comb and brush it into the finished style.

Tips and suggestions to improve blower styling

1. Always pick up wet hair with some dry hair as the warm air is applied.

2. For layered hair (graduated lengths), brush the hair forward and around the head to encourage volume. You must, however, do this quickly since you start brushing into the style line before the ends of the hair become dry.

3. The degree of root lift near the scalp is determined by the angle at which you hold the brush while the hair nearest to the scalp is blown dry.

4. To curve the ends, keep revolving the brush as you dry the hair.

5. The side hair is rolled back to give fullness and an away from the face look.

6. In order to achieve maximum volume, the hair at the back of the head is held outward while being rolled under.

7. The hair behind the ears is held forward while blow drying in order to blend it better with the nape area.

8. When blow styling begins at the nape area, a small brush is used to cup the hair up or under. You will find this cupping technique very easy if the hair has been cut well. Each additional section is then brought down and cupped up or under with a larger brush.

9. To puff the crown area, comb or brush the hair at the crown forward. Lift up with a comb or brush and direct medium air at the base. Then, direct it over the top of the comb. Lifting each section of hair at the crown with the comb will give you the maximum amount of height (volume).

10. If the patron has bangs, the bang hair is blown back, up and to the side with a small round brush before shaping it into the desired style of bang.

11. Always hold a round brush in the same position as you would a hair roller. The different diameters of brushes produce different degrees of curl and form depending on the length of the hair.

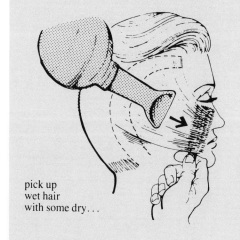

pick up
wet hair
with some dry. . .

Hairstyling

125

12. Large quantities of hair around the brush can produce poor results. In addition, each section will take longer to dry.

13. Resistant hair should be very moist.

14. In order to make a style last longer, finish it with cool air.

15. Never apply the hot air flow directly to the scalp because it will be too hot and may cause discomfort.

Unit 28
Air waving

Air waving with the hot air comb was introduced in the United States about 1950. It is a technique of drying and styling the hair in a single process. The hot air curl comb is an electric hair dryer. It is small enough to be held in one hand and has a special head to receive attachments. Most models can be fitted with several attachments. The most popular are the:

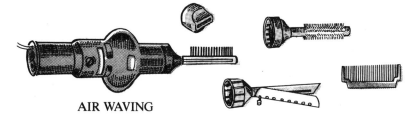

AIR WAVING

1. Coarse tooth comb

2. Roller iron

3. Curling (round) brush

4. Nozzle

The coarse tooth comb is used to mold, shape and curl the hair into the desired hairstyle. The fine tooth comb is used for teasing or back combing. The round brush smooths and finishes the hairstyle. The nozzle is for pin-point drying. The roller iron is for hair that is difficult to curve or curl while drying. Use the following procedure:

1. Shampoo the hair and towel dry.

2. Apply cream or lotion.

3. Attach the coarse tooth comb.

4. Start at the top of the head. Lift a small amount of hair and place it on the hot air comb. Turn it under.

5. Use your left hand as a guide and dry the entire head into style by lifting small amounts of hair and placing them on the hot air comb. Turn and hold each strand under for a few seconds. Repeat this procedure several times until the hair is thoroughly dry.

6. For the patron's comfort, change the position of the hot air comb on each strand frequently.

General objectives-student goals:
After study, instruction, practice and completion of this unit, you will be able to display understanding of air waving by giving a brief description of air waving and by demonstrating the procedure. You must have the proper implements and supplies in order to complete this unit successfully.

Hairstyling

7. When the hair is completely dry, tease or back comb it as necessary. Use the fine tooth comb attachment on the hot air comb.

8. Smooth and finish the style with the round brush attachment. Use a conventional comb for the final touches.

Unit 29
Lamp sets

Lamp sets are ideal for men and women whose hair has a natural tendency to wave or who have naturally wavy or curly hair. It is the preferred way of styling this type of hair after a haircut. By placing the hair into the style and drying it with infrared lamps with reflectors, the hair is permitted to remain undisturbed while drying. It will maintain its natural direction.

Procedure

1. Drape the patron. Shampoo the hair and blot it to remove excess moisture.

2. Cut the hair to style if a haircut is required.

3. Apply conditioner if required.

4. Relax or blouse the hair so that you can observe cowlicks, where the hair parts naturally and the grain and growth of the hair.

5. Place the hair into a style pattern without using hair rollers or pin curls.

6. Secure waves, molded lines, shapings or feathered edges with hair pins.

7. Use heat lamps (infrared lamps). Adjust the lamp according to the thickness of the hair but never closer than 15 inches (38.10 cm.) to the head. A three lamp unit will give you faster drying and provide even heat distribution around the head.

8. Check frequently to see how the hair is drying.

9. Remove the lamps and hair pins.

10. Relax the lamp set pattern into a style line.

11. The hair may be back combed where necessary. Use only a fine mist of hair spray.

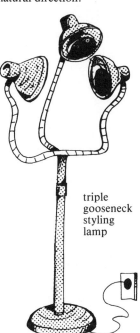

triple
gooseneck
styling
lamp

Unit 29
Lamp sets

General objectives-student goals:
After study, instruction, practice and completion of this unit, you will be able to display understanding of lamp sets by giving a brief description of lamp setting and by demonstrating the technique and procedure. You must have the proper implements and supplies in order to complete this unit successfully.

Hairstyling

Unit 30
Hairstyling to the individual

General objectives-student goals:
After study, instruction and completion of this unit, you will be able to demonstrate understanding of individual hairstyling by giving a brief overview of the subject and by identifying four facial structures, three profile shapes and three added observations.

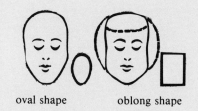

oval shape   oblong shape

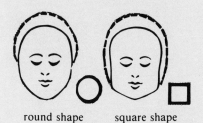

round shape   square shape

Hairstyling

Unit 30
Hairstyling to the individual

Hairstyling to the individual can be a complex art if a large number of unnecessary areas of consideration are the criteria for establishing a hairstyle design suitable for each patron. This unit simplifies the procedure by setting out the necessary considerations for styling hair to the individual:

1. Facial structure

2. Profile

3. Hairline

4. Neck shape

5. Stature

6. Hair texture

OPTICAL ILLUSION
makes one appear larger...

both lines are the same length...

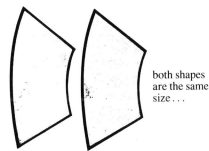

both shapes are the same size...

How well a hairstyle suits an individual is the ultimate test of its success. The stylist seeks to achieve perfect balance. This balance is achieved through optical illusion.

The perfect facial structure is oval. The perfect profile is straight. Therefore, the hairstylist seeks to combine hairstyle and profile in order to create the illusion of an oval face and a straight profile.

There are many facial types but upon close observation they fall into one of four categories:

1. Oval

2. Round

3. Square

4. Oblong (Rectangular)

Oval is the perfectly shaped face, and almost any hairstyle may be adapted to it.

Round and square facial shapes require similar style lines. Arranging the hair high on top of the head and close on the sides will help create an illusion of ovalness.

Oblong facial structures require a fringe or bangs. The hair should be styled with fullness on the sides and broad side-swept lines on top. There should be minimum height.

The straight profile is the ideal, and any line may be adapted. The concave profile requires that the hair be dressed close to the head with fullness at the nape and below the ears. A full bang over the forehead is also helpful. The convex profile requires light short bangs. The hair on the sides and at the nape should be styled close to the head.

Added observations

1. **Hairlines:** If the hairline recedes, style the hair close to the face. If the hairline is close to the face, style by combing away from the face.

2. **Long neck:** Avoid styling the hair up, short or close at the neck. Take the opposite approach for a short neck.

3. **Short stature:** Avoid long hair and flat hairstyles. Use the opposite for a tall stature.

4. **Hair texture:** Fine hair requires a hairstyle which creates an illusion of fullness and body. Coarse hair requires styling with curved lines which do not exaggerate the density of the hair.

A hairstylist should consider facial structure, profile and the added observations carefully when adapting modern hairstyles to the needs of the individual.

PROFILES

straight   concave   convex

Review questions

1. What is hairstyling?

2. Do good fingerwavers use aids when fingerwaving?

3. By what other names is a pin curl known?

4. What is a pin curl?

5. What degree of mobility does a pin curl made firmly within its base without a stem have?

6. What is a carved curl?

7. What is a skip wave?

Hairstyling

129

8. What is a roller curl?

9. What is curvature hairstyling?

10. What shape roller base is used in conjunction with conoid hair rollers?

11. What are the natural parts at the back of the head called?

12. Describe the difference between teasing and back combing.

13. What is the controlling factor for hairstyling to the individual?

14. Is it possible to maintain pressure on the hair between the irons with all types of thermal irons?

15. What is the best method for setting hair after it has been pressed?

16. What is blow dry styling?

17. What is a physiognomical haircut?

18. How can you curve ends while blow drying?

19. How close to the head can an infrared lamp be placed?

20. How can you increase the volume of a hairstyle when using the blow dry styling technique?

21. Is it always better to pick up wet hair with some dry hair during a blow dry styling?

Wigs, wiglets, switches and falls

Wigs, wiglets, switches and falls: Various types of hairpieces are designed to cover an individual's entire head of hair or for use in special areas of the head. These hairpieces will blend with the individual's own hair.

Overview: This chapter will provide you with the knowledge and skill required to become part of the lucrative field of wiggery.

Behavioral objectives-student goals: After completion of this chapter, and after instruction, study and practice, you will be able to perform and demonstrate competency in servicing wigs, wiglets, switches and falls by demonstrating the following techniques and procedures as they relate to hairpieces: cleaning, cutting, thinning, setting, combing, and placing and securing a hairpiece on the natural hair of an individual. You will also be able to demonstrate competency by identifying, explaining and/or listing the types of hairpieces, the technique for making wig measurements, making size adjustments and the procedure for coloring hairpieces.

Hairpieces are an important and dramatic part of the world of hairstyling. People wear wigs for many different reasons including but not limited to:

1. Covering baldness

2. Changing hairstyles without affecting the length or shape of their own hair

3. Having a well-groomed appearance when time does not permit a visit to the beauty salon

4. Protecting a bald head from strong sun

5. Adhering to religious custom

The sale and styling of hairpieces is an important part of the progressive hairstylist's income.

It is very important that you develop the knowledge and skill required to become part of the lucrative field of wiggery. The areas discussed in this chapter include:

Wigs, wiglets,
switches and falls

131

1. Types of wigs and hairpieces

2. Quality of wigs and hairpieces

3. Machine-made and hand-tied wigs

4. Wig measurements

5. Wig block measurements

6. Cleaning hairpieces and wigs

7. Cutting and thinning a wig

8. Setting a wig

9. Temporary color rinses and permanent tints for wigs and hairpieces

10. Wig size adjustments

   A. Shrinking a wig

   B. Reducing wig size by tucking

Wigs trace their history back to ancient Egypt. The most expensive wigs are those made from human hair. Hairpieces and wigs started to become popular in America in the year of 1957. The sales and services of wigs reached their peak in 1966. They are, however, still popular today. The introduction of modacrylic, kanekalon and dynel synthetic fibers for making wigs made caring for wigs and hairpieces easy. Wigs made with synthetic fibers retain their styling even after they are washed with shampoo and water. Some wigs and hairpieces are made of a blended mixture of human hair and synthetic fibers. If a wig or hairpiece is not properly labeled, the hair can be tested in order to determine if there are synthetic fibers present. Test by placing several strands of hair in a clean ashtray and light the strands with a match. If the hair burns quickly, has no odor and leaves small hard beads of fiber in the ashes, it is synthetic hair. Human hair gives off an odor and burns slowly.

The use of wigs and hairpieces in hairstyling has become an important and exciting part of a hairdresser's and cosmetologist's practice.

Sanitary and safety precautions for wigs, wiglets, switches and falls

1. Use wig cleaners in a well-ventilated room.

2. Liquid dry wig shampoo may be flammable. If so, keep it away from any flame.

3. Use a commercial nonflammable wig cleaner whenever possible.

4. Always strand test color before doing a complete application.

5. Always use a plastic covering over a wig block.

6. Allow $1/2$ inch (1.27 cm.) extra length when cutting bangs on a wig.

7. Always use the correct size wig block. This will prevent shrinking or stretching.

8. Avoid having the teeth of the comb touch the wig foundation because this can tear the wig easily.

9. Do not allow cleaning fluid to come into contact with your skin.

10. Avoid pulling the hair from the hairpiece foundation.

Wigs, wiglets, switches and falls

Unit 1
Types of hairpieces

1. A **wig** is designed to cover 95 – 100% of the patron's own hair.

2. A **wiglet** is designed for use in special areas of the head. It will blend with the patron's own hair. More than one wiglet may be used in the same or different areas on the head.

3. A **cascade** has an oval-shaped base and is designed for use at the back area of the head. It covers a smaller area than a fall does but greater than that which a wiglet covers.

WIGLET

WIG

WIGLET

SWITCHES

FALL

Unit 1

Types of hairpieces

General objectives-student goals:
After study, instruction and completion of this unit, you will be able to demonstrate understanding of types of hairpieces by identifying and giving a brief description of a wig, a wiglet, cascade, switch and fall.

CASCADE

Wigs, wiglets,
switches and falls

4. A switch is usually constructed with three stems of hair ranging from 20 to 24 inches (50.80 to 60.96 cm.) in length. Switches are usually braided or draped to blend with the hairstyle.

5. A fall covers a smaller area than a wig does but greater than that which a wiglet covers. Generally, a fall is worn long and casual. A fall worn in a casual style requires no setting. However, a fall can be set and styled into more elaborate hairdos. A removable headband is sometimes part of the design.

Unit 2
Quality of wigs and hairpieces

The quality of hairpieces will vary with the type of hair used. Hairpieces may be made from human hair or synthetic fibers. Human hair falls into three broad categories in regard to quality.

1. First quality is European Caucasian hair. It is usually grown by professional hair growers where a combination of care, diet, heredity and climate produce hair that is luxuriant. It is found in all natural shades—white, blonde, red, brown, black—and has a soft texture and good luster. First quality European hair is getting difficult to obtain because most European women and girls no longer grow their hair for the purpose of selling it to hair goods dealers.

2. Second quality is Indonesian hair. It is limp, lacks vitality and is readily available in dark shades only. Lighter shades can also be obtained.

3. Third quality is Asiatic (Oriental) hair. This type is very popular because of its low price range. Here, too, the darker shades are most readily available although the lighter shades can also be obtained. Modern methods of processing have made the development of a complete range of colors with good setting qualities possible.

   Note: All three qualities can be classified as human hair, imported hair or real hair. However, there is a great difference between them in quality and price. Some manufacturers make hairpieces which have a blend of European, Indonesian or Asiatic hair.

4. Synthetic hair is a man-made fiber. It feels like thread or material and is quite inexpensive when compared to human hair. Its main drawback is its glassy surface shine. Synthetic hair is usually not used or recommended professionally. The most popular synthetic fibers are modacrylic, kanekalon and dynel. Synthetic hair retains its styling well. These wigs and hairpieces can be washed and dried easily and quickly without affecting the style. Synthetic hair lacks the elasticity of human hair. This makes it extremely difficult to change the hairstyle.

Unit 3
Machine-made and hand-tied wigs

Wigs generally fall into one of two categories: machine-made or hand-tied. The machine-made wig is also known as a wefted wig. Loose hair is sewn into long wefts which are sewn in a spiral fashion around the netting, starting at the center top,

---

Unit 2
Quality of wigs and hairpieces

General objectives-student goals: After study, instruction and completion of this unit, you will be able to demonstrate understanding of the quality of wigs and hairpieces by writing and/or giving a brief overview of the subject.

Unit 3
Machine-made and hand-tied wigs

General objectives-student goals: After study, instruction and comple-

> Wigs, wiglets, switches and falls

134

approximately ¹/₄ inch (0.64 cm.) apart. Machine-made wigs are heavier than hand-tied wigs. They are ventilated and contain more hair, cost less and wear longer than hand-tied wigs. In some machine-made wigs, the starting topknot is hand-tied in order to eliminate the bulk, and the front hairline is hand finished. Machine-made wigs do not have the versatility of styling which hand-tied wigs have but they can give good service for at least five years.

machine-made

hand-tied

The hand-tied wig is also called a ventilated wig. In a hand-tied wig, each hair is individually knotted to a mesh cap in the same manner and direction as it grows on the human head. This wig is lighter in weight and is easier to style than machine-made wigs because of the way the hair is placed throughout the wig. These wigs are usually higher priced and more fragile than machine-made wigs. They require proper care. The average life of a hand-tied wig is two to three years.

Unit 4
Wig measurements

Wig measurements are made in order to guarantee a comfortable and secure fit. Correct measurements must be made of the patron's head. Comb and brush the hair as close and flat to the head as possible. A properly fitted wig will feel secure and will not bind. Make flat measurements with a measuring tape. Hold the tape securely around the areas of measurement with the least amount of pressure.

Procedure

1. Comb and brush the hair down flat and as close to the head as possible.

2. Always hold the measuring tape flat and close to the head with slight pressure on the tape.

3. Measure the patron's head starting at the front hairline. Continue around the head above the ears and end at the starting point.

4. Measure from the center forehead hairline to the center napeline.

5. Measure from temple to temple around the back of the head.

6. Measure from temple to temple across the crown of the head.

tion of this unit, you will be able to demonstrate understanding of machine-made and hand-tied wigs by writing and/or giving a brief overview of the subject.

Unit 4
Wig measurements

General objectives-student goals:
After study, instruction, practice and completion of this unit, you will be able to show understanding of wig measurements by demonstrating the procedure for making measurements for a comfortable and secure fit. You must have the proper implements and supplies in order to complete this unit successfully.

Wigs, wiglets,
switches and falls

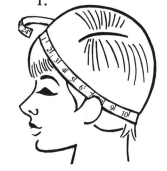

WIG

MEASUREMENTS

Wigs, wiglets, switches and falls

Unit 5

Wig block measurements

It is of utmost importance that a wig be placed on the correct size wig block while it is being serviced. This will prevent the wig from shrinking or losing its original size and shape.

Measure the patron's head. Start at the front hairline, continue around the head above the ears and end at the starting point. Canvas wig blocks come in various colors and sizes from 19 to 23 inches (48.26 to 58.42 cm.) including $\frac{1}{2}$ inch (1.27 cm.) sizes. Canvas blocks are color coded. The color of the canvas denotes the size of the block. If the head measures 21 inches (53.34 cm.: average size), a 21 inch (53.34 cm.) canvas wig block should be used. Using the measurements taken from the patron, measure the canvas wig block and mark the area on the block by placing pins in the same positions as the measurements.

Canvas blocks are used for cutting, styling, coloring and all work that has to be done on wigs. Styrofoam wig blocks are used for displaying or storing wigs. Styrofoam blocks are very lightweight and come in one size.

Unit 6

Cleaning wigs and hairpieces

Under normal conditions, it is not advisable to clean any hairpiece with soap and water. Although the human hair will wash well, the danger is that the netting will shrink and/or be torn when combing out matted hair. A commercial nonflammable wig cleaning solution should always be used in a well-ventilated room.

Procedure for cleaning a wig

1. Place the wig on a plastic covered canvas block and outline the wig along the hairline with small pins. Do not actually pin the wig to the block.

2. Pour 6 ounces (177.44 ml.) of wig cleaner into a large glass bowl.

3. Remove the wig from the block. Leave the outline of the pins in the block in order to ensure maintaining the correct size of the wig when the cleaning is complete and the wig is placed on the block again to dry.

4. Place the wig in the cleaning solution hair side down and allow the solution to saturate the wig cap and hair.

5. Dip the wig up and down and swirl it around in the solution for several minutes. Occasionally, squeeze the solution out of the hair.

6. Use a nail brush to clean the inside of the cap, particularly around the front hairline where make-up accumulates.

7. After the wig has been cleaned thoroughly, lift it from the bowl and squeeze out the solution. Blot the wig with a towel and place it back on the block. Match the wig to the previously outlined hairline in order to prevent shrinking. Pin the wig securely.

8. Comb the hair thoroughly. Set, allow to dry and comb out.

iglets and falls are cleaned by following steps 2, 4, 5 and 8 of the wig cleaning procedure. A switch is cleaned by following ps 2, 5 and 8 of the wig cleaning procedure.

> Note: Whenever the netting of a wig gets wet with water, follow the above procedure for pinning the wig in order to prevent shrinkage.

nit 7
utting a wig

wig may be cut on a canvas block or on the patron's head. It is recommended that cutting on the block be given preference cause the wig can be pinned to the block securely. This will prevent constant slipping of the wig during the cutting procedure. fore placing the wig on the block for cutting, the **elastic adjustment** in the nape area of the wig should be drawn up slightly d pinned. This will prevent cutting the nape area too short.

nter the wig on the correct size canvas block by pinning the center of the front hairline to the center of the block with both mple points even. Place two pins in the back, one on each side of the nape area.

hen cutting bangs, always allow $1/2$ inch (1.27 cm.) more length since the wig is usually placed $1/4 - 1/2$ inch (0.64 — 1.27 cm.) f the hairline when worn correctly.

it a wig by following the same procedure used in a basic haircut using the **blunt cut technique.**

1. Wet the hair and blot it.

demonstrating the procedure for cleaning a wig and by describing the procedures for cleaning wiglets, falls and a switch. You must have the proper implements and supplies in order to complete this unit successfully.

dip the wig
up and down
and swirl
around . . .

Unit 7
Cutting a wig

General objectives-student goals:
After study, instruction, practice and completion of this unit, you will be able to show understanding of how to cut a wig by demonstrating the technique and procedure. The hair on a wig is cut the same way as the hair on a human head. You must have the proper implements and supplies in order to complete this unit successfully.

> **Wigs, wiglets,**
> **switches and falls**

2. Comb the hair straight out from the crown in a circular fashion and allow it to fall in an umbrella shape around the entire head.

3. Cut to establish the hair length by placing the comb in your right hand and picking up a 1 inch (2.54 cm.) wide strand of hair at the center of the nape of the neck.

4. With the palm of your hand toward you, close the middle and index fingers of your left hand in a scissors position on the strand of hair at the point you would like to cut. Hold the hair straight down.

5. Transfer the comb to the palm of your left hand and blunt cut the hair immediately above the fingers of your left hand.

6. Pick up the next 1 inch (2.54 cm.) strand of hair to the left of the hair that has been cut, along with $^1/_2$ inch (1.27 cm.) of the cut hair to serve as a guide. Repeat steps 4 and 5.

7. Work to the left. Repeat step 6 until you reach the center of the forehead.

8. Return to the nape area and repeat step 6. Work to the right until the entire right side is cut.

9. After completing the full circle, check for evenness and trim any uneven ends.

10. Section the hair into five sections. Start by drawing a part all around the head 2 inches (5.08 cm.) within the hairline. Then, divide the hair within the circle into four equal sections with two parts: from the center front to the center rear and from side to side. Twist the hair within each of the four sections and fasten it out of the way.

11. Section 1 is the hair within the 2 inch (5.08 cm.) circle around the hairline. Section 2 is the patron's top front right section, and 3 is the top front left section. The back right section is 4, and the remaining back left section is 5.

12. Comb the hair in section 1 into its original umbrella shape. Again, start at the nape and subsection a $^1/_2$ inch (1.27 cm.) strand of hair vertically from the parting down to the hairline.

13. Grasp this strand firmly between the index and middle fingers of your left hand with the palm toward the head and the fingers pointing down.

14. Cut the hair according to the guideline which was cut for the established hair length by:

    A. Holding the hair directly outward

    B. Sliding your fingers along the strand until the hairs cut for the established hair length are just visible

    C. Blunt cutting the rest of the strands protruding through your fingers

15. Work around the left side of the head to the front. Repeat steps 12, 13 and 14. Each time, pick up some of the cut hair from the preceding vertical cut to serve as a guide.

Wigs, wiglets, switches and falls

16. Complete the left side. Return to the nape and shape the right side in the same way.

17. Unfasten section 2 and subsection a slender triangle which is $\frac{1}{2}$ inch (1.27 cm.) wide at the circular parting and narrowed down as it reaches the crown.

18. Secure the slender triangle of hair between the middle and index fingers of your left hand along with a few strands of hair from section 1 to act as a guide. Keep the palm turned towards the head with your fingers pointing towards the forehead. Cut the hair according to the guideline established in section 1.

19. Repeat this procedure until the entire section has been shaped. Always pick up part of the previously cut triangle as a guide.

20. Follow the same procedure for sections 3, 4 and 5. Always keep the fingers of your left hand pointing toward section 1.

21. Complete by checking the accuracy of the haircut by parting at random and taking up some hair on each side of this parting on the comb. Hold it directly out from the head at a right angle. Slide the comb through the hair to the hair ends and observe how the lengths of the cut ends blend together. Any uneven ends should be cut so that they conform to the overall lengths of the hair. There should never be more than $\frac{1}{4}$ inch (0.64 cm.) variation between any two neighboring strands of hair.

Unit 8
Thinning a wig

Thinning a wig is the same as thinning the hair. The objective is to remove the excess hair bulk from the wig. The purpose of this technique is to give shape to the wig hair by removing excess bulk without shortening its length. Distributing the bulk and weight of the hair helps to provide support for the completed hairstyle.

When thinning is necessary, it is usually needed in the back of the wig. Hold small vertical sections and place the thinning shears on a diagonal line approximately $1\frac{1}{2}$ — 2 inches (3.81 — 5.08 cm.) from the netting. Make two incomplete cuts into the strand. Incomplete cuts are when the tips of the blades do not come together during the cutting action. It is important to start the thinning $1\frac{1}{2}$ — 2 inches (3.81 — 5.08 cm.) from the netting in order to be sure that enough hair remains to cover the netting when the wig is combed out.

Removing hair bulk precedes cutting the hair. Hair texture, length of hair, hair density and the hairstyle to be designed are all factors that influence the amount of bulk removed from the wig hair.

1. Hair texture: Fine hair may be thinned closer to the netting than coarse hair. Coarse stubby ends will protrude from the top layer of hair whereas fine hair, being softer, will lie closer to the netting. Fine hair may be cut as close as 1 inch (2.54 cm.) from the netting. Coarse hair should be cut no closer than $1\frac{1}{2}$ inches (3.81 cm.) from the netting.

Unit 8
Thinning a wig

General objectives-student goals: After study, instruction, practice and completion of this unit, you will be able to show understanding of thinning a wig by demonstrating the procedure. You must have the proper implements and supplies in order to complete this unit successfully.

Wigs, wiglets,
switches and falls

2. **Length of the hair:** Hair cut with a wide variance in the lengths of the strands will require less thinning than hair cut with the strands essentially the same length over the entire wig.

3. **Density of the hair:** The average hair thickness of wigs varies from 100 to 400 hairs per square inch. Hair with greater density usually requires more bulk removal.

4. **Hairstyle:** If the finished hairstyle is one shaped to the contour of the head, the amount of bulk removed will be greater than one in a bouffant style.

Techniques for removing hair bulk

Hold a vertical subsection strand of hair $\frac{1}{2}$ inch by 2 inches (1.27 by 5.08 cm.) straight out from the block. Hold this and the wig between the fingers of your left hand. Place thinning scissors the correct distance from the net and cut once into the hair. Move out another 1 or $1\frac{1}{2}$ inches (2.54 or 3.81 cm.) on the same strand and cut again. Repeat a third time if the hair is long and thick enough. Remove the cut hairs by combing through the strand of hair. Repeat the procedure as necessary.

Unit 9
Setting a wig

Setting a wig is similar to setting a human head of hair. When the wig is cut properly, select a setting pattern which will bring about the desired hairstyle.

1. Pin the wig correctly and securely on the correct size canvas wig block.

2. Wet the hair. Caution should be used. You should avoid wetting the wig netting unnecessarily. Set the hair. Roller curls may be placed anywhere on the head and at almost any angle depending upon the hairstyle.

3. Section a rectangular base wherever rollers are required for the style.

4. Hold the comb in your right hand and the hair in your left. Comb the strand up.

5. Secure the strand between the index and middle fingers of your left hand. Use your right hand to fold up end paper over and under the strand. Slide the paper so that it extends at least $\frac{1}{2}$ inch (1.27 cm.) beyond the hair ends.

6. Hold the strand of hair and the paper with your left hand. Place the roller even with the end of the end paper.

7. Place the index and middle fingers of your right hand behind the roller to hold the hair in place and place your right thumb in front of the roller.

8. Repeat step 7 with your left hand. Turn the roller alternately with the fingers of your right and left hands until the roller is placed on its base.

Unit 9
Setting a wig

General objectives-student goals:
After study, instruction, practice and completion of this unit, you will be able to show understanding of setting a wig by demonstrating the technique and procedure. You must have the proper implements and supplies in order to complete this unit successfully.

Wigs, wiglets,
switches and falls

140

9. Fasten the roller securely on its base with a roller clip.

10. Repeat steps 3–9. Secure each additional curl roller to the previously secured one.

11. When time permits, it is best to dry a wig at normal room temperature.

12. Comb the wig on the block in the same manner as you would on a patron. When the hair has been set and dried, and the rollers, clips and pins have been removed from the hair, proceed as follows:

   A. Start at the lower back of the head and loosen all the curls row by row by combing through them.

   B. Use both the comb and brush in the direction in which the style is to be combed.

   C. Hold the comb in your right hand. Relax or drape the hair into the desired style with the fingers of your left hand.

   D. For a smooth finish of the ends, leave the hair fluffy. Smooth only the wispy ends.

   E. Use a fine mist of hair spray for the final touch.

   Note: If the hair is to be teased or back combed, this should be done between steps B and C.

Unit 10
Placing a wig and securing hairpieces

Place the finished wig on the patron's head after preparing her natural hair by making large flat pin curls around the sides and back of the head. The hair on top may be left loose but flat. Placing a stocking or wig cap over a head with short hair will keep the nape and side hair under the wig. The stocking or wig cap is placed on the head with the ears exposed. This is the best foundation on which to place a wig.

Place the wig on the patron's head. Allow the wig to slip over the head and set it $1/4$ — $1/2$ inch (0.64 — 1.27 cm.) off the front hairline. Adjust the sides to fit correctly over the ears. A properly fitted wig eliminates the need to use bobby pins in order to secure it to the head.

Wiglet and fall

To fasten a wiglet or a fall on a patron's head, set an area the same size as the netting into pin curls and secure the pin curls with bobby pins. The pin curls will serve as an anchor when pinning the wiglet or fall.

General objectives-student goals: After study, instruction, practice and completion of this unit, you will be able to show understanding of placing a wig on a patron's head and securing hairpieces by demonstrating the techniques and procedures for placing a wig and for securing a wiglet, fall and switch. You must have the proper implements and supplies in order to complete this unit successfully.

> **Wigs, wiglets, switches and falls**

1. Hold the wiglet or fall over the patron's head in several different positions until you find where it will fit best and look most becoming.

2. Place the wiglet or fall on the pin curls. Pin it securely with bobby pins.

3. Blend the wiglet or fall into the patron's hair.

Securing a switch

A switch is secured at the back or top area of the head by fastening it to one or two pin curls. These act as the main anchor. Then use sufficient hair pins and/or bobby pins around the edge of the hairpiece.

Unit 11
Temporary color rinses for wigs and hairpieces

Sunlight, air and normal wear will fade the color of any wig or hairpiece. A temporary rinse can make a wig look like new with a single application. Temporary rinses are safe and easy to use.

Procedure

1. Cover the canvas block with a plastic cover.

2. Pin the wig securely to the correct size canvas block and dampen it with water.

3. Pour color rinse into a bowl. Saturate a piece of cotton in the rinse and apply the rinse to one area at a time. Start at the back of the crown.

4. Hold a strand of hair firmly at the ends and start at the net area. Apply color with the saturated piece of cotton. Avoid getting rinse on the net.

5. As you work toward the hair ends, place the entire strand in the palm of your hand. Saturate the underside too.

6. Continue the same procedure on each strand until the entire wig is done.

7. Comb through the entire wig using a large tooth comb. This will ensure even color distribution.

Unit 11
Temporary color rinses for wigs and hairpieces

General objectives-student goals:
After study, instruction, practice and completion of this unit, you will be able to show understanding of temporary color rinses for wigs and hairpieces by demonstrating the technique and procedure. You must have the proper implements and supplies in order to complete this unit successfully.

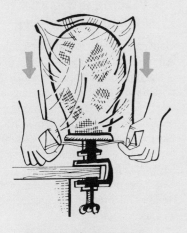

Wigs, wiglets,
switches and falls

8. Dry the wig in order to harden the color thoroughly before setting. This eliminates squeezing the color out of the hair during the setting process and helps avoid spots of demarcation from the perforations in the rollers.

9. Dampen the hair and set it.

Unit 12

Tinting wigs and hairpieces

Expert hair colorists always take a cautious position when it comes to using permanent tints or hair lighteners on hairpieces. Hair lighteners can weaken and even destroy the netting, threads and fabrics which are part of a wig. Even with precautions, color results are not always predictable. Because of the unknown quality of the hair and/or because the hair has been precolor treated, it is advisable to make strand tests to determine the formula and color to be used.

The finished color is always darker and drabber than the strand test. Although wig hair is difficult to lighten, it will absorb color easily. Adding water to the tinting formula will slow down the speed of the coloring action and give you full control. It will not change the color.

Procedure

1. Select the correct size block and protect the canvas with a plastic cover. Pin the wig securely.

2. Mix the color according to the results of the strand test.

3. Section the hair into four quadrants.

4. Start at the back right quadrant on a machine-made wig. Part off the wefts one by one. Apply tint on each side and work the color down the entire strand. On a hand–tied wig, use 1 inch (2.54 cm.) subsections.

5. Continue this procedure. Do the back left section next and then, the front two sections.

6. Work the color well into the hairline including the edge of the wig cap.

7. Distribute the color evenly by combing gently through the hair.

8. When the color is fully developed, place the wig in a shampooing position on the shampoo bowl. Rinse until the water runs clear. Shampoo the hair lightly. Do not rub the netting. Rinse again thoroughly.

9. Blot and prepare the hair for setting.

When tinting synthetic hair, the best results are obtained by using a fabric dye. Fabric dyes are available in many colors.

Unit 12
Tinting wigs and hairpieces

General objectives-student goals: After study, instruction, practice and completion of this unit, you will be able to show understanding of tinting wigs and hairpieces by giving a brief overview of the subject and by demonstrating the procedure. You must have the proper implements and supplies in order to complete this unit successfully.

Wigs, wiglets, switches and falls

Synthetic wigs and hairpieces tinted with a fabric dye will hold the color better than human hair wigs or hairpieces that are tinted with an aniline tint.

Unit 13
Wig size adjustments

Wig sizes can be adjusted two ways:

1. Shrinking

2. Tucking

Wig shrinking is recommended when the overall fit is too large. Tucking is recommended only when a specific area is too large or too bulky or when more adjustment is needed after shrinkage.

Shrinking procedure

1. Measure the patron's head according to the procedure for fitting a wig.

2. Use these measurements to measure a plastic covered canvas wig block. Place pins in the block to mark the identical measurements and positions.

3. Place the wig hair side down in a bowl with very hot water. Saturate the entire wig cap by leaving it in the bowl for several minutes.

4. Remove the wig from the bowl and allow the excess water to run off.

5. Blot with a towel and place the wig on the block. Pin the wig to fit the measurements previously outlined. Place enough pins all around the hairline in order to anchor the wig firmly to the measurements marked on the canvas block.

6. Comb the hair smoothly and thoroughly. Pin the top crown area securely to the block.

7. Shrinkage will take place throughout the loose areas.

8. Allow the wig to dry thoroughly.

9. If additional sizing is necessary, it should be done by tucking.

General objectives-student goals:
After study, instruction and completion of this unit, you will be able to demonstrate understanding of how to adjust the size of a wig when it is too large by writing and/or giving a brief overview of the shrinking and wig tucking procedures.

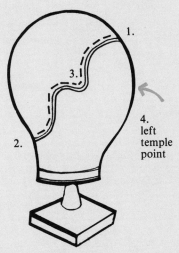

1.

3.

2.

4.
left
temple
point

mark identical measurements on block...

Wigs, wiglets,
switches and falls

Wig tucking

If the wig is too large in the crown area and rests on the patron's ears, make two crescent shaped tucks at the crown of the wig. In order to reduce the cap size from the forehead to the nape, make tucks in the nape wefts.

If the wig is too large at the crown, determine how much must be taken up and divide the amount equally on both sides of the wig. For example, if the wig is 1½ inches (3.81 cm.) too large, make two ¾ inch (1.90 cm.) tucks on the inside of each side of the cap.

If the area from the forehead to the nape is 1 inch (2.54 cm.) too large, make a 1 inch (2.54 cm.) tuck or two ½ inch (1.27 cm.) tucks across the back nape of the wig.

Note: Use linen thread and sew on the weft not the netting.

Unit 14
Postiche

Postiche is a French term for an **elaborate ornamental hairpiece**. A postiche is a highly styled hairpiece which becomes part of the hairstyle. A wiglet designed into an elaborate detailed effect and added to a hairstyle that has been completely combed is a postiche. Some postiches are ornamental in design; others are ornamental because of their bright theatrical colors. Animal hair, such as angora and yak, are tinted with bright elaborate colors and blended with human hair when making a hairpiece which is used for creative hairstyling. The postiche which has a combination of color and design is usually used during hairstyling competitions.

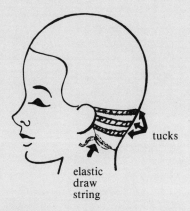

tucks

elastic
draw
string

Unit 14
Postiche

General objectives-student goals:
After study, instruction and completion of this unit, you will be able to demonstrate understanding of a postiche by writing and/or giving a brief overview of the subject.

Review questions

1. Why does a progressive hairstylist have special interest in hairpieces?

2. If a wiglet has an oval-shaped base, what is the base shape of a cascade?

3. On what part of the head is a cascade usually worn?

4. Which hairpiece covers the largest area of a woman's head: a wiglet, cascade or fall?

Wigs, wiglets,
switches and falls

145

5. Do all wigs and hairpieces have human hair?

6. What are the three broad categories of human hair in regard to quality?

7. Why is Asiatic (Oriental) hair the most popular type of hair for hairpieces?

8. What is synthetic hair?

9. Which lasts longer: a machine-made or a hand-tied wig?

10. Why do some machine-made wigs have a hand-tied topknot?

11. What is another name for a hand-tied wig?

12. Why are wig blocks color coded?

13. Is it advisable to clean human hair wigs and hairpieces with soap and water?

14. Should a wig be cut on a canvas block or on a patron's head?

15. How can you avoid cutting the nape area of a wig too short?

16. Why should an additional $1/_2$ inch (1.27 cm.) in length be allowed when cutting bangs on a wig?

17. How close to the netting can you start thinning a wig?

18. Is the procedure for setting a wig similar to the procedure for setting a human head of hair?

19. What is the best method for drying a wig after it has been set?

20. How can wig sizes be adjusted?

21. Why is European Caucasian hair rated first quality?

Wigs, wiglets,
switches and falls

Permanent waving — chemical waving

Permanent waving-chemical waving: A method of giving a lasting curl and/or wave to the hair by using chemicals that change the structure of the hair.

Overview: This chapter will provide you with all the methods of permanent waving, cold wave chemistry and safety measures.

Behavioral objectives-student goals: After completion of this chapter, and after instruction, study and practice, you will be able to perform and demonstrate competency in permanent waving by demonstrating: the complete cold wave procedure for both normal and tinted hair, test curl interpretation, instant and splash neutralizing methods, a body wave, curl control wave, spiral winding (flat, half and full twist), an end permanent and the piggyback double-rod method of wrapping hair. You will also be able to demonstrate competency by identifying, explaining and/or listing cold wave chemistry, acid perm chemistry, rod sizes, hair density, porosity and elasticity, types of cold wave lotions and neutralizers, curl control wave, instrument controlled processing time, safety measures, prepermanent wave procedures, curl reduction, Perm-A-Curl and perming frosted hair.

The permanent wave was invented by Charles Nessler in 1905, and he gave the first public demonstration in London in 1906. However, perming did not become popular until 1912. The hair was wrapped with tension on a spiral perm rod from the scalp to the hair ends. The permanent wave machine supplied the required heat with tube-like heaters that were attached to the machine with long adjustable electric wires. Each heater contained a heating element capable of supplying more than 212 degrees of heat. The tubes were placed over the rods in order to connect the patron to the machine during the processing period.

Late in 1930, the croquignole method of wrapping hair was introduced. This method involved wrapping the hair from the hair ends to the scalp. The heat was supplied with clamp-like heaters which attached the patron to the machine.

In 1931, the preheat method of perming was made available. The procedure and process were the same as the other perms except that the patron was not connected to the machine at any time. The machine was a tabletop model that preheated the wireless clamp-like heaters before they were placed over each individual rod. A moist protective pad was used with all these machine perms in order to keep the hair from drying while it was being processed with heat.

Machineless permanent waves were created in 1932 by Dr. Ralph L. Evans, Jr. and Dr. Everett G. McDonough. The permanent wave method required no wires or electricity. The heat was supplied by small flexible pads containing an exothermic chemical mixture which provided each pad with 212 degrees of controlled heat.

Permanent waving
chemical waving

straight
hair

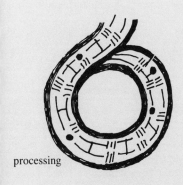

processing

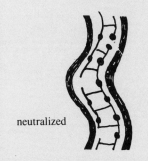

neutralized

**Permanent waving
chemical waving**

The cold wave method of permanent waving came into general use in 1940. The term cold wave is a misnomer. A more descriptive phrase for the cold wave method is the chemical method of permanent waving. The manufacturers chose to use the name cold wave in order to differentiate it from permanent waving procedures that involve the application of heat.

Although the cold wave perming process does not require electrical or chemical heat, it uses the normal body temperature of 98.6° and normal room temperature. Lower than normal temperature increases the processing time. Higher than normal body temperature decreases it. If the room temperature is cooler than normal because of air conditioning, a plastic or paper covering should be placed over the head during the processing time.

Chemicals (ammonium thioglycolate) are used to re-form the hair to the shape of the rod. The hair is wrapped without tension and other chemicals (neutralizer) are used to re-form and rebond the hair into its new shape. Cold wave lotions are highly alkaline.

Acid pH perming was introduced in 1970 but did not become popular until 1973. Acid balanced and acid pH wave lotions require some form of heat other than body heat in order to re-form the hair into a new shape. The hair is wrapped with tension. The pH of cold wave lotions ranges from about 8.5 to 9.5 but the pH of acid balanced perm lotions ranges from 7.5 to 8.2 and acid pH lotions have a value of up to 6.9. Both cold wave and acid wave lotions contain the same thioglycolic base. The ammonia content of acid balanced waving lotions is far below that of cold wave lotions. This is why these waving lotions must be activated with heat.

Neutralizing methods, techniques and procedures have not changed much over the years. Although on the rod neutralizing was introduced in 1952, the original splash method of soaking wrapped hair at the shampoo basin is still the best method for neutralizing long hair. Neutralizing is a part of perming hair that must be regarded as just as important as any other step in the permanent wave procedure.

Sanitary and safety precautions for permanent waving-chemical waving

1. The foundation of a permanent wave is the careful preshaping of the hair.

2. Always use gloves to protect your hands from irritation.

3. Apply protective cream around the hairline and neck. Cover them with a strip of absorbent cotton.

4. Avoid having waving lotion come in contact with the scalp. This will prevent skin irritation.

5. Wipe up any lotion that drips on the floor. This will prevent accidents.

6. Remove and replace cotton strips that become soaked with wave lotion.

7. Examine the hair and scalp before beginning a perm.

8. Do not brush the scalp area before a permanent wave.

9. Change the towel or protective covering around the patron's neck when it becomes wet.

10. Remove the rods carefully in order to prevent the hair and scalp from suffering undesirable reactions.

Unit 1
Cold wave chemistry

The components of hair (carbon, oxygen, hydrogen, nitrogen and sulfur) make up the **amino acids** that form the **protein keratin**. Hair is made of keratin. The linkages of amino acid are held together (bonded) by chemical bonds and physical bonds.

Chemical bonds are **peptide bonds** and **disulfide bonds**. These bonds can be broken (unlinked), re-formed and rebonded with the use of chemicals only. **Physical bonds** are **hydrogen bonds** and **ionic (salt) bonds**. They are easily broken by water or moisture. After being re-formed, they rebond by eliminating the water or moisture from the hair. The hair, however, can revert to its normal form with just the moisture in the air.

Peptide bonds secure the long chain of **end linkages** which run the full length of the hair fiber and form long chains of **polypeptides**. Disulfide bonds secure the cross linkages which connect with the end linkages like the cross pieces of a ladder.

When the alkaline waving solution is applied to the hair, it softens and swells the hair, lifts the cuticle and allows the solution to penetrate through the cuticle to the cortex which is made up of billions of long polypeptide chains. Once in the cortex, the chemical action of the perm lotion unlinks up to 70% of the disulfide bonds. This allows the polypeptide chain to rearrange and also permits the hair to take on a new form. 30% of the disulfide bonds remain unchanged.

After the hair is neutralized, only 50% of the broken bonds are re-formed and rebonded. Thus, 35% of the disulfide bonds were lost during the processing time. The swollen condition of the hair and water retention prevent the chemical bonds from being entirely relinked.

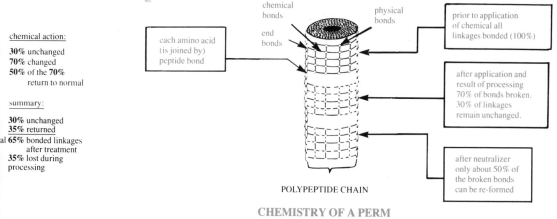

chemical action:

30% unchanged
70% changed
50% of the **70%**
    return to normal

summary:

30% unchanged
35% returned
al **65%** bonded linkages
    after treatment
35% lost during
processing

chemical bonds

physical bonds

end bonds

each amino acid (is joined by) peptide bond

prior to application of chemical all linkages bonded (100%)

after application and result of processing 70% of bonds broken. 30% of linkages remain unchanged.

after neutralizer only about 50% of the broken bonds can be re-formed

POLYPEPTIDE CHAIN

CHEMISTRY OF A PERM

Unit 1
Cold wave chemistry

General objectives-student goals:
After study, instruction and completion of this unit, you will be able to demonstrate understanding of the chemistry and theory of permanent waving by writing and/or giving a brief overview of the subject.

**Permanent waving
chemical waving**

Permanent waving
chemical waving

150

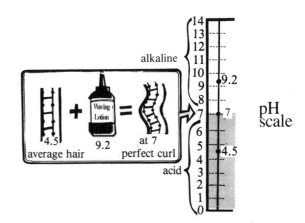

Unit 2
pH reaction

During the processing time of the permanent wave, the average hair, which has an acid mantle of pH 4.5–5.5, comes in contact with the waving lotion, which is alkaline and about pH 9.2. As the processing time continues, the pH of the acid mantle around the hair rises. 70% of the disulfide bonds are usually broken by the time the pH of the acid mantle rises to about 7. If the hair is permitted to process past the point of pH 7, it becomes overprocessed and damaged in texture and appearance. This may cause the peptide bonds, which are the strongest of the bonds, to break. Before more than 70% of the disulfide bonds can be broken, the peptide bonds will start to break. Once the peptide bonds are broken, there is no way of re-forming them. The hair will literally fall apart.

Unit 3
Cystine–cysteine

Disulfide bonds, which are sulfur cystine, are converted to cysteine through the application of waving lotion. The neutralizer oxidizes the cysteine back to cystine. Neutralizing the perm lotion after processing is complete is the final and most important cycle of the permanent wave procedure. The re-forming of the chemical bonds will affect the results: the lasting qualities and the strength of the curl. The greater the number of chemical bonds that are re-formed, the better the results. It is the swollen condition of the hair and the fact that hair retains a considerable amount of water that prevent the same number of chemical bonds that were unlinked from being linked again.

Unit 4
The cold wave

Cold waving involves two chemical actions:

1. Processing is the application of a waving lotion in order to soften the hair and permit rearrangement of its inner structure while the hair is wrapped around cold wave rods.

2. Neutralizing: When the processing time is complete, the hair is chemically neutralized. The neutralizing stops the processing action of the waving lotion and causes the hair to reharden in a new shape.

When waving lotions are manufactured to be self-neutralizing, follow the manufacturer's directions carefully.

Hair must be treated with extremely good care after a permanent wave. Hair is vulnerable to stretching, heat and moisture for at least 36 – 72 hours after the perm. Unnecessary stresses and applications to the hair should be avoided during the first 72 hours. Tell your patrons about these precautions and advise them not to brush their hair. They should comb it gently during this period.

Unit 5
Rod sizes

Rods vary in length and thickness. The use of the correct rod size helps to obtain the best results from any wave. Generally, the size of the rod is determined by the length of the hair, the finished hairstyle and the hair texture.

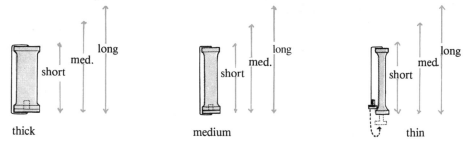

1. Length of the hair

    A. Hair 6 inches (15.24 cm.) or longer requires a large and thick rod.

    B. For a hair length from 3 to 6 inches (7.62 to 15.24 cm.), use a medium size and medium thick rod.

    C. For a hair length from 1 to 3 inches (2.54 to 7.62 cm.), use a thin short rod.

2. Style of the hairdo

    A. If the finished hairstyle is to have smooth lines or a casual appearance, large and thick rods must be used.

    B. If the hairstyle is to appear to have a lot of curl and body, use medium to thin rods.

tion of this unit, you will be able to demonstrate understanding of what cold waving involves by writing and/or giving a brief overview of the subject.

Unit 5
Rod sizes

General objectives-student goals: After study, instruction, practice and completion of this unit, you will be able to demonstrate understanding of perm rod sizes by identifying several rod sizes and the factors that determine rod size selection. You must have the proper supplies in order to complete this unit successfully.

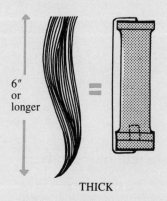

THICK

Permanent waving
chemical waving

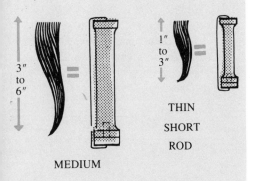

MEDIUM

THIN
SHORT
ROD

3. Hair texture

The texture of hair is classified as coarse, medium or fine. Feeling the hair with your fingertips will enable you to determine the general quality. Texture depends on three general characteristics:

1. Size (diameter)   2. Pliability   3. Growth variables

The texture, length of hair and hairstyle are judged together when determining the size of the perm rod used to produce the curls. Coarse hair usually requires a larger rod diameter and fine hair a smaller rod diameter. Fine hair is most difficult to perm because of its large proportion of moisture resistant cuticle which protects the cortex.

FINE HAIR

MEDIUM HAIR

COARSE HAIR

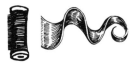

The size of the hair is measured by its diameter. The diameter of the hair shaft is not the same throughout its length. It is widest near the scalp area and tapers toward the hair ends. When checking for thickness or texture, examine the hair near the center of the shaft. Coarse hair has a large diameter. Fine hair has a much smaller diameter. The diameter ranges from 1/1500 of an inch (.0017 cm.) for fine hair to 1/400 of an inch (.0064 cm.) for coarse hair.

The pliability of hair is determined by its feel. It can be soft, harsh or resistant. The growth variables of hair include quality: wiry, silky or straight and stiff.

Unit 6
Scalp and hair analysis

Scalp analysis

Examine the scalp for abrasions, cuts, scratches, irritations or any signs of disease. If the patron has any of these conditions, do not permanent wave the hair. Minor irregularities should be protected with an application of a protective base cream.

Unit 6
Scalp and hair analysis

General objectives-student goals:
After study, instruction and comple-

Permanent waving
chemical waving

152

Hair analysis

A careful analysis of the hair is an important step in the permanent wave procedure. The hair's density, porosity, elasticity and overall condition will affect the results of a permanent wave. Each of these characteristics must be evaluated before giving the perm.

Hair density

The amount of hair selected for winding on each rod determines the width of the rod sections. The length of each rod section is about the same as the rod in most areas. When you have combined conditions calling for varying rod lengths in one section, it is correct to use a combination of rod sizes. Under normal conditions, special caution must be taken when permanent waving hair 6 inches (15.24 cm.) or longer. It is essential that complete penetration of both the waving lotion and the neutralizer take place. Appropriate care must be exercised in their application. Since long hair may have a tendency to soften and process faster, compensate for this by selecting the proper rod sizes and the proper amount of hair for winding on each rod in the various areas of the head.

size of rod
too short

rod size
too long

correct
rod size

use one small
rod in each
section on bottom...

combined conditions

tion of this unit, you will be able to demonstrate understanding of scalp and hair analysis as it applies to permanent waving by writing and/or giving a brief overview of the subject.

warning!
do not
give permanent...

SCALP CUT OR IRRITATION

**Permanent waving
chemical waving**

153

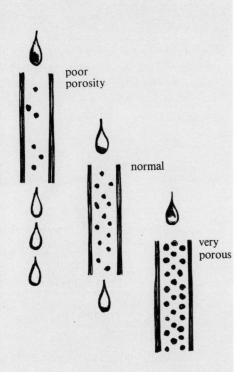

poor porosity

normal

very porous

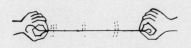

HAIR ELASTICITY

> **Permanent waving chemical waving**

Porosity

This is a guide for determining the proper waving lotion because hair that is porous absorbs liquids more readily.

1. The degree of porosity is determined by how quickly the hair absorbs liquids.

2. The greater the porosity, the milder the waving lotion that need be used.

3. Nonporous hair is resistant. This type of hair calls for a waving lotion for resistant hair.

Factors that indicate the degree of hair porosity:

1. Hair that dries quickly under the dryer has normal porosity. Overbleached hair and chemically (caustic) straightened hair are overporous and require longer drying time. Hair becomes overporous when its physical properties are damaged by the chemicals used on it. If the hair feels slimy to the touch when wet, it is overporous. Hair dries by the process of desorption. Hair with normal to good porosity will dry faster than overporous hair.

2. When the hair wets easily and thoroughly at the shampoo bowl, it has normal porosity.

3. If water does not roll freely off the hair when the patron is sitting up, it has normal porosity.

4. Naturally discolored hair is slightly overporous.

5. Bleached but not overbleached and tinted hair are slightly overporous.

6. Overbleached hair and hair straightened with caustic chemicals are overporous.

7. If water rolls freely off the hair when the patron is sitting up, it has poor porosity.

Elasticity

Elasticity is the ability of the hair to stretch and contract. It determines the processing time. Normal hair with good elasticity will achieve a perfect curl with a shorter processing time whereas hair with poor elasticity will need a longer processing time. If the hair has no elasticity at all, it will not take a permanent wave under any condition.

Factors that indicate the degree of elasticity:

1. Hair with good elasticity does not break when stretched and contracts after stretching.

2. This type of hair holds a setting well even without a permanent.

3. Poor elasticity is indicated by hair that tangles and is limp. It has very little stretch and does not contract easily. Hair with no elasticity breaks easily when stretched.

Unit 7
Permanent waving lotions

Cold wave lotions are alkaline waving lotions that have ammonium thioglycolate as their basic ingredient. This compound is obtained by combining ammonia and thioglycolic acid. Other materials which may be added are wetting agents, lanolin, proteins and other conditioners, and fragrances. Cold waves do not require applied heat and are given at room temperature. They utilize only the normal body temperature of 98.6°.

Cold waving solutions are manufactured in four different strengths:

1. Resistant is used for hair that is nonporous and difficult to wave.

2. Normal is used for hair that has good porosity.

3. Mild is used for tinted hair that is very porous.

4. Extra mild is used for overlightened, damaged or dry hair. These are overporous.

Acid pH waving lotions contain the same thioglycolic acid base as alkaline cold waves. However, they do not have the ammonia content which cold wave lotions have. Heat is required as part of the procedure in order to activate the perm lotion and start the processing time.

Unit 8
Neutralizers

Neutralizers are used to halt the action of permanent waving lotions and re-form the chemical cross bonds that were broken during the processing period. Neutralizing flattens the cuticle and rehardens the hair into the curled form.

Neutralizers are acetic oxidizing solutions. There are two types:

1. The instant lanolin type has a thick consistency. It contains sodium bromate, potassium bromate or hydrogen peroxide. It is applied with a plastic applicator bottle while the patron is in a normal sitting position at the styling station. This method of neutralizing is also called on the rod neutralizing.

Unit 7
Permanent waving lotions

General objectives-student goals: After study, instruction and completion of this unit, you will be able to demonstrate understanding of cold wave lotions and acid balanced lotions by giving a brief description of the two types of lotions, by identifying the four different strengths of waving lotions and by matching the hair characteristics to the proper strength waving lotion.

Unit 8
Neutralizers

General objectives-student goals: After study, instruction, practice and completion of this unit, you will be able to show understanding of cold wave neutralizers by giving a brief overview of their function by identifying the two methods of neu-

Permanent waving
chemical waving

tralizing and by demonstrating both methods. You must have the proper supplies in order to complete this unit successfully.

Unit 9
Sectioning and subsectioning hair

General objectives-student goals:
After study, instruction, practice and completion of this unit, you will be able to demonstrate understanding of sectioning and subsectioning hair by demonstrating and giving a detailed description of the procedure. You must have the proper implements and supplies in order to complete this unit successfully.

Unit 10
Wrapping the hair

General objectives-student goals:
After study, instruction, practice and completion of this unit, you will be able to show understanding of wrapping the hair for a permanent

---

Permanent waving chemical waving

156

---

2. The splash type is a more dilute water solution of oxidizing chemicals. It is applied from a glass or plastic bowl with absorbent cotton or a sponge. It is highly recommended when waving hair over 6 inches (15.24 cm.) in length. This type of neutralizer is applied at the shampoo bowl with the patron in the same position as for a shampoo.

Unit 9
Sectioning and subsectioning hair

Sectioning and subsectioning the hair is also known as blocking the head. The sectioning can be in any pattern since it is influenced by the hairstyle, haircut, hairline irregularity, hair density or manufacturer's instructions. The pattern shown here is specifically designed for the student in training and can be easily adapted to any State Board requirement. Sectioning and subsectioning:

1. Involve subdividing each section into partings of about the same size as the permanent wave rod used in a specific area of the head.

2. Help to distribute the hair evenly around the head.

3. Help to distribute the hair evenly among the rods. This ensures the same kind of curl over the entire head.

4. Allow for better control of the hair during the wrapping procedure.

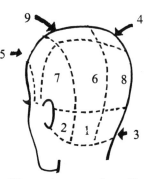

A good fundamental pattern for sectioning and subsectioning has nine basic sections. The sections must be uniformly arranged with clean uniform partings of equally subdivided rod sections. The rod sections must be about the same length as the rod used.

Unit 10
Wrapping the hair

Wrapping is the technique and procedure by which subsections of hair are croquignole wound around the perm rods, between one or two end papers, from the hair ends towards the scalp. The purpose of wrapping the hair around the rod is to have it conform to the rod shape and size during the processing procedure. In order to develop good waves, curls and ridges, the hair must be wrapped smoothly and neatly on each rod without stretching. Alkaline cold waves are wound without tension. Acid pH perms must be wound with a moderate amount of tension.

Winding the hair

In cold waving, when the hair is croquignole wound, the waving solution is used to soften and lift the cuticle by moistening each section before subsectioning and winding.

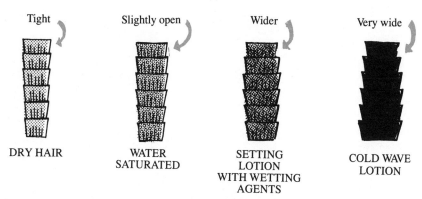

Tight — **DRY HAIR**

Slightly open — **WATER SATURATED**

Wider — **SETTING LOTION WITH WETTING AGENTS**

Very wide — **COLD WAVE LOTION**

wave by demonstrating the technique and procedure. You must have the proper implements and supplies in order to complete this unit successfully.

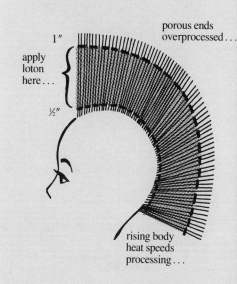

porous ends overprocessed . . .

1"

apply loton here . . .

½"

rising body heat speeds processing . . .

Apply the lotion from ½ inch (1.27 cm.) above the scalp to about 1 inch (2.54 cm.) from the ends using an applicator bottle, brush or a piece of cotton as an applicator. Comb the lotion thoroughly through the strand so that the complete hair strand is moistened with lotion. While you are a basic student, your instructor may suggest using water or water diluted lotion while wrapping and saturating with lotion after the entire head has been wound. In order to develop a uniform permanent wave, the hair must be wrapped neatly and smoothly across the rod without bulkiness and without stretching.

Procedure for wrapping

Subsection a strand of hair moistened with waving lotion. Comb the hair in the subsection up and out with all the hair evenly directed and distributed.

1. Place end papers near the hair ends.

   Note: End papers are used to help ensure smooth winding and to prevent fishhooks and straight ends.

2. Place the rod under the strand and draw the end paper and rod toward you until the hair ends are visible above the rod. Roll the end paper and hair under.

porous end paper
allows lotion to penetrate . . .

3. As the hair is wrapped, it should look outwardly firm and smooth. It must be wound on the rod without tension. **The rod should always be held in a position slightly ahead of the wrapping motion. This will prevent stretching and tension wrapping.**

 ①

 ②

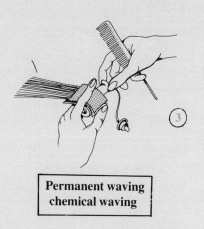 ③

Permanent waving chemical waving

don't
forget--
protective
gloves...

**APPLICATION OF
WAVING LOTION**

Unit 11

Processing time and the application of waving lotions

General objectives-student goals:
After study, instruction, practice and completion of this unit, you will be able to demonstrate understanding of processing perms and the application of waving lotions by writing or giving a brief overview of the subject.

**Permanent waving
chemical waving**

---

4. While rolling the hair under, use the thumb of each hand to maintain control of the strand. Wind smoothly without tension.

5. When the hair is wrapped and placed properly in the rod section, fasten the rod evenly across the hair with the fastener. Place the fastener a little above the center of the rod. A tight or twisted fastener can cause breakage.

The hands of the cosmetologist should never come in contact with the waving lotion. Protective gloves should always be worn. A protective cream should be applied around the patron's hairline and covered with a permanent wave cotton strip. When the application of cold wave lotion is complete and the dripping stops, remove the cotton strip and blot the area dry. Do not rub. Reapply protective cream if necessary.

Unit 11
Processing time and the application of waving lotions

The processing time is the period required for the hair wrapped around the rods to absorb the permanent waving lotion sufficiently to complete the rearrangement of the chemical bonds so that it may assume the pattern of the rod shape and size. The processing time for most permanents varies from one person to another. The ability of the hair to absorb moisture can also vary from time to time on the same individual even if all conditions are equal. It is always safe to anticipate the processing time being less than that of the previous wave and less than that suggested by the manufacturer's instructions. With time and experience, any cosmetologist can learn to determine the correct processing time through the use of test curls, a procedure explained later in this chapter.

The processing time will be influenced by:

1. Strength of the lotion

2. Porosity

3. Elasticity

4. Length of the hair

5. Condition of the hair

6. Patron's body temperature

7. Room temperature

Follow the manufacturer's instructions for prewrap wetting or moistening of the hair. Variations between products may be great. The rewetting or saturation procedure, however, is the same for all perms be they alkaline or acid pH.

Rewetting or saturation: When the entire head is wrapped thoroughly, rewet the entire head curl by curl with the waving lotion. Use a plastic applicator bottle. Begin at the nape area and work your way to the front of the head. Start by rewetting the curl that was wrapped first and end with the curl that was wrapped last.

Unit 12
Test curls

Test curls enable the cosmetologist to determine the speed of curl formation and the exact processing time. A good cosmetologist always makes test curls because every head of hair is different. Conditions even vary on the same head of hair and with each permanent wave.

Immediately after the rewetting application, a test curl should be made. The results of this test act as a guide for approximating the processing time. From this point on, frequent testing for curl development will prevent overprocessing.

Method 1

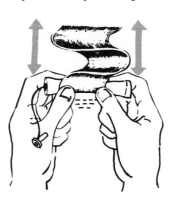

1. Loosen the rod fastener.

2. Unwind the rod 1¹/₂ turns without pulling on the strand.

3. Move the rod slightly toward the scalp.

4. Permit the hair to relax into a wave pattern without pushing.

5. Rewind and fasten the rod.

6. Continue testing for curl development at regular intervals. Test on different areas of the head each time.

7. Processing is complete when the wave forms a firm "S." The size of the rod controls the size of the "S" pattern. The peak is reached only once and if the processing is not stopped immediately, the hair will be overprocessed and damaged.

Method 2

1. Release the rod and hold it close to the scalp.

2. Unwind the hair two full turns. Allow a loop to form in the unwound hair.

3. Observe the hair at the lowest part of this loop.

Unit 12

Test curls

General objectives-student goals: After study, instruction, practice and completion of this unit, you will be able to show understanding of permanent wave test curls by demonstrating two techniques and procedures for making test curls and by giving a brief description of both techniques. You must have the proper implements and supplies in order to complete this unit successfully.

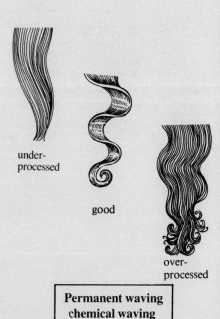

under-processed

good

over-processed

Permanent waving
chemical waving

4. If the processing is complete, the hair shaft will turn over completely and quickly. If the processing time is not complete, the hair fibers will not unwind completely, and the hair shaft will not turn over completely. You must learn how to look for the turnover of the hair shaft. When this procedure is practiced a few times, the turnover of the hair shaft is seen very easily.

5. If the processing time has not been completed, rewind and fasten the rod.

6. Continue testing for curl development at regular intervals and on different areas of the head.

7. The peak is reached only once and if the processing is not stopped immediately, the hair will be overprocessed and damaged. With time and experience, any cosmetologist can learn to determine the correct processing time through the use of test curls.

Unit 13
Neutralizing

Removing the waving lotion from the hair is a prerequisite to neutralizing a permanent wave. The waving lotion must be removed from the hair in order for the neutralizer to be effective. The waving lotion can be removed from the hair by:

1. Water rinsing

2. Blotting

Most manufacturers recommend that the waving lotion be removed by rinsing the hair with warm water because the water dilutes the waving lotion as it removes it from the hair. All areas of the head should be rinsed thoroughly with a gentle force of water spray, followed by blotting of each curl in order to remove excess wetness prior to the application of neutralizer. Blotting the hair prevents diluting the neutralizer and ensures proper penetration of the neutralizer into the hair ends.

Neutralizing without the preliminary water rinsing is accomplished by blotting each curl with highly absorbent paper towels after completion of the processing time. Carefully press the towel with your fingers between each curl while holding the rods firmly. Repeat the procedure until all excess wetness is removed.

When water is used to remove the waving lotion from the hair, there is a radical increase in the swelling of the hair shaft. This causes a smaller percentage of cross bonds to be re-formed. Longer lasting waves can only be developed by re-forming as many cross bonds as possible with complete and thorough neutralization.

Neutralizing is the process that produces the formation of curl by re-forming the broken cross bonds of the hair shaft into a new curled position. The neutralizer stops the action of the waving lotion completely, re-forms the chemical bonds and flattens the cuticle. There are two generally accepted methods of neutralization:

1. Instant method

2. Splash method

Unit 13
Neutralizing

General objectives-student goals:
After study, instruction, practice and completion of this unit, you will be able to demonstrate understanding of the effects of and procedure for neutralizing perms by writing or giving a brief description of the subject and by demonstrating both procedures. You must have the proper implements and supplies in order to complete this unit successfully.

Permanent waving chemical waving

160

Instant method (on the rod method)

1. Rinse the hair thoroughly in order to remove all waving lotion.

2. Blot each curl in order to remove excess moisture.

3. With the patron in a sitting position, place a cotton strip around the entire hairline. It will absorb drippings.

4. Use an applicator bottle and start by applying neutralizer to the curl that was wrapped last. Work backwards to the curl that was wrapped first. The length of time the neutralizer remains on the hair will vary from five to ten minutes depending on the brand used.

5. Rinse thoroughly. Allow to cool (complete neutralization) and remove the rods.

Splash method

Instant Method

1. Rinse the hair thoroughly and blot it lightly and completely.

2. Leave the patron in a lying position at the shampoo bowl.

3. Pour the entire neutralizer solution over all the rods and catch it in a plastic bowl in the basin. Continue to pour the neutralizer for five minutes.

4. The solution should remain on the hair for ten minutes.

5. Rinse thoroughly. Allow to cool (complete neutralization) and remove the rods.

Incomplete neutralization: Heat felt during the cooling period is an indication of incomplete neutralizing. Removing the rods from the hair while they are still warm will cause the hair to relax considerably and shorten the life of the permanent wave.

The best time to feel the hair on the rods and check for heat is about three minutes after the neutralizer has been water rinsed from the hair. The cooling period is used to ensure complete neutralization by allowing all of the heat to leave the hair while on the perm rods.

Overprocessed and overneutralized hair

It is possible to overprocess and/or overneutralize the hair during a perm. Overprocessing is caused by permitting the cold wave lotion to stay on too long. Overneutralizing is caused by applying a neutralizer which is too strong. When a neutralizer is chemically strong enough to neutralize the interior cortex completely, it is much too strong for the outer cortex. The outer part of the hair will be overneutralized. In both cases, the permanent wave will relax because of insufficient re-bonding of the chemical links.

Incomplete
Neutralizing

**Permanent waving
chemical waving**

Unit 14
Prepermanent waving steps

General objectives-student goals:
After study, instruction and completion of this unit, you will be able to demonstrate understanding of the four prepermanent waving steps by writing and/or giving a brief overview of all four steps.

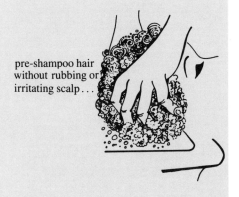

pre-shampoo hair without rubbing or irritating scalp . . .

Unit 15
Cold wave procedure

General objectives-student goals:
After study, instruction, practice and completion of this unit, you will

> **Permanent waving chemical waving**

Unit 14
Prepermanent waving steps

1. Examine the scalp. If the patron has cuts or scalp irritations, do not give him or her a permanent wave.

2. Determine

   A. Porosity

   B. Elasticity

   C. Density

   D. Style

Warning:
Do not give permanent . . .

3. Give one soaping with a mild shampoo and avoid hair brushing or massage. Wash the hair not the scalp.

4. Either a tapered or a blunt cut haircut can be given as a prepermanent haircut. Tapered ends curl easier and have more cur than blunt cut ends. The prepermanent haircut must be considered very carefully. The results must permit ease of wrappin, while conforming to style, type, texture and density of the hair.

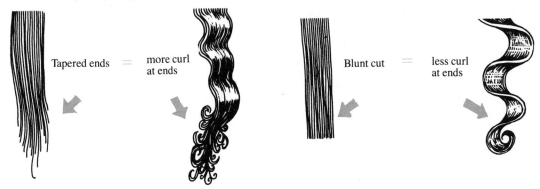

Tapered ends = more curl at ends   Blunt cut = less curl at ends

Unit 15
Cold wave procedure

Procedure

1. Drape the patron.

2. Shampoo. Use one light soaping.

3. Shape the hair.

4. Section the hair into nine sections while it is still damp from the shampoo.

5. Moisten the hair in section 1 with waving solution.

6. Subsection section 1 and wrap the hair on the rod.

7. Fasten the rod in the rod section.

8. Continue this procedure until the entire head is wrapped.

9. Protect the patron by using cotton strips and protective cream.

10. Rewet the entire head with waving lotion.

11. Process the hair. Make test curls.

12. When the hair is fully processed, rinse it thoroughly. Blot excess moisture.

13. Neutralize.

14. Rinse the hair thoroughly. Allow it to cool. Remove the rods.

be able to show understanding of the entire cold wave procedure by demonstrating the 14 step procedure. You must have the proper implements and supplies in order to complete this unit successfully.

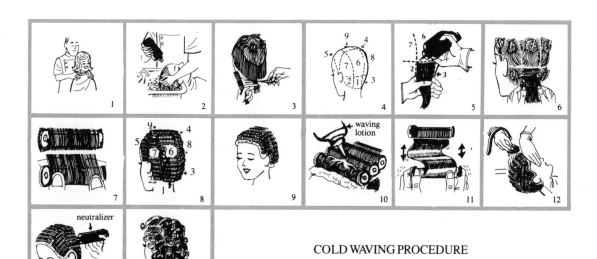

COLD WAVING PROCEDURE

Permanent waving
chemical waving

Unit 16

Body wave

Unit 16
Body wave

General objectives-student goals:
After study, instruction and completion of this unit, you will be able to demonstrate understanding of a body wave by writing and/or giving a brief overview of the subject.

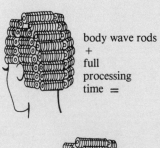

body wave rods
+
full
processing
time =

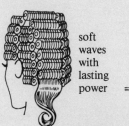

soft
waves
with
lasting
power =

sets
that
hold!

> **Permanent waving**
> **chemical waving**

164

The body wave is a permanent wave for the patron who definitely does not want straight hair yet wants her setting to hold up under most conditions and without a strong curl.

Body waves form wide, long lasting, full-bodied wave patterns of 1-2 inches (2.54 to 5.08 cm.). A conventional permanent produces a curl pattern varying from ½ inch to 1½ inches (1.27 to 3.81 cm.). A loose or soft permanent wave is not a true body wave. A loose or soft permanent wave, sold as a body wave, is usually underprocessed and will not have lasting power or hold a hair set from one shampoo to the next. This wave was developed **on** the hair not **in** the hair. The effect of the waving lotion was largely on the outer surface of the hair.

Both the hairstyle and texture of the hair determine whether a body wave is required. When the decision is difficult to make, a patron should try both a body wave and a conventional permanent wave to determine which she prefers.

If the texture of the hair is fine and soft, and the desired hairstyle calls for curls, a body wave is definitely not recommended.

The advantages of a body wave

1. The ends of the hair are full-bodied and respond instantly to the finger, comb or brush.

2. Moisture has a much less disturbing effect on the hairdo.

3. The wide, long lasting, strong and flexible waves hold their set from one shampoo to the next.

4. Relaxation is so slight that the effects of the body wave should last for a minimum of three months depending on the rate of growth.

5. It is difficult to kink or frizz the hair.

The basic procedure for a body wave is the same as for a cold wave with the following exceptions:

1. The most successful results are given on strands of hair 3½ – 7 inches (8.89 – 17.78 cm.) in length.

2. Use only nontapered rods of three sizes. The thinnest of these should be a minimum of ⁷/₁₆ of an inch (0.16 cm.) in diameter. The largest should be a minimum of ½ inch (1.27 cm.) in diameter. The lack of taper ensures even results across the entire strand.

3. The size of the rod is determined by the area on the head and the length of hair to be curled. Use a large diameter rod on long hair and at the top, crown and sides of the head. The smaller diameter is used on short hair and at the nape. The intermediate size is used in areas between the two.

4. Rods should be ventilated in order to ensure complete penetration of lotion and neutralizer. Injector type rods are preferred so that the lotion and neutralizer can be injected into the rod from the bottom end. This will allow the lotion and neutralizer to reach the hair ends. This will ensure complete penetration.

5. Using the correct cold wave lotions and neutralizers for body waves is of the utmost importance. Because of the large diameters of the rods, it is not enough to use a lotion which just weakens the hair links on the surface. The lotion used must penetrate deeply into the hair shaft. It must wave the hair from the inside out. The waved portion must dominate the hair shaft. Body wave neutralizers must also penetrate deeply and completely into the hair shaft. They must halt the action of the waving lotion completely. This permits all the linkages to re-form. The hair will regain its normal strength.

The **processing time** for a body wave is approximately ten minutes for most hair when using nontapered body wave rods. It is advisable to make test curls in order to determine the speed of the curl formation and the exact processing time. Check several different areas. Conditions vary on the same head of hair with each permanent wave. Follow the test curl procedure outlined in this chapter.

Neutralizing and cooling time

1. After rinsing the waving lotion from the hair, neutralizer should be applied to the hair thoroughly and timed for ten minutes.

2. Rinse well and blot dry.

3. Time another ten minutes before removing the rods.

4. The second ten minutes is the cooling period which ensures that all the heat has left the hair which is on the rods. The best time to feel the rods and check for heat is three minutes after the start of the cooling period.

5. Heat felt during the cooling period is an indication of incomplete neutralizing. Removing the rods from the hair while they are still warm will cause the hair to relax considerably and shorten the life of the body wave.

   Note: The cooling period and the effects of it apply to all methods of cold waving.

Unit 17
The curl control wave

The curl control permanent wave lies between the conventional cold wave and the body wave. It provides the support necessary to maintain the form and details of a hairstyle. It is not as strong as a conventional permanent nor as soft as a body wave. The best results are obtained on hair 2½ - 6 inches (6.35 - 15.24 cm.) in length.

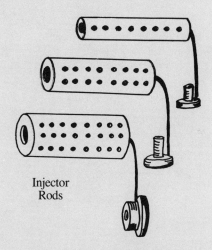

Injector
Rods

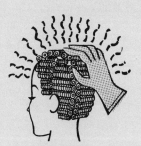

Incomplete
Neutralizing

Unit 17
The curl control wave

General objectives-student goals:
After study, instruction and comple-

Permanent waving chemical waving

tion of this unit, you will be able to demonstrate understanding of the curl control method of permanent waving by writing and/or giving a brief overview of the subject.

Unit 18
Perming color treated hair

General objectives-student goals:
After study, instruction and completion of this unit, you will be able to demonstrate understanding of perming hair that has been tinted, bleached or damaged by writing and/or giving a brief overview of the subject.

Permanent waving chemical waving

The procedure is the same as the conventional permanent wave with three exceptions:

1. Only two diameters of rods are used: large and medium.

2. The medium and large rods are alternated over the entire head. This provides good base support without excessive curliness.

3. Each strand is wound with three end papers which have been moistened with waving solution. The end papers act as a protective cushion for the expansion and contraction of the hair during the permanent wave process. When the hair ends portion of the hair strand expands against the perm rod, the three end papers cushion the hair ends. This results in a much softer curl at the hair ends.

only 2 diameters are used... alternate medium and large...

Unit 18
Perming color treated hair

Permanent waving tinted, bleached or damaged hair can be a problem. These types of hair are very porous and will process very quickly. It is important to analyze the hair properly. Depending on the hair analysis, special precautions and recommendations should be observed:

1. Always use a preperm conditioner.

2. Shampoo the hair with an acid balanced pH 6.5 shampoo before waving.

3. Use an acid pH perm lotion or a mild cold wave lotion. Both will be gentle to the hair. Both will preserve the color of the hair.

4. Use a winding lotion made with a mild waving lotion and conditioner before saturating with a mild waving lotion.

5. Make test curls. The size of the rods and the amount of hair wrapped on each rod is of great importance for achieving satisfactory curl formation with color treated or problem hair.

6. There is no room for error. Frequent checking is very important.

7. All color treated hair will have a degree of discoloration after a perm. The discoloration can be kept to a minimum by using a preperm conditioner at the time of the perm.

8. When a perm and a tint are given on the same day, always complete the perm procedure before starting the hair coloring procedure.

The desired results are added perm support or a body wave for the patron with color treated hair. A special size rod should be used to provide support for the unset type of hairstyle.

With comprehensive conditioning, careful wrapping techniques and professional judgment, perming color treated hair can create healthy, full of sheen, self-supporting and natural looking heads of hair. Always follow the instructions which accompany the product.

Unit 19
End permanents

End permanents are designed to give curl support only at the ends of the hair. They leave the hair near the scalp smooth. They are excellent for giving body and support to long hairstyles and for waving only the portion of the hair where curl is needed. If the hair is longer than 6–7 inches (15.24–17.78 cm.), the piggyback double-rod wrap should be used.

Procedure

1. Follow the conventional cold waving procedure up to and including sectioning the hair into nine sections.

2. Begin wrapping in the nape area.

3. The hair strand is directed downward, held at a low elevation and wound up toward the scalp. Do not wind more than 6 inches (15.24 cm.) of hair on each rod.

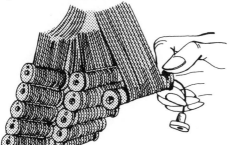

Do not wind more than
6 inches (15.24 cm.) on each rod . . .

4. Curls wound from the upper sections should be dropped. However, they should not overlap the rods below. They should be placed directly above the rod below them. If the hair is too long for this, stack the hair using chopsticks or plastic straws.

Chopsticks or
plastic straws

General objectives-student goals:
After study, instruction and completion of this unit, you will be able to demonstrate understanding of end permanents by writing and/or giving a brief overview of the subject.

END PERMANENT

Permanent waving
chemical waving

5. After wrapping the entire head, follow the conventional cold wave procedure to complete the permanent.

The piggyback double-rod method

When the hair is longer than 7 inches (17.78 cm.), the piggyback double-rod method of wrapping is the only method for perming long hair successfully. Unlike the conventional end permanent, the double-rod method can wave the entire strand up to the scalp and over the entire head. The general procedure is identical to the conventional cold wave with the exception of the wrapping.

End wrap papers allow space in which the hair can swell without touching another layer of hair. This prevents matting and a rough, dry feeling. For greater perfection, each rod section is wrapped to the end of the first end paper and then another paper is placed under the hair strand between the hair and the rod.

Procedure

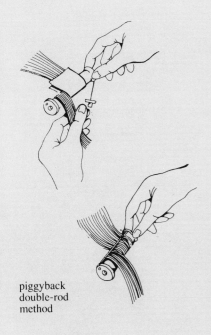

1. Use conventional cold wave rods of a preselected size. Start the wrap about halfway between the scalp and the hair ends. For the average hair type, the diameter of the rods used for this area should be at least one size larger than those used for wrapping the ends.

2. Use double end wrap papers: one on top and one underneath. Place the cold wave rod underneath the hair strand about midway between the ends and the scalp. Start the wrap by rolling the rod toward the scalp. At the same time, hold the hair ends to the left, away from the rod.

3. Secure the rod in the subsection at the scalp and allow the hair ends to hang from the rod.

4. Wrap the hair ends up to and above the first rod. Secure the end rod above or below the first rod in a piggyback position.

5. For better curl control, it is advisable to wrap each individual strand completely. Wrapping all the strands from the center to the scalp first and then wrapping all the hair ends is not recommended. The hair ends, which will have some lotion on them, should be expanding around the rod rather than hanging straight.

6. Test curls should be made from the hair end rods. This part of the strand curls easier and may need less processing time. The tightness of the perm near the scalp area may be controlled by using cold wave rods with a larger or smaller diameter.

piggyback
double-rod
method

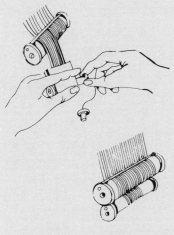

**Permanent waving
chemical waving**

Unit 20
Acid perming lotions: the heat wave

Acid waves contain thioglycolic acid base just as alkaline cold waves do but they do not have the ammonia content which cold waves have. The pH of acid wave lotions ranges from 3.7 to 6.7. These lotions do not chemically swell the hair. Their low pH requires that they be heat activated in order to lift the tiny overlapping imbrications on each hair shaft. This allows the lotion to penetrate. Unlike the conventional cold wave lotions which are formulated higher on the alkaline side of the pH scale and start their processing action upon contact with the hair, an acid pH permanent starts processing only when heat is applied. Once activated, the lotion penetrates the cuticle and gently dissolves most of the bonds between the sulfur atoms. This changes the cystine bonds (disulfide linkages of the hair) to cysteine.

The process will leave the keratin molecules free to move in relation to each other. During the neutralizing process, most but not all of these bonds are re-formed in a new curved position around the cold wave rod. Acid pH perming lotions re-form, fortify and secure additional primary bonds. These help strengthen the curl pattern and make it last for a longer period of time. When the neutralizing process is complete, the overlapping imbrications flatten. This allows the hair to return to its normal size. When an alkaline solution is used, a smaller number of primary bonds are re-formed, and the hair shaft never returns to its normal size because it was slightly damaged and suffered an increase in porosity during the swelling action. In general, the most important difference between a cold wave and an acid pH perm is that the condition of the hair after the acid pH permanent is better and the curl will be longer lasting with no early perm relaxation.

Acid pH perms work exceptionally well on most limp lifeless hair. This type of hair has fewer of the primary bonds that are essential to forming and holding a curl. Since there is no chemical swelling during this perming process, it is important to wrap with tension. Caution should be taken:

1. Not to stretch the hair while wrapping with tension

2. To use the correct rod tension when wrapping

3. To wrap the hair according to its texture

4. To wrap strong hair firmly with tension

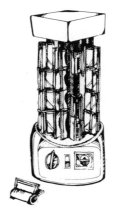

PERMING HEAT
UNIT

Delicate hair should be wrapped firmly but with less tension. It is important to wrap very little hair on each rod and to use as many cold wave rods as possible when using low pH lotions and neutralizers. If too much hair is wrapped on a single rod, the waving lotion and neutralizer will not penetrate thoroughly.

Unit 20

Acid perming lotions: the heat wave

General objectives-student goals: After study, instruction and completion of this unit, you will be able to demonstrate understanding of acid balanced perming by writing and/or giving a brief overview of the subject.

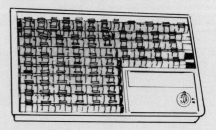

PERMING HEAT UNIT

Permanent waving chemical waving

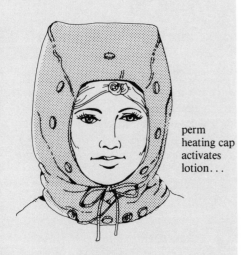

perm heating cap activates lotion...

Unit 21
Perming frosted hair

General objectives-student goals:
After study, instruction and completion of this unit, you will be able to demonstrate understanding of the chemistry that makes for successful perming of frosted hair by writing and/or giving a brief overview of the subject.

Permanent waving chemical waving

It is important for the heating equipment to be preheated while applying the perm lotion. The preheated equipment will ensure a uniform curl over the entire head. Self-heating lotions are exothermic perms which require no extra equipment or heat clamps. They produce a spontaneous gentle warmth by chemical reaction with no external heat of any kind. The perm lotion is usually mixed with a heat processing activator. This causes the lotion to become warm. A plastic cap may be placed on the head to ensure an even temperature around all the wound rods during the processing time. Always follow manufacturer's instructions.

Review:

Alkaline Perms: Curling lotions with a pH on the higher side of 7 on the pH scale. Utilizes natural body heat. Artificial heat not required.

Acid Balanced Perms: Curling lotions with a pH of 7 or slightly above 7 on the pH scale. Requires some form of artificial heat.

Acid pH Perms: Curling lotions with a pH below 7 on the pH scale. Requires some form of artificial heat.

Exothermic Perms: Alkaline curling lotions, when mixed with an additive, create heat by a chemical reaction. Mechanical heat not required.

Unit 21
Perming frosted hair

The science of permanent waving has expanded to include the successful permanent waving of hair which is made up of a mixture of lightened (bleached) hair, tinted hair and hair that has never received an application of any kind of a chemical.

All molecules contain a combination of both positive (cationic) and negative (anionic) electrical charges known as ions. Electrons and protons are elementary parts of a molecule. When there are more electrons than protons, a negative ion is formed. When a molecule has more protons than electrons, a positive ion is formed.

The number of negatively charged ions within the hair increases when the hair is damaged by natural causes or is treated with penetrating chemicals. The negative charge in the hair increases in direct proportion to the amount of abuse or damage.

In order to permanent wave frosted hair successfully, it is important to use a permanent wave lotion that has been formulated with specially developed proteins in which the molecules carry additional positive charges. These increase the electric attraction to the negatively charged tinted, colored or abused hair. The positively charged proteins act as a filler which buffers the waving lotion on the hairs that have been color treated or damaged. The ratio of the buffering action is equal to the amount of porosity. These energized molecules are drawn into the most porous sections of each hair strand. This reduces the activity rate in these areas and equalizes the porosity while processing. It is important to follow the manufacturer's instructions when perming frosted hair.

Unit 22
Perm-A-Curl

Perm-A-Curl, also known as Relax-A-Curl, is the method of perming naturally super curly hair. It is a method of relaxing super curly hair with a thio solution and immediately permanent waving the relaxed hair. The result will be larger and softer curls that do not require a basic foundation hair set.

The procedure requires that the super curly hair be relaxed to its highest degree of straightness and then given a perm with large diameter spool type perm rods. The length of the hair determines the size of the perm rod. The longer the hair, the larger the diameter of the rod. A minimum of $2\frac{1}{2}$ turns is necessary in order to develop a successful curl on short hair.

Technique and procedure

1. Arrange the equipment and supplies.

2. Prepare and drape the model just as for a regular hair relaxing treatment.

3. Shampoo the hair. Do not rub the scalp.

4. Towel dry. Leave the hair slightly damp.

5. Put on protective gloves.

6. Apply thio relaxer in the usual manner.

7. Set a timer. Continually comb the hair flat and smooth until the desired amount of relaxation is reached.

8. Avoid processing the hair for over 20 minutes. Without removing the lotion from the hair, section the hair for a regular perm and use plastic hair clips to hold each section of the hair securely in place.

9. Follow the exact procedure for giving a cold wave. Use larger diameter spool type perm rods.

10. When the wrapping is complete, saturate the hair on the rods and allow it to process. Then, neutralize the hair.

11. After the hair has been processed and neutralized completely, remove the rods and apply hair conditioner.

12. Comb the hair into a relaxed curly style and dry it under infrared heat lamps. Alternatively, set the hair in the usual manner.

   Note: The manufacturer's instructions may vary with each product. It is always advisable to follow the manufacturer's instructions.

General objectives-student goals: After study, instruction, practice and completion of this unit, you will be able to show understanding of the purpose, technique and procedure for perming super curly hair by demonstrating the procedure. You must have the proper implements and supplies in order to complete this unit successfully.

Permanent waving chemical waving

General objectives-student goals:
After study, instruction and completion of this unit, you will be able to demonstrate understanding of instrument controlled processing time by writing and/or giving a brief overview of the subject.

monitors the reaction of bond openings . . .

Permanent waving chemical waving

172

Unit 23
Instrument controlled processing time

Thioglycolic acid and ammonium thioglycolate are the most common reducing agents used in cold waving. Ammonium thioglycolate is the salt formed when ammonium hydroxide is added to thioglycolic acid. It is commonly called thio.

Most cold wave lotions consist of a dilute solution (7–9%) of thio with wetting agents and emulsifiers added. The pH ranges from 8.5 to 9.5. Although increasing the pH will shorten the processing time, it will increase the danger of overprocessing if the hair is porous.

When the waving lotion, the pH of which is approximately 8.5, is applied to the hair with an acid mantle of approximately 4.5, the chemical action begins. The lotion penetrates the cuticle, the hair swells, and the pH of the hair starts to rise. The perfect curl is obtained when the pH reaches 7, and the waving action is stopped.

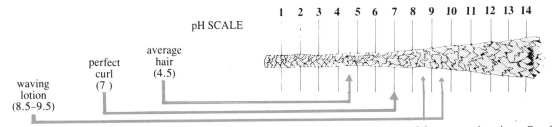

There are two conventional methods of testing for curl development and for completion of the processing time. One is human judgment. The other method uses instruments. There are instruments which can measure the pH change and signal when the perfect point (pH 7) has been reached. Test curls are unnecessary with this method provided that the manufacturer's instructions are followed.

There is more than one type of instrument available but the procedure is usually the same. The cold wave is given in the conventional manner and one rod—usually at the crown—is selected to carry the chemical change information directly to the instrument. A special sensitive probe is attached to the rod or wrapped along with the hair around the rod. A plastic cap is used on the patron's head to ensure even temperature. The probe cord is then attached or plugged into the instrument. The instrument panel may have one or more dials. It is possible to see the change take place by watching the needle on the dial move from the alkaline side toward the lower pH side of the scale. The instrument will signal when a pH of 7 has been reached.

There are six variables for successful perming:

1. Timing (processing)
2. Temperature (room, body and applied heat)
3. Lotion (strength and quality)
4. Porosity of the hair
5. Elasticity of the hair
6. pH of the lotion

Instrument controlled processing has some advantages over human judgment when working with hair of a delicate and sensitive quality. This type of instrument will signal when the six variables have reacted effectively.

Another type of machine measures the opening of the primary bonds in the hair. A probe is connected from the machine to the hair on one perm rod. The instrument with the probe monitors the bond openings as the lotion reacts with the hair. When the correct number of primary bonds are opened, the machine will indicate this. This eliminates guessing or misinterpretation of a test curl.

If the processing action is stopped before enough bonds have opened, the perm will be underprocessed. When there is an override of the processing time after the required amount of primary bonds are opened, the hair will be overprocessed. It will be dry, discolored and frizzy.

Unit 24
Perming with a spiral wind

The spiral method of winding hair is used successfully for both hairstyling and permanent waving. It is used for hairstyling when a super curly look without ringlet ends is desired on hair longer than 4 inches (10.16 cm.). Spiral winding is recommended for perming:

1. When the hair needs to be waved closer to the scalp

2. When the finished hairstyle will be in waves rather than curls

3. When the hair is longer than shoulder length, and the entire head will be permanent waved

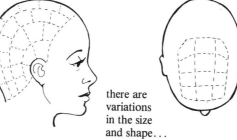

there are variations in the size and shape...

Sectioning

The scalp area is sectioned out into regular squares about $1\frac{1}{4}$ inches (3.18 cm.) on a side. Because of the natural variations in the size and shape of the skull, some sections and blocks must be a little uneven or in triangular form. The amount of hair in each block, however, should be approximately the same regardless of the size or shape of the subsection. There will be a noticeable difference in the appearance of the finished perm or style set if the amounts of hair in each subsection are not the same.

As in any other method of perming or setting hair, the total number of subsections cannot be specified because of variation in the size of the scalp area and hair density. The average head requires nine square subsections along the front hairline. It is recommended, therefore, that one square be made at the center of the front hairline and that four evenly spaced squares be made on each side. The individual with greater hair density or an extra large scalp area may require ten subsections along the front hairline. The nape area may require as little as three subsections. The size of the finished curl or wave depends on the number and diameter of the hairs within each subsection as well as on the diameter of the rod. Greater hair density requires smaller subsections.

Unit 24
Perming with a spiral wind

General objectives-student goals: After study, instruction and completion of this unit, you will be able to demonstrate understanding of spiral perming by writing and/or giving a brief overview of the subject.

SPIRAL WINDING

Permanent waving chemical waving

173

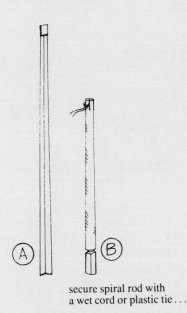

secure spiral rod with
a wet cord or plastic tie...

when spiral winding
during a hair set, the hair
may be wound slanted
down at an angle...

Permanent waving
chemical waving

174

The spiral wind

As soon as a 1¼ inch (3.18 cm.) subsection is marked off, the strand of hair should be combed free of tangles, drawn together directly at the center of the subsection and secured to the spiral rod either with a wet cord or between the slit of the rod depending on the type of spiral rod used. In most cases, the hair should be wound flat around the rod. For a kinky or frizzy look, the hair may be wound with a half twist or a full twist. The full twist will result in a super frizzy look.

flat wind   half twist   full twist

The flat wind

For convenience, the spiral winding is done toward the cosmetologist, counterclockwise around the rod (i.e., over the left side as you look down the rod). The strand of hair should be held firmly and guided like a flat horizontal band around the rod with one turn overlapping the other by about one quarter to one half the width of the strand. The index finger of your left hand should follow each turn and hold the hair securely against the rod as the winding moves down. Continue to hold the wound strand tightly and secure the ends of the strand securely with a piece of wet cord or a plastic tie.

the index finger of the
left hand should follow
each turn...

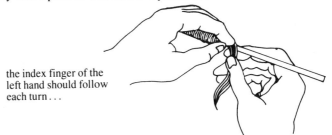

The full or half twist

The full or half twist spiral wind is not recommended for perming. It can, however, be used successfully for developing and setting hair into a style with a super fuzzy-kinky look.

The technique for winding is the same as for the flat wind with the exception of twisting the strand halfway or completely around as you direct the strand up around the rod toward you. The hair is twisted with each complete turn around the rod. When using these rods for a perm, the procedure is identical to any conventional perm method except for the winding.

Sparse ends of long tapered hair tend to result in an uncontrollable fuzzy look because the decreased bulk makes the winding proportionately closer. To prevent this, work in a little wool crepe and wind the last few turns back and over the previously wound hair. If the ends are noticeably thin, irregular, short or stubby, they can be kept under control and in place by winding the last few turns with a flat wisp of wool crepe. When spiral winding during a hair set, the hair may be wound flat, twisted or slanted down the rod at an appreciable angle.

Automatic spiral cold wave

The principle of the spiral method is winding a strand of hair in equal circles from the scalp to the hair ends. Winding with the imbrications of the hair makes spiral waving the most perfect method of permanent waving. It results in a curl that starts closer to the scalp, is uniform along its entire length and is softer at the hair ends than a croquignole wind. Spool type rods are available in a variety of sizes and are semiautomatic. They:

1. Eliminate kinky ends completely

2. Completely eliminate the use of end papers

3. Completely eliminate the ringlet curl from hair ends

4. Make it possible to give a tapered haircut before the permanent without having kinky ends

5. Permit winding to start from any section of the head

6. Allow the use of any conventional cold wave lotion and neutralizer

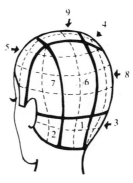

remember: 1½" by 1½" squares (3.81 cm. by 3.81 cm.)...

Procedure

1. Shampoo the hair. Rinse it thoroughly. Towel dry.

2. Divide the hair into nine basic sections.

3. Start in any section and wet the hair with the waving lotion. Be careful to observe the same precautions as in conventional cold waving.

4. Make an oblong panel within the section. Then, subsection it into squares. The size of the square is dictated by the size of the spool rod used. The size of the spool rod, in turn, is determined by the thickness of the rod which is required for the permanent wave. (The average subsection is a 1½" by 1½" [3.81 cm. by 3.81 cm.] square.)

5. Use a square section of hair for each spool rod.

6. Group the strands together and hold them straight up.

7. Keep the rod base open. Place the rod in the center of the square close to the scalp and lock it securely around the strand of hair.

8. Insert the hair into the spool. Hold the strand firm and turn the spool to wind the hair automatically onto the rod in a spiral fashion from the scalp to the hair ends.

start wind from scalp to hair ends...

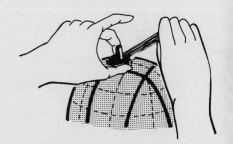

Permanent waving chemical waving

175

midst of winding
spiral wave...

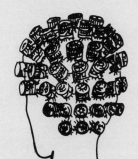

Unit 25

Curl reduction

General objectives-student goals:
After study, instruction and completion of this unit, you will be able to demonstrate understanding of the curl reduction technique and procedure by writing and/or giving a brief overview of the subject.

**Permanent waving
chemical waving**

spool type rods

9. Wind the entire head using the same technique. Use smaller spool rods where the hair is short. Selecting the right size spool rod is important. Too much hair will not fit within the spool and too little hair will cause the rod to loosen.

10. Saturate the hair on all the spool rods and process. The processing time for automatic spiral cold waves is somewhat longer than for conventional cold waving. This is because hair wound on spool rods does not sit directly on the scalp. It gets little benefit from body heat and is wrapped with less tension than when conventional rods are used.

11. Make test curls at three minute intervals.

12. After the hair is processed, neutralize it thoroughly. Use instant neutralizer for hair up to 5 inches (12.70 cm.) long. For hair lengths over 5 inches (12.70 cm.), use the splash or bath method of neutralizing.

13. When the neutralizing has been completed, rinse thoroughly. Wait ten minutes (cooling period) before removing the spool rods from the head. This cooling period may be used in all cold waving in order to prevent curl relaxation.

14. Remove the spool rods and set the hair.

Unit 25
Curl reduction

When a permanent wave results in too tight a curl, the curl can be relaxed at any time after the perm is completed. It should, however, be remembered that all perms relax within two shampoos. Under normal conditions, the degree of relaxation is related to the texture of the hair. Fine hair can relax up to 20% of its curl within two shampoos. Coarse hair has the least amount of curl reduction.

Any cold wave lotion may be used to relax a perm curl. Mix equal parts of perm lotion and alkaline shampoo. Carefully apply the mixture to the hair areas where the curl is to be widened and loosened. Work quickly. For normal relaxation, manipulate the treated hair lightly until it is sufficiently relaxed. For a faster and greater degree of relaxation, comb the mixture through the hair several times. The hair is then rinsed, towel blotted and neutralized. All curl relaxing treatments should be followed by an acid pH conditioning treatment. This will improve the appearance and feel of the hair.

Review questions

1. Does a low pH perm lotion require heat?

2. What is a more descriptive term for the cold wave method of perming?

3. Is the pH of a cold wave lotion on the acid or alkaline side of the scale?

4. Are all cold wave rods about the same size?

5. Which size cold wave rod does hair 6 inches (15.24 cm.) or longer require?

6. Should the length of each cold wave rod section be larger or smaller than the size of the rod?

7. Is it possible to have combined conditions calling for varying lengths of cold wave rods in one section?

8. What is hair elasticity?

9. Can a perm be given to hair that has no elasticity?

10. What is the main waving agent in a cold wave lotion?

11. What type of hair requires the splash method of neutralizing a perm?

12. When cold waving, how can you be certain that each hair strand is completely moistened with lotion?

13. When is it necessary to wrap a cold wave with water or water diluted lotion?

14. Why is it necessary to use end papers when wrapping a perm?

15. Why is it necessary for a cosmetologist to wear protective gloves while wrapping a cold wave?

16. Why are test curls necessary when giving a cold wave?

17. Does the curl formation of a cold wave reach its peak more than once during the processing period?

18. Does a blunt cut haircut curl more easily than a tapered haircut?

19. Why must body wave rods be ventilated and of the injection type?

Permanent waving
chemical waving

Permanent waving
chemical waving

Hair coloring

Hair coloring: The science of changing the color of hair by either removing and/or adding color to hair with chemicals.

Overview: This chapter provides you with detailed information concerning all three categories (temporary, semipermanent and permanent) of hair coloring.

Behavioral objectives-student goals: After completion of this chapter, and after instruction, study and practice, you will be able to perform and demonstrate competency in hair coloring by demonstrating the application of and procedure for: temporary hair coloring, semipermanent hair coloring, permanent hair coloring (tint and bleach, single and double process, retouch and virgin applications), a hair coloring accelerating machine, a predisposition test, a strand test, applying tint with both a tint brush and a plastic applicator bottle and frosting hair using the cap method and the weaving needle. You will also be able to demonstrate competency by identifying, explaining and/or listing: the requirements and procedures for a lash and brow tint, the tint back to natural, tint removers, hair color fillers, toners, the selection of hair lighteners, all seven stages of hair lightening, special coloring techniques for tipping, halo lightening, streaking, corrective hair coloring, blonde on blonde, illuminizing, nuancing and monochromatics as well as treating hair discoloration. You will also show understanding of permanent rinses, coloring with henna, carcinogens and hair coloring as well as the need for patron release and record cards.

Hair coloring is the science of changing hair color by either removing and/or adding color. Artificial color (tinting) may be applied to the natural pigment of the hair, to hair tinted previously or to hair that has been prelightened. Hair lightening can remove natural pigment from the hair or color from tinted hair.

The application of hair coloring is an art. Timing the development of the color is most crucial. Hair coloring is a challenging subject because no two individuals respond to color in the same manner. Product knowledge is just as important as the required expertise in application and procedure. Hair coloring is not a luxury. It has become a necessity for both men and women.

The natural pigment of hair can be lightened, highlighted, rinsed, toned and tinted. Hair coloring requires the cosmetologist to have thorough knowledge of the complete range of hair coloring products, the available shades of color offered by the leading manufacturers and their various methods of application. The cosmetologist must also be able to perform a hair analysis in order to determine the patron's needs, the texture of the hair, the condition of the hair and scalp, the natural pigment and the patron's taste for color. The successful hair colorist must also have a thorough understanding of color harmony and an eye developed and trained for variations in shade. Thorough training in hair coloring is necessary for the hair colorist in order to develop the ability to give a consultation and do the required hair analysis. The ability of the colorist to consult with and advise a patron is the most important aspect of hair coloring. It is the foundation for establishing the patron's faith in the judgment and skill of the hair colorist.

Hair coloring

Hair coloring is classified into three categories:

1. Temporary color

2. Semipermanent color

3. Permanent hair color

    A. Adding color (tinting)

    B. Removing color (lightening and bleaching)

Single process hair coloring (tinting) accounts for almost 50% of the hair coloring business. Double process hair coloring (bleaching and tinting) accounts for about 10%. Special effects coloring (frosting, streaking, tipping, blonde on blonde) semipermanent coloring and temporary coloring account for about 40% of the hair coloring business. The most recent advances in hair coloring techniques are in strand by strand, special effects and application procedures.

When a hair coloring application and a permanent wave or any other chemical process are to be given at the same time, question arises: which should be given first? Either can go first but each sequence has advantages and disadvantages. Observation and experience give preference to giving the permanent wave first.

Sanitary and safety precautions for hair coloring

1. Drape the patron correctly in order to protect her clothing.

2. Examine the scalp for cuts and abrasions or any other problem that may require you not to give the hair coloring service requested.

3. Give a predisposition test before each coloring service if a product containing an aniline derivative is to be used.

4. Mix the color preparation immediately before use.

5. Avoid overlapping during a retouch application.

6. Always wear protective gloves.

7. Always follow the manufacturer's instructions for each product used.

Hair coloring

Unit 1
Chemistry of hair coloring

Natural hair color is caused by tiny grains of pigment in the cortex layer of the hair. This pigment is called melanin and it can produce black, brown, yellow or red colors. The absence or lack of melanin causes white and gray hair.

If you wish to lighten hair color, you must oxidize the melanin pigment by using a bleaching agent which penetrates the cuticle layer and changes the melanin. If you wish to color the hair, an amino dye is commonly used. It passes through the cuticle and is developed in the cortex into a larger molecule of artificial pigment. This developing is also an oxidation process.

In both bleaching and developing color, the oxidation job can be done by the simple yet versatile oxidation agent hydrogen peroxide. Pure hydrogen peroxide is a colorless, syrupy, violently active liquid much too strong for ordinary use. It is always used in diluted forms. Its formula indicates that it has extra oxygen atoms which it is anxious to give up. After the available oxygen is released and oxidizes the substance it contacts, only water remains.

$$2H_2O_2 = 2H_2O + O_2$$

Bleaching (hair lightening)

Most bleaching agents contain hydrogen peroxide in liquid form or a chemical which will produce hydrogen peroxide to liberate oxygen (e.g., powdered bleaches). Hydrogen peroxide is usually used in a 6% solution. This liberates 20 volumes of oxygen from each volume of itself. Higher concentrations are available but are dangerous to use. Stabilized hydrogen peroxide contains small amounts of acids which lower the pH and reduce decomposition before use. When using hydrogen peroxide, a few drops of ammonia water (usually sold as a 28% solution) will neutralize any stabilizer and release the oxygen faster.

Hydrogen peroxide is available in liquid or creme form with a wide variety of additives. In creme form, it is often called a developer. Lanolin derivatives are used for clouding, thickening and emulsifying the clear hydrogen peroxide solution for appearance (cosmetic elegance), ease of application and hair and scalp protection. Other conditioners are often added to creme lighteners.

Oil bleaches contain sulfonated oil and ammonia. They may be neutral or contain some diluted tints. The addition of hydrogen peroxide activates them.

Powdered bleaches generally contain oxygen releasing agents such as sodium perborate plus magnesium carbonate and surface active agents. They are usually mixed with hydrogen peroxide to form a bleaching paste. This paste is powerful and, if desired, can be applied to specific areas of the hair as, for example, in frosting and streaking.

Dyes (hair tinting)

Some of the early products of organic chemistry were synthetic dyes. They were first used on hair in France in 1883 and have been gradually developed and improved to the point that they are used almost exclusively. These synthetic organic dyes have

General objectives-student goals: After study, instruction and completion of this unit, you will be able to demonstrate understanding of the chemistry of hair coloring by writing and/or giving a brief overview of the subject.

Hair coloring

supplanted vegetable dyes, like Egyptian henna, and metallic dyes. They are known by several names, all of which refer to the same group of products: aniline dyes since many are derived from aniline; amino dyes since they contain an amino group in their formula; oxidation dyes because they require oxidation by the peroxide developer; para dyes because the most common type is paraphenylenediamine.

These aniline derivative, or oxidation dyes, work on the theory that colorless intermediate dye compounds have small molecules which can pass through the cuticle into the cortex of the hair. In the cortex, they join with oxygen from hydrogen peroxide to form large molecules of colored dye. These molecules are too large to pass out through the cuticle and are, therefore, locked in the cortex.

The intermediate dye is usually mixed with a soapless detergent. This increases cuticle penetration. When the dye color is developing, the oxidizing agent (liquid, powdered or creme hydrogen peroxide) gives up its available oxygen. This leaves water and the dye. The tint and the developer must be mixed just before the product is applied to the hair in order to make sure that the developing does not take place until the dye is in the cortex. The action of hair tint is such that the small molecules in the tint enlarge when mixed with the developer. The mixture must be applied to the hair as soon as it is mixed so that when the molecules enlarge they become trapped in the hair. This causes the color to be fixed in the hair permanently.

The cuticle of the hair is raised by alkalinity. The base formula (the complete color formulation minus the dye) is the vital vehicle which carries the dye intermediates into the cortex where they are converted into permanent color. The swollen, raised, uneven cuticle allows the chemicals to penetrate deep within the hair shaft. The actual color is formed inside the hair and is reflected through the cuticle which is the translucent layer of the hair.

Light is color. Objects have color because they have the ability to absorb some elements of color while reflecting others. The reflection of light increases as the hair becomes lighter (bleaching). Prebleached hair reflects light and, therefore, will reveal variations of even slight color change. The final color which you see is the color level of the hair caused by the reflection of light.

The permanence of the shade produced depends on how well the hair is prepared to receive the dye and the treatment to which it is subjected. Aniline dyes, regardless of shade, are most effective on hair that has been softened or prebleached.

Aniline dyes are available in several forms:

1. Bleach-dye combinations which, through the addition of various surface active agents, can produce the desired shade in one operation. For lighter shades, the bleaching action occurs just before the coloring effect although they appear to act almost simultaneously.

2. Shampoo tints which are combinations of dye and shampoo with thickening agents. These require a preliminary softening or prebleaching with hydrogen peroxide.

3. Color shampoos are intended to impart just a tinge of color to hair of any shade.

4. Cream dyes which have the color incorporated in a soft creamy emulsion. These are usually sold in sealed tubes.

Hair coloring

Unit 2
Color theory

All colors originate from three primary colors: red, yellow and blue. When any of the primary colors is mixed with equal amounts of another primary color, they form a secondary color. When a secondary color is mixed with an equal amount of a primary color, an intermediate color is produced. This breakdown and mixture of color can be continued in order to produce an infinite number of colors. It is essential that the cosmetologist be able to select and mix colors intelligently. To do this, a basic understanding of the principles of color is necessary. All color comes originally from light be it natural or artificial. White light is a mixture of light rays of all colors. Pigment has no color of its own but has the ability to absorb certain rays and reflect others. The reflected colors are those responsible for the pigment's characteristic color. Red hair, for example, absorbs all light rays except red ones. It reflects these. This makes the hair look red.

The three terms used to designate distinct color characteristics are hue, intensity and value. The hue of a color is the name by which we know it, e.g., red, yellow, green, or blue. These are all brilliant colors. Rose and pink are both variations of the basic red hue and gold is a variation of yellow. When hues which are somewhat similar are placed next to each other, the progression of color can be seen easily. The color wheel demonstrates this.

The intensity of a color is the degree of color and brilliance less than maximum. An orange-red is still red in hue but it is very different from the color red. Although the colors are of the same hue, the orange-red has a lower intensity. Colors near the center of the color wheel are less brilliant and of lower intensity than those near the outer edge. Colors along the outward bounds of the color wheel are the most brilliant and of a higher intensity.

The value of color is the lightness or darkness of it, e.g., a light orange-red, medium orange-red or dark orange-red. A light value is high; a dark value low. Orchid is a high value of violet and green is a low value of olive green.

Unit 3
Types of hair coloring

Temporary hair coloring

Temporary hair coloring adds highlights and color to hair and will have no lasting effect on the natural color. It is easily removed by shampooing. Temporary colorings are also used to highlight gray hair, banish yellow from gray hair, cover a limited amount of gray hair, fill in porous hair and color blend hair discoloration. A patch test is not required for temporary hair colors that contain only certified colors.

Types of temporary color:

1. Color rinses: Available in liquid or powder (concentrate) for all shades of hair including gray and white.

Unit 2
Color theory

General objectives-student goals:
After study, instruction and completion of this unit, you will be able to demonstrate understanding of the theory of color by writing and/or giving a brief overview of the subject.

Unit 3
Types of hair coloring

General objectives-student goals:
After study, instruction and completion of this unit, you will be able to demonstrate understanding of the many types of hair coloring by writing and/or giving a brief overview of:

1. Temporary hair coloring

2. Semipermanent hair coloring

3. Permanent hair coloring

Hair coloring

2. Color shampoos: These are a combination of color rinse and shampoo. They highlight and impart color tones to the hair during the shampoo. They are available in all shades. A color filler may be substituted for a color shampoo.

3. Hair crayons: These are used between color treatments to color new hair growth. They are available in all colors.

4. Hair color creams: These are used in the same manner as hair crayons. They have a cream base, are packaged in small jars and are easier to apply than crayons. They are available in most colors.

5. Hair color sprays and powders: These are used for exotic effects and to compliment high fashion coiffures. A limited selection of colors, such as gold, silver, and purple, is available.

Semipermanent hair coloring

Semipermanent hair coloring requires no peroxide developer and has a mild penetrating and coating action. The color is retained for several weeks. Semipermanent color requires a patch test and is available in all shades. They are recommended to blend gray hair partially and to highlight the natural color of the hair.

Permanent hair coloring

This type of hair coloring remains in the hair until:

1. The hair grows out and the tinted hair is cut off.

2. Changed by a hair lightening process.

3. Treated with a tint remover. Permanent hair coloring cannot be removed completely or washed out of the hair.

There are two types of permanent hair color:

1. Penetrating tints: All professional permanent hair coloring is done with penetrating tints. These are also known as aniline derivative dyes or oxidation tints. These tints penetrate through the cuticle of the hair into the cortex where the color is developed by the peroxide. Penetrating tints are available in all shades and require a patch test.

2. Coating tints: These do not penetrate the hair but deposit a thin coating on the hair with each application. Their continued use will render the hair unfit for perming and will make it difficult to lighten or tint.

There are two basic types of coating tints:

1. Vegetable tints such as Egyptian henna or any pure natural organic henna are produced from healthy henna bushes grown in western Asia. The henna bush produces three basic colors: the roots produce black, the leaves red and the stems a natural nondescript color. These colors can be mixed to produce many shades. The black can be used on

coating tints   penetrating tints

Hair coloring

black and brown hair. The natural is very popular and adds body, luster and shine to the hair without changing the natural color. Henna appeals to the beauty salon customer who wants both the benefits of colored hair and the benefits of a natural looking color from a natural product.

2. **Metallic or compound dyes:** The colors obtained by using compound dyes are better than those which come from vegetable tints because the compound dye is composed of metallic salts and organic henna. However, the color does not hold and it is impossible to lighten the hair as it colors. Metallic dyes are progressive and color builds up with each successive application. With straight metallic dyes, daily applications must be made until the proper shade has developed. The darker colors require longer periods of application. Regardless of the basic shade or the shade desired, there is only one prepared mixture. This type of product is used by many patrons who wish to color their hair in the privacy of their own homes without the problems of retouching.

The Food and Drug Administration announced its intention to approve lead acetate for use as a color additive in hair dyes. Lead acetate, the ingredient in some dyes that progressively darken gray hair, has been on the list of color additives provisionally approved by the agency. The FDA requires that the label of all hair coloring products containing lead acetate bear a statement that the product contains lead acetate.

Unit 4
Accelerating machines

Hair coloring accelerating machines are used to shorten the processing time of hair lightening and coloring by up to 80%. These machines utilize photon units of energy in a range which is both effective and harmless. A reflective surface disperses the energy to all parts of the hair. Processing time is reduced because the energy from the bulbs speeds the pace of molecular motion and induces the chemical substances on the hair to work faster. These machines are designed for use with hair lighteners, tints and toners. Most powdered lighteners should not be used with these machines.

Color development with the machine should be checked after the first five minutes, which is equal to 30 minutes of normal processing time, and once each minute thereafter.

Accelerating machines are used successfully for all hair coloring including lightening virgin hair, stripping hair, tints, toners, frosting, tipping and streaking.

Unit 5
Allergy and predisposition test

The predisposition test is also called a patch test or a skin test. The test is given 24 hours before every application. The purpose is to ascertain whether or not a person is allergic to the contents of the product. Allergy is an unpredictable condition, and some patrons may react to a product after using it for many years without a reaction. If a patron is allergic to a particular type of product, she may have the same reaction with any other brand. It is the aniline derivative (coal tar) that causes allergic reactions.

Unit 4
Accelerating machines

General objectives-student goals: After study, instruction and completion of this unit, you will be able to demonstrate understanding of accelerating machines by writing and/or giving a brief overview of the subject.

Unit 5
Allergy and predisposition test

General objectives-student goals: After study, instruction, practice

Hair coloring

185

and completion of this unit, you will be able to show understanding of the importance of the predisposition test by writing and/or giving a brief overview of the subject and by demonstrating the procedure. You must have the proper implements and supplies in order to complete this unit successfully.

Unit 6

Release statement and hair coloring record cards

General objectives-student goals:
After study, instruction, practice and completion of this unit, you will be able to demonstrate understanding of the importance of the release statement and hair coloring record

> **Hair coloring**

186

The patch test is given either on the inner fold of the elbow or behind either ear extending into the hairline.

1. Select and wash a test area about the size of a quarter with soap and water. Then, dry it with absorbent cotton.

2. Prepare a test solution that consists of 12 drops of the actual tinting mixture. If a mixture of colors is used, the test solution must be prepared to duplicate the actual tinting mixture.

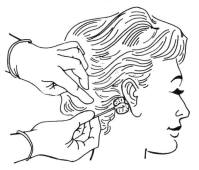
apply solution to either test area...
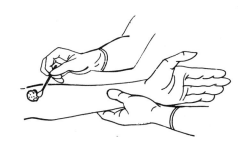

3. Use a cotton tipped applicator to apply enough test solution to cover the selected test area. Allow it to dry and leave the area uncovered and untouched for a 24 hour period.

   Note: Although most patrons show a reaction within a few hours after the test, there are many who do not show hypersensitivity until the 23rd or 24th hour of the test period.

4. After 24 hours, examine the test area. If the results are negative, i.e., the skin shows no sign of inflammation, proceed with the application of tint.

5. If the test shows a positive reaction, i.e., reddening of the skin, burning, itching, swelling or eruption, in or around the test area at any time during the test period, the person is allergic and must not use the product. A product which causes a positive reaction may also cause headaches and vomiting.

Unit 6
Release statement and hair coloring record cards

Record keeping is an important responsibility for the cosmetologist. There are many reasons for keeping accurate records. The most important reason is to avoid difficulties encountered in previous treatments. All information of significance should be recorded. The card should contain the patron's name, address, telephone number, date, patch test results, hair condition, hair color, scalp condition as well as a description of the hair, case history of corrective treatments, results of previous treatment, charges, operator, formula, timing and all special instructions.

RELEASE
NAME_____ TELEPHONE _____
ADDRESS_____ ZIP CODE_____
CITY_____ STATE _____
CONDITION OF HAIR_____
TYPE OF COLORING_____
OPERATOR_____ DATE _____
I understand fully that the haircoloring which I am about to receive is ordinarily harmless to normal hair but may damage my hair because of its condition.
I accept all responsibility for any damage that may result to my hair.
Signature of patron_____

SAMPLE RELEASE STATEMENT

Name _____ Date _____
Address _____ Zip Code _____
City _____ State _____
Telephone _____
PATCH TEST ☐ Negative ☐ Positive
CONDITION OF HAIR COLOR
% of gray ☐ streaked ☐ faded ☐ oily ☐ dry
CONDITION OF SCALP
☐ dandruff ☐ cuts ☐ irritation ☐ scalp disease
DESCRIPTION OF HAIR
Form_____ Texture_____ Porosity_____ Color_____ Length_____
Sample attached ☐ Yes ☐ No

FRONT ← **SAMPLE HAIR COLORING RECORD** → **BACK**

CORRECTIVE TREATMENTS
Case History:
Protein Filler ☐   Color Filler____ Pre Color Treatment _____
COLOR PROCESS
☐ Whole Head ☐ Retouch ☐ Corrective ☐ Double Process
☐ Single Process ☐ Pre-softened
RESULTS
☐ Good or____

DATE	PRICE	OPERATOR	FORMULA, TIMING & SPECIAL INSTRUCTIONS

The release card is used to release the salon owner and operator from the responsibility for accidents and/or damages because of the condition of the hair at the time the service is given. Release statements are also used for all chemical services such as permanent waving and hair straightening. The patron signs the release prior to the beginning of the service. If all the hair and scalp conditions are normal, the patron is not asked to sign a release card.

Unit 7
Temporary color rinses

Temporary color rinses are widely used in beauty salons. This is because these rinses shampoo from the hair with a single soaping and have a wide variety of uses. These include:

1. Highlighting any shade of hair

2. Use between touch ups

3. Toning down overlightened hair

4. Restoring faded hair to its natural shade

5. A color refreshener after shampooing tinted or toned hair

6. Beautifying white or gray hair

7. Covering discoloration of white and gray hair

There are two methods of applying temporary rinses. Both require that the hair be shampooed and blot dried:

Method 1

1. Keep the patron in a sitting position at the styling station. Use a plastic applicator bottle to apply the rinse in the same

cards by writing and/or giving a brief overview of the subject and by completing a record card with information about yourself. You must have the proper supplies in order to complete this unit successfully.

Unit 7
Temporary color rinses

General objectives-student goals: After study, instruction, practice and completion of this unit, you will be able to show understanding of temporary hair colors by writing and/or giving a brief overview of the subject and by demonstrating the procedure for an application at the shampoo basin. You must have the proper implements and supplies in order to complete this unit successfully.

Hair coloring

manner as setting lotion. Alternatively, it may be applied with a spray attachment. This type of rinse does not have to be water rinsed from the hair.

2. The prepared color rinse diluted according to instructions may be applied from a bowl with a brush, cotton or sponge at the shampoo basin.

The procedure outlined in method 1 requires no special instructions. The procedure for method 2 is as follows:

1. Prepare the color rinse according to the manufacturer's instructions.

2. Wear protective gloves.

3. After the hair is towel dried after the shampoo, apply the prepared color rinse with a brush, cotton or sponge. While the patron is still at the shampoo bowl and in the same position as for a shampoo:

    A. Start the application around the front hairline.

    B. Work your way around to the nape hairline.

    C. Apply the rinse from the nape area up to the crown in $1/4$ inch (0.64 cm.) layers.

    D. Make sure all the strands are saturated.

    E. If the ends are porous, dilute the mixture just before applying it to the ends.

4. The development time is from two to five minutes. Follow the manufacturer's instructions.

5. Rinse the hair until the water runs clear.

6. Blot the hair and style it in the usual manner.

Unit 8
Permanent rinses

Permanent rinses are not manufactured. They are the result of human error. The use of any temporary rinse, progressive or semipermanent coloring, as well as a soap cap, illuminizing color or French fluff can result in permanent discoloration of the natural hair color under certain conditions. Two of the most common causes are:

1. The use of any of the above material full strength on extremely damaged or porous hair. Some types of hair are naturally porous while others become very porous and/or damaged because of a normal or improper application of cold wave lotion, hair lightener or chemical hair straightening cream, constant hair pressing or the continued use of a thermal iron.

Unit 8
Permanent rinses

General objectives-student goals:
After study, instruction and completion of this unit, you will be able to demonstrate understanding of why rinses can create a permanent color change by writing and/or giving a brief overview of the subject.

Hair coloring

2. The repeated application of semipermanent color or progressive hair color on hair before all traces of the color deposit from a prior application are no longer visible.

Although most manufacturers of semipermanent hair color suggest a repeat application within six to eight weeks, you will find that a large number of cases result in permanent discoloration if the hair holds the color deposit longer than eight weeks and a new application is made on the hair.

Discoloration can be observed by checking the new growth area for a line of demarcation. It must also be remembered that under normal conditions, hair ends are the most porous part of the hair strand and will hold color much longer than the hair near the scalp or at the center of the strand.

Temporary rinses, brightening rinses and semipermanent rinses are not designed for permanent hair color but when a semipermanent hair color is not used correctly, it can become progressive because of build-up. When any brightening or temporary rinse is not used correctly, it can become a permanent rinse because of absorption and/or too frequent applications. When this happens, the way to remove the temporary color permanently from the hair is to cut that part of the hair from the strand. The alternative is to tint back or lighten the hair to its natural shade. However, because of normal oxidation of color on tinted or lightened hair, it will be difficult to maintain the color.

Unit 9
Preparation for hair coloring

In order to ensure successful hair coloring results, consult with the patron and determine her color preference before starting to tint her hair. Use these three basic rules as a guide to help you and your patron make a good color selection within a very short period of time.

1. When hair loses its pigment and starts to change to gray or white, the skin is also losing its pigment. Therefore, lighter shades of color should be considered in order to compliment the new lighter skin tones.

2. Use a color chart to show the range of colors.

3. Try real hairpieces (wiglets) along the front hairline in order to help the patron determine if the color is becoming.

Preparation for tinting:

1. Drape the patron correctly for a hair coloring.

2. Examine the scalp carefully in order to make certain that there are no open cuts or abrasions. If there are any, do not proceed with the coloring.

3. Preparation:

Unit 9
Preparation for hair coloring

General objectives-student goals: After study, instruction and completion of this unit, you will be able to demonstrate understanding of the requirements for preparation for hair coloring by writing and/or giving a brief overview of the subject.

examine hair and scalp...

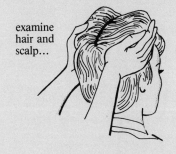

Hair coloring

A. Towels

B. Tint cape

C. Protective gloves

D. Applicator bottle or tint brush and glass dish

E. Combs appropriate for hair coloring

F. Absorbent cotton

G. Shampoo

H. Selected tint and peroxide

I. Timer

J. Hair coloring record card

K. Skin stain remover

L. After-shampoo rinse

4. The preliminary strand test: No two heads of hair react to a color application in the same manner. This is because no two individuals have the same:

A. Balance of red pigment

B. Resistant spots

C. Porosity

D. Timing requirements

A strand test is the only sure way to determine what the finished results will be like. It enables you to foresee any possibility of breakage or discoloration and to determine the correct timing for proper color development.

Unit 10
Preliminary strand test

A strand test is given in order to determine the outcome of a color application. It is used to help determine the correct formula and developing time. Guesswork is time-consuming and dangerous. A strand test can forecast such problems as discoloration, breakage and the presence of undesirable substances. The strand test is always given at the back of the head.

Procedure for the preliminary strand test

1. Section and secure all the hair out of the way with the exception of one strand at the back right side of the patron's head, about 3 inches (7.62 cm.) up from the nape.

2. Mix small quantities of the materials to be used and apply them to the full strand of hair. Use a brush or a plastic applicator bottle.

Unit 10
Preliminary strand test

General objectives-student goals:
After study, instruction, practice and completion of this unit, you will be able to show understanding of the strand test by writing and/or giving a brief overview of the subject and by demonstrating the technique. You must have the proper implements and supplies in order to complete this unit successfully.

Hair coloring

190

3. Allow the solution to develop until the desired shade has been reached. Follow the timing instructions recommended by the manufacturer.

4. Wash and dry the test strand. Examine the results.

5. If the results are not exact, make another strand test. Make the necessary corrections in either the mixture or the timing.

6. When the test strand shows the desired results, have the patron sign a release if necessary and fill in the hair tint record.

Unit 11
Semipermanent hair coloring

A self-penetrating type of coloring that requires no peroxide developer and has a mild penetrating action is called a semipermanent hair color. There is no lightening action on the hair. Color is retained for several weeks. Semipermanent color requires a patch test and is available in all shades. It is recommended to blend gray hair partially and to highlight the natural color of the hair. Each time that hair with semipermanent color is shampooed, the color fades. Continued fading allows the natural hair color to show through so that there is no line of demarcation to emphasize the new growth.

Developing time for most products ranges from 15 to 60 minutes depending on the product used and the hair to which it is applied. Some semipermanent hair colors require that the head be covered with a plastic cap in order to utilize normal body temperature as part of the color developing procedure. Follow the manufacturer's instructions concerning whether a preliminary shampoo is required. All semipermanent hair coloring should be as close to the patron's natural hair color as possible. The results obtained will depend on the original hair color, the hair texture and the length of the developing time. If there is any doubt about the outcome, a preliminary strand test should be given before the color is applied to the entire head. There are many shades specifically designed for heads with 5 to 100% gray hair.

Semipermanent tints can:

1. Add color and highlights to hair that has no gray.

2. Cover gray hair 100% without a visible change in the natural color of the hair.

3. Make gray hair more beautifully gray. The selection of colors ranges from white to slate smoke gray.

Semipermanent tints are formulated to last from three to five weeks depending on the porosity of the hair. The color is self-penetrating and is applied the same way each time. This eliminates retouching. The color cannot rub or wash off because it has light penetrating power. This type of product requires a predisposition test.

Procedure and application of semipermanent tints

The preparation for semipermanent tints is the same as outlined for permanent tints. The following outline lists the basic rules to follow. However, some products vary in their application, and the manufacturer's instructions should be followed:

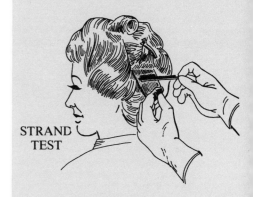

STRAND
TEST

Unit 11
Semipermanent hair coloring

General objectives-student goals: After study, instruction, practice and completion of this unit, you will be able to show understanding of semipermanent hair coloring by writing and/or giving a brief overview of the subject and by demonstrating the procedure. You must have the proper implements and supplies in order to complete this unit successfully.

Hair coloring

191

1. Give a light shampoo if required.

2. Dry the hair thoroughly.

3. Wear protective gloves and apply the color to the hair without sectioning. Start where there is a difference in color (gray, streaked or faded).

4. Apply the tint to the scalp area and work through the entire head of hair. Saturate all the hair thoroughly.

5. Pile the hair loosely on top of the head.

6. Use a head covering if recommended.

7. Make a strand test following the manufacturer's instructions as a guide for correct timing.

8. When the color has developed, rinse well. Shampoo if required.

9. Apply an after-shampoo rinse.

10. Blot the hair and set it.

> Note: In some heads of hair, the color from semipermanent tints is retained in the hair longer than in others, and subsequent applications could cause a build-up of color. This type of hair would then require a retouch. Adapt the procedure used in retouching permanent tints to the requirements of the product being used.

Unit 12
Single process tint (virgin hair)

The term **virgin hair** is used to describe hair that has been neither lightened nor tinted.

Single application tints have two effects on hair. They lighten and add color to the hair in a single application. Preshampooing is not necessary, and the hair can be colored lighter or darker than the patron's natural shade. It is also possible to blend in gray or white hair and leave no line of demarcation.

Unit 12

Single process tint (virgin hair)

General objectives-student goals: After study, instruction, practice and completion of this unit, you will be able to show understanding of the application of a single process tint on virgin hair by demonstrating the procedure with both a plastic applicator bottle and a tint brush. You must have the proper implements and supplies in order to complete this unit successfully.

Hair coloring

Application with a plastic applicator bottle

1. Section the hair into four quadrants and put on protective gloves.

2. Mix the selected tint in a plastic applicator bottle.

3. Outline the partings of the four quadrants with tint only if the hair is gray in the area nearest the scalp.

4. Subsection each quadrant into $1/4$ inch (0.64 cm.) strands. Use the nozzle of the bottle to part the hair and apply the tint.

5. Start the application where the gray is most prevalent. When no gray hair is present, start the application at the crown area. Work the back quarters first.

6. Pick up a strand of hair with one hand while the other holds the plastic applicator bottle. Hold the hair strands up and away from the head so that the subsection parting is exposed.

7. Place the nozzle point on the hair strand $1/2$ – 1 inch (1.27 – 2.54 cm.) above the part and gently squeeze the applicator. Apply the mixture. Distribute it liberally and evenly along the hair strand using the thumb of the hand holding the strand. The mixture in the applicator bottle is applied from left to right. Make new partings with a return motion from right to left.

8. Apply the mixture to the hair strand by strand. Work outward to within 1 inch (2.54 cm.) of the hair ends.

9. When the application to the quadrants is complete, either apply the tint to the area nearest the scalp and to the hair ends directly or comb it through.

10. Start the timing.

11. When the desired color has developed, rinse with warm water in order to remove free color.

12. Shampoo.

13. Remove stains from the neck, hairline and ears.

14. Apply an after-shampoo rinse. Blot and set the hair.

Hair coloring

When a tint brush is used, the color is mixed in a glass bowl. Begin the application by subsectioning each quadrant with a tail comb or with the back end of the tint brush. Apply tint to each strand, first on the topside and then below. Apply the tint liberally first about ½ – 1 inch (1.27 – 2.54 cm.) from the scalp. Then, work outward to within 1 inch (2.54 cm.) of the hair ends.

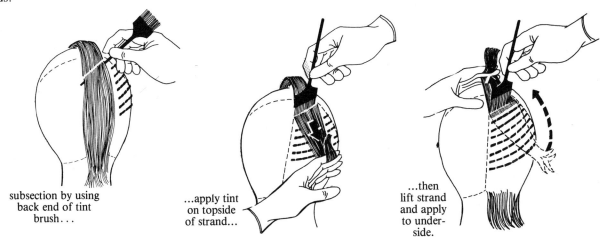

subsection by using
back end of tint
brush . . .

. . . apply tint
on topside
of strand . . .

. . . then
lift strand
and apply
to under-
side.

Unit 13
Retouch procedure and the application of a single process tint

A **tint retouch** is the application of color to new hair growth after it has been previously tinted. Hair grows approximately ½ inch (1.27 cm.) each month. To avoid having the hair appear neglected, you will have to advise your patrons to retint (retouch) the new growth every 2½ – 4 weeks, depending on the color contrast and the rate of growth.

To retouch the new hair growth, follow the procedure for coloring virgin hair in a single process with these differences:

1. Apply the tint to new growth (scalp area) only. Distribute it liberally and evenly along the partings. Use the thumb of the hand holding the hair strand.

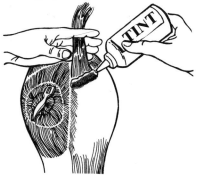

apply to the
new growth only

Unit 13

**Retouch procedure and
the application of a
single process tint**

General objectives-student goals:
After study, instruction, practice and completion of this unit, you will be able to show understanding of a single process retouch procedure by demonstrating the procedure. You must have the proper implements and supplies in order to complete this unit successfully.

Hair coloring

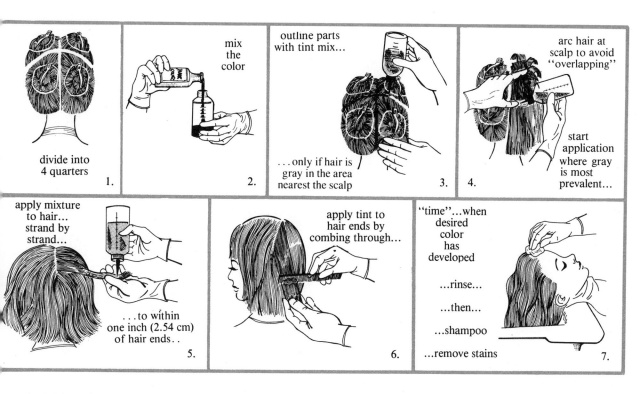

1. divide into 4 quarters

2. mix the color

3. outline parts with tint mix... ...only if hair is gray in the area nearest the scalp

4. arc hair at scalp to avoid "overlapping" start application where gray is most prevalent...

5. apply mixture to hair... strand by strand... ...to within one inch (2.54 cm) of hair ends..

6. apply tint to hair ends by combing through...

7. "time"...when desired color has developed ...rinse... ...then... ...shampoo ...remove stains

2. When the developing time is complete, apply a soap cap made by mixing the remaining color with an equal amount of shampoo or water to the rest of the hair, or comb the tint applied to the root area through the entire head of hair.

3. After the color has been thoroughly distributed, allow it to remain on the hair from one to three minutes depending on the porosity of the hair.

4. Shampoo and finish in the same manner as outlined for a single process application for virgin hair.

Application with a plastic applicator bottle

1. Section the hair into four quadrants and put on protective gloves.

2. Mix the selected tint in a plastic applicator bottle.

3. Outline the partings of the four quadrants with tint only if the hair is gray in the area nearest the scalp.

4. Subsection each quadrant into ¼ inch (0.64 cm.) strands. Use the nozzle of the bottle to part the hair and apply tint.

Hair coloring

195

5. Start the application where gray is most prevalent. When no gray hair is present, start the application at the crown area. Work the back quarters first.

6. Pick up a strand of hair with one hand while the other holds the plastic applicator bottle. Hold the hair strands up and away from the head so that the subsection parting is exposed.

7. Place the nozzle point at the scalp area. Gently squeeze the applicator bottle and apply the formula to the new growth to a fraction below the line of demarcation. This line is where the new growth and the previously tinted hair meet. This technique avoids overlapping of color since the application of tint tends naturally to spread downward on the hair strand.

8. Apply to all four sections and set the timer.

9. Recheck for spots missed or insufficient tint application.

10. Strand test the root area. When the color is developed, blend the tint through the ends by combing. Apply a soap cap.

11. Rinse all the tint from the hair with warm water. Shampoo and apply an after-shampoo acid pH rinse.

12. Remove tint stains from the face, neck, ears and along the hairline.

13. Complete the hair coloring record card.

Unit 14
Presoftening

Presoftening lifts the cuticle layer of the hair and allows the tint to penetrate the cortex.

Presoftening is recommended for gray or white hair that is resistant and will not readily absorb tint completely. Presoftening this hair makes it porous and more receptive to the tint and ensures 100% coverage of gray or white hair with little or no change in color during the period in which the presoftener is retained. Presoftening may be achieved by using prepared products such as cream lightener or oil lightener (blue or clear). It is mixed in a 4 to 1 ratio, i.e., mix ¼ ounce (7.39 ml.) of prepared bleach product and 1 ounce (29.57 ml.) of 20 volume peroxide. A mixture of 2 ounces (59.15 ml.) of hydrogen peroxide and eight drops of 28% ammonia is also used as a presoftener.

Procedure for presoftening

Apply a presoftener in the same way as a tint. Use a brush or a cotton swab applicator. No preshampooing of the hair is required. Apply the softener from the hair nearest the scalp to the hair ends on virgin hair or to the new growth only on a retouch. Allow it to remain on for 20 minutes. Shampoo lightly in order to wash out the softener but do not irritate the scalp. Dry the hair thoroughly and proceed with the application of the tint.

Unit 14

Presoftening

General objectives-student goals:
After study, instruction and completion of this unit, you will be able to demonstrate understanding of presoftening the hair in order to increase porosity and overcome resistance to hair tint by writing and/or giving a brief overview of the subject.

Hair coloring

196

Unit 15
Hair lightening

Lightening the color of hair (bleaching) involves removing pigment from the hair. It is usually a preliminary treatment which prepares the hair for the application of a tint or toner. However, it is sometimes used as a color treatment by itself.

A mild prelightening treatment is usually followed by the application of a tint. A high degree of prelightening is followed by the application of a toner. The higher the degree of prebleaching, the lighter the color of toner that may be applied. In order to lighten from black to pale yellow, the hair must go through seven color changes. The degree of color change and the length of time it will take to lighten depend on the type of hair lightener chosen and the pigmentation of the hair. The seven color changes are:

1. Black   4. Red-gold   6. Yellow

2. Brown   5. Gold   7. Pale yellow

3. Red

Stages of
hair lightening

The hair lightening process makes the hair more porous. The higher the degree of porosity, the better the toner's color penetration.

A patron with naturally very light hair who wishes to use a toner must prelighten her hair in order to achieve the necessary degree of porosity for toner penetration and retention.

The root area always requires less time for lightening than the hair shaft because of rising body heat. The shaft of the hair usually requires double the amount of time which the hair nearest the scalp requires.

The term double process is used to identify a double application that involves two separate services which use different products. The first process involves the use of a bleaching agent to lighten the hair. After the hair is lightened and the bleaching agent is shampooed from the hair, the second process, which adds color to the hair, is the application of a toner or tint.

General objectives-student goals:
After study, instruction and completion of this unit, you will be able to demonstrate understanding of hair lightening by writing and/or giving a brief overview of the subject.

Hair coloring

197

General objectives-student goals:
After study, instruction and completion of this unit, you will be able to demonstrate understanding of three types of hair lighteners by writing and/or giving a brief overview of the subject.

Unit 16
Selection of hair lighteners

A hair lightening product is selected because of its use. It must be determined where, how and for what purpose you are going to use it. Creme lighteners and mild oil base lighteners can make direct contact with the scalp. High intensity hair lighteners (powdered or liquid) should not come in contact with the skin around the face, ears and scalp area.

Creme lighteners have a thick consistency. They do not run or drip. They always remain moist. The bluing agent helps drab red and gold tones while lightening. The addition of one to three envelopes of powdered peroxide accelerators will increase the lightening action.

Oil base hair lighteners have a mild lightening action which can be accelerated by adding powdered boosters.

Powdered and liquid lighteners used for high bleaching contain built-in substances for faster and stronger lightening action. Most powdered hair lighteners should never come in contact with the scalp or skin or be used with accelerating machines. They are recommended only when extensive lightening is required and the hair is strong and in good condition. For example:

1. Stripping hair
2. Frosting, tipping or streaking
3. Removing tint
4. Extremely resistant hair

General objectives-student goals:
After study, instruction and completion of this unit, you will be able to demonstrate understanding of the required preparation for lightening virgin hair by writing and/or giving a brief overview of the subject.

Unit 17
Preparation for lightening virgin hair

A preliminary lightening strand test is necessary in order to determine the correct lightening mixture and the length of time t leave the mixture on the hair. It is also an opportunity to evaluate the reaction of the hair to the lightening mixture. It is advisabl and timesaving to make the preliminary strand test on several full strands of hair. Use a mixture proportionately equivalent to th mixture that will be used in the final lightening process. Time accordingly.

Check list for the strand test

1. If the hair is not light enough, increase the strength of the mixture and/or increase the lightening time depending on th desired results.

2. If the hair is too light, decrease the lightening time or consider a milder mixture.

3. If the hair is very dark and resistant, it may not lighten sufficiently in one application. When additional lightenin treatments are required, it is advisable to allow a day to elapse between applications.

Hair coloring

4. The strand test should be observed carefully for breakage or discoloration. If the hair shows damage, reconditioning and retesting are required before proceeding.

5. When the desired color is obtained, and if the condition of the hair remains good, proceed with the full color application.

Preparation for lightening virgin hair

1. Towels

2. Tint cape

3. Protective gloves

4. Plastic applicator bottle or applicator brush and glass bowl

5. Shampoo

6. Absorbent cotton

7. After-shampoo rinse*

8. Combs appropriate for hair coloring

9. Clips to secure the hair

10. Record card

11. Peroxide and lightening agents

12. Measuring cup

13. Timer

14. Protective skin cream

    * After a hair lightening, one of two types of after-shampoo rinse may be used:

        1. When lightening is a color treatment in itself, use an acid rinse, e.g., vinegar or creme.

        2. When lightening is a treatment preliminary to the application of a tint or toner, use a peroxide neutralizing rinse.

Hair coloring

Unit 18
Procedure for lightening virgin hair

General objectives-student goals:
After study, instruction, practice and completion of this unit, you will be able to show understanding of the procedure for lightening virgin hair by giving a brief overview of the subject and by demonstrating the procedure. You must have the proper implements and supplies in order to complete this unit successfully.

when hair shafts are lightened well into halfway mark, apply lightener to root area and hair ends... use applicator or brush...

Hair coloring

Unit 18
Procedure for lightening virgin hair

1. Drape the patron for a hair lightening.

2. Examine the hair and scalp for abrasions or open wounds. Do not make an application if the scalp is not normal.

3. Section the hair into four quadrants.

4. Apply protective cream on the skin area around the entire hairline.

5. Prepare the lightening mixture.

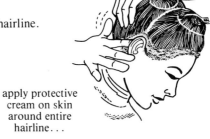

apply protective cream on skin around entire hairline...

6. Wear protective gloves. Apply the lightener. Start where the hair seems darkest and/or most resistant. This area is usually at the crown, and it is advisable to start the application there, at the back of the head.

7. Make ¼ inch (0.64 cm.) subsections and apply the mixture generously to each strand on both the top and underside. Start inch (2.54 cm.) away from the scalp and work to 1 inch (2.54 cm.) of the hair ends.

8. Continue ¼ inch (0.64 cm.) subsections and the application until all four quadrants are covered. Keep the hair moist.

9. When the hair shafts are lightened more than halfway, wipe off all excess hair lightener with a damp towel and begin the root application. The excess hair lightener is wiped off in order to make a cleaner and easier root application.

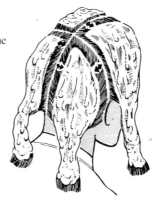

apply lightener one inch (2.54 cm.) away from scalp and hair ends...

rising body heat causes the root area to lighten faster than the hair shaft...

10. Apply the mixture to the area nearest the scalp. Start at the darkest part of the hair and use ⅛ inch (0.32 cm.) partings. Apply the mixture thickly to the 1 inch (2.54 cm.) area near the scalp, to the hair ends left uncovered earlier and to the previously lightened hair from which the excess lightener was removed.

11. When the application is complete, pile the hair loosely on top of the head and allow it to process for the required amount of time. Do not rub the lightening mixture into the scalp.

12. When the desired shade is obtained, rinse and shampoo the hair.

Note: If the desired shade does not develop from the initial application, it is advisable, as a safety measure and for the patron's comfort, to wait 24 hours before repeating the application.

When the hair is lightened to the gold, yellow or pale yellow stages, a toner may be used as the second application in order to obtain the desired color. If the hair was lightened only to the brown, red or red-gold stages, a tint should be used to obtain the desired color.

Unit 19
Hair lightening retouch application

Retouching involves applying hair lightening mixture only to new hair growth. This hair must be lightened to match the previously lightened hair.

When retouching, the lightening mixture is applied only to the new growth unless a new color is desired or there has been a build-up of color after many toner applications. If this is the case, wait until the new growth has lightened sufficiently. Then, apply the remainder of the lightener to the rest of the hair shaft as a soap cap.

Hair lightening retouch procedure

1. Divide the hair into four quadrants.

2. Use a plastic applicator bottle and subsection the hair. Make ⅛ inch (0.32 cm.) partings starting at the top of the right back quadrant.

3. Hold the applicator firmly in the palm of your hand while making partings with the tip of the nozzle.

4. Pick up a strand of hair with your free hand and hold it away from the head at an angle that will expose the new growth.

5. Place the nozzle point over the new growth and gently squeeze the applicator.

6. Apply the mixture in the applicator only to the new growth. Go from left to right. Make a new parting on the return motion from right to left.

Unit 19
Hair lightening retouch application

General objectives-student goals: After study, instruction, practice and completion of this unit, you will be able to show understanding of a hair lightening retouch application by demonstrating the procedure. You must have the proper implements and supplies in order to complete this unit successfully.

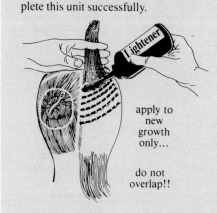

apply to new growth only...

do not overlap!!

Hair coloring

7. Apply the lightener to the new growth in all four quadrants. Do not overlap the previously lightened hair.

8. Set the timer. When the desired lightness and porosity have been obtained, rinse, shampoo and towel dry.

9. The hair is now ready for the application of tint or toner.

Application with a coloring brush

When a coloring brush is used, the mixture is kept in a glass bowl. Begin the application by subsectioning each strand with a ta comb or with the back end of the coloring brush designed for subsectioning. Hold the hair strand straight up with your free ha and apply the mixture generously to the new growth, first on the topside and then on the underside. Do not overlap t previously lightened hair.

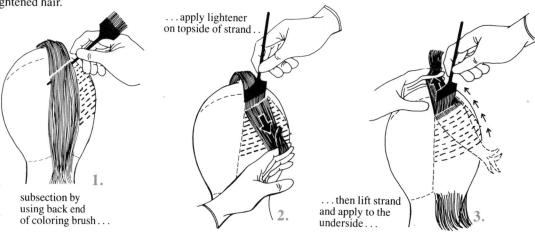

...apply lightener on topside of strand..

1.

subsection by using back end of coloring brush...

2.

...then lift strand and apply to the underside...

3.

Unit 20
Toners

A toner is an oil shampoo tint. It is a penetrating type of permanent hair coloring that is mixed with equal parts of peroxic before it is used. Toners are most effective when used on highly prelightened hair.

The delicate high fashion blonde shades of toners depend on the preliminary lightening leaving the hair sufficiently lightene and porous enough to accept and retain the toner. If hair is lightened to the pale yellow stage but is not porous, it will not reta the color of a toner. Toners require a predisposition test 24 hours before application. A strand test can predetermine the fin color.

Unit 20

Toners

General objectives-student goals:
After study, instruction, practice and completion of this unit, you will be able to show understanding of toners by giving a brief overview of the subject and by demonstrating the application procedure. You must have the proper implements and supplies in order to complete this unit successfully.

Hair coloring

202

Procedure for the application of a toner

1. After the shampoo, towel dry the hair.

2. Section the hair into four quadrants while it is wet.

3. Prepare the mixture.

4. Use a plastic applicator bottle to outline each quadrant along the partings with the mixture.

5. Start at the crown of the right rear quadrant. Apply the mixture to the root area. Use the tip of the nozzle to subsection each section with ⅛–¼ inch (0.32–0.64 cm.) partings.

6. Immediately after the root application is complete, use the comb to blend the mixture through the entire head. Apply enough additional mixture to saturate the hair.

   Note: When the strand test shows porous ends, do not comb the mixture through until the last few minutes of developing time.

7. Pour the remaining mixture on the hair and blend it throughout.

8. Comb the hair loosely on top of the head. This will permit circulation of air for better color development.

9. Time for 20–30 minutes or according to the manufacturer's instructions. If necessary, reapply along the hairline where the toner has a tendency to dry too quickly.

10. When the desired color is reached, rinse thoroughly and shampoo.

11. Apply an after-shampoo rinse.

12. Blot and set the hair.

Unit 21
Illuminizing

Illuminizing is a hair coloring technique which allows you to gently lighten the natural color of hair which may be dull and/or drab. The results are obtained by using a mild hair lightener over the entire head for a few minutes. If extreme care is taken with the application and timing of the lightener, the hair will not require retouch applications.

Procedure

1. Prepare a mild hair lightening mixture in a glass bowl. Use reduced volume peroxide.

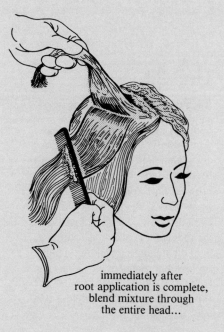

immediately after
root application is complete,
blend mixture through
the entire head...

Unit 21
Illuminizing

General objectives-student goals: After study, instruction and completion of this unit, you will be able to demonstrate understanding of illuminizing by writing and/or giving a brief overview of the subject.

Hair coloring

General objectives-student goals:
After study, instruction, practice and completion of this unit, you will be able to show understanding of creative hair coloring by giving a brief overview of the subject and by demonstrating the techniques and procedures for frosting, tipping, halo lightening, streaking, blonde on blonde and nuancing. You must have the proper implements and supplies in order to complete this unit successfully.

FROSTING

TIPPING

Hair coloring

204

2. Seat the patron in a lying position at the shampoo basin. The mixture must be applied quickly.

3. Apply the mixture to the hair with absorbent cotton. Avoid having the mixture come into contact with the hair at the scalp area until the application to all full length strands has been completed.

4. Comb the mixture through in order to ensure complete coverage.

5. Time from 30 seconds to three minutes depending on the desired results. Caution: extended processing time can result in the need for retouch applications.

Unit 22
Creative hair coloring

Creative hair coloring is the individualized process of lightening or darkening preselected hair strands in limited proportions and areas of the head. The purpose of this process is to add contrasting color to the existing hair color. The range of the color effect can be from soft color tones to exciting dramatic color effects. The methods used for creative hair coloring vary according to the desired effect, the patron's hair and the hairstyle.

Beyond perfecting the timing which is so crucial to hair coloring, the greatest advances have been made with creative strand-by-strand color application. These techniques make the new growth at the scalp area less conspicuous. The need for retouch applications is reduced drastically.

Frosting, tipping, halo lightening, streaking, blonde on blonde, echoing, mutation blonding and nuancing

All these hair coloring treatments lighten all or parts of the hair so that there is contrast of color.

1. Frosting: One method uses a plastic perforated cap and a crochet needle. The other is the weaving method, a technique of wrapping each section to be lightened in aluminum foil. Frosting gives a lightened effect to the hair by lightening small strands throughout the head. These are then blended with the darker hair. The entire length of each strand is colored. Frosting does not require retouching. Entirely new strands of hair can be lightened when the previously frosted hair grows out provided that all the old coloring has been cut off or tinted back.

2. Tipping: Unlike frosting, tipping involves lightening just the ends of preselected hair strands from the front area only. It does not require retouching.

3. Halo lightening: Only the crown hair is lightened to a shade slightly lighter than the remainder of the hair. Retouch applications are required.

4. Streaking: This method produces strips of lighter color (usually one to four streaks) which are in contrast with the remainder of the hair. Retouch applications are required.

HALO LIGHTENING

STREAKING

BLONDE ON BLONDE
(Mutation & Echoing)

5. **Blonde on blonde:** This is also called **echoing** and **mutation blonding**. It produces the same effect as sun bleaching blonde hair. It can be retouched but this requires a skillful and careful application.

Frosting: cap method

For a quick method of frosting, use a **frosting cap**. These plastic caps come with ready made perforations. Use the following procedure:

1. Comb and brush the hair smooth but loose. Give special attention to the front hairline. No preshampoo is necessary.

2. Place the plastic cap on the head and secure it.

3. Pull the hair gently through the holes with a fine crochet needle. The density of the hair determines the number of the crochet needle used. The more hair per square inch, the larger the hook on the crochet needle.

4. Start drawing the strands through the holes, along the front hairline. Work toward the back of the head.

5. The hairs along the front hairline should be drawn from directly under the holes in the cap so that the strand will be lightened as close to the scalp as possible.

6. When all the hairs have been drawn through the cap, comb them smooth.

7. Wear protective gloves. Apply the hair lightening mixture thoroughly to each strand. Use a flat brush.

8. Wrap the entire head with a large sheet of aluminum foil or a plastic cap.

9. When the strands are lightened to the desired shade, remove the head covering. Rinse the lightener off while the plastic bleaching cap is still on.

10. If a toner is to be used, apply it in the usual manner before removing the cap.

FROSTING:
Cap Method

pull hair "gently" through the holes...

Hair coloring

205

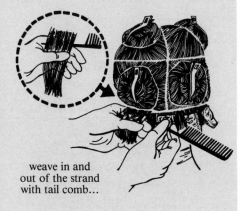

FROSTING:
Weaving Method

weave in and
out of the strand
with tail comb...

11. Remove the cap. Shampoo and apply an after-shampoo rinse.

12. Blot and set the hair.

Frosting: weaving method

1. Comb the hair into nine sections. A preliminary shampoo is not necessary.

2. Secure each section so that all the hair is out of the way. Leave a 1 inch (2.54 cm.) section across the nape.

3. Start at the right back side of the nape section and proceed to part off a subsection that measures approximately 1 inch (2.54 cm.) square. When the hair is less dense, the subsection should measure 2 inches (5.08 cm.) square. Every other subsection should be pinned out of the way. Only the hair remaining will be woven.

4. Use a fine tail comb and a darning movement to move in and out. Pick up about ten strands of hair from within the subsection. Each strand should consist of about ten hairs. As you weave in and out, hold the hair to be bleached as the top layer.

5. Place a piece of aluminum foil beneath the selected hairs as close to the scalp as possible.

6. Apply the hair lightening mixture to the hair strands.

7. Flatten the foil by first overlapping both sides so that they cover the strands. Then, roll the strands up as close to the scalp as possible.

8. Continue across the bottom row of hair strands.

9. Repeat steps 3 to 8 by preparing 1 inch (2.54 cm.) subsections just above the bottom row of hair. Continue to pattern the rows in a checkerboard fashion until the entire head has been completed.

10. When the hair has been completely wrapped, start timing.

11. Test for color every 15 minutes until the desired shade is obtained. To hasten the action, place a hair net over the entire head and place the patron under a hot hair dryer.

12. Treat each subsection individually by removing the aluminum foil, rinsing thoroughly and applying toner if it is to be used. Repeat the procedure for each individual subsection. For uniform results, the toner should be allowed to remain on the lightened strands for at least ten minutes.

13. If the toner is to be used over the entire head instead of on individual strands, it must be removed within three minutes.

14. Shampoo. Apply an after-shampoo rinse. Blot and set the hair.

Tipping

1. Determine the size of the area (front only) in which the hair is to be tipped.

2. Section the hair to be treated and secure the remaining hair neatly out of the way.

3. Use a checkerboard pattern. Pin every other subsection out of the way. The ends of the remaining strands are the hairs which will be lightened. The density of the hair determines the size of the checkerboard pattern. An average section is ¾ inch (1.90 cm.) square.

4. Protect the hair around each strand by applying a heavy layer of protective cream.

5. Place a piece of aluminum foil beneath the strand.

6. Apply the hair lightening mixture only to the ends of the hair.

7. Fold both sides of the foil over the strand. Roll the strand up close to the scalp.

8. Repeat the procedure for the remaining strands.

9. The lightening action may be hastened by placing a hair net on the patron and seating her under a hot hair dryer.

10. Check the lightening action frequently. When the desired color has been obtained, rinse each strand individually. Remove the foil from each individual strand.

11. If a toner is to be used, apply it to the lightened ends only.

12. Shampoo. Apply an after-shampoo rinse. Blot and set the hair.

Halo lightening

1. Section by securing all the hair except that at the crown section. No preliminary shampoo is required.

2. Apply the hair lightening mixture to the entire crown section from the scalp to the ends. Use the procedure for lightening virgin hair.

3. When the desired shade has developed, rinse the lightener off.

4. Apply toner to the lightened hair.

5. Shampoo. Apply an after-shampoo rinse. Blot and set the hair.

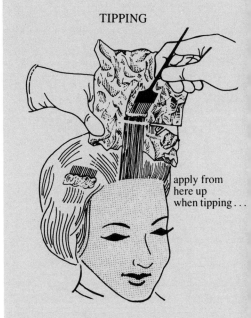

TIPPING

apply from here up when tipping...

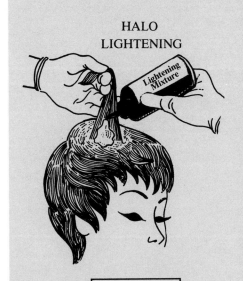

HALO LIGHTENING

Hair coloring

207

6. Retouch by following the same procedure as for a double process retouch. Use this procedure only for the lightened hair.

Streaking

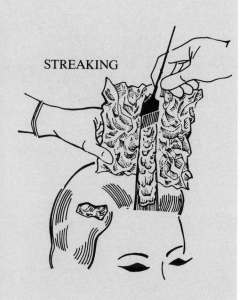

STREAKING

1. Determine where the streak or streaks are to be placed. No preshampoo is necessary.

2. Secure all the hair neatly out of the way except the hair which is to be treated.

3. Depending on the density of the hair, most strands to be lightened are placed in subsections of about ¾ inch (1.90 cm.) square.

4. Place the proper size aluminum foil underneath the hair to be lightened.

5. Apply the lightening mixture to both sides of the strand.

6. Wrap the hair by folding both sides of the foil over the strand. Roll the strand up close to the scalp.

7. When the desired shade has been obtained remove foil and rinse off one strand at a time. Apply toner to the strands if required.

8. Shampoo. Apply an after-shampoo rinse. Blot and set the hair.

Blonde on blonde: Also known as echoing and mutation blonding

1. The entire head should be prelightened. The higher the degree of prelightening, the better the results.

2. Shampoo and then apply the lightest of the toners to be used to the entire head of towel dried hair. Develop for 20 minutes. Rinse the toner off. This is the first and lightest color.

3. Section and subsection the hair into a checkerboard pattern. The size of the subsections depends upon the density of the hair and the desired results.

4. Wrap every other section with aluminum foil by folding both sides of the foil over each individual strand. Roll the strands up to the scalp.

5. Apply the next darker shade of toner to the unwrapped hair on the front half of the head.

6. Apply the darkest shade of toner to the unwrapped hair on the back half of the head. Develop for 20 minutes.

7. When the color development is complete, rinse the toner from the hair thoroughly. Remove all the foil and shampoo the hair.

8. Apply an after-shampoo rinse. Blot and set the hair.

BLONDE ON BLONDE

TONER

be sure to apply toner under wrapped strands, too...

Hair coloring

Blonde on blonde (echoing and mutation blonding) may be retouched when the new growth at the scalp area needs to be lightened. After lightening the hair at the scalp area, follow the procedure outlined on the previous page.

Nuancing: The multiple color technique

Nuancing is the application of a hair tint or bleach that has been mixed with full and reduced volume peroxide. The hair tint or bleach is applied in limited proportions in selected areas over the entire head. Nuancing results in many subtle or slight variations of one color. It creates a multi-color effect. This effect is obtained by adding hair lightener or tint to several strands of natural color hair or tinted hair. Each individual strand is colored to a greater or lesser degree.

The technique involves peroxide reduction. Create light, medium and dark color reflections for the most natural looking effects. Use full volume peroxide in the tint or lightener for the lightest color. Reduce by 5 volumes for a medium color and by 10 volumes for the dark shades.

Procedure

1. Section the hair into four quadrants.

2. Subsection the hair according to its density. Use smaller subsections for hair with greater density.

3. Prepare a light mixture and apply it to all the subsections where the lightest hair color is desired. Wrap each strand in aluminum foil and fold them securely into place.

4. Prepare the reduced volume peroxide mixture and apply it to the subsectioned strands selected for the medium color change. Wrap each subsection in aluminum foil.

5. Prepare a mixture with the greatest peroxide volume reduction and apply it to the strands in those areas where the least amount of color change is desired. Wrap all the strands in aluminum foil.

6. Set a timer and allow all three applications to process for the same amount of time.

7. Strand test as necessary.

8. When the color change is complete, unwrap each of the low volume foil wrappings first. Water rinse them thoroughly at the shampoo basin. Blot any excess water.

9. Remove the medium wrappings next and water rinse. Then, remove the light hair color wrappings.

10. Water rinse the entire head. Shampoo.

11. Apply an acid pH rinse.

Monochromatic is another term for nuancing: the shading of one hair color from dark to light.

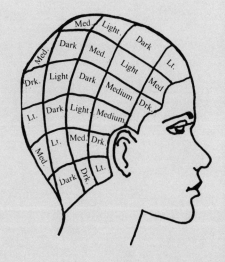

SECTIONING
FOR
NUANCING

Hair coloring

209

Reduction of peroxide

Volume	Percentage	Peroxide	Water
2½ volume	¾%	¼ ounce (7.39 ml.)	1¾ ounces (51.75 ml.)
5 volume	1½%	½ ounce (14.20 ml.)	1½ ounces (44.36 ml.)
7½ volume	2¼%	¾ ounce (22.18 ml.)	1¼ ounces (36.97 ml.)
10 volume	3%	1 ounce (29.57 ml.)	1 ounce (29.57 ml.)
12½ volume	3¾%	1¼ ounces (36.97 ml.)	¾ ounce (22.18 ml.)
15 volume	4½%	1½ ounces (44.36 ml.)	½ ounce (14.20 ml.)
17½ volume	5¼%	1¾ ounces (51.75 ml.)	¼ ounce (7.39 ml.)
20 volume	6%	2 ounces (59.15 ml.)	0

To calculate the volume, multiply the percentage by 10 and divide by 3.

Unit 23
Hair color fillers

Hair color fillers come in a wide variety of colors. They are used to build-up color on damaged and overporous hair and to equalize color take from the hair nearest the scalp all the way to the ends of the hair.

Unit 23

Hair color fillers

General objectives-student goals:
After study, instruction and completion of this unit, you will be able to demonstrate understanding of hair color fillers by writing and/or giving a brief overview of the subject.

Hair coloring

210

Hair color fillers are used for:

1. Faded ends

2. Uneven color

3. Hair that does not hold color

4. Tinted hair that has streaked

5. Color refreshener between touch ups

Hair color fillers may be:

1. Mixed with tints or toners

2. Applied directly to the hair

3. Used full strength or diluted with water

Products of different manufacturers vary in color selection and application. Therefore, follow the manufacturer's instructions carefully.

Unit 24
Tint removers

Commercially prepared tint removers are used to remove penetrating tints from the hair. The use of these color removers is always followed by the application of a new color. The removal of penetrating tints can never be handled routinely. Each treatment must be handled individually because:

1. The degree of color removal will vary on each head.

2. The condition of the hair may limit the number of applications.

With some tint removers, a 24 hour waiting period should elapse between the removal of color and the new color application. The manufacturer's directions for the product should be followed carefully.

There is a difference between stripping color and lifting color. Although the word stripping is used rather loosely in relation to hair coloring, it is generally accepted throughout the industry and by most State Boards that:

1. Stripping is the removal of permanent artificial color from the hair.

2. Lifting or lightening color is the removal of natural color from the hair.

Unit 24
Tint removers

General objectives-student goals:
After study, instruction and completion of this unit, you will be able to demonstrate understanding of tint removers by writing and/or giving a brief overview of the subject.

Hair coloring

Unit 25

Tint back to natural hair color

General objectives-student goals:
After study, instruction and completion of this unit, you will be able to demonstrate understanding of the requirements for tinting a head of hair that has been lightened or tinted back to its natural color by writing and/or giving a brief overview of the subject.

Unit 26

Lash and brow tint

General objectives-student goals:
After study, instruction, practice

Hair coloring

Unit 25
Tint back to natural hair color

There are many reasons why a patron will find it necessary to color his or her hair back to its natural color. The procedure requires a predisposition test. Each head of hair must be considered individually. The following list of rules may be used as a guide:

1. Check the hair nearest the scalp for the true hair color.

2. Evaluate the present condition and color of the hair.

3. Select the appropriate hair color filler if necessary.

4. Select the shade of tint to be used.

5. Give a predisposition test.

6. Make strand tests in order to determine the proper timing, color and mixture.

Procedure

1. When necessary, apply an appropriate hair color filler over the entire head.

2. Allow the filler to remain on the hair for 20 minutes.

3. Rinse and towel dry.

4. Section the hair into four quadrants. Subsection into ¼ inch (0.64 cm.) partings for the tint application.

5. Apply the appropriate tint to both sides of the hair strand from the hair nearest the scalp to the ends.

6. Make a strand test immediately after the application has been completed. When the desired shade is obtained, shampoo.

7. Give an after-shampoo rinse. Blot and set the hair.

Unit 26
Lash and brow tint

Use only products specially prepared for coloring the eyelashes and eyebrows. Aniline derivative tints should never be used for coloring eyebrows or eyelashes. The application of them in this area may cause injury to the eye. The application procedure varies with each product. However, the following is a good guide:

1. The patron must lie down in a facial or shampoo chair with a headrest. A straight or sitting position is dangerous.

2. Drape properly including a clean towel across the chest.

3. Remove all traces of cosmetic make-up from the lashes and brows.

4. Apply petroleum jelly lightly around the eyes and on the paper eye shields.

5. Adjust the eye shields and close the eyes gently.

6. Apply number 1 solution to the lashes and brows with a cotton tipped applicator. Discard the cotton tipped applicator once it is used. **Never redip an applicator into the bottle**

7. Three minutes after applying number 1 solution, apply number 2 solution in the same manner as number 1 solution. Allow it to remain on for 60 seconds.

8. Remove all skin stains with the special stain remover (solution number 3) which comes with the lash and brow tint.

9. Remove the eye shields. Wash the brows and lashes with water on a piece of absorbent cotton.

wash lashes with cold water...

Stain Remover

...and use stain remover if necessary...

10. Place moist eye pads over the eyes and rewash the brows with soap and water on a piece of absorbent cotton.

11. Remove the eye pads and wash the eyelashes.

12. Place witch hazel pads over the eyes for two minutes as a final touch.

Unit 27
Advanced hair coloring and chromatics related to hair discoloration

Sodium thiosulfate is indispensable to the hair colorist. It can be purchased at drug or surgical supply stores. Thiosulfate is a chemical that can improve bleaching and tinting results in many ways. Thiosulfate removes:

   1. Yellow streaks from white and gray hair.

and completion of this unit, you will be able to show understanding of the technique and procedure for giving a lash and brow tint by demonstrating the procedure. You must have the proper implements and supplies in order to complete this unit successfully.

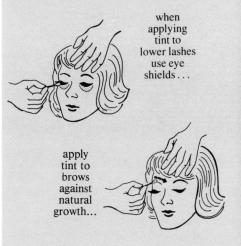

when applying tint to lower lashes use eye shields...

apply tint to brows against natural growth...

Unit 27
Advanced hair coloring and chromatics related to hair discoloration

General objectives-student goals:
After study, instruction and comple-

Hair coloring

213

tion of this unit, you will be able to demonstrate understanding of hair discoloration by writing and/or giving a brief overview of the subject.

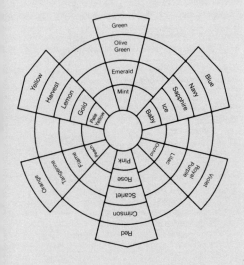

COLOR WHEEL

214

2. Ugly brownish casts in iron gray hair.

3. Yellow and gold casts from bleached hair. It is especially useful for virgin bleaching.

4. Any discoloration in white hair caused by hair straightening which cannot be removed even by deep bleaching.

5. Most temporary hair colorings or rinses from any hair color. For example, white hair takes on an undesirable blue shade which shampooing will not remove.

Thiosulfate can also be used to lighten tints and dyes without leaving telltale red or orange casts.

Dissolve two tablespoons of thiosulfate in 4 ounces (118.30 ml.) of water. Add two teaspoons of citric acid. Apply the mixture to the troubled area and watch closely until the desired result is obtained. Always follow this procedure.

Unwanted green in ash blondes or browns: Green is a secondary color resulting from the combination of blue and yellow. It can be corrected by adding red. Add one to three caps of any red tint of equal tone value to the tint being used.

Unwanted orange in redheads: Orange is red and yellow. Add blue to eliminate the orange.

Unwanted purple in silvers and pastels: Purple is red and blue. Therefore, add yellow to eliminate the purple.

Unwanted yellow in natural grays or silvers: The missing primary colors are red and blue. Red and blue combined are purple. Use a filler with a purple base because the purple is needed to eliminate the yellow.

Yellow + blue = green   Red **eliminates** green

Red + blue = violet   Yellow **eliminates** violet

Red + yellow = orange   Blue **eliminates** orange

Use this principle to neutralize and change any undesirable shade by adding its opposite color. Use the color wheel as a guide.

It is a simple color theory. All colors begin with three primary colors: blue, yellow and red. Mix them and you have secondary colors: green, violet and orange. It is the base color that will determine the final shade. A toner with a blue base applied to hair lightened only to the gold or yellow stage will have a green cast. The hair must be lightened to a pale yellow stage so that the blue will dominate the yellow. A strand preview test is the best way to prevent mistakes.

Unit 28
Hair coloring with henna

There are two kinds of henna. One is an organic coloring agent. The other, which is known as white henna, is used to thicken liquid hair lightening mixtures. White henna is a powdered magnesium carbonate that does not have any effect on lightening or changing the color of hair. Henna for hair coloring was one of the first organic coloring agents used for beauty. It dates back to the ancient Egyptians, Africans and Persians. Henna is a vegetable dye prepared from the powdered leaves, roots and stems from a thorny bush known in botanical terms as the lawsonia inermis. The henna plant is grown mainly in the Middle East and on the coast of Mediterranean Africa. Today, most of the plants come from Morocco, Iran and India.

This bush produces three basic colors. The powdered leaves produce red, the roots black and the stems a nondescript natural color. These colors may be mixed to produce many shades. The black can be used on black and brown hair. The natural is very popular. It is used to condition, thicken, strengthen, add body, luster and shine to the hair without changing its color.

Henna appeals to the young customer and to beauty salon patrons who want to maintain a natural color and have all the benefits of henna as well as most of the benefits of colored hair.

When henna powder is mixed with the correct amount of water, it becomes a paste. When it is applied to the hair, it seals the cuticle layer and coats the shaft with color. The sealed cuticle gives the hair a high gloss and a polished finish.

Compound henna is organic henna to which metallic salts have been added. Compound dyes achieve better colors than pure vegetable tints, but the colors do not hold. Compound henna is not compatible with modern hair coloring and permanent waving materials.

Although henna was originally used for coloring the hair, a very large percentage of the henna used has the nondescript natural shade. A predisposition test is not required with most henna products.

Implements, supplies and materials

1. Shampoo cape, neck strip, towels, acid balanced shampoo, comb, hair clips

2. Rubber gloves, plastic bowl, wooden spoon, a 2 inch (5.08 cm.) wide paint brush, porcelain or heat resistant glass double boiler, electric heater

3. Plastic cap, dryer, timer

Procedure

1. Select the shade and mix it in a clean plastic bowl. Add enough very hot water to thicken the mixture to a pasty consistency or, depending on the specific manufacturer's instructions, the mixture may be prepared in the top of a double boiler and kept hot on an electric heater throughout the entire procedure.

General objectives-student goals: After study, instruction and completion of this unit, you will be able to show understanding of hair coloring with henna by writing and/or giving a brief overview of the subject.

this is the henna plant "lawsonia inermis" . . .

Hair coloring

the mixture may be
mixed in the top
of a double boiler...

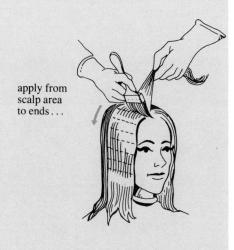

apply from
scalp area
to ends...

2. While the mixture is heating, drape the patron and shampoo her hair with an acid balanced shampoo. Towel the hair dry.

3. Section the hair into quadrants. Wear gloves. Use a clean brush to apply the mixture like a tint. However, you must use much larger subsections.

4. Start at the nape. Apply from the scalp area to the ends. Work deeply into the hair using the brush and your fingers so that the pasty mixture adheres to the shaft.

5. Work upward until you reach the crown area. Continue by completing the application to the second half of the back section in the same manner.

6. Use the same size subsections and apply the mixture to the two front sections. Start at the top of the head and work your way down toward the hairline around the ear. Always apply the mixture sparingly around the facial hairline.

7. Pack the henna mixture thoroughly so that all the hair shafts are covered.

8. Bring all the hair up toward the crown with your fingers and the brush. Apply the balance of the mixture over the entire head.

9. Place some absorbent cotton around the hairline and over the ears. Cover the patron's head with a plastic cap.

10. Place the patron under a hot hair dryer, heating cap or infrared lamps for 30 minutes. If a deeper color is desired, leave the mixture on the hair for an additional 30 minutes. The patron remains under the heat source for this additional period of time.

11. Remove the plastic cap and allow the patron to remain under the dryer or infrared lamps for an additional 15 minutes.

12. Rinse the hair thoroughly with warm water until all the henna mixture has been rinsed from the hair.

13. Shampoo the hair with an acid balanced pH 6.5 shampoo.

Henna coloring treatments are not recommended for prelighted hair or for hair that has more than 10% gray.

Hair coloring

216

Unit 29
Henna removal process

To remove some henna coloring from the hair or if a lighter final shade is desired, follow this procedure:

1. Apply rubbing alcohol (about 70%) to clean dry hair. Saturate well, but not to the point of dripping.

2. Let the hair stand 10 minutes.

3. Apply about 3½ ounces (3.51 ml.) of castor oil over the hair wet with alcohol. Work the oil well over all the hair shafts.

4. Cover with a plastic cap and place under a hot hair dryer for 30 minutes.

5. Shampoo the hair with a soapless oil shampoo.

6. If further removal or reduction of color is desired, repeat the procedure.

Unit 30
Carcinogens and hair coloring

Over the years, there have been several unfavorable reports regarding permanent hair coloring, but they have never been substantiated with actual proof. Most questions arise concerning one particular ingredient: **4-Methoxy-M-Phenylenediamine**, also known as **2, 4-DAA** and **4-MMPD**.

The following six points of information have been recorded in this book because teachers, students and clinic patrons have been asking questions since the information on 4-Methoxy-M-Phenylenediamine was released by the Environmental Defense Fund.

1. The safety of hair dyes and 4-MMPD has been established by extensive painting studies on animals and by a number of studies of human experience by scientists at the American Cancer Society, Yale University, Oxford University and Toronto University. All these studies show no difference in cancer rates between people heavily exposed to hair dyes and those who are not.

2. A 13 year study conducted by Dr. E. Cuyler Hammond of the American Cancer Society showed no difference in cancer mortality between a group of 5,000 cosmetologists and a matched group whose members are not cosmetologists.

3. A substantial body of research sponsored by the hair coloring industry and by respected outside scientists confirms the safety of hair dyes.

4. The results of human experience and a 60 year history of safe use by millions of women also confirm the safety of hair dyes.

Unit 29
Henna removal process

General objectives-student goals:
After study, instruction and completion of this unit, you will be able to demonstrate understanding of how to remove henna coloring from hair by writing and/or giving a brief overview of the subject.

Unit 30
Carcinogens and hair coloring

General objectives-student goals:
After study, instruction and completion of this unit, you will be able to demonstrate understanding of how carcinogens relate to hair coloring by writing and/or giving a brief overview of the subject.

Hair coloring

5. The tests conducted by the National Cancer Institute (NCI) were on rats and mice. They were fed massive doses of hair dyes at a level equivalent to a woman drinking 25 bottles of hair dye a day every day of her life. This level must compared to the typical user's external application of 30 minutes once a month or less.

6. The same NCI studies show no effect when the same chemical is fed to rats and mice at a level lower ($\frac{1}{2}$ or $\frac{1}{4}$) than t maximum dose tested.

The safety of hair dyes is an important issue, and authorities believe that humans can use them safely. Most authorities also agr that the conclusions of the NCI are hasty and incorrect.

The unfavorable publicity is just a continuation of the occasional stories which appeared in the press over the past years. It c also be expected that public-interest groups will ask the Food and Drug Administration to require that many hair dyes carry warning that a chemical ingredient can cause cancer in animals.

Although there may be a repetition on this type of publicity for various other products used in the practice of cosmetology, should not give serious consideration to eliminating or making substitutions for any of the products we are presently using unle they are proven unsafe. **Another important factor is that most temporary rinses, tints and some permanent colors do n contain the ingredient 4-MMPD.**

Most manufacturers have modified their tint and toner formulas to eliminate a questionable ingredient which may require t warning labels and notices proposed by the Food and Drug Administration.

The new formulas appear lighter and clearer in the bottle. In most cases, the shades are comparable with the old colors. Co development time, coverage of gray and color fading are not affected by the formula change.

Some shades take on a bluer or more blue-violet cast during the oxidation period but this does not affect the color results. In sor cases, it may be necessary to make some color adjustment when retouching hair which had been colored with the old formu The red shades will be of new red colors. A few minor adjustments of mixtures will be necessary during the transition perio

Unit 31
Corrective hair coloring

A hair coloring specialist has the knowledge and expertise required to practice corrective hair coloring. Corrective hair colori is the art of rectifying undesirable results which arise from the application of hair color. Each problem must be treat individually. Only with time and experience can expertise be developed. The corrective work most often needed is to:

1. Remove red, gold or green color casts from the hair

2. Remove sharp lines of color demarcation along the front hairline

3. Remove color from overporous hair ends

Unit 31
Corrective hair coloring

General objectives-student goals:
After study, instruction and completion of this unit, you will be able to demonstrate understanding of corrective hair coloring by writing and/or giving a brief overview of the subject.

Hair coloring

4. Lighten hair to a higher stage, without breakage, in order to eliminate a gold cast from the color

5. Create an ash color without having the hair appear gray

Above average skills, product knowledge and knowledge of hair chemistry are the credentials required for performing corrective hair coloring.

Review questions

1. Does hair lightening remove only the natural pigment from the hair?

2. Is peroxide used as a developer for semipermanent hair coloring?

3. Does a semipermanent hair coloring require a predisposition test?

4. Can a tint remover remove permanent hair color from the hair?

5. Does a coating tint penetrate the hair?

6. What are the three colors produced by the henna bush?

7. Why are accelerating machines used for hair coloring?

8. What is another name for a patch test?

9. What are the best areas for a predisposition test?

10. What type of hair is considered virgin hair in regard to hair coloring?

. Can hair be lightened with a single process tint?

. What effect does presoftening have on the hair before the application of a tint?

. Is preshampooing required before the application of a presoftener?

14. Do semipermanent tints require retouching?

15. Is a temporary color rinse available in more than one color?

16. Are hair lightening and bleaching the same?

17. Does a hair lightener make the hair more porous?

18. Does the hair shaft require more processing time than the hair near the scalp area?

19. Do toners require a predisposition test?

20. Is there more than one method of frosting hair?

21. What are the effects of the hair coloring treatment called frosting?

22. Does frosted hair require retouching?

23. What is tipping?

24. What is halo lightening?

25. What is streaking?

26. Is the effect of blonde on blonde, mutation blonding and echoing the same?

27. May blonde on blonde hair coloring be retouched?

28. What are the uses of hair color fillers?

29. Is it necessary to recolor the hair after using a color remover?

30. Is a waiting period required between a color removing treatment and a new color application?

Hair coloring

Hair straightening

Hair straightening: The process of changing the natural hair forms so that the hair becomes straight. There are two methods: a chemical method which straightens the hair permanently and a method which is called hair pressing. Pressing straightens the hair temporarily.

Overview: This chapter provides you with detailed information, methods, applications and procedures for straightening, relaxing or straightening curly hair temporarily.

Behavioral objectives-student goals: After completion of this chapter, and after instruction, study and practice, you will be able to perform and demonstrate competency in hair straightening by demonstrating the complete procedure for chemical hair straightening, hair pressing, the retouch procedures for both methods of hair straightening and Relax-A-Curl. You will also be able to demonstrate competency by identifying, explaining and/or listing: the difference between chemical hair straightening and hair relaxing, the composition and effects of the supplies used for thioglycolate and sodium hydroxide formulas and procedures, the soft and hard press methods of straightening hair temporarily and the chemical blowout.

Chemical hair straightening is a process of permanently changing the natural hair forms so that the hair becomes straight. Thereafter, only the new growth needs to be treated. Chemical hair relaxing is basically the same as chemical hair straightening, but milder ingredients are used to transform naturally curly or kinky hair forms to soft wavy hair.

The methods for removing undesirable curl from super curly hair are known by many different names, such as relaxing, straightening, permanent waving, reverse permanent waving and the chemical blowout. The terms straightening and relaxing are the ones which are used most often. A hair straightener is capable of making wavy, curly and kinky hair forms completely straight. A hair relaxer will remove some, but not all, of the natural curl, wave, kink or frizz from the hair. How straight the hair becomes depends on the amount of curl or kink present, the product used, the condition of the hair, the processing time and the technique and procedure used by the cosmetologist.

The two chemicals which are most commonly used to straighten hair are:

1. Ammonium thioglycolate

2. Sodium hydroxide

There are some products that contain ammonium sulfite

More than 57% of beauty salons offer hair relaxing and hair straightening services. Each performs an average of six chemical hair straightenings per month. There are some salons that specialize in hair straightening, and over 90% of their services are related to chemical hair straightening. A survey has determined that 49% of the hair straightening services were for hair relaxing, 47% for hair straightening and 4% for hair pressing.

Sanitary and safety precautions for hair straightening

1. Always examine the hair and scalp.

2. Wear protective gloves on both hands.

3. Always make a strand test to determine the results to be expected.

4. Protect the patron's eyes when water rinsing relaxer from his or her hair.

5. Do not apply sodium hydroxide straightener to hair that was previously treated with ammonium thioglycolate or ammonium sulfite. The reverse is also true. Do not apply ammonium thioglycolate or ammonium sulfite to hair that was previously treated with sodium hydroxide.

6. Be certain to remove all the chemical from the hair.

7. When retouching the new growth, do not allow the chemical to overlap on the previously straightened hair.

8. When pressing hair, avoid excessive heat on the pressing comb or irons.

9. Avoid the use of an excessive amount of pressing oil or cream.

10. Keep pressing combs free from carbon build-up.

11. Test the temperature of the heated comb before applying it to the hair.

12. Never exceed the processing time recommended by the manufacturer.

13. Clean and remove chemical deposits from the work area, shampoo cape and chair used for the chemical process.

14. Be careful not to scrape the patron's scalp with a comb.

15. Do not allow any chemical to come in contact with unprotected skin.

16. Use an automatic timer during the processing.

17. Smooth and spread the chemical in one direction. Go towards the hair ends only.

Hair straightening

18. Keep the hair away from the patron's face in a straight back position.

19. Have the patron remove neck and ear jewelry prior to treatment. This will help prevent the possibility of a chemical reaction with the material of the jewelry.

20. Never give a predisposition test with a caustic hair straightener.

Unit 1
Ammonium thioglycolate

A thioglycolate hair straightener contains ammonium monoethanolamine thioglycolate or thioglycolic acid adjusted to the desired pH with ammonia or monoethanolamine. A heavy creme base is used to make the material easier to apply.

The action of the thioglycolate is the same in straightening as in cold waving. The disulfide links of the keratin are broken down. This softens the hair. The hair is then smoothed to a straightened shape with a comb and/or with the hand technique.

When the hair has been straightened satisfactorily, the action is stopped by a neutralizer which usually contains an oxidizing compound. The neutralizer is left on the hair long enough to penetrate the hair shaft and stop the action of the thioglycolate. Complete neutralization, followed by rinsing, removes all the straightening agent from the hair and restores the hair to its original chemical state. Although 4 ounces (118.30 ml.) of 20 volume hydrogen peroxide mixed with 28 ounces (828.07 ml.) of water will act as a neutralizer, solid oxidizing agents (potassium bromate and sodium perborate) have been found to be more suitable.

Typical formula for a thioglycolate hair straightener

Glyceryl monostearate	15.0%
Stearic acid	3.0%
Ceresin	1.5%
Paraffin	1.0%
Sodium lauryl sulfate	1.0%
Distilled water	61 to 70%
Thioglycolic acid	5% to 10% (normal hair)
	2% to 5% (tinted hair)

Unit 1
Ammonium thioglycolate

General objectives-student goals: After study, instruction and completion of this unit, you will be able to demonstrate understanding of hair relaxing with thio hair straightening and ammonium sulfite products by writing and/or giving a brief overview of the subject including a typical formula for a thioglycolate hair straightener.

Hair straightening

Ammonium hydroxide (26° Bé)	0.5 to 2.5%
Perfume	Q.S.*
pH value	9.2 to 9.5

*Qualitative scale

The chemical reactions are as follows:

Softening action

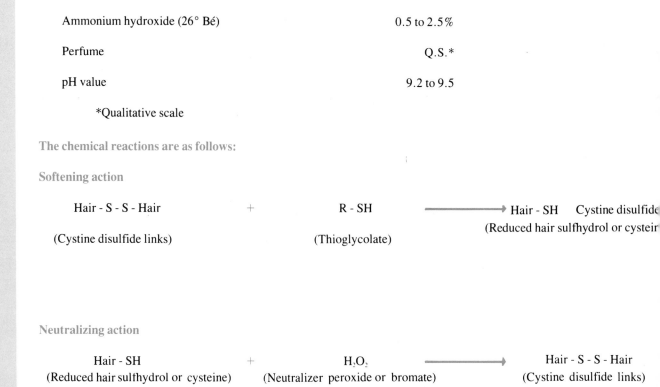

$$\text{Hair - S - S - Hair} \quad + \quad \text{R - SH} \quad \longrightarrow \quad \text{Hair - SH} \quad \text{Cystine disulfide}$$

(Cystine disulfide links) (Thioglycolate) (Reduced hair sulfhydrol or cysteine)

Neutralizing action

$$\text{Hair - SH} \quad + \quad \text{H}_2\text{O}_2 \quad \longrightarrow \quad \text{Hair - S - S - Hair}$$

(Reduced hair sulfhydrol or cysteine) (Neutralizer peroxide or bromate) (Cystine disulfide links)

As the equations show, the hair is restored to its original structure after the treatment. However, the hair is now straight.

Unit 2
Procedure for a thio relaxer

1. Examine the scalp for sores or abrasions. If there are any, do not proceed with the straightening.

2. Examine the hair. If the hair is hard, dry or brittle, a strand test should be given.

3. Shampoo the hair. Do not rub the scalp. Towel dry.

4. Section the hair into four quadrants: down the center from the forehead to the nape and across behind the ears from ear to ear.

Unit 2
Procedure for a thio relaxer

General objectives-student goals:
After study, instruction, practice and completion of this unit, you will be able to show understanding of the procedure for giving a thio relaxer by demonstrating the procedure. You must have the proper implements and supplies in order to complete this unit successfully.

Hair straightening

224

5. Protect the ears and the skin along the hairline.

6. Prepare neutralizer.

7. Wear protective gloves. Apply hair straightening creme to each ¼ inch (0.64 cm.) section. Start at the nape of the back section and work up toward the crown. Apply creme to the entire strand, starting ¼ inch (0.64 cm.) from the scalp on each subsection in order to avoid direct contact between the chemical and the scalp.

apply straightener with comb . . .

8. Repeat the procedure in all four sections. Work in a clockwise rotation around the head.

9. Let the hair soften for 5-15 minutes. Then, comb through each section once to straighten the hair. Be certain to smooth the hair nearest the scalp.

10. Allow the hair to continue processing for the time recommended by the manufacturer. Make a strand test at three minute intervals.

11. Rinse thoroughly using warm water until the creme has been completely removed from the hair. Blot the hair dry.

12. Neutralize. Pour the prepared neutralizer into a glass or plastic container and set it in the shampoo basin. Keep the patron in position at the shampoo basin and pour the prepared solution through the hair. Collect it in a bowl. Pour the solution through the hair six to ten times in order to be sure that the hair has been neutralized completely.

13. Rinse thoroughly with water in order to remove the neutralizer. Blot and set the hair into the desired style.

ways follow the product manufacturer's instructions. There are many variations of products and procedures.

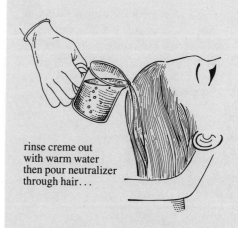

rinse creme out
with warm water
then pour neutralizer
through hair . . .

Hair straightening

225

Ammonium sulfite

Ammonium sulfite is also used as a hair relaxer. Some products containing ammonium sulfite may require the application of mild heat. Always follow the manufacturer's instructions.

Ammonium sulfite softens the disulfide cross-linkages. The hair becomes softened and will yield to a change of formation. If the change is to remain, the new form must be made stable while the hair is in its softened state. This is accomplished by re-forming the disulfide linkages through chemical oxidation (neutralization).

Reaction

Hair - S - S - Hair	+	HSO_3		Hair SH + Hair SSO_3H
(Disulfide links)		(Sulfite ion)		(Reduced hair)

This formulation of sulfite functions at a nearly neutral pH in the range of pH 7 to 7½ in a moderately viscous base. Rinsing and the use of a neutralizer after the softening step drives the above reaction to the left. This relinks most of the disulfide bonds and allows the hair to be rebuilt to its original chemical state but in a straightened configuration.

Unit 3
Sodium hydroxide

Sodium hydroxide is also called caustic. When it is mixed in a solution with stearic and oleic acids, it is used for hair straightening. In fact, it was the first chemical used for straightening hair. Different products have different levels of sodium hydroxide. The percentage of sodium hydroxide in various products ranges from 5 to 10 percent. The pH value goes from 7.5 to 14. The greater the percentage of sodium hydroxide, the higher the pH value. In addition, the reaction of the chemical on the hair proceeds more quickly. However, there is a drawback with the quicker reacting chemicals. They are more likely to damage the skin and hair.

Sodium hydroxide causes the hair fibers to swell. It softens the main disulfide bonds which link the polypeptide chains of the hair. This action should be complete within eight minutes. During this process, the disulfide links lose one molecule of sulfur. After rinsing, they rejoin as lanthionine links between the polypeptide chains. This stabilizes the hair. Hair treated with thioglycolate will return to its original structure but hair treated with sodium hydroxide will not do so.

Chemical reaction

Hair - S - S - Hair	+	NaOH		Hair - S - Hair
(Cystine disulfide link)		(Sodium hydroxide)		(Lanthionine link)

Unit 3
Sodium hydroxide

General objectives-student goals:
After study, instruction and completion of this unit, you will be able to demonstrate understanding of sodium hydroxide as a hair straightener by writing and/or giving a brief overview of the subject including two examples of formulas using sodium hydroxide.

Hair straightening

226

You should protect the patron's skin with a base. This is especially true during the rinsing procedure. Sodium hydroxide can burn the skin and scalp. It should also be noted that if you leave sodium hydroxide on the hair for too long a period, it may cause discoloration, make the hair brittle and cause breakage.

Two examples of formulas using sodium hydroxide

Formula 1

Sodium hydroxide	5%
Glycerine monostearate	15%
Glycerol	5%
Water	75%
Perfume	Q.S.*
pH value	10-14

Formula 2

Stearic acid	15%
Oleic acid	5%
Glycerol	5%
Sodium hydroxide	10%
Water	65%
Perfume	Q.S.*
pH value	10-14

*Qualitative scale

Although a predisposition test is recommended for most products that come in contact with the skin, do not give the test with a caustic hair straightening product. A caustic straightener must never come in contact with the skin. A caustic chemical hair straightener can burn the skin immediately on contact.

Hair straightening

Unit 4

Procedure for a sodium hydroxide hair straightener

General objectives-student goals:
After study, instruction, practice and completion of this unit, you will be able to show understanding of hair straightening with a caustic by demonstrating the entire procedure. You must have the proper implements and supplies in order to complete this unit successfully.

apply base to scalp, ears and skin around hairline

Hair straightening

228

Unit 4

Procedure for a sodium hydroxide hair straightener

1. Examine the scalp for sores or abrasions. If there are any, do not proceed with the straightening.

2. Examine the hair and make a strand test. The procedure for making a strand test requires the application of the chemical to a hair strand in the back area of the head. The application and procedure are made in the same manner as you would when applying the chemical to the entire head.

3. Do not brush or shampoo the hair.

4. Section the hair into four quadrants: down the center from the forehead to the nape and across behind the ears from ear to ear.

5. Apply a protective base evenly. Cover the scalp completely. Start with the back left section and work counterclockwise around the head. Subsection each quadrant into ¼ inch (0.64 cm.) horizontal partings from ear to ear. Apply the base to the scalp with the middle and index fingers or index finger only across the top parting of each strand and press down.

   Note: When the protective base is applied correctly, each parting, when lifted, will show base cream on the back of the strand. The base is placed on the scalp and pressed in. It is not spread or rubbed on. Protect the ears and skin along the hairline with protective base.

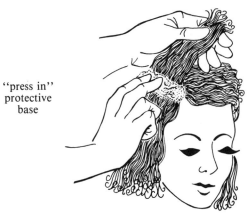

"press in" protective base

6. Divide the hair into four quadrants again. Wear protective gloves and apply hair straightening cream. Start at the crown of the back left section and lay the chemical straightener on the hair shaft starting about ½ inch (1.27 cm.) from the scalp area. When applying the straightener, the hair is subsectioned in the same manner as when applying the protective base cream. Complete the application to all four sections.

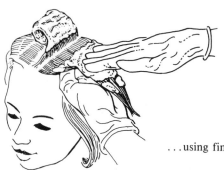

apply straightener
starting ½" (1.27 cm.)
from scalp...

...using fingers or a comb

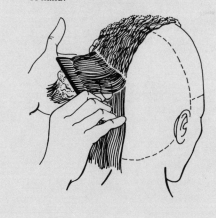

When using comb:
comb hair over palm
of hand.

7. Again, apply straightener to the hair closest to the scalp. Begin to straighten and smooth the hair in the root area and at the hairline with a comb or your fingers. Then, comb through the hair shaft. Add more chemical as needed. The processing time will range from two to eight minutes depending on the degree of excess curl, the texture of the hair and the amount of time used for the application.

Strand test the hair while spreading the chemical. Observe the reaction of the hair to the chemical by stretching and spreading the strands in order to see how fast the natural curl or kink is relaxing and straightening. When the desired results have been obtained, continue to step 8. If, however, the action is too fast in any one area, water rinse the relaxer from that section and then continue with the procedure.

8. Rinse thoroughly with warm water. Hold the spray 4-5 inches (10.16-12.70 cm.) from the head. The straightener should be removed from the hair by the force of the water not with your hand.

Important:
carefully smooth
hair around
entire hairline...

9. Shampoo the hair thoroughly. Do not rub the scalp.

10. Blot the hair.

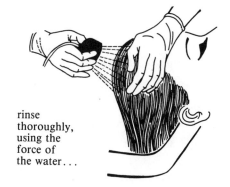

rinse
thoroughly,
using the
force of
the water...

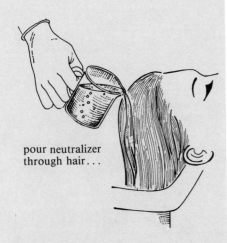

pour neutralizer
through hair...

11. Neutralize according to the product and the manufacturer's directions. Set the hair into the desired style.

> Note: Some sodium hydroxide hair straighteners do not require the application of a protective base because the base is built into the hair straightening cream. These no-base products are usually hair relaxers rather than hair straighteners because the chemical action is retarded by the base cream.

Students who are still in training should always apply a protective base at the scalp, around the ears and around the skin at the hairline even when using a no-base product.

You should use a hair filler and a conditioner before straightening or relaxing tinted, bleached or damaged hair. These products will fill the cuticle scales of the hair shaft. This will prevent porous hair from breaking and will permit even penetration of the straightening lotion. Protein hair fillers are usually the most effective.

You should not give a hair straightening or hair relaxing treatment to a patron who has received a hair coloring treatment on that same day. You should allow at least 72 hours to elapse between a tint and straightening or relaxing treatments. It is preferable to straighten hair before tinting it. This will prevent the removal of tint color from the hair. It should be noted that some chemical combinations are not compatible and may leave deposits.

Hair ends should be blunt cut before a hair straightening treatment. You should not use slither cutting because this may lift or destroy some of the hair imbrications. If this happens, the hair may become more porous. As you acquire professional skills and abilities, you will be able to judge when the hair has been straightened sufficiently so that it is becoming to each individual patron. Sometimes, however, it is necessary to perform a second straightening or relaxing treatment. If this is the case, allow five days to elapse between applications.

The chemical action of straightening hair resembles that of coloring hair. The straightening chemical lifts the cuticle layer of the hair. It then enters the cortex. Chemical hair straighteners cause a separation of the hair's cystine bonds. Sometimes, this may cause a visible discoloration of the hair.

Improper use of hair straightening chemicals may cause scalp irritation. If this happens, treat the condition at once with an acetic acid (vinegar) rinse. Use a solution of 8 ounces (236.59 ml.) of water to 1 ounce (29.57 ml.) acetic acid (vinegar concentrate). If the concentrate is not available, and you must use household vinegar as a neutralizer, prepare a mixture of equal parts of vinegar and warm water.

You should use a release statement for hair straightening treatments. This form can be the same as that used for hair coloring. If you have any doubts concerning the results of a hair straightening treatment, make a strand test before beginning the procedure. It will serve as a guide for determining the final results.

Retouching: The retouch procedure is exactly the same as the procedure for a regular chemical hair relaxing or straightening treatment. However, you apply the chemical only to the new growth. You do not comb the straightening cream through previously treated hair. It must be noted that you apply protective cream not only to the scalp but also to previously treated hair.

Hair straightening

Unit 5
Chemical blowout

The chemical blowout is a combination of chemical hair straightening and hairstyling. It is a specialized service for people with super curly hair. It removes a small amount of curl by means of chemical relaxation. The procedure makes the hair more manageable and allows it to serve as a foundation for softer and smoother hairstyles. You can use either a thio relaxer or a sodium hydroxide hair straightener for the chemical blowout. You should take care not to overrelax the natural curl. The result would be an unintended hairstyle.

Procedure for a chemical blowout using ammonium thioglycolate

1. Drape the patron for a chemical treatment.

2. Examine the scalp for sores and abrasions. If there are any, do not proceed.

3. Examine the hair. If it is hard or brittle, you should make a strand test.

4. Shampoo the hair and towel it dry. Do not rub.

5. Section the hair into four quadrants: down the center from the forehead to the nape and across the head from behind the ears from ear to ear.

6. Protect the patron's ears and the skin along the hairline by applying a protective base.

7. Prepare the neutralizer.

8. Wear protective gloves. Apply the relaxer to each ¼ inch (0.64 cm.) section. Start at the nape of the back section and work up toward the crown. Apply the relaxer to the entire strand of hair as quickly as possible.

9. Repeat the procedure in all four sections. Work in a clockwise rotation around the entire head.

10. Manipulate the hair with your fingers for three to five minutes. Do not comb the relaxer through the hair. Do not stretch the hair. Stop the relaxing procedure while the hair still shows a wave and curl formation. Avoid overrelaxing.

11. Rinse the relaxer from the hair.

12. Neutralize.

13. Rinse the neutralizer out. Blot the hair dry.

Unit 5
Chemical blowout

General objectives-student goals: After study, instruction and completion of this unit, you will be able to demonstrate understanding of a chemical blowout by writing and/or giving a brief overview of the subject.

Hair straightening

231

14. Apply an acid pH conditioner with moisturizing agents and a light emollient. The emollient can provide a barrier against moisture loss.

15. Style the hair. Use a hair lifter or a hair pick in an upward manner while you dry the hair with a hand dryer and/or infrared lamp.

16. Shape the hair if necessary.

17. After the hair has been cut and combed to style, fluff and smooth it with the hair lifter or hair pick.

The chemical blowout procedure using sodium hydroxide is almost the same as the procedure using ammonium thioglycolate There are two differences.

1. When using sodium hydroxide, do not give the hair a preliminary shampoo. The hair is shampooed after it has been relaxed.

2. When you use sodium hydroxide, the processing time is much shorter. Sodium hydroxide is strongly alkaline. It can relax super curly hair twice as fast as ammonium thioglycolate.

Always follow the manufacturer's instructions because they vary with each product.

Unit 6
Relax-A-Curl for recurling

Relax-A-Curl is also called Perm-A-Curl. This procedure uses a thio solution to relax super curly hair. The relaxed hair is then immediately permanent waved. The result is larger and softer curls which do not require a basic foundation hair set.

Relax-A-Curl is a twofold procedure. First, the super curly hair is relaxed to its highest degree of straightness. Then, the straightened hair receives a perm. You must use large diameter spool type perm rods. The length of the hair determines the size of the perm rod. The longer the hair, the larger the diameter of the rod. A successful curl cannot be developed on short hair unless you use at least two and one-half turns of the rod.

Technique and procedure

1. Arrange the equipment and supplies.

2. Prepare and drape the model just like for a regular hair relaxing treatment.

3. Shampoo the hair. Do not rub the scalp.

4. Towel dry. Leave the hair slightly damp.

General objectives-student goals:
After study, instruction, practice and completion of this unit, you will be able to show understanding of the procedure for relaxing hair and then recurling it by demonstrating the procedure. You must have the proper implements and supplies in order to complete this unit successfully.

Hair straightening

5. Put on protective gloves.

6. Apply thio relaxer in the normal manner.

7. Set a timer. Keep combing the hair flat and smooth until the desired amount of relaxation is obtained.

8. Avoid processing the hair for more than twenty minutes. Section the hair for a regular perm. Use plastic hair clips to hold each section of hair securely in place. Do not remove the lotion when you perform this step.

9. Follow the exact procedure for giving a cold wave. Use larger diameter spool type perm rods than those which you would have used to give the same hair a conventional perm.

10. When the wrapping has been completed, saturate the hair on the rods. Allow the hair to process and then neutralize it.

11. After the hair has been processed completely and neutralized, remove the rods and apply hair conditioner.

12. Comb the hair into a relaxed curly style. Dry it by using infrared heat lamps or set it in the usual manner.

You should always follow the manufacturer's instructions because they may vary with each product.

Unit 7
Temporary hair straightening

Hair pressing is a method of straightening curly and/or kinky hair temporarily. The procedure involves the use of a hot comb. Hair pressing is also called silking. The problem with this technique is that the hair will revert to its original curliness if it is exposed to moisture. Hair pressing is usually a preliminary service. It prepares the hair for a thermal roller curl or a croquignole curl hair set.

Implements and material

1. Two pressing combs and/or pressing irons

2. Electric or gas heater

3. Pressing oil or cream press

4. Tail or styling comb, brush and hair clips

5. Lanolin hairdressing and hair spray

midget pressing
comb

pressing
comb

IMPLEMENTS USED
IN HAIR PRESSING

General objectives-student goals:
After study, instruction and completion of this unit, you will be able to demonstrate understanding of temporary hair straightening by writing and/or giving a brief overview of the subject.

electric iron heater

Hair straightening

233

You must examine the patron's hair and scalp before a hair pressing treatment. If you find any scalp abrasion or injury, do not proceed with the pressing. If you find hair damage because of improper coloring or improper pressing treatments, you should recommend a series of hair reconditioning treatments.

Hair with a coarse wiry texture has the greatest tolerance for heat. It is also the most difficult to press. Hair with medium texture responds easily to hair pressing. You must give a great amount of care to hair with fine texture because this type of hair burns and breaks easily. Practice will help the technician learn the correct temperature for all pressing instruments. It will also teach you what degree of pressure different hair textures can tolerate without breakage.

A pressing treatment exerts pressure on the scalp. You should always try to press the hair in the direction in which it grows. If the patron's scalp is tight, there may be some pain and discomfort during the pressing procedure. When the patron's scalp is loose, it is difficult to apply pressure. You can obtain satisfactory results if you use smaller subsections and light pressure.

You should keep a record card with all necessary information. This information will help you to improve the results of future pressing treatments. A good record card includes information such as:

1. The condition of the hair and scalp

2. Flexible or tight scalp

3. Lightened or tinted hair

4. Identification of the area in which the hair is or has been damaged

5. Hard press or soft press

6. Date of the last pressing

7. High, medium or low heat used for the comb or irons

8. The patron's history of chemical straightening treatments

A pressing comb is usually made from stainless steel, brass or a combination of brass and copper. There are different size combs. Some combs have more teeth than other combs do. The teeth of some combs are spaced further apart than the teeth of others. It helps to use a small pressing comb for short ends. Some pressing combs retain heat for a longer period than others do.

The rods of pressing irons come in various thicknesses. The thickness of the prongs varies from very thin to extra large. They are constructed of either white or blue steel. They hold heat evenly. There are irons with revolving handles or with insulated stationary handles.

Pressing combs and irons must be kept free from carbon deposits. You may use any one of many commercially prepared products for cleaning combs and irons. It is very safe to use electric hot combs and irons. They perform their job in an extremely effective manner. Most have controls for varying the temperature. The settings are low, medium and high.

Hair straightening

234

Do not use irons which are too hot on gray, tinted or bleached hair. The result may be discoloration or hair breakage. Avoid excessive heat and pressure when working near the ends of fine, gray, tinted or bleached hair. Do not use excessively hot irons and combs when pressing short fine hairs along the hairline. It is easy to damage fine hair. If an accidental burn occurs, apply 1% gentian violet or a similar product directly to the burn immediately.

Unit 8
Procedure for pressing hair

There are two techniques for pressing hair.

1. The soft press is a single complete pressing application.

2. The hard press utilizes a second application which is made over the soft press. You must use caution and skill when performing the hard press. It can cause injury to the hair.

Procedure

1. Shampoo and dry the hair thoroughly under a hair dryer.

2. Apply a small amount of pressing oil over the entire head for dry, brittle or damaged hair. You can also use cream press over the entire head. Use the lanolin type for normal hair.

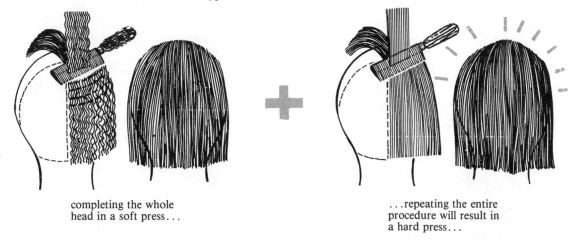

completing the whole
head in a soft press...

...repeating the entire
procedure will result in
a hard press...

3. Comb the hair. Section it into four main quadrants. Pin three sections. Leave the back right section ready for subsectioning.

4. Heat the pressing comb. If you use a gas heater, the teeth of the comb should face upward away from the flame.

General objectives-student goals: After study, instruction, practice and completion of this unit, you will be able to demonstrate understanding of straightening curly hair temporarily by demonstrating the technique and procedure. You must have the proper implements and supplies in order to complete this unit successfully.

Hair straightening

235

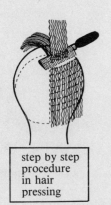

insert comb with teeth toward operator approximately ½″ (1.27 cm) from scalp...

1.

turn comb and maintain pressure on back rod of comb...

2.

Hair straightening

236

5. Start at the top of the right back section. Subsection the hair into short ¼ inch (0.64 cm.) partings. Work from the crown to the nape. Complete one quadrant at a time.

6. Test the temperature of the heated pressing comb by touching it to a piece of lightweight paper. If the paper shows any sign of scorching, allow the comb to cool.

7. Hold the ends of a strand from a small subsection with the index finger and thumb of your left hand. Direct the hair upward and away from the scalp.

8. Insert the teeth of the pressing comb into the topside of the hair section. Make the insertion close to the scalp. Hold the hair strand firmly against the back rod of the comb.

9. Keep a firm pressure on the hair around the back rod of the pressing comb. Turn it away from you slowly. Draw the rod up through the entire hair strand until the hair ends pass through the teeth. It is the back rod of the comb that actually presses the hair.

10. Repeat this pressing motion twice on top of the strand and once underneath it.

11. Each completed subsection should be placed up or to one side in order to keep it away from the work area.

12. Continue over the entire head until all the sections have been pressed.

13. For a hard press, repeat the hot comb procedure a second time.

14. Comb and style the hair. Finish by applying hairdressing and/or hair spray.

It is necessary to perform touch ups on new growth and between shampoos because the hair reverts to its original form when it comes into contact with moisture. You can perform a spot touch up when a small area reverts to its original form. If you must perform a touch up over the entire head, the touch up involves the same procedure as a regular pressing treatment with one exception. You do not shampoo the patron's hair

maintain constant pressure on comb while drawing it to the hair ends...

3.

press each strand twice topside with teeth toward you and once underside with teeth facing away from you...

4.

1. What is chemical hair straightening?

2. What is the difference between chemical hair relaxing and chemical hair straightening?

3. Is the action of thioglycolate the same in straightening and cold waving?

4. How often should a strand test be made when straightening hair with thioglycolate?

5. Does hair straightened with sodium hydroxide return to its original structure like it does when straightened with thioglycolate?

6. Can sodium hydroxide burn the skin and scalp?

7. Is it necessary to protect the skin when the hair is being water rinsed after being straightened with sodium hydroxide?

8. Should hair be straightened chemically if there are sores or abrasions on the scalp?

9. What is the technique for applying protective base to the scalp?

10. Should the hair be stretched or pulled during the sodium hydroxide hair straightening procedure?

11. Are no-base hair straighteners as effective as those that require a base?

12. Why is it important to wait at least 72 hours between hair coloring and hair straightening services?

13. What waiting period is required before making a second hair straightening application?

14. Does chemical hair straightening cause discoloration of the hair?

15. Can household vinegar be used as a neutralizer after a sodium hydroxide hair straightening treatment?

16. What is hair pressing?

17. Why is hair pressing considered a preliminary service?

18. What is the difference between pressing oil and cream press?

19. Under normal conditions, what is the size of the average subsection used during the hair pressing procedure?

20. Why is a record card for pressing treatments important?

21. What is the difference between a soft press and a hard press?

Super curly hair

Super curly hair: Kinky, frizzy or woolly hair is most characteristic of Black people. It is also found among many Caucasians.

Overview: This chapter provides you with the techniques and methods for servicing super curly hair.

Behavioral objectives-student goals: After completion of this chapter, and after instruction, study and practice, you will be able to demonstrate competency in super curly hair services by demonstrating the following techniques for servicing super curly hair: combing the hair while it is wet, combing the hair when it is dry, hair brushing, cutting and shaping, wet setting, chemical blowout, Perm-A-Curl, thermal roller curling, hair pressing, chemical hair straightening with a sodium hydroxide formula (whole head and retouch), corn rowing and French braiding. You will also be able to demonstrate competency by identifying, explaining and/or listing the requirements and procedures for shampooing and conditioning super curly hair, relaxing super curly hair with a thioglycolate relaxer and the retouch procedure for a hair press.

Kinky, frizzy or woolly hair is sometimes called **super curly hair or Afro-American hair.** Although super curly hair is not restricted to Black races, the extreme degree of curl pattern and kinks observed in Afro-American hair is almost nonexistent in other races. Chemically, Afro-American hair is the same as Caucasian hair. There are, however, some major structural differences which limit the styles in which Afro-American hair can be worn. Altering the hair structure by either chemical or mechanical means in order to overcome the excessive degree of curliness and kinkiness can result in extreme damage.

All the styling methods for super curly hair which are in common use today cause some degree of damage to the hair. The most widely used techniques utilize curl relaxers and chemical hair straighteners. The relaxers are used to:

1. Soften and control tight kinky hair

2. Remove some but not all of the excess curliness so that there will be greater styling versatility and manageability

Chemical hair straighteners are used to remove all traces of curl from the hair. These products are extremely alkaline and cause considerable damage to the hair and some degree of breakage. The greatest damage associated with chemical hair relaxers and straighteners is excessive dryness, structural weakness and cuticle abrasion.

Damage by mechanical means includes hair pressing services, thermal curl styling, braiding (corn rowing) and the use of hair picks. Heat styling causes dryness and weakness of the hair shafts. Braiding and hair picks cause cuticle abrasion.

Super curly hair

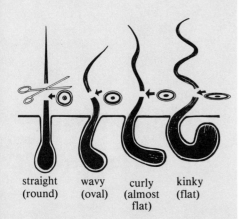

straight
(round)

wavy
(oval)

curly
(almost
flat)

kinky
(flat)

Super curly hair is flat in structure, and the sharp angle of the follicle results in the hair growing in the form of a tight spiral. It grows straight up and away from the scalp. The spiral form and its lack of weight make the hair stand out from the head. The outer layer of cells lies extremely close to the cuticle. The function of these cells is to protect the cuticle which, in turn, protects the cortex. These cells are constantly removed from the hair by normal brushing.

Super curly hair does not retain moisture like other types of hair. When it is not brushed or combed thoroughly, most of the cuticle protective cells remain, become hardened and are more difficult to remove. If this condition is permitted to continue, the hair will appear dull and coarse. This condition can cause breakage.

The sebaceous gland next to the hair follicle secretes sebum which mixes with the water and salts excreted from the sweat glands and forms the acid mantle around the hair shaft. The acid mantle acts as a waterproof barrier and provides the lubrication which minimizes friction between the hair strands. Individuals with super curly hair have fewer sebaceous glands. This accounts for their dry fragile hair.

Afro-American super curly hair contains more protein and less water than Caucasian hair. The number of layers in the hair cuticle of Caucasians is as few as seven. Super curly hair has as many as 15 cuticle layers.

Sanitary and safety precautions for super curly hair

1. Use a hair clipper (fine blade: 0000) to cut the hair at the back of the neck and hairline. Do not use a razor.

2. Sanitize hair clippers and electric scissors after each use.

3. Always cut super curly hair while dry not when it is wet.

4. Do not spread protective base on the hair.

5. Do not brush the hair excessively prior to a relaxing treatment or a chemical blowout.

6. Do not interrupt chemical services once they are started.

7. Use a timer to clock the processing time.

8. Protect your hands with protective gloves when using strong chemicals.

9. Adjust the water temperature so that it is warm and comfortable.

10. Test the temperature of pressing combs and thermal irons before they make contact with the hair.

Super curly hair

Unit 1
Combing super curly hair when wet

Most super curly hair is very porous and has very poor elasticity. The hair is fragile and becomes matted and entangled with neighboring hairs. In extreme cases, when the hair is quite long, it becomes knotted.

To disentangle the hair after a shampoo, use an after-shampoo rinse and damp dry the hair using a towel. Be certain that all excess water is removed from the hair before proceeding. Use a shampoo-tangle comb. Begin by combing the hair at the nape area. Start at the ends of the hair and work up toward the hair nearest the scalp. Comb through small sections until all the hair is free of tangles and ready to dress.

A wire bristle hair brush with a rubber back is also an excellent tool with which to disentangle wet hair. If this hair brush and the shampoo-tangle comb are not available, a conventional comb may be used. You must use the wide teeth of the comb and work with exceptionally small sections around the entire head.

Procedure

1. Remove excess water from the hair. Use a towel.

2. Comb the hair. Start at the nape area.

3. Use a wire bristle brush, a shampoo-tangle comb or the wide teeth of a conventional comb.

4. Begin combing small subsections of hair at the nape area. Start at the hair ends.

5. Place the comb or brush further back on the hair strand with each disentangling motion and comb forward toward the hair ends.

6. Continue to work through small sections until all the hair is free of tangles and ready for the next service.

Unit 2
Combing super curly hair when not wet

When super curly hair is to be combed while in a dry state, the technique is to lift the comb through the hair rather than pull the comb back and over the hair. The lifting technique will help free the hair with the least amount of stress and will avoid pulling the hair and breakage. Start by applying a lubricant to the hair. Massage in a circular motion at the scalp up through the hair. Loosen the tangles with your fingers spread apart.

Unit 1
Combing super curly hair when wet

General objectives-student goals: After study, instruction, practice and completion of this unit, you will be able to show understanding of how to comb super curly hair correctly, without discomfort to the patron, while the hair is wet by giving a brief overview of the subject and by demonstrating the procedure. You must have the proper implements and supplies in order to complete this unit successfully.

WIRE BRUSH

TANGLE COMB

Unit 2
Combing super curly hair when not wet

General objectives-student goals: After study, instruction, practice and completion of this unit, you will

Super curly hair

be able to show understanding of how to comb super curly hair while it is in a dry state by giving a brief overview of the subject and by demonstrating the procedure. You must have the proper implements and supplies in order to complete this unit successfully.

Unit 3
Brushing super curly hair

General objectives-student goals: After study, instruction, practice and completion of this unit, you will be able to show understanding of the technique for brushing super curly hair by giving a brief overview of the subject and by demonstrating the procedure. You must have the proper implements and supplies in order to complete this unit successfully.

rotate brush in this manner..

Super curly hair

242

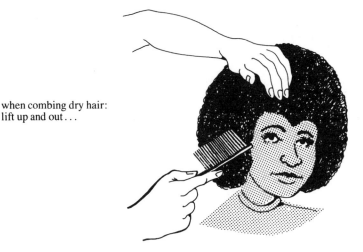

when combing dry hair:
lift up and out . . .

To lift the comb through the hair, select a wide tooth comb and hold it firmly in your hand. Avoid turning motions of the comb. Start on either side of the head. Insert the comb with the teeth upward to the hair against the scalp along the lower hairline over the ear. Follow the contour of the head at the scalp. Comb through the hair in a circular manner by turning the wrist while lifting up and out. Continue this motion around the head until the hair is completely disentangled. Then, comb into place according to style.

Unit 3
Brushing super curly hair

When brushing hair for hair hygiene, always use a natural bristle hair brush. Natural bristle has many tiny imbrications which clean and polish the hair. Nylon and plastic bristles are smooth and recommended only for dressing the hair. Brushing the hair with a good natural bristle hair brush will stimulate the scalp, clean, polish and strengthen the hair so that there will be less breakage. The hair will be able to grow longer. The outer layer of cells of super curly hair lies extremely close to the cuticle. The function of these cells is to protect the cuticle which, in turn, protects the cortex. These cells, however, should be removed from the hair constantly by normal brushing. If the cells are allowed to harden and are not removed, they will cause breakage.

Super curly hair should always be brushed in line with its growth pattern which is up and away from the scalp. Authorities agree that the best manner of brushing is always up, starting on the hair close to the scalp. This gives mild massage by gently pulling on the various muscles. It is also advisable to brush the hair forward, parting off small sections with a finger or a comb, and forcing the bristles well down on the hair close to the scalp. The brush should be held firmly, and the wrist moved with each stroke so that the brush goes through a semicircular motion. The outside bristles should touch the hair at the scalp first, and the whole area of the bristles should pass over it so that the inside bristles almost touch the scalp before the brush is passed over and through the strand of the hair. The purpose of a hair brush is to brush the hair not the scalp.

Unit 4
Shampooing and conditioning super curly hair

The principle and procedure for shampooing super curly hair are identical to the principle and procedure for shampooing straight or wavy hair. The type of shampoo is determined by the condition of the hair and scalp. Whenever possible, an acid balanced low pH shampoo should be used.

Hair conditioners for super curly hair are not as easy to select as shampoos. Very few conditioners work well with super curly hair. There are three basic types from which to select:

1. A conditioner which is applied to the hair and remains on it for a few minutes before it is rinsed with water.

2. A conditioner which is applied to the hair and not rinsed. A styling lotion may be applied over the conditioner if needed.

3. A combined conditioner and styling lotion. This product does not require rinsing.

These three types of conditioners are available in many different formulas.

The type of conditioner used depends on the condition of the hair and how the hair will respond. Conditioners with moisturizers usually do a better job than high protein conditioners when the hair does not need much protein. If a high protein conditioner is used on hair that cannot absorb it, the hair will feel dry and brittle. Several conditioners should be tried, a different one at each sitting, in order to determine the type and formula best suited for the type and condition of the super curly hair.

The objective of conditioning is to restore compactness to the cuticle and restore some natural sheen to the hair. All hair care products used on super curly hair should be of a low acid pH. They should contain light emollients, protein and moisturizing agents which aid the restoration of hair fiber strength.

Although super curly hair is quite fragile, it is usually damaged mechanically and/or chemically. Pressing combs and curling irons cause dryness, split ends, dullness and an abraded cuticle.

The hair pick used to style and comb the natural hairstyle abrades the cuticle. Although the abraded cuticles interlock with one another and create a fuller look, the hair will be damaged and appear dull.

Corn row braiding can damage super curly hair shafts severely because of the extreme tension which braiding places on each individual hair shaft. Braiding hair that has been chemically treated can result in severe damage including breakage.

Conditioners and treatments for super curly hair should return the hair to an acid pH state, give the hair shaft internal strength, provide moisture and a barrier to atmospheric moisture.

Unit 4
Shampooing and conditioning super curly hair

General objectives-student goals: After study, instruction and completion of this unit, you will be able to demonstrate understanding of shampooing and conditioning super curly hair by writing and/or giving a brief overview of the subject.

Super curly hair

Unit 5
Cutting super curly hair

General objectives-student goals:
After study, instruction, practice and completion of this unit, you will be able to show understanding of cutting super curly hair by writing and/or giving a brief overview of the subject and by demonstrating the procedure. You must have the proper implements and supplies in order to complete this unit successfully.

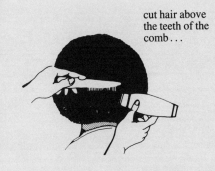

cut hair above the teeth of the comb . . .

Super curly hair

244

Unit 5
Cutting super curly hair

Most people whose hair is super curly are reluctant to cut or shape their hair because curly hair generally grows more slowly than the usual ½ inch (1.27 cm.) per month. Continued shaping will, however, help strengthen the hair and keep it looking well-groomed.

Cutting the natural and Afro is accomplished by using a large tooth comb with an electric hair clipper and/or scissors. There are many types of electric hair clippers, but the cordless clipper with interchangeable blades is highly recommended as the most professional tool for cutting super curly hair.

When giving a full haircut and shaping, start by cutting with a large tooth blade and follow by using a smaller tooth blade. When trimming and shaping hair that has been cut recently, start the shaping with one of the finer tooth blades. The extremely fine blade (0000) is used to cut the hairs at the back of the neck and to shape the hairline.

CUTTING SUPER CURLY HAIR
(Afro - natural)

Super curly hair should always be cut when it is dry, before or after the shampoo. Whenever possible, give the haircut before the shampoo.

Cutting super curly hair (Afro-natural)

1. Drape the patron.

2. Disentangle the hair.

3. Determine the style line according to the hair, head shape and facial features.

4. Comb the hair up and out, away from the head.

5. Determine the length by the nape guideline. Never cut above the natural hairline at the nape.

shape the hairline . . .

6. Begin at the nape. Cut upward the back of the head to the crown. Insert the comb into the hair with the teeth down. Comb the hair out from the head and let the hair to be cut extend beyond the teeth of the comb.

7. Hold the electric clipper in the same horizontal position as the comb and trim over the teeth of the comb. This will ensure an even cut. After cutting the back to the crown area, cut both sides in the same manner up toward the top of the head. Trim across the top of the head, from side to side. Blend with the crown and sides. Curve this shaping action in order to avoid a square look. Use hair clippers around the face to shape the style line. Start at the temple area on one side and taper toward the center of the forehead. Curve this shaping action in order to avoid a square look. Continue to outline around the face until the shaping is complete.

8. Comb the hair up and out once again and use the electric scissors to cut only the uneven ends.

curve the
shaping...

the
electric
scissors

9. Spray with light lubricant and use your hands to shape the contour. The hand shaping is important because each time super curly hair is combed, there will be uneven lengths of hair which need to be put back in place.

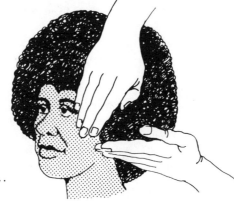

use hands
to shape...

10. Use a light hair spray to hold the style line, control the ends and maintain the natural look.

Super curly hair

245

Unit 6

Wet setting super curly hair

General objectives-student goals:
After study, instruction, practice and completion of this unit, you will be able to show understanding of wet setting super curly hair by demonstrating the technique and procedure. You must have the proper implements and supplies in order to complete this unit successfully.

Super curly hair

246

Unit 6
Wet setting super curly hair

Roller setting super curly hair is exactly the same as roller setting wavy or straight hair. End papers should be used when working with unruly hair ends. It is of the utmost importance not to remove the rollers from the hair before it is completely dry. The hair must, in addition, be allowed to cool after the hair dryer has been turned off.

The hair will not revert to its normal state unless it becomes exposed to moisture or dampness. If the result of the setting is too tight, it can be blown out with a blow dryer. This will produce a softer and looser hair set before combing it into style.

When wet setting chemically treated hair, it is best to use wire mesh hair rollers without a brush insert or plastic covered wire mesh hair rollers. The large mesh design permits faster air circulation and quicker drying.

Roller curls

A roller curl is a broad curl formed by winding a wet strand of hair around a cylindrical object and securing it in position until dry. Roller curls are used to achieve height, fullness and smoothness. Speed in setting and shorter hair drying time are among the advantages of roller setting.

Rollers come in many shapes, sizes and compositions. The circumference of the roller to be used depends on several considerations. The following is a basic guide:

1. Use a roller with a large circumference for long hair.

2. Use a roller with a large circumference for a casual hairstyle.

3. Use a roller with a smaller circumference when a style is detailed with waves or ridges.

4. Use a roller with a smaller circumference when the hairstyle needs body.

End papers

Complete control over the hair ends can be obtained best by using end papers when winding the hair around a roller. After sufficient practice, the use of end papers can be discontinued. A rectangular curl base is used with roller settings. The use of zigzag partings for the curl bases along the front hairline will help prevent separations during the combout. The size of the base is determined by the size of the roller. The larger the roller, the larger the base required. When the hair is wound, the roller is placed on its base and secured with a roller clip, curl clip, roller pin or bobby pin.

Roller setting technique

Depending on the hairstyle, roller curls may be placed anywhere on the head and at almost any angle.

1. Section a rectangular base wherever rollers are required for the style.

2. Hold the comb in your right hand and the hair in your left. Comb the strand up.

3. Secure the strand between the index and middle fingers of your left hand. Use your right hand, still holding the comb, to fold the end paper over and under the strand. Slide the paper so that it extends at least $\frac{1}{2}$ inch (1.27 cm.) beyond the hair ends.

4. Hold the strand of hair and the paper in your left hand. Place the roller even with the end of the end paper.

5. Place the index and middle fingers of your right hand behind the roller to hold the hair in place. Place your right thumb in front of the roller.

6. Repeat step 5 with your left hand. Turn the roller alternately with the fingers of your right and left hand until the roller is placed on the base.

7. Fasten the roller securely on its base. Use a roller clip or a roller pick when using wire mesh rollers.

8. Repeat steps 1-7. Secure each additional roller in the same manner as the previously secured roller.

Unit 7
Thermal roller curling super curly hair

Thermal roller curl irons come in many different types and circumferences. Some roller curl irons may be fitted with adapters that change their circumference. Others have perforations for steaming oils back into the hair with vapors. Some are designed to be heated by gas flames or small electric heaters. It is possible to maintain pressure between the shell and the rod with this type of iron. Others have a built-in heating element and operate from an electric outlet. The hair fits freely between the blade and the barrel. Pressure cannot be applied to the hair with this type of iron. The roller iron with the built-in heating element is lightweight and thermostatically controlled to maintain constant heat throughout the setting process. Some irons have a low, medium and high heat control. The heat control becomes important when setting bleached, dry or abused hair because these types of hair require mild heat.

The roller iron saves time for both the stylist and the patron. Once the entire head is set, the hair is ready to be combed into a style. Controlled mild heat makes the hair more supple, gives it body and allows it to be shaped into any hairstyle.

Procedure

1. Shampoo the hair.

2. Apply cream or styling lotion in order to eliminate static electricity. All hair has a natural negative charge. This can be eliminated by using a styling cream or lotion which contains positive molecules.

Unit 7
Thermal roller curling super curly hair

General objectives-student goals: After study, instruction, practice and completion of this unit, you will be able to show understanding of thermal curling by writing or giving a brief overview of the subject and by demonstrating both the roller curl and croquignole curl techniques and procedures. You must have the proper implements and supplies in order to complete this unit successfully.

Super curly hair

247

NOTE: Bob curling is a technique for setting short hair with a thermal curling iron. The method and technique are the same as for curling long and medium length hair with two exceptions:

1. *The diameter of the rod and shell or barrel and blade of the thermal iron is much smaller.*
2. *The ends of a hair strand do not have to be directed and pulled over the rod or barrel to form a curl.*

The bob curl requires only that you slide the iron down the hair strand to the ends, guide the ends of the strand into the center of the thermal iron, and form the curl by rotating the curl towards the scalp.

Super curly hair

248

3. Dry the patron's hair. While the hair is drying, heat the roller curling iron.

4. Use the same sectioning and subsectioning used for roller setting.

5. Subsection one strand of hair and comb it smoothly. Hold the strand of hair at an angle of at least 90 degrees from the head.

6. Hold the strand and the comb in your left hand. Place the barrel of the thermal iron 1½ inches (3.81 cm.) from the scalp so that the strand of hair is between the barrel and the curved blade.

7. Rotate the iron half a turn.

8. Open the curved blade and wind the strand one complete turn around the barrel of the iron.

9. Close the iron.

10. Rotate the iron half a turn until the curved blade is close to the scalp. Direct the strand in the same direction as the rotation of the iron.

11. Open the curved blade.

12. Wind one more turn of the strand around the barrel.

13. Close the curved blade.

14. Rotate a fraction of a turn in order to bring the curl closer to the scalp.

15. Hold in position for a few seconds.

16. Rotate back to the position with the curved blade down.

17. Open the curved blade and repeat steps 12-16 until the strand is wound completely. Rotate while opening and closing the curved blade until the hair ends are between the curved blade and the barrel.

18. Roll the curl to the scalp. Protect the scalp from the hot iron by placing a comb on the scalp underneath the iron and curl. Hold this position long enough to develop a firm curl.

19. Slide the comb through beneath the iron. Open the curved blade and direct the curl off the barrel with the large teeth of the comb. Withdraw the hot iron at the same time.

20. Repeat steps 12-19 on all the strands until the entire head is curled.

21. After the last curl has cooled, comb and brush the hair.

Thermal croquignole curling

Thermal curling is a popular method of setting hair that has been pressed. It is also used as a foundation setting for all types of hair. It eliminates working with wet hair, the use of hair rollers and drying hair after it is set. When thermal curling is done properly, the foundation can be used for brushing and combing the hair into any hairstyle.

There are two methods of thermal curling:

1. Thermal roller curling

2. Thermal croquignole curling

Thermal croquignole curling produces a stronger foundation than thermal roller curling does. It also requires more skill. Croquignole curling is recommended for hairstyles with a soft, casual or draped effect.

Thermal curling irons are manufactured in many thicknesses. They are made of either blue or white steel. They hold heat evenly. Irons are available with revolving handles or insulated stationary handles. The thickness of the prongs varies from very thin to large, bouffant and extra large. The extra large iron has a 1¹/₄ inch (3.18 cm.) diameter. It is called a directional iron.

Procedure for thermal croquignole curling

1. Shampoo the hair. Dry it under a dryer.

2. Press the hair if required.

3. Apply cream or oil to the hair sparingly.

4. Heat the irons to the correct temperature.

5. Comb the hair smooth. Part it on the right side.

6. Start at the front hairline below the part on the patron's right side. Part off an oblong hair strand ³/₄ inch (1.90 cm.) wide by 1¹/₂ inches (3.81 cm.) long.

7. Hold the hair strand with the thumb and index finger of your left hand. When the iron is heated to the correct temperature, direct the points away from the patron's face and insert the iron with the shell on top about 1 inch (2.54 cm.) from the scalp.

8. Hold the iron firmly and roll it under one complete turn. The technique of clicking the iron constantly during the operation permits the hair to glide easily over the iron.

9. Draw the end of the hair strand toward the points of the iron with your left hand.

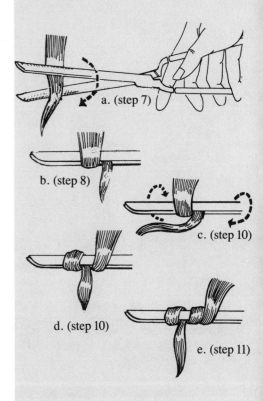

a. (step 7)

b. (step 8)

c. (step 10)

d. (step 10)

e. (step 11)

Super curly hair

10. Loop the strand underneath the tip of the iron. Hold the iron tightly and direct it slightly forward toward the face.

11. By directing the iron forward and pulling the hair with your left hand, two loops are formed around the iron with the ends of the strand between the loops.

12. Roll and click the iron under until the ends of hair disappear, and the iron rolls freely within the hair.

13. Roll the curl to the scalp. Protect the scalp from the hot iron by placing a comb on the scalp underneath the iron and curl. Hold the curl on the iron and allow heat to penetrate.

14. Slide the comb from beneath the iron and direct the curl off the iron with the large teeth of the comb. At the same time, draw the hot iron out.

15. Continue the procedure on all strands until the entire head has been curled.

16. Comb and brush the hair into the desired style.

Unit 8
Hair pressing

Hair pressing with a hot comb is a method of straightening curly and/or kinky hair temporarily. The main disadvantage is that the straightened hair will revert to its original curly appearance if it is exposed to any type of moisture. Hair pressing is usually a preliminary service which prepares the hair for a thermal roller curl or a croquignole curl hair set.

The implements and material required are:

1. Two pressing combs and/or pressing irons

2. Electric or gas heater

3. Pressing oil or cream press

4. Tail or styling comb, brush and hair clips

5. Lanolin hairdressing and hair spray

When preparing the patron for hair pressing, it is mandatory to examine the scalp and hair. If the patron has any abrasion or injury to the scalp, the pressing treatment should not be given. If examination of the hair shows damage because of hair coloring or improper pressing treatments, a series of hair reconditioning treatments should be recommended.

Unit 8
Hair pressing

General objectives-student goals:
After study, instruction, practice and completion of this unit, you will be able to show understanding of hair pressing super curly hair by writing or giving a brief overview of the subject and by demonstrating the procedures for a soft press and a hard press. You must have the proper implements and supplies in order to complete this unit successfully.

Super curly hair

Procedure

1. Shampoo and dry the hair thoroughly under a hair dryer.

2. Apply a small amount of pressing oil for dry, brittle or damaged hair or cream press (lanolin type for normal hair) over the entire head of hair.

3. Comb the hair and section it into four main quadrants. Pin only three sections. Leave the back right section ready for subsectioning.

4. Heat the pressing comb. If a gas heater is used, the teeth of the comb should face upward away from the flame.

5. Start at the top of the right back section. Subsection the hair into short $1/4$ inch (0.64 cm.) partings. Work from the crown to the nape and complete one quadrant at a time.

6. Test the temperature of the heated pressing comb on a piece of lightweight paper before applying it to the hair. If the paper shows signs of scorching, allow the comb to cool.

7. Hold the ends of the strand of a small subsection with the index finger and thumb of your left hand and direct the hair upward and away from the scalp.

8. Insert the teeth of the pressing comb into the topside of the hair section close to the scalp. Hold the hair strand firmly against the back rod of the comb.

9. Keep the hair pressed firmly against the back rod of the pressing comb and turn it slowly away from you. Draw it up through the entire hair strand until the hair ends pass through the teeth. It is the back rod of the comb that actually presses the hair.

10. Repeat this pressing motion twice on top of the strand and once underneath.

11. Each completed subsection should be placed up or to one side in order to keep it away from the work area.

12. Continue over the entire head until all the sections have been pressed.

13. Comb and style the hair. Finish with an application of hairdressing and/or hair spray.

Two basic techniques are used in hair pressing:

1. Soft press: One complete pressing application using the pressing comb as described above.

2. Hard press: Achieved by means of a second application over the soft press. If caution and skill are not used, a hard press could cause injury to the hair.

Super curly hair

251

With practice, a technician will learn what the correct temperature for all pressing instruments should be and the degree of pressure which different hair textures can tolerate without breakage. Coarse wiry hair can tolerate the most heat and is the most difficult to press. Hair of a medium texture responds easily to hair pressing. Hair of a fine texture requires the most care since it burns and breaks easily.

A hair press exerts a definite amount of pressure on the scalp during the pressing action. Whenever possible, hair should be pressed in the direction in which it grows. A tight scalp may cause some pain and discomfort during a pressing treatment. When pressing hair on a loose scalp, it is difficult to apply pressure. Satisfactory results may be obtained by using smaller sections and light pressure.

A record card listing all necessary information is important for improving the results of future pressing treatments. A good record includes information such as:

1. The condition of the hair and scalp

2. Flexible or tight scalp

3. Lightened or tinted hair

4. Identification of the area where the hair is or has been damaged

5. Hard press or soft press

6. Date of last pressing

7. High, medium or low degree of heat for the comb or irons

8. Any history of chemical straightening treatments

A pressing comb is usually constructed of stainless steel, brass or a combination of brass and copper. Combs are available in different sizes. Some have more teeth than others, and some teeth are spaced further apart than others. A small pressing comb is handy for short ends and some pressing combs will hold heat longer than others. Pressing irons are available with rods of various thicknesses. They are made of either white or blue steel and hold heat evenly. Irons are available with revolving handles or insulated stationary handles. The thickness of the prongs may vary from very thin to large and extra large diameters.

Pressing combs and irons must be kept free from carbon build-up at all times. There are many good commercially prepared products that may be used for cleaning purposes.

Discoloration or breakage may occur when pressing gray, tinted or bleached hair if the irons or combs are too hot. When pressing these types of hair and fine hair, avoid excessive heat and pressure near the hair ends. When pressing short fine hairs along the hairline, the irons and combs must not be too hot because excessive heat may damage fine hair.

For accidental burns, apply 1% gentian violet or a similar ingredient directly to the burn immediately.

Super curly hair

252

Touch ups are necessary for new growth and between shampoos when the hair reverts to its original form because of moisture. When a small portion of an area reverts, a spot touch up may be successful. When the entire head of hair reverts, the touch up involves the same procedure as a regular pressing treatment except that the hair is not shampooed.

Note: Electric hot combs and irons are safe and extremely effective. Most of them are thermostatically controlled with low, medium and high degrees of heat.

Unit 9
Chemical straightening super curly hair with ammonium thioglycolate

Chemical hair straightening is a process of permanently changing natural hair forms so that the hair which was treated becomes permanently straight. Thereafter, only the new growth needs to be treated.

Chemical hair relaxing is basically the same as chemical hair straightening, but milder ingredients are used to transform naturally curly or kinky hair forms to soft wavy hair. The two chemicals most commonly used to straighten hair are:

1. Ammonium thioglycolate

2. Sodium hydroxide

A thioglycolate hair straightener contains ammonium or monoethanolamine thioglycolate or thioglycolic acid adjusted to the desired pH with ammonia or monoethanolamine. A heavy creme base is used to make the material easier to apply.

The chemical action of the thioglycolate is the same in straightening as in cold waving. The disulfide links of the keratin are broken down. This softens the hair. The hair is then smoothed to a straightened shape with a comb and/or with a hand technique.

When the hair has been straightened satisfactorily, the action is stopped by a neutralizer, which usually contains an oxidizing compound. This neutralizer is left on the hair long enough to penetrate the hair shaft and stop the action of the thioglycolate. Complete neutralization, followed by rinsing, removes all the straightening agent from the hair and restores it to its original chemical state. Although 4 ounces (118.30 ml.) of 20 volume hydrogen peroxide mixed with 28 ounces (828.07 ml.) of water will act as a neutralizer, solid oxidizing agents (potassium bromate and sodium perborate) have been found to be more suitable.

Procedure for thioglycolate

1. Examine the scalp for sores or abrasions. If there are any, do not proceed with the straightening.

2. Examine the hair. If the hair is hard, dry or brittle, a strand test should be given.

3. Shampoo the hair and towel it dry. Do not rub the scalp.

Unit 9
Chemical straightening super curly hair with ammonium thioglycolate

General objectives-student goals: After study, instruction, practice and completion of this unit, you will be able to show understanding of chemical straightening by demonstrating the technique and procedure using ammonium thioglycolate. You must have the proper implements and supplies in order to complete this unit successfully.

Super curly hair

4. Section the hair into four quadrants: down the center from the forehead to the nape, and across behind the ears from ear to ear.

5. Protect the ears and the skin along the hairline.

6. Prepare neutralizer.

7. Wear protective gloves and apply the hair straightening creme to each $1/4$ inch (0.64 cm.) section. Start with the back section at the nape and work up toward the crown. Apply creme to the entire strand. Start $1/4$ inch (0.64 cm.) from the scalp in each subsection in order to avoid direct contact between the chemical and the scalp.

8. Repeat the procedure in all four sections. Work in clockwise rotation around the head.

9. Let the hair soften for 5-15 minutes. Then, comb through each section once to straighten the hair. Be certain to smooth the hair nearest the scalp.

10. Allow the hair to continue to process for the time recommended by the manufacturer. Make a strand test at three minute intervals.

11. Rinse thoroughly using warm water until the creme has been removed from the hair completely. Blot the hair dry.

12. Neutralize. Pour the prepared neutralizer into a glass or plastic container and set it in the shampoo basin. Keep the patron in position at the shampoo basin and pour the prepared solution through the hair. Collect it in a bowl. Pour the solution through the hair from six to ten times in order to be certain that it is completely neutralized.

13. Rinse thoroughly with water until the neutralizer has been removed. Blot and set the hair into the desired style.

Unit 10
Chemical straightening super curly hair with sodium hydroxide

Sodium hydroxide (caustic) in a solution with stearic and oleic acids was the first chemical cosmetic used for straightening hair. The sodium hydroxide content of different products varies from 5% to 10%. The pH value goes from 7.5 to 14. The more sodium hydroxide, the higher the pH and the quicker the reaction of the chemical on the hair. The chances of the quicker reacting chemicals damaging the skin or hair are also greater.

Sodium hydroxide functions as a hair straightener by swelling the fibers and softening the main disulfide bonds which link the polypeptide chains of the hair structure together. The hair should be completely softened within eight minutes. During the chemical action, the disulfide links lose one molecule of sulfur. After rinsing, they rejoin as lanthionine links between the polypeptide chains and stabilize the hair. Unlike thioglycolate, hair treated with sodium hydroxide does not return to its original structure.

General objectives-student goals: After study, instruction, practice and completion of this unit, you will be able to show understanding of chemical straightening by demonstrating the technique and procedure using sodium hydroxide. You must have the proper implements and supplies in order to complete this unit successfully.

Super curly hair

The patron's skin should be carefully protected with base, especially when the hair is being rinsed. Sodium hydroxide can burn the skin and scalp. If sodium hydroxide is left on the hair too long, it may discolor the hair, make it brittle and cause breakage.

Procedure for sodium hydroxide

1. Examine the scalp for sores or abrasions. If there are any, do not proceed with the straightening.

2. Examine the hair. If the hair is hard, dry or brittle, a strand test should be given.

3. Do not brush or shampoo the hair.

4. Section the hair into four quadrants: down the center from the forehead to the nape and across the head behind the ears from ear to ear.

5. Apply a protective base evenly in order to cover the scalp completely. Start with the back left section and work counterclockwise around the head. Subsection each quadrant into $1/4$ inch (0.64 cm.) horizontal partings (ear to ear). Apply the base to the scalp with the middle and index fingers or index finger only across the top parting of each strand and press down.

   Note: When the protective base is applied correctly, each parting, when lifted, will show base cream on the back of the strand. The base is placed on the scalp and pressed in. It is not spread or rubbed on. Protect the ears and skin along the hairline with a protective base.

6. Divide the hair into four quadrants again. Wear protective gloves. Apply the hair straightening cream. Start in the back left section at the crown and lay the chemical straightener on the hair shaft starting about $1/2$ inch (1.27 cm.) from the scalp area. When applying the straightener, the hair is subsectioned in the same manner as in the application of the protective base cream. Complete the application to all four sections.

7. Again, apply straightener to the hair closest to the scalp. Use your comb or fingers to straighten and smooth the hair in the root area and along the hairline. Then, comb through the hair shaft. Add more chemical as needed. The processing time will range from two to eight minutes depending on the texture of the hair and the amount of time used for the application.

8. Rinse thoroughly with warm water. Hold the spray 4-5 inches (10.16-12.70 cm.) from the head. The straightener should be removed from the hair by the force of the water, not with your hand.

9. Shampoo the hair thoroughly. Do not rub the scalp.

10. Blot the hair.

11. Neutralize according to the manufacturer's directions. Set the hair into the desired style.

    Note: Some sodium hydroxide hair straighteners do not require the application of a protective base because the base

Super curly hair

255

is built into the hair straightening cream. These no-base products are usually hair relaxers not hair straighteners. This is because the chemical action is retarded.

Always apply a protective base around the ears and the skin around the hairline.

Before straightening or relaxing tinted, bleached or damaged hair, a hair filler as well as a conditioner should be used. This will protect porous hair from breakage and permit even penetration by filling the cuticle scales of the hair shaft. Protein hair fillers are usually the most effective.

Hair coloring and hair straightening or relaxing treatments should not be given to the patron on the same day. Waiting at least 72 hours after tinting is recommended. A hair straightening treatment should be given first in order to avoid removing tint color from the hair. Some chemical combinations are not compatible and may leave deposits.

Hair ends should be blunt cut prior to a hair straightening treatment. Slither cutting may lift or destroy some of the imbrications of the hair. This can cause the hair to become more porous.

It requires professional ability to learn to judge when the hair has been sufficiently straightened for each individual patron. If, for any reason, a second hair straightening or relaxing treatment is required, wait five days before the second application is made.

The chemical action of hair straighteners resembles that of coloring agents. The cuticle layer of the hair is lifted and the chemicals enter the cortex layer. Chemical hair straighteners separate the cystine bonds or molecular connections and may sometimes cause a visible discoloration of the hair.

Scalp irritation because of improper use of hair straightening chemicals can be treated with an acetic acid (vinegar) rinse. Use a solution of 8 ounces (236.59 ml.) of water to 1 ounce (29.57 ml.) acetic acid (vinegar concentrate). If you use household vinegar as a neutralizer, prepare a mixture of equal parts of vinegar and warm water.

The same type of release statement used for hair coloring should be used for hair straightening treatments. Whenever there is any question concerning what the results will be, always make a strand test before straightening as a guide for determining the final results.

Retouching

Follow all the steps for a regular chemical hair relaxing or straightening treatment, but apply the chemical only to the new growth. The hair straightening cream is not combed through previously treated hair. Protective cream is applied to the hair which was previously treated and also to the scalp.

Unit 11
Chemical blowout

The chemical blowout is a specialized service for people with super curly hair. It is a combination of chemical hair straightening and hairstyling. The procedure involves the removal of a small amount of curl by relaxing the hair chemically and leaving it in a

Unit 11

Chemical blowout

General objectives-student goals:
After study, instruction, practice

Super curly hair

256

more manageable condition. The chemical blowout permits the hair to serve as a foundation for softer, smoother hairstyles. The chemical blowout can be accomplished with either a thio hair relaxer or a sodium hydroxide hair straightener. Caution should be taken not to overrelax the natural curl. To do so would result in a hairstyle that was not intended.

Chemical blowout using the ammonium thioglycolate procedure

1. Drape the patron for a chemical process.

2. Examine the scalp for sores and abrasions. If there are any, do not proceed.

3. Examine the hair. If the hair is hard or brittle, a strand test should be given.

4. Shampoo the hair. Do not rub. Towel dry.

5. Section the hair into four quadrants: down the center from the forehead to the nape and across the head behind the ears from ear to ear.

6. Protect the ears and the skin along the hairline by applying a protective base.

7. Prepare neutralizer.

8. Wear protective gloves. Apply the relaxer to each $1/4$ inch (0.64 cm.) section. Start with the back section at the nape and work up toward the crown. Apply relaxer to the entire strand of hair as quickly as possible.

9. Repeat the procedure in all four sections. Work in a clockwise rotation around the head.

10. Manipulate the hair with your fingers for three to five minutes. Do not comb through or stretch the hair. Stop the relaxing procedure while it still shows a wave and curl formation. Avoid overrelaxing.

11. Rinse the relaxer from the hair.

12. Neutralize.

13. Rinse out the neutralizer and blot the hair dry.

14. Apply an acid pH conditioner with moisturizing agents and a light emollient. These can provide a barrier against moisture loss.

15. Style the hair by using a hair lifter or hair pick in an upward manner while drying the hair with a hand dryer and/or infrared lamp.

16. Shape the hair if necessary. Use either scissors or hair clippers.

and completion of this unit, you will be able to show understanding of a chemical blowout by writing or giving a brief overview of the subject and by demonstrating the procedure. You must have the proper implements and supplies in order to complete this unit successfully.

Super curly hair

257

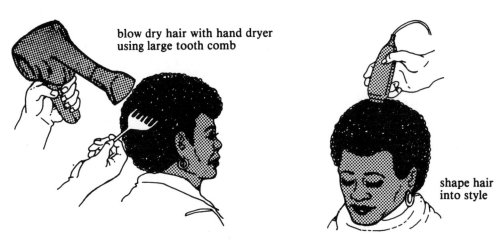

blow dry hair with hand dryer using large tooth comb

shape hair into style

17. After the hair has been cut and combed to style, fluff and smooth it with a hair lifter or hair pick.

The chemical blowout procedure with sodium hydroxide is exactly the same as that with ammonium thioglycolate with the following two exceptions:

1. The hair does not receive a preliminary shampoo. When sodium hydroxide is used, the hair is shampooed after the hair is relaxed.

2. The chemical processing time is much shorter. Sodium hydroxide is a strong alkaline chemical which can relax super curly hair in about half the time it takes with ammonium thioglycolate.

Always follow the product manufacturer's instructions because they vary with each product.

Unit 12
Perm-A-Curl

Perm-A-Curl is the method of perming hair that is naturally super curly. It is a method of relaxing super curly hair with a thio solution and immediately permanent waving the relaxed hair in order to form larger and softer curls that do not require a basic foundation hair set.

The procedure requires that the super curly hair be relaxed to its highest degree of straightness and then given a perm with large diameter spool type perm rods. The size of the perm rod is determined by the length of the hair. The longer the hair, the larger the diameter of the rod. A minimum of $2\frac{1}{2}$ turns is necessary in order to develop a successful curl on short hair.

Unit 12

Perm-A-Curl

General objectives-student goals:
After study, instruction, practice and completion of this unit, you will be able to show understanding of the purpose, technique and procedure for perming super curly hair by demonstrating the procedure. You must have the proper implements and supplies in order to complete this unit successfully.

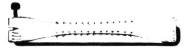

Super curly hair

258

Technique and procedure

1. Arrange the equipment and supplies.

2. Prepare and drape the model just like for a regular hair relaxing treatment.

3. Shampoo the hair. Do not rub the scalp.

4. Towel dry. Leave the hair slightly damp.

5. Put on protective gloves.

6. Apply thio relaxer in the usual manner.

7. Set a timer. Comb the hair flat and smooth until the desired amount of relaxation is obtained.

8. Do not process the hair for more than 20 minutes. While the lotion is still on the hair, section the hair for a regular perm and use plastic hair clips to hold each section of hair securely in place.

9. Follow the exact procedure for giving a cold wave using spool type perm rods of a larger diameter than those which would have been used to give that same hair a conventional perm.

10. When the wrapping has been completed, saturate the hair on the rods and allow it to process. Then, neutralize.

11. After the hair has been completely processed and neutralized, remove the rods and apply hair conditioner.

12. Comb the hair into a relaxed curly style. Dry it with infrared rays heat lamps or set it in the usual manner.

The manufacturer's instructions may vary with each product. It is always advisable to follow the manufacturer's instructions.

Unit 13
Braiding-corn rowing

The techniques for corn rowing and French braiding involve a close-to-the-head braiding technique and are exactly the same. French braid styling usually has one or two large thick braids lying close to the scalp. With corn rowing, the braids are very thin and are arranged in narrow rows over the entire head. This type of close-to-the-head braiding is especially effective on short hair. There are two effects: the **standard braid** in which the strands overlap underneath and a projected braid forms on top, and the **inverted braid** in which the strands overlap on top and the braid forms on the underside. This gives the topside of the braid a flat appearance.

Unit 13
Braiding-corn rowing

General objectives-student goals:
After study, instruction, practice

Super curly hair

259

and completion of this unit, you will be able to show understanding of corn rowing and French braiding by writing or giving a brief overview of the subject and by demonstrating the standard braiding technique. You must have the proper implements and supplies in order to complete this unit successfully.

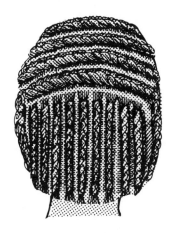

CORN ROWING

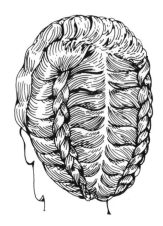

FRENCH BRAID

Standard braiding technique for French braiding and corn rowing (See next page for illustration)

1. Comb and section the hair into the required rows.

2. Start at the top of one row and part a triangular section. Divide it into three even strands. (Figure 1)

3. Start to braid by crossing strand 1 on the left under strand 2. Draw the strands tightly. (Figure 2)

4. Cross strand 3 under strand 1. Tighten the strands. (Figure 3)

5. Pick up another strand from the left: strand "L." Add it to strand 3 and then turn strand 2 under strand 3. (Figure 4)

6. Pick up another strand from the right: strand "R." Add it to strand 2 and then turn strand 1 under strand 2. (Figure 5)

7. Continue picking up strands from the left and right sides until the entire row has been completed. The ends may be secured by back combing, with a small rubber band or with sewing thread that matches the hair color.

   Note: Always add the picked up hair to the center strand. The strand that crosses under becomes the center strand with each braid crossing action.

Inverted braid

The procedure for the inverted braid is exactly the same as for the regular braid with the exception that the strands are crossed over rather than under and the picked up strands are added to the strand nearest the pick up side.

Super curly hair

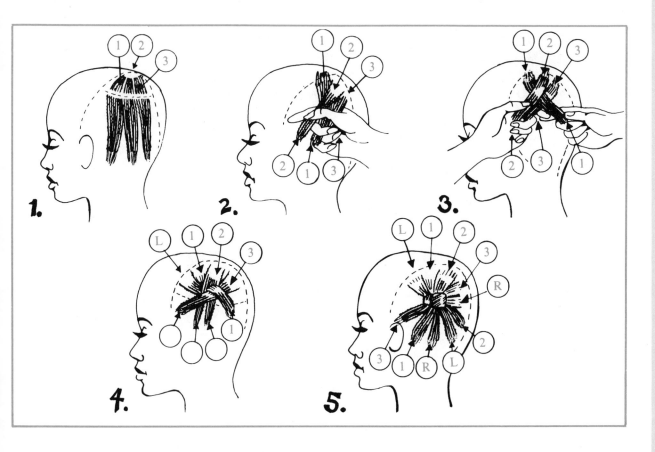

Review questions

1. Is super curly hair found only on Black people?

2. What is the structural shape of super curly hair?

3. What is the best type of shampoo for super curly hair?

Super curly hair

4. Does super curly hair grow straight up from the scalp or at an angle?

5. Does super curly hair retain moisture?

6. Are the principle and procedure for shampooing super curly hair identical to the principle and procedure used for straight or wavy hair?

7. Should people with super curly hair cut and shape their hair frequently?

8. When is a hair clipper with an extremely fine blade (0000) used?

9. Is it best to cut super curly hair when it is wet or when it is dry?

10. What is the best way to determine the length of a natural or Afro haircut?

11. How can you prevent a square look when cutting the natural or Afro?

12. When is it best to use electric scissors on super curly hair?

13. Can super curly hair be wet set with hair rollers?

14. Should hair rollers be removed while the hair is damp?

15. Are the techniques and procedures for permanently or temporarily straightening super curly hair the same as those used for straightening curly or wavy hair?

16. Are the techniques for corn rowing and French braiding the same?

17. Does the hair have to be long in order to develop a good French braid or a style with corn rowing?

18. What causes super curly hair to grow in the form of a tight spiral?

19. Does super curly hair become matted easily?

20. Is a wire bristle hair brush with a rubber back a good tool for disentangling super curly hair?

Super curly hair

Skin care, esthetics and facial massage

Skin care, esthetics and facial massage: The art and science of deep skin cleansing, muscle toning, increasing circulation and exercising the muscles of the face.

Overview: This chapter provides you with the preventative and corrective methods, applications and procedures for treating the skin.

Behavioral objectives—student goals: After completion of this chapter, and after instruction, study and practice, you will be able to perform and demonstrate competency in skin care, esthetics and facial massage by demonstrating the application and procedure for: 15 facial massage movements, the acne facial, facial pack, facial mask, eyebrow shaping, peelings and a cosmetic face lift. You will also be able to demonstrate competency by identifying, explaining and/or listing the implements, supplies and equipment required for professional skin care.

Facial massage is an effective means of exercising the muscles of the face and increasing circulation. The cosmetologist is limited to the following skin treatments:

1. Cleansing the skin

2. Massage

3. Preventive treatment, such as maintaining healthy skin by cleansing, increasing circulation, activating skin glands and relaxing nerves.

4. Corrective treatment of minor conditions, such as blackheads, whiteheads, acne, oiliness and dryness.

Massage is one of the most effective therapeutic treatments practiced in cosmetology. It should never be undertaken by anyone who does not have a thorough knowledge of the anatomy affected. The correct names of all muscles and nerves should be learned so that they will always be recognized. In order to become familiar with the sensations produced by scientific massage, cosmetologists should practice the movements on themselves and locate all the motor points with a sure touch. The accuracy with which the operator can locate a motor point and induce the proper stimulation contributes substantially to the patron's relaxation.

Facial treatments may be given once a week. The facial area in the salon should be as quiet as possible so that the patron can enjoy the relaxation and stimulation of the massage.

Skin care, esthetics
and facial massage

SKIN CARE SERVICES

Unit 1
Skin analysis

General objectives-student goals:
After study, instruction, practice and completion of this unit, you will be able to demonstrate understanding of skin analysis by making an analysis of your own skin. You must have the proper implements and supplies in order to complete this unit successfully.

> **Skin care, esthetics and facial massage**

264

The cosmetologist does not treat skin diseases. However, he or she must be able to recognize the various skin conditions for which the cosmetologist can provide treatment. All other skin conditions should be referred to a medical doctor.

All full service salons provide skin care services but less than 50% of the salons use specialized skin care equipment for the deep cleansing treatments employed in the practice of esthetics.

Sanitary and safety precautions for skin care, esthetics and facial massage

1. Use only sanitized towels.

2. Do not treat sensitive skin tissue.

3. Do not put alcohol or astringent on eye pads.

4. Avoid hard or heavy stroking movements in bony areas.

5. Protect the patron's eyes with cotton pledgets when using the infrared lamp.

6. Use tweezers that have been sanitized.

7. Tweeze one hair at a time.

8. Do not allow tweezed hairs to fall into the patron's eyes.

9. Maintain a clean and orderly arrangement of supplies.

10. Fingernails should be kept short.

11. Avoid using lotions containing alcohol on dry skin.

Unit 1
Skin analysis

The cosmetologist must know what type of facial treatment will be of the most benefit to the patron. In order to determine the best treatment for a particular type of skin or skin condition, the cosmetologist must make an analysis of the skin and recognize the different skin conditions.

Analysis of the skin will determine:

1. Skin type: normal, oily, dry
2. Skin condition: comedones, whiteheads, large pores, infection, broken capillaries, disease

3. Skin pH: the combination of natural body fluids (sebum and perspiration) on the surface of the skin

4. Elasticity: the flexibility of the skin

5. Skin texture: soft, harsh, velvety, rough

The analysis can be made with a naked eye under natural light or with a magnifying glass. This instrument enlarges the skin many times and provides greater detail of the skin texture and condition.

Before analyzing the skin, remove all make-up and cleanse the skin. The results of the analysis will provide the information necessary for choosing lotions and creams and for determining the areas that need extra attention, the type of equipment required, the amount of pressure to apply during massage movements and the color of make-up to apply.

Skin type is determined by pinching small portions of flesh between your thumb and index fingers. Thick skin indicates oiliness and thin skin dryness. The skin pH is tested by using Squibb nitrazine test paper. Rub the strip of paper on a small portion of skin which was wet with water. However, the pH reading of the skin is of little value to the cosmetologist and esthetician because the skin's pH is always changing according to surrounding conditions and activities.

The pH readings do not change the method or procedure of treatment. They do, however, help you to use products with the proper pH. Skin, like hair, has a normal acid pH, and the creams and lotions used should maintain the pH range of the skin: between pH 3.7 and pH 5.5.

The elasticity of the skin is tested by pinching small portions of flesh between your thumb and index finger and stretching them outward. The more the skin stretches and bounces back, the greater the elasticity. If the skin does not regain its normal shape instantly, it is beginning to lose elasticity.

The skin texture is determined by touch. A rough texture and/or flakiness means dry, dehydrated skin. Large pore openings, shine and a sallow color indicate an oily skin condition. Broken capillaries cannot be corrected by salon treatments. These treatments can, however, be very effective in preventing broken capillaries. There are specialized physicians who treat broken capillaries but the results of these treatments are limited.

Unit 2
Implements and supplies

1. Reclining chair with footrest and headrest.

2. Washable gown and head covering.

3. Low stool.

4. Towels, tissues and cotton.

Unit 2
Implements and supplies

General objectives-student goals: After study, instruction and completion of this unit, you will be able to demonstrate understanding of the implements and supplies required for facial massage by identifying the implements and supplies. You must have the proper implements and supplies in order to complete this unit successfully.

> **Skin care, esthetics and facial massage**

5. Comedone extractor used to remove blackheads after manipulations.

6. Spatula, paper cups and small bowls.

7. Cosmetic preparations.

8. Infrared lamp used during manipulations to warm the skin.

9. Antiseptic solution.

10. Facial steamer used to open pores, for oily skin and prior to using a comedone extractor.

11. Violet ray for superficial stimulation which leaves the skin with a warm healthy glow. It is used after manipulations w treating skin conditions.

12. Vibrator which is used in place of the violet ray when treating dry skin conditions.

Unit 3
Massage movements

Digital stroking is performed with the fingers. The fingers are curved so that just the cushions of the fingertips touch the skin

Circular effleurage is a light stroking movement in a circular fashion using only the fingertips.

Digital friction uses the fingertips, knuckles or the ball of the thumb to press firmly at the stopping points.

Nerve friction is a movement in which the thumb and one or two fingers follow the nerve tract, pressing or squeezing the flesh a regular intervals.

Palmar stroking is performed with the whole hand. The hand is held loosely with the fingers curved to conform to the shape of the area under treatment. Palmar stroking is employed on the forehead, chest, back and arms.

Heavier nerve friction is another form of nerve friction which consists of sliding over the skin with the finger exerting pressur at regular intervals. This is used over the shoulders and back. It is very effective along the spine when two fingers of the left han are drawn down the back and pressed between each vertebrae from the neck to the waist. Full weight and pressure is provided a the right hand bears down on the left without bending at the elbows.

Clapping is a movement in which the whole palm is used to strike the skin. The hand is cupped to create a deep sound. When th hand is held open, the sound is higher. Clapping is used principally in massage of the back and shoulders.

Knuckling is a movement similar to a tapping movement in which the fingers are curled so that the knuckles of the four finger strike the skin. When performing this movement, the hand should be rolled slightly from the wrist so that the knuckles will strik the skin in the same spot.

Tapotement is performed with fingers held flexibly and firmly while fingertips are brought against the skin in rapid successior

---

Unit 3
Massage movements

General objectives-student goals:
After study, instruction, practice and completion of this unit, you will be able to show understanding of massage movements by demonstrating digital stroking, circular effleurage, digital friction, nerve friction, palmar stroking, heavier nerve friction, clapping and knuckling. You must have the proper implements and supplies in order to complete this unit successfully.

MASSAGE MOVEMENTS

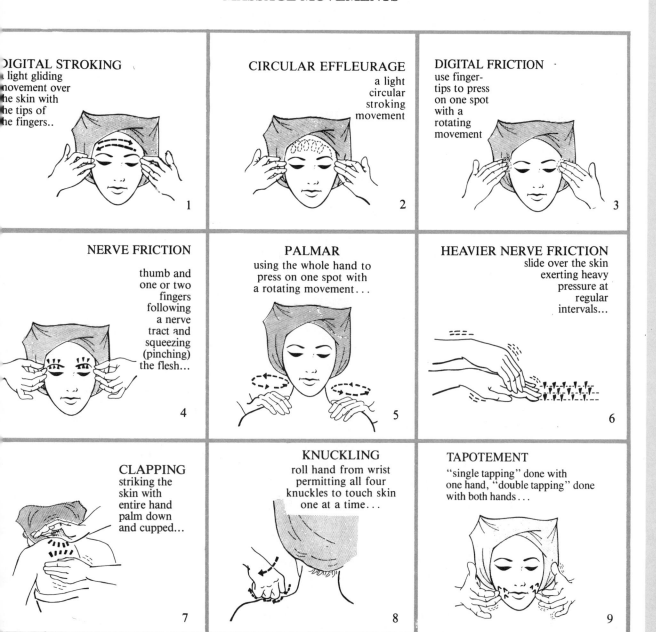

DIGITAL STROKING
a light gliding movement over the skin with the tips of the fingers..

1

CIRCULAR EFFLEURAGE
a light circular stroking movement

2

DIGITAL FRICTION
use finger-tips to press on one spot with a rotating movement

3

NERVE FRICTION
thumb and one or two fingers following a nerve tract and squeezing (pinching) the flesh...

4

PALMAR
using the whole hand to press on one spot with a rotating movement...

5

HEAVIER NERVE FRICTION
slide over the skin exerting heavy pressure at regular intervals...

6

CLAPPING
striking the skin with entire hand palm down and cupped...

7

KNUCKLING
roll hand from wrist permitting all four knuckles to touch skin one at a time...

8

TAPOTEMENT
"single tapping" done with one hand, "double tapping" done with both hands...

9

Skin care, esthetics
and facial massage

Unit 4

Preparation and procedure for facial massage

General objectives-student goals:
After study, instruction, practice and completion of this unit, you will be able to show understanding of the preparation and procedure for facial massage by demonstrating the preparation and procedure. You must have the proper implements and supplies in order to complete this unit successfully.

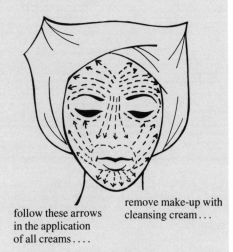

follow these arrows in the application of all creams....

remove make-up with cleansing cream...

Skin care, esthetics and facial massage

Unit 4

Preparation and procedure for facial massage

1. Help the patron dress appropriately and remove all the patron's jewelry.

2. Cover the back of the chair with a clean towel and place a paper towel on the footrest.

3. Adjust the towel across the patron's chest and secure the head covering.

4. Lower the facial chair to a reclining position and adjust the headrest.

5. Wash your hands and rinse them in an antiseptic solution.

Procedure

1. Remove make-up by first spreading cleansing cream over both your palms and all your fingers and then by applying it to the patron's face. Start at the chin. Work out and up toward the ears and cheeks. Continue around the eyes, nose, forehead, along the hairline and down and out on the neck and chest.

2. Remove the cream with tissues folded into mittens and placed around both of your hands.

3. Analyze the skin in order to determine:

   A. If it is oily or dry

   B. If comedones or acne are present

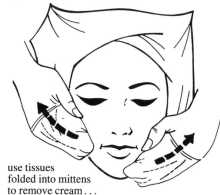

use tissues folded into mittens to remove cream...

4. Based on your observations, determine the correct preparations to use including creams and astringents.

5. Apply emollient cream in the same manner as the cleansing cream.

6. Adjust an infrared lamp at a comfortable distance and start the facial manipulations.

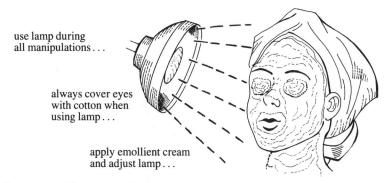

use lamp during
all manipulations . . .

always cover eyes
with cotton when
using lamp . . .

apply emollient cream
and adjust lamp . . .

7. Each movement is performed five times with an even rhythm and tempo. Without removing your hands from the patron's face, start with the middle three fingers of both your hands firmly under the chin and slide up over the cheeks and temples to the middle of the forehead.

8. Disconnect the infrared lamp.

9. Remove the cream with tissues folded into mittens and placed around both of your hands.

10. Sponge the patron's face with skin toning lotion (astringent). Use cotton pledgets. Wipe the face dry.

11. Apply make-up if required.

12. Return the chair to an upright position and remove the draping from the patron.

13. Discard the used materials and supplies. Clean the work area.

Unit 5
Program of facial movements

There is no one set facial massage routine. Many excellent ones have been designed by prominent experts. Your school or instructor may suggest modifications for the program set out here. It is important that you follow a set of movements which are designed to stimulate the structures in the regions on which you work. The precise routine can vary.

Movement 1: This is used to stimulate the frontalis and to make transverse wrinkles less conspicuous. Use the cushion of the middle and index fingers of both your hands. Alternate short strokes without pressure as you make a hand-over-hand movement from the upper side of the nose to the hairline. Move across the forehead toward the left temple gradually. Return all the way across to the right temple and back to the middle of the forehead. After completing this movement for the fifth time, stop at the right temple.

Unit 5
Program of facial movements

General objectives-student goals: After study, instruction, practice and completion of this unit, you will be able to show understanding of the 15 facial movements by demonstrating all 15 movements and by giving a brief description of each one. You must have the proper implements and supplies in order to complete this unit successfully.

> **Skin care, esthetics and facial massage**

Anatomy affected: Muscles: frontal portion of the epicranius, temporal fascia. Nerves: supraorbital, supratrochlear, temporalis. Vessels: frontal and supraorbital arteries and veins. Bones: frontal.

Movement One

LIGHT
DIGITAL
STROKING
AND
EFFLEURAGE

Movement 2: This is used to intensify movement 1. Move the middle and index fingers of both your hands back across the forehead in a semicircular effleurage (light stroking) toward the left temple. Return to the right temple and finish the movement at the middle of the forehead.

Anatomy affected: Muscles: frontal portion of the epicranius, temporal fascia. Nerves: supraorbital, supratrochlear, temporalis. Vessels: frontal and supraorbital arteries and veins. Bones: frontal.

Movement 3: This is used to stimulate the muscles around the eyes and nose. Slide your fingers to the supratrochlear nerve which is between the eyes on both sides of the upper part of the nose. Press and rotate once. Slide your fingers down the sides of the nose in a circular effleurage .Press and rotate on the tip of the nose and on the nasalis nerve, which is on both sides above the tip of the nose. Move back up to the supratrochlear nerve.

Anatomy affected: Muscles: corrugator supercilli, procerus nasalis. Nerves: supratrochlear, infratrochlear, nasal. Vessels: angular, external nasal. Bones: frontal, nasal.

Movement Three

CIRCULAR EFFLEURAGE

Movement 4: This is used to stimulate muscles around the eyes. Slide your fingers down so that they take firm hold under the chin. Hold your thumbs at the supratrochlear nerve at the inner end of the eyebrow area. Move your thumbs out along the rim of the eyebrow line. Press at four points. Rotate five times at the temples and slide back lightly under the eyes to the supratrochlear nerve.

Movement Two

SEMI-CIRCULAR
EFFLEURAGE

**Skin care, esthetics
and facial massage**

Anatomy affected: Muscles: corrugator, orbicularis oculi, temporal. Nerves: supraorbital, supratrochlear, temporal. Vessels: middle temporal, supraorbital, frontal arteries and veins, nasal veins. Bones: frontal, zygomatic.

Movement Four

NERVE FRICTION,
DIGITAL FRICTION
AND
EFFLEURAGE

Movement 5: This is used to stimulate the muscles of the chin and cheeks. Slide your fingers to the jawbone. Separate your fingers above and below the jawbone and lead toward the left ear with heavy friction. Press and rotate the middle finger five times on the motor point of the facial nerve (upper part of the cheekbone below the eye). Return around the chin with a light stroke (right hand leading) and continue toward the right ear with heavy friction. Press and rotate on the facial nerve.

Anatomy affected: Muscles: platysma, triangularis, quadratus labii inferioris, mentalis, masseter. Nerves: branches of the facial, mental and cutaneous colli. Vessels: external maxillary, transverse facial, posterior auricular arteries; anterior facial, inferior labial, external jugular veins. Bones: mandible.

Movement 6: This is used to stimulate various muscles of the cheeks. Slide toward the right ear and separate the index and middle fingers of your left hand. Hold the skin in front of the ear firmly. Use the fingers of your right hand to rotate five times on the auriculo-temporal nerve in front of the right ear. Slide lightly to the lower cheek. Separate and press your fingers against the maxilla and mandible and rotate five times at the corner of the mouth. Slide lightly up to the temple and repeat the rotation on the temporal nerve. Reverse your hands and repeat the entire movement on the left side of the face.

Anatomy affected: Muscles: masseter, zygomaticus, risorius, orbicularis oris. Nerves: trigeminal, masseteric, buccal, auriculo-temporal, infraorbital. Vessels: external maxillary artery; superficial temporal, transverse facial superior and inferior labial arteries and veins. Bones: mandible, maxilla, zygomatic.

Movement Six

NERVE FRICTION
AND
DIGITAL FRICTION

Movement 7: This is used to stimulate and raise the corners of the mouth. Hold the head steady with your left hand and slide your right hand under the chin. Bring your thumb and middle fingers up to the corners of the mouth and do a circular effleurage five times. Continue around the mouth to the side of the cleft in the upper lip. At the same time, press the side of your index finger into the cleft and pinch the two sides together.

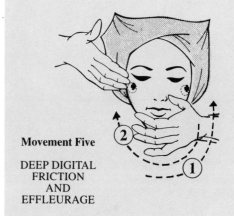

Movement Five

DEEP DIGITAL
FRICTION
AND
EFFLEURAGE

Skin care, esthetics
and facial massage

271

Anatomy affected: Muscles: orbicularis oris, risorius, triangularis, mentalis, quadrati labii inferioris and superioris, caninus, depressor septi. Nerves: facial, mental, buccal. Vessels: superior and inferior labial arteries and veins. Bones: maxilla and mandible.

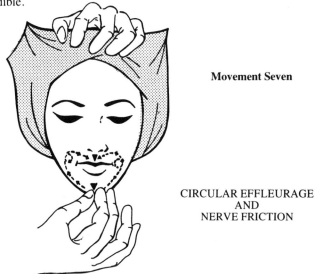

Movement Seven

CIRCULAR EFFLEURAGE
AND
NERVE FRICTION

Movement 8: This is used to stimulate and tighten the muscles of the cheeks. Slide the fingers of both hands firmly to the point of the chin and slide with friction toward the right ear. Press the four points along the mandible (jawbone). Press your middle finger on the motor point for the facial nerve (below the ear at the end of the jawbone) and rotate twice. Return with a light stroke to the chin. Slide to the corner of the mouth and repeat the friction. Press four times across the cheek toward the ear. Press and rotate twice on the motor point for the 5th nerve in front of the ear. Return with a light stroke to the mouth and slide to the corner of the nose. Repeat the friction. Press four times across the cheek toward the temple. Press and rotate twice on the temporal nerve at the temple. Repeat the same movements on the left side.

Anatomy affected: Muscles: masseter, zygomaticus, risorius, orbicularis oris. Nerves: trigeminal, masseteric, buccal, auriculo-temporal, infraorbital. Vessels: external maxillary artery; superficial temporal, transverse facial, superior and inferior labial arteries and veins. Bones: mandible, maxilla, zygomatic.

Movement Eight

NERVE
FRICTION AND
DIGITAL
FRICTION

**Skin care, esthetics
and facial massage**

272

Movement 9: This is used to stimulate and tighten the muscles of the cheeks. Follow the same lines as in movement 8 and tap the face with a lifting and dropping movement on both sides of the face at the same time. There are no rotations at the terminal points and the hands return to the starting points through the air.

Anatomy affected: Muscles: masseter, zygomaticus, risorius, orbicularis oris. Nerves: trigeminal, masseteric, buccal, auriculo-temporal, infraorbital. Vessels: external maxillary artery; superficial temporal, transverse facial, superior and inferior labial arteries and veins. Bones: mandible, maxilla, zygomatic.

Movement Nine

SINGLE
TAPOTEMENT

Movement 10: Tapotement is used to stimulate and tighten the muscles of the cheeks by tapping over the same lines as movement 9. Use both hands rapidly on the same side of the face.

Anatomy affected: Muscles: masseter, zygomaticus, risorius, orbicularis oris. Nerves: trigeminal, masseteric, buccal, auriculo-temporal, infraorbital. Vessels: external maxillary artery; superficial temporal, transverse facial, superior and inferior labial arteries and veins. Bones: mandible, maxilla, zygomatic.

Movement Ten

DOUBLE
TAPOTEMENT

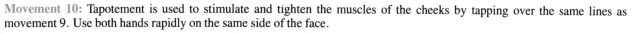

Movement 11: This is used to stimulate and tighten the muscles of the cheeks. With your hands partially closed, grasp the flesh at the chin between your thumb and the knuckle of your first finger. Work up the face with a plucking movement. Work both sides of the face at the same time:

A. From the chin to the inner corner of the eye

B. From the chin to the outer corner of the eye

C. From the chin to the ear

Anatomy affected: Muscles: masseter, zygomaticus, risorius, orbicularis oris. Nerves: trigeminal, masseteric, buccal, auriculo-temporal, infraorbital. Vessels: external maxillary artery; superficial temporal, transverse facial, superior and inferior labial arteries and veins. Bones: mandible, maxilla, zygomatic.

Movement Eleven

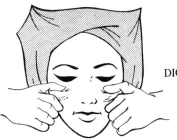

DIGITAL KNEADING

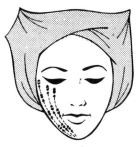

NERVE FRICTION

Movement 12: This is used to stimulate and tighten the muscles of the cheeks. Go over the same lines as in movement 11 with sharp, stinging taps of the fingertips. Keep your wrists and fingers loose.

Anatomy affected: Muscles: masseter, zygomaticus, risorius, orbicularis oris. Nerves: trigeminal, masseteric, buccal, auriculo-temporal, infraorbital. Vessels: external maxillary artery; superficial temporal, transverse facial, superior and inferior labial arteries and veins. Bones: mandible, maxilla, zygomatic.

Movement 13: This is used to break up fatty deposits under the chin. Place three fingers of both your hands under the chin and iron a double chin by employing firm friction back under the chin and under the line of the mandible (jawbone) toward the ear. Alternate the stroking toward opposite sides.

Anatomy affected: Muscles: platysma. Nerves: mental, mandibular, cutaneous colli. Vessels: external maxillary artery, common facial, external jugular veins. Bones: mandible.

Movement Thirteen

PALMAR
FRICTION AND
STROKING

Movement Twelve

DOUBLE
TAPOTEMENT

Skin care, esthetics and facial massage

Movement 14: This is used to tighten the platysma (neck area) and stimulate the pectoral muscles. Place the fingertips of both your hands together under the chin and slide them down the neck with a firm stroke until they lie flat on the chest. Use a light touch over the middle of the throat. Press and rotate three times.

Anatomy affected: Muscles: platysma, pectoralis minor. Nerves: supraclavicular, mental, cutaneous colli, mandibular. Vessels: subclavian. Bones: mandible, clavicle, sternum, upper ribs.

Movement Fourteen

DIGITAL STROKING,
PALMAR STROKING
AND
DIGITAL FRICTION

Movement 15: This is used to coordinate all movements and give final impetus to more rapid circulation. Keep the patron in a sitting position. Slide your hands back to the side of the neck. Then, apply heavy friction down and out to the shoulder. Rotate the deltoid muscle at the end of the shoulder three times. Slide your hands along the scapulae (along the shoulder blades) to the spine, up over the cervical vertebrae (bones in the neck) to the base of the cranium (back of the skull). Press up against the occipital nerve at the base of the skull.

Anatomy affected: Muscles: sternocleidomastoid, platysma, deltoid, trapezius. Nerves: spinal accessory, cutaneous colli, three occipitals, acromial, brachial plexus, supraclavicular. Vessels: axillary, subclavian. Bones: clavicle, scapulae, vertebrae.

Unit 6
Acne facial

Acne is the most common and annoying of the skin conditions which the cosmetologist is called on to assist in treating. Acne is an inflammatory condition of the sebaceous (oil) glands. It is characterized by papules (dry pimples), pustules (pimples containing pus) and comedones (blackheads). Acne lesions are produced on the face, neck, back and chest.

The cosmetologist should refer the patron to a competent physician. The physician may treat acne with medicine, x-ray or ultraviolet light. He may recommend a diet that eliminates foods high in fats, sugars and starches.

Dirt and oil on the surface of the skin do not cause acne. However, individuals with acne should keep their skin as clean as possible in order to avoid aggravating the condition.

Movement Fifteen

PALMAR FRICTION,
ROTATION AND
CIRCULAR EFFLEURAGE

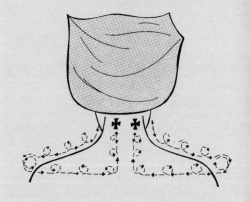

Unit 6
Acne facial

General objectives-student goals: After study, instruction, practice and completion of this unit, you will be able to show understanding of

---
Skin care, esthetics and facial massage

275

acne facials by writing and/or giving a brief overview of the subject and by demonstrating the procedure. You must have the proper implements and supplies in order to complete this unit successfully.

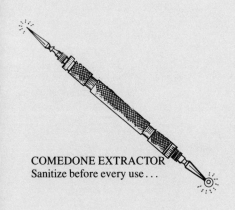

COMEDONE EXTRACTOR
Sanitize before every use . . .

Unit 7

Facial pack

General objectives-student goals:
After study, instruction, practice and completion of this unit, you will

> **Skin care, esthetics and facial massage**

276

The real cause of acne is the hormonal change which occurs during adolescence in both the male and the female. The reaction of the genetic predisposition to these changes generates acne lesions but only in some individuals. No one is responsible for causing the condition. Those affected are victims of biology. Medical science has treatments which will control acne within a short period of time.

The cosmetologist is limited to the cosmetic treatment of acne. This is very helpful. When treating acne, the cosmetologist cleans the skin, treats oiliness of the skin by local application, removes blackheads and uses special medicated preparations.

Procedure

1. Prepare the patron for a plain facial.

2. Cleanse the face with a medicated soap (tincture of green soap).

3. Apply acne cream over the face and neck.

4. Apply high frequency current with a facial electrode for a maximum of five minutes and/or use a facial steamer.

5. Remove the acne cream.

placing index finger on electrode when applying or removing avoids giving patron an uncomfortable sensation . . .

6. Remove blackheads and cleanse any pustules that may have ruptured. Use a comedone extractor for the blackheads and the needle point for the whiteheads.

7. Apply acne lotion and leave it on for five minutes.

8. Remove the acne lotion and apply a cold wet towel for one minute.

9. Saturate cotton pledgets with antiseptic lotion and apply with a blotting movement over the entire face and neck.

Unit 7
Facial pack

Face packs and masks can be used as part of a facial or as an entirely separate treatment. Face packs stimulate and refresh the skin of the face. Ordinarily, a cream is applied which creates a sensation of slight tingling while it tightens the skin. A bleach pack produces mild lightening of the area over which it is applied. A bleach pack reduces the contrast of freckles. Therefore, it is a popular treatment for autumn. It also makes the skin appear fresh and clear. Five to six treatments may be required for a noticeable improvement of freckles. A bleach pack has no effect on birthmarks. Oily skin responds well to clay and lemon packs.

Facial packs are recommended for normal or oily skin. They should not be given to dry skin. A facial mask is recommended for dry skin.

Procedure for facial packs

1. Give a plain facial, including manipulations, up to the point of applying foundation make-up.

   Note: If a bleach facial pack is to be given, substitute a good bleaching cream as the emollient during the massage and protect the eyebrows with a plain emollient cream.

2. Use either high frequency current with a facial electrode and/or a facial steamer for five minutes.

3. Apply pack-lemon, clay or bleach. Keep it away from the eyes, nostrils and mouth.

4. Place cotton pads moistened with witch hazel over the eyes.

5. Allow the pack to remain on the skin until it is dry. The action may be quickened by using an infrared lamp.

6. Remove the pack with hot but comfortable wet towels.

7. Pat dry. Apply foundation make-up.

Unit 8
Facial mask

Facial masks (hot oil mask) are part of a facial treatment for dry skin. They are applied directly to the skin with the aid of layers of gauze with openings for the eyes, nostrils and mouth. A facial mask softens, smooths, refreshes, reconditions and lubricates dry skin.

The formula for the hot oil mask varies from a prepared massage oil and plain olive oil to an equal mixture of massage oil and massage cream which is heated until liquified.

Procedure

1. Give a plain facial, including vibrator and manipulations, up to the point of applying foundation make-up.

2. Cover the eyes with pads moistened with witch hazel.

3. Apply two layers of gauze saturated in warm oil as a neck covering.

4. Apply two layers of gauze saturated in warm oil to the face. Leave openings for the eyes, nostrils and mouth.

be able to show understanding of facial packs by giving a brief overview of the subject and by demonstrating the procedure. You must have the proper implements and supplies in order to complete this unit successfully.

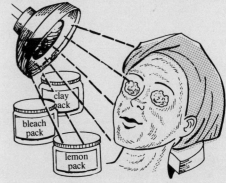

...for normal and oily skin...

Unit 8
Facial mask

General objectives-student goals: After study, instruction, practice and completion of this unit, you will be able to show understanding of facial masks by giving a brief overview of the subject and by demonstrating the procedure. You must have the proper implements and supplies in order to complete this unit successfully.

Skin care, esthetics and facial massage

277

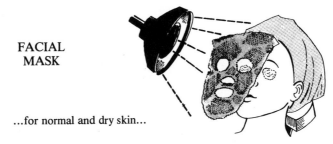

FACIAL
MASK

...for normal and dry skin...

5. Time for 15 minutes without a lamp or apply an infrared lamp for five minutes.

6. Remove the gauze. Apply hot but comfortable wet towels. Use these to remove the oil.

7. Pat dry. Apply foundation make-up.

Unit 9
Eyebrow shaping

Well-shaped eyebrows add to the beauty of a face. The natural growth pattern of the eyebrows is very often shapeless, but this condition may be corrected by tweezing, shaving or by using a wax depilatory.

The most recommended method is **tweezing** (epilation) because the hairs which are pulled out take longer to appear again and do not form the stubble which usually results from shaving. The disadvantage of a wax depilatory is that the fine light hairs are unavoidably removed with the heavy dark hairs.

In order to determine the proper shape for a patron's eyebrows, observe if the patron has:

1. **Square facial structure:** Help to create a more oval illusion by tweezing a high arch slightly toward the ends of the eyebrows. Begin the arch line above the inside corner of the eye.

square
shape

WRONG   RIGHT

Unit 9
Eyebrow shaping

General objectives-student goals:
After study, instruction, practice and completion of this unit, you will be able to show understanding of eyebrow shaping by giving a brief overview of the subject and by demonstrating the technique and procedure. You must have the proper implements and supplies in order to complete this unit successfully.

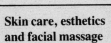

Skin care, esthetics
and facial massage

278

2. **Oblong facial structure:** A shorter illusion can be created by making the eyebrows archless and almost straight.

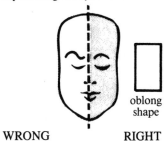

oblong shape

WRONG   RIGHT

3. **Round facial structure:** The same high arch used for the square facial structure helps create an illusion of ovalness.

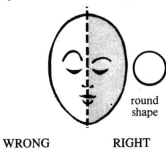

round shape

WRONG   RIGHT

4. **Close set eyes:** Create the illusion of wider spaced eyes by shortening the eyebrows over the nose.

The actual technique for removing any single hair is simple.

1. Press the thumb and third finger of your left hand down firmly on both sides of the hair. Spread them a little in order to stretch the skin. This will cause the hair to stand up straighter. This will make it easier to grasp the hair and lessen any pain from the tweezing.

2. Grasp the hair firmly in the tweezer, which is held between the thumb and index fingers of your right hand, and pull it along the line of the growth direction from the skin.

finishing touches are done above the eyebrow . . .

most of the shaping is done under the eyebrow...

close set eyes

(‿)   wrong

(‿)   right

pull in direction of natural hair growth

Skin care, esthetics and facial massage

279

1. Prepare the patron.

2. Determine the correct type of arch.

3. Cover the patron's eyes with cotton moistened with witch hazel.

4. Soften the eyebrows with cotton pledgets containing hot water, emollient cream or a desensitizing preparation.

5. Remove the hair between the eyebrows.

6. Remove the hairs from under the eyebrow line by pushing them upward before removing.

7. Remove the hair from above the eyebrow line by pushing them downward first. Remove as few hairs as possible from this area. Most of the shaping is done under the eyebrow line.

8. Remove the cotton from the patron's eyes.

9. Apply emollient cream and massage the eyebrows to restore normal circulation. Remove the cream with a tissue.

10. Apply astringent to the eyebrows and surrounding skin.

11. Use an eyebrow pencil as necessary.

Unit 10
The art of esthetics

Bioesthegenics is the scientific study of organic skin care. The words bioesthegenics and esthetician were coined in Europe because this field of practice was mainly European until early 1966. It did not gain popular recognition in the United States until 1972.

Estheticians practice the professional art of esthetics. Estheticians who are professionally trained and licensed usually maintain a practice in a skin care center, a full service beauty salon, a health salon or a spa. Their expertise is the care and treatment of skin.

The esthetician's knowledge and practice is far beyond that of the cosmetician, who uses facial make-up to correct and beautify the skin. Esthetics is not, however, as advanced or complete as the skill which a dermatologist has. The dermatologist is a medical doctor and treats the skin medically. The esthetician limits his or her practice to the scientific study of the effects and results of the natural organic substances used to treat and aid the skin.

Unit 10
The art of esthetics

General objectives-student goals:
After study, instruction and completion of this unit, you will be able to demonstrate understanding of the art of esthetics by writing and/or giving a brief overview of the subject.

Skin care, esthetics
and facial massage

280

Skin analysis and the practice of esthetics require additional training and special skills as well as special equipment. A professional esthetician is also required to have knowledge of the products which are applied to the skin.

It is important to have the basic knowledge of the cosmetologist's facial treatments before starting a practice in esthetics. The esthetician must also have:

1. A completely equipped booth, no smaller than 7 feet by 7 feet (2.13 by 2.13 m.), with a wash basin and electrical outlets.

2. The minimum equipment which includes:

   A. The cold-light magnifying lamp

   B. A standard body facial treatment chair with matching revolving stool

   C. A complete set of apparatus on a self-contained, wheel mounted stand which is self-sufficient and easily movable. The apparatus should consist of:

      1. Spray atomizer used to prepare the skin for cleansing and for acne and seborrhea.

      2. Skin cleanser: The brushing machine, also known as an electric peeling machine, and the asperation machine remove dead cells and clean the pores.

      3. Ultraviolet lamp for tanning and for treating acne.

      4. A wand for the application of astringent lotion or a filiform shower spray.

      5. Black light lamp: The glow at a particular wave length shows foreign matter which cannot normally be seen.

      6. Short wave electrolysis: An epilation needle or tweezer for the permanent removal of superfluous hair.

      7. High frequency equipment with assorted electrodes for increased blood circulation and for stimulation of muscle tone.

      8. Vacuum (aspiration-suction) for the removal of blackheads.

      9. Wax melting heater for the temporary removal of superfluous hair.

3. A complete line of professional skin care products which are perfectly pH balanced for each type of skin. They are made from natural organic materials, have a low pH, are acid balanced and do not contain alcohol or mineral oil. There are many specialized creams, lotions, moisturizers, oils, astringents, packs and masks. A complete series of products for both normal skin and conditions such as acne, oily skin, dry skin, sensitive skin and mature skin is needed for skin

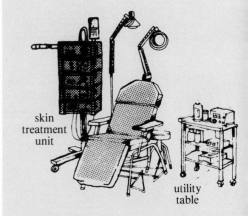

skin treatment unit

utility table

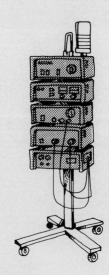

skin treatment unit

Skin care, esthetics and facial massage

281

care services. The products should be intermixable. This allows the esthetician to use the products as is or to create individualized mixtures for any skin condition. Treatments vary from a 15 minute facial to clean, refresh, tone, firm, smooth, soften and nourish to the most sophisticated treatment which requires a minimum of one hour and 30 minutes.

Peelings

Peelings are used to deep clean the pores and remove dead cells from the surface of the skin. Peelings are used at the beginning of a treatment, after the preliminary cleansing. This prepares the skin for penetration by other treatment products. It ensures immediate and maximum results. Depending on the skin condition and the product to be used, a peeling can be accomplished with any combination of cream, mask, pack, suction, vapor, infrared lamp or the brushing machine.

Note: Chemical skin peeling should be practiced by competent dermatologists only.

The esthetician should also have a knowledge of cosmetic surgery as it relates to the art of esthetics. Areas of interest are rhytidectomy (face lift and excision of wrinkles), rhinoplasty (nose), blepharophryplasty (eyelids) and dermabrasion (chemical peeling of the skin surface).

Cosmetic face lift

A face lift without surgery or chemical peeling is a popular skin care service that can give a patron a more youthful appearance.

The cosmetic face lift is not a type of facial mask. You can feel and see improved results with the first treatment. It cleans the pores, helps to tighten and tone the skin and muscle tissues, and penetrates to the lower surfaces in order to lubricate and moisturize the skin.

Cosmetic face lifts have a cumulative effect. The treatments should be given at least twice a week until the optimum results have been obtained. Treatments should then continue once a week in order to maintain these results.

The application and procedure vary with each product, and the manufacturer's instructions should be followed. The procedure outlined here is a basic one.

Procedure

1. Cleanse the skin of the neck and face areas thoroughly. Include the area around the ear.

2. Rinse well with cool water and pat dry.

3. Use a small facial brush to start the application of the cosmetic lift at the lower part of the neck. Use upward strokes. Work toward the chin line and over to the area behind the ear.

4. Use upward strokes and proceed from the chin to the hairline and from the corner of the eye to the hairline.

start at the
lower part of the
neck and work
toward the chin line..

Skin care, esthetics
and facial massage

5. Use the brush gently around the eye areas. Do not apply the lift too close to the eyelash line.

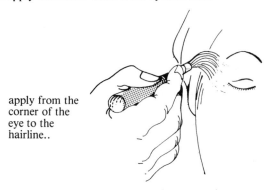

apply from the corner of the eye to the hairline..

6. Complete the application over the entire face.

7. The lift becomes tacky within a few minutes. If a second application is needed for problem skin or problem areas, now is the time to apply it.

8. After the application has been completed, the patron must lie flat with no pillows. You must keep the feet elevated. The patron must remain totally relaxed without talking or smoking for 45 minutes. As the lift dries and the nutrients work their way into the layers of the skin, the patron will feel a slight pulsing, a warm tingling or a pulling or tightening sensation because of the increased flow of blood.

9. After 45 minutes, remove the lift. Use the special mixture and water. The lift is water soluble. The special mixture helps to soften the lift for easy removal.

10. Use water soaked towels and gently remove the lift by patting. Do not rub.

11. Pat the skin dry. Apply oil and/or moisture cream over the entire face and neck. Blot any excess.

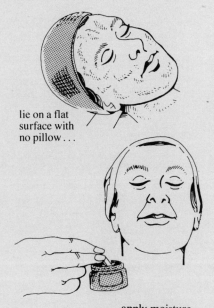

lie on a flat surface with no pillow . . .

apply moisture cream and/or oil..

Review questions

1. What is a facial massage?

2. Why is it important to learn the correct names of all the muscles, nerves, vessels and bones involved in the massage technique?

3. How often can facial treatments be given?

Skin care, esthetics and facial massage

4. Can any reclining chair be used for a facial?

5. What is a comedone extractor?

6. When is the best time to use the violet ray during a facial?

7. Can a vibrator be used to treat both an oily and dry skin condition during a facial treatment?

8. Is it necessary to cover the patron's eyes with cotton when using an infrared lamp during a facial?

9. How many times should facial massage movements be repeated?

10. Do you press on the occipital nerve at the base of the cranium during a facial treatment?

11. What is the most common skin condition which the cosmetologist is asked to treat?

12. Why should a cosmetologist refer a patron with acne to a competent physician?

13. How can you avoid giving the patron an uncomfortable sensation when using a high frequency electrode during a facial?

14. What is a good medicated soap for cleansing a face with an acne condition?

15. How does a bleach pack affect the skin?

16. Should facial packs be given for dry skin conditions?

17. Should a facial mask be given for oily skin conditions?

18. How can you protect the patron's eyes when using an infrared lamp during a facial?

19. How many layers of gauze are required for a facial mask?

20. What is the technique for removing hairs from under the eyebrow line?

21. To what is the esthetician's skin care practice limited?

22. What is the minimum size of an esthetician's skin care booth?

23. The brushing machine, which is used as a skin cleanser, is also known as an electric peeling machine. Can it be used for the asperation technique which roughens the skin?

24. What is a black light lamp used for during a skin care treatment?

Facial make-up

Facial make-up: The art of improving one's appearance and physical attractiveness by applying facial cosmetics.

Overview: This chapter provides the information necessary in order to gain the knowledge required for practicing the art of creating a magnified illusion of beauty by using cosmetics.

Behavioral objectives—student goals: After completion of this chapter, and after instruction, study and practice, you will be able to perform and demonstrate competency in the art of facial make-up by demonstrating the application and procedure for a complete facial make-up, individual eyelash application and corrective make-up techniques. You will also be able to demonstrate competency by identifying, explaining and/or listing: the required implements and supplies, details about the color wheel, hints on facial make-up, evening make-up, balmasque make-up and theatrical make-up.

Good facial make-up is an art that requires constant study and wide practical experience. Hairstyling and make-up are natural mates because the creation of an illusion of improved beauty is the main object of both. Once trained in the basic knowledge of line, movement, direction and color, the cosmetologist can elaborate on these factors and offer a wider range of personal services.

BEFORE

AFTER

A facial make-up can be applied at any time but is usually given after a facial massage. The patron should be in a reclined or semireclined position, and the cosmetologist may work from the side or from the back of the patron while applying the cosmetics.

When the application of cosmetics is done correctly, it will accent good features and minimize poor ones. A make-up artist must have a good understanding of product information, skin conditions, complexion tones, facial structure and the basic principles of optical illusion.

Facial make-up

Sanitary and safety precautions for facial make-up

1. Always sanitize mascara, eyebrow and lip brushes after each use.

2. Do not get mascara in the eyes.

3. Do not point the tweezers toward the patron's eyes when applying artificial eyelashes and when tweezing eyebrows. Always work with clean tweezers.

4. Sharpen the eyebrow and eye-liner pencils after each use.

5. Discard all used sponges.

6. Always recap eyelash adhesive bottles as soon as possible.

7. Discard any unused solution. Do not pour it back into the bottle.

8. Remove all creams from jars using a sanitized spatula.

9. Keep eyelash adhesive from coming in contact with the eyelids.

10. Avoid getting creams and lotions in the patron's eyes, nose and mouth.

11. Sanitize all reusable materials and equipment after each use.

12. Work in well-lighted area.

13. Use light feathery strokes when blending cosmetics on the skin.

14. A make-up application should be made only on skin that has been cleansed properly.

Unit 1

Complexion tones

General objectives-student goals:
After study, instruction and completion of this unit, you will be able to demonstrate understanding of complexion tones by writing and/or giving a brief overview of the subject.

Facial make-up

286

Unit 1
Complexion tones

Complexion tones are classified as light, golden, pink, red, olive, tan, brown and black. A light complexion is described best as fair skin with pale pink undertones. Skin with a golden complexion has a predominant yellow cast. Pink skin has a very light red undertone. Red skin has very deep red undertones. An olive complexion is made up of a yellowish green color which can be classified as almost very light brown without red undertones. Tan skin can range from light to dark brown with red undertones. Brown skin can have red or yellow undertones and can range from light to dark brown. A black complexion is not jet black. It is a deep dark brown without yellow or red undertones.

Unit 2
Facial structures

There are many facial types but they all fall into one of four categories:

1. Oval

2. Round

3. Square

4. Oblong (Rectangular)

FACIAL STRUCTURE

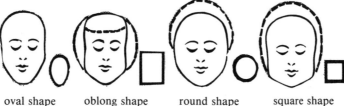

oval shape   oblong shape   round shape   square shape

Oval is the perfectly shaped face.

Round and square facial shapes require similar make-up techniques. These will help to create the illusion of ovalness.

Oblong facial structures are long. Here too, the object is to create an oval illusion.

Unit 3
Implements, supplies and procedure

Implements and supplies

1. Towels

2. Headband

3. Draping cloth

4. Cleansing cream and tissues

5. Cotton pledgets and spatula

6. Astringent lotion or skin freshener

7. Cream or liquid foundation bases

8. Disposable puffs and sponge

9. Rouge and loose or pressed powder

10. Eye-shadow, pencil, liner and mascara

Procedure

1. Wash your hands before preparing the patron.

2. Apply cleansing cream sparingly to the face and neck. Use the same technique as for facials with upward circular movements. Cleanse above and below the eyes and remove all mascara.

Unit 2
Facial structures

General objectives-student goals:
After study, instruction and completion of this unit, you will be able to demonstrate understanding of facial structures by writing and/or giving a brief overview of the subject.

Unit 3
Implements, supplies and procedure

General objectives-student goals:
After study, instruction, practice and completion of this unit, you will be able to show understanding of the implements, supplies and procedure for the application of facial make-up by identifying the implements and supplies required for a basic make-up application and by demonstrating the procedure. You must have the proper implements and supplies in order to complete this unit successfully.

Facial make-up

3. Thoroughly remove the cleansing cream. Apply astringent or skin freshener, if necessary, to remove all traces of cleansing cream.

4. Apply moisturizer base to protect against the drying effects of facial cosmetics.

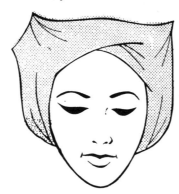

apply moisturizer base

5. Shape the eyebrows whenever possible. The high point of the arch should generally be toward the outer part of the eyebrows.

6. Before the application of cosmetics, remove excess moisturizer base from the skin in order to achieve an even application of make-up. Apply astringent to oily skin. Concentrate on the oily areas around the nose and forehead. Use skin freshener on dry or normal skin. Blot dry. Eliminate this step if excessive moisturizer base is not present.

for dry or normal skin

apply astringent or skin freshener according to skin condition...

for oily skin

7. Apply liquid or cream base. A thin coating of base is applied with a disposable sponge. Create a soft satin look for day wear and a glowing look for evening. The base is not for color, but is used to smooth the skin. The base color should harmonize with the color of the skin.

8. Test the color of the base on the patron's neck for true blending effects. If the base blends to zero with the skin, it is correct.

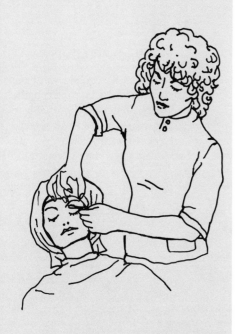

Liquid Base

base selected should blend with skin color...

PASTE

sponges should not be used from one patron to another...

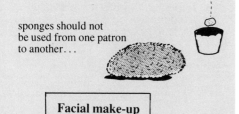

Facial make-up

288

9. Shadow and highlight the skin and facial features as needed. Use eye-shadow sticks, creamy base or pressed powder. To highlight, use any color lighter than the skin. To minimize, use any color darker than the skin.

10. Apply translucent powder with very little pigment in order to set the make-up.

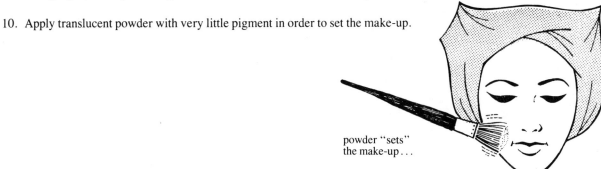

powder "sets" the make-up . . .

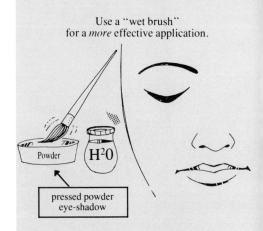

Use a "wet brush" for a *more* effective application.

Powder   H²0

pressed powder eye-shadow

11. Apply eye-shadow. If pressed powder eye-shadow is used, apply it with a brush and a little water for a stronger color which will hold better.

12. Apply eye-liner. The eye-liner is applied in a very fine line along the entire lid as close to the lashes as possible. This makes the eyes appear larger. If the line is made above the crease on the upper eyelids, it will give the eyes more depth. The patron must keep the eyes closed. Start at the inner point. Make a thicker line as you go out to the corner. To create a lift, make an extension line at the end of the eyes. The eyes should be open during this part of the procedure.

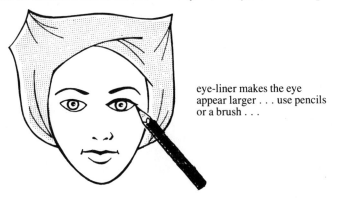

eye-liner makes the eye appear larger . . . use pencils or a brush . . .

13. Apply lashes. Follow the manufacturer's instructions. Some basic rules for applying lashes are:

A. Measure the lash against the eye from the inner corner and cut it to the measurement.

B. Seal the cut end with colorless nail polish. This will prevent unraveling.

C. Curl the lash and add mascara before applying.

EYELASH STRIPS

Facial make-up

289

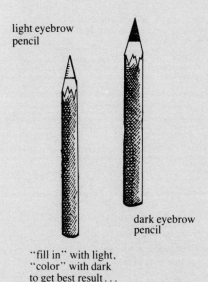

light eyebrow
pencil

dark eyebrow
pencil

"fill in" with light,
"color" with dark
to get best result . . .

Facial make-up

290

D. While the adhesive is drying, shape the lash to the curve of the eyelid.

E. Use a wig cleaning liquid to clean false eyelashes.

14. Use two eyebrow pencils: a light one to fill in the eyebrow line and a dark one to color the hairline strokes.

15. Apply powder over the face, neck and eyelids to seal the make-up.

16. If artificial lashes are not used, apply mascara to the lashes. The eyes should be open during this procedure. Apply the mascara and brush upward on the underside of the upper lashes. Apply lightly from the topside of the lower lashes.

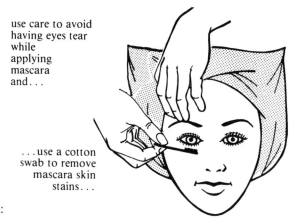

use care to avoid
having eyes tear
while
applying
mascara
and . . .

. . . use a cotton
swab to remove
mascara skin
stains . . .

17. Two shades of lip rouge should be applied:

A. Deep color to outline the lips.

B. Lighter color to fill in and blend with the outline and the lips.

The outline is made with a fine point applicator. The lips should be closed and in a relaxed position. The lips should be in a stretched position when filling in. This will ensure smooth coverage. Blot any excess with a tissue.

18. Apply blush rouge to the forehead, upper eye bone and cheeks. Never apply rouge high on the temples, under the eyes or in a hard circle on the cheeks. When the make-up treatment has been completed, the center of the face should appear highlighted and the balance shaded. Make-up can change color on oily skin within a short time after the application.

Hints for facial make-up

1. Apply foundation in sparing dabs all over the face. Then, blend it thoroughly.

2. A dot of eye-shadow is placed on the center of the lid. Then, it is blended up and out until the outline disappears.

3. For an oval face, place a dab of rouge on the cheekbones and blend out. For a long face, place rouge high on the cheekbones and blend out. For a round face, place the rouge on line with the center of the eye and blend out and down.

4. Shape the eyebrows from underneath in order to produce a larger skin area. This will make the eyes appear larger. The brows should be allowed to grow near the nose. This will make the bridge appear narrow.

5. Apply lipstick from the upper center to the outer corner. The lower lip should match the upper one in fullness except at the bow in the center.

6. Extend the eyelash line slightly beyond the outer corner in order to give the illusion of a longer lash. Apply mascara from the outer corner.

7. After the application of lipstick, blot the lips with a tissue. Test the evenness of the application by checking the imprint.

Unit 4
Corrective make-up techniques

Corrective make-up involves slight adjustments of the facial features. This may mean changing the curve of the eyebrows, the shape of the mouth, lowering the forehead or shortening the nose. The two sides of the face are never the same. If the two sides are so different that the face appears asymmetrical, the less attractive side should be made up to match the better one.

The ideal face can be divided horizontally into three equal parts, from the:

1. Hairline to the eyebrows

2. Eyebrows to the bottom of the nose .

3. Bottom of the nose to the tip of the chin

When these three areas of the face are not equal, the cosmetician should create an optical illusion which makes them appear as nearly equal as possible.

Unit 5
Corrective make-up: forehead

To create an illusion of a lowered forehead, darken the forehead near the hairline with a fairly wide stripe of color three shades darker than the base color. Blend downward gradually into the base foundation color to avoid a sharp line of demarcation.

A forehead that is too low can be made to appear higher by means of a color three shades lighter than the base foundation color originally applied at the hairline.

Unit 4
Corrective make-up techniques

General objectives-student goals: After study, instruction and completion of this unit, you will be able to demonstrate understanding of corrective make-up techniques by writing and/or giving a brief overview of the subject.

Unit 5
Corrective make-up: forehead

General objectives-student goals: After study, instruction, practice and completion of this unit, you will be able to show understanding of

Facial make-up

corrective make-up techniques for the forehead by demonstrating the techniques. You must have the proper implements and supplies in order to complete this unit successfully.

Unit 6
Corrective make-up: nose

General objectives-student goals:
After study, instruction, practice and completion of this unit, you will be able to show understanding of corrective make-up techniques for the nose by demonstrating the techniques. You must have the proper implements and supplies in order to complete this unit successfully.

Unit 7
Corrective make-up: jawline and chin

General objectives-student goals:
After study, instruction, practice and completion of this unit, you will be able to show understanding of corrective make-up techniques for the jawline and chin by demonstrating the techniques. You must have the proper implements and supplies in order to complete this unit successfully.

Facial make-up

292

If the frontal lobes are too prominent, they can be toned down with shadow, and depressed areas between the frontal lobes and the area just above the eyebrows can be brought forward with highlight.

The forehead can be narrowed or widened by shadows or highlights at the temples. The shadows or highlights blend with the forehead. Shadow will create a narrow illusion.

Unit 6
Corrective make-up: nose

If the nose is too long, an illusion can be created which makes it appear shortened. Apply a deeper color under the tip of the nose and blend it up over the tip. If the nose is too short, use a highlight three shades lighter than the basic foundation under and over the tip of the nose.

In order to widen a narrow nose, apply a broad highlight down the center and the wings of the nostrils. To make a broad nose narrower, shadow the nostrils and sides of the nose and apply a very narrow highlight down the center.

in make-up... shadow and light are used to create optical illusions...
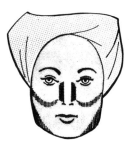

Remember that in corrective make-up, shadows and highlights are usually three shades darker or lighter than the base. If the nose is too bulbous at the tip, shadow the tip on either side of the highlight. If the nose is not straight, apply a narrow highlight down the nose. Blend it in the direction opposite to the natural bend and shadow it on either side.

Shadows and highlights should always be blended carefully. Although shadows and highlights are usually three shades darker or lighter than the base, it is sometimes necessary to use stronger contrasts in order to achieve the desired effect.

Unit 7
Corrective make-up: jawline and chin

When the chin is too long, shadow the lower part of it. If the chin is too short, highlight it and blend carefully.

When the jawline appears too square or too prominent, shadow the part which needs to be rounded off and toned down. Apply the shadow both under and over the jawbone. If the chin is too prominent, shadow the whole chin. If the chin recedes, highlight it. A pointed chin can be flattened with a square shadow. Minimize a double chin by shadowing it.

Unit 8
Corrective make-up: wrinkles

Wrinkles, like frontal lobes and depressions, cannot be disguised any more completely than a double chin. They can, however, be minimized by brushing in a highlight where you normally find a shadow and shadowing the projecting part of the wrinkle. It is the projecting part that normally catches the highlight that should be shadowed. This illusion tends to flatten the wrinkle.

Unit 9
Corrective make-up: eyes

Corrective eye make-up always adds emphasis to the eye. This is accomplished by means of colored eye-shadow, eye-liner, mascara and sometimes by means of false lashes.

Eye-shadow: Eye-shadow is used to beautify and project the eye. Conservative colors are blue, blue-gray, blue-green and brown. Brown is always used for corrective eye make-up for men. Violet may tend to age.

Eye-shadow is placed on the upper eyelid only and is heaviest next to the eye. It should not extend up to the eyebrow. Eye-shadow will create an optical illusion which spreads the eyes apart. If the eyes are too far apart, they can be brought together by moving the eye-shadow in toward the nose. To make the eyes more prominent, the eyelid is highlighted instead of shadowed. A touch of rouge on the bone just below the outer end of the eyebrow will add a sparkle to the eye.

Eye-lining: Eye-lining is used as an accent to emphasize the eyes further. It is the technique of drawing a line along the upper lid close to the lashes with a sharp black or brown eyebrow pencil. The line starts about two-thirds of the way in toward the nose. If the eyes are too close together, start at the tear duct. The line follows the lash line and extends about ¼ inch (0.64 cm.) beyond the outer corner of the eye. The line should fade out and not end abruptly. A similar line is drawn on the lower lid from about one-third of the way in from the outer corner outward toward the top line. Make this line fade out before it meets the top line.

If the eyes are too close together, the eye-lining accents are made strongest at the outer ends and are carried farther beyond the corner of the eye than usual. When the eyes are too far apart, the accents are placed in the inner corners and do not extend to the outer corners (illustration 1).

illustration one

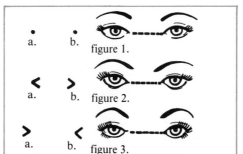

a. b. figure 1.

a. b. figure 2.

a. b. figure 3.

Unit 8
Corrective make-up: wrinkles

General objectives-student goals: After study, instruction, practice and completion of this unit, you will be able to show understanding of corrective make-up techniques for wrinkles by demonstrating the procedures. You must have the proper implements and supplies in order to complete this unit successfully.

Unit 9
Corrective make-up: eyes

General objectives-student goals: After study, instruction, practice and completion of this unit, you will be able to show understanding of corrective make-up techniques for the eyes by demonstrating the techniques. You must have the proper implements and supplies in order to complete this unit successfully.

Facial make-up

illustration two

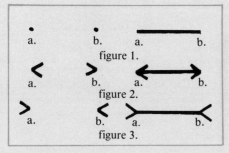

figure 1.

figure 2.

figure 3.

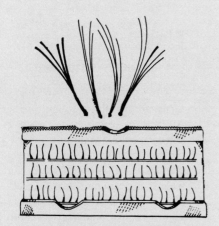

**INDIVIDUAL EYELASH
APPLICATION**

Facial make-up

294

Illustration 2: The space between the two points A and B in figures 1, 2 and 3 are equal in length. In figure 2, the space and line both appear to be shorter in length than do those in figure 1. This illusion is created by the two arrows placed at either end. They restrict the vision to a smaller area. In figure 3, the reverse is true. Here, the distance between points A and B appears longer. The arrows at either end lead the eye outward beyond the limits of the actual distance between A and B.

Mascara and eyelashes: The female's lashes are always darkened with mascara, usually black. Occasionally, blue and green may be effective. If men's lashes are very light, they can be tinted or treated with a very sparse application of brown or black mascara. Women can use false lashes if their eyes need additional definition.

Individual eyelash application

Individual eyelash application is the technique of applying permanently curled individual eyelashes, one at a time, to the patron's natural eyelashes. The lashes last two to five weeks, depending on the care that the patron gives them. A retouch (the reapplication of a few lashes) can be given when some of the lashes fall out. The wearing of individual eyelashes requires special protective maintenance. The patron should be told to:

1. Keep away from the eyes by going around them when washing the face.

2. Avoid sleeping on the face. Lashes are easily lost during sleep.

3. Avoid tight clothing going over the face. Place a scarf over the head and face when pulling tight clothing over the head.

Eyelashes are available in both four and six ply lash and in three sizes: short, medium and long. For the most natural looking effects, a combination of all three lengths is advisable. The short lengths are used at the inner corners, and the longer lengths are applied to the outer lashes. Although individual lashes may be applied to the lower lashes, the latter are generally too weak to hold the artificial lashes as well as the natural upper lashes. Work from behind the patron when applying the upper lashes. Stand in front of the patron when applying the bottom lashes.

Preparation

1. Lash scissors	4. Absorbent cotton	7. Adhesive solvent
2. Eyelash brush	5. Eyelid and eyelash cleaner	8. Eyelashes
3. Tweezer	6. Adhesive	9. Adjustable light

Procedure

1. Have the patron recline in a facial chair.

2. Adjust the lighting so that it lights the facial area.

3. Apply some eyelash cleaner to the lids and lashes with a cotton tipped swab. Blot and wipe them clean.

4. Brush the upper lashes with an eyelash brush in order to separate them.

5. Stand behind the patron. Select a lash of the correct length and ply and, using the tweezer, take the lash bulb from the tray. Dip the bulb in adhesive and spread it on the existing eyelash.

6. Place the first lash at the top center of the existing eyelash of the left eye. Place it near the base. The patron must keep the eyes half open and looking down.

7. Lay the new lash on. The eyelid should not be touched at any time.

8. Apply a lash on both sides of the center lash. Continue to add lashes.

9. If the eye starts to tear, blot the tears and continue the application on the other eye.

10. When the application is complete, check for lashes that may be out of line. If necessary, remove them with a cotton tipped swab and adhesive solvent. Then, replace the lash removed.

11. If necessary, trim the lashes for evenness with eyelash scissors.

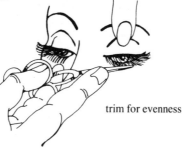

trim for evenness

Depending on the desired fullness, as many as 75 lashes may have to be used for each eye.

Note: The adjustable light should be placed behind the facial chair and adjusted so that there is no direct lighting in the cosmetologist's or patron's eyes.

Unit 10
Corrective make-up: eyebrows

The eyebrow line must follow the line of the eye. Eyebrows that are too straight, too arched, too slanted, too thin, too thick, too close together, too far apart or too shaggy are less attractive than they should be and need to be corrected. If the brow is well-formed and well-placed, it can be darkened with a black or brown pencil. Use short, quick, light strokes in the direction of the hair growth. Eyebrows should not be darkened by drawing a heavy line. Darken the hairs not the skin underneath the hairs. The exception, however, is when the natural brow needs to be filled out. In most cases, eyebrows do not need darkening. If there

start in center and alternate from one side of the center to the other side..

lay it on...at no time should you ever touch the eyelid...

it takes as many as 75 lashes for each eye...

Unit 10
Corrective make-up: eyebrows

General objectives-student goals:
After study, instruction, practice and completion of this unit, you will

| Facial make-up |

be able to show understanding of corrective make-up techniques for the eyebrows by demonstrating the techniques. You must have the proper implements and supplies in order to complete this unit successfully.

Unit 11
Corrective make-up: cheeks

General objectives-student goals: After study, instruction, practice and completion of this unit, you will be able to show understanding of corrective make-up techniques for the cheeks by demonstrating the techniques. You must have the proper implements and supplies in order to complete this unit successfully.

Unit 12
Corrective make-up: lips

General objectives-student goals: After study, instruction, practice and completion of this unit, you will be able to show understanding of corrective make-up techniques for the lips by demonstrating the techniques. You must have the proper implements and supplies in order to complete this unit successfully.

Facial make-up

are unnecessary hairs between the eyebrows, pluck them out. Beware of plucking too much. If the eyes and eyebrows are too close together, the inner ends can be plucked and the outer ends extended with an eyebrow pencil. If they are too far apart, they should be penciled in toward the center. It is not necessary to achieve an ideal classic brow. If the line of the brow is too straight or too slanted, it can be reshaped a little by plucking. If the result is not satisfactory, further shaping is possible using the eyebrow pencil.

Unit 11
Corrective make-up: cheeks

If the cheeks are too prominent, the part of the cheek to be made less outstanding should be shaded with a base three shades darker than that used on the rest of the face. If the cheeks are too sunken or hollowed, the colors are reversed by using a base three shades lighter.

Rouge should be placed on the cheekbone not low on the cheek. If the effect is to sink the cheeks in, use the rouge as a shadow below the cheekbone.

Rouge should not be placed too near the eye or nose. The best guide is never to let it come nearer the nose than an imaginary line dropped vertically from the center of the eye. A narrow face requires that the rouge be kept even further from the nose and placed nearer the ears. If the face is too wide, keep the rouge away from the ears and apply it in a semivertical pattern rather than horizontally. Avoid round spot applications and always apply rouge lightly.

Unit 12
Corrective make-up: lips

The shape of lips should not be made to conform to a set pattern. They should be shaped so that they complement the individual face.

Thin lips can be corrected by overpainting. Drawing new lips of the desired size and shape makes the lower lip lighter than the upper. This makes the mouth appear fuller. Highlighting over the upper lip will also help correct thin lips.

Thick lips are difficult to conceal because the edges are nearly always very definite. They can be minimized by covering the lips with a base. Then, use color only toward the inside of the lips and fade it outward into the base color.

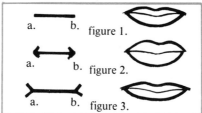

a.　b.　figure 1.

a.　b.　figure 2.

a.　b.　figure 3.

Wide lips require color application toward the center of the lips. Cover the outer corners with the base.

Narrow lips require that the color be carried to the extreme corners. Do not carry the color much beyond the natural corners of the mouth. The artificial line will become apparent as soon as the mouth is opened.

A heavy upper lip with a thin lower one requires overpainting the lower lip to match the upper one. For the mouth with a thin upper lip, it is necessary to overpaint the upper lip to match the lower one.

Normally, it is best not to carry the color to the extreme corners of the mouth except for the purpose of widening it. The technique for overpainting is to define the lips by outlining them with a dark red pencil. The outline should not be left as a distinct line. It should be blended toward the center of the lip.

Unit 13
The color wheel

The color wheel is used for selecting suitable colors for cosmetics used in facial make-up. It is essential that the cosmetologist be able to select and mix colors intelligently. To do this, a basic understanding of color principles is necessary.

1. There are three primary colors:

   A. Red

   B. Yellow

   C. Blue

2. There are three secondary colors:

   A. Orange

   B. Green

   C. Violet

3. There are six intermediate colors:

   A. Red-orange

   B. Yellow-orange

   C. Red-violet

   D. Blue-violet

   E. Yellow-green

   F. Blue-green

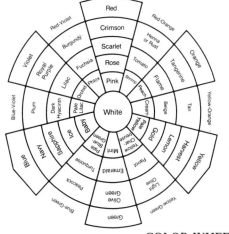

COLOR WHEEL

Unit 13
The color wheel

General objectives-student goals: After study, instruction and completion of this unit, you will be able to demonstrate understanding of the color wheel by writing and/or giving a brief overview of the subject.

neighbors on the color wheel are good harmonies

opposites on the color wheel are good contrasts

Facial make-up

297

Neighboring colors on the wheel are good harmonies. Colors directly opposite each other on the color wheel are good contrasts. Intensify color by using contrasting color. For example, orange lipstick with blue eyes or a green ribbon on red hair.

All color comes from the source of light be it natural or artificial. White light is a mixture of light rays of all colors. Pigment has no color of its own but has the ability to absorb certain rays and reflect others. The reflected colors are those responsible for the pigment's characteristic color. Red hair, for example, absorbs all light rays except red ones which it reflects. This makes the hair look red.

The three terms used to designate distinct color characteristics are hue, intensity and value. The hue of a color is the name by which we know it, e.g., red, yellow, green or blue. These are all brilliant colors. Rose and pink are variations of the basic red hue, and gold is a variation of yellow. When similar hues are placed next to each other, the progression of color can be seen easily. The color wheel demonstrates this.

The intensity of a color is the degree of color brilliance less than maximum. An orange-red is still red in hue, but is far different from the color red. Although the colors are of the same hue, the orange-red has a lower intensity.

Colors nearer the center of the color wheel are less brilliant and have lower intensity than those near the outer edge. Colors along the outward bounds of the color wheel are the most brilliant and have a higher intensity.

The value of a color is the lightness or darkness of that color, e.g., a light orange-red, medium orange-red or dark orange-red. A light value is high; a dark value is low. Orchid is a high value of violet, and green is a low value of olive green.

Unit 14
Evening make-up

Make-up colors are intensified for evening wear. The foundation base should have extra depth of color. Glowing pearlized cosmetics add drama and extra excitement to the skin tone. Eye make-up should be of the same colors as worn during the day. However, the application should be heavier and more exaggerated. False lashes should be considered and trimmed accordingly.

Unit 15
Balmasque make-up

Balmasque make-up is an application of facial make-up in which the cosmetics are applied with exaggerated detail and in colors which match the costume, gown or dress. The colors used, the products applied and the technique will change according to each individual situation. The application of false lashes is a must. Some additional training, beyond that which is needed for the application of conventional make-up, is required in order to develop the skills necessary to apply make-up with exaggerated detail.

Unit 14
Evening make-up

General objectives-student goals:
After study, instruction and completion of this unit, you will be able to demonstrate understanding of evening make-up by writing and/or giving a brief overview of the subject.

Unit 15
Balmasque make-up

General objectives-student goals:
After study, instruction and completion of this unit, you will be able to demonstrate understanding of balmasque make-up by writing and/or giving a brief overview of the subject.

Facial make-up

Unit 16
Theatrical make-up

Theatrical make-up starts with the basic principles of the art and technique of basic make-up application. These principles are used creatively in the design and execution of facial make-ups which go far beyond that for day, evening or balmasque make-up. The practice of theatrical make-up requires additional training, special skill and special equipment.

The study of theatrical make-up involves such subjects as: character analysis, physiognomy (eyes, nose, mouth, eyebrows), facial anatomy, color in make-up (grease paint and cake make-up), optical illusions, shadow and light, three dimensional make-up (nose putty, derma wax), rubber prosthesis, beards, mustaches and wigs, lighting and make-up, character make-up and achieving a likeness of real people.

The principles of make-up for photography, television and platform appearances are essentially the same as for theatrical make-up except that the finished product must be a mirror image and not for an audience many feet away.

Review questions

1. Is it best for a patron to be in a sitting position when you are applying facial make-up?

2. Is the face cleansing technique for a facial make-up treatment the same as that for a standard facial?

3. At what point during the facial make-up treatment do you shape the eyebrows?

4. On what type of skin should a skin freshener be used?

5. On what type of skin should an astringent be used?

6. Where is it best to test the color of the base in order to see if there is true blending?

7. What cosmetic is best for setting facial make-up?

8. Why is it necessary to use two eyebrow pencils during a facial make-up treatment?

General objectives-student goals: After study, instruction and completion of this unit, you will be able to demonstrate understanding of theatrical make-up by writing and/or giving a brief overview of the subject.

Facial make-up

9. Is mascara applied to the lashes with the patron's eyes open or closed?

10. Is it necessary to apply two shades of lip rouge?

11. In what areas of the face should blush rouge be applied during a facial make-up treatment?

12. Does the color of facial make-up hold well on oily skin?

13. How can you make the eyes appear larger by shaping the eyebrows?

14. When the lips appear too long, how can a shortening effect be created with lip rouge?

15. What is the opposite color of red?

16. Name the three primary colors.

17. Can individual eyelashes be replaced when some of the lashes fall out?

18. Can individual lashes be applied to the lower lashes?

19. Should the new lash touch the eyelid during the application of individual eyelashes?

20. Approximately how many individual eyelashes may be required for an individual eyelash application to one eye?

21. Does facial make-up require constant study?

22. Why are hairstyling and facial make-up natural companions?

23. Should the cosmetologist work from the front of the patron when applying facial make-up?

24. Can both an astringent and a skin freshener be used on the same individual during a facial make-up treatment?

Facial make-up

Fingernail and hand care: manicuring

Fingernail and hand care: manicuring: The art of improving the appearance and condition of the fingernails and hands.

Overview: This chapter provides you with the information necessary in order to gain the knowledge and skill required for practicing the art of manicuring, hand care and pedicare.

Behavioral objectives-student goals: After completion of this chapter, and after instruction, study and practice, you will be able to perform and demonstrate competency in manicuring by demonstrating the application and procedure for: a manicure table setup, a short manicure, barber shop manicure, oil or lanolin manicure, hand and arm massage and a pedicare treatment with foot massage. You will also be able to demonstrate the technique for: smoothing a smudge, finger massage, Mend-A-Nail and the application of artificial fingernails. You will also be able to demonstrate competency by identifying, explaining and/or listing: the types of manicures, the required implements, supplies and equipment, typical fingernail shapes, the electric manicure, pedicare implements and equipment, disorders of the nails and all details concerning the many types of artificial nails.

Manicuring is the art of caring for the fingernails and hands. A good manicure improves the appearance of the fingernails and hands. Manicuring can be the finishing touch which complements a hairstyle. It is also an additional source of income.

The nails are fairly reliable indicators of general body health. Simple fingernail irregularities come within the province of cosmetology and can be treated by the manicurist.

Full service beauty salons, barber shops and full service unisex salons also provide such related services as pedicare, which is care for the toenails and feet, and artificial fingernails.

Manicuring requires a working knowledge of nail cosmetics and understanding of the basic anatomy and physiology of the arms, hands, fingernails, legs and feet.

Types of manicures

1. The long manicure is a standard manicure which includes hand, finger and arm massage.

2. The short manicure is a standard manicure which does not include finger or arm massage.

3. The barber shop manicure is a man's manicure. The nails are filed round and buffed or polished with a clear liquid nail enamel.

4. The booth manicure is a woman's manicure done under the same physical conditions as the barber shop manicure. The nails are manicured while the patron is receiving other services.

5. The oil or lanolin manicure substitutes hot oil or lanolin in place of the water used during the soaking period.

A proficient manicurist must:

1. Acquire the necessary manicuring skills to give:

   A. A short manicure within 15 to 20 minutes.

   B. A long manicure within 30 minutes.

   C. A barber shop manicure within 15 minutes. These procedures must be completed neatly and professionally within the specified time.

2. Learn how to use the manicuring time for selling other services performed in the salon.

3. Be able to recognize the different nail shapes and know how each should be treated in order to make it most attractive.

Sanitary and safety precautions for fingernail and hand care: manicuring

1. Never work on diseased nails, fingers or toes.

2. Clean, sanitize and dry all implements after each manicure or pedicare.

3. Discard all articles that cannot be used.

4. Do not spill nail enamel remover. It will damage clothing and most furniture finishes.

5. Avoid filing too deeply into the corners of the nails.

6. Never apply artificial nails where there is an active case of fungus.

7. Avoid excess pressure at the base of the nail (matrix). This may damage the nail.

8. Avoid excess friction while buffing nails.

9. Apply an antiseptic to all cuts.

10. Label all containers.

11. Do not work on a nail when the surrounding skin is infected or inflamed.

12. Avoid excess contact between nail enamel remover and skin.

Unit 1
Equipment, implements and supplies

The items referred to as equipment and implements are permanent. Supplies are consumed and replaced. The following are needed for a manicure:

Equipment

1. Manicure table, patron's chair and manicurist's stool

2. Finger bowl with a paper cup and soapy solution

3. Electric heater for the hot oil or lanolin manicure

4. Supply tray

5. Table cushion for use as a patron's armrest

6. Sanitizing solution in the container holding the manicure implements

7. Container for clean absorbent cotton

Implements

1. Long, thin, flexible metal file for shaping extra long or hard nails.

2. Emery boards: The coarse side is used for shaping; the fine side for beveling.

3. A metal pusher for loosening the mantle and cleaning the cuticle.

4. Two orangewood sticks for cleaning and working around the nails and applying creams and liquids.

5. A nail brush for scrubbing the nails and fingertips.

6. Cuticle nippers for cutting the cuticle and trimming the area around the nails.

7. A buffer for dry polishing.

   Note: Eliminate the nail buffer when its use is not permitted by law.

Unit 1
Equipment, implements and supplies

General objectives-student goals: After study, instruction, practice and completion of this unit, you will be able to show understanding of manicuring equipment, implements and supplies by identifying them. You must have the proper implements and supplies in order to complete this unit successfully.

Fingernail and hand care: manicuring

303

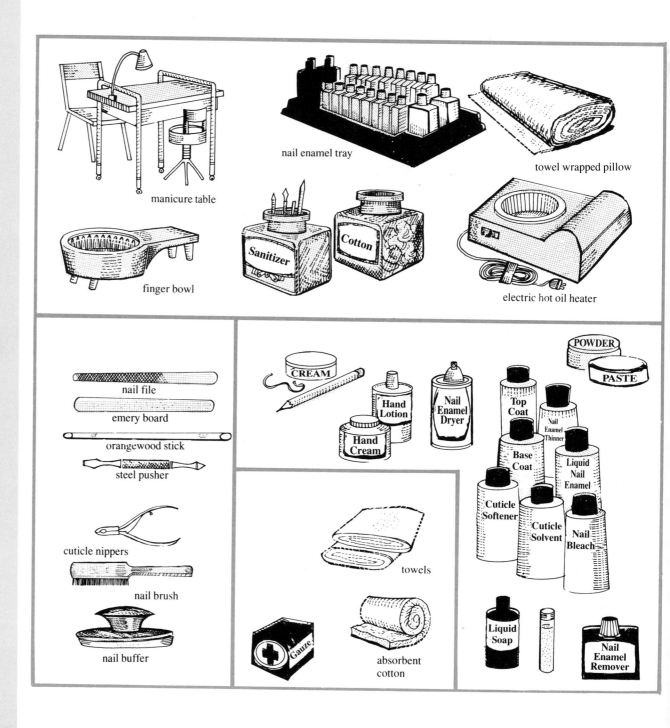

manicure table

nail enamel tray

towel wrapped pillow

finger bowl

Sanitizer

Cotton

electric hot oil heater

nail file

emery board

orangewood stick

steel pusher

cuticle nippers

nail brush

nail buffer

CREAM

Hand Lotion

Hand Cream

Nail Enamel Dryer

Top Coat

Base Coat

Nail Enamel Thinner

POWDER

PASTE

Liquid Nail Enamel

Cuticle Softener

Cuticle Solvent

Nail Bleach

towels

Gauze

absorbent cotton

Liquid Soap

Nail Enamel Remover

Supplies

1. Soap and water to clean the fingernails and soften the cuticle.

2. Hot oil or lanolin to soften the cuticle and the skin around the nails.

3. Cuticle softener: This is an oil or cream used to lubricate the skin around the nails.

4. Cuticle solvent: This softens and removes the cuticle.

5. Nail bleaches: These contain hydrogen peroxide and are used to remove stains.

6. Pumice powder: This is used with a buffer to smooth uneven nail ridges or to prepare the surface of a fingernail before applying an artificial nail.

7. Pumice stone: This is used to smooth the edge of the skin around the nails and to remove light skin stains.

8. Nail whiteners: These are applied under the free edge of the nail to keep the tips looking white.

9. Nail enamel remover: This is used to dissolve the old enamel on the nails.

10. Hand cream and lotions are used during the long manicure for hand, arm and finger massage.

11. Dry nail polish: This is a powder or paste that imparts a shine to the nail when used with a buffer.

12. Base coat: This is applied before the application of nail enamel.

13. Enamel thinner is a solvent used to thin out thickened nail enamel.

14. Clear or colored liquid nail enamel.

15. Liquid nail enamel drier: This is applied from a spray can for instant drying of nail enamel.

16. Top coat is applied as a nail enamel after the application of the nail enamel.

Disposable supplies

1. One or two small towels. Use one for the short manicure, two for the long manicure.

2. Absorbent cotton: This is used to remove nail enamel at the start of the manicure. It is also used with the orangewood stick when cleaning around the nail after the application of new nail enamel.

3. A small piece of gauze for removing nail enamel from the nail tips.

Fingernail and hand care: manicuring

Unit 2
Fingernail shapes

General objectives-student goals:
After study, instruction and completion of this unit, you will be able to demonstrate understanding of fingernail shapes by writing and/or giving a brief overview of the subject.

SLENDER TAPERING NAIL

correct

average

...avoid shortening this nail... keep it slim and tapered...

AVERAGE OVAL NAIL

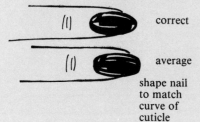

correct

average

shape nail to match curve of cuticle

Fingernail and hand care: manicuring

306

Unit 2
Fingernail shapes

A graceful and flattering nail shape adds beauty to the hands. The manicurist will show skill and professional knowledge of manicuring by producing exactly the right nail shaping for each patron.

In general, nails may be divided into four types:

1. Slender tapering nail
2. Average oval nail
3. Square nail
4. Broad clubbed nail

The slender tapering nail is most frequently found on the thin or fragile hand. The tapered appearance of the fingers should be carried out into the fingernail shaping. This type of shaping can usually be worn longer. A shorter nail is not flattering and may give the fingertip a stubby appearance.

The average oval nail has the ideal nail contour. This type of nail is usually found on the average size hand with well-molded fingers. In order to maintain the oval nail contour, the tip of the nail should be shaped to follow the curve of the cuticle at the base of the nail.

The square nail generally has a flat structure. For this reason, it is unwise to allow the nail edge to protrude far beyond the fingertip. It is usually best to round the fingernail into an arc just beyond the tip of the finger.

SQUARE NAIL

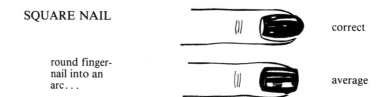

round fingernail into an arc...

correct

average

The broad clubbed nail is wider than it is long. It is difficult to treat this type of nail and impossible to give it the illusion of an oval shape. A tip which extends only slightly beyond the cushion of the finger will produce the most becoming appearance.

BROAD CLUBBED NAIL

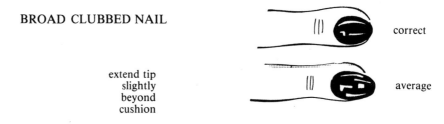

extend tip slightly beyond cushion

correct

average

Unit 3
Setup for the manicure table

1. Towel wrapped pillow

2. Wet sanitizer containing manicure implements

3. Finger bowl with paper cup

4. Fingernail brush

5. Nail enamel tray with cuticle solvent and enamel remover

6. Cotton and cotton pledget container

7. Alcohol

1. Gauze

2. Electric heater for oil or lanolin manicures

3. Dry polish

4. Pumice stone

5. Pumice powder

6. Nail whitener

7. Enamel thinner

8. Container for soiled and waste materials

   Note: This container is cleaned after each manicure.

9. White iodine

10. Peroxide

8. Emery board

9. Steel file

10. Buffer

11. Instant nail enamel drier

12. Patron's chair

13. Manicurist's stool

Unit 3
Setup for the
manicure table

General objectives-student goals: After study, instruction, practice and completion of this unit, you will be able to show understanding of the setup for the manicure table by setting the manicure table for a manicure. You must have the proper implements and supplies in order to complete this unit successfully.

Fingernail and hand care: manicuring

307

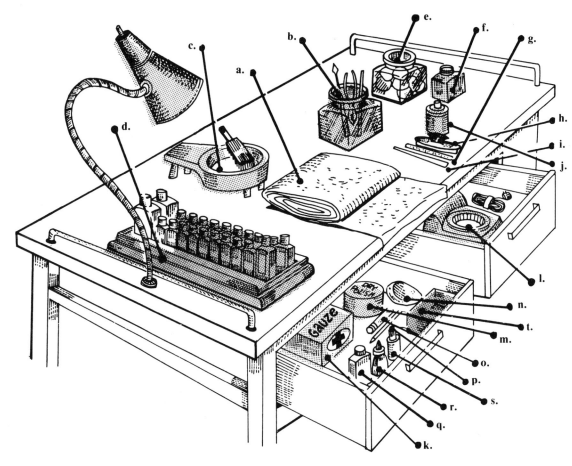

SETUP FOR A MANICURE TABLE

a. towel wrapped pillow
b. wet sanitizer containing
   manicuring implements
c. finger bowl, paper cup and
   nail brush..
d. nail enamel tray with cuticle
   solvent and remover..
e. absorbent cotton
f. alcohol
g. emery board
h. buffer
i. steel file

j. instant dry enamel
k. gauze
l. electric oil heater
m. dry polish
n. pumice stone
o. pumice powder
p. nail whitener
q. thinner
r. white iodine
s. peroxide
t. empty box
   (for soiled & waste materials)

Unit 4
Preparation and procedure for a short manicure

Preparation: Careful compliance with all sanitary precautions is of the utmost importance. The manicurist must wash her hands with a disinfecting soap before working on each patron. Caution must be taken not to cut the skin. The manicurist should always have hydrogen peroxide and white iodine on hand for treating any accidental injury immediately.

Procedure

1. Wash your hands with a disinfectant soap.

2. Seat the patron comfortably with her arm resting on the edge of the table.

3. Place the manicuring bowl containing warm water, soap and disinfectant by the patron's right hand.

4. Remove old enamel from the fingers of the right and left hands. Work from the little finger toward the thumb.

   A. Moisten a cotton pledget with nail enamel remover.

   B. Press the pledget against the nail firmly for a few moments in order to soften the nail enamel.

   C. When the enamel begins to dissolve, wipe the nail clean.

   D. Press firmly and direct the cotton pledget from the base of the nail to the tip.

   E. Fresh cotton should be used as needed. Do not smear the old enamel on the cuticle.

   F. Dip a cotton tipped orangewood stick in the enamel remover and clean around the cuticle.

5. Shape the nails. Start with the right hand.

   A. Determine the type of nails the patron has and the shaping that will make them look most becoming.

   B. Allow the patron's fingers to rest relaxed over your hand.

   C. Use a file or emery board as required.

   D. Start by filing the nail of the little finger of the right hand. Continue towards the thumb. Release each finger as it is finished.

   E. File only the free edge. Hold the patron's finger between the thumb and first two fingers of your left hand.

Unit 4
Preparation and procedure for a short manicure

General objectives-student goals: After study, instruction, practice and completion of this unit, you will be able to show understanding of the preparation and procedure for a short manicure by demonstrating the procedure. You must have the proper implements and supplies in order to complete this unit successfully.

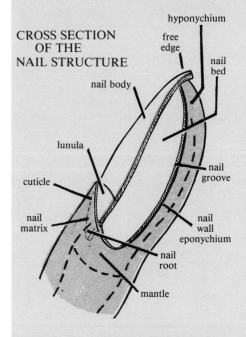

CROSS SECTION OF THE NAIL STRUCTURE

hyponychium
free edge
nail bed
nail body
lunula
nail groove
cuticle
nail matrix
nail wall
eponychium
nail root
mantle

Fingernail and hand care: manicuring

309

F. Hold the file or emery board in your right hand. Tilt it so that the filing is done mainly to the underside of the free edge of the nail. Do not rub the skin.

G. Work from the corners toward the center. Do not saw back and forth. This causes splitting. File each nail going from right to left and then from left to right. Use two short and one long sweeping stroke on each side of the nail. The nails will look better longer and will wear better if they are not filed deep in the corners.

6. Soften the cuticle by placing the fingertips of the patron's right hand into the finger bowl containing soap and warm water. Do this after completing the filing of the entire right hand and two fingers of the left (small and ring fingers).

7. While the right hand is soaking, complete the filing of the nails of the left hand. Work toward the thumb. Then, remove the right hand from the finger bowl.

8. Dry the fingertips, the hand and the area between the fingers. Hold the manicure towel with both hands. During this process, loosen and push the cuticle and adhering skin on each nail back. Use the cushion of your fingers over the towel.

9. Wrap a thin layer of cotton around the blunt edge of an orangewood stick. You will use this as an applicator. Apply the cuticle solvent all around the mantle of the fingers of the right hand. The orangewood stick can be dipped in the soapy water in the manicure bowl and/or in bleaching preparation and used to cleanse under the free edge.

10. The spoon end of the cuticle pusher is held in a flat position and used carefully to loosen the dead skin from around the sides and base of the nails without scratching the nail plate. Too much pressure on the live tissue at the root of the nail can cause injury to the nail.

11. Always start with the little finger and work toward the thumb. Keep the cuticle moist while working.

12. Keep the towel over the index finger and push the cuticle back.

13. Use nippers to remove excess cuticle, bits of loose skin and hangnails. The cuticle should be cut and removed as a single segment.

14. When cutting the cuticle of the middle finger of the right hand, place the fingertips of the left hand into the manicure bowl.

15. Apply bleaching preparation under the free edge of each nail of the right hand with the cotton tipped orangewood stick.

16. Apply cuticle oil or cream around each finger with the orangewood stick and work it well into the mantle and groove by rubbing it in a circular motion with your thumb.

17. Remove the left hand from the manicure bowl. Dry each finger as outlined in step 8 and continue to step 16.

Fingernail and hand
care: manicuring

18. Cleanse the nails of both hands by holding the patron's right hand over, not in, the manicure bowl and by brushing in a downward movement to clean the nails and fingers of excess cream or oil.

19. Repeat the same procedure for the left hand. Start with the little finger. Dry the hands carefully and check the nails for any flaws.

20. Remove any bits of cuticle that remain and eliminate possible rough spots on the free edge with light strokes of the fine side of the emery board. This technique also helps to give the nails a smooth beveled edge.

21. If required:

    A. Repair any split or broken nails.

    B. Give a finger massage.

    C. Give an arm and hand massage.

22. Apply base coat first to the right hand and then to the left. Start with the little finger and work toward the thumb. Use long strokes. Allow the base coat to dry before applying enamel.

23. Apply liquid nail enamel. Start with the little finger of the right hand.

    A. Remove the brush from the nail enamel and as you move up and out remove all excess enamel by pressing the brush gently against the sides of the opening of the bottle.

    B. Apply the enamel lightly and quickly in long even strokes.

    C. When the entire nail is to be covered, apply the enamel with one stroke along the left side of the nail. Then, follow the line of the cuticle across the base of the nail. Then, apply two strokes from the base to the free edge.

    D. Completely cover the nail with four strokes. Control the width of the stroke by putting pressure on the brush.

    E. If a half-moon is desired, apply the enamel in a half-circle across the base. Expose the matrix or develop a crescent-shaped area at the base of the nail. Then, cover the rest of the nail with two strokes toward the free edge.

    F. When the first coat of enamel has dried, a second coat may be applied.

24. Remove excess polish with a cotton tipped orangewood stick dipped into nail enamel remover. Clean carefully around the cuticle and nail edges.

25. Apply top coat in the same manner as the nail enamel.

Fingernail and hand
care: manicuring

311

26. Spray nail enamel drier directly on the nail enamel for quick drying. Hold the can 6 inches (15.24 cm.) away from the nails and spray freely.

> Note: The application of the top coat is usually eliminated when the enamel is sprayed with nail enamel drier.

> Note: Always keep the nail enamel thin enough to flow freely. Add enamel solvent when the enamel thickens.

Unit 5
Smoothing a smudge

The ability and skill to smooth smudged nail enamel without removing all of it from the nail can be an important timesaver.

Procedure

1. Remove the brush from the nail enamel bottle—allowing some enamel to remain on the brush. Dip the brush into the bottle of nail enamel remover.

2. Apply the remover to the nail in front of the smudge. It will lift the nail enamel so that it covers the smudge.

3. Do not stroke. Dab the brush lightly over the smudge. Allow the liquid to dry.

> Note: The acetone acts as a softener and permits you to smooth the enamel without removing it from the nail. A reapplication of enamel is not necessary.

Unit 6
Barber shop manicure

The barber shop manicure for men can be given at the barber chair or manicure table and involves the same procedure as a standard manicure from step 1 to step 20. At this point, the nails are either buffed (dry polish), or clear neutral liquid enamel is applied.

Procedure

1. Wash your hands with disinfectant soap.

2. Seat the patron comfortably with his arm resting on the edge of the table.

3. Place the manicuring bowl containing warm water, soap and disinfectant by the patron's right hand.

4. Remove old enamel from the fingers. Start with the little finger of the right hand and work toward the thumb.

General objectives-student goals:
After study, instruction, practice and completion of this unit, you will be able to show understanding of the technique for smoothing smudged nail enamel on fingernails by demonstrating the technique. You must have the proper implements and supplies in order to complete this unit successfully.

General objectives-student goals:
After study, instruction, practice and completion of this unit, you will be able to show understanding of a barber shop manicure by demonstrating the technique and procedure. You must have the proper implements and supplies in order to complete this unit successfully.

> **Fingernail and hand care: manicuring**

MANICURE
PROCEDURE

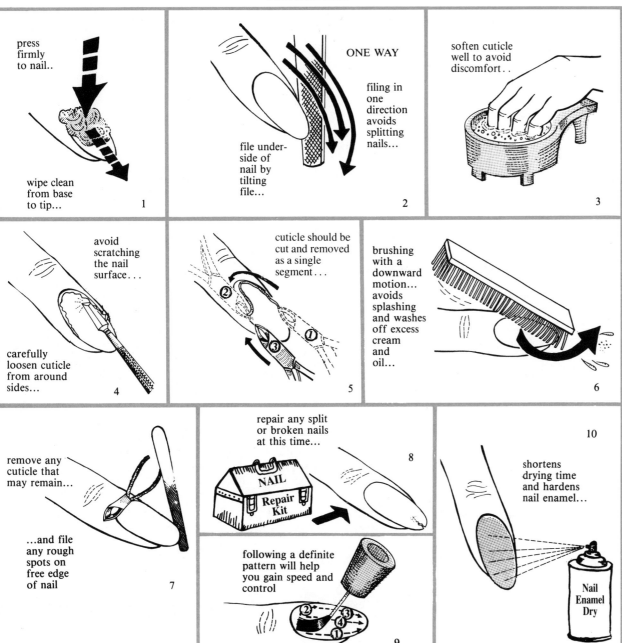

press firmly to nail..

wipe clean from base to tip...

1

ONE WAY

file under-side of nail by tilting file...

filing in one direction avoids splitting nails...

2

soften cuticle well to avoid discomfort..

3

avoid scratching the nail surface...

carefully loosen cuticle from around sides...

4

cuticle should be cut and removed as a single segment...

5

brushing with a downward motion... avoids splashing and washes off excess cream and oil...

6

remove any cuticle that may remain...

...and file any rough spots on free edge of nail

7

repair any split or broken nails at this time...

8

NAIL Repair Kit

following a definite pattern will help you gain speed and control

9

10

shortens drying time and hardens nail enamel...

Nail Enamel Dry

Fingernail and hand care: manicuring

A. Moisten a cotton pledget with nail enamel remover.

B. Press the pledget against the nail firmly for a few moments in order to soften the nail enamel.

C. When the enamel begins to dissolve, wipe the nail clean.

D. Press firmly and direct the cotton pledget from the base of the nail to the tip.

E. Fresh cotton should be used as needed. Do not smear the old enamel on the cuticle.

F. Dip a cotton tipped orangewood stick in enamel remover and use it to clean around the cuticle.

5. Shape the nails. Start with the right hand.

A. Determine the type of nails the patron has and the shaping that will make them look most becoming.

B. Allow the patron's fingers to rest relaxed over your hand.

C. Use a file or emery board as required.

D. Start by filing the nail of the little finger of the right hand. Continue towards the thumb. Release each finger as it is finished.

E. File only the free edge. Hold the patron's finger between the thumb and first two fingers of your left hand.

F. Hold the file or emery board in your right hand. Tilt it so that the filing is done mainly to the underside of the free edge. Do not rub the skin.

G. Work from the corners toward the center. Do not saw back and forth. This causes splitting. File each nail going from right to left and then from left to right. Use two short and one long sweeping stroke on each side of the nail. The nails will look better for a longer time and will wear better if they are not filed deep in the corners.

6. Soften the cuticle by placing the fingertips of the right hand into the finger bowl containing soap and warm water. Do this after completing the filing of the entire right hand and two fingers of the left hand (small and ring fingers).

7. While the right hand is soaking, complete the filing of the nails of the left hand. Then, remove the right hand from the finger bowl.

8. Dry the fingertips, the hand and the area between the fingers. Hold the manicure towel with both hands. During this process, loosen and push the cuticle and adhering skin on each nail back. Use the cushion of your fingers over the towel.

9. Wrap a thin layer of cotton around the blunt edge of an orangewood stick. You will use this as an applicator. Apply the cuticle solvent all around the mantle of the fingers of the right hand. The orangewood stick can be dipped in the soapy water in the manicure bowl and/or in bleaching preparation and used to cleanse under the free edge.

10. The spoon end of the cuticle pusher is held in a flat position and used carefully to loosen the dead skin from around the sides and base of the nails without scratching the nail plate. Too much pressure on the live tissue at the root of the nail can cause injury to the nail.

11. Always start with the little finger and work toward the thumb. Keep the cuticle moist while working.

12. Keep the towel over the index finger and push the cuticle back.

13. Use nippers to remove excess cuticle, bits of loose skin and hangnails. The cuticle should be cut and removed as a single segment.

14. When cutting the cuticle of the middle finger of the right hand, place the fingertips of the left hand into the manicure bowl.

15. Apply bleaching preparation under the free edge of each nail of the right hand with a cotton tipped orangewood stick.

16. Apply cuticle oil or cream around each finger with the orangewood stick. Work it well into the mantle and groove by rubbing it in a circular motion with your thumb.

17. Remove the left hand from the manicure bowl. Dry each finger as outlined in step 8 and continue to step 16.

18. Cleanse the nails of both hands by holding the patron's right hand over, not in, the manicure bowl and by brushing in a downward movement to clean the nails and fingers of excess cream or oil.

19. Repeat the same procedure on the left hand. Start with the little finger. Dry the hands carefully and check the nails for any flaws.

20. Remove any bits of cuticle that remain and eliminate possible rough spots on the free edge with light strokes of the fine side of the emery board. This technique also helps to give the nails a smooth beveled edge.

21. At this point, the nails are either buffed (dry polish), or clear neutral liquid enamel is applied.

   A. Buffed nails: Apply powder or paste nail polish to the entire length of the chamois part of the buffer and to the nail. Hold the patron's finger between your thumb and index finger. Buff the nail with downward strokes from the base to the free edge. Buff each nail until a smooth clean gloss has been obtained. Lift the buffer from the nail on each stroke. This prevents a hot or burning sensation.

   B. Liquid enamel: When clear liquid enamel is used for men's manicuring, apply a colorless base coat and top coat. Follow the standard procedure.

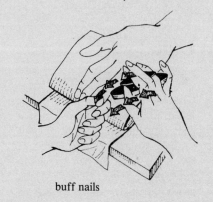

buff nails

Fingernail and hand care: manicuring

Unit 7
Oil or lanolin manicure

General objectives-student goals:
After study, instruction, practice and completion of this unit, you will be able to show understanding of the effects and procedure for an oil or lanolin manicure by giving a brief overview of the subject and by demonstrating the procedure. You must have the proper implements and supplies in order to complete this unit successfully.

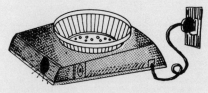

HOT OIL MANICURE HEATER

Unit 8
Finger massage

General objectives-student goals:
After study, instruction, practice and completion of this unit, you will be able to show understanding of finger massage by demonstrating the technique. You must have the proper implements and supplies in order to complete this unit successfully.

> **Fingernail and hand care: manicuring**

Unit 7
Oil or lanolin manicure

The oil or lanolin manicures are designed to help replace natural oil and moisture lost because of the use of detergents. They are recommended for brittle nails and dry rough skin around the fingertips. If the nails are ridged, buff with pumice powder at the beginning of the manicure.

Procedure

1. Heat the liquid lanolin, olive oil or prepared commercial product in an electric heater designed especially for this type of manicure.

2. The procedure is the same as for the standard manicure but it substitutes the heated product for the soap and water and eliminates the use of cuticle remover and massage cream.

3. After the cuticles have been treated, give a finger massage.

4. Remove the oily preparation with a warm damp towel or a wash 'n dri towel.

5. Repair any split or broken nails.

6. Wipe each nail with a cotton pledget moistened with enamel remover. This removes all traces of the oily preparation before the application of the base coat and nail enamel.

Unit 8
Finger massage

1. Start with the little finger of each hand. Hold the patron's fingertip between your thumb and first two fingers. Lift each finger in turn by the tip and make as large a circle as possible in the air. Repeat five times in both directions with each finger.

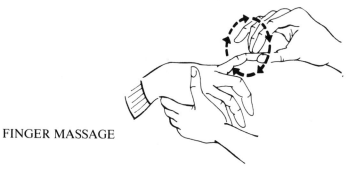

FINGER MASSAGE

2. Grasp each fingertip in turn between your thumb and first two fingers. Pinch it hard and slide off the tip with a snap. Repeat five times on each finger.

Unit 9
Hand and arm massage

Hand and arm massage is a special service which may be added to the standard manicure procedure for an extra fee. Hand and arm massage helps to keep the hands and fingers flexible and the skin smooth.

Procedure

1. Start with the little finger of each hand. Hold it with your thumb and next two fingers. Lift each finger in turn by its tip and make as large a circle as possible in the air. Repeat five times in both directions with each finger. Give the tip a slight pinch as it is released.

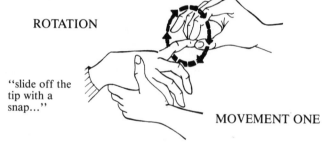

ROTATION

"slide off the tip with a snap..."

MOVEMENT ONE

2. Keep the thumbs together toward the outer side of the hand. Start at the wrist and work down toward the fingers in a semicircular effleurage. Return to the wrist with one stroke. Move to the middle of the wrist and repeat the movement down the hand. Repeat the same movement down the inner side of the hand.

3. Start at the palm and knead each finger by rolling and twisting the flesh between the thumb and first finger of your right hand. Work toward the fingertips and return with a single stroke. Repeat five times on each finger.

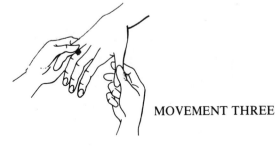

knead by twisting the flesh working toward fingertips...

MOVEMENT THREE

Unit 9
Hand and arm massage

General objectives-student goals: After study, instruction, practice and completion of this unit, you will be able to show understanding of hand and arm massage by demonstrating the procedure. You must have the proper implements and supplies in order to complete this unit successfully.

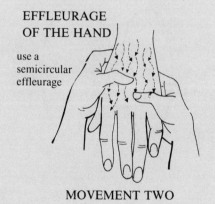

EFFLEURAGE OF THE HAND

use a semicircular effleurage

MOVEMENT TWO

Fingernail and hand care: manicuring

317

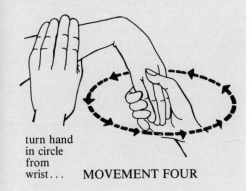

turn hand
in circle
from
wrist...   MOVEMENT FOUR

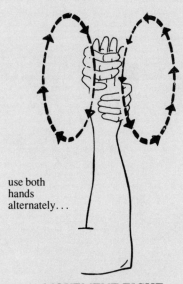

use both
hands
alternately...

MOVEMENT EIGHT

**Fingernail and hand
care: manicuring**

318

4. Hold all the fingers together and turn the hand in a circle from the wrist, five times in each direction.

5. Hold your palm against the patron's and bend her hand back at the wrist against the resistance. Repeat five times.

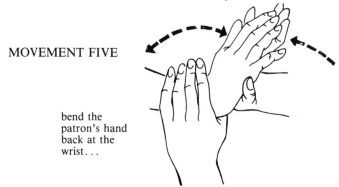

MOVEMENT FIVE

bend the
patron's hand
back at the
wrist...

6. Grasp all the patron's fingers in yours and hold the hand straight. Flex it down or forward toward the wrist, against the resistance. Repeat five times.

7. Grasp each fingertip in turn between the thumb and first two fingers of your hand. Pinch it hard and slide off the tip with a snap. Repeat five times on each fingertip.

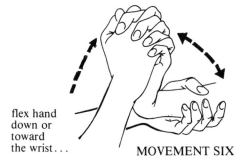

flex hand
down or
toward
the wrist...   MOVEMENT SIX

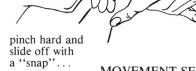

pinch hard and
slide off with
a "snap"...   MOVEMENT SEVEN

8. Hold the patron's hand straight up in both your hands. Stroke it firmly with both hands alternately. Move rapidly from the tips to the wrist as if you were working on a tight glove. Give five double strokes on each hand.

9. Grasp the patron's hand firmly with one hand at the wrist. Keep the patron's hand turned downward. Massage the arm from the wrist to the elbow using a chucking (pinching) motion in which the flesh is grasped firmly and moved up and down along the arm bones. Repeat five times.

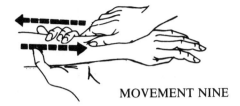

massage up and
down along the
arm bones...

MOVEMENT NINE

10. Use a firm circular motion from the wrist to the elbow. Hold the patron's arm with both hands and apply pressure with the thumb. Repeat five times on both sides of the patron's arms.

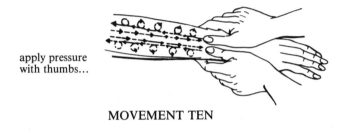

apply pressure
with thumbs...

MOVEMENT TEN

11. Bend the patron's arm at the elbow and hold it firmly at the wrist. Put the other hand into the elbow joint and massage the elbow using a circular motion and a slight pressure with your thumb and index fingers. Repeat five times.

Unit 10
Mend-A-Nail

Broken or split nails can be mended so that they appear normal. This procedure allows the damaged area to grow out until it can be trimmed off and does not detract from the appearance of the hands.

Procedure

use orangewood stick
to tuck end paper under
free edge of nail...

split
nail

tear end paper
do not cut...

1. Remove all nail enamel.

2. File and shape the nail.

3. Tear a piece of end paper so that it overlaps the broken or split nail area. The tissue is torn in order to create an irregular edge. This prevents a sharp line of demarcation. Do not cut the paper with scissors or leave a straight edge.

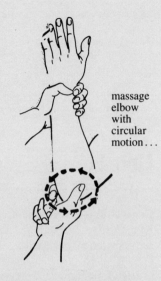

massage
elbow
with
circular
motion...

MOVEMENT ELEVEN

Unit 10

Mend-A-Nail

General objectives-student goals: After study, instruction, practice and completion of this unit, you will be able to show understanding of Mend-A-Nail by demonstrating the technique. You must have the proper implements and supplies in order to complete this unit successfully.

| Fingernail and hand care: manicuring |

319

4. Apply clear nail enamel on the split and on both sides of the paper. Place the paper on the nail so that it covers the split and extends over the nail edge.

5. Tuck the tissue under the free edge of the nail with an orangewood stick. Apply clear enamel under the free edge.

6. Smooth the surface of the patch with the cushion of your finger. Your finger must be moistened with nail enamel remover. Direct your finger away from the nail edge while smoothing.

7. If required, add a second patch for reinforcement.

8. Dry the patch thoroughly before applying base coat, nail enamel and top coat.

Unit 11
Artificial fingernails

General objectives-student goals:
After study, instruction, practice and completion of this unit, you will be able to show understanding of artificial fingernails by giving a brief overview of the subject and by demonstrating the procedure, application and removal of artificial nails applied with nail molds. You must have the proper implements and supplies in order to complete this unit successfully.

> **Fingernail and hand care: manicuring**

Unit 11
Artificial fingernails

The subject of manicuring is not limited to the traditional manicure procedures nor to the application of artificial nails with a nail mold. Manicurists should be trained and knowledgeable in all methods and techniques. Nail caps, nail extenders, nail tips, nail transplant and nail wrapping are some of the many manicure related services available in most full service beauty salons.

With the exception of the application of artificial fingernails with nail molds, detailed step-by-step procedures for the specialized manicuring services have been omitted because of the wide variations between the methods and techniques recommended by various manufacturers. You should follow the manufacturer's instructions for each product.

Nail caps: This is the application of a full size shell-like fingernail on top of and bonded to the natural nail.

Nail extenders: This is the use of silver foil nail forms fitted around the outer nail and slightly under the nail tip. The premixed material is applied at the juncture of the nail tip and form. It is then spread so that it blends with the newly formed nail tip.

Nail tips: Artificial nail tips are like nail caps but are applied only to the tip of the natural nail. They are very good for patrons whose nails chip easily or grow irregularly. They are easily removed with a nail clipper.

Nail transplant: When a very long fingernail is broken and not lost, it is quick and easy to cement it to the natural nail. Apply fast drying nail glue only to the fragment and press it into place. Hold until dry. File the glue ridge formed at the joint down.

Nail wrapping (the hard wrap): This is a service for patrons with broken or bitten nails. The wrap protects the nail until it has grown out. The nail wrap paper is preglued and placed on the nail. The overlapping paper is cut into thin strips and tucked under the free edge of the nail so that it lies flat. A protective ceramic glaze is applied to both the top and underside of the nail.

Nail molds

Artificial nails are recommended for the patron who wants beautiful nails when her own are very short and/or badly shaped. They can also be used to conceal broken nails and to help overcome the habit of nail biting.

Implements and Supplies

1. A selection of nail molds (17 sizes)
2. Liquid
3. Powder
4. Eyedropper
5. Buffer

6. Pumice powder
7. Emery board
8. Plastic strips to remove excess mixture
9. Nail enamel

Procedure

1. Complete the manicure but do not apply nail enamel.

2. Buff the surface of the nails with pumice powder or with the fine side of an emery board.

3. Select the proper size nail mold.

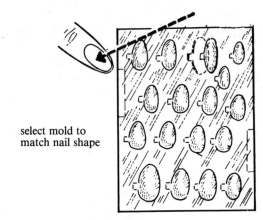

select mold to
match nail shape

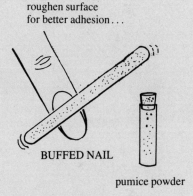

roughen surface
for better adhesion . . .

BUFFED NAIL

pumice powder

4. If the mold needs adjustment in order to fit the nail, reshape it with an emery board. If the curvature of the nail is greater than the mold, pinch the sides of the mold together.

5. Fill approximately two-thirds of the nail mold with powder.

6. Slowly saturate the powder drop by drop with the liquid from an eyedropper.

7. Tilt the mold up and down to blend the powder and liquid properly.

8. Place the mold on the base of the nail first and then on the rest of the nail.

**Fingernail and hand
care: manicuring**

9. Hold the mold in place for several seconds. Do not press down on the mold.

10. Wipe away excess solution immediately.

11. Allow the mold to remain on the nail for 15 minutes.

12. Hold the tab of the mold and gently lift it off the nail.

13. File the artificial nails to the desired length. Apply nail enamel.

Removing artificial nails

1. Cut the artificial nails to approximately $\frac{1}{8}$ inch (0.32 cm.) beyond the nail tip.

2. Press both the artificial and natural nails down toward the fingertip.

3. This releases the artificial nail from the base of the nail.

4. Apply a little oil under the break. Then, gently lift the artificial nail off.

Unit 12
Electric manicure

The electric manicure follows the same procedure as a standard manicure except that special implements are used. These implements are attachments for an electric device designed to do a faster and more efficient job.

Some of the attachments are:

1. Coarse and fine emery wheels which are used to file the nails.

2. A cuticle pusher for loosening the cuticle.

3. A cuticle brush for removing excess cuticle.

4. A buffer for buffing the nails with dry polish or pumice powder.

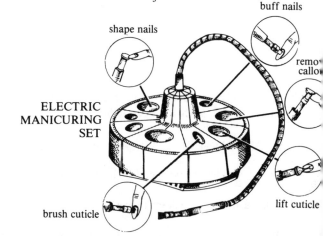

ELECTRIC MANICURING SET

shape nails

buff nails

remo callo

brush cuticle

lift cuticle

use oil at base to help free nail...

to remove: press nail down at fingertip...

Unit 12
Electric manicure

General objectives-student goals:
After study, instruction, practice and completion of this unit, you will be able to show understanding of electric manicuring by giving a brief overview of the subject and by identifying the implements that are attached to the electric device. You must have the proper implements and supplies in order to complete this unit successfully.

Fingernail and hand care: manicuring

Unit 13
Pedicare

A pedicare, the art of caring for the toenails and feet, is recommended for improving the appearance and comfort of the feet. A complete pedicare treatment includes care of the feet, legs and toenails. The foot massage extends to a little above the ankle.

Diseases of the foot and abnormal foot conditions like corns, ingrown toenails and callouses are not treated by the manicurist. Depending on the condition, a podiatrist and/or a medical doctor is best qualified to give the proper treatment. Ringworm of the foot is an infectious disease which can spread over the sole and between the toes. Fungus infections of the feet and nails are usually chronic. Fungal organisms, like athlete's foot, are contagious and spread by skin contact with another person. The resistance of a person's body to these infections plays the most important role in catching and/or spreading the organism.

Equipment and supplies: The items used are essentially the same as for manicuring but with several additions:

1. Two enameled or plastic basins of warm water for the foot bath and rinse

2. An ottoman on which to rest the patron's foot

3. A plastic apron to protect the operator's uniform

4. Toenail clipper

5. Three Turkish towels

6. A low stool for the operator

7. Cotton pledgets

8. Antiseptic solution

9. Astringent

10. Foot powder

11. Paper towels

12. An extra orangewood stick

13. Emery boards

14. Cuticle pusher

15. Nail enamel

16. Manicure brush

17. Cuticle nipper

18. Emollient cream

low stool

ottoman

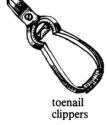
toenail clippers

enamel basin

PEDICARE IMPLEMENTS & EQUIPMENT

General objectives-student goals: After study, instruction, practice and completion of this unit, you will be able to show understanding of a pedicare treatment by giving a brief overview of the subject, by identifying the equipment and supplies and by demonstrating the preparation and procedure. You must have the proper implements and supplies in order to complete this unit successfully.

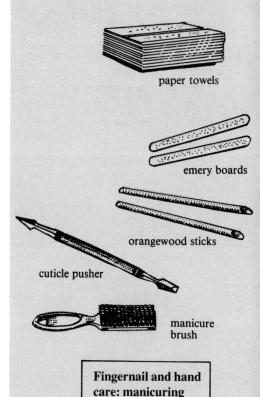

paper towels

emery boards

orangewood sticks

cuticle pusher

manicure brush

Fingernail and hand care: manicuring

AVOID INGROWN TOENAILS

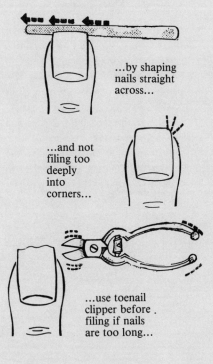

...by shaping nails straight across...

...and not filing too deeply into corners...

...use toenail clipper before filing if nails are too long...

Fingernail and hand care: manicuring

Preparation

1. Seat the patron comfortably in a facial chair.

2. Have the patron remove shoes and hose.

3. Place a clean folded Turkish towel on the ottoman.

4. Wash your hands thoroughly and rinse them in a disinfecting solution. This will protect them against infection.

5. Assemble the instruments on your right side and place the foot tub containing warm water and antiseptic on your left side. Spread two Turkish towels over your lap, one to protect you and the other for use on the patron.

6. Rinse both feet in the basin by swirling water lightly over them. Remove the feet from the water and dry them.

7. Add 2 inches (5.08 cm.) of hot water to the basin and about 1 ounce (29.57 ml.) of soap solution.

Procedure

1. Remove old nail enamel from the nails of both feet. Start from the little toe and work toward the big toe.

2. Shape the nails straight across with a file or with the coarse side of an emery board. Unevenly cut or filed corners may cause ingrown toenails. Use a toenail clipper first if the nails are too long.

3. Soak the right foot. Allow the water to rise to the ankle.

4. Shape the nails of the left foot.

5. Remove the right foot from the water and dry it. Use an orangewood stick to apply cuticle solvent around the mantle and under the free edge of the nails.

6. Start with the little toe and push back and raise the cuticle with the round end of a metal pusher.

7. Dry the toe and carefully use nippers to snip off only the hangnails and loose bits of skin.

8. Apply an emollient cream with cotton on a second orangewood stick. Massage the cream into the groove and mantle with a circular motion of the thumb.

9. Repeat steps 6, 7 and 8 on each toe. While working on the third toe, have the patron place the left foot in the tub.

10. Repeat steps 5–9 on the left foot.

11. Use a nail brush with soap and water to remove grease and oils from the nails.

12. Rinse the feet and dry them. Separate the toes by placing cotton pledgets between them. Apply nail enamel.

Unit 14
Foot massage

When foot massage is used, it is applied after step 10 of the pedicare procedure. Start with the right foot.

1. Place some emollient cream on the arch of the foot and spread it over the entire foot and slightly above the ankle.

2. Steady the foot by holding it firmly around the metatarsal arch with your left hand. Rotate the toes three times in each direction.

MOVEMENT ONE

...hold foot firmly around metatarsal...

3. Keep the patron's foot upright. Make your thumbs meet on the sole. Keep the fingers on top. Knead the foot thoroughly. Work from the heel and ankle toward the toes. Repeat the movement three times.

4. Hold the toes steady in your left hand and cup the heel in your right. Rotate the foot firmly. Repeat five times.

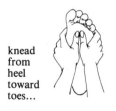

knead from heel toward toes...

MOVEMENT TWO

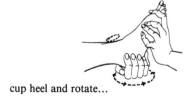

cup heel and rotate...

MOVEMENT THREE

5. Hold the foot steady at the arch. Double your right hand into a fist and roll the knuckles from side to side across the sole. Work gradually from the heel to the toes.

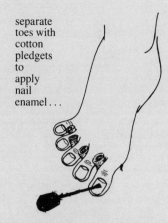

separate toes with cotton pledgets to apply nail enamel...

Unit 14
Foot massage

General objectives-student goals: After study, instruction, practice and completion of this unit, you will be able to show understanding of foot massage by demonstrating the technique and procedure. You must have the proper implements and supplies in order to complete this unit successfully.

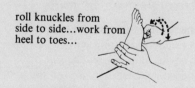

roll knuckles from side to side...work from heel to toes...

MOVEMENT FOUR

Fingernail and hand care: manicuring

325

6. Knead and twist each toe between the knuckles of your bent fingers. Slide off with a light pull. Repeat three times.

7. Start at the instep. Apply firm sliding rotary movements down to the center of the toes. Use both hands. Repeat five times.

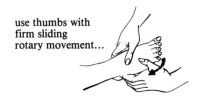

knead
toes
between
knuckles...

use thumbs with
firm sliding
rotary movement...

MOVEMENT FIVE   MOVEMENT SIX

8. Shift both your hands to the ankle bones and wring the flesh around and above them. Use a twisting movement and slide your right hand down to the toes with each twisting movement. Repeat five times.

9. Repeat steps 1-7 on left foot.

10. Remove the cream from both feet with a towel. Wet the feet with warm water.

11. Apply astringent to the feet with a cotton pledget.

12. Dust the feet lightly with talcum or foot powder.

13. Wipe the toenails with nail enamel remover in order to remove any traces of cream.

14. Separate the toes by inserting cotton pledgets between them. Apply nail enamel.

Unit 15
Disorders of the nails

Nail diseases should never be treated by the cosmetologist. A manicure should never be given if the nails show any inflammation or infection.

Cosmetologists and manicurists should be concerned only with simple nail conditions: those that are harmless and painless variations of the normal nail shape or structure. It is important to know which of these are temporary and which are permanent, as well as those which are simple cosmetic defects.

The most common nail disorders are:

1. Hangnails

---

slide right hand down to
toes with each twisting movement...

MOVEMENT SEVEN

Unit 15

Disorders of the nails

General objectives-student goals:
After study, instruction and completion of this unit, you will be able to demonstrate understanding of the disorders of the nails by writing and/or giving a brief overview of the subject.

> **Fingernail and hand care: manicuring**

2. Ingrown nails

3. Split nails

4. Furrows

5. Eggshell nails

6. Spotted nails

7. Misshapen nails

Hangnail (agnail) is a term which applies to two conditions:

1. A sliver of the epidermis

2. A sliver of the nail

A sliver of the epidermis is skin which becomes detached from the mantle at the sides of the nail. The cause of this condition is neglect of the nails. This permits the cuticle to grow fast over the nail instead of being kept apart from it. The skin remains attached to the nail growing out with it. This condition can be extremely painful. Hangnails must be treated carefully in order to prevent further splitting of the skin.

A sliver of the nails is when part of the nail grows away from the main body after splitting. This is caused by improper filing of the nails or by tearing the nail rather than filing or cutting it.

Treatment of hangnails consists of removing the cause of the condition. This prevents its recurrence. Regular manicure and pedicare routines are recommended.

Ingrown nails (onychocryptosis) are caused by a sliver of nail that becomes enveloped in the mantle. It grows into the flesh instead of toward the tip. It is more common in the toes because of the pressure of shoes which can distort normal growth.

Split nails (onychorrhexis) may occur either in the form of flaking up of layers at the free edge or lengthwise in the lines of the lamellae in the body. Splitting may result from an injury to the finger. It is often associated with dryness and brittleness of the hair when there is a glandular disorder. Excessive use of cuticle solvents and nail enamel remover or careless filing or lack of beveling can also help cause splitting.

Treatment of split nails depends on the cause of the condition and discontinuing the use of drying chemicals. The application of softening oily preparations will improve the nails rapidly. Proper filing of the nails will prevent splitting if there is no underlying cause for it.

HANGNAILS!

If *not* given proper care they can become extremely painful …

sliver of skin

sliver of nail

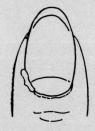

ingrown nails

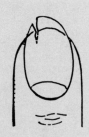

brittle or split nails

Fingernail and hand care: manicuring

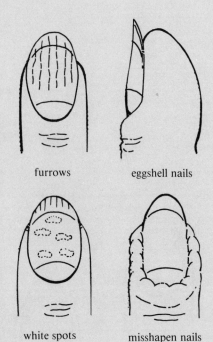

furrows   eggshell nails

white spots   misshapen nails

Fingernail and hand care: manicuring

Furrows are depressions in the nails which may be of constitutional origin or merely the disturbance of nail cells near the matrix. An injury can cause this. Furrows may also owe their origin to mechanical maltreatment during a manicure. Pressing too hard or scraping too deeply with a metal instrument may injure the cells near the base. Repeated application of cuticle solvents also produces both furrows and roughness in the nails.

Eggshell nails (onychotrophia) are a condition in which the nail substance is noticeably whiter, thinner and more flexible than in normal healthy nails. The plates tend to separate from the nail bed and curve upward at the free edge. This condition is usually found among persons who are ill. It presents no particular difficulty but should always be handled carefully when manicuring.

Spotted nails have white spots (leuconychia) which are said to be air bubbles within the nail layers. How the bubbles gain access to the inner layers of the nails has not been determined. On some nails, the whiteness appears in strips across the entire width. This has been ascribed to pressure used when loosening the nail fold during a manicure. Black or brown spots in the nail are usually the result of any injury which causes bleeding in the nail bed. The dried blood attaches itself to the nail and grows out with it. It drops off when it reaches the free edge.

When the entire nail is badly injured, and the generating cells are not destroyed, a new nail starts to grow at once. It may either push the dead one ahead of it as it grows out or grow out underneath it.

Misshapen nails may owe their origin to any one of a number of causes. Internal disturbances may produce the stunted enlargement called onychauxis. Picking the nails, especially around the base, may cause a claw-like overgrowth at the tip (onychogryposis). Biting the nails is one of the most common causes of misshapen nails. In persons of all ages, this habit (onychophagia) is traceable to constant or occasional nervousness.

Nail fungus is a problem that has grown at the same rate as the fingernail business and industry. The number of manicurists and nail salons has more than tripled since 1981.

Sculptures, nail caps, nail extenders, nail tips, overlays and anything else (except nail enamel) that cover the nail body (nail plate) can cause fungus. This type of fungus is usually seen as a green discoloration of the nail plate. The degree of discoloration can range from pale to dark green.

Nail fungus is caused by the combination of moisture and lack of air between the nail and that which covers the nail. The moisture and lack of air cause the nail bed to soften, become spongy, tender and green in color. Dampness and the lack of air create mold, deterioration and a buildup of bacteria. The degree of discoloration indicates the length of time the condition has existed. It is when the nail covering becomes loose or if it has had any degree of lifting that a fungus infection can develop.

There is no instant or magic cure for nail fungus. In most cases, the nail with fungus requires anywhere from several weeks to several months to grow out. Once a fungus infection has set in, the nail cover should be removed completely and the nail(s) given protein nail treatments until the nail has strengthened and grown out.

Early detection (light green discoloration) of a nail fungus can be treated with several light applications of mild medicinal peroxide (*USP 3%) to remove some of the green discoloration. The peroxide treatment will also destroy any bacteria on the infected nail. Nail fungus can be avoided by using nail glue only and by immediately resealing the artificial nail cover to the nail plate when it becomes loose, thereby eliminating the damage caused by the presence of moisture. All moisture must be eliminated from a lifted nail (nail dryer, blow dryer, fan) before resealing, and the resealed nail(s) should not come in contact with water for one hour after resealing.

*United States Pharmacopeia

Review questions

1. What is the purpose of a manicure?

2. Can manicuring be a profitable beauty salon service?

3. Does the condition of the fingernails indicate the general health of an individual?

4. Is there more than one type of manicure and more than one procedure for giving a manicure?

5. How long does it take to give a short manicure?

6. Is a sanitizing solution container an important piece of manicuring equipment?

7. For what is the long, thin, flexible nail file used during a manicure?

8. Do you use a nail buffer with liquid nail polish or dry polish?

9. Do Board of Health regulations always permit the use of a nail buffer during a manicure?

10. What effect does a cuticle solvent have on the cuticle?

11. What is a dry nail polish?

12. Is a manicurist required to take sanitary precautions?

13. Is a manicurist required to wash her hands before working on each patron?

14. Is a back and forth sawing motion with a nail file good for the fingernails?

15. At what point during a manicure are broken or split nails repaired or finger, arm or hand massages given?

16. How many strokes are required to cover the fingernail completely with nail enamel?

17. Can smudged nail enamel be smoothed without removing all of it from the fingernail?

18. Why is it necessary to lift the fingernail buffer from the nail with each stroke during the nail buffing procedure?

19. What is best to use for removing the oily preparation from the fingers during the oil or lanolin manicure?

20. What is the main reason for mending a broken or split nail?

Fingernail and hand care: manicuring

Fingernail and hand
care: manicuring

Men's haircutting, hairstyling and hair care

n's haircutting, hairstyling and hair care: **The** long hairstyles of the 1970s triggered men to go to the cosmetologist instead the barber for their haircuts and hair services.

erview: **This** chapter provides you with the details concerning the similarities and differences in the methods and techues for servicing men's and women's hair.

havioral objectives-student goals: **After** completion of this chapter, and after instruction, study and practice, you will form and demonstrate competency in men's haircutting, hairstyling and hair care by: demonstrating a man's haircut, manent wave, hair conditioning treatment, hair tint, chemical hair straightening process and manicure. You will also be e to demonstrate competency by identifying, explaining and/or listing the requirements and procedures for tinting mushes and beards, wig services and hairpieces.

e longer hairstyles of the late 1960's have triggered men to go to the cosmetologist instead of the barber for their haircuts I their hair services. This move was inevitable because cosmetologists were accustomed to handling hair of all lengths.

le licensed cosmetologist was trained to cut and shape long and short hair, style hair and emphasize the patron's best features ile minimizing poor ones. Blow dry styling services, hair conditioning, hair coloring, hair straightening, permanent ving, wig services and manicuring have all been part of cosmetology and were rapidly available for men in all beauty ons offering men's hairstyling services. Barbers did not have experience with long hairstyles in those days. Their skills re limited to cutting short hair and basic barbering services. This, however, is not true today. Barbers are known as stylists, men's stylists, or barber stylists. Most State regulations permit barbers to provide the same full service as cosmetologists I some states are requiring cosmetologists to know how to give a shave in order to hold a "combination" or "unisex" ense. The principle physical and chemical actions, basic requirements, and procedures in permanent waving, hair conditioning, hair coloring, hair straightening, wig services and massage movements for servicing men are the same as for women.

anitary and safety precautions for men's haircutting, hairstyling and hair care, etc.

1. Use a rolling motion with a described semicircle in order to avoid making steps when cutting a graduated neckline.

2. Buff the nails in only one direction in order to prevent a hot or burning sensation.

3. Comb and brush wigs and hairpieces carefully in order to avoid pulling the hair from its foundation.

4. Make strand tests. Avoid guessing.

5. Make test curls frequently until the hair is fully processed.

6. Do not give scalp treatments immediately before chemical hair treatments.

7. Protect the patron's clothing with the proper draping.

8. Protect the patron's ears and the skin around the hairline when using strongly alkaline or caustic products.

Unit 1
Men's haircutting

Unit 1
Men's haircutting

General objectives-student goals:
After study, instruction and completion of this unit, you will be able to demonstrate understanding of men's haircutting by writing and/or giving a brief overview of the subject.

Procedures for shaping and cutting men's hair into a contemporary style are quite similar to those for shaping and cutting women's hair. The average man who goes to the cosmetologist to have his hair styled is not one who has long long hair nor is he one who wants a conventional barber haircut. He is usually a man who must maintain a well-groomed image, is style conscious and wants the longer hair look.

Hair shaping is an important basic hairdressing skill because it is the foundation for all hairstyling. The durability of any hairstyle is influenced by the shape of the hair. There are different types of haircuts—a basic circular haircut, a basic five section haircut and the multi-level cut—but the important thing is that hair bulk and length, properly shaped to the contour of the head or into a definite style pattern, help you achieve professional results in the final hairstyle.

The circular haircut is almost foolproof. It is a blunt-cut method of shaping hair and can be used for shaping any hairstyle except the cap-shaped neckline cut. This requires an added cutting technique at the neckline.

Although a razor or scissors can be used for this haircut, it is suggested that the scissors be your first choice until you have confidence in your ability to control your hands and the hair at the same time.

The only difference between a scissors haircut and a razor haircut is the implement used to cut the hair. There is no difference in the results if the implements are used correctly. Both blunt cutting and slithering techniques are practiced professionally with a razor and a scissors.

The basic five section haircut is another time-tested method of cutting hair. Hair may also be cut with a razor using this technique. Again, it is suggested that the scissors be your first choice until you have confidence in your ability to control your hands and the hair at the same time.

Men's hair may be cut either wet or dry when using conventional haircutting scissors. However, the hair must be thoroughly wet when cutting with a razor. For best results, it is advisable to use thinning scissors on hair that has not been made wet.

Unit 2
Procedure for men's haircutting

1. Drape the patron.

2. Comb and analyze the hair. Determine the growth pattern, hair texture, density and natural hair tendencies.

3. Shampoo the hair and blot excess water.

4. Section the hair accordingly, i.e., for a multi-level cut, a basic circular haircut or a five section haircut. Proceed to cut the hair to style.

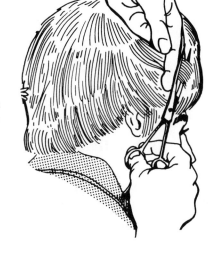

back and sides must blend . . .

5. The section behind the ears must blend in length with both the back and side areas.

6. Sideburns are an important feature of men's hairstyling and should blend with the total style. Do not exaggerate the sideburns excessively. The hair immediately above the sideburns is tapered to blend with the sideburns. The low part of the sideburn is tapered by using the same technique used in basic neckline shaping (rolling motion). Sideburns are defined with an electric trimmer.

7. Apply styling lotion and conditioner.

Unit 2
Procedure for men's haircutting

General objectives-student goals: After study, instruction, practice and completion of this unit, you will be able to show understanding of the techniques and procedure for men's haircutting by demonstrating a man's haircut. You must have the proper implements and supplies in order to complete this unit successfully.

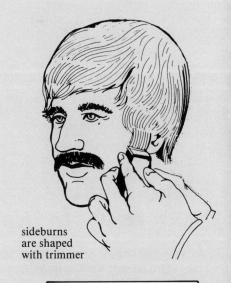

sideburns are shaped with trimmer

> **Men's haircutting, hairstyling and hair care**

Unit 3
Permanent waving for men

General objectives-student goals:
After study, instruction, practice and completion of this unit, you will be able to show understanding of what is required for permanent waving men's hair by demonstrating the technique and procedure. You must have the proper implements and supplies in order to complete this unit successfully.

Men's haircutting, hairstyling and hair care

334

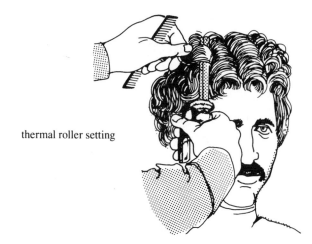

thermal roller setting

8. Blow dry in order to finish the style. If the hair is exceptionally straight and/or the growth pattern is such that it would n respond to blow drying, the hair should be styled by roller setting or thermal roller curling.

9. Final styling details are placed with a comb.

10. A light application of hair spray holds the style lines and maintains a natural look.

Unit 3
Permanent waving for men

Permanent waving for men gives added body and fullness to the hair and helps to maintain a styled line. The procedure is identical to the one used for perming women's hair. When perming men's hair, exceptional consideration should be given to the diameter of the rod. Large diameter rods should be used for casual hairstyles. It is important to have $1\frac{1}{2}$ full turns of hair on a perm rod for a satisfactory curl. Use smaller diameter rods on short hair. The principle physical and chemical actions, basic requirements and procedures in permanent waving men's hair are the same as for women.

Sectioning and subsectioning of the hair

Good sectioning is a definite aid to good permanent waving. Choose the sectioning pattern after considering all of the following:

1. Hair density

2. Any hairline irregularity

3. Head contour

4. Desired style

A good fundamental pattern for sectioning and subsectioning has nine basic sections. The sections must be arranged uniformly with clean and uniform partings of equally subdivided rod sections. The rod sections must be about the same length as the rod used.

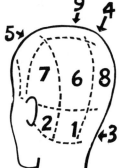

Procedure for wrapping

Subsection a strand of hair moistened with waving lotion. Comb the hair in the subsection up and out with all the hair evenly directed and distributed.

1. Place an end paper near the hair ends.

    Note: End papers are used to help assure smooth winding and to prevent fishhooks and straight ends.

2. Place a rod under the strand and draw the end paper and rod toward you until the hair ends are visible above the rod. Roll the end paper and hair under.

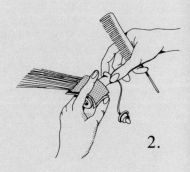

3. As the hair is wrapped, it should look outwardly firm and smooth and be wound on the rod without tension. The rod should always be held in a position slightly ahead of the wrapping motion to avoid tension wrapping.

4. While rolling the hair under, use the thumb of each hand to keep control of the strand. Wind smoothly without tension.

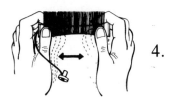

5. When the strand is wrapped and placed properly in the rod section, fasten the rod evenly across the hair with the fastener. Place the fastener a little above the center of the rod. A tight or twisted fastener can cause hair breakage.

Men's haircutting, hairstyling and hair care

Processing time

Processing time is the period required for the hair to absorb the permanent waving lotion sufficiently to loosen its chemical bonds. This will allow the hair to assume the new pattern of the rod. The following factors influence the processing time.

1. Strength of the lotion

2. Porosity

3. Elasticity

4. Length of the hair

5. Condition of the hair

6. Patron's body temperature

7. Room temperature

Test curl method

test curl

1. Loosen the rod fastener.

2. Unwind the rod $1\frac{1}{2}$ turns without pulling on the strand.

3. Move the rod slightly toward the scalp.

4. Permit the hair to relax into a wave pattern without pushing.

5. Rewind and fasten the rod.

6. Continue testing for curl development at regular intervals. Test on different areas of the head.

7. Processing is complete when the wave forms a firm "S" The size of the rod controls the size of the "S" pattern. The peak is reached only once. If the processing is not stopped immediately, the hair will be overprocessed and damaged.

Neutralizing

The neutralizer is the chemical solution which stops the action of the waving lotion and rehardens the hair in its new curled form.

Procedure

1. Rinse the hair thoroughly in order to remove the waving lotion.

2. Blot each curl in order to remove excess moisture.

3. Keep the patron in a sitting position and place a cotton strip around the entire hairline. The cotton will absorb drippings.

4. Use an applicator bottle and start by applying neutralizer to the curl that was wrapped last. Work backwards to the curl that was wrapped first. The length of time during which the neutralizer remains on the hair will vary from five to ten minutes depending on the brand used.

5. Rinse thoroughly, allow to cool and remove the rods.

Cold waving procedure

1. Drape the patron.

2. Shampoo. Apply one light soaping.

3. Shape the hair.

4. Section the hair into nine sections while it is still damp.

5. Moisten the hair in section 1 with waving solution.

6. Subsection section 1 and wrap the hair on the rod.

7. Fasten the rod in the rod section.

8. Continue this procedure until the entire head is wrapped.

9. Protect the patron with cotton strips and protective cream.

10. Rewet the entire head with waving lotion.

11. Process the hair. Make test curls.

12. When the hair is fully processed, rinse it thoroughly. Blot excess moisture.

13. Neutralize.

14. Rinse the hair thoroughly. Allow to cool. Remove the rods.

The above procedures may vary with some products. Always follow the manufacturer's instructions.

Unit 4
Hair conditioning, scalp treatments, hair treatments

Hair conditioning and scalp massage are very beneficial. Hair conditioners are designed to improve the condition of the hair as well as to give it body and sheen. Scalp manipulations stimulate the nerves, muscles and glands in the scalp. It is an excellent means of increasing blood circulation which nourishes the scalp tissues. The procedures, products and techniques are the same for men and women.

Scalp treatments help preserve the health and beauty of both the hair and scalp. Healthy hair needs frequent brushing, scalp manipulations and shampooing. Brushing the hair with a good natural bristle hair brush will stimulate the scalp and clean and polish the hair. Remember that the purpose of a hair brush is indicated by its name. Use it to brush the hair not the scalp.

Unit 4
Hair conditioning, scalp treatments, hair treatments

General objectives-student goals: After study, instruction, practice and completion of this unit, you will be able to show understanding of men's hair and scalp conditioning treatments by demonstrating the scalp treatment procedure and the procedure for hair treatments. You must have the proper implements and supplies in order to complete this unit successfully.

> **Men's haircutting, hairstyling and hair care**

A natural bristle hair brush is recommended for hair hygiene and professional hair and scalp treatments. Natural bristle has many tiny imbrications which clean and polish hair. Nylon bristle is shiny and smooth. It is recommended only for hairdressing and blow dry styling.

Scalp manipulations

Scalp manipulations stimulate:

1. The circulation of blood to the scalp

2. The muscles

3. The scalp glands

Correct manipulations stimulate the flow of blood through the capillaries. The additional nutriment secreted by the papilla contributes toward a healthier hair and scalp condition. It also relieves itching, a very common scalp complaint.

Pulling the hair at the scalp helps to stimulate the scalp and prevent shedding. The correct hair pulling technique is to grasp a small amount of hair between the thumb and forefinger about 1 inch (2.54 cm.) above the scalp, hold tightly and pull firmly. Repeat over the entire head area. The hair pulling technique to stimulate the scalp is an excellent substitute for the scalp exercise usually obtained by hair brushing. This technique should be used daily if the hair is not brushed.

Basic scalp movements

Scalp manipulations utilize modifications of two basic movements:

Stroking: A smooth light gliding stroke (effleurage), without pressure, over the surface of the skin in linear or circular motion.

Compression:

1. Friction: Pressure applied to the tissues with the fingers or hand along the nerve tracts.

2. Kneading: Grasping the skin and flesh with the hand and fingers, lifting the tissues and squeezing them.

Procedure for scalp treatments

1. Drape the patron and brush the hair.

2. Section the hair into four quadrants. Fasten three of these out of the way. Leave one loose.

3. Hold the comb between your middle and index fingers. Hold a cotton pledget between your thumb and index finger. Subsection each quadrant with partings from $\frac{1}{4}$ to $\frac{1}{2}$ inch (0.64 – 1.27 cm.) apart. Apply tonic or lotion. Rub it on the scalp along the lines of the partings.

4. If a pomade or cream is to be applied, place a small dab on the back of your left hand. Hold the comb between the index and middle fingers of your right hand. Apply the pomade with the tips of these fingers.

5. Adjust an infrared lamp or other heating device over the patron's head.

6. Give scalp manipulations 1–9 as illustrated.

7. Shampoo the hair and towel it dry.

8. Use direct or indirect high frequency equipment.

9. Apply the appropriate scalp tonic or pomade.

10. Set, dry and comb the hair into the desired style.

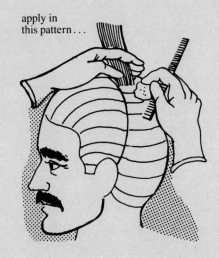

apply in this pattern . . .

Hair treatments

Hair treatments are intended to treat the hair shaft not the scalp. Corrective hair treatments are recommended for dry, abused and damaged hair. They are also recommended before and/or after a permanent wave, hair tinting, bleaching or straightening treatment.

There are many different types of hair conditioning treatments. Select the one manufactured for the specific condition to be treated. Most of these preparations have penetrating value and show excellent results after the first treatment.

Procedure

1. Drape the patron.

2. Brush the hair.

3. Shampoo the hair and blot it dry.*

4. Apply hair conditioner on the scalp area. Use the same technique as for a scalp treatment. When the application to the scalp is complete, apply the conditioner to the entire hair shaft.

5. Apply movements 3–7 of the scalp treatment procedure.

6. Use a heating cap or accelerating machine according to the manufacturer's instructions.

7. Remove the heating cap or accelerating machine and section the hair into four quadrants. Subsection each quadrant with $\frac{1}{4} - \frac{1}{2}$ inch (0.64 – 1.27 cm.) partings. Hold the comb in your right hand. Use the thumb, index and middle fingers of both hands. The fingers slide over the entire length of each strand of hair. Begin with the hair nearest the scalp and slide towards the ends. This is achieved with a circular motion. Start with your left hand. Pull and slide upward towards yourself. As the left hand reaches the ends of the strand, the right hand starts again at the scalp area. This is repeated three times on each strand over the entire head.

8. Rinse the hair.* Blot it dry and set.

   *If the preparation is not water soluble, eliminate shampooing as the third step and shampoo instead of water rinse as the eighth step. Always follow the product manufacturer's instructions.

The scalp treatment procedure for all scalp conditions including baldness (alopecia areata), premature baldness, unnatural fall, dry dandruff and oily dandruff is the same. It is important to select and use hair preparations, tonic, lotion or cream manufactured for the condition to be treated.

Unit 5
Men's hair coloring

Men are enjoying the benefits of hair coloring. Modern coloring agents are used widely and openly. The results are natural looking and give mature men a more youthful appearance.

Young men also color their hair. Men's hair coloring is not limited to covering gray hair. Many males are sufficiently fashion-oriented to illuminize (lighten) their hair as well as to streak, tip and frost it. Nuancing is also very popular with men. Nuancing is also called monochromatic hair coloring. It is the technique of creating many subtle or slight variations of one color. This produces a multi-color effect. Nuancing involves lightening several fine strands of either natural or dyed hair. Each individual strand is lightened to a greater or lesser degree. No two strands are lightened to the same stage.

Nuancing techniques usually require the use of less than 20 volume peroxide. The result is subtle or slight variations of one color and the creation of a multi-color effect. These techniques produce a natural look, one which simulates the look which frequent and prolonged sun exposure gives to the hair.

Hair coloring is the science of changing the color of hair by either removing and/or adding color. Artificial color (tinting) may be applied to the natural pigment of the hair, to previously tinted hair or to hair that has been prelighted. Hair lightening can remove natural pigment from the hair or color from tinted hair. There are three categories of hair color.

General objectives-student goals:
After study, instruction and completion of this unit, you will be able to demonstrate understanding of men's hair coloring by writing and/or giving a brief overview of the subject.

Men's haircutting,
hairstyling and hair care

1. Temporary hair color

2. Semipermanent color

3. Permanent hair color

    A. Adding color (tinting)

    B. Removing color (lightening-bleaching)

Temporary hair coloring will add highlights and color to the hair. It will have no lasting effect on the hair color. It is easily removed by shampooing. Temporary colorings are also used to highlight gray hair, banish yellow from gray hair, cover a limited amount of gray hair, fill in porous hair and color blend hair discoloration. A patch test is not required for temporary hair colors which contain only certified colors.

Semipermanent hair coloring requires no peroxide developer and has a mild penetrating action. Color is retained for several weeks. Semipermanent color requires a patch test and is available in all shades. They are recommended to blend gray hair partially and to highlight the natural color of the hair.

Permanent hair coloring: This type of hair coloring remains in the hair until:

1. The hair grows out and the tinted hair is cut off.

2. Changed by a hair lightening process.

3. Treated with a tint remover. Permanent hair coloring cannot be completely removed or washed out of the hair.

Tinting mustaches and beards: A gray mustache and/or beard is more aging than gray hair. Men are likely to tint their mustaches before they start tinting their hair. An **aniline derivative tint** should never be used for tinting mustaches or beards. Special products, such as those used for tinting eyebrows and eyelashes, are used for coloring mustaches and beards. The choice of colors is limited to light brown, dark brown and black. These three colors usually satisfy the color range for mustaches and beards. Mustaches and beards may be lightened with any liquid hair lightener when little or no gray hair is involved. The resulting color—various shades of blonde and/or red—will be determined by the natural color and pigment of the hair. Men's hair coloring is basically the same as women's hair coloring.

Unit 6
Men's hair straightening

Unruly, curly, overcurly and kinky hair have long plagued men because these conditions limit the way the hair may be combed. It is almost impossible to style these types of hair. When the humidity is high and there is moisture in the air, the problem increases.

lighten hair strands

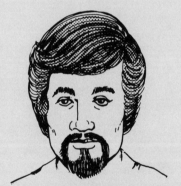

TINTING MUSTACHES AND BEARDS

Unit 6
Men's hair straightening

General objectives-student goals:
After study, instruction and comple-

Men's haircutting, hairstyling and hair care

tion of this unit, you will be able to demonstrate understanding of men's hair straightening by writing and/or giving a brief overview of the subject.

There are two methods to straighten hair. One is temporary; the other is permanent. The degree of straightening required is determined by how the hair is to be styled. The degree of straightening ranges from loosening a kink and relaxing a curl to the highest degree to straightening the hair completely.

Hair pressing

Hair pressing with a hot comb is the professional method of straightening curly and/or kinky hair temporarily. The main disadvantage is that the straightened hair will revert to its original curly appearance if it is exposed to any type of moisture.

The implements and materials required are:

1. Two pressing combs and/or pressing irons

2. Electric or gas heater

3. Pressing oil or cream press

4. Tail or styling comb, brush and hair clips

5. Lanolin hairdressing and hair spray

When preparing the patron for a hair pressing, it is mandatory to examine the patron's scalp and hair. If the patron has any abrasion or scalp injury, the pressing treatment should not be given. If examination of the hair shows damage because of hair coloring or improper pressing treatments, a series of hair reconditioning treatments should be recommended.

Chemical hair straightening

Chemical hair straightening is a process of permanently changing natural hair forms so that the treated hair becomes permanently straight. Thereafter, only the new growth needs to be treated.

Chemical hair relaxing

Chemical hair relaxing is basically the same as chemical hair straightening but milder ingredients are used to transform naturally curly or kinky hair forms to soft wavy hair. The two chemicals most commonly used to straighten hair are:

1. Ammonium thioglycolate: A thioglycolate hair straightener contains ammonium monoethanolamine thioglycolate or thioglycolic acid adjusted to the desired pH with ammonia or monoethanolamine. A heavy creme base is used to make the material easier to apply. The action of the thioglycolate is the same in straightening as in cold waving. The disulfide links of the keratin are broken down. This softens the hair. The hair is then smoothed to a straightened shape with a comb and/or the hand technique.

The chemical action of hair straighteners resembles that of coloring. The cuticle layer of the hair lifts and the chemicals enter the cortex layer. Chemical hair straighteners separate the cystine bonds or molecular connections and may cause a visible discoloration of the hair.

When the hair is straightened satisfactorily, the action is stopped by a neutralizer which usually contains an oxidizing compound. This neutralizer is left on the hair long enough to penetrate the hair shaft and stop the action of the thioglycolate. Complete neutralization, followed by rinsing, removes all the straightening agent from the hair and restores it to its original chemical state. Although 4 ounces (118.27 ml.) of 20 volume hydrogen peroxide mixed with 28 ounces (828.07 ml.) of water will act as a neutralizer, solid oxidizing agents (potassium bromate and sodium perborate) have been found to be more suitable.

2. Sodium hydroxide: Sodium hydroxide (caustic) in a solution with stearic and oleic acids was the first chemical used for straightening hair. The sodium hydroxide content of different manufacturers' products varies from 5% to 10%. The pH value goes from 7.5 to 14. The more sodium hydroxide, the higher the pH value and the quicker the reaction of the chemical on the hair. The chances of the quicker reacting chemicals damaging the skin or hair are also greater.

As a hair straightener, sodium hydroxide functions by swelling the fibers and softening the main disulfide bonds which link the polypeptide chains of the hair structure. The hair should be softened completely within eight minutes. During the chemical action, the disulfide links lose one molecule of sulfur. After rinsing, they rejoin as lanthionine links between the polypeptide chains and stabilize the hair. Unlike thioglycolate, hair treated with sodium hydroxide does not return to its original structure. The patron's skin should be carefully protected with a base, especially when the hair is being rinsed. Sodium hydroxide can burn the skin and scalp. If sodium hydroxide is left on the hair too long, it may discolor the hair, make it brittle and cause breakage.

Always apply a protective base around the ears and the skin around the hairline.

Before straightening or relaxing tinted, bleached or damaged hair, a hair filler and a conditioner should be used. They will protect porous hair from breakage and permit even penetration by filling the cuticle scales of the hair shaft. Protein hair fillers are usually the most effective.

Hair coloring and hair straightening or relaxing treatments should not be given to the patron on the same day. Waiting at least 72 hours after tinting is recommended. Some chemical combinations are not compatible and may leave deposits.

Hair ends should be blunt cut prior to a hair straightening treatment. The slither cutting may lift or destroy some of the imbrications of the hair. This could cause the hair to become more porous. It requires professional ability to judge when the hair has been sufficiently straightened for the individual patron.

If, for any reason, a second hair straightening or relaxing treatment is required, wait five days before the second application is made.

Scalp irritation because of improper use of hair straightening chemicals should be treated with an acetic acid (vinegar concentrate) rinse immediately. Use a solution of 8 ounces (236.59 ml.) of water to 1 ounce (29.57 ml.) of acetic acid (vinegar concentrate).

chemical
hair straightening

Men's haircutting,
hairstyling and hair care

In order to use household vinegar as a neutralizer, prepare a mixture of equal parts of vinegar with warm water.

The same type of release statement used for hair coloring should be used for hair straightening treatments.

Whenever there is a question concerning what the results will be, make a strand test before straightening. This test will serve as a guide for determining the final results.

The technique and procedures for straightening men's hair are basically the same as the technique and procedures for straightening women's hair.

Unit 7
Men's wigs and hairpieces

Wig services

Men's wig servicing is an important part of the cosmetologist's trade. Men do not wear wigs only to cover a lack of hair. Some men wear them to cover an abundance of hair. Men who must wear short hair to meet the required image of their business or profession, but who personally prefer longer hairstyles, will wear a short wig to cover up their own hair.

Men's wigs, just like women's wigs, must be adapted to the individual by proper fitting, shaping and styling. They require the same type of servicing as women's wigs, i.e., cleaning, setting and coloring.

It is very important that you develop the knowledge and skill required to become part of the lucrative field of wiggery. The important areas are:

1. Types of hairpieces
2. Quality of hairpieces
3. Machine made and hand tied wigs
4. Wig measurements
5. Wig block measurements
6. Cleaning hairpieces

7. Cutting a wig
8. Setting a wig
9. Temporary color rinses and permanent tints for wigs
10. Wig size adjustments
   A. Shrinking a wig
   B. Reducing wig size by tucking

Men's hairpieces

The servicing, care and fitting of men's hairpieces (toupees) require additional training and special skills. Some of these skills are: measurement for hairpieces, pattern making, hair color matching, preliminary haircutting, and cutting and blending the

---

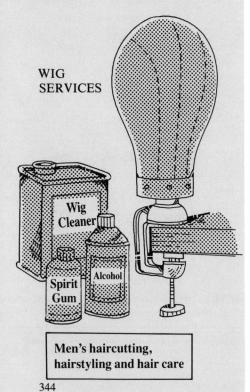

Unit 7
Men's wigs and hairpieces

General objectives-student goals:
After study, instruction and completion of this unit, you will be able to demonstrate understanding of men's wigs and hairpieces by writing and/or giving a brief overview of the subject.

WIG
SERVICES

Wig Cleaner

Spirit Gum   Alcohol

Men's haircutting, hairstyling and hair care

airpiece. Application and removal of the hairpieces, especially those with a lace front, also require special attention and raining.

Hairpieces are available for full head coverage as well as partial (front, crown or top). Facial hairpieces, i.e., mustaches, sideburns and beards, are also part of this specialized service.

Unit 8
Men's manicuring

A good manicure improves the appearance of the fingernails and hands. It is a part of personal hygiene. It is wrong to think that men prefer a conservative manicure (cleaning and filing only). It is important to follow the procedure for the standard women's manicure up to the point at which nail enamel is applied. At this point, the nails are buffed (dry polish powder or paste) or clear liquid nail enamel is applied.

Manicuring is an important service and it reflects the quality of all the other services which the cosmetologist offers. A men's manicure should be completed within 15 to 20 minutes.

Procedure

1. Wash your hands with disinfectant soap.

2. Seat the patron comfortably with his arm resting on the edge of the table.

3. Place the manicuring bowl containing warm water, soap and disinfectant by the patron's right hand.

4. Remove any old clear enamel from the fingers. Start with the little finger of the right hand.

   A. Moisten a cotton pledget with nail enamel remover.

   B. Press the pledget firmly against the nail for a few moments. This will soften the nail enamel.

Unit 8
Men's manicuring

General objectives-student goals:
After study, instruction and completion of this unit, you will be able to demonstrate understanding of men's manicuring by writing and/or giving a brief overview of the subject.

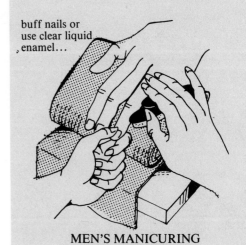

buff nails or use clear liquid enamel...

MEN'S MANICURING

Men's haircutting, hairstyling and hair care

345

C. When the enamel begins to dissolve, wipe the nail clean.

D. Press firmly and direct the cotton pledget from the base of the nail to its tip.

E. Fresh cotton should be used as needed. Do not smear the old enamel on the cuticle.

F. Dip a cotton tipped orangewood stick in enamel remover and clean around the cuticle.

5. Shape the nails. Start with the right hand.

A. Determine the type of nail the patron has and the shaping that will make them look most becoming.

B. Allow the patron's fingers to rest relaxed over your hand.

C. Use a file or emery board as required.

D. Start by filing the nail of the little finger of the right hand. Continue towards the thumb. Release each finger as it is finished.

E. File the free edge only. Hold the patron's finger between the thumb and first two fingers of your left hand.

F. Hold the file or emery board in your right hand. Tilt it so that the filing is done mainly to the underside of the free edge of the nail without rubbing the skin.

G. Work from the corners toward the center. Do not saw back and forth. This causes splitting. File each nail going from right to left and then from left to right. Use two short and one long sweeping stroke on each side of the nail. The nails will look longer and wear better if they are not filed deep in the corners.

6. After completing the filing of the right hand and two fingers of the left hand, soften the cuticle by placing the fingertips of patron's right hand into the finger bowl containing soap and warm water.

7. While the right hand is soaking, complete the filing of the nails of the left hand. Then, remove the right hand from the finger bowl.

8. Dry the fingertips, the hand and the area between the fingers. Hold the manicure towel with both hands. During this process, loosen and push the cuticle and adhering skin on each nail back. Use the cushion of your fingers over the towel.

9. Wrap a thin layer of cotton around the blunt edge of an orangewood stick for use as an applicator. Apply the cuticle solvent all around the mantle of the fingers of the right hand. This same orangewood stick can be dipped in the soapy water of the manicure bowl and/or bleaching preparation and used to cleanse under the free edge.

10. The spoon end of the cuticle pusher is held in a flat position and carefully used to loosen the dead skin from around the sides and base of the nails without scratching the nail plate. Too much pressure on live tissue at the root of the nail can cause injury to the nails.

11. Always start with the little finger and work toward the thumb. Keep the cuticle moist while working.

12. Keep the towel over the index finger and push the cuticle back.

13. Use nippers to remove excess cuticle, bits of loose skin and hangnails. The cuticle should be cut and removed as a single segment.

14. When cutting the cuticle of the middle finger of the right hand, place the fingertips of the left hand into the manicure bowl.

15. Use the cotton tipped orangewood stick to apply bleaching preparation under the free edge of each nail of the right hand.

16. Apply cuticle oil or cream around each finger with the orangewood stick and work it well into the mantle and groove by rubbing in a circular motion with your thumb.

17. Remove the left hand from the manicure bowl. Dry each finger as outlined in step 8 and continue to step 16.

18. Cleanse the nails of both hands by holding the patron's right hand over not in the manicure bowl. Brush in a downward movement to clean the nails and fingers of excess cream, oil and other substances.

19. Repeat the same procedure for the left hand. Start with the little finger. Dry the hands carefully and recheck the nails for any flaws.

20. Remove any bits of cuticle remaining and eliminate possible rough spots on the free edge by using light strokes with the fine side of the emery board. This technique also helps to give the nails a smooth beveled edge.

21. Buff (dry polish powder or paste) the fingernails or apply clear liquid nail enamel.

Review questions

1. Why were cosmetologists more successful than barbers when cutting men's hair during the early 1970s?

2. Is the procedure for cutting men's hair different from the procedure for cutting women's hair?

3. Are sideburns an important feature of men's hairstyling?

4. Why is perming recommended for men?

5. When cutting men's hair, must the length of the section behind the ears blend with the back and side areas?

6. Is the procedure for perming men's hair different from the procedure used to perm women's hair?

7. When should large diameter permanent wave rods be used for perming men's hair?

8. When is it advisable to use smaller diameter perm rods for perming men's hair?

9. Is there any difference between the physical or chemical actions of perming men's and women's hair?

10. Name some of the services which the cosmetologist offers male patrons.

11. Is men's hair coloring limited to covering gray hair?

12. Which is more aging: a gray mustache and/or beard or gray hair?

13. Why do men who do not have gray hair color their hair?

14. What benefits does coloring hair give men?

Superfluous hair

Superfluous hair: Unwanted hair on the face, legs and arms.

Overview: This chapter provides you with the information, knowledge and skill necessary for treating the problem of superfluous hair.

Behavioral objectives—student goals: After completion of this chapter, and after instruction, study and practice, you will be able to perform and demonstrate competency in treating superfluous hair by demonstrating the application and procedure for: removing superfluous hair with a wax depilatory and lightening the color of the hair with a hair lightening preparation. You will also be able to demonstrate competency by identifying, explaining and/or listing: the types of treatment for superfluous hair, the general procedure for electrocoagulation, the procedure for inserting an electrolysis needle and general information about the electronic tweezer.

Thousands of women devote much of their time and money to the treatment and removal of unwanted hair on the face, legs and arms. The professional cosmetologist should have the knowledge and skill necessary for treating the problem of superfluous hair. What to do about superfluous hair is one of the most common problems brought to cosmetologists everywhere. Every well-trained cosmetologist should know the best methods of treatment for the various forms of this condition, and every beauty salon should be equipped to remove unwanted hair. The scientific name for excess hair is hypertrichosis. Other terms used to describe excessive hair are:

Hirsute: Hairy, having coarse long hair, shaggy.

Hirsuties: Growth of an unusual amount of hair in unusual locations, e.g., on the faces of women or the backs of men.

Hirsutism: Excessive growth or abnormal distribution of hair.

There are two types of treatment for superfluous hair:

1. Lighten the hairs by bleaching

2. Remove the hairs

Superfluous hair

The simplest treatment for superfluous hair is lightening it by bleaching. This should be recommended only if the offending hairs are merely an excess growth of the slightly pigmented hair on the face, arms and legs.

There are two methods of hair removal, one temporary and the other permanent.

1. Temporary: Repeated treatments are necessary as new hair grows.

2. Permanent: The papilla is dissolved, and there is no regrowth.

There are two methods for removing hair temporarily:

1. Depilation: The process of removing hair at or near the level of the skin. Examples are:

    A. Shaving

    B. Rubbing the hair off with abrasives

    C. Chemical depilation

2. Epilation: The process of removing hair by breaking its contact with the papilla and pulling it out of the skin. Examples are:

    A. Tweezing

    B. Wax depilatories

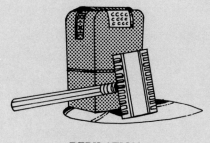

DEPILATION

Superfluous hair

350

The permanent method of removing superfluous hair is called electrology. There are three methods:

1. Electrocoagulation

2. Electrolysis

3. Electronic tweezer

Electrocoagulation is the single needle method, a process of dissolving tissues by means of the heat of high frequency currents. It requires only one needle, and the patron is not part of the circuit.

Electrolysis is the multiple needle method. This is the process of dissolving tissues by means of the chemical action of galvanic current. The patron is part of the circuit.

The electronic tweezer uses the same short wave radio frequencies as electrolysis. It glides the waves along the hair shaft to the papilla and destroys it.

Sanitary and safety precautions for superfluous hair

1. Always read the manufacturer's instructions when using products that remove superfluous hair.

2. Always apply an antiseptic solution to the areas in which superfluous hair has been removed.

3. Do not treat areas with signs of abrasions, inflammation, eruptions, cuts or infection.

4. Do not remove hairs from the nostrils, eyelids and ears.

5. Do not use depilatories on hairs growing from moles or warts.

Unit 1
Lightening hair by bleaching

Lighten the hair by using a mixture of prepared oil bleach and two parts of peroxide. Apply the mixture with a hair coloring brush or a large swab. Cover all the hair thoroughly. Repeat the application so that the hair is continuously wet until it has been lightened completely. The time varies from 15 minutes to one hour depending on the pigment and the texture of the hair. Dark pigment and coarse hair require more time. The hair lightening treatment is most effective on lanugo hair. This type of hair is softer and lighter than other types. Bleaching treatments may be continued as long as the results are satisfactory.

Unit 1
Lightening hair by bleaching

General objectives-student goals:
After study, instruction and completion of this unit, you will be able to demonstrate understanding of lightening superfluous hair with a hair lightener by writing and/or giving a brief overview of the subject.

Superfluous hair

Unit 2
Depilation

General objectives-student goals:
After study, instruction and completion of this unit, you will be able to demonstrate understanding of three depilation treatments by writing and/or giving a brief overview of the subject.

Unit 3
Epilation

General objectives-student goals:
After study, instruction, practice and completion of this unit, you will be able to show understanding of epilation by writing and/or giving a brief overview of tweezing superfluous hair and by demonstrating the procedure for the application of wax depilatories. You must have the proper implements and supplies in order to complete this unit successfully.

> **Superfluous hair**

352

Unit 2
Depilation

Depilation is recommended when the offending hairs cover a large area, when the skin is extremely delicate and when the patron is sensitive to pain or discomfort.

1. **Shaving:** Wash the area. Apply shaving cream. Use a safety razor with a sharp blade. With an electric razor, use a preelectric shave lotion to keep the skin dry during the operation.

2. **Abrasives** may be in the form of a block, powder or glove. They are used to rub the hair shaft above the skin level away. This method of hair removal is not popular and is not practiced in beauty salons today.

3. **Chemical depilatories** are available in cream or paste form. Their use is usually limited to the arms and legs. A skin test is recommended when treating the face or any area where the skin may be sensitive. Always follow the manufacturer's instructions.

Unit 3
Epilation

Epilation is recommended when the patron does not mind its discomfort and does not have sensitive skin. Hairs which are pulled out take longer to appear again and do not form stubble.

A. **Tweezing** is recommended whenever the offending hairs are few in number or scattered over a clear area. It is also satisfactory for eyebrow shaping. The hairs in the nostrils and on the eyelids and ears should never be plucked because of the danger of infection. For complete comfort during a tweezing operation, the use of special products with an analgesic effect is recommended.

B. **Wax depilatories** are used successfully over large areas including the face, armpits, back, arms and legs.

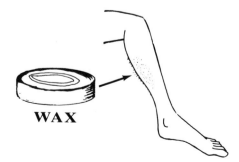

WAX

Procedure for wax depilatories

1. Melt the wax on a stove or hot plate.

2. Wash the skin area to be treated.

3. Dust the skin area with talcum powder.

4. Test the temperature and consistency of the heated wax by applying a little of it to the inner side of your wrist.

5. Apply the melted wax with a spatula or brush. Spread it over the skin in the same direction as the hair growth.

6. Permit the wax to cool and harden.

7. Draw the skin tight and pull the wax off quickly. Pull against the direction of the hair growth.

8. Apply an antiseptic lotion to the area treated.

Note: When extra large areas are to be treated, it may be more convenient to apply the wax in 2 inch (5.08 cm.) wide strips rather than in one large patch.

Unit 4
Electrology

Electrology is the professional practice of using electricity to remove hair permanently.

Electrocoagulation

Electrocoagulation employs the heat of high frequency current to destroy tissues. It requires only one needle. Always follow the manufacturer's instructions.

General procedure for electrocoagulation

1. Sanitize the tweezer, needle and skin area.

2. Observe the angle of the hair follicle carefully. Insert the needle at the same angle. The depth of insertion will vary according to the coarseness of the hair. It will usually be from $1/8$ to $1/4$ of an inch (0.32 to 0.64 cm.). The needle does not touch the papilla.

3. Apply the current.

General objectives-student goals: After study, instruction and completion of this unit, you will be able to demonstrate understanding of electrology by writing and/or giving a brief overview of electrocoagulation, electrolysis and the electronic tweezer.

Superfluous hair

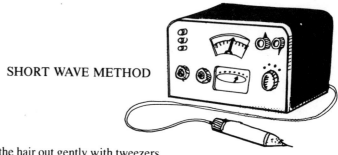

SHORT WAVE METHOD

4. Remove the needle and lift the hair out gently with tweezers.

   Note: If the hair does not slide out easily, repeat the procedure a second time or as often as required.

5. Sponge the area with antiseptic and apply medicated foundation or antiseptic powder.

Electrolysis

Electrolysis is the multiple needle method developed in 1916. It is not in much use today. The patron immerses four fingers of one hand into an electrode cup filled with water. Needles are inserted one at a time, starting with the needle farthest from you. Insert the needle to the papilla until you meet slight resistance. The current is increased with each needle insertion. Some machines have 10 needles. When the last needle is inserted, the first needle is ready for removal. Lift the needle out and remove the hair without pulling it. Most hair will lift out easily but a second insertion may be necessary if the hair does not slide out. Occasionally, a hair will not respond even after a second insertion. In this case, remove the hair forcibly with a tweezer and repeat the procedure again at the next treatment.

Procedure for inserting a needle

1. Grasp the needle holder with the thumb and index finger of your right hand.

2. Stretch the skin around the hair to be removed with the thumb and middle finger of your left hand.

3. Hold the needle lightly and slide it into the opening of the hair follicle at the same angle as the hair grows.

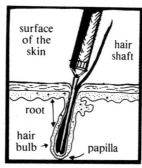

surface
of the
skin

hair
shaft

root

hair
bulb

papilla

needle inserted
correctly destroys
papilla...
eliminates regrowth...

incorrectly inserted
needle does not
affect papilla
and hair will
regrow...

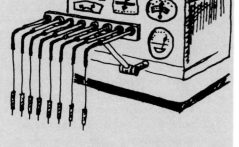

GALVANIC METHOD

Superfluous hair

354

Note: Insertions during an electrocoagulation treatment are made in the same manner as electrolysis insertions. However, they are not as deep. During the electrolysis insertions, the needle touches the papilla. The depth of the insertion with electrocoagulation varies according to the coarseness of the hair. It is usually $^1/_8$-$^1/_4$ inch (0.32-0.64 cm.).

The electronic tweezer

The electronic tweezer is an epilator which removes superfluous hair by means of high frequency current. The skin tissue is not affected because there is no contact with it.

The electronic tweezer, which uses the same short wave radio frequencies as electrolysis does, glides the waves along the hair shaft to the papilla. This destroys it. When the papilla is destroyed, the hair it nourished will never grow again. All methods of permanent hair removal destroy the papilla. If, however, the papilla is not completely destroyed, regrowth may begin to appear in about eight weeks. Although the electronic tweezer is the most comfortable method of permanent hair removal, it can be used only when there is enough hair above the surface of the skin for tweezing.

The fast intense internal heat destroys the papilla. The current reaches the papilla through a wire. Radio frequency energy plus the moisture of the hair make up the heat process which ultimately dries up the papilla.

Procedure for the electronic tweezer

1. Clean the area to be treated.

2. Use the electronic tweezer to grasp a superfluous hair close to the skin. Do not touch the skin.

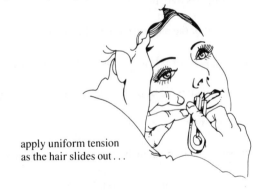

apply uniform tension
as the hair slides out . . .

3. Gently lift the hair up and back in order to open the follicle. Then, return to the original position.

4. Apply current by means of a foot switch. Keep the current on until the hair slides out.

5. Remove your foot from the foot switch.

6. Continue this procedure until the treatment has been completed.

7. Apply a soothing lotion.

There is no irritation to the skin and no swelling or scabs. The patron may use make-up and treat the face area normally without side effects.

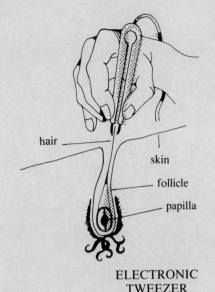

hair

skin

follicle

papilla

ELECTRONIC TWEEZER

Superfluous hair

355

1. Is it important for a cosmetologist to acquire the knowledge and skill required for the removal of superfluous hair?

2. What are the most common areas of the body which require treatment for unwanted hair?

3. Name the two treatments for superfluous hair.

4. Why is there no regrowth of hair with a permanent hair removal method?

5. Name the two methods of temporary hair removal.

6. What is the depilation method of hair removal?

7. Give three examples of depilation.

8. Is the patron part of the electric circuit when you remove hair with the single needle method?

9. What type of applicator is best for applying a bleaching mixture to superfluous hair on the face, arms or legs?

10. Can chemical depilatories be used on the face, arms and legs?

11. Why is epilation more effective than depilation for the removal of superfluous hair?

12. Should the superfluous hairs in the nostrils and ears be plucked with tweezers?

13. Can wax depilatories be used successfully for removing superfluous hair?

14. Can a melted wax depilatory be removed while it is still warm?

15. Should a melted wax depilatory be removed in the direction of the hair growth?

16. What is electrocoagulation?

17. What is the usual depth of the needle insertion when using electrocoagulation for the removal of superfluous hair?

18. Does the electrocoagulation needle touch the papilla during the removal of superfluous hair?

Cosmetic dermatology of the skin, scalp and hair

Cosmetic dermatology of the skin, scalp and hair: This is an area of dermatology which treats healthy skin, its appendages and the correction of minor conditions and diseases.

Overview: This chapter provides you with data about certain disorders of the skin, scalp and hair. This information will teach you to recognize disorders which may be treated by the cosmetologist.

Behavioral objectives-student goals: After completion of this chapter, and after instruction and study, you will be able to perform and demonstrate competency in cosmetic dermatology of the skin, scalp and hair by identifying, explaining and/or listing detailed information concerning the following areas: classes of skin diseases, common terms, lesions of the skin, pigments and growth of the skin, dandruff, common diseases, disorders and allergies.

Cosmetic dermatology is a division of dermatology which treats healthy skin, its appendages and the correction of conditions and minor diseases.

Since the skin, hair and nails are the principal areas with which the cosmetologist deals, it is important to know the simple facts about the disorders which may be encountered. In addition to recognizing certain hair, scalp and skin conditions, the cosmetologist should know what procedures to follow when treating a specific condition. Any condition which the cosmetologist does not recognize or is not permitted to treat should be referred to a medical doctor. To protect the health of the cosmetologist and the public, patrons with contagious skin diseases or infections should not be serviced in the beauty salon until the condition has cleared.

Physicians who specialize in the treatment of various skin conditions are called dermatologists. Every physician makes a study of skin during training. However, a dermatologist makes an intensive study of the skin and the treatment of its diseases.

The purpose of all cosmetic dermatology treatments is the improvement of appearance. This goal is realized by treatments for prevention and treatments for correction. Experienced cosmetologists know that the diagnosis of pathological conditions and the prescription of remedies are beyond their province. They practice only what comes within the limits of the practice of cosmetology.

Cosmetic dermatology of the skin, scalp and hair

Sanitary and safety precautions for cosmetic dermatology of the skin, scalp and hair

1. Always use sanitary precautions when making an analysis and diagnosis of diseases and disorders of the skin and hair.

2. Never treat skin or hair conditions which are outside the province of a cosmetologist.

3. Never prescribe remedies which are outside your province.

4. Never prescribe or give treatments for conditions which are not readily recognizable as one of the common cosmetic conditions which come within the practice of a cosmetologist.

5. Always refer unrecognizable conditions to a competent physician.

Unit 1
Classes and causes of skin disease

Classes of skin disease

1. Diseases of the skin proper

2. Diseases of the appendages

    A. Disorders of the glands

    B. Diseases of the hair

    C. Disorders of the nails

Causes of skin disease

Diseases of the skin and its appendages are traceable to three basic causes:

1. Influences on the external cells of the skin

2. Influences on the nerves

3. Influences on the nutrient fluids (blood or lymph) and metabolism

---

General objectives-student goals:
After study, instruction and completion of this unit, you will be able to demonstrate understanding of the classes and causes of diseases by writing and/or giving a brief overview of the subject.

Cosmetic dermatology of the skin, scalp and hair

The causes of skin diseases can be direct or predisposing. The direct causes are easily identified as:

1. Actinic from rays of heat, light, X-ray

2. Bacteriological from fungus growths

3. Chemical from acids, alkalies, poisons

4. Mechanical from rubbing or scratching

5. Parasitic from insect parasites

The predisposing causes of skin disease lie in some inherited tendency in the individual or possibly in some peculiar set of conditions within the organism. Because of the important relationship between this condition and the use of cosmetic preparations and treatments, cosmetologists should learn all they possibly can about allergy as it relates to their work.

Unit 2
Allergy

Allergy is a condition characterized by extreme sensitivity to certain substances which do not affect the average person adversely. Unfavorable reaction to the offending substance shows up as an irritation of the skin or mucous membranes.

Substances that cause an unfavorable reaction of the skin or membranes are called allergenic substances or allergens. Individuals are said to be allergic to, have an idiosyncrasy toward, or be predisposed to the offending substances. Cosmetologists should learn these terms and know how to use them.

There are two types of allergies. An allergy of a kind is caused by certain substances when they are applied to the skin, hair or nails. They may cause reactions such as redness, itching, swelling, burning, small water blisters and watering of the eyes and nose. Allergic reactions can be prevented by giving the patron a predisposition test with the cosmetic products to be used. An allergy of a degree is caused by excessiveness: too much of anything.

Some persons are susceptible to only one substance, food, chemical or drug while others are affected by several substances which may or may not be related to one another.

Unit 3
Definition of common terms

Words that relate to the practice of cosmetology and are used commonly in the language of dermatology should be understood and used correctly by cosmetologists. Some of them are:

Unit 2
Allergy

General objectives-student goals:
After study, instruction and completion of this unit, you will be able to demonstrate understanding of allergy by writing and/or giving a brief overview of the subject.

Unit 3
Definition of common terms

General objectives-student goals:
After study, instruction and comple-

Cosmetic dermatology of
the skin, scalp and hair

359

tion of this unit, you will be able to demonstrate understanding of the definition of common terms by writing and/or giving a brief overview of the subject.

Unit 4
Lesions of the skin

General objectives-student goals:
After study, instruction and completion of this unit, you will be able to demonstrate understanding of lesions of the skin by writing and/or giving a brief overview of the subject.

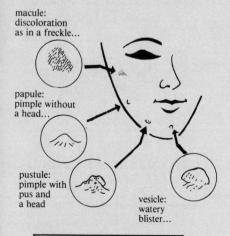

macule:
discoloration
as in a freckle...

papule:
pimple without
a head...

pustule:
pimple with
pus and
a head

vesicle:
watery
blister...

Cosmetic dermatology of the skin, scalp and hair

Dermatitis: Any inflammation of the skin.

Dermatosis: Any specific disease or condition of the skin.

Inflammation: A process common to many diseases and conditions of the skin. It shows itself in redness, eruption on the skin surface and inner swelling (edema).

Erythema: This is a redness of the skin which disappears under pressure and returns when the pressure is removed.

Hyperemia: This is redness of the skin because of an excessive rush of blood to the area.

Symptom: This is a sign of disease and helps identify it. Symptoms may be:

    1. **Subjective:** These can be felt only by the person experiencing them.

    2. **Objective:** These can be seen or felt by both the person experiencing them and others.

    3. A combination of both.

Unit 4
Lesions of the skin

Lesions are important in the diagnosis of skin disease. Their existence often allows a disease to be discovered and identified. To simplify classification, lesions are grouped as:

    1. Primary

    2. Secondary

Primary lesions are those seen in the early stages of an abnormal condition. These are:

    Macule: A spot or discoloration level with the skin, such as freckles.

    Papule: A small solid elevated spot in the skin, such as a pimple without a head.

    Pustule: An elevated spot in the skin containing pus, such as a pimple with a head.

    Vesicle: A small elevated spot in the skin containing watery fluid, such as a blister.

    Bulla: This is the same as but larger than a vesicle.

Nodule: This is the same as but larger than a papule.

Wheal: A temporary itchy swollen lesion, such as hives or an insect bite.

Tumor: This is the same as but larger than a nodule.

Secondary lesions are marks in the skin which develop in the later stages of a disease. These are:

Scale: A horny layer of epidermis of any size, such as dandruff.

Crust: A dried mass of substance which forms a covering for an area of skin.

Excoriation: This is also called a scratch, a raw spot on the skin produced by scraping or scratching. It heals without a scar.

Scar: Scar tissue is the result of an injury or skin condition which has penetrated the dermal layer.

Fissure: A split in the skin penetrating into the derma, such as chapped lips.

Ulcer: An open sore of the skin with a loss of skin depth. It may or may not contain pus.

Cicatrix: This is a mass of fibrous tissue which has grown in order to replace lost skin. It remains as a permanent disfigurement, such as a burn, ulcer or deep cut.

Stain: An abnormal permanent discoloration in the skin because of certain conditions, diseases or a birthmark.

Unit 5
Common terms applied to skin disease

Skin disease: An infection of the skin.

Chronic disease: A disease of long duration.

Acute disease: A disease of short duration.

Contagious disease: A disease which is communicable from one person to another.

Congenital disease: A disease which is present at birth.

Infectious disease: A disease caused by a pathogenic microorganism taken into the body.

Unit 5
Common terms applied to skin disease

General objectives-student goals: After study, instruction and completion of this unit, you will be able to demonstrate understanding of the common terms applied to skin disease by writing and/or giving a brief overview of the subject.

> **Cosmetic dermatology of the skin, scalp and hair**

361

Parasitic disease: A disease caused by parasites, such as pediculosis or ringworm. There are two types of parasites: vegetable and animal. Ringworm owes its origin to vegetable parasites.

Epidemic: This is when a disease or condition attacks great numbers of people in a particular locality.

Unit 6
Pigment anomalies and growths

Pigment anomalies and growths are conditions such as freckles, moles, warts, birthmarks and other discolorations of the skin. Most of these anomalous conditions are simple disorders which do not denote any serious pathological condition. Others may be signs of serious diseases. The cosmetologist, therefore, should know how to distinguish them.

Lentigo: The little spots called freckles owe their origin to uneven distribution of melanin in the skin. Freckles occur mostly in persons with light complexions. They are part of the protective mechanism of the skin. They are brought out by exposure to sunlight. The process is similar to tanning except that the development of the pigment is not even. The cause of freckles is not completely known. It has been suggested that freckles accumulate over the nerve endings in order to protect the nerves from strong light rays.

Freckles are more conspicuous during the summer months and may disappear entirely during the winter. They are likely to recur year after year.

The treatment of freckles includes the use of cosmetic make-up and bleaching. Since the pigment is in the skin at the base of the epidermis, there must be penetration of the outer layers of the skin in order to bleach freckles. Strong bleaches, which can penetrate the skin, can also injure it. Preventive measures are the best. Keep the face, arms and hands well shaded in order to avoid these skin blemishes.

Chloasma: This is also called moth patches or liver spots. It is increased deposits of pigment in the skin. They are similar to freckles but larger and darker in color. They generally occur on the face, neck and hands. They may be oval, round or irregular in shape. The cause of chloasma is unknown. There is no connection between the spots and any disorder of the liver. They are not malignant and are treated in the same manner as freckles.

Leucoderma is a condition in which the skin lacks pigment and shows irregular patches that may be completely white or lighter than the color of the surrounding skin. This condition is also known as vitiligo. It is the exact opposite of freckles and chloasma. The skin spots do not have the usual amount of pigment.

The cause of leucoderma is unknown. Corrective make-up affords temporary covering, and carefully implanted color by means of tattooing results in a more permanent color which is much less conspicuous than the white patches.

Naevi is a general term covering all types of birthmarks, such as:

1. Moles which are harmless growths and may consist of an accumulation of tissue which may or may not contain an excess of pigment and/or hair. Small moles are considered beauty spots.

Unit 6
Pigment anomalies and growths

General objectives-student goals:
After study, instruction and completion of this unit, you will be able to demonstrate understanding of pigment anomalies and growths by writing and/or giving a brief overview of the subject.

2. Stains which are reddish-purple irregular patches. They are sometimes called wine stains because of their characteristic color.

Stains owe their origin to some irregularity in the blood and vascular system. They may cover a large area of the face or neck. The dermatologist is the person best qualified to treat naevi. Moles are usually removed by using electrolysis or high frequency current. The cosmetologist does not treat moles. Deeply pigmented moles should never be touched.

There is no successful treatment for stains. The cosmetologist should not treat stains beyond the application of cosmetics which will make them less conspicuous.

Verruca (wart): These small growths are usually located on the face, neck and hands. They should cause no alarm since they frequently disappear as mysteriously as they came. The structure of a wart may be broad, round, flat or raised. It consists of a group of elongated papillae covered with a hardened epidermis.

The cause of warts is a filterable virus which is so small that it can pass through the pores of the finest filter paper. Warts are considered contagious. The treatment of warts includes cutting them off when possible, burning them with chemicals and drying the tissue by means of high frequency current (electrodesiccation). All these methods should be practiced by the physician, not by the cosmetologist.

Keratoma (callus): This is an acquired thickened patch of epidermis resulting from pressure and friction. Continued friction on the same spot will cause the formation of a callus which is likely to remain as a hardened spot for some time. The hardened callus formation on the toe, which is called a corn, is caused by the pressure of a shoe which is too tight, too short or too loose. Calluses are part of nature's automatic defense mechanism that protects the underlying tissues.

Unit 7
Inflammatory conditions of the skin

Most of the skin conditions brought to the attention of the cosmetologist are forms of simple inflammation accompanied by redness, swelling and/or scaly lesions. These symptoms help to identify the conditions. All the rules of sanitation and hygiene should be observed when examining the skin. Correct diagnosis is the foundation for successful treatment.

Dandruff

The medical term for dandruff is pityriasis. This is the most common disease of the skin which the cosmetologist sees.

Pityriasis is a common, widespread, contagious disorder of the scalp. It is characterized by the shedding of a large number of fine white scales from the epidermis. Severe cases of dandruff produce scabbing, itching, swelling and redness of the scalp. The possible causes of dandruff include: malfunction of the oil glands, scalp bacteria, a tight dry scalp or an imbalance of hormones.

Unit 7
Inflammatory conditions of the skin

General objectives-student goals: After study, instruction and completion of this unit, you will be able to demonstrate understanding of inflammatory conditions of the skin by writing and/or giving a brief overview of the subject.

Cosmetic dermatology of the skin, scalp and hair

OILY DANDRUFF:
is yellowish and
clings to the scalp...

**PITYRIASIS
STEATOIDES**

DRY DANDRUFF:
is white,
flaky and
loose...

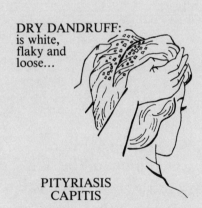

**PITYRIASIS
CAPITIS**

**Cosmetic dermatology of
the skin, scalp and hair**

Until medical authorities define the nature of dandruff clearly, you should treat it as any other contagious disorder. Cosmetologists and barbers who give hair and scalp treatments must maintain high standards of salon and shop hygiene in order to avoid the risk of transfer.

Dandruff is an undesirable and incurable disorder. Fortunately, it is controllable. Some of these techniques will be discussed later in this unit. Most dandruff problems improve with warm weather because people tend to wash their hair more often than in the cold months.

The results of several surveys indicate that 80 to 95% of all adults experience some degree of dandruff. This disorder has been observed in children as young as six years old. Dandruff is practically nonexistent after the age of seventy five. This disorder is more common among males than among females.

Pityriasis steatoides (oily dandruff) is characterized by yellowish scales which are larger than dry dandruff. The scales mix themselves with sebum. This causes them to stick to the scalp in patches and to cling to the hair. These scales are not easy to remove by means of simple brushing or shampooing. When you treat the scalp and remove the scales, you will notice that the epidermis of the scalp is reddened and inflamed. In most cases, oily dandruff is accompanied by considerable itching. This type of dandruff is more difficult to control than dry (common) dandruff

Pityriasis capitis simplex (dry dandruff) is characterized by small, white, powdery scales and an itchy scalp. These scales are attached to the scalp and hair loosely. They usually fall to the shoulders. Shampooing and regular hair brushing will help the scalp and hair appear cleaner and prevent build-up of an unsightly appearance.

In order to control dandruff, it is important to remove dandruff scales regularly. You must prevent a build-up of bacteria and fungi. Here are some techniques and basic facts to help you treat and control dandruff:

1. Brush and fine comb the hair. This procedure removes excess scales from the scalp and hair. Remember, you should treat the scalp with greater care than you would normally. Avoid irritating the healthy part of the scalp.

2. Shampoo the hair frequently. The use of nonprescription medicated and antiseptic shampoos is essential in order to destroy bacteria and microorganisms found in the scalp. These may be contributing to a dandruff disorder. Medications or shampoos containing sulfur-salicylic acid as an active ingredient are very effective. They gently peel the surface layers of the scalp and remove dandruff scales. Prescription shampoos are the most effective and should be used according to the physician's instructions.

3. Change brands of medicated shampoos occasionally. This is important because the hair may gradually become resistant to the active ingredients. This will make the shampoo ineffective.

4. When using medicated shampoos, give the hair an initial soaping and follow it with a second lathering. Leave the second lathering on the scalp and hair for a minimum of five minutes before rinsing.

5. The epidermis normally sheds scales on the body area and the scalp about every thirty days. This normal flaking is usually invisible because bathing and normal rubbing of the skin removes the scales. When a dandruff condition exists, the peeling increases considerably.

6. Concentrated or full strength medications used to treat the scalp or dissolve the flakes from the hair will also harm the scalp. This occurs because the epidermis and scales of the scalp are made of soft keratin. They are sensitive to various chemicals. The hair is made of hard keratin. It is not as sensitive as the scalp.

Psoriasis

Psoriasis is a common inflammatory skin disease which is chronic. The characteristic lesion of psoriasis is a whitish scaling of the skin mounted on well-defined red patches. The scales often appear imbricated. It is not contagious. The cause is not known, and there is no known cure. It is usually found on the scalp, elbows, knees, chest and lower back.

Eczema

Eczema is the most common of all the diseases of the skin. It is estimated to account for almost 40% of all skin conditions observed. The specific cause is unknown. The condition may be either acute or chronic. It is not contagious. It is recognized by its many forms of dry or moist lesions. Diagnosis is difficult and should be made by a physician.

Herpes simplex

Herpes simplex is a virus infection. It is commonly called fever blisters or cold sores. The blisters usually appear in the area of the lips or nostrils. The condition is contagious. The cause is unknown. The blisters usually disappear within one week.

Parasitic conditions

Pediculosis, commonly called lice, is a contagious condition caused by animal parasites infesting the hair of the scalp. A single application of a specially prepared preparation can cure this condition.

Scabies is a highly contagious skin disease. Vesicles and pustules may form because of the irritation of the parasites and because of scratching.

Tinea

Tinea is the disease known as ringworm. It is most commonly seen in the beauty salon as athlete's foot. It is a contagious and infectious disease of the skin caused by the invasion of a fungus (vegetable growth). In its early stages, ringworm appears as reddened patches of little blisters.

Cosmetic dermatology of the skin, scalp and hair

Unit 8
Disorders of the sebaceous glands

Unit 8
Disorders of the sebaceous glands

General objectives-student goals:
After study, instruction and completion of this unit, you will be able to demonstrate understanding of disorders of the oil glands by writing and/or giving a brief overview of the subject.

Seborrhea is a skin condition which owes its origin to overstimulation of the sebaceous glands. It is characterized by a shiny appearance and greasy feeling on the face. On the scalp, it is indicated by the unusual amount of oil on the hair.

Overstimulation of the sebaceous glands leads to the secretion of an excess amount of oil. Lack of tone in the muscles and poor elasticity of the skin around the hair follicles also causes this. These conditions allow the oil to ooze continuously. Many leading authorities believe that the indirect causes of seborrhea are digestion, elimination and diets high in fat content.

Comedones or **blackheads** are masses of hardened **sebum** which form tiny pointed plugs. They are found on the face, especially around the cheeks, nose and mouth. They are also seen down the chest and the middle of the back. They vary considerably in appearance. On the forehead and chin, the comedones may be raised slightly. Around the nose, the tops may be depressed. This gives the skin a pitted appearance. The most common form is that which is level with the skin. Comedones are removed with an extractor or by gentle pressure with the fingers.

Milia or **whiteheads** are a disorder caused by the accumulation of sebaceous matter beneath the skin. They may or may not occur with comedones. Milia are **tiny white** or **yellowish nodules**. They are found around the eyes, cheeks, lobes of the ears and across the forehead. They seem to be more prevalent in persons with dry skin who would normally not have comedones. The treatment of milia consists of pricking them with a sanitized pointed implement in order to release the hardened masses, and then contracting the tissues with an astringent.

Acne is an inflammatory condition of the sebaceous glands characterized by **papules, pustules** and **comedones**. Acne is one of the most common diseases that will be observed in the beauty salon. This condition affects millions of people of all ages and does not have a definite cause or cure. **Excessive oiliness** is one of the many factors responsible for the development of acne. The sebum secreted by the sebaceous glands and the moisture of the skin make up the acid mantle. Natural acidity protects against invading germs. If the mantle is not acidic enough, infection can come easily. **Deep cleansing** is the key factor for preventing or correcting acne.

Steatoma is also called a **wen** or a **sebaceous cyst**. They are smooth prominences which vary in size. Usually, a follicle is found where they occur. On the scalp, steatomas are usually hairless and rarely become malignant. However, because they are constantly exposed to the actions of a comb and brush, they should be removed by a physician.

Asteatosis is a condition characterized by an almost complete lack of oil in the skin. This condition is rare in persons who patronize beauty salons. It is associated with an **endocrine deficiency**. This condition should not be confused with dryness of normal skins. The latter respond readily to cosmetic treatments.

Cosmetic dermatology of the skin, scalp and hair

Unit 9
Disorders of the sudoriferous glands

The sudoriferous glands are also known as sweat glands. They collect toxins accumulated in the skin and eliminate them in the form of sweat. The amount and rate of sweating depend on the climate, physical exertion expended and the degree of an individual's nervous temperament.

Hyperhidrosis is a condition characterized by excessive perspiration. It is common in persons of nervous temperament. Although it is ordinarily confined to the forehead and armpits, excessive perspiration may cause the hands and feet to feel clammy. If the sweat is hyperacidic, it will discolor clothing. Astringent preparations and antiperspirants are helpful and effective.

Miliaria rubra, commonly known as prickly heat, usually occurs in warm weather on anyone who perspires profusely. It is an acute inflammatory disorder of the sweat glands. The affected surface always becomes inflamed and sometimes itches. It must be treated carefully in order to avoid infection from scratching. Anti-perspirants are used to prevent excessive perspiration, and fine powders are used to keep the skin dry.

Other sudoriferous conditions are: anidrosis, chromidrosis, hematidrosis, bromidrosis and uridrosis. These pathological conditions are considered rare and will probably never be seen by the cosmetologist.

Unit 10
Diseases and defects of the hair

A cosmetologist must be able to distinguish between healthy and unhealthy hair. The characteristics of unhealthy hair are:

1. Lack of sheen
2. Brittleness
3. Excessive oiliness
4. Excessive dryness
5. Excessive split ends
6. Abnormal shedding
7. Poor color
8. Excessive thinness

Hypertrichosis

Hypertrichosis is the presence of superfluous hair. It is the growth of hair on areas of the body normally bearing only downy hairs. The condition is most frequently associated with glandular disturbances and occurs in some women around the time of menopause. Superfluous hair can be removed by various physical and chemical treatments, such as epilation, depilation, electrolysis and electrocoagulation.

Unit 9
Disorders of the sudoriferous glands

General objectives-student goals:
After study, instruction and completion of this unit, you will be able to demonstrate understanding of sweat glands by writing and/or giving a brief overview of the subject.

Unit 10
Diseases and defects of the hair

General objectives-student goals:
After study, instruction and completion of this unit, you will be able to demonstrate understanding of diseases and defects of the hair by writing and/or giving a brief overview of the subject.

HYPERTRICHOSIS

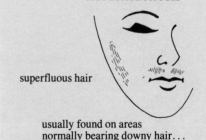

superfluous hair

usually found on areas
normally bearing downy hair...

Cosmetic dermatology of
the skin, scalp and hair

367

Alopecia

Alopecia (baldness) is generally characterized by the lack of hair follicles. There are many forms and causes of alopecia. Some of the factors known to cause this condition are:

1. Heredity (excessive male hormones)
2. Infections
3. Systemic diseases
4. Medications
5. Mechanical stress
6. Radiation

Male pattern baldness is the result of heredity. It owes its origin to an excessive supply of male hormones or at least a lack of female hormones. Because the female hormone normally predominates, most women will not suffer permanent hair loss.

Infections which cause hair loss can be fungal, bacterial (staphylococcal, streptococcal), viral (herpes zoster) or ringworms. Early diagnosis and treatment are important for preventing permanent hair loss.

Systemic diseases which may lead to baldness include allergies to drugs, advanced diabetes, influenza, scarlet fever, syphilis, pituitary disorders, leukemia and cancer. Drugs or chemicals with toxic effects can also cause hair loss. Permanent loss of hair has occurred after accidental ingestion of insecticides. Temporary loss (breakage) has occurred when chemicals such as hair lighteners, straighteners or cold wave lotions were used improperly.

Medications which may cause alopecia are: chemotherapy, penicillin, sleeping pills, birth control pills, blood pressure pills and excessive use of aspirins. Mechanical stress is a cause of temporary hair loss. Securing rollers too tightly, barrettes, bobby pins, braids and a tight ponytail are some of the things which can pull hair from the scalp. Radiation from atomic accidents, explosions, radium, X-rays and radioisotopes can cause either temporary or permanent baldness.

Some causes of baldness are still unknown. One morning you can awaken and find one or more circular bald spots. The name for this particular type of baldness is alopecia areata. In this case, hair will usually regrow spontaneously without any treatment.

Alopecia prematura is a form of baldness which begins at any age. It is a slow thinning process. The hairs fall out and are replaced by a regrowth of successively weaker hairs until even these are gone.

Alopecia congenita is total absence of hair at birth. This may be because of some defect in the structure of the hair follicles.

Alopecia senilis is the form of baldness which develops after middle life.

Canities

Canities is the term used to describe gray hair. The immediate cause is the loss of natural pigment in the hair. Canities may be congenital or acquired. When it is congenital, it exists before birth. Acquired canities may owe its origin to either old age or prematurity if it develops in early adult life. It may also be the result of nervous shock or some serious illness.

Another condition is called **accidental canities**. Hair can suddenly turn white overnight. Many cases of this condition have been documented over the past 40 years. However, there is no scientific proof that the condition exists. It is difficult to understand how the entire length of hair can suddenly lose all its pigment within hours. Several reasonable explanations exist. Two of them are:

1. Air bubbles enter the normal pigmented hair. The hair appears white because the air bubbles reflect light. This phenomenon has been observed through the microscope.

2. Individuals with natural dark hair mixed with white hair can, for some medical reason, quickly lose large amounts of the hair which contains the natural color. The remaining white hairs create the illusion that all the hairs turned white overnight. People may not notice the actual hair loss. Some recognized and accepted causes for this type of hair loss are:

    A. Mental stress

    B. Fright

    C. Excitement

    D. Acute illness

Scientists, who have researched the disorder of white hair, agree that pigmented hair can lose all of its melanin within a few months but not within a few hours. A large number of follicles that had produced hair with melanin suddenly develop unpigmented gray or white hairs.

Albinism is the hereditary lack of melanin in the hair, skin or eyes. As a result, albinos have light yellow hair, pale skin and colorless or pink eyes. The condition is caused by the lack of the enzyme which produces melanin. There is no cure for this disorder. Albinos may receive the same hair treatments given to patrons whose pigmentation is normal.

Trichoptilosis

Trichoptilosis (split ends) is the number one hair problem. This disorder develops at the end of a hair fiber. It is characterized by: jagged edges of the cuticle, slightly lifted scales and tiny cracks in the fiber. The splitting of a hair end is rapid when the cuticle layer has been removed completely. As the splitting progresses, it widens and becomes visible on the hair. Split ends result from worn-out hair. Normal grooming can cause this disorder. The end of the hair fiber is the oldest part of the hair and endures a considerable amount of physical and abrasive wear on its surface. Long hair can rub against the back of a chair and develop split ends faster than short hair. Its stronger bounce and movement while walking and in the wind can also cause the ends to split.

The best method to eliminate split ends is cutting. Be sure to use well-sharpened scissors because dull scissors can cause split ends. A special haircutting technique can remove all split ends without shortening the length of the hair. Tinting the hair can hide split ends. Special products designed to repair split ends produce only temporary results. There is no cure for split ends. The best way to handle the problem is to prevent it.

TRICHOPTILOSIS
(Split Ends)

Cosmetic dermatology of
the skin, scalp and hair

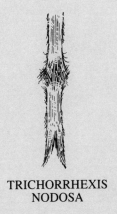

**TRICHORRHEXIS
NODOSA**

Trichorrhexis nodosa

Trichorrhexis nodosa is a rare disorder of the hair. It is characterized by nodular swellings emerging along the hair shaft. The nodes are usually found near the ends of the hair, around the upper third portion of its length. The hair is exceedingly brittle. It breaks spontaneously or when combed. The hair usually breaks through one of the nodes. This results in a peculiar brush-like spread of the hair fibers from the broken hair.

You can observe this disorder by pulling the hair through your fingertips. The hair will either feel irregular and knotty or it will break easily through the node and look ragged. If you examine the hair shaft under a microscope, you will find one or more whitish, shiny, transparent nodular swellings covering the circumference of the hair. There are usually one to five nodes on a single hair.

The single cause of this disorder has not been firmly established. Some of the popular beliefs regarding the cause of trichorrhexis nodosa are:

1. An accumulation of gas within the hair

2. A fatty infiltration of the medulla at certain points

3. Nutritional disturbance

4. Degeneration of the medulla

5. Swelling of the cells of the medulla

This disorder can be eliminated by long continued treatment. Treatment consists of stimulating the scalp with massage, ointments and/or solutions and lubricating the hair.

Fragilitas crinium

Fragilitas crinium refers to brittle hair which may split easily anywhere along the hair length. Extreme brittleness of the hair is usually traceable to careless treatment or neglect. The use of strong alkaline soaps, lotions, and many other hair preparations and chemical treatments may make the hair brittle. The damage to the hair shaft has no effect on the new growth. Correcting the cause will prevent the recurrence of brittleness.

1. What is cosmetic dermatology?

2. What is allergy?

3. Can a cosmetologist treat an individual who has an allergy?

4. Define the term acute disease.

5. What kind of skin condition is lentigo?

6. What is the medical term for dandruff?

7. Is dandruff contagious?

8. Is psoriasis an acute skin disease?

9. Is it possible to perm, tint, lighten or chemically straighten the hair of a patron who has severe psoriasis of the scalp?

10. What is the most common of all skin diseases?

11. What is pediculosis?

12. Is athlete's foot a form of ringworm?

13. Is tinea contagious?

14. What are the characteristics of comedones?

15. What are the characteristics of alopecia areata?

16. What is the term for gray hair?

17. Is canities acquired only because of old age, prematurity, nervous shock or some serious illness?

18. To what does the term trichoptilosis refer?

Cosmetic dermatology of
the skin, scalp and hair

Histology

Histology: This is the study of the minute anatomical structures which are beyond the reach of the naked eye.

Overview: This chapter introduces you to a branch of science which provides information concerning anatomical structures capable of being seen only with the aid of lenses.

Behavioral objectives-student goals: After completion of this chapter, and after instruction and study, you will be able to perform and demonstrate competency and understanding of histology by identifying, explaining and/or listing the fundamental information about cells, skin, glands of the skin and nails.

Histology is the study of the minute anatomical structures which are beyond the reach of the naked eye and can be seen only with the aid of lenses. It is sometimes called microanatomy. The study clarifies the structure and activities of cells as well as their arrangement in tissues.

The treatment of cells, skin, glands of the skin and nails in this chapter is a study of histology as it relates to the cosmetologist. This subject has been treated in a concise, comprehensive manner without unnecessary technical terms. The cosmetologist is expected to have only a fundamental knowledge of this subject.

Unit 1
Cells

A cell is a microscopic unit of a living substance called protoplasm. It is known that a cell contains a large number of specialized macromolecular structures which bring about the chemical reactions required for the cell to exhibit the properties of life.

The cosmetologist's knowledge of cells is important if his or her practice includes esthetics and scalp treatments because cells are the foundation of all living structure. Every part of the human body is composed of cells.

A cell is a structural unit of living substance. Although cellular activity may take place at a normal pace in healthy skin, the cosmetologist can increase the activity with proper treatment. Sluggish cells may require more frequent treatment and deep stimulation.

Unit 1
Cells

General objectives-student goals: After study, instruction and completion of this unit, you will be able to demonstrate understanding of cells by writing and/or giving a brief overview of the subject.

$\boxed{\text{Histology}}$

A cell repairs and produces tissue. Except for nerve cells, almost all body cells are capable of self-repair after injury. Only an existing cell can produce another cell. Cells grow by absorbing the surrounding tissue fluid and lymph.

The most noticeable structure within a cell is the functional center called the nucleus. It is the life producing part of a cell. The nucleus participates in cell reproduction. The nucleolus is a small spherical body within the cell nucleus. The substance which surrounds the nucleus is called cytoplasm. Cytoplasm contains the essentials for self-repair, growth and reproduction.

Constant cell reproduction is required in order to keep tissue healthy. Mitosis is the process of human cell reproduction. A cell divides in half and becomes two separate cells during the indirect cell division process.

Cell shapes can be elongated, flat, round or cubical. Their size ranges from 1/3000 to 1/300 of an inch (0.0085 to 0.085 mm.) in diameter. The mean is probably somewhere between these two measurements.

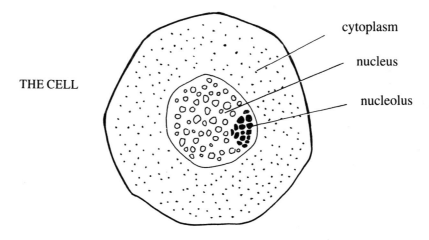

THE CELL

cytoplasm

nucleus

nucleolus

The cosmetologist can stimulate cellular activity:

1. By massaging. Cells are exceedingly responsive to the external stimulus of facial massage movements and scalp manipulations.

2. With heat applications from infrared lamps or heating caps.

3. By using high frequency current when deep stimulation is required.

All treatments which increase cellular activity should be concluded with cold applications (towels in iced water) and the application of an astringent.

Histology

Physiological properties

Some cells become specialized and perform one kind of function. Other cells perform other functions. Some physiological properties of cells are:

Respiration: Cells absorb oxygen which is used to bring about the oxidation of food substances in order to provide energy.

Growth: Growth is attained by cells staying about the same size and multiplying in numbers instead of becoming larger. Cells become inefficient if they exceed a certain size.

Irritability: Cells are sensitive to certain stimuli, e.g., massage, light, chemicals and electric current. Irritability is at its highest state of development in nerve cells.

Absorption and assimilation: Cells take in and utilize food and other substances from their surface. Cells are active in the process of nutrition. This follows digestion and occurs after absorption.

Contractility: The structural components within muscle cells are manifested by a cell shortening in response to a stimulus. Contraction is because of thin filaments sliding between thick filaments and interlocking. There is no contraction in relaxed muscles.

Secretion: Substances which certain cells absorb can synthesize new substances and deliver these through their surrounding membranes as useful secretions which have specific functions elsewhere.

Excretion: All cells can rid themselves of waste that results from utilizing food and oxygen.

Circulation: This is the flowing of protoplasm within the cell. By this means, nutritive material and oxygen may be distributed gradually to all parts of the protoplasm, and waste substances are gradually brought to the surface for elimination.

Cell division: In all living organisms, each cell grows and produces other cells. Since the cells of the body are constantly wearing out and leaving the body in the excretions, the need for constant reproduction of cells is apparent. Cells usually divide by indirect cell division (mitosis). The new cell is like the parent cell except in size. Some cells are thought to divide directly (amitosis). In direct division, the cell elongates, the nucleus and cytoplasm become constricted in the center, and the cell divides, forming two cells which grow to the size of the original cell.

Tissue fluid

All cells lie in a liquid environment known as tissue fluid. This fluid is only the medium of exchange between blood plasma and the cells. Substances needed by cells for maintenance, growth and repair diffuse from the plasma to the tissue fluid and then to the cell.

MITOSIS

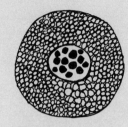

Diagram of Cell

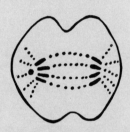

Cell Beginning to Divide

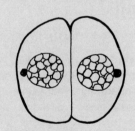

Cell Division Completed

Histology

Tissue fluid derives from the plasma of the blood. It is formed by the process of diffusion and filtration. Its composition is similar to that of blood plasma. Because of the varying needs and wastes of different tissues, the tissue fluid must vary in composition in different parts of the body.

The tissue fluid bathes all cells of the body. It delivers the material needed to maintain functional activity. It picks up and returns the products of this activity to the blood. This interchange is effected by means of diffusion.

Blood cells

Blood cells are not attached to each other or to any other kind of cells. When they enter the blood stream, they are suspended by and carried along in blood plasma. Plasma is the fluid portion of the blood. There are two types of blood cells: red and white. Red cells are called erythrocytes. White cells are called leukocytes. Red cells perform their function while they are in the blood. Most white cells perform their function only when they leave the blood and enter the loose connective or other tissues of the body.

Epithelial tissue

The cells which form epithelial tissue create a protective covering for the outer surface of the body and for the linings of many internal parts. This tissue also absorbs, e.g., in the lungs and intestines. It secretes, e.g., in the glands, and excretes, e.g., in the kidneys and liver.

Unit 2
Skin

The skin is a loose elastic outer covering of the body. It is an organ and consists of groups of cells and tissues. It is the largest organ of the whole body. It has an estimated area of about 20 square feet (1.85 m.^{2}), and weighs about six pounds (2.72 kg.). The appendages of the skin include the hair, nails, sweat and oil glands. Thick skin is found on the palms of the hands, the soles of the feet, the knees and elbows. Thin skin covers the rest of the body. Thick skin has a thick layer of keratin on its outer surface, and thin skin has a relatively thin layer of keratin. The distribution of skin over the total body surface area is approximately as follows:

Head and neck	10%
Anterior trunk	18%
Posterior trunk	18%
Upper extremities ($9\% \times 2$)	18%
Lower extremities ($18\% \times 2$)	36%
Total	100%

Unit 2
Skin

General objectives-student goals:
After study, instruction and completion of this unit, you will be able to demonstrate understanding of skin by writing and/or giving a brief overview of the subject.

Histology

The skin has many functions. It covers the body and protects the deeper tissues from drying and injury. It is very important when an individual is burned. It protects against invasion of infectious organisms. It contains end organs with many sensory nerve fibers. It is important for temperature regulation. It has excretory functions which eliminate water and various salts. It has secretory functions which produce sebum. The skin needs sebum for lubrication. The skin also has absorbing powers.

Protection: The skin serves to cover and protect all deeper tissues, organs, blood vessels and nerves from the invasion of bacteria and from blows or other external injuries. The skin is waterproof. This permits a fluid body to exist in what is often a very dry atmosphere. The keratin layer of the outer layer of the skin makes it possible to have a bath or dive into a pool without becoming swollen with water or shrinking. Because the epidermis contains certain cells that produce the dark pigment melanin, it protects the body from the harmful effects of too much ultraviolet light.

Sensation: The skin is the principal organ for the sense of touch because it is richly endowed with sensory nerve endings. All sensations of heat, cold, texture and pressure are conveyed to the brain by these nerve endings. Sensation is keenest at the fingertips.

Regulation of temperature: Nerve endings in the skin regulate body temperature by causing the blood vessels to dilate or contract and by means of secretions from the sudoriferous (sweat) glands.

Heat generated in the body is lost directly through the skin. When the temperature of the air is lower than that of the body, the rate of heat loss can be decreased or increased by the degree to which the capillaries of the papillary regions of the skin are open to circulation. If the temperature in the air is close to or higher than that of the body, the sweat glands pour fluid on the surface of the body, where it evaporates and cools the outer part of the skin. Hence, blood circulating through the papillary regions of the skin, from which sweat is evaporating, looses heat.

Excretion: The sweat glands eliminate waste matter produced by some cells. These glands play an important role in the regulation of body temperature. The activity of these glands is the result of either direct stimulation of the nerve endings in the glands or indirect stimulation through the sensory fibers of the skin. The usual cause of excretion is a high external temperature or muscular exercise.

Secretion: The sebaceous glands of the skin produce sebum which the skin needs for lubrication in order to preserve its softness. It also serves to protect the hairs from becoming too dry and brittle as well as from becoming too easily saturated with moisture. It also prevents undue absorption or evaporation of water from the skin. Oil glands are located over the entire surface of the skin except on the palms of the hands and the soles of the feet.

Absorption: The skin can be considered an organ of absorption only in the most limited sense. True absorption is a biochemical process by which substances are taken up into the blood stream. Selected substances may actually be absorbed. Penetration of the skin should not be confused with the absorptive function of the skin. The skin can be penetrated with a sharp implement. However, it does not absorb water and other solutions freely.

A red dermal light, infrared lamp or steam is used to aid the absorption of fatty substances, such as creams, oils and ointments. Steam is also used to aid the absorption of alcoholic solutions, such as antiseptics, astringents and tonics.

Histology

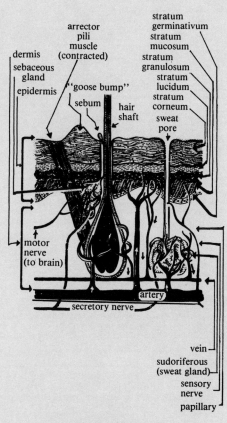

arrector pili muscle (contracted)

dermis
sebaceous gland
epidermis

"goose bump"

sebum

hair shaft

stratum germinativum
stratum mucosum
stratum granulosum
stratum lucidum
stratum corneum

sweat pore

motor nerve (to brain)

artery

secretory nerve

vein
sudoriferous (sweat gland)
sensory nerve
papillary

STRUCTURE
OF
SKIN

Histology

378

Structure of the skin

The skin consists of two distinct layers:

1. Epidermis which is the outer layer of the skin.

2. Dermis which is the lower layer of the skin.

    Note: Some histologists refer to the subcutaneous tissue as a third layer. Others consider it part of the dermis.

The epidermis is the outer layer of the skin and consists of four layers:

1. Stratum corneum: This is the outermost layer of the skin. It consists of flat scales which overlap to make a practically waterproof covering for the whole skin. During the normal growth process, this outer layer flakes off constantly.

2. Stratum lucidum: This layer is seen only in the skin of the palms and soles where the epidermis is the thickest.

3. Stratum granulosum: This layer consists of cells that have a distinctly granular appearance. These cells are practically dead, and those nearer the top show signs of cornification. The red color of lips and the pinkish color of the skin under the nails is noticeable because the granular layer is absent.

4. Stratum mucosum: This layer is composed of layers of cells whose shape ranges from oblong to square. The square cells constitute the main body of the mucous layer. The lowest row of cells in this layer is called the stratum germinativum. Only in this area is there any sign of the usual properties of living cells.

The dermis is the lower layer of the skin. It is sometimes called the true skin and consists of two layers:

1. The papillary layer is directly below the epidermis. It is characterized by the papillae which are tiny finger-like projections that exist in large numbers all over its upper surface. These papillae contain blood vessels and tactile corpuscles. These are the nerve endings which create the sense of touch.

2. The reticular layer contains most of the nerves and blood vessels of the skin. The meshes of this part of the skin connect it to the underlying tissues. The glands and hair follicles that penetrate to the surface of the skin are embedded in this layer.

Nutrition of the skin

The skin is nourished by the blood just as every other organ of the body is. The total area of the capillary network is so large that it holds from one-half to two-thirds of the total blood supply of the body. The dermis is also well supplied with lymph.

Muscles of the skin

The skin has both voluntary and involuntary muscles. The platysma is the principal voluntary muscle. The involuntary muscles are the arrectores pilorum which cause the formation of goose flesh.

Nerves of the skin

The skin has three types of nerves:

1. Sensory

2. Motor

3. Secretory

Sensory nerves transmit all sensations of touch, temperature, pressure and pain to the brain or spinal cord.

Motor nerves act on the arrector muscles and also cause the dilation and contraction of the blood vessels.

Secretory nerves stimulate the activity of the sweat and oil glands.

The skin contains the terminations of many nerve fibers and receptors. The fibers and receptors are classified as:

1. Motor nerve fibers

2. Touch and pressure receptors

3. Temperature sense receptors

4. Pain receptors

Motor nerve fibers are distributed among the blood vessels and arrector muscles.

Touch: The sensation of touch is served by three types of receptors:

A. Meissner's corpuscles affect the fingers, lips and margins of the eyelids.

B. Merkel's disks affect the borders of the tongue and certain other sensitive epithelium which form the epidermis and line hollow organs and all passages of the respiratory, digestive and urinary systems.

C. Naked nerve endings: The cornea of the eye is sensitive to touch and contains only naked nerve fibers.

Histology

379

Pressure receptors are distributed in the deep regions of the subcutaneous tissue, in connective tissues, in membranes of the le and forearm, and in the muscles. These receptors are specialized structures of sensory nerve terminals which are excited b specific stimuli.

Temperature sense receptors are hot and cold receptors. Skin is not equally sensitive in regard to detecting objects, th temperature of which is either colder or warmer than the skin. There are spots where cold is detected more easily and other spo where warmth is detected more easily. The receptor of warmth is called the corpuscle of Ruffini. It lies deep in the skin. Th cold receptor is called the Krause end-bulb. These end-bulbs are most prevalent in the connective tissue of the dermis.

Pain receptors in the skin rise from the nerve plexus deep in the corium by means of thin fibers. These naked fibers branc freely and end in fine beaded terminals beneath and between the cells of the deep layers of the epidermis. Naked endings are als present in many of the connective tissues of the body, but not in all of them. The pain endings respond to all types of stimuli b they chemical, mechanical or thermal. The sensation of pain serves as a warning against the injurious nature of the stimulus.

Glands of the skin

There are two types of glands in the skin:

1. Sudoriferous or sweat glands: These excrete sweat.

2. Sebaceous or oil glands: These secrete sebum.

The sweat glands are tightly coiled organs located far down in the dermis layer of the skin, with a tube or duct of microscopic size extending to the surface of the skin. The minute opening at the surface of the skin is called a pore. The sweat works its way out through the pore. These glands are of different sizes and types. The total number in the skin is estimated to be two to three million. They occur all over the body. They are most numerous on the forehead, armpits, palms and soles. The sweat glands play an important part in the temperature regulating function of the skin.

The sebaceous glands aid in the protective function of the skin. The sebum which they secrete helps keep the skin soft and supple. They consist of little sacs whose ducts usually open into the hair follicle. They also exist on nonhairy surfaces. These glands are found in all parts of the body except for the palms and soles.

If sebum hardens and clogs the openings at the surface of the skin, it forms blackheads. Sebum can have a most profound effect on the appearance and properties of the skin. Oil glands are affected by sex hormones, diet, drugs, x-rays and cosmetic formulations. Sweating has no effect on sebum secretion, and the rate of sebum production is not influenced by the amount of sebum on the skin.

Skin color

Some authorities say that there are only three basic strains: white, yellow and black. Others recognize five: white, yellow, black, red and brown. The color of skin depends mostly on the melanin pigment. The blood supply also plays a role. The color of the skin is a hereditary trait. Albinism is the absence of pigment. This condition may occur in the skin, hair, eyes, or in all three places. Persons with this condition are called albinos.

Skin elasticity

Normally, the skin is elastic and stretches slightly over the body frame. The tension is evident in the gaping of a cut which frequently must be forcibly held or sewn together to ensure proper healing. The elasticity of the skin is definitely limited. Healthy skin expands and then regains its former shape almost immediately. The loss of elasticity is a characteristic of aged skin.

Elastic fibers (elastin and collagen) are cross-linked into a three dimensional network which gives the skin and its larger blood vessels elasticity. Elasticity is a quality of all the layers of the skin.

Loss of elasticity is easily demonstrated when the stretched skin does not regain its former conformation rapidly. The skin will also appear grossly thinner, and the underlying blood vessels become prominently visualized. Wrinkling is also a characteristic of loss of elasticity. This is especially true in aging skin.

Unit 3
Nails

Nails are horny, translucent, plate-like appendages of the skin, which protect the tips of the fingers and toes. The technical term for the nail is onyx, and the study of nails is onychology.

Nails, like hair, are outgrowths of the epidermis. They are composed mainly of the substance called keratin. Keratin in this form is whitish and translucent. This permits the pink color of the dermis to show through. It is tough and not affected by ordinary chemical agents. Strong alkaline solutions may have an effect on the nails, and hair tints and some rinses will stain the nails deeply.

The nails vary in thickness. The nail is heaviest on the thumbs and big toes. The nail plate is constructed in layers which are welded together and called lamella.

Nails do not contain nerves or blood vessels. The lack of vessels indicates that blood does not circulate through the nails.

Structure of the nails

Nails consist of two parts:

1. Nail root

2. Nail body including the free edge

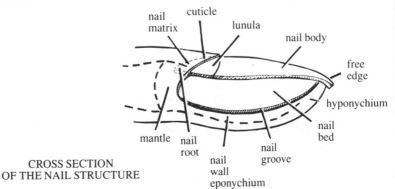

CROSS SECTION
OF THE NAIL STRUCTURE

Unit 3
Nails

General objectives-student goals:
After study, instruction and completion of this unit, you will be able to demonstrate understanding of nails by writing and/or giving a brief overview of the subject.

Histology

The nail root is the base of the nail and is entirely embedded beneath the skin. It originates from the matrix under the nail fold.

The nail body or nail plate is the entire exposed portion of the nail. It is attached to the nail bed and terminates at the free edge.

Nail growth

Toward the end of the third month of embryonic life, nails begin to grow. The health and growth of the nails, like that of the hair, is influenced by nutrition, health and disease. The average rate of growth is about ½ inch (1.27 cm.) every four months. Depending on its length from the root to the free edge, a nail may require two to four months to replace itself. The nail of the middle finger grows fastest. The thumb nail grows slowest.

Like hair, nails grow faster in warm weather. They are an end product of the body, and as such, can be cut off without causing injury. Toenails grow more slowly than fingernails. They are also thicker and harder. Children's nails grow more rapidly than those of elderly persons.

If a nail is torn off accidentally or lost through disease, it will be replaced if the matrix is not damaged. The nail growth process involves the soft keratin epidermal tissue of the nail bed which moves forward with the growth of the nail root. When the cells are bonded, they move out as the pressure of the nail fold builds. The epidermal tissue of the cuticle hyponychium and eponychium protects the nails from damage and infection.

Associated nail structures

Nail bed: This is the skin upon which the nail body rests. It has many blood vessels and nerves. The blood vessels supply nourishment. The nail bed consists of the deeper layers of the epidermis.

Mantle: This is the deep fold of skin in which the nail root is embedded.

Matrix: This produces the nail through a cell reproduction and hardening process. The matrix contains nerves and blood vessels. It is located beneath the nail root.

Lunula (half-moon): This is the light crescent at the base of the nail.

Eponychium (nail wall): This is where the nail is firmly embedded in the skin by a continuous fold of epidermis at the sides and base.

Cuticle: This is the overlapping skin around the nail.

Hyponychium: This is the portion of the skin on which the nail body rests.

Nail groove: This is the recess in which the nail moves as it grows.

Free edge: This is the portion of the nail which extends beyond the fingertip.

The fingernail, like the hair, has no blood vessels or nerves. It consists of dead cells which are not able to send pain messages to the brain. This is why you can cut and file nails without pain.

Review questions

1. What is histology?

2. Are fingernails considered part of the epidermis?

3. On which fingers and toes are the nails the thickest?

4. What is the average rate of growth for fingernails?

5. Do toenails grow faster than fingernails?

6. Will a fingernail replace itself if it is torn off accidently or lost because of disease?

7. What is the skin?

8. Is the skin the largest organ of the body?

9. How is the skin nourished?

Histology

NOTES

Trichology

Trichology: The technical term for the scientific study of the hair.

Overview: This chapter provides you with knowledge of the structure, functions and characteristics of hair. It also provides you with a good understanding of its growth and regrowth.

Behavioral objectives-student goals: After completion of this chapter, and after instruction and study, you will be able to perform and demonstrate competency in and understanding of trichology by identifying, explaining and/or listing: the functions of hair, the structure of hair, the cycles of hair growth, hair forms, hair textures, physical properties of hair, hair elasticity, hair porosity, tensile strength, surface tension, characteristics of healthy and unhealthy hair, causes of unhealthy hair, scalp disorders, hair disorders and superfluous hair.

Hair is the most important subject with which the cosmetologist is concerned. Every cosmetologist and barber must have an excellent understanding of hair. When a cosmetologist or barber has knowledge of the structure, functions and characteristics of hair and understands its growth and regrowth, he or she will have the foundation required for hair care and scientific hair services.

Trichology is the technical term for the scientific study of hair. In order to make an accurate analysis of the hair, you must:

1. Learn the structure and chemistry of hair

2. Study the growth and regrowth of hair

3. Learn the functions of hair

4. Learn to determine the characteristics of unhealthy hair

5. Learn to determine the causes of unhealthy hair

6. Learn to determine the characteristics of healthy hair

7. Learn to determine the fundamental requirements of hair

Trichology

Unit 1

The function of hair

General objectives-student goals:
After study, instruction and completion of this unit, you will be able to demonstrate understanding of the function of hair by writing and/or giving a brief overview of the subject.

long hair

short hair

lanugo hair

Trichology

Hair is the cylindrical, threadlike outgrowth of the epidermis in man and other mammals. Most hair is considered dead matter because it does not contain nerves or blood vessels except in a small area which includes the bulb.

Hair analysis is a prerequisite for all hair services. When you know what to look for, your practical experience in cosmetology and/or barbering will provide you with the proper approach for selecting the correct hair products and the proper hair service. It will also help to ensure the safe and effective use of all professional products. A hair analysis record card should be kept on file for every patron. The results of the original analysis should be reviewed and/or updated whenever a service requires a hair analysis.

Unit 1

The function of hair

Hair covers the entire surface of the skin except the palms, soles, lips and eyelids. It serves as an adornment and as protection for the skin and various structures of the body. Healthy hair and an appropriate hairstyle may improve an individual's appearance and self-image.

There are three types of hair. These are found on specific areas of the body:

1. Long hair

2. Short hair

3. Lanugo hair

Long hair grows from the scalp. Its maximum length may reach 3-5 feet (0.91-1.5 m.) if left uncut. The hair at the top and back of the head may grow longer than the hair at the sides of the head. Long hair also grows on men's faces. Long hair protects the scalp against injury, the rays of the sun and cold weather.

Short hair grows in the regions of the axilla and pubis as well as in the nostrils and on the ears, eyebrows and eyelids. Eyebrows keep sweat from running into the eyes. Eyelashes keep excessive light and dust out of the eyes. Nostril hairs filter impurities and dust from the air. Dust is also filtered by the hairs in the ears.

Lanugo hair is soft, down-like and frequently, though not always, colorless. Except for those surfaces of the body entirely devoid of hair (palms, soles, lips and eyelids) or covered with other varieties, lanugo hair is found over the entire surface of the body.

Lanugo eyebrow and eyelash hairs as well as all other lanugo hair do not have an arrector pili muscle. The term lanugo characterizes very small, fine, soft hairs which have a long tapering point. If lanugo hair becomes longer and/or coarser, its anatomical structure will change to that of the long soft hair. Lanugo hair has a shaft with no medulla. It grows out of a small short follicle, and the sebaceous gland is proportionately very large. Some minute lanugo hairs are simply an appendage of the gland.

Unit 2
Hair structure

A hair has two parts. The hair root is the invisible portion of a hair. It is located beneath the surface of the skin. The hair shaft is the visible portion of the hair. It extends above the surface of the skin or scalp. During hair growth, new root cells develop. The root pushes up and out of the skin's surface and becomes part of the hair shaft. More root cells develop and the process continues.

Hair looks like a stiffened thread emerging from the skin's surface. It actually contains thousands of epithelial cells. Instead of becoming flat scales, these cells fuse together into a long spine by forcing themselves through a tiny tube in the skin. The root and a small section of the hair shaft lie in a sac beneath the surface of the skin. This structure is called the hair follicle. Follicles are found on the entire surface of the scalp and skin except on the palms and soles.

There are approximately 1,000 hair follicles per square inch (2.54 cm.²) and 120 square inches (774.19 cm.²) of area on the average scalp. Therefore, most scalps contain 120,000 hairs. This quantity varies according to the texture of the hair. A head with coarse hair will have more scalp hairs than a head with fine hair. Hair color will also influence the number of hairs on the scalp. People with blond hair usually have the most hairs per square inch (2.54 cm.²). Brunettes have the second highest count, and people with red hair have the fewest hairs per square inch (2.54 cm.²).

The size, shape and direction of the follicle determine the size, shape and direction of the hair. Hair follicles may grow in various directions on some areas of the scalp. This causes the condition known as cowlicks.

At the extreme base of each follicle, there is a projection called the papilla. This structure produces the cells from which the hair develops. The papilla is composed of about 90% water. The papilla has nerves. It has a rich blood supply which nourishes the root and makes the growth of the hair possible. Any disease or injury, which destroys either the papilla or the follicle, will cause the hair to stop growing in that area.

A soft moist substance composed of soft growing cells surrounds the papilla. This structure is called the bulb. The bulb is popularly called the root. However, the root is every part of the hair below the skin.

A sweat pore is a minute opening at the surface of the skin. It denotes the outlet of a sudoriferous gland. The openings are tubes of microscopic size. They are formed from a single layer of epithelial tissue. The total number of pores is estimated to be two to three million. When the skin of some regions of the body is highly magnified and examined closely, the sweat pores become distinctly visible between the papillary ridges.

The sebaceous glands (oil glands) are located near each hair follicle. There are from one to six oil glands per follicle. These glands secrete a substance called sebum which lubricates the hair and protects the skin and hair against loss of moisture. The

Unit 2
Hair structure

General objectives-student goals: After study, instruction and completion of this unit, you will be able to demonstrate understanding of the structure of hair by writing and/or giving a brief overview of the subject.

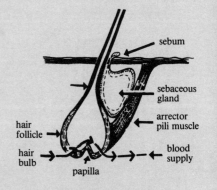

HAIR STRUCTURE

Trichology

387

ducts of these glands are connected to the hair follicles, and the sebum travels along the outside of the hair shaft. The activity of the sebaceous glands is influenced by changes in the endocrine glands within the body as well as by diet, blood circulation, drugs and emotional disturbances.

The arrector pili muscle is located alongside and attached to each hair follicle. Lanugo hairs, eyebrows and eyelashes do not have an arrector pili muscle. Fear or cold can contract these muscles. This contraction causes the hair to stand on end and causes bumps to develop on the skin. This condition is commonly known as gooseflesh or goose bumps. The arrector pili muscles also aid in perserving body heat when the skin is exposed to cold.

Unit 3
Layers of hair structure

The cell structure of the hair is arranged in three circular layers:

1. Cuticle

2. Cortex

3. Medulla

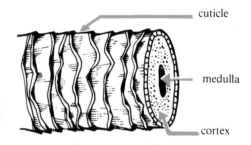

THE HAIR FOLLICLE

cuticle

medulla

cortex

The cuticle is the outer layer of the hair. It is composed of several thin, curved, colorless layers. The entire surface is broken up into tiny, overlapping, flat, scale-like cells which cover the circumference of the hair. Their free ends face up toward the pointed end of the hair. The cuticle protects the other layers of the hair.

Keratin acts as a bond and holds the layers of the cuticle together. Tension and continuous abrasion of the hair caused by brushing, combing or braiding can loosen or detach the outer layers of the cuticle. The inner layers of the cuticle remain together and protect the keratin from abrasion. Chemicals or improper care and handling of the hair may weaken or loosen the bonds between the layers. When this happens, the cuticle may become detached from the hair shaft. This causes damage to the hair.

The cortex is the middle layer of the hair. It makes up most of the hair mass (about 75%). It is composed of spindle-shaped, elongated cells which unite to make flattened fibers.

the cells in the cortex layer are long, spindle shaped . . .

General objectives-student goals:
After study, instruction and completion of this unit, you will be able to demonstrate understanding of the three hair layers by writing and/or giving a brief overview of the subject.

the cells in the cuticle layer are flat . . .

Trichology

Hair strength and elasticity are determined by the fibers in the cortex. The weaving and interlacing of the many lengthwise fibers cause the entanglement which creates the overall strength. The cortex contains the pigment melanin. This substance gives color to the hair. The cells in the cortex are more sensitive to the effects of alkalies and other chemicals than the cells of the cuticle. The cuticle is, in fact, so strong that chemicals which will destroy the cortex will not affect the cuticle.

The medulla is the inner layer of the hair. It extends from the bulb to a short distance below the bulb. It consists of round cells, air bubbles and some pigment. If the medulla does not receive nourishment from the bulb, it does not take form. The space is then taken up by the fibers in the cortex. The medulla may not exist at all in very fine hair and rarely extends for the entire length of the hair. Lanugo hairs have the shortest medulla.

Unit 4
Growth and regeneration of hair

Hair is an inert, horny substance without any nerves or blood vessels. Individual hairs, therefore, must obtain their nourishment from the blood vessels in the papilla. The healthy condition of the hair is intimately dependent on the general condition of the skin and on proper superficial stimulation of the glands and muscles.

Proper hygienic care helps increase the length of the hair. This is probably because the stimulated scalp muscles contract and keep the hairs in contact with their papillae for a longer time. Sooner or later, however, every hair reaches the time when it breaks away from its papilla and drops out of the skin. The total length of all hairs is not equal because when the individual hairs reach a certain length, the ends split and wear off. This creates an average length. On women, this average varies from 12 to 36 inches (30.48 to 91.44 cm.). However, there are many cases of hair 4-6 feet (1.22-1.83 m.) long. Men average a maximum length of 8-12 inches (20.32–30.48 cm.). Sometimes, beard hair grows longer.

Hairs live for a certain time and are then lost. An old hair is not out of the skin before a new one has begun to grow in its place. Human hair sheds regularly throughout the year. The periods of greatest loss are during the spring and autumn. The reasons for this loss pattern are not understood clearly.

Some authorities claim that each hair can support only a certain weight and that the hair loosens and falls out when it reaches that weight. Others believe that as hair ages it atrophies, or hardens slightly, so that it cannot take up its proper nourishment. Regardless of the theories, when hair reaches the end of its natural life, it detaches itself. It moves away from the papilla gradually as a new shoot begins to push the older hair out of the follicle.

Hair cells

The papilla is the productive organ of the hair. Its proper function depends on nourishment and oxygen from the blood stream. Hair grows as a result of mitosis (indirect cell division) and the multiplication of the soft cells in the papilla. The bulb and root are formed from these cells. These cells also cover the papilla.

Hair cells originate in the portion of the bulb that fits over the top and sides of the papilla. Growth starts at the top of the papilla. This process forms the medulla. The sloping sides of the papilla give birth to the cortex. The cuticle originates where the outer

the cells in the medulla layer are round . . .

General objectives-student goals: After study, instruction and completion of this unit, you will be able to demonstrate understanding of how hair grows by writing and/or giving a brief overview of the subject.

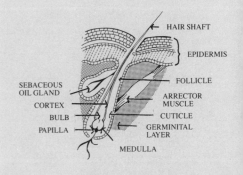

Trichology

389

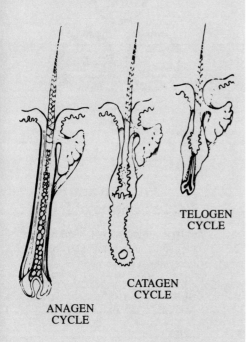

Hair Growth Cycle

ANAGEN
CYCLE

CATAGEN
CYCLE

TELOGEN
CYCLE

the first hair
covering is wool-like

Trichology

rim of the bulb lies along the base of the papilla. Cells just above the papilla are the youngest. The cells at the point of the hair shaft are the oldest.

Cycles

Hair growth is a discontinuous process because periods of growth alternate with periods of rest. Hair grows in three cycles:

　　1. Anagen　　　2. Catagen　　　3. Telogen

Anagen is the first cycle of hair growth. It is the period of hair development. This is the time when the hair bulb stretches and moves upward into the hair follicle. Hard keratin begins to synthesize in the follicle. This process forms the horny layer of the shaft. It is called keratinization.

Catagen is the second cycle of hair growth. It is the slow growth period. It occurs between hair growth and the cessation of activity in the hair follicle. Keratinization does not take place during this period. A club hair is formed, and thin threads of keratin anchor it to a contracted follicle.

Telogen is the third cycle of hair growth. It is the dormant period. This is the final stage in which new hair starts to loosen the old hair. It lasts until the fully grown hair has been shed. Then, a new anagen cycle begins.

It is difficult to observe the actual process of hair regeneration. Therefore, it cannot be explained in absolute terms. Different hairs, even in the same area, do not have the same life cycle or starting and ending cycle periods. The generally accepted theory states that once a new shoot starts to generate, the old hair reaches the end of its natural life. The old hair detaches itself from the papilla and gradually moves away from the papilla. It appears as if the new hair is pushing the old hair from the follicle. As some hairs shed, others form. Still others are growing. The shedding of up to 75 hairs a day is considered normal. The greatest loss takes place in the spring and autumn. After shedding, a new hair begins to form within 20 to 42 days. It takes from 41 to 72 days for a new hair to grow from the papilla to the surface of the scalp. Most scalp hair is replaced every two to seven years. Eyebrows and eyelashes are replaced every four to five months.

Stages

There are three stages in the development of the hair covering of the human head. The first covering is wool-like. It is called baby hair. Baby hair usually lasts from one to three years, rarely up to five years. This type of hair must be cut with very sharp scissors because it is very fine, soft and contains considerable moisture.

The secondary stage of the hair covering lasts until about the age of twelve. As this stage advances, the cuticle begins to lose moisture. It gets harder and coarser.

The third stage is the permanent hair covering. The texture, elasticity, porosity and density of the hair will vary according to the sex, race and the individual.

Rate of growth

The hair on the scalp grows at an average rate of $1/2$ inch (1.27 cm.) a month. The rate varies according to the:

1. Length of the hair

2. Location of the hair

3. Season

4. Time of day

5. Sex

Short hair grows faster than long hair. The longer hair is allowed to become, the slower it grows. It has been noted that medulla cells are missing near the base of long hair, and that the imbrications are not visible in the cuticle. It is the lack of proper natural nourishment that slows the rate of growth as the hair grows longer. The hair at the crown grows faster than the hair along the hairline. Hair grows faster during warm weather and during the day. Scalp hair grows faster in women than in men.

Pattern

You should examine and analyze the pattern of hair growth and the natural fall of the hair. These factors will help you determine how to shape and style the hair so that it enhances the natural form. The natural fall position varies as the hair grows longer than 3 inches (7.62 cm.). Close observation, continued practice and experience can ensure accurate judgment.

The parting of the patron's hair may be determined by one or more of the following:

1. Shape of the head

2. Direction of the hair growth in particular areas (i.e., cowlicks, whorls)

3. Hairstyle

4. Facial structure

5. Special hair partings

Unless it is the exception to the rule, the natural growth pattern over the entire head is as follows:

1. The hair on top of the head, from a little above the temple line on both sides of the head and from the front hairline back to the crown, grows straight up and out from the scalp. This makes it possible to comb the hair in this area in any direction without going against the natural growth pattern.

Trichology

391

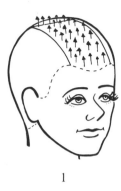 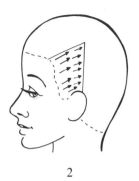 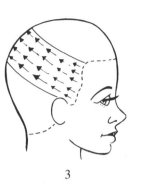 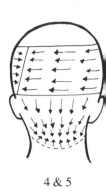

| 1 | 2 | 3 | 4 & 5 |

2. The hair on the left side of the head, from a little above the temple line down to the ear and from the front hairline back to about 1 inch (2.54 cm.) behind the ear, grows back away from the face.

3. The hair on the right side of the head, from a little above the temple line down to the ear and from the front hairline back completely across the back of the head to about 1 inch (2.54 cm.) behind the left ear, grows from right to left. This region includes the back of the head from the crown to about 1 inch (2.54 cm.) below the top of the ears.

4. The hair across the back of the head, from about 1 inch (2.54 cm.) below the top of the ears to the nape, grows downward toward the nape.

5. At the nape, the hair may grow in many various directions.

Approximately the first 3 inches (7.62 cm.) of hair lie in the growth pattern position. As the hair grows and acquires more length, it also increases its weight. The extra weight and length affect the natural fall of the hair. This will shift its position. The position of short hair is influenced by the natural growth pattern. The position of long hair is influenced by its weight.

Hair growth on the nape of many people is often claimed to be the result of previous shaving, clipping or cutting. This is a false statement. It is not based on fact. Outside forces cannot create hair or hair follicles.

Unit 5
Hair forms

The form or shape of hair provides an excellent method for classifying types. Scientific research has shown that human hair falls into one of four general forms. Hair may be classified as:

1. Straight
2. Wavy

3. Curly
4. Super curly

Unit 5
Hair forms

General objectives-student goals:
After study, instruction and completion of this unit, you will be able to demonstrate understanding of the typical hair forms by writing and/or giving a brief overview of the subject.

> **Trichology**

The shape of the follicle determines the shape of the hair. Thus, there is a relationship between the hair follicle, the hair form and the hair shape.

Hair form	Hair follicle	Cross-section of the hair shape
Straight	Perpendicular	Round
Wavy	Slanted	Oval
Curly	Curved	Almost flat
Super curly	Curved	Flat

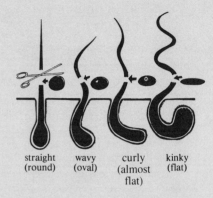

straight (round)   wavy (oval)   curly (almost flat)   kinky (flat)

Note: There is always the exception to the rule. Sometimes, these shapes and forms do not apply.

Super curly hair

Kinky, frizzy or woolly hair is sometimes called **super curly hair**. Although super curly hair is most characteristic of Black people, it is also found among many Caucasians.

Super curly hair is flat in shape. The sharp angle of the follicle results in the hair growing in the form of a tight spiral. It grows straight up and away from the scalp. The spiral form and its lack of weight enable it to stand out from the head.

The outer layer of cells on super curly hair lies extremely close to the cuticle. The function of these cells is to protect the cuticle. Normal brushing of the hair constantly removes these cells from the hair. When the hair is not brushed or combed thoroughly, most of the protective cells of the cuticle remain intact. They harden and are more difficult to remove. If this condition continues, the hair will appear dull and coarse. Breakage may also occur.

Super curly hair does not retain moisture like other forms of hair do. Most super curly hair is not very porous and has poor elasticity. The hair is fragile. It becomes matted and entangled with neighboring hairs. When the hair is quite long, it becomes knotted.

Trichology

393

Physical properties of hair

Unit 6
Physical properties of hair

General objectives-student goals:
After study, instruction and completion of this unit, you will be able to demonstrate understanding of the physical properties of hair by writing and/or giving a brief overview of the subject of hair texture, absorption, desorption, adsorption, porosity, elasticity, tensile strength, surface tension, color and natural moisturization of the scalp and hair.

Texture

The texture of hair is classified as coarse, medium or fine. You can determine the texture by feeling the hair with your fingertips. Texture depends on three general characteristics:

1. Size (diameter)

2. Pliability

3. Growth variables

fine hair

medium hair

coarse hair

The size of hair is measured by its diameter. The diameter of the hair shaft is not the same throughout its length. It is widest near the scalp area and tapers towards the hair ends. When checking for thickness or texture, examine the hair near the center of the shaft. Coarse hair has a large diameter. Fine hair has a much smaller diameter. The diameter ranges from 1/1500 of an inch (.0017 cm.) for fine hair to 1/400 of an inch (.0064 cm.) for coarse hair. The pliability of hair is determined by its feel. It can be soft, harsh or resistant. The growth variables of hair include quality: wiry, silky or straight and stiff.

Absorption

Absorption occurs when moisture or a substance passes through or into the hair, and is then retained. Sometimes, people will use the term porous to mean absorption. This can be misleading because people may assume that absorption takes place because of pores in the hair.

Hair has the ability to absorb and retain moisture. It is hygroscopic. Steam and chemicals increase hair's hygroscopic ability. Hair absorbs moisture from the atmosphere or from the perspiration of the skin. Hair will absorb an amount of water which equals not more than 30% of its own weight.

ABSORPTION

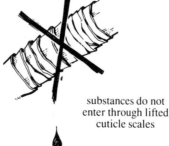

substances do not enter through lifted cuticle scales

substances pass through the outer cells and penetrates the entire hair structure

Trichology

It is sometimes said that as absorption takes place, the cuticle scales lift and allow substances to enter between them. Actually, the substances pass directly through the cuticle cells and penetrate the entire hair structure.

The rate of absorption differs in hairs from the same area of the body and along the shaft of the same hair. The absorption rate increases towards the hair ends. When normal untreated hair is completely immersed in water, it takes from about fifteen to twenty minutes for the hair to absorb its maximum amount of water.

The diameter of hair expands after absorption of water has taken place. The degree of hair swelling depends on the amount of water absorbed. After absorption is complete, the diameter can only increase about 20%, and the length of the hair can increase only about 1%.

Desorption

Desorption occurs when water passes out of the hair. Hair is reluctant to release its moisture content. It may take several days for the hair to release moisture when it is exposed to a constant, normal room temperature. Whenever moisture has been desorbed from the hair, the hair will reabsorb the moisture when exposed to normal room temperature.

Adsorption

Adsorption, as understood by cosmetologists, occurs when substances adhere to the outside of the hair. Many substances, such as oil, fat and wax, have the ability to adsorb to hair. The degree of adsorption varies with different substances. Products containing animal or vegetable oils adsorb better than those containing mineral oils. Some of the vegetable oils used in hair products are: olive oil, castor oil, corn oil, peanut oil and hydrogenated oil. Animal fats used in hair products include lanolin and a few others.

Porosity

Hair porosity is a measure of the ability of hair to absorb moisture from hair products. This ability can be classified as good, average or poor. Porosity affects such things as the timing in hair coloring and the strength of permanent waving lotion. If the hair feels slimy when wet, it is probably overporous. Hair becomes overporous when its physical properties are damaged by the chemicals used on it. Overporous hair can owe its origin to overbleaching, tints, chemical hair relaxers and waving lotions. Although the essential chemical elements in hair are replaced by new blood reaching the papilla, damaged physical properties are not easy to rebuild. Hair dries by the process of desorption. Therefore, hair with normal to good porosity will dry faster than overporous hair.

Elasticity

Elasticity is the ability of the hair to stretch and contract back to its original shape without breaking. The cuticle and the entanglement of individual fibers in the cortex control the strength and elasticity of the hair. Moisture is an important factor in hair's elastic behavior. Good elasticity is an indication of normal to excessive moisture content. Hair with poor elasticity is brittle, lacks moisture and is inclined to break.

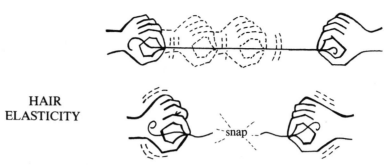

HAIR
ELASTICITY

When a hair is held at its length and stretched in water, it will return to its original length only as long as it is still wet. If a hair is stretched and allowed to dry while it is held at its length, it will remain stretched. Dry hair remains at its new length because it does not have the opportunity to reabsorb moisture. If it is exposed to moisture or water, the stretched hair will automatically and immediately revert to its original length.

Normal hair will usually stretch approximately 20% of its normal length. Then it will spring back. Wet hair can generally be stretched 40% of its length. When hair is stretched 50% or more, it will break. Hair with good porosity will stretch more than hair with poor porosity.

Elasticity and hair setting

Elasticity is extremely important in hair setting. It is generally understood by cosmetologists that good quality hair holds a curl better than hair of poor quality because of the former's ability to stretch. It is actually the contractile ability of the hair which determines the quality of the set.

Poor quality hair will stretch, but will not contract as easily as good quality hair. After poor quality hair has been set, the pulling force of brushing or combing stretches the curl to some degree. However, it does not spring back. Good quality hair will bounce back after brushing or combing because of its strong contractile power.

Tensile strength

The tensile strength of hair is determined by the amount of weight or tension required to cause its rupture. Fine hair will not support as much weight or tension as medium or coarse hair of the same quality. A normal untreated hair will support from 2 to 6 ounces (56.70 to 170.10 g.) of weight depending upon its diameter and quality.

The tensile strength of a single hair on an individual may vary considerably. The portion of the hair closest to the scalp will usually show greater tensile strength than the portion farthest from the scalp. The upper layers of hair will be much weaker than those underneath. This is because the upper layers are exposed to sunlight.

The tensile strength of a hair may be less than normal without any specific cause. Under certain physical conditions, hair may grow abnormally weak in tensile power. This results from any condition which deprives the hair of important amino acids, especially cystine.

In general, low tensile strength indicates excessive loss of protein and/or a breakdown of cystine between keratin molecules. Bleaches, tints, exposure to the sun and improper hair care oxidize the cystine. This causes a weak hair structure. Damaged hair, which cannot support at least 1½ ounces (42.52 g.) of weight, is considered unsatisfactory for chemical hair straightening, perming, hair pressing and other treatments. High tensile strength is the result of sufficient protein in the hair.

Surface tension

Surface tension is the attraction between solid and liquid surfaces. The molecules in drops of water and most shampoos are too large to penetrate the hair follicle. They roll off the surface of the hair. A single drop of most chemical products which contain wetting agents is approximately 2½ times smaller than a drop of water. These agents create a capillary action and permit the product to cling to and penetrate the hair shaft.

Color

Natural hair color is caused by the number and color of the tiny grains of pigment in the cortex layer of the hair. This pigment is called melanin. It can produce black, brown, yellow or red colors. The source of these pigments is the blood stream. Its characteristic color is hereditary. The absence or lack of melanin causes white and gray hair. These conditions may be the result of natural aging, illness, nervous shock or emotional tension.

Natural hair color is usually associated with the density of hair. Generally, blondes have the greatest density (140,000 hairs per square inch [2.54 cm.²]). Brunettes have a smaller density (110,000 hairs per square inch [2.54 cm.²]). Those with natural red hair have the smallest density (90,000 hairs per square inch [2.54 cm.²]).

Natural moisturization of the scalp and hair

The scalp tissue and the hair are covered with an acid mantle. This is a combination of sebum and the watery fluid excreted by the sudoriferous glands. This half-aqueous, half-greasy film protects the skin and hair against atmospheric changes. It prevents the loss of natural moisture. The elasticity of the hair, which is directly affected by hydrogen bonds and salt bonds, is totally dependent on the hair's own natural moisturization. Elasticity and proper moisturization are responsible for flexibility and for the bouncy qualities of the hair fibers.

Unit 7
Hair and scalp disorders and conditions

As a cosmetologist or barber, you must be able to identify hair that is healthy or unhealthy. Hair care techniques and services depend on the condition of your patron's hair.

SURFACE TENSION

| no wetting agents | some wetting agents | correct amount of wetting agents |

Unit 7
Hair and scalp disorders and conditions

General objectives-student goals:
After study, instruction and completion of this unit, you will be able to

Trichology

demonstrate understanding of hair and scalp disorders and conditions by writing and/or giving a brief overview of healthy and unhealthy hair, scalp disorders, hair disorders, and hair and scalp conditions.

The characteristics of healthy hair are:

1. Glossiness
2. Elasticity
3. Normal density
4. Freedom from trichoptilosis
5. Normal growth
6. Good color

The characteristics of unhealthy hair are:

1. Lack of sheen
2. Brittleness
3. Excessive oiliness
4. Excessive dryness
5. Excessive split ends
6. Abnormal shedding
7. Poor color
8. Excessive thinness

It is also important to identify the causes of unhealthy hair so that you can administer treatment or refer your patron to a medical doctor.

Some causes of unhealthy hair are:

1. Neglect
2. Insufficient circulation
3. Disorders of the oil glands
4. Illness
5. Chemical irritation

Scalp disorders

Pityriasis (Dandruff)

Pityriasis is common and widespread. It is a contagious disorder of the scalp. The shedding of a large number of fine white scales from the epidermis is its symptom. Scabbing, itching, swelling and redness of the scalp may result from severe cases of dandruff. There are many possible causes of dandruff. They are a malfunction of the oil glands, scalp bacteria, a tight dry scalp or an imbalance of hormones.

Cosmetologists and barbers who give hair and scalp treatments must maintain high standards of salon and shop hygiene in order to prevent the transfer of unhealthy conditions. Therefore, treat dandruff as a contagious disorder until medical authorities define the nature of the disorder clearly.

Trichology

398

Although dandruff is an undesirable and incurable disorder, it is controllable. Most dandruff problems lessen in intensity during warm weather. This is because people tend to wash their hair more often than during periods of cold temperatures.

Several surveys indicate that 80 to 95% of all adults experience some degree of dandruff. Children as young as six years in age have also been observed with this disorder. Dandruff is rarely found on persons over the age of seventy five. This disorder is more common among men than among women.

The technical term for oily dandruff is pityriasis steatoides. Its characteristic is yellowish scales which are larger than dry dandruff scales. The scales mix with sebum and stick to the scalp in patches. They also cling to the hair. It is not easy to remove the scales by means of simple brushing or shampooing. The epidermis of the scalp is likely to become reddened and inflamed when you treat the scalp and remove the scales. Generally, considerable itching accompanies oily dandruff. Oily dandruff is more difficult to control than dry dandruff.

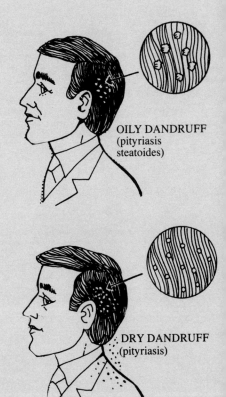

OILY DANDRUFF
(pityriasis steatoides)

DRY DANDRUFF
(pityriasis)

Pityriasis capitis simplex is the medical term for dry dandruff, which is also called common dandruff. Its characteristics are small, white, powdery scales and an itchy scalp. The scales are loosely attached to the scalp and hair. They usually fall to the shoulders. Shampooing and regular hair brushing help make the scalp and hair appear cleaner. They prevent the accumulation of unsightly scales.

In order to control dandruff, you must remove the scales regularly. You must prevent the growth of bacteria and fungi. Give attention to the following basic facts and techniques for treating and controlling dandruff.

1. Brush and fine comb the hair. This procedure removes excess scales from the scalp and hair. Since dandruff is a disorder, you must treat the scalp with greater care than you would normally. Avoid irritating the healthy part of the scalp.

2. Shampoo the hair frequently. You should use a nonprescription medicated or antiseptic shampoo. These will help destroy bacteria and microorganisms found on the scalp. These may be contributing to the dandruff condition. Medications or shampoos that contain sulfur-salicylic acid as an active ingredient are very effective for controlling dandruff. They gently peel the surface layers of the scalp. In this way, they remove dandruff scales. The most effective shampoos are those dispensed only by prescription. Remember, you must use them only according to the physician's instructions.

3. On occasion, change the brand of your medicated shampoo. It is important to do this because the hair may gradually become resistant to the shampoo's active ingredients. If this happens, the shampoo will not be effective.

4. When you use medicated shampoos, follow a double procedure. First, give the hair an initial soaping. Follow this by a second lathering. Leave the second lathering on the hair for at least five minutes. Then, rinse it from the hair.

5. About every thirty days, the epidermis sheds scales over the entire body and scalp. Bathing and normal rubbing of the skin remove the scales. This is why you cannot see this normal flaking. When a dandruff condition exists, this peeling increases considerably. The epidermis peels in a period less than the normal thirty days.

Trichology

6. Concentrated or full strength medications,which are used to treat the scalp or dissolve the flakes from the hair, can harm the scalp. The reason for this is the fact that both the epidermis and the scales of the scalp are made of soft keratin. These medications do not harm the hair because hair is made of hard keratin. It is not as sensitive as the scalp.

Three scalp disorders are sometimes wrongly identified as dandruff. This is because they are also characterized by scales. These conditions are:

1. Psoriasis

2. Tinea (Ringworm)

3. Seborrhea

When large areas of the scalp are affected by psoriasis or seborrhea, it is possible for the scales to block the follicle openings and interfere with the natural flow of sebum. The result of these disorders may be a dry scalp.

Psoriasis

Psoriasis is a common, inflammatory and chronic disorder of the skin. The lesion of psoriasis is characterized by whitish scales of the skin mounted on red, well-defined patches. It often appears as imbricated scales. It is usually found on the scalp, elbows, knees, chest and lower back.

We still do not know the cause of or the cure for psoriasis. Psoriasis is not contagious. No one knows why certain people are afflicted by the disorder, but we do have some understanding of what happens when the disease occurs. Under normal conditions, everyone sheds millions of dead skin cells every day. To balance this steady loss, deeper skin layers produce replacement cells that migrate to the surface. In psoriasis, this orderly process does not operate. New cells are formed at an abnormally high rate and reach the surface many times faster than in normal skin. Psoriatics simply make too much skin too fast. The result is psoriasis plaque, a skin area with well-defined borders. The outer skin layer, which is normally as thin as tissue paper, becomes markedly thickened and reddened. Dead skin cells mass at the plaque to form layers of silvery scales that flake off constantly. The disease does not interfere with physical activities or cosmetic services. Patrons with psoriasis can receive permanent waves and hair coloring treatments without any problems.

Home treatment for psoriasis consists of:

1. Coal tar remedies. The coal tar is in shampoo, creams, lotions, baths and gels.

2. Moisturizers. These products contain ingredients that seal in water already in the skin and keep it from evaporating. Moisturizers are not sold as psoriasis remedies, but they help make the patient look and feel better. They also have some therapeutic value. The main benefit of a moisturizer is that it helps remove scales. This makes the skin less flaky. It also lessens the temptation to pick off the scales, which may cause bleeding and irritation. Most important, removing scales enhances the action of most of the other treatments which must penetrate to the underlying skin.

Professional treatment consists of:

1. **Topical steroids:** These are creams and lotions which are applied to the skin.

2. **Injected steroids:** These are reserved for isolated patches that resist other treatments.

3. **Anthralin:** This is a topical medication that is especially good for thick stubborn psoriasis plaques. It is not very popular because it stains the skin, hair and nails.

4. **Methotrexate:** This is a drug taken internally. It has been in use since 1950.

5. **Light therapy:** Whether ordinary sunlight or ultraviolet light, it is one of the best treatments for psoriasis.

Seborrhea

Seborrhea is a disorder of the skin and scalp. It is characterized by **excessive shininess** and **greasiness** on the face. On the scalp, seborrhea is characterized by an **unusual amount of oil on the hair**. Its scales are generally thicker and more abundant than the scales found in dandruff. Seborrhea causes inflammation of the oil glands beneath the scalp. The inflammation owes its origin to overstimulation and secretion of sebum from the sebaceous glands. This produces a reddened scalp from which the scales arise.

Tinea (Ringworm)

Tinea is a contagious and infectious disorder of the skin and scalp. In its early stages, ringworm appears as **reddened patches**. It is caused by the invasion of **fungus** (vegetable growth). Ringworm is not commonly seen in the beauty salon or barber shop. It requires medical attention.

Hair disorders

Trichoptilosis (Split ends)

The **number one hair problem** is trichoptilosis. Trichoptilosis occurs at the end of a hair fiber, at the point farthest from the scalp. Jagged edges of the cuticle, slightly lifted scales and tiny cracks in the hair fiber characterize trichoptilosis. When a hair's cuticle layer has been removed, the splitting of a hair end becomes rapid. As the splitting progresses, it widens and becomes visible. Split ends are symptoms of worn-out hair. They can be the result of normal hair grooming. The hair end is the oldest part of the hair. It must endure considerable physical and abrasive wear. Long hair develops split ends faster than short hair. It is more likely to rub against the back of a chair than short hair is. Long hair has stronger bounce and movement when walking and when blowing in the wind than short hair does. Its bounce and movement can cause split ends.

The best method for eliminating split ends is **cutting them**. You must use very sharp scissors. **Dull scissors can cause split ends**. There is a special haircutting technique for removing split ends without shortening the length of the hair.

You can hide split ends by tinting them. There are special products that are designed to repair split ends. However, their results are only temporary. There is no cure for trichoptilosis. The best way to handle the problem is to prevent it.

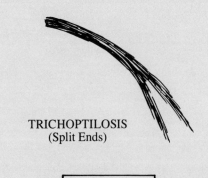

TRICHOPTILOSIS
(Split Ends)

Trichology

Trichorrhexis nodosa is a rare hair disorder. Its symptom is nodular swellings along the hair shaft. The nodes are usually found on the upper third portion of a hair and near the ends of the shaft. This disorder causes the hair to become extremely brittle. It breaks either spontaneously or when being combed or brushed. The breakage usually occurs through one of the nodes. The result is a peculiar brush-like spread of hair fibers from the broken hair.

TRICHORRHEXIS NODOSA

This disorder can be observed if you pull the hair through your fingertips. The hair may feel irregular and knotty. It may break easily through the node and look ragged. One or more whitish, shiny, transparent nodular swellings covering the circumference of the hair will appear under a microscopic examination. You will usually find one to five nodes on a single hair.

The cause of trichorrhexis nodosa has not been established firmly. Some of the popular beliefs concerning its cause are:

1. An accumulation of gas within the hair shaft

2. A fatty infiltration of the medulla at certain points of the hair shaft

3. A nutritional disturbance

4. A degeneration of the medulla

5. A swelling of the cells of the medulla

Long and continued treatment can eliminate this disorder. The treatment consists of stimulating the scalp by means of massage, ointments and/or solutions, and lubricating the hair.

Albinism

Albinism is a hereditary condition. It is a deficiency of melanin in the hair, skin or eyes. Those who suffer from albinism are called albinos. They have light yellow hair, pale skin and colorless eyes which appear pink. The cause of the condition, as noted, is a melanin deficiency. The lack of melanin owes its origin to the absence of the enzyme which produces melanin. There is no cure for this disorder. Albinos can receive the same hair treatments as persons with normal pigmentation can receive.

White hair

Hair can turn white suddenly and overnight. There is ample documentation of this phenomenon. However, there is no scientific proof of its existence. The problem is that it is difficult to understand how the entire hair shaft, which is a nonliving structure, can suddenly lose all its pigment within several hours. There are a few reasonable explanations.

1. Air bubbles can enter the normal pigmented hair. The bubbles reflect light. This creates the appearance of whiteness. It is possible to observe this phenomenon through the microscope.

2. Some individuals have naturally dark hair mixed with white hair. For some reason, these people can lose large amounts of their dark hair very quickly. The result is an illusion that all the hairs have turned white overnight. The actual hair loss may not be noticeable. Some of the recognized and accepted causes for this type of hair loss are:

   A. Mental stress

   B. Fright

   C. Excitement

   D. Acute illness

There is agreement within the scientific community that pigmented hair can lose all its melanin within a few months. However, those who have researched the disorder of white hair do not believe that hair can turn white within a few hours. They do not believe that a large number of follicles, which had produced hair with melanin, can suddenly produce only hair which is an unpigmented gray or white.

Scalp and hair conditions

Pediculosis capitis (Head lice)

Pediculosis capitis is a contagious condition characterized by lice on the scalp and hair. Lice usually attack the occipital region of the scalp. People whose hygiene is poor or who live in unsanitary environments are the most likely to contract this condition. Pediculosis capitis can be transferred from one individual to another by using the same brush, comb or other personal object.

The prime symptom of this condition is itching of the scalp. An irritation is produced when the louse tries to obtain its nourishment from the skin of the scalp. The louse inserts its long snout into the hair follicles, sucks its food from the deeper parts and moves about the scalp. It attaches ova (reproductive cells) to the hair. The amount of itching varies according to the sensitivity of the individual, the number of lice present, and the extent and duration of the condition. Scratching will cause lesions of the scalp.

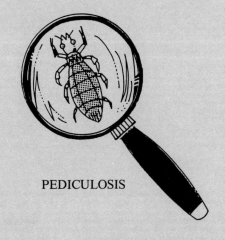

PEDICULOSIS

Trichology

female louse

The male head louse is about 1.5 mm. long and about one-half as broad. The female louse is slightly larger than the male. Lice have a triangular-shaped head, two fine-jointed antennae, an elongated oval body, strong claws and three pairs of legs. The color of the louse is light gray. The ova or nits are very small, oval-shaped and gray in color.

The female louse can lay from fifty to sixty eggs. The young lice hatch in six days and can multiply within twenty days. This rapid rate of reproduction is the reason why the condition spreads so quickly. One louse is capable of producing 8,000 lice in eight weeks. Head lice can lay their eggs on the scalp and/or attach themselves to the hair shaft. One hair can carry from one to five ova. The distance of the ova from the scalp may determine the extent of the condition. The youngest cells lie nearest to the scalp. The oldest cells are found at the hair ends.

Many nonprescription drugs and prepared chemical products will destroy lice with one treatment. After the treatment, fine comb the hair to remove the destroyed lice and ova.

Pityriasis (dandruff) can be mistaken for pediculosis. If a patron's only complaint is itching of the scalp, you should examine the condition very closely. You may find small, grayish bodies similar to lice on the hair. They may just be perforated dandruff scales, not lice. If they are dandruff, remove the scales by brushing and treat the scalp for dandruff.

Hypertrichosis (Superfluous hair)

Hypertrichosis is superfluous hair growth on areas of the body that normally bear downy hairs. The papilla, at the bottom of each hair, supplies nourishment to the growing hair. Unless the papilla is destroyed or does not function, the hair will continue to grow.

The end of a hair that has been plucked may appear to have a root on it, but this is actually the bulb of the follicle wall. Tweezing a hair can energize the papilla and strengthen the growth of a new hair. Regrowth of the hair may appear within two to six weeks.

Electrolysis or the **electronic tweezer** completely destroys the papilla and prevents hair regrowth. The electronic tweezer is an excellent tool for the permanent removal of superfluous hair. Damaging or destroying a papilla can cause a neighboring dormant hair follicle to spring to life and produce a new hair. Sometimes, however, the papilla is only damaged and not completely destroyed. In this case, regrowth may appear in about eight weeks. Because a damaged papilla provides less nourishment to the growing hair, the new hair will be lighter and finer than the original one.

Depilation is removal of hair above the skin. Temporary hair removal is usually accomplished with a razor or hair clipper. A shaved or clipped hair is removed at the skin's surface. Therefore, the hair end appears blunt, stubby and thicker than before. Removing hair with a razor or hair clipper will not cause thicker, coarser or darker hair to grow back in its place. The use of any cutting implement does not affect the hair follicle in a permanent manner or the future growth of the hair.

Epilation is removal of a hair below the skin. Hair waxing and chemical depilatories can remove hair from beneath the surface of the skin temporarily. Depending on an individual's normal rate of hair growth, these methods of epilation are effective for up to four weeks. Chemical depilatories are not recommended for delicate skin or sensitive areas of the body.

Tweezing or pulling excess hairs from the nose, ears and eyelash areas can be dangerous. Cut these hairs with a small special scissors with blunt rounded tips.

Trichology

Alopecia (Baldness)

A lack of hair follicles is the general characteristic of alopecia. There are many types of alopecia and numerous causes of it. Some of the causes of this disorder are:

1. Heredity (Excessive male hormones)
2. Infections
3. Systemic diseases
4. Medications
5. Mechanical stress
6. Radiation

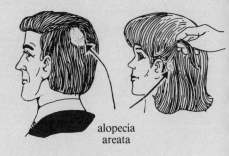

alopecia
areata

alopecia

Male pattern baldness is the result of heredity. Its cause is a generous supply of male hormones or at least a lack of female hormones. Most women will not suffer permanent hair loss because the female hormone dominates the male one.

The male hormone dehydrotestosterone surfaces on the scalp along with natural oils. If this hormone accumulates and gets reabsorbed, it acts on the hair follicles. It slows or halts hair growth. The depositing of the male hormone is the precipitating factor in genetic hair loss. Although shampooing helps wash away some of the male hormone deposits, some doctors apply low doses of female hormones directly to the scalp in order to neutralize the male hormone in an attempt to arrest rapid hair loss.

Of all the cosmetic methods of coping with baldness, hair transplant remains the one most widely accepted by doctors. They have been moving hair from where it is to where it is not for about thirty years. Transplantation is performed in the doctor's office. It involves anesthetizing the donor and recipient areas, and cutting out cylindrical plugs of skin from the hairy sections of the scalp. The plugs measure ³⁄₁₆ inch (0.48 cm.) wide and ¼ inch (0.64 cm.) long. Each donor graft contains about a dozen follicles from which hair grows. Cylinders of tissue of the same size are punched out of the bald scalp, and a hairy plug is inserted into each hole. No sutures are needed because blood clots around the plug and holds it in place as the skin grows. The donor sites also heal and disappear.

Doctors usually do forty or fifty grafts in a two hour session. There is a month interval between sessions. A balding crown or a moderately receding hairline requires about 150 plugs. A large bald area may need 400 to 600, depending largely on the width and thickness of the remaining fringe.

You cannot keep taking hair from one area and transplanting it to another. You must leave enough hair to cover the areas from which the donor graft was taken.

There are certain infections which can cause hair loss. They can be fungal, bacterial (staphylococcal, streptococcal), viral (herpes zoster) or ringworms. Early diagnosis and treatment are important for preventing permanent hair loss.

Systemic diseases often lead to baldness. These conditions include allergies because of drugs, advanced diabetes, influenza, scarlet fever, syphilis, pituitary disorders, leukemia and cancer. Hair loss can also be the result of ingestion or application of drugs or chemicals with toxic effects. The ingestion of insecticides has been observed to cause permanent hair loss. The improper use of chemicals such as hair lighteners, straighteners and cold wave lotions has been known to cause temporary hair loss (breakage).

Trichology

405

Medications that may cause alopecia are: chemotherapy, penicillin, sleeping pills, birth control pills, blood pressure pills and aspirins in excessive numbers.

Mechanical stress can also cause temporary hair loss. This type of hair loss is called traction alopecia. It can result from securing rollers too tightly, barrettes, bobby pins, braids and a tight ponytail.

Radiation from atomic accidents, explosions, radium, x-rays and radioisotopes can cause either temporary or permanent baldness.

Some of the causes of alopecia are unknown. You can awaken in the morning and find one or more circular bald spots. This particular type of baldness is called alopecia areata. This is not a condition about which you should worry. Usually, the hair will regrow spontaneously without any treatment.

There are many forms of alopecia. Here are some common terms and definitions:

Alopecia adnata: This is an uncommon form of baldness. It is apparent at birth and owes its origin to an absence of hair follicles. It is also called alopecia congenitalis

Alopecia cicatrisata: This is circular and irregular patches of alopecia which are caused by closely set points of inflammation and atrophy of the skin. It is a permanent condition.

Alopecia circumscripta: This is loss of hair in circumscribed patches with little or no inflammation. The beard area as well as the scalp can be involved.

Alopecia congenitalis: This is an uncommon form of baldness. It is present at birth and owes its origin to an absence of hair follicles. It is also called alopecia adnata

Alopecia mucinosa: This is circumscribed patches of hair loss on the face. It is accompanied by degeneration of the structure of the hair follicle.

Alopecia prematura: This is baldness which occurs in young people. The hair gradually thins and falls out.

Alopecia senilis: This is baldness which occurs in old age in the form of a gradual thinning of the hair.

Alopecia syphilitica: This is transient baldness occurring in the second stage of syphilis in the form of a moth-eaten appearance in the temporoparietal regions.

Alopecia totalis: This is complete baldness of the scalp.

Alopecia unguium: This is the falling off of the nails.

Alopecia universalis: This is loss of hair from all parts of the body.

Ten technical terms used to describe some hair and scalp conditions

1. **Pityriasis amiantacea:** This is a skin disorder of the scalp characterized by oily, scaly dandruff that clings to the hair and by an inflamed scalp.

2. **Neurodermatitis:** This is a scalp disorder that results from a nervous temperament. It is characterized by a dry scaly scalp.

3. **Morphoea:** This is a thickening and hardening of the connective tissue of the scalp. It is also called scleroderma.

4. **Discoid lupus erythematosus:** This is a scalp and skin disorder of unknown cause.

5. **Pseudopelade:** This is irregular patches of alopecia which arise because of closely set points of skin inflammation.

6. **Folliculitis decalvens:** This is an inflammatory condition of the hair follicles of the scalp. It causes baldness.

7. **Pili annulati:** This is ringed hair.

8. **Pilica polonica:** This is a matted condition of hair caused by neglect.

9. **Monilethrix:** This is beaded hair. It is a congenital hair defect characterized by dryness, fragility and nodes.

10. **Ichthyosis follicularis:** This is a hereditary skin disease associated with baldness and the absence of eyebrows and eyelashes.

Unit 8
Chemistry of the hair

Organic substances

Protein is one of the three most important organic constituents of living matter. It represents almost one-half of the body's dry matter. The other two principal organic constituents are fats and carbohydrates.

Protein is a compound which contains five chemical elements: carbon, oxygen, nitrogen, hydrogen and sulfur. To form a protein, these elements develop into small molecular chains or units called amino acids. These acids are linked lengthwise and held together by peptide bonds.

About twenty different amino acids are found in proteins. All of them are not necessarily present in the same protein molecule. An almost unlimited variety of proteins may be formed by rearranging the amino acid sequence and by changing the total number of amino acids in the sequence. Large proteins can have several hundred amino acids.

Unit 8
Chemistry of the hair

General objectives-student goals: After study, instruction and completion of this unit, you will be able to demonstrate understanding of the chemistry of hair by writing and/or giving a brief overview of organic substances, the chemical composition of hair, physical and chemical bonds, cystine and cysteine, the amphoteric quality of hair and the chemistry of a permanent wave.

Trichology

407

Protein is water soluble. It can, therefore, be an ingredient in cosmetic products such as hair conditioners. Water alone can remove water soluble protein conditioners from the hair.

Except for a small area which includes the bulb, hair is dead matter. You cannot feed dead matter. Protein is not hair food. Protein hair conditioners are compatible with the hair. They are used to protect the hair from chemical and environmental influences. They provide a thin protective film for normal hair. They fill the vacant spaces and damaged sections of damaged hair.

All living cells contain nucleic acid. Once the hair is formed in the follicle, the nucleic acid no longer functions. Many cosmetic formulations contain nucleic acid as a conditioning agent. There are opposing viewpoints regarding the effectiveness of nucleic acids in cosmetics. Some authorities claim that nucleic acids aid in reconstructing the hair, imparting moisture to dry hair and improving its elasticity and tensile strength. Others believe that hairdressing products and conditioners containing nucleic acids are not very effective. According to this group, the high molecular weight and large size of the amino acids make it difficult for the cosmetic preparation to penetrate the hair shaft. They also believe that these products do not repair or reconstruct broken hair bonds.

Chemical composition of hair

A single human hair is composed of approximately 97% protein, .03% trace elements and 2.97% water, lipids and pigment. The percentages vary according to the moisture content of the hair. Hair contains varying amounts of the same elements found in all proteins. The following percentages are usually found in medium to dark hair:

Carbon: 50%

Oxygen: 21%

Nitrogen: 18%

Sulfur: 4%

Hydrogen: 6.7%

Trace elements: .03%

The chemical composition will vary according to the color of the hair. Dark hair usually contains the highest percentage of carbon and the lowest percentage of sulfur. Light hair contains less carbon and more oxygen and sulfur.

There are many different kinds of amino acids in the hair. Some of them are acidic and some are alkaline. It is the amine group in amino acids that, depending on the medium they are in, function as an alkaline. The acid portion of an amino acid is stronger and more active than the alkaline portion.

Trichology

Average percentages of identifiable amino acids in human hair

The percentages vary according to the total number of amino acids present in the hair. Large proteins can have as many as several hundred amino acids which are formed according to the protein molecule size.

Amino acid	Human hair	Amino acid	Human hair
Alanine	5.0	Lysine	3.0
Arginine	10.0	Methionine	1.5
Aspartic acid	6.0	Phenylalanine	3.0
Cystine	18.0	Proline	5.0
Glutamic acid	13.0	Serine	8.0
Glycine	5.0	Threonine	1.0
Histidine	1.5	Tyrosine	3.0
Isoleucine	4.0	Valine	6.0
Leucine	7.0		

Although it has been definitely established that hair products designed for use on all forms of hair can be used just as successfully on super curly hair, it must be noted that super curly hair requires thorough brushing on a regular basis in order to prevent the outer layer of cells from hardening. Super curly hair needs a deep cleansing shampoo and products that add, maintain or seal in hair moisture.

Protein lipids, moisture, carbohydrates and pigment coexist in a single strand of hair. The proteins that are linked to carbohydrates are called glycoproteins. Glycoproteins keep the natural moisture inside the cortical cells by binding these cells together. They also protect the surface of the cuticle cells. Fine limp hair has a very thin diameter with a high proportion of moisture-resistant cuticle. This makes it difficult to work with. It is physically unable to hold a hair set or perm as well as coarse, normal or medium fine hair.

Trichology

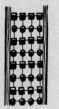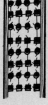

solid
cross-
linkage
formation

broken
cross-
linkages

**POLYPEPTIDE CHAIN IN THE
KERATIN MOLECULES**

Physical and chemical bonds

A bond is the linkage between two atoms which form a molecule. The hair structure is held together by molecular bonds. Hair contains physical and chemical bonds.

Physical bonds are made of hydrogen and ionic salt bonds. They exist between the peptide chain. They are weak and easily broken by water, stretching or cutting. After being re-formed, they rebond by eliminating the water and moisture from the hair. There are more hydrogen bonds in the hair than any other type of bond. Chemical bonds are disulfide (sulfur-cystine) and peptide bonds. Disulfide bonds are cross-linkages. They secure the long chain of end linkages which run full length of the hair fiber and form long chains of polypeptides. The cross-linkages connect with the end linkages like cross-pieces on a ladder. These bonds are strong. Only chemicals can break them.

Peptide bonds are end bonds which join each amino acid in the form of a chain. End bonds are the strongest bonds in the cortex. Once the end bonds are broken, they cannot be repaired.

Hydrogen and sulfur cystine bonds are cross bonds. They hold the long chains of amino acids together. Cross bonds form a link between the parallel chains of amino acids. These bonds play a vital role during the permanent wave process.

Cystine-Cysteine

Cystine is a crystalline amino acid which contains the element sulfur. About 18% of normal hair is cystine. The amount of cystine in the hair affects elasticity, strength, gloss, coloring and waving. The sulfur in cystine reacts with the chemicals in cosmetics and allows the hair to change its form or color. There is a higher percentage of cystine in the hair than in the skin. Therefore, a peroxide or penetrating dye will color the hair permanently. It will not affect skin color.

Cysteine is also an amino acid which contains sulfur. Cysteine is an oxidized form of cystine. The oxidation process is important during a permanent wave. The application of the cold wave lotion (thioglycolate) destroys and changes the cystine bonds to cysteine. This chemical change softens the hair. After the application of the neutralizer, the cysteine is oxidized back to its original cystine bonds.

Amphoteric quality of hair

Amphoteric refers to substances that react with either acids or alkalies. Because keratin contains acid and alkaline amino acids, hair can react to either acid or alkaline substances. Most hair preparations used in the practice of cosmetology are neutral, acidic or basic (alkaline).

If an acidic substance is applied to the hair, the basic amino acids in the hair will react with the acid in the substance. If an alkaline substance is applied to the hair, the acid amino acids in the hair will react with the alkali in the substance. The application of an acidic or alkaline substance or solution will flatten and tighten the cuticle and create a different feel or behavior of the hair. For example, after a soap shampoo (alkali), a final rinse of vinegar (acid) always improves the feel of the hair.

Trichology

Chemistry of a permanent wave

The components of hair (carbon, oxygen, hydrogen, nitrogen and sulfur) make up the amino acids which form the protein keratin. The amino acids are held together (bonded) by chemical bonds and physical bonds.

When alkaline waving solution is applied to the hair, it softens and swells the hair and lifts the cuticle. This allows the solution to penetrate to the cortex which is made up of billions of long polypeptide chains. Once in the cortex, the chemical action of the perm lotion unlinks up to 70% of the disulfide bonds. This allows the polypeptide chain to rearrange. The hair takes a new form. 30% of the disulfide bonds remain unchanged.

After the hair has been neutralized, only 50% of the broken bonds are re-formed and rebonded. Thus, 35% of the disulfide bonds were lost during the processing time. The swollen condition of the hair and retention of water prevent the chemical bonds from being relinked entirely.

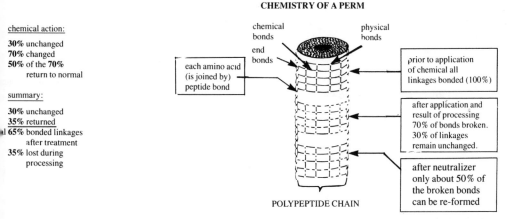

CHEMISTRY OF A PERM

chemical action:

30% unchanged
70% changed
50% of the **70%**
    return to normal

summary:

30% unchanged
35% returned
65% bonded linkages
    after treatment
35% lost during
    processing

chemical bonds
physical bonds
end bonds

each amino acid (is joined by) peptide bond

prior to application of chemical all linkages bonded (100%)

after application and result of processing 70% of bonds broken. 30% of linkages remain unchanged.

after neutralizer only about 50% of the broken bonds can be re-formed

POLYPEPTIDE CHAIN

pH reaction

During the processing time of the permanent wave, the average hair, which has an acid mantle of pH 4.5-5.5, comes in contact with the waving lotion, which is alkaline and about pH 9.2. As the processing time continues, the pH of the acid mantle around the hair rises. 70% of the disulfide bonds are usually broken by the time the pH of the acid mantle rises to about 7. If the hair is permitted to process past the point of pH 7, it becomes overprocessed, and damaged in texture and appearance. This may cause the peptide bonds, which are the strongest of the bonds, to break. Before more than 70% of the disulfide bonds can be broken, the peptide bonds will start to break. Once the peptide bonds are broken, there is no way of re-forming them. The hair will literally fall apart.

Cystine-Cysteine

Disulfide bonds, which are sulfur cystine, are converted to cysteine by means of waving lotion. The neutralizer oxidizes the cysteine back to cystine. Neutralizing the perm lotion after processing has been completed is the final and most important

Trichology

411

cycle of the permanent wave procedure. The re-forming of the chemical bonds produces the lasting qualities and strength of the curl. The greater the number of chemical bonds that are re-formed, the better the results. It is the swollen condition of the hair and the fact that hair retains a considerable amount of water that prevent the same number of chemical bonds which were unlinked from linking once again.

Overprocessing and overneutralization

It is possible to overprocess and/or over neutralize the hair during a perm. Overprocessing is caused by permitting the cold wave lotion to stay on too long. Overneutralizing is caused by applying a neutralizer which is too strong. When a neutralizer is chemically strong enough to neutralize the interior cortex completely, it is much too strong for the outer cortex. The outer part of the hair becomes overneutralized. In both cases, the permanent wave will relax because of insufficient rebonding.

Chemical symbols

S–S: A chemical symbol for the chemical bonds in the hair prior to the application of permanent wave lotion.

S–H–H–S: A chemical symbol for broken S–S bonds.

S–H–O–H–S: A chemical symbol for chemical bonds in the hair during the neutralizing process. This process allows the bonds to re-form. Cysteine is oxidized back to cystine.

H: A symbol used to identify hydrogen bonds.

Unit 9
Hair analysis

Structural analysis of the hair

The microscope is a very impressive instrument which can be used to determine the general condition of hair by means of color reflection. If green, blue, red or yellow is reflected from the hair, it is an indication of whether the hair is in excellent, fair, poor or damaged condition. The interpretation of what one sees is the critical part of hair analysis with a microscope.

The experienced trichologist or cosmetologist can determine the exact condition of hair without using a microscope. He or she can view the hair closely with the naked eye, feel it with the fingertips and test the tensile strength (elasticity) by stretching it. This type of analysis can be as accurate as that with a microscope.

The most important part of a hair analysis is not the microscope, it is product knowledge. One must know the correct product and method of application in order to treat a specific condition. The successful trichologist and cosmetologist is required to make the study of product knowledge an important part of their practice.

General objectives-student goals:
After study, instruction and completion of this unit, you will be able to demonstrate understanding of hair analysis by writing and/or giving a brief overview of the subject.

Trichology

412

Although microscopy has little value to the practicing cosmetologist or trichologist, he or she can consider the microscope a sales tool for selling hair conditioning treatments when it is used to show patrons before and after hair samples or pictures of how the cuticle of the hair becomes flat and tight to the shaft after the application of a low pH hair conditioner. In research, however, it will help the entire hair cosmetic industry to improve its understanding of the structure of human hair. This knowledge will aid in the development of better quality hair care products.

Parts of a compound microscope

Eyepiece

Monocular tube

Prefocusing gage

Coarse focusing knob

Nosepiece

Objectives

Stage

Disc diaphragm

Inclination joint

Fine focusing knob

Mirror

Base

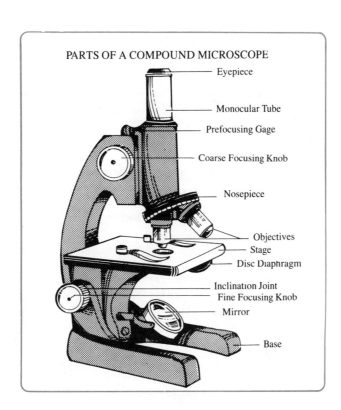

PARTS OF A COMPOUND MICROSCOPE

- Eyepiece
- Monocular Tube
- Prefocusing Gage
- Coarse Focusing Knob
- Nosepiece
- Objectives
- Stage
- Disc Diaphragm
- Inclination Joint
- Fine Focusing Knob
- Mirror
- Base

Trichology

413

a single hair
magnified
1,000 times

a single hair
magnified
100,000 times

a single hair
magnified
500,000 times

Trichology

The chart below defines the characteristics of the three microscopy techniques used for hair analysis.

Microscopy techniques	Degree of magnification	How it magnifies	Treatment of hair samples	Output
Optical	Up to 1,000 times	Light rays	Natural form and color No coating or chemical treatments	Color pictures
Electron	Up to 100,000 times	Electron beam	Chemically prepared	Black and white pictures only
Scanning electron	Up to 500,000 times	Electron beam	Coated with substance which reflects electrons and produces images No chemical treatments	Larger and clearer black and white pictures

Mineral analysis of the hair

The human body needs well-balanced minerals for good health. Hair is extremely sensitive to the body's deficiencies and excesses of minerals, such as magnesium, potassium, calcium, sodium and lead. A laboratory analysis of the hair detects mineral imbalances in the body. Only one gram (0.04 ounce) of hair cuttings is required for a complete analysis. A mineral analysis of the hair is valuable to doctors and nutritionists. It is of little practical value to the practicing trichologist, cosmetologist or barber.

Important nutrient minerals are: calcium, magnesium, sodium, potassium, copper, zinc, iron, manganese, chromium, cobalt, lithium, molybdenum, phosphorous, selenium, silicon and vanadium. Toxic minerals are: lead, arsenic, mercury, cadmium, aluminum, nickel and beryllium. Nutrient minerals become toxic at sufficiently high levels. Toxic minerals are essential at extremely low levels. For some minerals, the margin between the level that is beneficial and the level that is harmful may be relatively small.

Mineral analysis of hair gives information about mineral levels in tissues. The hair, nails and teeth are tissues in which trace materials are sequestered and/or stored. Hair mineral tests measure a different aspect of the body system than blood or urine tests do. The relative level of stored minerals provides an indication of the minerals that are available for catalyzing various enzyme reactions. The degree of accuracy of a hair mineral analysis is dependent on quality control, the hair sample and laboratory procedures. The proper utilization of a mineral hair analysis requires the expertise of a physician who can correlate the test results with the individual's other medical tests, laboratory tests and general health history. This physician should be a specialist in preventative medicine and nutrition.

Practical hair analysis

A practical hair analysis as detailed on the hair analysis record card enables the cosmetologist to select the correct products and the correct application method for treating specific conditions.

How to use the hair analysis record card

Item 1 Insert the patron's name, the date, the patron's complete address and telephone number.

Item 2 Inquire about the general health of the patron. Record the word average, poor or excellent.

Item 3 Record any specific illness and information which the patron mentions to you.

Item 4 Inquire about any medication taken internally by the patron. It is not necessary to be specific about the kinds of medicine used, but it may be helpful to know when the medication was taken last. Put a check in the space provided if medication is being taken. Illness and medication have a definite effect on the hair. If an individual is in poor health, the hair will not be in good condition or respond satisfactorily to treatment. Antibiotics and other medicaments taken internally will reach the hair within 48 to 72 hours and spread throughout the hair shaft in about 12 days. It takes approximately 19 days before the antibiotics are eliminated from the hair completely. To remove the effects of antibiotics or other medicaments from the hair shaft, apply acetone to the shaft and distribute it evenly with a comb. Leave the acetone on the hair for five minutes. Then, shampoo the hair. The acetone absorbs the medicaments. The acetone and the medicaments are removed by shampooing and rinsing the hair. If the medicine is left on the hair, it would react unfavorably with perm lotion and affect the processing time of a permanent wave.

Item 5 Texture plays a large part in the appearance, feel, design and treatment of the hair. The sense of touch is the common test for hair texture. Record the texture of your patron's hair.

Item 6 The porosity determines the amount and speed of liquid absorption into the hair shaft. This is an influential factor in permanent waving, hair tinting and many other services. The porosity can be good, average or poor. Record the porosity in the space provided.

Item 7 Structural strength represents the elasticity of the hair. Elasticity affects the amount of stretch and contraction in the hair. Indicate the structural strength of your patron's hair. Classify it as good, average or poor.

Item 8 Record the color of the patron's hair. State if it is natural or tinted.

Item 9 Use Squibb Nitrazine test paper to test the pH of the hair. Wet a few strands of the hair near the scalp area with a small amount of water and rub the hair with a piece of Nitrazine paper. You may also wet the paper and rub it on a few strands of dry hair. Observe the color change of the paper. For a true reading of the Nitrazine paper, match the color to the paper color guide on the container. Setting lotion, hair spray and other cosmetics will have a slight effect on the pH reading. Record the pH number in the space provided.

Item 10 The density of the hair is the amount of hair per square inch (2.54 cm.^{2}) on the head. The average measurement is 1,000 hairs per square inch (2.54 cm.^{2}). The density of the hair usually determines the amount of hair to be placed on each roller, the number of rollers on a head and the number of perm rods.

Trichology

Item 11 Most items listed under the condition of the hair are self-explanatory. It should be noted that a patron with psoriasis of the scalp may have permanent waving and hair coloring treatments under most conditions. Trichoptilosis is split hair ends and should be recorded. Alopecia areata in women is common. It is usually temporary and clears by itself. This condition is very common after childbirth and in people who are extremely nervous.

Item 12 Chemically treated or pressed hair always requires special attention. It is important to record these services correctly.

Item 13 The form of the hair—straight, wavy, curly or super curly—is determined by the hair type: round, oval, almost flat, flat. Hair type indicates the degree of tension to put on the hair while setting and how to cut it.

Item 14 Examine the surface of the scalp for cuts, scratches or abrasions. If you notice any of these scalp conditions, act as required. The flexibility of the scalp is directly related to hair chemicals and/or pressing treatments.

Item 15 Prior to performing most services on a patron, a hair analysis should be made. Make your recommendations for specific services in this section of the card.

Hair analysis record

1. Name_____ Date_____

   Address_____ Telephone_____

   City_____ State_____ Zip Code_____

2. General health_____

3. Illness_____

4. Medication_____

5. Texture   Coarse____   Medium____   Fine____   6. Porosity   Good____   Average____   Poor____

7. Structural strength (Elasticity)_____

8. Color_____   9. pH_____   10. Density_____

11. Condition of the hair or scalp: Normal_____   Psoriasis_____
                                       Dry_____   Trichoptilosis (Split ends)_____
                                       Oily_____   Alopecia areata (Bald spots)_____
                        Pityriasis (Dandruff)_____   Other_____

(FRONT)

Trichology

416

12. Chemical treatments:

A. Color: Single_____   Double_____   Other_____

B. Chemical straightener: Caustic_____   Thioglycolate_____   Other_____

C. Permanent wave: Acid balanced_____ __   Cold wave_____   Other_____

D. Pressed hair_____   Other_____

13. Hair type: Round_____   Oval_____   Flat_____

14. Condition of the scalp: Cut_____   Scratch_____   Abrasion_____   Other_____
                            Tight_____   Loose_____   Normal_____

15. Recommendations: _____
_____
_____
_____
_____
_____

Unit 10
Frequent questions about hair

1. **Do all scalp hairs develop a cuticle, cortex and medulla?**

Only about 85% of the scalp hair becomes full-fledged hair with all three layers. The rest, even in old age, remain downy hairs.

2. **What is the hygroscopic ability of hair?**

The ability of hair to absorb moisture makes it hygroscopic. It is made more readily hygroscopic by such agents as steam and chemicals. In hair coloring, the hair is made more absorbent by peroxide.

3. **Is salt water injurious to hair?**

No, salt water is not injurious to hair. Salt water does not contain injurious ingredients.

Unit 10
Frequent questions about hair

General objectives-student goals: After study, instruction and completion of this unit, you will be able to demonstrate understanding of the answers to some of the most frequent questions about hair by writing and/or giving the answers to 24 questions related to hair.

Trichology

4. It is often said that hair grows after death. Is this a fact?

No, hair does not grow after death. The shrinking of tissues causes the hair to project above the skin. This produces the illusion of growth.

5. Should hair be shampooed daily?

Frequent shampooing is not necessary and should be avoided. Hair should be washed only when it is not free from oil, dust and dirt.

6. Can hair be nourished with topical applications?

No, hair is nourished by the blood, not by external means.

7. What causes hair to swell?

Hair swells in strong acids, alkali and water. The swelling action lifts the scales of the cuticle. When hair swells too fast, it loses its structural strength. The cuticle tightens with the application of a mild acidic rinse. The acidic rinse applied after a tint not only ensures a tight cuticle but it also ensures against loss of color. Although normal hair contains approximately 30% moisture, water will cause hair to swell about 20% and lengthen up to 1%.

8. Which of the hair bonds is the hardest to disrupt?

The hair structure is held together by many types of molecular bonds. The disulfide bond is the hardest to disrupt. The other bonds will react easily when the hair is wet with water.

9. Are protein hair conditioners effective for all types of hair?

A protein hair conditioner must have the proper pH and the correct molecular size in order to be absorbed into the hair shaft. If the pH of the protein is too high and/or the molecules are too large, the application of the protein will be ineffective. A protein conditioner should have a pH of about 4.7 and a small molecular size.

10. Is the strength of the hair controlled by the cortex layer?

Yes, the total strength of hair is divided between the cuticle and the cortex with about 65% controlled by the cortex layer and 35% by the cuticle layer.

11. Is it possible for hair strands to unravel?

No, protein (keratin) keeps a strand of hair from unravelling.

Trichology

12. Is the practice of hair transplant limited to the medical profession?

Hair transplantation is the process of transplanting individual hairs from a given area of a person to another area, more specifically to the scalp. This process is restricted to the medical profession.

13. Why does hair break easily?

Easy breakage of hair that has not been damaged indicates insufficient protein and lack of moisture.

14. Can hair conditioners and/or hair treatments repair damaged hair instantly?

The natural laws of nature do not permit instant healing of broken bones or cuts. The same is true with hair. It is not possible to repair damaged hair instantly. When hair is damaged, it is from the inside, out.

15. How do alkaline products affect the hair?

Continuous exposure of the hair to alkaline products or mixtures results in a lack of the important disulfide bonds. When large amounts of these bonds are missing, the results of a cold wave or a set and the general appearance of the hair will be unsatisfactory.

16. Is hair with excessive elasticity a problem?

Yes, hair with excessive elasticity will not hold a set or respond to a chemical processing of any type successfully.

17. Is hair with low elasticity better than hair with excessive elasticity?

Hair with low elasticity is brittle and inclined to break. Both types are a problem.

18. What types of hair are considered resistant?

Most coarse, gray and natural red hair are classified as resistant.

19. What percentage of waving agents is used in a permanent wave solution?

Resistant hair requires a perm lotion with a 10% solution of active waving agents. Normal hair requires an 8% solution; damaged or tinted hair a 5-6% solution.

20. Does hair contain water?

Yes, hair contains some amount of water under normal conditions. Hair absorbs moisture from the surrounding atmosphere or from the perspiration of the skin.

Trichology

21. Is moisture important to the elastic behavior of hair?

If the normal water content is removed from the hair through the use of a hair dryer for a definite period, the hair will show no inclination to stretch. It will break before an appreciable extension is obtained. This demonstrates the extreme importance of moisture in the elastic behavior of hair.

22. How can a curl be produced on hair without moisture?

When using thermal irons on dry hair, we produce a curl because the heat of the iron causes a release of the normal moisture content from the hair in the form of steam. In this way, the moisture required to form the wave or curl on the curvature of the iron is readily obtained. The amount of steam produced is slight and most times invisible. However, it is sufficient to bring about the desired result.

23. Is moisture the important factor that enables hair to stretch?

Moisture is not only important in enabling hair to stretch, it is just as important in causing its contraction. For example, if a hair of any definite length is stretched in water while under tension, it will return to its original length only while it is still wet. However, if hair is stretched and then allowed to dry while held at its length, it will remain stretched. As long as the hair is not given the opportunity to reabsorb moisture, it will remain at its newly stretched length. Exposing the stretched hair to moisture or water will cause it to return automatically and immediately to its original length.

24. Why does short hair grow faster than long hair?

The theory is that as hair grows longer, it ages naturally and atrophies, or hardens slightly, so that it cannot take up its proper nourishment. It has been noted that medulla cells are missing near the base of long hair and that the imbrications are not visible in the cuticle. It is the lack of proper natural nourishment that slows the rate of growth as the hair grows longer.

Review questions

1. For what is trichology the technical term?

2. What is the name of the form in which peptides join amino acids?

3. What is the name of the linkage between two atoms which form a molecule?

Trichology

4. Physical bonds are made of hydrogen. Chemical bonds are disulfide and what else?

5. By what type of bonds is the hair structure held together?

6. What is the first cycle of hair growth called?

7. What is the chemical symbol for the chemical bonds in the hair prior to the application of a permanent wave lotion?

8. Until what age does the secondary stage of the hair covering last?

9. What is the chemical symbol for the broken S-S bonds?

10. There is a term which refers to hair's ability to react with both acidic and alkaline substances. What is this term?

11. What is the chemical symbol for the chemical bonds in the hair during the neutralization process?

12. What is the symbol used to identify hydrogen bonds?

Trichology

Trichology

Bacteriology and sanitizing

Chapter

20

Bacteriology and sanitizing: The study of bacteria and sanitization as they relate to the practice of cosmetology.

Overview: This chapter informs you about a branch of science which provides information about bacteria and an understanding of the importance of sanitization.

Behavioral objectives-student goals: After completion of this chapter, and after instruction and study, you will be able to perform and demonstrate competency and knowledge of bacteriology and sanitizing by identifying, explaining and/or listing: the forms of bacteria, infection, immunity, methods of sterilization and sanitary regulations pertaining to the beauty salon, implements, supplies and equipment, and the cosmetologist.

Bacteriology is the branch of science that deals with the study of microorganisms called bacteria, and their relation to health and disease. The cosmetologist must have knowledge of bacteriology in order to understand the importance of sanitization. He or she must become familiar with the precautions which must be taken in order to protect health.

Bacteria exist everywhere. They vary in size and shape. They are invisible to the naked eye. They are so small that when magnified one thousand times, they may appear no larger than a pin head. The origin of bacteria is unknown, and like all living things, they multiply. They exist in:

1. Earth
2. Foods
3. Air
4. Water

5. Human body
   A. Mouth
   B. Intestines
   C. Hands
   D. Skin

There are over twelve hundred species of bacteria. They are divided into two general classes:

1. Pathogenic
2. Nonpathogenic

Bacteriology and sanitizing

423

Pathogenic bacteria (pathogens) cause disease. Nonpathogenic bacteria are either harmless or, in some cases, beneficial to man. Over 70% of bacteria are of the nonpathogenic type. They live on the dead remains of living things and act as agents in putrefaction (decay). They keep the earth free of substances that might cause harm to other living things.

Pathogenic bacteria are undesirable because they breed and spread disease, produce poisons and toxins, cause infection and consume body foods needed for normal health.

Soiled linen, dirty hands, air, dust, breathing, dirty fingernails, dirty implements and flies are transmitters of bacteria in beauty salons. The conditions necessary for bacterial growth are filth, warmth, moisture and food. Bacteria multiply every half hour. A bacterium divides into two halves and becomes two bacteria. Each bacterium reproduces in the same manner. Bacteria can be destroyed by intense heat, sunlight, strong alkalies, strong acids and by sterilization. Freezing cannot destroy bacteria. Freezing merely puts them into an inactive state.

Sanitary and safety precautions for bacteriology and sanitizing

1. Store all sanitizing and cleaning chemicals in a cool dry area.

2. Label all containers.

3. Always wash your hands after using chemicals.

4. Wipe all spilled chemicals up at once.

5. Never use liquids in unlabeled containers. Discard all unknown chemicals.

6. Keep all containers tightly covered.

7. Always follow the manufacturer's instructions when mixing and/or using chemicals.

8. Avoid hand contact with the skin or eyes while using chemicals.

9. Wear a washable uniform.

10. Keep stations, drawers, cabinets and equipment clean and neat.

11. Do not keep soiled implements in the drawer in which you keep clean implements.

12. Deposit soiled towels in a covered container.

13. Sanitize implements and equipment after each use.

Unit 1
Forms of bacteria, infection and immunity

Forms of bacteria

Cosmetologists are most concerned with pathogenic bacteria. Bacteria are identified by their distinct shapes.

1. **Cocci** are ball or egg-shaped cells. The germs of pneumonia and spinal meningitis are of this type. Included in this group are:

    A. **Diplococci** which grow in pairs and cause pneumonia.

    B. **Staphylococci** which grow in clusters and are present in abscesses and boils.

    C. **Streptococci** grow in curved lines resembling a string of beads; and are found in blood poisoning.

2. **Bacilli** are rod-shaped cells found in tuberculosis and lockjaw.

3. **Spirilla** are coil-shaped cells found in Asiatic cholera, rat bite fever and other virulent diseases.

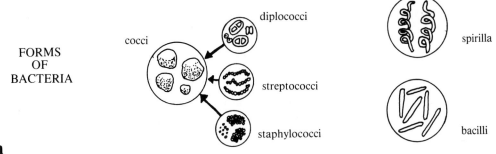

FORMS OF BACTERIA

cocci — diplococci — streptococci — staphylococci — spirilla — bacilli

Infection

Bacteria exist all around us. When a person is chilled, run down or has poor resistance, the germs can easily infect the body through:

1. The air during respiration. Coughing and sneezing spread germs.

2. Food may become contaminated if left exposed. Raw foods need special care. Milk must be pasteurized.

3. Inanimate objects: Contaminated objects used or handled by a diseased person.

Unit 1
Forms of bacteria, infection and immunity

General objectives-student goals:
After study, instruction and completion of this unit, you will be able to demonstrate understanding of the forms of bacteria, infection and immunity by writing and/or giving a brief overview of the subject.

Bacteriology and sanitizing

4. Direct contact: Kissing, hand shaking or touching an infected person.

5. Water: Drinking, washing or bathing.

6. Animals: A direct bite from an insect that has bitten an infected person, or direct contact with an infected animal.

Infection may be either local or general. Local infection is limited to one region of the body such as an abscess or a boil. General infection passes from one organ to another. Local infections, if neglected, may easily lead to general infections. These can spread in three ways:

1. Continuity of tissue: A cold can travel along the mucous membrane of the nose and throat into the bronchial tubes and lungs.

2. Through the blood stream: For example, blood poisoning, caused by streptococci which invade the body through a cut or abrasion, travels through the blood stream.

3. Lymph vessels: A condition that may cause inflammation in the lymph nodes. It may also travel to various parts of the body through the vessels of the lymphatic system.

Immunity

Immunity is the ability of the body to resist and overcome infection. Resistance is a measure of the body's ability to withstand infection. Resistance may exist in varying degrees. Susceptibility is the opposite of resistance. It indicates how prone the body is to infection.

1. Natural immunity may be inborn.

2. Acquired immunity takes place when one attack of a disease serves to prevent a recurrence.

3. Artificial immunity can be acquired by introducing certain biochemical substances into the body.

Unit 2
Sanitization and sterilization

The information, formulas and disinfectants mentioned in this unit are widely used and accepted for the practice of cosmetology. A broad review of all available information, however, indicates that the hygiene and sanitization laws vary in each state. Consult the Health Department and the State Board of Cosmetology in your state for a list of approved formulas and disinfectants. Always use them according to the manufacturer's instructions.

Sanitization is the branch of applied science that deals with practical measures designed to promote public health and prevent disease.

Unit 2

Sanitization and sterilization

General objectives-student goals:
After study, instruction and completion of this unit, you will be able to demonstrate understanding of

---

Bacteriology and sanitizing

Sterilization is the process by which all bacterial life is removed from an object. Health Departments and State Boards of Cosmetology realize that it is impossible to sterilize—in the true sense of the word—all the implements and equipment in a beauty school or salon. Although methods of sterilization are employed, the implements and equipment can only be considered sanitized. They are not sterilized.

Methods of sterilization

Sterilization can be achieved by using physical or chemical agents. **Physical sterilizing agents** are:

1. **Dry heat:** The process involves exposure to constant high temperature (300°-320°F).

2. **Moist heat:** This is immersion in boiling water for 20 minutes.

3. **Ultraviolet radiation:** In a sanitizer, this is an excellent method for keeping sanitized implements sterile.

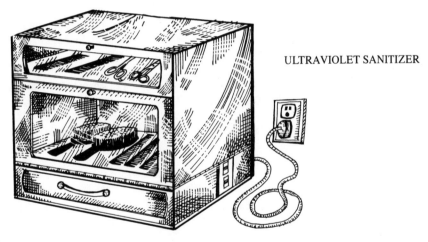

ULTRAVIOLET SANITIZER

Chemical sterilizing agents are:

1. Antiseptics and disinfectants:

   A. **Antiseptics** retard the growth of bacteria without destroying bacterial life. They may be applied to the skin.

   B. **Disinfectants** destroy pathogenic bacteria. They are used to sanitize equipment and implements. There are many prepared chemical disinfectants which are approved by the Boards of Health and State Boards of Cosmetology. Some of the popular ones are:

      1. **Alcohol** below 70% serves as an antiseptic for the skin. A 95% solution may be used as a disinfectant to sanitize implements.

Bacteriology and sanitizing

2. Formaldehyde: A 40% solution is a good disinfectant and fumigant (vapors). A 5% solution is a good antiseptic. To sanitize implements and prevent rust, a 25% solution should be prepared as follows:

2 parts formaldehyde

5 parts water

1 part glycerine

Some authorities claim that the use of formaldehyde for barber and beauty shop equipment sterilization needlessly threatens the health of cosmetologists and patrons. The results of a study indicate that the concentration of formaldehyde in the air is too high during sanitizing. Formaldehyde may cause cancer. In most states, current regulations favor dry sterilizers for equipment sanitization. However, they allow the use of liquid formaldehyde.

3. Quaternary ammonium compounds: These are powerful germicides (disinfectants) used to sanitize implements. They are inexpensive, odorless, nonirritating to the skin and stable. When mixing, always follow the manufacturer's instructions.

4. Hydrogen peroxide: A 3% solution may be used as an antiseptic and a mild disinfectant. Peroxide without U.S.P. on the label is not pure. It may cause an infection if it is used on an open cut.

2. Vapors are used in a drawer or cabinet sanitizer in order to keep implements sterile. Formaldehyde may be used for this purpose.

Procedure for sterilizing

1. Objects which will be sterilized should be washed thoroughly with soap and water in order to remove all foreign matter.

2. Immerse the implements in a wet sanitizer containing a disinfectant solution.

3. Remove the implements after the specified amount of time. Rinse them in clean water. Wipe them dry and place them in a storage cabinet sanitizer until ready for use. If the sanitizer cabinet is the fumigant type, use a 40% solution of formalin (formaldehyde) in a small tray or cup with a sponge or blotter.

Unit 3
Sanitary regulations for beauty salons, implements, supplies and equipment, and the cosmetologist

Beauty salons

1. Walls, ceilings, floors and equipment must be free from dust. They must be washable.

Unit 3

Sanitary regulations for beauty salons, implements, supplies and equipment, and the cosmetologist

General objectives-student goals:
After study, instruction and comple-

Bacteriology and sanitizing

428

2. The working area must be well lighted, heated and ventilated.

3. There must be an adequate supply of hot and cold running water.

4. All plumbing fixtures must be installed properly.

5. All electrical connections and equipment must be installed and grounded properly.

6. Drinking facilities and paper cups should be provided.

7. A lavatory should be equipped with hot and cold running water, liquid soap and paper towels.

8. Dogs, cats and birds are not permitted in a beauty salon.

Implements, supplies and equipment

1. Change the covering on the headrest for each patron.

2. Shampoo boards and bowls must be kept clean.

3. Linens and towels must be clean. They are to be used only once. Then, they are deposited in a covered container for soiled linens.

4. Any article which is dropped on the floor is not to be used again until it has been sterilized.

5. All waste materials, including hair regularly swept from the floor, must be deposited in covered containers.

6. Creams and all other semisolid substances must be dipped from the original container with a sterile spatula and transferred to a receptacle for use during a treatment.

7. Lotions or fluids must be poured into a container and then applied to the individual by means of a cotton pledget or a sterilized applicator.

8. Provide an individual paper cup for the finger bowl used during manicures.

9. Shampoo capes must not come in contact with the patron's neck skin.

10. Soiled combs, brushes and other used materials must be removed from the top of the work station immediately after use.

11. All implements must be sanitized.

tion of this unit, you will be able to demonstrate understanding of the sanitary regulations for beauty salons and cosmetologists by writing and/or giving a brief overview of the subject.

Bacteriology and sanitizing

12. Clips and pins must not be placed in the mouth.

13. Hair nets must be washed after each use.

14. Implements must not be carried in the pockets of your uniform.

Cosmetologists

1. All cosmetologists must observe all the rules of personal hygiene.

2. No person suffering from an infectious or communicable disease is permitted to work in any establishment devoted to cosmetology.

3. Each cosmetologist is required to wear a washable uniform while working on patrons. The uniform should not be sleeveless.

4. The cosmetologist's hands should be washed with soap and running water both before and after serving a patron, and after leaving the toilet.

5. No work shall be performed on any person having a visible infection or any other indication of a contagious or communicable disease.

6. Cosmetologists must not treat any inflammatory disease or condition of the skin, scalp, face or hands.

Review questions

1. What is bacteriology?

2. If bacteria exist everywhere and vary in size and shape, why are they invisible to the naked eye?

3. Can pathogenic bacteria cause disease?

4. Are nonpathogenic bacteria harmless?

5. How do germs infect the body?

6. Can a local infection lead to a general infection?

7. What is immunity?

8. What is resistance?

9. Is it possible for a cosmetologist to sterilize—in the true sense of the word—all the implements and equipment which he or she uses regularly?

10. Is sanitizing implements and equipment instead of sterilizing them acceptable?

11. Can antiseptics be applied to the skin?

12. Can chemical vapors be used as sterilizing agents?

13. Name a chemical agent which can be used for sterilizing with vapors.

14. How is a fumigant type of disinfectant solution used in a sanitizer cabinet?

NOTES

Chemistry for cosmetologists

Chapter

21

Chemistry for cosmetologists: Chemical processes and the many ways in which they relate to the practice of cosmetology.

Overview: This chapter provides you with knowledge of chemistry as it relates to daily salon operations.

Behavioral objectives-student goals: After completion of this chapter, and after instruction and study, you will be able to perform and demonstrate competency and knowledge of chemistry by identifying, explaining and/or listing: mixtures and chemical compounds, physical and chemical changes, the pH scale, acids, bases and salts, solutions and emulsions, cosmetics for the hair, skin and hands, the chemistry of sterilization, and biochemistry.

Many people believe that chemistry is a mysterious world of test tubes and strange apparatus. They think that it is practically impossible for the average cosmetologist to know anything about or understand chemistry. Chemistry is the science that deals with the composition of substances and the many ways in which they change or react with other substances. Cosmetologists are constantly utilizing chemicals and chemical processes in their daily salon operations. An understanding of elementary chemistry and chemical terms can be helpful in regard to selecting and using the best products for a particular beauty service and condition. Understanding the chemistry of products is a very important part of the practice of hairdressing and cosmetology.

This chapter deals with some basic, useful facts in areas of chemistry that are of interest to the cosmetologist. It is designed for students who have no formal background in chemistry but who need a working understanding of the science as it applies to the practice of hairdressing and cosmetology.

Chemistry is concerned with the substances existing in nature and with those which can be compounded from or react with other substances (synthetic–not of natural origin). Chemistry allows scientists the ability to make accurate measurements of the properties of matter. Matter is any substance that occupies space and has mass. It exists in these forms:

1. Solid

2. Liquid

3. Gas

Chemistry for
cosmetologists

433

Solid objects have fixed volumes and rigid shapes. Liquids have fixed volumes, flow and assume the shapes of their containers. Gases resemble liquids in their ability to flow. Gases, however, have the distinctive property of expanding or contracting to fill the volume of their containers. A gas has neither a fixed shape nor volume and can be compressed and pressurized.

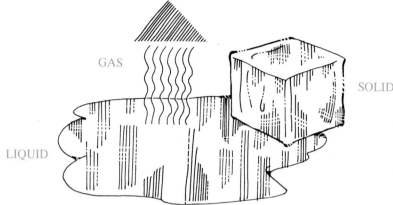

GAS

SOLID

LIQUID

Unit 1
Elements, their symbols and atoms

Every known substance is composed of one or more of the chemical elements. An element is a simple building block of substance matter which cannot decompose or separate into any other substance by ordinary chemical changes or unions. The smallest quantity of an element is called an atom.

Scientists have identified 106 elements. Robert Boyle was the first to recognize the nature of a chemical element in 1661. By 1789, the first list of elements was published. Each one of them has been given a symbol. The symbol is an abbreviation for the element. These symbols are used as a form of shorthand to describe the element. They are usually the first letter, or the first two letters, of the Latin name for the element.

Elements can combine with one another to form a wide variety of more complex substances called molecules and compounds. Compounds number in the millions. More are being discovered or created every day.

Atoms bond together in order to form elements, molecules and compounds. A molecule is the smallest particle of a compound. It is composed of two or more atoms joined together. When all the atoms in the molecule are of the same kind, the molecule is an element. If any one of the atoms in the molecule is of a different kind, the result is a molecule or compound.

Atoms are made up of protons, electrons and neutrons. The protons and electrons contain electric charges. A single dissociated atom of sodium becomes sodium ion and has an electrical charge. The protons have a positive charge, and the electrons have a negative charge. The neutrons do not have an electric charge. An atom has equal numbers of protons and

Unit 1

Elements, their symbols and atoms

General objectives-student goals:
After study, instruction and completion of this unit, you will be able to demonstrate understanding of elements, their symbols and atoms by writing and/or giving a brief overview of the subject.

Chemistry for cosmetologists

434

electrons. When the number of protons and electrons is not equal, the atom becomes an ion. A bond formed between two ions, excluding hydrogen (H) or hydroxyl (OH) ions, is called a salt bond or an ionic bond. Salt bonds are found in the hair. They help to stabilize the hair's protein chains.

A complete list of elements and related information is provided on the following pages. Attention should be given to the following notes.

1. The atomic weights are the 1979 IUPAC (International Union for Pure and Applied Chemistry) values.

2. ( ) around atomic weights indicates that the number is the atomic weight of the most stable isotope.

3. A – indicates that the data is not known.

4. A = Atmospheric indicates that the natural form of the element can change when exposed to factors other than ordinary pressure and temperature.

Unit 2
Mixtures and chemical compounds

A mixture is any combination of substances in which the ingredients are mixed and held together mechanically without a chemical reaction between the substances. Some mixtures can be quite complicated like solutions, suspensions and emulsions. However, there is still no chemical reaction between the ingredients.

A mixture may be a combination of elements which still resembles the original elements. For example, combining vegetable dyes with metallic salts forms a hair coloring mixture in which the original elements are still easily identified.

Mixtures differ from pure substances because they can be separated into their component parts by a physical process. For example, table salt can be obtained when evaporation separates water from a mixture of table salt and water or other compounds in seawater.

A chemical compound is a combination of elements which are united chemically in definite proportions. Although the number of elements is only 106, these elements can join together in almost limitless combinations. This results in hundreds of thousands of chemical compounds.

A chemical compound is formed by an interaction between the elements involved. This chemical change results in the formation of an entirely new substance. Nearly everyone is familiar with the compound sodium chloride. This is ordinary table salt. However, the two elements which unite to form salt are entirely different. Sodium is an extremely active silvery metal which reacts violently with water and other substances. Chlorine is a poisonous gas which is also extremely active. However, the chemical combination of these two elements results in the safe stable compound sodium chloride. (Text continued on page 448)

Unit 2
Mixtures and chemical compounds

General objectives-student goals: After study, instruction and completion of this unit, you will be able to demonstrate understanding of mixtures and chemical compounds by writing and/or giving a brief overview of the subject.

Chemistry for cosmetologists

435

TABLE

OF

ELEMENTS

Element	Symbol	Atomic Number	Atomic Weight	N = Nature or L = Laboratory	Radio-active	State A = Atmospheric L = Liquid G = Gas S = Solid	Specific Gravity/ Density
Actinium	Ac	89	(227)	N	Yes	S	—
Aluminum	Al	13	26.9815	N		S	2.70
Americium	Am	95	(243)	L	Yes	S	11.72
Antimony	Sb	51	121.75	N		S	6.62
Argon	Ar	18	39.948	N		G/A	1.00178
Arsenic	As	33	74.9216	N		S	5.727
Astatine	At	85	(210)	N		S	—
Barium	Ba	56	137.33	N		S	3.5
Berkelium	Bk	97	(247)	L	Yes	S	—
Beryllium	Be	4	9.0122	N		S	1.86
Bismuth	Bi	83	208.980	N		S	9.80
Boron	B	5	10.811	N		S	2.45
Bromine	Br	35	79.909	N		L	3.12
Cadmium	Cd	48	112.41	N		S	8.65
Calcium	Ca	20	40.08	N		S	1.55
Californium	Cf	98	(251)	L	Yes	S	—
Carbon	C	6	12.01115	N		S	2.26
Cerium	Ce	58	140.12	N		S	3.37

Melting Point	Boiling Point	Discoverer	Year	Country
1050 C	—	André de Bierne	1899	France
660	2057	Hans C. Oersted	1825	Denmark
1100	—	G.T. Seaborg, R.A. James, L.O. Morgan, A. Ghiorso	1945	United States
630.5	1380	Known to the ancients	—	—
-189.2	-185.7	Sir William Ramsay, Baron Rayleigh	1894	Scotland
817	613	Known to the ancients	—	—
302 C	—	D.R. Carson, K.R. MacKenzie, E. Sergé	1940	United States
714	1640	Sir Humphry Davy	1808	England
—	—	G.T. Seaborg, S.G. Thompson, A. Ghiorso	1949	United States
1277	2770	Friedrich Wöhler, A.A. Bussy	1928	Germany, France
271.3	1560	Known to the ancients	—	—
2300	2550	H. Davy, J.L. Gay-Lussac, L.J. Theward	1808	England, France
-7.2	58.78	Antoine J. Balard	1826	France
320.9	765	Friedrich Stromeyer	1817	Germany
838	1440	Sir Humphry Davy	1808	England
—	—	G.T. Seaborg, S.G. Thompson, A. Ghiorso, K. Street, Jr.	1950	United States
3726	4830	Known to the ancients	—	—
795	3468	W. Von Hisinger, J. Berzelius, M. Klaproth	1803	Germany, Sweden

TABLE

OF

ELEMENTS

Chemistry for cosmetologists

Element	Symbol	Atomic Number	Atomic Weight	N=Nature or L=Laboratory	Radio-active	State A=Atmospheric L=Liquid G=Gas S=Solid	Specific Gravity/ Density
Cesium	Cs	55	132.905	N	Yes	L	1.90
Chlorine	Cl	17	35.453	N		G	1.56
Chromium	Cr	24	51.996	N		S	7.1
Cobalt	Co	27	58.9332	N	Yes	S	8.9
Copper	Cu	29	63.54	N		S	8.92
Curium	Cm	96	(247)	L	Yes	S	—
Dysprosium	Dy	66	162.50	N		S	8.56
Einsteinium	Es	99	(254)	L	Yes	S	—
Element 106*	—	106	—	L	Yes	**	—
Erbium	Er	68	167.26	N		S	9.16
Europium	Eu	63	151.96	N		S	5.24
Fermium	Fm	100	(253)	L	Yes	S	—
Fluorine	F	9	18.998403	N		G	0.0017
Francium	Fr	87	(223)	N	Yes	S	—
Gadolinium	Gd	64	157.25	N		S	7.95
Gallium	Ga	31	69.72	N		L	5.9
Germanium	Ge	32	72.59	N		S	5.36
Gold	Au	79	196.967	N		S	19.3

*The International Union for Pure and Applied Chemistry has not adopted an official name or symbol for this element.

**Information is unavailable at time of printing.

Melting Point	Boiling Point	Discoverer	Year	Country
28.5	690	Gustov Kirchhoff, Robert Bunsen	1860	Germany
-101	-34.7	Carl Wilhelm Scheele	1774	Sweden
1890	2200	Louis Vauquelin	1797	France
1495	2900	George Brandt	1737	Sweden
1083	2336	Known to the ancients	—	—
—	—	G.T. Seaborg, R.A. James, A. Ghiorso	1944	United States
1407	2600	Paul Émile Lecoq de Boisbaudran	1886	France
—	—	Argonne	1952	United States
—	—	G. Flerov, A. Ghiorso	1974	Soviet Union, United States
1497	2900	Carl Mossander	1843	Sweden
1439	826	Eugene Demarcay	1901	France
—	—	Argonne	1953	United States
-223	-188	Henri Moissan	1886	France
—	27	Marguerite Perey	1939	France
1312	3000	Jean de Marignac	1880	Switzerland
29.78	2237	Paul Émile Lecoq de Boisbaudran	1875	France
958.5	2700	Clemens Winkler	1886	Germany
1063	2970	Known to the ancients	—	—

TABLE

OF

ELEMENTS

Chemistry for cosmetologists

TABLE

OF

ELEMENTS

Element	Symbol	Atomic Number	Atomic Weight	N=Nature or L=Laboratory	Radio-active	State A=Atmospheric L=Liquid G=Gas S=Solid	Specific Gravity/ Density
Hafnium	Hf	72	178.49	N		S	13.3
Hahnium	Ha	105	(260)	L	Yes	**	—
Helium	He	2	4.0026	N		G/A	.126
Holmium	Ho	67	164.930	N		S	8.76
Hydrogen	H	1	1.00797	N		G	.071
Indium	In	49	114.82	N	Yes	S	7.3
Iodine	I	53	126.9044	N		S	4.93
Iridium	Ir	77	192.2	N		S	22.4
Iron	Fe	26	55.847	N		S	7.89
Krypton	Kr	36	83.80	N		G/A	2.6
Lanthanium	La	57	138.91	N		S	6.17
Lawrencium	Lr	103	(256)	L	Yes	S	—
Lead	Pb	82	207.19	N	Yes	S	11.34
Lithium	Li	3	6.939	N		S	0.534
Lutetium	Lu	71	174.97	N		S	9.84
Magnesium	Mg	12	24.312	N		S	.97
Manganese	Mn	25	54.9380	N		S	7.2
Mendelevium	Md	101	(258)	L	Yes	S	—

**Information is unavailable at time of printing.

Melting Point	Boiling Point	Discoverer	Year	Country
2222	5400	Dick Coster, Georg von Hevesy	1923	Denmark
—	—	G. Flerov, A. Ghiorso	1968, 1970	Soviet Union, United States
-272.2	-268.9	Nils Langlet, P.T. Cleve, Sir William Ramsay	1895	Sweden, Scotland
1461	2600	J.L. Soret	1878	Switzerland
-259.14	-252.8	Henry Cavendish	1766	England
156.4	2000	Ferdinand Reich, H. Ritcher	1863	Germany
113.7	184.35	Bernard Courtois	1811	France
2454	(5300)	Smithson Tennant, A.F. Fourcroy, L.N. Vauquelin, H.V. Collet-Descotils	1804	England, France
1535	3000	Known to the ancients	—	—
-156.6	152.9	Sir William Ramsay, M.W. Travers	1898	Great Britain
920	(3470)	Carl Mossander	1839	Sweden
—	—	A. Ghiorso, T. Sikkeland, A.E. Larsh, R.M. Latimer	1961	United States
327.4	1620	Known to the ancients	—	—
108.5	1336	Johann Arfvedson	1817	Sweden
1625	3327	Georges Urbain	1907	France
651	1107	Sir Humphry Davy	1808	England
1260	1900	Johann Gahn	1774	Sweden
—	—	G.T. Seaborg, A. Ghiorso, B. Harvey, G.R. Choppin, S.G. Thompson	1955	United States

TABLE

OF

ELEMENTS

Chemistry for cosmetologists

TABLE

OF

ELEMENTS

Element	Symbol	Atomic Number	Atomic Weight	N=Nature or L=Laboratory	Radio-active	State A=Atmospheric L=Liquid G=Gas S=Solid	Specific Gravity Density
Mercury	Hg	80	200.59	N		L	13.55
Molybdenum	Mo	42	95.94	N		S	10.2
Neodymium	Nd	60	144.24	N		S	6.9
Neon	Ne	10	20.183	N		G/A	1.2
Neptunium	Np	93	(237)	L	Yes	S	19.5
Nickel	Ni	28	58.71	N		S	8.90
Niobium	Nb	41	92.906	N		S	8.4
Nitrogen	N	7	14.0067	N		G	0.00125
Nobelium	No	102	(255)	L	Yes	S	—
Osmium	Os	76	190.2	N		S	22.57
Oxygen	O	8	15.9994	N		G	1.14
Palladium	Pd	46	106.4	N		S	12.16
Phosphorus	P	15	30.9738	N		S	1.83
Platinum	Pt	78	195.09	N		S	21.37
Plutonium	Pu	94	(244)	L	Yes	S	19.82
Polonium	Po	84	(210)	N	Yes	S	9.2

Melting Point	Boiling Point	Discoverer	Year	Country
-38.87	356.58	Known to the ancients	—	—
2620	5560	Carl Wilhelm Scheele	1778	Sweden
840	—	C.F. Auer von Welsbach	1885	Austria
-248.7	-245.9	Sir William Ramsay, M.W. Travers	1898	England
640	—	E.M. McMillian, P.H. Abelson	1940	United States
1455	2900	Axel Cronstedt	1751	Sweden
2345	3800	Charles Hatchett	1801	England
-209.9	-195.8	Daniel Rutherford	1772	Scotland
—	—	Nobel Institute For Physics	1957	Sweden
2700	5500	Smithson Tennant	1804	England
-218.4	-182.96	Carl Wilhelm Scheele, Joseph Priestley	1774	Sweden, England
1549	3980	William Wollaston	1803	England
44.1	280	Hennig Brand	1669	Germany
1773	4300	Julius Scaliger	1557	Italy
639.5	3508	G.T. Seaborg, J.W. Kennedy, E.M. McMillian, A.C. Wahl	1940	United States
254	—	Pierre and Marie Curie	1898	France

TABLE

OF

ELEMENTS

Chemistry for cosmetologists

Element	Symbol	Atomic Number	Atomic Weight	N=Nature or L=Laboratory	Radio-active	State A=Atmospheric L=Liquid G=Gas S=Solid	Specific Gravity/ Density
Potassium	K	19	39.0983	N		S	0.86
Praseodymium	Pr	59	140.907	N		S	6.5
Promethium	Pm	61	(145)	L	Yes	S	—
Protactinium	Pa	91	(231)	N	Yes	S	15.37
Radium	Ra	88	(226)	N	Yes	S	5.0
Radon	Rn	86	(222)	N	Yes	G/A	0.00973
Rhenium	Re	75	186.2	N		S	20.53
Rhodium	Rh	45	102.905	N		S	12.5
Rubidium	Rb	37	85.47	N		S	1.53
Ruthenium	Ru	44	101.07	N		S	12.2
Rutherfordium	Rf	104	—	L	Yes	**	—
Samarium	Sm	62	150.35	N		S	7.7
Scandium	Sc	21	44.956	N		S	3
Selenium	Se	34	78.96	N		S	4.8
Silicon	Si	14	28.0855	N		S	2.4
Silver	Ag	47	107.870	N		S	10.5
Sodium	Na	11	22.9898	N		S	0.97
Strontium	Sr	38	87.62	N		S	2.6

**Information is unavailable at time of printing.

Melting Point	Boiling Point	Discoverer	Year	Country
62.3	760	Sir Humphry Davy	1807	England
940	3127	C.F. Auer von Welsbach	1885	Austria
1027	—	J.A. Marinsky, Lawrence E. Glendenin, Charles D. Coryell	1945	United States
1230	—	Otto Hahn, Lise Meitner, John Cranston, Fredrick Soddy	1917	Germany, England
960	1140	Pierre and Marie Curie	1898	France
-71	61.8	Friedrich Ernst Dorn	1900	Germany
3160	5900	Walter Noddack, Ida Tacke, Otto Berg	1925	Germany
1985	4500	William Wollaston	1803	England
38.5	700	R. Bunsen, G. Kirchhoff	1861	Germany
2500	4900	Karl Klaus	1844	Russia
—	—	G. Flerov, A. Ghiorso	1964, 1969	Soviet Union, United States
1072	(1900)	Paul Émile Lecoq de Boisbaudran	1879	France
1539	2730	Lars Nilson	1879	Sweden
220	685	Jöns Berzelius	1817	Sweden
1420	2600	Jöns Berzelius	1823	Sweden
960.8	2210	Known to the ancients	—	—
97.5	892	Sir Humphry Davy	1807	England
(768)	1380	A. Crawford	1790	Scotland

TABLE

OF

ELEMENTS

Chemistry for cosmetologists

TABLE

OF

ELEMENTS

Element	Symbol	Atomic Number	Atomic Weight	N=Nature or L=Laboratory	Radio-active	State A=Atmospheric L=Liquid G=Gas S=Solid	Specific Gravity/ Density
Sulfur	S	16	32.064	N		S	2.0
Tantalum	Ta	73	180.948	N		S	16.6
Technitium	Tc	43	(79)	L		S	11.5
Tellurium	Te	52	127.60	N		S	6.24
Terbium	Tb	65	158.924	N		S	8.27
Thallium	Tl	81	204.37	N		S	11.85
Thorium	Th	90	232.038	N	Yes	S	11.2
Thulium	Tm	69	168.934	N		S	9.05
Tin	Sn	50	118.69	N		S	7.3
Titanium	Ti	22	47.90	N		S	4.5
Tungsten	W	74	183.85	N		S	19.3
Uranium	U	92	238.03	N	Yes	S	19.07
Vanadium	V	23	50.942	N		S	5.96
Xenon	Xe	54	131.30	N		G/A	308
Ytterbium	Yb	70	173.04	N		S	6.98
Yttrium	Y	39	88.905	N		S	4.47
Zinc	Zn	30	65.37	N		S	7.14
Zirconium	Zr	40	91.22	N		S	6.4

Chemistry for cosmetologists

Melting Point	Boiling Point	Discoverer	Year	Country
112.8	444.6	Known to the ancients	—	—
3027	5425	Anders Ekeberg	1802	Sweden
2200	—	Carlo Perrier, Émillo Sergé	1937	Italy
452	990	Franz Muller von Reichenstein	1782	Romania
1356	2800	Carl Mossander	1843	Sweden
302	1457	Sir William Crookes	1861	England
1750	3850	Jöns Berzelius	1828	Sweden
1145	1727	Per Theodor Cleve	1879	Sweden
231.9	2270	Known to the ancients	—	—
1668	3280	William Cregor	1791	England
3370	5900	Fausto and Juan Jose de Elhuyar	1783	Spain
1133	3818	Martin Klaproth	1789	Germany
1900	3450	Nils Sefstrom	1830	Sweden
112	108	Sir William Ramsay, M.W. Travers	1898	England
824	1427	Jean de Marignac	1878	Switzerland
1509	(2927)	Johann Gadolin	1794	Finland
419.5	907	Andreas Marggraf	1746	Germany
1852	3580	Martin Klaproth	1789	Germany

TABLE

OF

ELEMENTS

Chemistry for cosmetologists

Formulas are abbreviations for chemical compounds. They give the symbols of all the elements, which compose the molecules of the compound, and the proportions in which they are combined. Some common formulas for compounds used in making cosmetic products are:

Chemical compound	Formula	Uses
Ammonia	NH_3	Making amino dyes and detergents
Ammonium hydroxide	NH_4OH	Cold wave lotion, bleaching, smelling salts
Calcium carbonate	$CaCO_3$	Talcum powder-component of chalk
Hydrogen peroxide	H_2O_2	Bleaching, oxidation of tints and neutralizing cold wave lotions
Magnesium carbonate	$MgCO_3$	Talcum powder, bleaching paste
Nitric acid	HNO_3	Dyes and explosives
Sodium carbonate	Na_2CO_3	Water softener, bath salts
Sodium hydroxide	$NaOH$	Soap making, hair straightening
Water	H_2O	Chemically: production, solution and dilution of other products

Unit 3
Physical and chemical changes

A physical change takes place when a substance is altered in form or state without a change in composition. For example, water can exist in all three physical states: as a solid (ice), as a liquid (water) or as a gas (steam). However, its atomic composition does not change. When a stretched rubber band or a piece of glass breaks, it is a physical change. We still recognize both the rubber and the glass.

A chemical change results in the formation of one or more new substances, each having its own properties. In a chemical change, two or more elements or compounds combine to form a more complex substance or break down to form simpler substances.

Unit 3
Physical and chemical changes

General objectives-student goals:
After study, instruction and completion of this unit, you will be able to demonstrate understanding of physical and chemical changes by writing and/or giving a brief overview of the subject.

Chemistry for cosmetologists

A chemical change is expressed in a shorthand method called an equation. For example, the equation for the formation of table salt (sodium chloride) is:

$Na + Cl = NaCl$
Sodium + chlorine = salt

The same sodium chloride compound could also be produced by combining sodium hydroxide with hydrochloric acid. This equation would be:

$NaOH + HCl = NaCl + H_2O$
Sodium hydroxide + hydrochloric acid = salt + water

Hydrogen peroxide decomposes readily into water and oxygen gas. The equation for this reaction is:

$2H_2O_2 = 2H_2O + O_2$
Hydrogen peroxide = water + oxygen

Heat or light can cause this reaction. This is the reason why unstabilized hydrogen peroxide should be stored in a cool dark place and in containers or brown bottles which do not admit light.

If hydrogen peroxide does decompose in the salon, it turns into water and cannot perform its job. The function of hydrogen peroxide is to release oxygen during the bleaching and hair coloring processes. It is also used to stop the action of cold wave lotions (neutralization). All of these processes are called oxidation. Conversely, when hydrogen is introduced, the process is called reduction.

Equations involving complicated molecules are sometimes expressed in words rather than in the shorthand method. For example, the action of hydrogen peroxide with an aniline dye, also called "amino" or "coal tar" dye, can be expressed as follows:

dye base + hydrogen peroxide = colored dye compound

Another example could be the preparation of castile soap from olive oil with glycerine as a by-product. This equation could be written:

olive oil + sodium hydroxide = olive oil soap + glycerine

Unit 4
Acids, bases and salts

Many of the substances used in cosmetology fall into one of the following categories of chemical compounds: acids, bases or salts.

PHYSICAL CHANGE: when cup is broken pieces are still recognizable...

Unit 4
Acids, bases and salts

General objectives-student goals:
After study, instruction and completion of this unit, you will be able to demonstrate understanding of acids, bases and salts by writing and/or giving a brief overview of the subject.

Chemistry for cosmetologists

An acid is a compound which ionizes in solution to give H ions that are positively charged hydrogen atoms. These are called hydrogen ions. They give the acid its properties. The word acid comes from the Latin acidus, meaning sour. An acid has a sour taste and turns litmus paper red.

A base, also called an alkali, is the hydroxide of a metal which ionizes in water to give hydroxyl-ion (OH). In other words, a base is a combination of a metal and a hydroxide ion (chemical symbols: OH). Bases are bitter tasting, corrosive to the skin, soapy to the touch. They turn litmus paper from pink to blue.

A salt is a compound formed by the union of an acid and a base. The hydrogen of the acid is replaced by a metal. The other product formed is always water.

Alkaline substances are usually used in hair cosmetic products because of their softening (perms and relaxers) and cleansing (shampoos) powers. Alkalies are compounds composed of hydroxide ions. Acids have hydrogen ions. The strength of these compounds is measured in terms of the number of ions that they supply in a water solution. The scale for measuring this concentration of ions is called the pH (potential of hydrogen) scale.

Unit 5
The pH scale

The relative acidity or alkalinity of a solution is given in terms of the hydrogen ion concentration. This is calculated on the pH scale (potential of hydrogen) which goes from 0 to 14. Pure water has a pH of 7. Therefore, 7 is considered neutral. The higher the number above 7, the more alkaline the solution. The lower the number below 7, the more acidic the solution.

It is very important for the cosmetologist to know the pH of the various products used in the salon. If a product is strongly acidic (with a pH of 4 or lower) or strongly alkaline (a pH higher than 10), it may be harmful to the skin or hair. The pH value should be obtained from the manufacturer of any product with which you are not familiar. It can also be determined by colorimetric indicators, such as pH papers or the universal indicator.

The average pH values of some common products are:

Product	Average pH
Ammonium thioglycolate (used in cold wave lotions)*	9
Boric acid	5
Soapless shampoo*	6–7
Soap*	8–9

Unit 5
The pH scale

General objectives-student goals:
After study, instruction and completion of this unit, you will be able to demonstrate understanding of the pH scale by writing and/or giving a brief overview of the subject.

Chemistry for cosmetologists

Sodium bicarbonate (baking soda)	8–9
1% sodium hydroxide (used in hair straighteners)*	12
Hair conditioners	2.5–7.0
Hair bleach	9.4
Powder bleach	9.6–11.0
Tints and toners	9.5

*The pH of commercial products varies according to the manufacturer.

Since the pH can be determined by colorimetric indicators or electrometric instruments, there is no need for the cosmetologist to study the scientific basis for the pH scale. The pH meter is an electronic device with two electrodes. They are immersed in an aqueous solution and generate a signal which is registered on the meter. Measuring pH with a pH meter is not for the cosmetologist. It is much more practical to use pH papers or a liquid universal indicator. It should be noted, however, that the pH meter is much more precise and can be used in colored solutions. The color of a solution may interfere with the observation of color indicators, both liquid and paper.

pH Meter

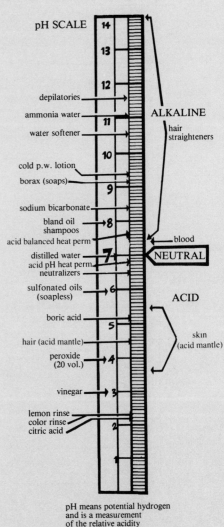

pH means potential hydrogen and is a measurement of the relative acidity or alkalinity of a solution...

Chemistry for cosmetologists

Mathematically, the pH number is a measurement of the hydrogen-ion concentration expressed in terms of the number of gram-ions in a liter (1.06 quarts) of solution. Pure water is neutral and contains equal amounts of equally active hydrogen (H) and hydroxyl (OH) ions. There is one of these gram-ion units in every 10,000,000 parts. The number of zeros indicates the pH. In the case of water, it is 7. In a neutral solution, there is an equal number of active hydroxide ions (OH) and active hydrogen ions

451

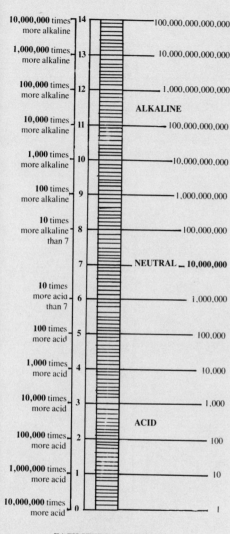

10,000,000 times more alkaline	14	100,000,000,000,000
1,000,000 times more alkaline	13	10,000,000,000,000
100,000 times more alkaline	12	1,000,000,000,000
		ALKALINE
10,000 times more alkaline	11	100,000,000,000
1,000 times more alkaline	10	10,000,000,000
100 times more alkaline	9	1,000,000,000
10 times more alkaline than 7	8	100,000,000
	7	**NEUTRAL** — 10,000,000
10 times more acid than 7	6	1,000,000
100 times more acid	5	100,000
1,000 times more acid	4	10,000
10,000 times more acid	3	1,000
		ACID
100,000 times more acid	2	100
1,000,000 times more acid	1	10
10,000,000 times more acid	0	1

**EACH STEP INCREASES
BY MULTIPLES OF 10**

**Chemistry for
cosmetologists**

452

(H). The number of zeros for both the H ions and the OH ions must total 14. In acid solutions, the active H ion concentration goes up as the active OH ion concentration goes down. The result is that any pH less than 7 is acidic. Alkaline solutions work in an opposite manner. The OH ion concentration goes up as the active H ion concentration goes down. Any pH number above 7 indicates that the OH ions outnumber the H ions. The solution is alkaline.

The number of zeros indicates the pH.

1. Neutral: Pure water has a pH of 7. It contains one gram-ion unit in every 10,000,000 parts (7 zeros: pH of 7).

2. Acid: A solution with a pH of 5 would have one gram-ion unit in every 100,000 parts (5 zeros). A pH of 3 would mean one gram-ion unit in every 1,000 parts (3 zeros). As the pH number decreases below 7, the solution becomes more and more acidic.

3. Alkaline: A solution with a pH of 9 would have one gram-ion unit in every 1,000,000,000 parts (9 zeros). As the pH number goes above 7, the solution becomes more and more alkaline.

Hair and skin do not have a pH value. We can only measure the pH of liquids. We cannot measure the pH of oily products or solids. Water must be present in order to determine pH. The liquid mantle of the hair, about 4.5, is a combination of the natural body fluids (sebum and perspiration) that surround and are absorbed into the hair. Sweat or perspiration is a colorless, watery liquid. It is slightly turbid (i.e., not clear). It has a salty taste and a characteristic, though variable, odor. When it forms and passes off quickly, it is alkaline or neutral. Under normal circumstances, it becomes acidic from contamination with sebum and other waste material on the skin.

All alkaline products are not bad for the hair. Some products, like perms, tints, hair straighteners and hair relaxers, require a high pH in order to be effective and provide good results. Acid pH shampoo and hair conditioners help tighten the cuticle and return the hair to its original composition prior to the alkaline treatment(s). It is not the high pH of a product that can cause damage to the hair. It is the degree of free alkali in the product which causes the problem. Most reliable manufacturers use quality control methods to produce alkaline products with a very low level of free alkali.

The pH value of hair products affects the diameter and sheen of the hair. Slightly acidic products do not create swelling. Neutral products (pH 7) create a small degree of swelling which increases the diameter of the hair slightly. Alkaline products lift the cuticle and cause extreme swelling of the hair. They increase the diameter of the hair greatly. Hair has more sheen when the cuticle scales retain their natural, smooth, flat form. Alkaline solutions raise the cuticle. The cuticle will tighten and return to its flat form when acid balanced preparations are used as the final product on the hair.

All shampoo products tend to strip tinted hair color. The pH value and the concentration of the active ingredients in the shampoo control the degree of stripping. Shampoos which are slightly acidic (lower pH) will strip less color than alkaline shampoos (higher pH). An acid shampoo can also strip color if the ingredients include large amounts of suds-creating agents (alkaline).

The original pH of the hair and scalp are restored naturally within two to seven hours after the use of alkaline products. The skin has the ability to regenerate its acidity through the secretion of the sebaceous glands and the excretion from the sudoriferous glands.

Unit 6
Solutions and emulsions

A solution is a homogeneous mixture of one or more substances dissolved into another. For example, when sugar is dissolved in water, the sugar crystals break down into such fine particles that they are invisible and form a clear, transparent solution of uniform composition. The dissolved substance, sugar in this case, is called the solute, and the substance in which the solute is dissolved, water in this case, is called the solvent.

If the particle size of the solute is rather coarse, like the particles in muddy water, and if they will eventually settle out if left standing, the mixture is called a suspension.

If the particles are smaller than in a suspension but larger than in a solution, and if they stay suspended in a translucent solution, the mixture is called a colloid.

Finally, if a colloidal suspension of a liquid in another liquid has an emulsifying agent (or binder) added to it, this mixture is called an emulsion. Emulsions are very common in cosmetology because they make the compounds involved easier and/or safer to apply. Some examples of emulsions are: hair conditioners, cream shampoos and a multitude of cosmetic creams and lotions for both the hair and skin.

The strength of a solution is determined by the amount of solute dissolved in it. It is expressed in terms of the percentage of the solution that consists of the dissolved substance. If the solute is a solid, the percentage is determined by weight. For example, if you dissolve 10 pounds (4.53 kg.) of sugar into 90 pounds (40.82 kg.) of water, the result would be a 100 pound (45.36 kg.) solution, 10% of which is sugar. It would be called a 10% sugar solution. If the solute is a liquid dissolved in another liquid, the strength of the solution would be the percentage of the total liquid volume that is solute. For example, 6 liquid ounces (177.44 ml.) of pure hydrogen peroxide dissolved in 94 ounces (2.78 l.) of water would be called a 6% hydrogen peroxide solution. If the solution gives off a gas, a way of describing its strength is by the volume of gas given off. If a pint of solution can release 20 pints (9.46 l.) of gas, it is called a 20 volume solution. Using hydrogen peroxide as an example, 20 volume hydrogen peroxide means a solution that can give off 20 times its own volume in gas.

Unit 7
Shampoo

Shampoo molecules have a double action. They attract and hold grease, dirt and other particles of foreign matter. They also have a strong attraction for water. This allows the shampoo to remove grease, dirt and particles of foreign matter during the water rinsing part of the shampoo.

Although there are many variations, there are three basic types of shampoos:

1. Soap shampoos
2. Soapless shampoos and detergents
3. Dry shampoos

Unit 6
Solutions and emulsions

General objectives-student goals:
After study, instruction and completion of this unit, you will be able to demonstrate understanding of solutions and emulsions by writing and/or giving a brief overview of the subject.

Unit 7
Shampoo

General objectives-student goals:
After study, instruction and completion of this unit, you will be able to demonstrate understanding of shampoo chemistry by writing and/or giving a brief overview of the subject.

Chemistry for cosmetologists

Soap shampoos are made by mixing an alkali, usually sodium hydroxide or potassium hydroxide, with an oil or fat. The oil or fat may be a vegetable oil like olive oil or coconut oil or an animal fat like tallow or lanolin. Shampoos made with olive oil are better for the hair and skin but produce little lather. Olive oil shampoos are called castile shampoos. However, some manufacturers now use the term castile for blended shampoos. Coconut oil shampoos lather profusely but may be harsh on the scalp and hair. Therefore, blends of olive oil and coconut oil shampoos, hydrogenated coconut oil shampoos or olive oil shampoos with an added lathering agent are often recommended.

The pH of a shampoo is important and should be available on request. For cosmetologists who prefer to make their own quick and easy test of pH, sets of pH papers are available at many supply houses. Soap shampoos with a higher pH may clean better. However, they may be too harsh and drying to the hair and scalp. Soap shampoos with a pH from 8.5 to 9.5 are generally satisfactory. Those with a pH above 9.5 may be too strong.

Soap shampoos are usually purchased in concentrated form (jellies, granules or liquid) and diluted with water prior to use. When diluting, add just enough hot water to keep the solution liquid when it cools. When it is used, the shampoo solution should be diluted again with warm water. The solution should not be boiled since this would hydrolyze the soap and release alkali.

In order to overcome some of the disadvantages of soap shampoos, particularly the lack of lather and/or the residue formed in hard water, chemists have developed products which are commonly called soapless shampoos. These shampoos are made by a process similar to that used for soap shampoos except the oils or the alcohols related to fatty acids are treated with sulfuric acid first. These ingredients are called wetting agents. The resulting soapless detergent is called a surfactant.

The advantages of soapless shampoos include the fact that they work equally well with hard or soft water, clean both the hair and scalp thoroughly, and usually have a neutral pH of about 7.

The disadvantages of soapless shampoos revolve around the fact that they are powerful detergents. Repeated applications may cause the hair to become very dry and extra absorptive of dyes or cold wave solutions. In addition, they may strip the color from dyed hair.

don't let the label on
soapless shampoos mislead you!!
(synthetic or detergent)

An anionic detergent is the main ingredient found in most synthetic detergent shampoos. This detergent ion carries a negative electrical charge. A nonionic detergent is used as a neutral additive. It does not carry a positive or a negative charge. Its main function is to make the shampoo lather and rinse freely and leave the hair in better condition. Amphoteric detergents have neutral molecules which contain an equal number of positive and negative charges. Shampoos with amphoteric detergents will irritate or sting less if they drip into the eyes during the shampoo procedure. This type of shampoo is excellent for shampooing children's hair.

Chemistry for
cosmetologists

Synthetic detergent shampoos do not form an insoluble curd when used with hard water. They lather well and rinse easily and freely without dulling the hair. Synthetic shampoos have a greater cleansing efficiency than soap shampoos, but they leave the hair feeling harsher, more unmanageable and with a considerable amount of static electricity (the flyaway look).

Cream shampoos are usually emulsions containing sulfonated products. They have the same advantages and disadvantages as soapless shampoos. However, they are often more expensive to use. The emulsifier used to thicken the shampoo adds cost but does not increase the cleansing power. Cream shampoos aid uniform distribution and are sometimes easier to apply, particularly if they contain an antiseptic ingredient or another additive that may be irritating to the eyes.

Oil shampoos may refer to a treatment with hot oil followed by a shampoo or to a shampoo containing some extra oil or lanolin which is supposed to penetrate the hair and leave lasting results.

If a cosmetologist wishes to clean a patron's hair without using water, he or she can use a dry shampoo. These are not shampoos in the strict sense, but rather cleansing or absorptive products. For example:

1. Liquid dry shampoos are liquid solvents similar to the dry cleaning agents used on clothes. The solvent, such as benzine or carbon tetrachloride, dissolves the greasy coating on the hair which is holding the tiny particles of dirt. They should not be used regularly because they extract natural oil from the hair. Also, some of these products are highly inflammable and must be used cautiously.

2. Powdered dry shampoos are mixtures of such products as orris root, talc, chalk and starch. They absorb the greasy material that is holding the dirt, and then the resulting substance is removed by thorough brushing.

When selecting shampoos, the first consideration should be the type of water available. Hard water is caused by the solution in the water of certain salts of calcium, magnesium and other metals. Such water can be softened by using chemicals or zeolite tanks. The water is passed through a mineral ion-exchange material that exchanges the calcium and magnesium for sodium ions.

If the salon has soft water, the first choice of shampoo should probably be a plain soap shampoo since it is relatively inexpensive, will cleanse most hair satisfactorily, and leaves the hair in good condition. However, the salon must also have soapless shampoos available for situations requiring extra cleansing power, such as oily hair or scalp conditions, or for after a salon service which may leave an oil or grease residue on the hair. In addition, specialty shampoos are desirable for certain tinted, bleached or damaged hair and dandruff conditions.

Unit 8
Waving preparations

There are two general classes of waving preparations:

1. Fluids for setting hair temporarily

2. Solutions for waving the hair permanently

Unit 8
Waving preparations

General objectives-student goals: After study, instruction and completion of this unit, you will be able to demonstrate understanding of hair setting lotions and permanent waving lotions by writing and/or giving a brief overview of the subject.

Chemistry for cosmetologists

455

Hair setting lotions are composed mainly of fluids of gelatinous substances obtained from Irish moss, pectin and other sources. These ingredients are mixed with arabic, tragacanth or similar gums, perfume and coloring. The quick drying setting lotions contain mostly gums in perfumed alcohol. Because of their high alcohol content, they may be drying to the hair and scalp. Some setting lotions also contain wetting agents which increase their ability to penetrate the hair. This helps the hair to hold a set longer. Lotions containing a hygroscopic resin can be reactivated by moisture or by rewetting.

Chemical waving lotions initiate a chemical reaction which changes the hair structure. The function of the chemical waving lotion is to break the cross-linkages, or bonds, between the polypeptide chains in the keratin molecules of the hair. These bonds can then be re-formed on a rod. Two sulfur atoms constitute the bonds which are called disulfic links or sometimes simply sulfur bonds. The cold waving solution breaks the bonds by adding hydrogen to the sulfur atoms. The solution acts as a reducing agent.

Thioglycolic acid and ammonium thioglycolate are the reducing agents used most frequently in cold waving. Ammonium thioglycolate is the salt formed when ammonium hydroxide is added to thioglycolic acid. It is commonly called thio. Most cold waving lotions are composed of a dilute solution (7-9%) of thio with wetting agents and emulsifiers added. The pH ranges from 8.5 to 9.5. Increasing the pH will shorten the processing time. It will also increase the danger of overprocessing if the patron's hair is porous. The general and quantitative analysis of permanent wave lotions is complex. The following brief outline will give you a better understanding of the products you use.

There are basically three types of permanent wave lotions:

1. The conventional cold wave lotion

2. The two bottle cold wave (acid balanced heat perm)

3. The three bottle acid pH perm (acid pH heat perm)

1. The conventional cold wave lotion is composed of approximately 7% thioglycolic acid to which 1.2%-1.3% free ammonia has been added. The combination of these two chemicals produces ammonium thioglycolate. The thioglycolic acid content of lotions for tinted and bleached hair is much lower (4¼%). These mixtures also contain oils, perfume, conditioning agents and an emulsifier, all of which are compatible. In addition to the chemicals, all lotions contain water. The pH value of a cold wave lotion for normal and high test goes from 9.3 to 9.4. The pH value of lotions for tinted and bleached hair ranges from 9.1 to 9.2. This uses normal body temperature for activation of lotion.

2. The two bottle heat wave lotion is basically the same as the conventional cold wave lotion except that the thioglycolic acid content is higher (9%). The free ammonia, however, constitutes only about ½%. It is the low percentage of the free ammonia which brings the pH value down to only 7.5-8.2. This lotion must be activated with mechanically produced heat because of its low pH.

3. The three bottle acid pH perm process involves the following chemicals:

   1. Approximately 75% glyceryl monothioglycolate and 25% glycerine

2. Water solution containing ammonia

3. Neutralizer

Glyceryl monothioglycolate will not produce a wave by itself. It cannot be bottled together with water. If these two chemicals were bottled together, they would break up. The results would be thio and water.

A very small amount of free ammonia is added to these two chemicals. This brings the pH value up to 6.9. This product also has the necessary amount of perfume, emulsifier and other substances added to it. This low pH lotion will not lift the cuticle of the hair unless it is processed with mechanically produced heat.

Unit 9
Chemical hair straighteners and relaxers

A hair straightener eliminates 100% of the curl from the hair. A relaxer does not eliminate all the curl.

Sodium hydroxide or caustic hair straighteners are more powerful than thio straighteners. They cause the hair to expand. They change the disulfide bonds. These bonds lose one molecule of sulfur. They rejoin in a different combination when the chemical action is stopped by thorough rinsing.

The sodium hydroxide is usually in an emulsion or cream solution with stearic and oleic acids so that it can be applied carefully to the hair strands and not be so liquid that it runs on the scalp and skin. The percentage of sodium hydroxide in the product is extremely important. Products with a higher percentage will work faster and straighten very curly hair. However, they are more dangerous.

The majority of chemical hair straighteners, apart from thio types, contain sodium hydroxide. Regardless of variations in names and formulations, the only difference is the percentage of caustic which they contain. The following precautions should always be observed. The patron's hair and scalp must be in good condition. Do not brush or shampoo the hair. Use a protective base cream on the scalp, ears and hairline. Wear gloves. Keep the caustic away from unprotected skin and eyes. Time carefully. Rinse thoroughly.

Most no-base straighteners or relaxers, except thios, are still caustic. The base is usually included in the emulsion, and the hydroxide is in a lower concentration. All precautions, except the use of a protective base, must be observed.

Ammonium sulfite solutions are sometimes used as straighteners. These will soften the disulfide bonds. These sulfite solutions function at a nearly neutral pH (7-7.5) in a moderately viscous base.

Thioglycolate

Thioglycolate cosmetics used to straighten hair contain ammonium or monoethanolamine thioglycolate, or thioglycolic acid adjusted to the desired pH with ammonia or monoethanolamine. A heavy creme base is used to hold the hair in a straightened position.

Unit 9
Chemical hair straighteners and relaxers

General objectives-student goals:
After study, instruction and completion of this unit, you will be able to demonstrate understanding of hair straighteners and relaxers by writing and/or giving a brief overview of the subject.

Chemistry for cosmetologists

457

The action of the thioglycolate is the same as in cold waving. The disulfide links of the keratin are broken down. This results in softening of the hair. The hair is then smoothed to a straightened position using a comb or your hands.

The following is a typical formula for a thioglycolate straightener:

Formula 9

Glyceryl monostearate	15.0%
Stearic acid	3.0%
Ceresin	1.5%
Paraffin	1.0%
Sodium lauryl sulfate	1.0%
Distilled water	61–71%
Thioglycolic acid	5–10% for regular lotion 2–5% for use on tinted hair
Ammonium hydroxide (26° Bé)	0.5–2.5%
Perfume	Q.S.*
pH	9.2–9.5

*Qualitative scale; also quantity sufficient for compatibility—the amount needed to arrive at 100% of a formula.

When the hair is straightened, the action is stopped by a neutralizer which contains an oxidizing compound. This neutralizer is left on the hair long enough to penetrate the hair shaft and stop the action of the thioglycolate. Neutralization serves two functions: (1) removal of the straightening agent from the hair, (2) restoration of the hair to its original condition. The second function gives the hair the desired permanence.

Sodium hydroxide

Sodium hydroxide in combination with stearic and oleic acids was the first chemical cosmetic used for straightening hair. The sodium hydroxide content of various products varies from 5 to 10%. The pH value goes from 10 to 14. In general, the more sodium hydroxide and the higher the pH value, the quicker the reaction of the chemical on the hair.

Sodium hydroxide functions by swelling the hair fibers and softening the main disulfide bonds which link the polypeptide chains together. The hair should be completely softened within eight minutes. If it is not, the action should be stopped by rinsing the sodium hydroxide from the hair. During the chemical action, the disulfide links lose one molecule of sulfur. After rinsing, the links rejoin as lanthionine links between the polypeptide chains. The hair is now stabilized. The following is a schematic diagram of the chemical reaction.

Hair - S - S - Hair   +   NaOH   →   Hair - S - Hair
(Cystine disulfide link)   (Sodium hydroxide)   (Lanthionine link)

Extreme care must be taken to prevent the chemical from coming into contact with the skin because sodium hydroxide will burn the skin and scalp. If sodium hydroxide is left on the hair too long, there is the danger that the hair will dissolve.

The following are examples of formulas using sodium hydroxide:

Formula 1		Formula 2	
Sodium hydroxide	5%	Stearic acid	15%
Glycerine monostearate	15%	Oleic acid	5%
Glycerol	5%	Glycerol	5%
Water	75%	Sodium hydroxide	10%
Perfume	Q.S.*	Water	65%
		Perfume	Q.S.*
pH	10–14	pH	10–14

*Qualitative scale; also quantity sufficient for compatibility—the amount needed to arrive at 100% of a formula.

Ammonium bisulfite softens the disulfide cross-linkages. The hair becomes more plastic (softened) and will yield to a change of direction. If the change in direction is to remain, the new position must be made stable while the hair is in its softened state. This is accomplished by re-forming the disulfide linkages by means of chemical oxidation (neutralization). The reaction may be written as follows:

Hair - S - S - Hair   + HSO_3 ⟶   Hair SH + Hair SSO_3H
(Disulfide links)   (Bisulfite ion)   (Reduced hair)

This sulfite reaction functions at a nearly neutral pH (7-7½) in a moderately viscous base. Rinsing and the use of a neutralizer after the softening step drives the above reaction to the left. This relinks the disulfide bonds. The hair is then rebuilt to its original chemical state. However, it is in a straightened configuration.

Unit 10
Hair lighteners and hair coloring

Unit 10
Hair lighteners and hair coloring

General objectives-student goals:
After study, instruction and completion of this unit, you will be able to demonstrate understanding of hair lighteners and hair coloring by writing and/or giving a brief overview of the subject.

Natural hair color is caused by tiny grains of pigment in the cortex layer of the hair. This pigment is called melanin. It can produce black, brown, yellow or red colors. The absence or lack of melanin causes white and gray hair.

If you wish to lighten hair color, you must oxidize the melanin pigment by using a bleaching agent which penetrates the cuticle layer. If you wish to color the hair, an amino dye is generally used. It passes through the cuticle and is developed in the cortex by oxidation into a larger molecule of artificial pigment. This developing is an oxidation process.

In both bleaching and developing color, the oxidation job can be done by using hydrogen peroxide. Pure hydrogen peroxide is a colorless, syrupy, violently active liquid much too strong for ordinary use. Hydrogen peroxide, written H_2O_2, is made up of two hydrogen atoms and two oxygen atoms. It is an oxidizing agent that causes the release of oxygen when mixed with tint, toner, or lightener. After the available oxygen is released and the substance it contacts is oxidized, only water remains.

$$2H_2O_2 = 2H_2O + O_2$$

Most bleaching agents contain hydrogen peroxide in some liquid form. Alternatively, they contain some chemical which produces it (e.g., powdered bleaches). Hydrogen peroxide is usually used in a 6% solution. This will liberate 20 volumes of oxygen gas for each volume of itself. Stabilized hydrogen peroxide contains small amounts of acids which lower the pH and reduce decomposition before use. When using hydrogen peroxide, a few drops of ammonia water (usually sold as a 28% solution) will neutralize any stabilizer and release the oxygen faster.

Hydrogen peroxide is available in liquid or creme form with a wide variety of additives. In creme form, it is often called a developer. Lanolin derivatives are added for clouding, thickening and emulsifying the clear hydrogen peroxide solution for appearance (cosmetic elegance), ease of application, and hair and scalp protection.

Hydrogen peroxide, often referred to simply as peroxide, is found in clear liquid, creme, powder and tablet forms. Peroxide is relatively unstable. It must be kept in sealed containers and protected from strong light and heat.

When peroxide is mixed with an aniline derivative permanent hair color, the oxygen molecules in the peroxide combine with hair color molecules. This causes the coloring agent to develop and locks the color molecules within the hair shaft permanently. Hydrogen peroxide activates bleaching agents. The ingredients in the bleach solution attack the natural pigment content of the hair. They disperse and destroy the melanin. The result is a lighter colored hair.

Peroxide strength is usually measured in volumes of oxygen liberated per volume of solution. There is an easy way to convert peroxide volumes into percentages, and percentages into volume measures. Multiply the volume strength by .3 to arrive at the percentage of peroxide. For example, a 20 volume hydrogen peroxide multiplied by .3 equals a 6% strength peroxide solution. To calculate volume, multiply the percentage by 10 and divide by 3.

Volume and percentage of peroxide

5 Volume = 1.5%		60 Volume = 18.0%
10 Volume = 3.0%		70 Volume = 21.0%
20 Volume = 6.0%		80 Volume = 24.0%
30 Volume = 9.0%		90 Volume = 27.0%
40 Volume = 12.0%		100 Volume = 30.0%
50 Volume = 15.0%		

Peroxide may be diluted before it is used on the hair. When used as a developer with tint, 20 volume peroxide gives equal color lift and deposit of permanent hair color. As the strength of the peroxide is lowered, there is less lifting action and a greater deposit of color. When the strength of peroxide is increased, there is a greater lift of color and a smaller deposit of permanent hair color.

Reduction of peroxide

Volume	Percentage	Peroxide	Water
2½ volume	¾%	¼ ounce (7.39 ml.)	1¾ ounces (51.75 ml.)
5 volume	1½%	½ ounce (14.20 ml.)	1½ ounces (44.36 ml.)
7½ volume	2¼%	¾ ounce (22.18 ml.)	1¼ ounces (36.97 ml.)
10 volume	3%	1 ounce (29.57 ml.)	1 ounce (29.57 ml.)
12½ volume	3¾%	1¼ ounces (36.97 ml.)	¾ ounce (22.18 ml.)
15 volume	4½%	1½ ounces (44.36 ml.)	½ ounce (14.20 ml.)

Chemistry for
cosmetologists

17½ volume	5¼%	1¾ ounces (51.75 ml.)	¼ ounce (7.39 ml.)
20 volume	6%	2 ounces (59.15 ml.)	0

Each time you add an equal amount of water to any volume peroxide, it decreases the volume by half.

Color lift and color deposit

18% = 60 volume	Maximum to be used, not used on the scalp, total color lift
15% = 50 volume	Not used on the scalp, total lifting action, black hair only
12% = 40 volume	Can be used on the scalp, strong lifting action, no deposit
9% = 30 volume	Can be used on the scalp, greater color lift, less deposit of permanent hair color
6% = 20 volume	Standard volume usage, equal color lift, equal deposit of permanent hair color
3% = 10 volume	Diluted volume usage, less color lift, greater deposit of permanent hair color

Any volume used under 10 volume strength gives greater permanent hair color deposit and no color lift.

Oil bleaches contain sulfonated oil and ammonia. They may be neutral or contain some dilute tints. The addition of hydrogen peroxide activates them. Powdered bleaches generally contain oxygen releasing agents such as sodium perborate, magnesium carbonate and surface active agents. They are usually mixed with hydrogen peroxide to form a bleaching paste.

One of the early developments of organic chemistry was synthetic dyes. These synthetic organic dyes have supplanted vegetable dyes like Egyptian henna and metallic dyes. They are known by several names: aniline dyes, amino dyes, oxidation dyes and para dyes.

These aniline derivative, or oxidation dyes, work because the colorless dye intermediate compounds have small molecules which can pass through the cuticle into the cortex of the hair. In the cortex, they join with oxygen from hydrogen peroxide and form large molecules of colored dye. These molecules are too large to pass out through the cuticle. They are, therefore, locked in the cortex in a manner similar to natural pigment.

The intermediate dye is usually mixed with a soapless detergent. This increases the penetration of the cuticle. As the shade develops, the oxidizing agent (hydrogen peroxide) gives up its available oxygen. The result is water and dye. The tint and the developer must be mixed just before the product is applied to the hair so that the developing does not take place until the dye is in the cortex of the hair.

The permanence of the shade produced depends on how well the hair is prepared to receive the dye and the treatment to which it is subjected. Aniline dyes, regardless of shade, are most effective on hair that has been softened or prebleached but can be used on virgin hair as well.

Aniline dyes are available in several forms:

1. Bleach-dye combinations produce the desired shade in one operation. Surface-active agents must be added. For lighter shades, the bleaching action occurs just before the coloring effect although they appear to act almost simultaneously.

2. Shampoo tints are combinations of dye and shampoo with thickening agents added. These require a preliminary softening or prebleaching with hydrogen peroxide.

3. Color shampoos impart just a tinge of color to hair of any shade.

4. Cream dyes have the color incorporated in a soft creamy emulsion. They are usually sold in sealed tubes.

Unit 11
Hair and scalp products

Scalp lotions are used to prevent scaliness and dryness. They contain ingredients such as cholesterol, lecithin and pilocarpine. Antidandruff lotions may contain quaternary ammonium compounds or antiseptic compounds as ingredients. Scalp lotions for oily skin have a high percentage of alcohol and compounds with astringent properties.

Scalp pomades contain a high percentage of mineral oil and wax, vegetable oils, and resin. These substances act as bases for active ingredients such as sulfur, conditioners and PVP (Polyvinylpyrrolidone). The latter is a protein-like compound used to repair damaged hair.

Hair creams, both fluid (creme) and semisolid, are often used after a shampoo in order to make the hair glossy and easier to set. They are composed of emulsions of oils, waxes, fatty acids and lanolin products. Water and mild alkalies are added to them.

Hair sprays often contain PVP in solution with alcohol, glycerine, lanolin and water. Some hair sprays and setting lotions also contain a hygroscopic resin which is reactivated by moisture. Hair sprays are supposed to keep the hair in place even under damp conditions. The special propellant used in hair spray cans does not cause burning.

Hair rinses include acid rinses which are used to help the water rinse remove soap and other residue left on the hair after shampooing. Creme rinses have synthetic surface active agents as a base. These deposit a light film on the hair. The coating makes the hair feel soft and silky. It facilitates easy combing. Temporary color rinses often contain acids mixed with certified coloring modified with emulsifiers and wetting agents.

Unit 11
Hair and scalp products

General objectives-student goals: After study, instruction and completion of this unit, you will be able to demonstrate understanding of cosmetics for the hair and scalp by writing and/or giving a brief overview of the subject.

Chemistry for cosmetologists

Unit 12
Cosmetics for the skin

Unit 12
Cosmetics for the skin

General objectives-student goals:
After study, instruction and completion of this unit, you will be able to demonstrate understanding of cosmetics for the skin by writing and/ or giving a brief overview of the subject.

The cosmetologist uses a wide variety of preparations to beautify or recondition the skin. These include creams, lotions, powders, make-up and miscellaneous products used for personal hygiene.

Creams

Creams for the skin are generally emulsions which are combinations of two liquids of different character mixed until they break into minute globules. These globules are suspended in the solution by an emulsifying agent.

Cleansing creams are water-in-oil emulsions which melt at body temperature and spread readily over the skin. The oils should be light enough to penetrate into the follicles, clear them of impurities and flow away easily. Cleansing creams include cold creams which contain mineral oils and waxes, quick liquifying creams which are not really creams but rather mineral products-petrolatum, mineral oil, mineral wax, ceresin—which melt very quickly, and liquifying cleansing creams which may contain up to 75% water with synthetic detergents added for extra cleansing power.

Many types of sensitive skins should not be cleansed with soap and water. Only cleansing creams should be used. If the patron believes that she must use soap and water, use cleansing cream afterwards. Cleansing cream can remove a large amount of soil. Also, the softening effect of a good cleansing cream will leave the skin in better condition.

Massage creams, or emollient creams, lubricate the skin during massage. There are differences between massage creams and cleansing creams. The latter are heavier, thicker in consistency and contain ingredients that can penetrate and soften the skin. These ingredients include animal fats and waxes (beeswax, lanolin, spermaceti), vegetable fats and oils, synthetic waxes, surface-active agents, fatty acids, alcohols and mineral oils. Lanolin is active in emulsification and carries the substance that acts on the skin. Cholesterol, silicones and lecithin are organic substances which are particularly effective skin softeners.

Massage creams are sometimes called tissue creams, nourishing creams or antiwrinkle creams. Discretion and common sense should govern the recommendation of medicaments and other substances alleged to have special rejuvenating properties, such as turtle oil, vitamins and bee jelly. Some of the claims made for these substances have not been proven scientifically. However, substances applied superficially may effect local improvement by softening the skin and by stimulating circulation. Filling out of contours may be achieved by means of massage of the underlying structures. If any systemic improvement results from the use of one of these substances, it must be classified as a drug not a cosmetic.

Finishing creams include such preparations as powder base and foundation cream. They are used before make-up is applied. They contain up to 75% water, which evaporates quickly and leaves a thin protective film on the skin. Pure stearic acid is combined with a small quantity of alkali to form a soap. The soap serves as an emulsifying agent and stabilizer for the stearic acid and water. This emulsion constitutes the real cream.

Chemistry for cosmetologists

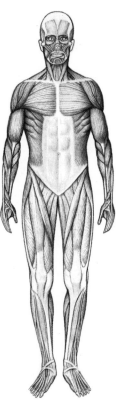

HUMAN ANATOMY

This transparent overlay illustrates four systems of the human body—skeletal, nervous, muscular and circulatory—and is designed to help you form a basic conception of the structures of the body. The various structures may be viewed in their exact locations and in relation to each other. By the use of the transparencies, you can identify these relationships and better understand how they work.

Plate A illustrates the skeletal system in grey tones with the nervous system (Plate B) overlayed in green. Plate D illustrates the muscular system in red and grey tones. The circulatory system (Plate C) overlays the muscular system with the veins in blue and the arteries in red. It should be noted that in an actual human body, the circulatory system runs through the muscular system; however, for illustrative purposes we have placed the blood vessels on top of the muscles.

SKELETAL SYSTEM

1 – Frontal	15 – Thoracic Vertebrae
2 – Parietal	16 – Lumbar Vertebrae
3 – Temporal	17 – Radius
4 – Sphenoid	18 – Ulna
5 – Ethmoid	19 – Metacarpals
6 – Lacrimal	20 – Phalanges
7 – Nasal	21 – Femur
8 – Zygomatic	22 – Patella
9 – Maxilla	23 – Tibia
10 – Mandible	24 – Fibula
11 – Cervical Vertebrae	25 – Talus
12 – Clavicle	26 – Calcaneus
13 – Sternum	27 – Metatarsals
14 – Humerus	28 – Phalanges

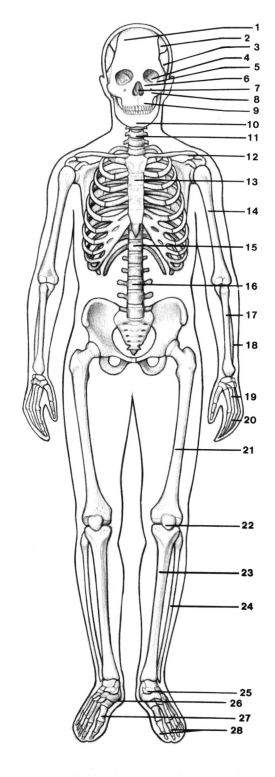

PLATE A
SKELETAL
SYSTEM

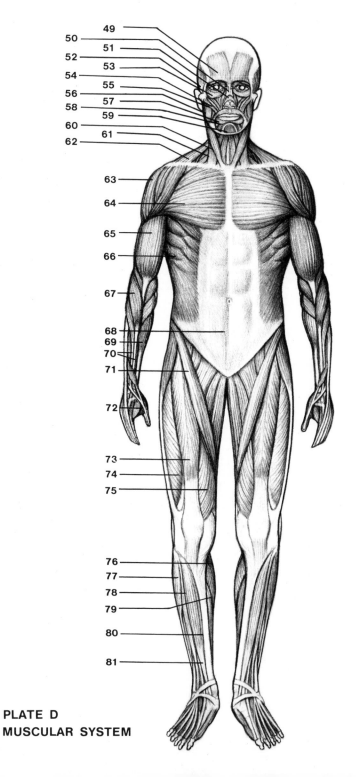

MUSCULAR SYSTEM

49 – Frontalis

50 – Procerus

51 – Nasalis

52 – Temporalis

53 – Orbicularis Oculi

54 – Quadratus Labii Superioris

55 – Zygomaticus

56 – Masseter

57 – Buccinator

58 – Orbicularis Oris

59 – Mentalis

60 – Sternocleidomastoid

61 – Quadratus Labii Inferioris

62 – Trapezius

63 – Deltoid

64 – Pectoralis Major

65 – Biceps

66 – Latissimus Dorsi

67 – Pronator

68 – Rectus Abdominus

69 – Flexor

70 – Extensors

71 – Sartorius

72 – Abductors

73 – Rectus Femoris

74 – Vastus Lateralis

75 – Vastus Medius

76 – Gastrocnemius

77 – Peroneus Longus

78 – Extensor Digitorum Longus

79 – Soleus

80 – Tibialis Anterior

81 – Peroneus Brevis

PLATE D
MUSCULAR SYSTEM

INDEX

Liquid foundation creams contain essentially the same ingredients as finishing creams with glycerine, alcohol or other liquids added. Finishing creams form a light, smooth film on the skin. They conceal roughness temporarily and aid the flattering effect of make-up.

Special creams for specific purposes include acne creams which contain medicaments such as benzoin, boric and salicylic acids, sulfur, zinc oxide and calamine (zinc carbonate); bleaching creams which lighten the color of the skin because they contain peroxide, sodium perborate and mild acids and hormone creams which contain estrogenic substances.

Lotions

A lotion is a water and alcohol solution of ingredients which have some special action on the skin. Some common types of lotion are:

1. Skin toning lotions, or skin fresheners, are antiseptic and slightly astringent solutions which may contain boric acid, menthol, witch hazel, alum or mild organic acids. They are used during a facial treatment to sponge the face after the removal of the massage cream.

2. Astringent lotions are useful in the treatment of oily skin and coarse pores. They contain mildly astringent compounds such as alum, zinc or magnesium sulfate, bethnaphthol and boric or salicylic acid in water solutions of both alcohol and glycerine.

Face powders

No single face powder is suitable for every type of skin. Even normal skin tends either towards oiliness or towards dryness. Therefore, a complete beauty salon should have various shades of two types of face powder. These are: a heavy powder for oily skins and a light powder for dry skins. The terms heavy and light refer to their covering power or opacity. The ingredients of the most commonly used face powders are:

1. Titanium dioxide and zinc oxide for covering power

2. Talc and starch for slip

3. Calcium, magnesium, zinc stearates and colloidal clay (kaolin) for adherence

The two types of colored substances used to vary the tint of face powders are: natural and synthetic metallic pigments; synthetic metallic compounds of certain dyes called lakes. A good powder has the coloring blended so perfectly with the other ingredients that no bright flecks of color are visible.

In addition to the vanishing foundation creams, grease paints and pastes are produced in several forms: a creamy cake (cake make-up) and a firm stick or a rich creamy fluid. These foundation products conceal minor blemishes effectively and impart a youthful bloom to the complexion. Cake foundations cover best but leave a flat finish. The cream types, usually sold in tubes, leave a matte finish. Liquid foundations, which are generally easier to use but may not cover as well, are produced in both oil types and emulsion types. The latter contain a small quantity of water in suspension.

Make-up

Skilled make-up artists use an amazing variety of rouges to achieve specific effects. The types used include:

1. Cream rouge which is usually made with a petrolatum base to which lanolin, oils or waxes have been added. This rouge has more lasting quality than some of the other types. It is good for dry skin. These rouges can be reduced in color if mixed with additional base or foundation.

2. Liquid rouge consists of a dye in a solution of various waxes in water or alcohol and glycerine. It is easy to use and excellent for evening wear.

3. Powdered rouge has some of the ingredients of face powder with the coloring ground into the mixture.

4. Cake rouge is similar to powdered rouge except that moisturizers and binders are added so that it can be molded or pressed into shape. It is usually recommended for oily skin.

5. Special purpose rouges include blushers for highlighting and glimmer which imparts a gloss for evening wear.

The base used for a lipstick is essentially the same as that for cream rouge. However, it has a higher percentage of easy melting ingredients. A good lipstick should melt at body temperature. It should soften the lips as well as color them. The lipstick must go on smoothly, show no unevenness in shade or texture and penetrate sufficiently so that the color does not come off. The shade should blend with the rouge used. Indelible lipstick generally contains a soluble bromo-acid dye which is a derivative of the synthetic organic dye eosin.

Eye-shadow is composed of a base mixture of waxes and oils containing zinc oxide and the appropriate colorings. Many eye-shadows also contain metallic colors. They must be used with care in order to avoid irritation. Eye-shadow comes in powder, cake, stick and cream form.

Colorings for eyebrows and eyelashes may be either temporary or permanent. Temporary colorings come in the form of crayons encased in wood (eyebrow pencil) or as mascara. Mascara, which is available in cream, liquid and cake form, contains synthetic waxes or triethanolamine soaps plus lampblack (carbon) or natural metallic oxide dyes. Some mascaras have additives which make the lashes appear longer. Permanent dyes for the eyebrows and eyelashes are usually solutions of silver nitrate combined with a developer. Silver nitrate darkens when exposed to light and combines with the keratin of the hair. This process creates a permanent dark stain.

Unit 13
Cosmetics for the hands

Manicure preparations include products designed to cleanse, soften, bleach or polish the nails. Cleansers are usually soaps in convenient forms such as flakes, beads or drops of concentrated shampoo.

Softeners are also called cuticle removers or cuticle solvents. They are composed of a 2.5% solution of some alkali (potassium hydroxide, sodium carbonate, trisodium phosphate) with about 20% glycerine in water. They loosen the dead cuticle around the base of the nail. Another type of cuticle softener is called nail cream. It is composed of a creamy base containing lanolin, cocoa butter, cholesterol and other products. It is designed to keep the skin around the nails from becoming too dry and to prevent the nails from becoming too brittle.

Hand bleaches can come in a liquid form containing hydrogen peroxide or dilute organic acids. It is also available as an opaque white paste containing titanium or zinc whitening agents. Bleaches may be used for removing nicotine stains and other discolorations from the fingers and under the free edge of the nail. Whitening agents in the form of pencils or sticks are not recommended for sanitary reasons.

Enamels are available in the form of a lacquer which imparts a shiny varnish-like coating to the nails. They are composed of camera cellulose compounds, resins, pigments, plasticisers and other substances dissolved in a mixture of organic solvents which evaporate quickly. Many compounds and additives are being developed constantly. These are designed to give translucent, frosted, pearl and other effects.

Nail enamel removers are composed of organic solvents, such as acetone, and various additives, such as oil, lanolin and cholesterol. These negate the drying effect of the solvent on the nail. The same solvents without additives are sold as nail enamel thinners.

Artificial nails is a term that may refer to several methods of repairing broken or abused nails, or improving the appearance of nails. The simplest method is to use a premanufactured plastic nail which is placed over the natural nail and secured with a quick-drying adhesive. Another method is to mix a powdered plastic compound, usually methyl methacrylate, with a liquid chemical that converts it immediately into a firm continuous plate of hardened plastic. The cosmetologist is actually building an artificial nail as this mixture is applied. The third method involves the use of nail molds and a plastic compound. A nail mold which fits the natural nail is selected, and the plastic powder compound is placed in this mold. A few drops of conversion liquid are then used to saturate the powder. The mold is quickly inverted and placed on the natural nail.

Hand creams and lotions: Disappearing hand creams consist of an oil and water emulsion with substances added to soften the skin and relieve irritation. Such substances include fatty acids, lanolin, silicones, cholesterol, lecithin and healing agents. Glycerine and related compounds are also excellent in hand creams because they first take up superficial moisture after the hands are washed, and yet leave a film that helps to retain natural moisture in the skin.

Hand lotions are composed of thin emulsions of stearic acid and water with the addition of the same compounds used in hand creams.

General objectives-student goals: After study, instruction and completion of this unit, you will be able to demonstrate understanding of cosmetics for the hands by writing and/or giving a brief overview of the subject.

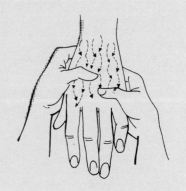

HAND CREAM & LOTION

Chemistry for cosmetologists

467

Unit 14

Hair conditioners

Reconditioning the hair by using hair conditioners is a service practiced by cosmetologists for restoring and improving the texture, appearance and manageability of normal, damaged or chemically processed hair. The improved hair condition is, however, only temporary.

The reconditioning process consists of the application of an acid pH hair conditioner or after-shampoo rinse. These products restore cuticle strength and sheen to the hair. The ingredients of hair conditioners do not become a permanent part of the cuticle surface. The cuticle provides a flexible covering for the hair shaft, and the spaces between them contain some sebum which is secreted by the sebaceous glands. The sebum forms a moisture resistant film which maintains flexibility and prevents moisture loss from within the hair shaft.

The cortex constitutes the major portion of the hair fiber. Conditioners are absorbed into the cortex. However, the results cannot last because the hair components are dead and cannot function biologically. Therefore, shampooing the hair will remove any and all deposits made through the conditioner's processes of absorption and adsorption.

Hair conditioners are used after shampooing the hair. A good hair conditioner will:

1. Help prevent damage to the hair

2. Help protect damaged hair from further damage

3. Help restore damaged hair to a normal or less damaged condition

4. Leave the hair untangled, easy to comb, supple and glossy

5. Add more body to limp or fine hair

Many hair conditioners contain the organic, water soluble substance called protein. Protein hair conditioners are compatible with hair. They protect it from chemical and environmental influences. They also provide a thin protective film on normal hair and fill the voids and damaged sections of the hair. Water alone can remove protein conditioners from the hair.

A good hair conditioner is composed of substances which have positive charges. These will neutralize the negative charges in the hair. The positive charges are called cationic, and the hair, with its negative charges, is called anionic. When a cationic conditioner is rinsed through the hair, the cationic substance binds itself to the hair on contact. The positive nitrogen atom of the cationic substance combines with the negative carboxyl radical of the hair. This is known as eletrophilic attraction. The bond made is not permanent. However, it is very strong and can resist removal by ordinary hair brushing. Conditioners cannot resist removal by shampooing because most shampoos are anionic.

Unit 15
Jojoba oil

Jojoba oil is appearing as an ingredient in both hair and skin products, such as shampoo, conditioners, hand lotions and body lotions. The jojoba plant is a hardy desert plant. It grows freely in the unfertile desert and survives high heat, winds and lack of water. It takes about ten years for the plant to reach maturity. It produces a crop of 5-10 pounds (2.27-4.54 kg.) of nuts per year once it reaches maturity, and continues to produce for more than 100 years. The nut is small and brown in color. Approximately 15 pounds (6.80 kg.) of nuts are required to produce 1 gallon (3.79 l.) of jojoba oil. The oil is a clear, odorless and tasteless polyunsaturated liquid.

Jojoba oil is being considered as a remedy for hair loss. Tests indicate that jojoba oil dissolves scalp sebum readily. This removal of the fatty secretion of the sebaceous glands, which tends to block the normal hair growth cycle when it becomes encrusted on the scalp, frees the clogged hair follicles from debris and stimulates the germinating cells in the epidermis to renew hair growth.

Jojoba oil is a good moisturizer for dry skin and provides a smooth, nongreasy emollient feel. Shampoo cannot contain large amounts of jojoba oil because it will prevent the shampoo from foaming. Duplicating jojoba oil synthetically will provide an expanded line of jojoba products. Jojoba oil has joined the ranks of lanolin, protein and vitamin E in the world of hair and skin products.

Unit 16
Sterilization

Ideally, sterilization means the destruction of all forms of bacterial life. In practice, however, it is accepted to mean surgical cleanliness and the destruction, temporarily or permanently, of the bacteria that may cause disease. This is accomplished by depriving the bacteria of the conditions they need to survive such as food and moisture. Sterilization can be accomplished by either physical or chemical methods.

Physical sterilization can be brought about through the use of dry heat (hot air ovens), boiling water, steam (autoclaves) and ultraviolet radiation. These physical means are not usually available in a beauty salon. Chemical sterilization can be accomplished through the use of germicides, which include antiseptics, disinfectants and fumigants.

An antiseptic is a chemical used to check the growth of bacteria, thus preventing the development of disease or decay. An antiseptic is temporary in action. It can be used on the skin because it is not as strong as a disinfectant. Antiseptics include oxidizing agents, such as hydrogen peroxide, chloramine—T (chlorazene), sodium hypochlorite (clorox) and iodine. Other antiseptics are alcohol in solutions of 50-70% water and boric acid in 3% solutions.

A disinfectant is a substance that destroys bacteria completely. Disinfectants can be diluted to form antiseptics. However, all antiseptics are not disinfectants. Disinfectants are too corrosive or poisonous to apply to the skin.

Unit 15
Jojoba oil

General objectives-student goals:
After study, instruction and completion of this unit, you will be able to demonstrate understanding of jojoba oil by writing and/or giving a brief overview of the subject.

Unit 16
Sterilization

General objectives-student goals:
After study, instruction and completion of this unit, you will be able to demonstrate understanding of sterilization as a means to destroy all forms of bacterial life by writing and/or giving a brief overview of the subject.

Chemistry for
cosmetologists

Probably the most popular disinfectants are quaternary ammonium compounds. When diluted these are nontoxic, odorless and yet powerful. They are available under many brand names from various manufacturers. However, since they lose their beneficial effect when they come in contact with organic matter, all soil and grease must be removed from articles to be sanitized, and the solution should be changed regularly.

Other disinfectants include hexylresorcinol, cresol (Lysol, CN, Pinesol) and phenol. The latter two are poisonous and have an offensive odor. They are no longer recommended by most State Boards of Cosmetology.

A fumigant is a gaseous substance capable of destroying pathogenic bacteria. The fumigant process was formerly employed in beauty salons. Formaldehyde was used in cabinets. This has been discouraged by most State Boards because of the unfavorable publicity related to formaldehyde.

Unit 17

Biochemistry

Biochemistry deals with chemical compounds and processes occurring in living organisms. It is an interesting and vigorously expanding branch of science. Many of the organic products mentioned in this chapter were introduced by biochemists. Revolutionary new cosmetology products and processes are constantly being researched and developed. Therefore, the cosmetologist who wants to be a leader in the exciting beauty world of tomorrow needs some knowledge of this field and alertness to new biochemical developments.

Biochemistry can be considered a combination of biology and chemistry. It involves the study of the intricate composition and behavior of the substances responsible for living matter. The basic unit of the living organism is the cell. This is composed largely of water in which organic compounds such as proteins, carbohydrates, salts of nucleic acid and lipids are dissolved or suspended.

Proteins are the most complex components of living matter. Great progress has been made in understanding them. The unit from which all proteins are constructed is amino acid. Molecules of amino acid combine with each other into long chains with cross-linkages. As we know from cold waving, these chains can be broken and rearranged through the use of thioglycolates. This is one of the developments of biochemistry which is used every day in the salon. Similar discoveries are leading to new products for treating and conditioning hair.

Interesting studies are also being conducted on the manner in which protein in nature links itself to dye groups. For example, the protein in hemoglobin is oxidized in the lungs to form oxyhemoglobin pigment. This gives arterial blood its bright red color. As the oxygen content is taken up by the tissues, the color becomes the dull red of the blood in the veins. Note how similar this procedure is to the action described previously in this chapter in regard to aniline (amino) dyes. As more is learned about proteins, there will undoubtedly be breakthroughs in hair coloring procedures.

Enzymes break down food proteins into their component amino acids. These acids are then rebuilt into new proteins by other enzymes. Research concerning enzymes should result in products of great value for improving skin tone and hair growth.

Unit 17

Biochemistry

General objectives-student goals:
After study, instruction and completion of this unit, you will be able to demonstrate understanding of biochemistry by writing and/or giving a brief overview of the subject.

Chemistry for cosmetologists

Even some of the hormones, or chemical regulators of body functions, have now been recognized as proteins or chains of amino acids. An example is thyroglobulin. This hormone regulates the rate of oxidation in the organism through a small portion of its large molecule amino acid thyroxine. This is the actual thyroid hormone. It can be made commercially. Another protein hormone made commercially is insulin, the regulator of sugar oxidation. There is, in fact, a whole series of hormones which regulate body functions. Further research in this area will develop regulatory hormones for the skin and hair.

Another important chemical group of cell constituents is the lipids. We are all familiar with the fats, which are combinations of glycerine and various acids. When fats are split, or saponified, by alkali, the acid components combine with them to form soaps. Fats may also be split by enzymes called lipases. These play a prominent role in digestion. The phospholipids, which contain both phosphorus and nitrogen, are also of great importance to life processes. Of these, lecithin and cephalin are found in tissues. Another lipid, present in the tissues of all animals and an important blood constituent, is cholesterol. This is a complex substance which contains only carbon, hydrogen and oxygen. Cholesterol is an important substance used in hair conditioners and massage creams.

Another aspect of biochemistry concerns itself with yeasts, molds and both useful and harmful bacteria. The study of viruses and infection has led to the development of vaccination procedures (immunization) and antibiotic drugs produced by molds and bacteria.

Biochemistry is also deeply concerned with vitamins, some of which are proving to be very important in regard to the condition of the hair, scalp and skin. There will certainly be further developments in all areas of biochemistry which are of interest to cosmetologists.

Review experiments

The following experiments are designed to help cosmetology students understand some theories advanced by the teacher in the classroom.

Experiment 1: Testing the pH values of:

1. Liquid shampoo

2. Vinegar

3. Ammonia

4. Water

Chemistry for cosmetologists

1. Alkaline shampoo
2. Acid pH shampoo
3. White vinegar (acetic acid)
4. Ammonia water 28%
5. Water

6. pH indicator (paper tape)
7. pH color comparison chart
8. Test tubes
9. Strips of test tube labels

General objectives-student goals: To demonstrate understanding of pH indicators by illustrating the use of pH paper tape indicators as follows:

1. Pour equal amounts of the liquids to be tested in separate test tubes. Label each test tube.

2. Test the pH of water and note the pH value.

3. Add a little water to each of the other liquids.

4. Test the pH of the liquid in each tube and match the color changes to the colors on the chart.

5. Note the pH value of each liquid.

Results: Water has a neutral pH value. When mixed with other liquids, its pH value changes accordingly. Testing the pH value of a solution will reveal its acid or alkaline strength. The cosmetologist will have a better understanding of how to use the product.

Experiment 2: Neutralizing an alkaline solution with an acid

Equipment and supplies:

1. Perm lotion (cold wave thio)
2. Perm neutralizer
3. Three test tubes

4. pH indicator (paper tape)
5. Stirring rod

General objectives-student goals: To demonstrate understanding of how an alkaline solution is neutralized with an acid as follows:

1. Pour a small amount of perm lotion into a test tube.

2. Test and record the pH value of the lotion.

EXPERIMENT 2

Chemistry for cosmetologists

3. Measure an equal amount of neutralizer (acid) into the second test tube.

4. Test and record the pH value of the neutralizer.

5. Pour equal amounts of perm lotion and neutralizer into the third test tube and stir.

6. Test and record the pH value of the mixture.

Results: The perm lotion has an alkaline pH value. The neutralizer has an acid pH value. When mixed together, the two chemicals produce a neutral pH solution. All chemical solutions are either neutral, alkaline or acid. Neutralizing is a means of stopping the action of a solution.

Experiment 3: Relaxing an overprocessed perm

Equipment and supplies:

1. A sample of hair with an overprocessed curl

2. Thio perm lotion

3. Three 1¹/₂ ounce (44.36 ml.) glass containers

4. Protective gloves

5. Neutralizer

6. Water

7. Towels

General objectives-student goals: To demonstrate understanding of how an overprocessed permanent curl can be relaxed by using the following procedure:

1. Dip the overprocessed hair sample into a glass containing a small amount of thio perm lotion.

2. Wear protective gloves. Squeeze the excess lotion from the hair sample and manipulate the hair strand for 30 seconds.

3. Rinse the hair sample by dipping it into the second glass containing a small amount of water.

4. Blot the hair sample with a towel.

5. Dip the hair sample into the third glass containing the neutralizer. Allow it to neutralize for five minutes.

6. Replace the water in the second glass. Rinse the neutralizer from the hair sample.

7. Observe the results of the reduced curl.

Results: Frizziness and too much curl can be reduced in overprocessed hair by means of the process set out above.

Chemistry for
cosmetologists

Experiment 4: Color mixing

Equipment and supplies:

1. Pure food liquid colors: A. Red   B. Yellow   C. Blue

2. Three small $1^1/_2$ ounce (44.36 ml.) glass containers

3. Water

4. Stirring rod

General objectives-student goals: To demonstrate understanding of how the three primary colors can be blended to produce other colors by using this procedure:

1. Fill the three small glass containers half full with water.

2. Measure equal amounts of pure liquid food colors into each of the three containers as follows:

   Container 1: Red and yellow

   Container 2: Yellow and blue

   Container 3: Blue and red

3. Observe the color change.

Results: The mixture of equal parts of red and yellow produces an orange color. Yellow and blue produce green. Blue and red produce violet. Different proportions of the primary colors produce different colors. Mixing more than two colors produce additional colors.

Experiment 5: Peroxide volume testing

Equipment and supplies:

1. 20 volume peroxide

2. Test tube

3. Hydrometer

General objectives-student goals: To demonstrate understanding of how peroxide volume can be tested whenever there is doubt concerning the actual volume of a peroxide as follows:

1. Pour a small amount of 20 volume peroxide (enough to allow the hydrometer to float) into the glass hydrometer container.

2. Place the hydrometer in the container and allow it to float.

3. The peroxide volume is noted by reading the number on the hydrometer which is level with the surface of the peroxide in the glass container.

Results: There is never any doubt concerning the volume of the peroxide you use. Peroxide volume should always be tested when:

1. The cap of the bottle or gallon of peroxide has been left off the container for an extended period of time.

2. Any bottle of peroxide has not been used for an extended period of time.

3. Peroxide volume is reduced for creating special color effects.

Review questions

1. What is chemistry?

2. Why is an understanding of elementary chemistry and chemical terms important to the cosmetologist?

3. What does the word synthetic mean?

4. What is the smallest part of an element?

5. Is there any special format used for assigning a symbol to an element?

6. What is a mixture?

Chemistry for
cosmetologists

7. What is a chemical compound?

8. Explain what a physical change is. Use water as an example.

9. What is a chemical change?

10. What does the abbreviation pH mean? What does it represent?

11. Are chemical hair straighteners alkaline or acid products?

12. Is it necessary for cosmetologists to know the pH of the products they use?

13. What is the general term for all chemical products used on the hair, skin and nails?

14. Can hard water be softened?

15. Of what are quick drying setting lotions composed?

16. Why do some setting lotions contain wetting agents?

17. How do you neutralize a stabilizer in peroxide so that it releases oxygen faster?

18. What type of solution is used as permanent dye for the eyebrows and eyelashes?

19. Why are quaternary ammonium compounds the most popular disinfectants?

20. What is biochemistry?

21. Does biochemistry concern itself with vitamins?

22. What is stabilized hydrogen peroxide?

23. Why are lanolin derivatives added to hydrogen peroxide?

24. What type of oil is used in oil bleaches?

25. How are oil bleaches activated?

26. What types of hair coloring have synthetic organic dyes supplanted?

27. Why are aniline dyes most effective on the hair?

Anatomy and physiology in beauty culture

Anatomy and physiology in beauty culture: The study of the structure and function of organisms as it relates to the practice of cosmetology.

Overview: This chapter introduces you to a branch of science that provides information from which you will gain knowledge about anatomy as it relates to the treatments practiced by the cosmetologist.

Behavioral objectives-student goals: After completion of this chapter, and after instruction and study, you will be able to perform and demonstrate competency and knowledge of anatomy and physiology by identifying, explaining and/or listing: the bones of the head, neck, thorax, extremities, blood circulation, the circulatory system, muscular system, nervous system, digestive system, excretory system, respiratory system and the procedure for rescue breathing.

Anatomy is the branch of science that deals with the structure and function of organisms. For correct treatment of the outer surface of the body, the cosmetologist must know the anatomy of the region that is treated. In this way, every muscle, nerve, bone and blood vessel that comes within any kind of beauty treatment will become as real to the cosmetologist as if it were actually visible on the surface of the skin.

Physiology is a branch of biological science which treats the functions of the various parts of the living body. Its primary concern is the means by which the body carries on various processes which keep it in good working order. The signs of life in any body are expressed in the ability to move, take nourishment, grow and reproduce. Plants and animals have these characteristics. They are organic. Objects such as stones are lifeless and are inorganic.

The constant operation of the fundamental activities known as the biological processes keeps every living body alive. The biological processes are circulation, respiration, digestion, excretion and reproduction.

The human body is composed of nine systems, or groups of organs, which are of varying degrees of importance to the cosmetologist. They are the:

1. Skeletal system

2. Muscular system

3. Nervous system

4. Circulatory (vascular) system

5. Endocrine system

6. Excretory system

7. Respiratory system

8. Digestive system

9. Reproductive system

> Note: The endocrine and reproductive systems do not come within the province of the cosmetologist. The cosmetologist is not obliged to learn the names, locations and functions associated with these systems.

Organs are made up of two or more tissues. An organ performs a specific function. When two or more organs are grouped together, a system is created.

It should be noted that although the illustrations in this chapter identify many of the muscles, veins and arteries of the head, face and neck, only those that are involved in treatments performed by a cosmetologist are described in this chapter.

Unit 1
The skeletal system

The study of the bones, their structure and functions is called osteology. The bony framework of the body is called the skeletal system or skeleton. It consists of over 200 bones that hold the body upright and allow it to move into different positions. The muscles are attached to the skeleton. The skeletal system supports the body and protects the internal organs. Its function is entirely mechanical.

A joint is where two bones come together. The joints are supported best by developed muscle power. Loose joints may be strengthened by developing the muscle's power by means of exercise.

The shape and structure of the bones vary according to their function. Bones are classified according to shape.

1. Long bones have a shank and two knob-like ends. They are found in the arm, leg, hand and foot.

2. Flat bones are found in the skull.

3. Irregular bones are found in the wrist, ankle and other areas.

General objectives-student goals:
After study, instruction and completion of this unit, you will be able to demonstrate understanding of the skeletal system by writing and/or giving a brief overview of the subject.

Anatomy and physiology in beauty culture

Cartilage, ligaments and tendons are three forms of connective tissue:

1. Cartilage is a firm and tough elastic substance. It is similar to bone but it does not have bone's mineral content. It serves to:

    A. Cushion the bones at the joints

    B. Prevent jarring between bones while they are in motion

    C. Give shape to certain external features, such as the nose, ears and throat

2. Ligaments are bands or sheets of fibrous tissue which help to support the bones at the joints.

3. A tendon is a band of dense fibrous tissue. It forms the termination of a muscle and attaches the muscle to a bone.

The number of bones in the various parts of the skeletal system are:

Skull	22	Thorax (chest)	25
Accessory to the skull	7	Upper extremities	64
Spinal column (sacrum and coccyx: 1 each)	26	Lower extremities	62
		Total	206

Bone is made up of one-third organic matter and two-thirds inorganic matter. The organic matter found in bone tissue consists of bone cells, blood vessels and other connective tissue. Phosphorus and calcium are the two major minerals in bone. Their presence accounts for the hardness of the bone tissue. The center of the bone contains a soft, fatty substance called marrow. Marrow is responsible for the production of blood cells and gives nourishment to the bone. Periosteum is the tough fibrous membrane that serves as a point of attachment for muscles, tendons and ligaments. It produces new bone tissue after injury and during normal growth.

The spinal column is the only part of the skeletal system that extends through the whole body. Because a human stands in an upright position, the weight of the head, trunk and the entire body are put directly on the spinal column and legs. The spinal column is located exactly in the middle of the body and should be perfectly straight from top to bottom. The vertebrae are shaped like disks which have a solid portion on one side and a hole on the other side. The holes are the dorsal cavity of the spinal cord, and the outermost projection can be seen and felt up and down the back as little bumps. The bones of the spinal column are separated by flat disks of cartilage but held together by ligaments and muscles. Cosmetologists are interested in the structure and function of the spinal column because it governs their own comfort during long periods of standing. It is the factor that controls correct posture under all conditions.

Anatomy and physiology
in beauty culture

SKELETAL SYSTEM

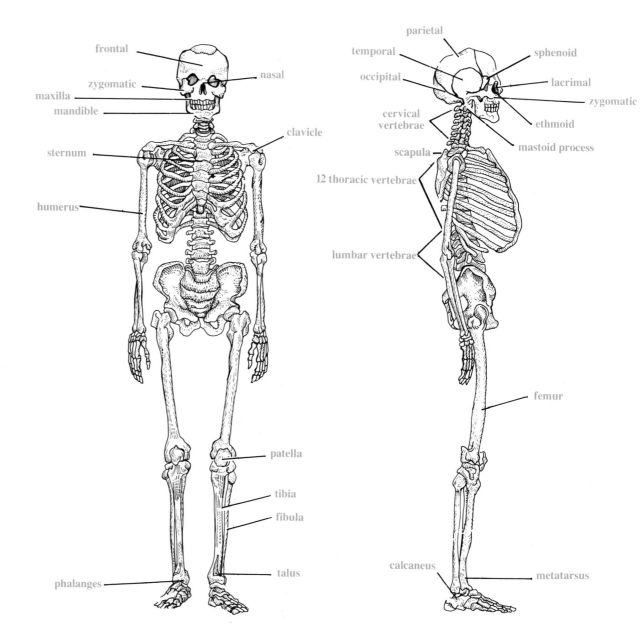

frontal

zygomatic

nasal

maxilla

mandible

sternum

clavicle

humerus

patella

tibia

fibula

talus

phalanges

parietal

temporal

sphenoid

occipital

lacrimal

zygomatic

cervical vertebrae

ethmoid

scapula

mastoid process

12 thoracic vertebrae

lumbar vertebrae

femur

calcaneus

metatarsus

Unit 2

Bones of the head and face

The bony casing of the head is called the skull. It consists of 22 connected bones, divided into two portions:

1. The cranium comprises the whole top and back of the skull. It serves as a safe, protective receptacle for the brain.

2. The face comprises the front lower part of the skull. It contains several noticeable cavities (eyes, nose, ears and mouth) and some invisible cavities called sinuses.

The cranium is made up of eight bones:

1. Occipital	1		4. Temporal	2	
2. Frontal	1		5. Sphenoid	1	
3. Parietal	2		6. Ethmoid	1	
				Total	8

The cranial bones, with the exception of the ethmoid bone, are of interest to the cosmetologist because they are important in scalp massage.

1. The occipital bone forms the back and base of the head.

2. The frontal bone forms the bulge of the forehead from the crown down into the eye sockets.

3. The two parietal bones form the back and sides of the skull.

4. The two temporal bones complete the formation of the sides and base of the skull.

5. The sphenoid bone forms the front part of the base of the cranium. It completes the eye sockets and the nose, and binds all the other cranial bones together.

The face is made up of 14 bones but only seven of them are usually affected during a massage:

1. Nasal	2		3. Maxillae	2
2. Zygomatic	2		4. Mandible	1

Unit 2

Bones of the head and face

General objectives-student goals: After study, instruction and completion of this unit, you will be able to demonstrate understanding of the bones of the head and face by writing and/or giving a brief overview of the subject.

Bones of Head, Neck & Thorax

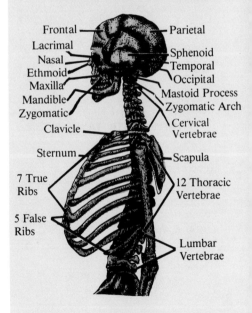

Frontal
Lacrimal
Nasal
Ethmoid
Maxilla
Mandible
Zygomatic
Clavicle
Sternum
7 True Ribs
5 False Ribs

Parietal
Sphenoid
Temporal
Occipital
Mastoid Process
Zygomatic Arch
Cervical Vertebrae
Scapula
12 Thoracic Vertebrae
Lumbar Vertebrae

Anatomy and physiology in beauty culture

481

Those not usually affected during massage are:

1. Vomer	1	3. Lacrimal	2
2. Nasal conchae	2	4. Palatine	2
		Total	14

The hyoid bone is in the throat area. It supports the tongue.

The cosmetologist need only be concerned with those bones of the face that are affected by massage.

1. Nasal bones form the bridge of the nose and determine its shape. Cartilage forms the foundation at the tip of the nose.

2. Zygomatic bones form part of the eye sockets. They extend out from the temporal bones and form an arch on each side of the face.

3. Maxillae bones form the entire upper jaw, the lower part of the sides of the nose and the remaining segment of the eye sockets. The forward edge holds the upper teeth. The angle at which the teeth are placed determines the shape of the upper lip.

4. The mandible bone forms the chin and entire lower jaw.

Unit 3
Bones of the neck and thorax

The seven bones in the neck are called cervical vertebrae. One supports the head. A second serves as a pivot which allows the free movement of the head. Only the remaining five come within the scope of face and scalp massage. Their knobs can be seen and felt when the neck is bent sharply forward.

The bones of the thorax, or chest, serve as a protective covering for the organs found in the upper ventral cavity. Those that come within the region of massage are:

1. The dorsal vertebrae: They number 12 and extend from the neckline to the waist.

2. The ribs: These are 24 curved bones extending around the sides of the chest. Knowing the location of the ribs and their associated ligaments, muscles and nerves is important for correct massage of the back and chest.

3. The sternum, or breastbone, is a narrow flat bone in the middle of the chest.

General objectives-student goals:
After study, instruction and completion of this unit, you will be able to demonstrate understanding of the bones of the neck and thorax by writing and/or giving a brief overview of the subject.

Anatomy and physiology in beauty culture

4. The clavicles, or collarbones, are two long curved bones extending across the top of the thorax from the sternum to the shoulders.

5. The two scapulae, or shoulder blades, are two broad, flat, triangular bones which cover about half the depth of the back part of the thorax.

Unit 4
Bones of the extremities

The arms and legs are called the extremities. They are almost identical in structure.

Upper extremities

Upper arm	1	Palm	5
Lower arm	2	Digits (fingers)	14
Wrist	8	Total	30

Lower extremities

Thigh	1	Arch	5
Lower leg	2	Digits (toes)	14
Instep	7	Accessory	1
		Total	30

Note: In our first summary of the bones of the skeletal system (Unit 1), the total number of bones in the upper extremities is given as 64. This includes the two collarbones and both shoulder blades which, for the subject matter of beauty culture, have been considered with the bones of the thorax. The count for the lower extremities is given as 62. This figure includes the two hipbones which are not directly related to cosmetology.

Bones of the arm

There are three bones in the arm:

1. Humerus: This is the long bone of the upper arm.

General objectives-student goals: After study, instruction and completion of this unit, you will be able to demonstrate understanding of the bones of the extremities by writing and/or giving a brief overview of the subject.

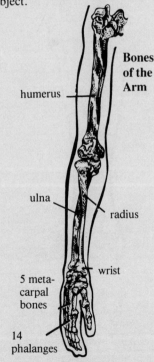

Bones of the Arm

humerus

ulna

radius

5 meta-carpal bones

wrist

14 phalanges

Anatomy and physiology in beauty culture

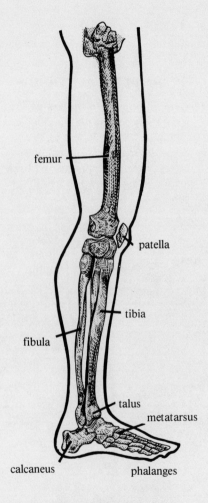

femur

patella

tibia

fibula

talus

metatarsus

calcaneus

phalanges

Bones of the Leg

2. Ulna: This is the large bone on the little finger side of the forearm.

3. Radius: This is the smaller bone on the thumb side of the forearm.

The carpus, or wrist, is a flexible joint composed of eight small irregular bones. They are held together by ligaments.

The bones of the hand are divided into two categories:

1. Metacarpi: These are the five long, slender bones which form the palm of the hand.

2. Phalanges: There are two of them in the thumb and three in each of the other fingers.

Bones of the leg

From the knee down, the bones of the lower leg are the:

1. Patella: This is the knee cap (accessory bone).

2. Tibia: This is the shinbone, the larger bone on the inner side of the leg.

3. Fibula: This is the smaller bone on the outer side of the leg.

The instep consists of seven bones. The three most important of these to the cosmetologist are the:

1. Talus: This is the ankle.

2. Calcaneus: This is the heel.

3. Malleolus: These are the rounded projections of the ankle.

The bones of the foot are divided into two categories:

1. Metatarsi: These are the five slender bones which form the arches of the foot. The curve from the heel to the toes is called the longitudinal arch. The curve across the foot behind the toes is called the metatarsal arch.

2. Phalanges: These number 14, two in the big toe and three in each of the others.

The top of the foot is called the dorsal surface, and the sole is called the plantar surface.

Table of bones which are of varying degrees of importance to the cosmetologist

Bone	Location
Atlas	The first cervical vertebra
Calcaneus	The heel bone; the largest tarsal bone
Calvaria	The skullcap; the upper part of the skull
Capitate	The largest carpal bone in the distal row of carpal bones
Carpus	The wrist; the eight bones of the wrist
Cervical vertebrae	The seven upper bones of the vertebral column, which are located in the neck region
Clavicle	The collarbone
Coccyx	The last bone in the vertebral column
Cranium	The bones of the head excluding the bones of the face; the bony case of the brain
Dorsal vertebrae	The bones of the vertebral column, which are located in the region of the middle back
Ethmoid	A bone forming part of the walls of the nasal cavity
Femur	The proximal bone of the hind or lower limb
Fibula	The splint bone; the lateral bone of the leg
Frontal	Either of a pair of membrane bones that form the forehead
Hamate	A bone of the wrist
Humerus	The long bone of the upper arm extending from the shoulder to the elbow
Hyoid	A bone which is shaped like the letter "U" and situated at the base of the tongue; supports the tongue and its muscles
Lacrimal	A small thin bone, resembling a fingernail, situated in the anterior medial wall of each orbit
Lumbar vertebrae	The bones of the vertebral column, which are located in the region of the lower back
Lunate	A bone of the wrist
Malleolus	The rounded projection of the ankle
Mandible	The lower jawbone
Mastoid process	A conical nipple-like projection of the temporal bone
Maxilla	The jawbone
Metacarpus	The bones of the palm of the hand
Metatarsus	The bony structure that forms the instep of the foot
Nasal	Two bones that form the bridge of the nose

Anatomy and physiology
in beauty culture

485

Bone	Location
Navicular	Scaphoid of the hand; scaphoid of the foot
Occipital	A compound bone that forms the posterior part of the skull
Palatine	Bones situated at the back part of the nasal fossae
Parietal	Bones which form the side and roof of the cranium
Patella	The kneecap
Phalanges of the foot	14 bones: 2 for the great toe, 3 for each of the other toes
Phalanges of the hand	14 bones: 2 for the thumb, 3 for each of the other fingers
Pisiform	Most medial of the proximal row of the carpus; smallest carpal bone
Radius	The outer and smaller bone of the forearm
Scaphoid of the foot	A navicular bone of the foot
Scaphoid of the hand	Largest bone of the proximal row of carpal bones
Scapula	Shoulder blade; flat triangular bone of the posterior part of the shoulder
Sphenoid	The compound bone that forms the anterior base of the skull
Sternum	The flat bone of the breast
Talus	The anklebone
Tarsus	The posterior portion of the foot
Temporal	The bone forming the side and base of the skull
Tibia	The shinbone; the large medial bone of the leg
Trapezium	The first bone of the distal row of the carpus; the greater multangular bone
Trapezoid	The smallest bone in the distal row of the carpus; the lesser multangular bone
Triquetrum	One of the proximal row of carpal bones
Turbinate	
Inferior turbinate	Nasal concha; an irregular scroll-shaped bone, situated on the wall of the nasal cavity
Middle turbinate	Middle nasal concha of the ethmoid bone
Superior turbinate	Superior nasal concha of the ethmoid bone
Ulna	Medial bone of the forearm, located on the little finger side
Vomer	The thin plate of bone between the nostrils
Zygoma	A bone of the skull that extends along the front or side of the face below the eye; the malar; the cheek bone

Unit 5
The circulatory system

The vascular, or circulatory, system consists of two systems:

1. The blood vascular system circulates the blood. It includes the heart, arteries, veins and capillaries.

Unit 5

The circulatory system

General objectives-student goals:
After study, instruction and comple-

Anatomy and physiology in beauty culture

2. The lymph vascular system parallels the venous system and supplies each cell with whatever it needs from the blood.

The blood vascular system

The blood vascular system circulates the blood in the body. Blood is a bright red fluid, thicker than water and slightly sticky. Its normal temperature is about 100°F, and its pH reaction is slightly alkaline. It makes up about 1/20 of the body weight.

Blood is the nutrient fluid of the body. Its functions include:

1. Carrying food to the cells

2. Carrying oxygen to the cells for the consumption of food and the production of heat and energy

3. Carrying internal secretions necessary for chemical activity within the body

4. Carrying waste products away from the cells

5. Equalizing the water content of the body

6. Equalizing the temperature of the body

7. Protecting the body against infections

Blood is composed of a clear fluid called plasma. Millions of tiny individual cells float in the plasma. There are three distinct cell structures which float in the blood stream.

1. Red cells   2. White cells   3. Platelets

The function of the red cells is to carry oxygen. They outnumber the white cells by about 700 to 1. The white cells are the active agents in the defense against bacteria and in the repair of tissues. The platelets aid in the coagulation, or clotting, of the blood.

The heart is a hollow muscular organ which serves as the vital center of the body. It keeps the blood pumping through the body by rhythmic movements of its muscular walls.

The arteries are organs of the circulatory system which carry blood from the heart to other parts of the body.

The capillaries are minute tubes which carry the blood to each tiny cell of the body.

The veins are organs which carry impure blood from other organs and tissues back to the heart. They are relatively thin walled tubes near the surface of the body.

Anatomy and physiology
in beauty culture

The circulation of the blood from the heart through the arteries to other principal organs of the body and back to the heart through the veins is called systemic or general circulation.

The circulation of blood from the heart to the lungs for oxigenation and then back to the heart is called pulmonary circulation.

Two Systems of

Blood Circulation

(Systemic & Pulmonary)

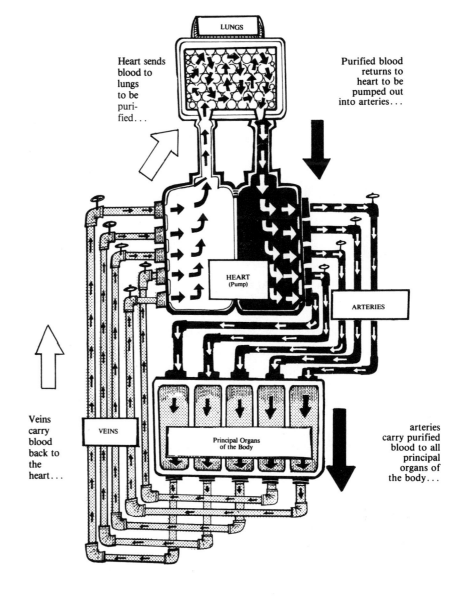

Heart sends blood to lungs to be puri- fied...

Purified blood returns to heart to be pumped out into arteries...

LUNGS

HEART (Pump)

ARTERIES

Veins carry blood back to the heart...

VEINS

Principal Organs of the Body

arteries carry purified blood to all principal organs of the body...

The lymph vascular system

The venous part of the blood vascular system and the lymph vascular system parallel each other very closely.

Lymph is a watery fluid derived from the blood plasma. It serves as a medium of exchange between blood and body tissues. It is constantly oozing out through the capillary walls by means of the process of osmosis.

Lymph supplies each cell with whatever is needed from the blood for proper activity. The blood never comes into direct contact with the body cells. Therefore, lymph is needed.

Lymphatics: Corresponding to the network of capillaries are minute tubes with closed ends called lymph capillaries. These form another network of larger and still larger branches called lymphatics. These correspond to the veins.

Lymph nodes: These are spongy masses scattered in the network of lymphatics. They filter lymph and clear it of bacteria and other foreign substances. They also produce white corpuscles. Lymph nodes are usually found near important blood vessels. They are especially numerous in the neck, thorax, armpits, groin and the upper parts of both arms and legs.

Vascular supply of the head, face and neck

The common carotid arteries slant upward from the root of the neck. They are the main sources of blood supply to the head, face and neck. At the level of the thyroid cartilage, each artery divides into:

1. External carotid arteries

2. Internal carotid arteries

The external carotid artery has eight branches, each of which supplies blood to the various regions of the cranium, face, ears and tongue.

1. External maxillary: This passes over the lower jaw and rests on the muscles of the face. Some branches are:

    A. Submental: This branch supplies blood to the region of the chin and lower lip.

    B. Inferior labial: This branch supplies blood to the lower lip.

    C. Superior labial: This branch supplies blood to the upper lip and septum of the nose.

    D. Angular: This branch supplies blood to the side of the nose.

2. Occipital: This passes to the back of the head and scalp and up to the vertex (crown) of the skull. Some of its branches are:

    A. Auricular: This branch supplies blood to the skin behind the ear.

B. Sternocleidomastoid: This branch supplies blood to the sternocleidomastoid muscle.

C. Posterior auricular: This branch passes over the scalp and head, behind and above the ears.

D. Superficial temporal: This is a direct continuation of the external carotid. It passes in front of the ear and over the temples. Some of the branches of the superficial temporal artery are:

1. Frontal: This branch supplies blood to the forehead.

2. Parietal: This branch supplies blood to the sides and crown of the head.

3. Transverse facial: This branch supplies blood to the masseter muscle and skin.

4. Middle temporal: This branch supplies blood to the temples and eyelids.

5. Anterior auricular: This branch supplies blood to the external ears.

6. Zygomaticoorbital: This branch supplies blood to the orbit and orbicularis.

The internal carotid artery has several branches, most of which are inside the skull. One, which extends into the superficial layers of the muscles, is the ophthalmic. It passes into and around the eye. One of its branches is the supraorbital. This branch supplies blood to the orbit, eyelids, sides of the nose and forehead.

Veins of the head, face and neck

The deeper veins that draw the blood from the head, face and neck correspond in position and name to the arteries just described. The blood from the internal regions of the cranium flows into the internal jugular vein. The superficial veins converge around and below the ear into the external jugular vein.

Vascular supply of the thorax, arm and hand

All the arteries of the upper thorax and arm are branches or direct continuations of one main trunk. Its divisions, in order, are:

1. Subclavian artery: This extends under the collarbone as far as the line of the armpit. Its branches supply blood to the brain, neck, chest and upper part of the back.

2. Axillary artery: This extends through the armpit into the upper arm. Its branches supply blood to the chest, shoulder and arm.

3. Brachial artery: This extends down the arm to just below the elbow, where it branches into the:

   A. Radial artery   B. Ulnar artery

These branches supply blood to all parts of the hand.

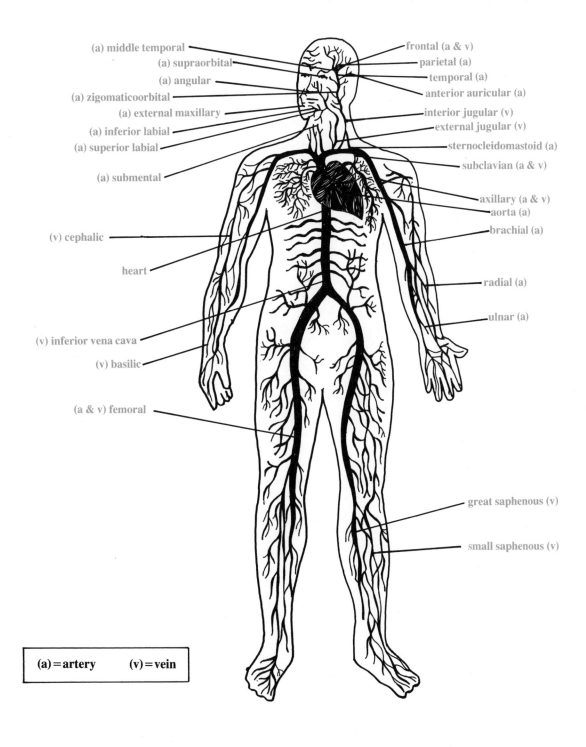

(a) middle temporal

(a) supraorbital

(a) angular

(a) zigomaticoorbital

(a) external maxillary

(a) inferior labial

(a) superior labial

(a) submental

(v) cephalic

heart

(v) inferior vena cava

(v) basilic

(a & v) femoral

frontal (a & v)

parietal (a)

temporal (a)

anterior auricular (a)

interior jugular (v)

external jugular (v)

sternocleidomastoid (a)

subclavian (a & v)

axillary (a & v)

aorta (a)

brachial (a)

radial (a)

ulnar (a)

great saphenous (v)

small saphenous (v)

(a) = artery   **(v) = vein**

**CIRCULATORY
SYSTEM**

**Anatomy and physiology
in beauty culture**

Veins of the thorax and arm

From one complicated network at the back of the hand and from another at the front, the blood flows into the radial and ulnar veins in the forearm. These veins then form the:

1. Cephalic vein: This extends up the arm on the radial side (front).

2. Basilic vein: This extends up the ulnar side (outside) of the arm. Under the shoulder, these veins join to form the axillary vein.

3. Axillary vein: This continues as the subclavian vein.

4. Subclavian vein: This meets the jugular veins from the head. It finally empties into the innominate veins.

The arteries of the leg are unimportant to the cosmetologist. However, two veins of the leg are markedly affected during massage of the leg:

1. Great saphenous: This extends along the inner side of the front of the leg.

2. Small saphenous: This extends up the back of the leg.

Table of arteries which are of varying degrees of importance to the cosmetologist

Artery	Blood supply
Angular	Lacrimal sac and the eye muscle
Aorta	After leaving the heart, supplies blood to the various arteries for circulation throughout the body
Auricular	
Anterior auricular	Anterior part of the ear
Posterior auricular	Scalp and parotid gland
Axillary	Armpit
Brachial	Upper arm
Buccal	Buccinator muscle, cheeks and upper gums
Carotid	
Common carotid	Head, face and neck
External carotid	Anterior portion of the neck, face, scalp, ear and side of the head
Internal carotid	Forehead, nose and internal ear

Artery	Blood supply
Cerebral	
Posterior cerebral	Cortex of the temporal and occipital bones
Cervical	
Ascending cervical	Muscles of the neck, the membrane of the spinal cord and the vertebrae
Deep cervical	Deep neck muscles and spinal cord
Digital	Fingers and toes
Frontal	Forehead and upper eyelid
Genicular	
Lateral inferior genicular	Knee joint
Interosseous	
Anterior interosseous	Deep anterior forearm
Posterior interosseous	Muscles of the skin and posterior forearm
Labial	
Inferior labial	Lower lip
Superior labial	Upper lip and nose
Masseteric	Masseter
Maxillary	Lower region of the face, mouth and nose and deep structures of the face
Mental	Lower lip and chin
Occipital	Scalp, the back of the head up to the crown and the muscles of the neck
Opthalmic	Upper muscles of the eye and the eyelid
Palmar arch	Joints, bones and skin of the palm and fingers
Palpebral	
Lateral palpebral	Upper and lower eyelids
Parietal	The crown and side of the head
Peroneal	Shaft of the fibula, the ankle joint and the dorsum of the foot
Plantar	
Lateral plantar	Toes, heel and related muscles
Medial plantar	Skin on the surface of the sole of the foot
Plantar arch	Muscles of the toes
Radial	Muscles of the forearm, elbow, wrist and skin of the hand and fingers
Sternocleidomastoid	Sternocleidomastoid muscle
Subclavian	Neck and upper extremities
Submental	Chin and lower lip
Supraorbital	Forehead and upper eyelid

Artery	Blood supply
Suprascapular	Muscles of the shoulder joints
Supratrochlear	Anterior scalp
Tarsal	Surface of the foot and tarsal joints
Temporal	
Deep temporal	Temporal muscle, orbit and skull
Middle temporal	Temporal muscle and eyelids
Superficial temporal	Muscles of the head and the scalp
Thyrocervical trunk	Muscles of the neck, upper back and cervical spinal cord
Tibial	
Anterior tibial	Knee, muscles of the leg and skin on the front of the leg
Anterior-Recurrent	Knee joint and overlying muscles and skin
Posterior tibial	The sole of the foot and the muscles of the lower leg
Posterior-Recurrent	Ankle joint, the posterior part of the leg and foot, and the sole of the foot
Transverse facial	Skin of the face, the parotid gland and the masseter
Vertebral	Muscles of the neck
Zygomaticoorbital	Orbit and orbicularis

Table of veins which are of varying degrees of importance to the cosmetologist

This table includes only those veins which have no corresponding artery of the same name. The names of veins which have corresponding arteries of the same name can be deduced from the names of the arteries listed in the table of arteries.

Vein	Location
Ascending lumbar	Near the lumbar spinal column
Basilar plexus	At the basilar part of the occipital bone
Basilic	Medial side of the biceps brachii
Brachiocephalic	Root of the neck
Cephalic	Radial side of the hand and forearm
Diploic	Inside the frontal, temporal, parietal and occipital bones
Emissary	Small openings of the skull
External vertebral plexuses	Anterior and posterior to the vertebral column
Facial	Anterior side of the face

Vein	Location
Jugular	
Anterior jugular	Begins near the hyoid bone and descends to the lower part of the neck
External jugular	The side of the neck
Internal jugular	Begins in the occipital region and extends to the upper and back part of the neck
Saphenous	
Great saphenous	Medial side of the leg and thigh
Small saphenous	Back of the leg

Unit 6
The muscular system

The scientific study of the structure and function of the muscles is called myology. The muscular system covers and shapes the skeleton. It contains over 500 muscles which constitute about 45% of the total weight of the body. Muscles vary in length from a fraction of an inch (2.54 cm.) to nearly 24 inches (60.96 cm.). They differ greatly in shape.

There are three types of muscular tissue:

1. Striated (voluntary)

2. Nonstriated (involuntary)

3. Cardiac

Striated muscle gets its name from its horizontal cross-strips. It is controlled by the will. It is voluntary muscle.

Nonstriated muscle is smooth. It does not have strips. It is not under the control of the will. It is involuntary muscle. It is controlled by the sympathetic nervous system. It constitutes the wall of the arteries and internal organs.

Cardiac muscle tissue is found only in the heart. Its action is involuntary.

A typical muscle is composed of a thick contracting portion called the body and two ends which attach the muscle to the skeleton or other tissues. One end of the muscle is called its origin; the other is called its insertion. The origin of a muscle is the more fixed attachment. The insertion is the more movable attachment.

A tendon is fibrous tissue which attaches muscles to bones.

Unit 6
The muscular system

General objectives-student goals:
After study, instruction and completion of this unit, you will be able to demonstrate understanding of the muscular system by writing and/or giving a brief overview of the subject.

Anatomy and physiology in beauty culture

MUSCULAR
SYSTEM

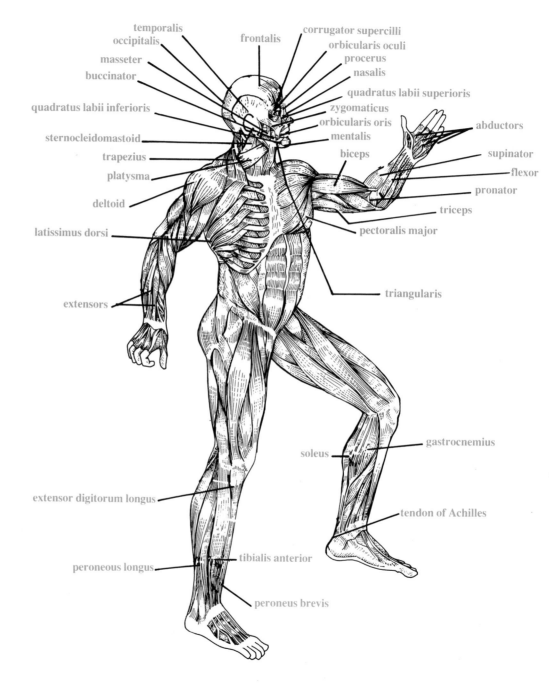

temporalis
occipitalis
masseter
buccinator
quadratus labii inferioris
sternocleidomastoid
trapezius
platysma
deltoid
latissimus dorsi
extensors
extensor digitorum longus
peroneous longus

frontalis
corrugator supercilli
orbicularis oculi
procerus
nasalis
quadratus labii superioris
zygomaticus
orbicularis oris
mentalis
biceps
abductors
supinator
flexor
pronator
triceps
pectoralis major
triangularis
gastrocnemius
soleus
tendon of Achilles
tibialis anterior
peroneus brevis

There are four characteristics that distinguish muscle tissue from other forms of tissue:

1. Excitability: This is the ability to respond to stimulus or irritation.

2. Contractility: This is when muscular tissue becomes shorter and thicker in response to stimulus.

3. Extensibility: This is a muscle's ability to stretch beyond its original length.

4. Elasticity: This quality allows muscular tissue to return to its original form and position after contracting or extending.

When the skeletal muscles are well nourished and developed, muscle tone is noticeable in their ready reaction to stimulus. Muscle tone also keeps the muscles firm and the joints in place. It also aids the regulation of body temperature.

Movement in a muscle—contracting and extending—is always the result of some outside stimulus. The stimulus may be:

1. Chemicals: A change in nutrition

2. Mechanical: Exercise or massage

3. Nerves: Impulses through the nervous system

4. Physical: The application of electricity, heat or light

Muscles of the head and face

The muscles of the head and face are numerous. They are studied best when grouped according to their location and function. The cosmetologist is primarily concerned with the muscles that lie nearer the skin and are more directly affected by massage.

Muscles of the scalp

The epicranius covers the entire top and back of the head from the eyebrows to the neck. It is composed of two muscles:

1. Occipital: This muscle originates in the back part of the epicranius. Its action draws the scalp backward.

2. Frontal: This muscle originates in the front part of the epicranius. Its action raises eyebrows and draws the scalp forward.

Muscles of the nose

The muscles of the nose are affected only slightly during facial massage. Consideration is given only to the more important ones.

1. Procerus: This muscle covers the bridge of the nose. It draws the eyebrows down.

2. Nasalis: This muscle has two parts:

A. Compressor narium

B. Depressor alae nasi

These are small muscles at the tip of the nose which contract and expand the opening of the nostril.

3. Depressor septi: This muscle is located at the lower part of the nose. It draws the entire tip of the nose down. This action compresses the nostrils.

Muscles of the eyes

Only two of the external orbital muscles are affected by cosmetology treatments:

1. Orbicularis oculi: This muscle has two parts. It forms a complete circle around the eye. It has a double action which closes the eye forcibly and involuntarily. It wrinkles and draws the surrounding skin down.

2. Corrugator supercilli: This is a small narrow muscle which originates at the inner end of the eyebrow. It puckers the eyebrow.

Muscles of the mouth

The various muscles surrounding the mouth are often referred to as the muscles of expression. They are superficial and readily affected by the movements of massage. They can be easily located on charts or on the face itself.

1. Quadratus labii superioris: This muscle consists of three strips which surround the upper part of the lip. It raises the wing of the nose and lip, draws them back and widens the nostril.

2. Orbicularis oris: This muscle is formed by the extension and interlacing of several of the muscles surrounding the mouth. It holds the mouth closed. When forcibly contracted, it puckers the lips.

3. Caninus: This muscle originates in the maxilla. It lifts the corner of the mouth and helps keep it closed.

4. Zygomaticus: This muscle originates in the outer arch of the zygomatic bone. It draws the upper lip upward and back.

5. Buccinator: This muscle is located directly at the side of the face between the jaws. Its action compresses the cheeks when they are distended.

6. Risorius: This muscle originates in the fascia near the ear. It is inserted at a right angle slightly below the corner of the mouth. Its action draws the corner of the mouth out and back.

7. Triangularis: This muscle originates in the lower line of the mandible. Its action draws the corner of the mouth down.

8. Quadratus labii inferioris: This muscle originates in the lower part of the lip. Its action draws the lower lip down and a little to one side.

9. Mentalis: This muscle originates in the mandible and is inserted into the skin of the chin. Its action raises the lower lip, pushes it forward and causes wrinkling of the chin.

Muscles of mastication

These muscles aid the action of the jaws in chewing food. Even with deep manipulations, only two of these muscles are affected by massage:

1. Temporalis: This muscle originates in a large oval area in the temporal bone. It closes the jaws.

2. Masseter: This muscle has two layers. It originates in the arch of the zygomatic bone. Its action closes the jaws.

Muscles of the neck

1. Platysma: This is a broad flat muscle which extends from the chest and shoulder muscles to the side of the chin. It draws the lower lip down and holds the skin of the neck smooth and taut.

2. Sternocleidomastoid: This is a large thick muscle which extends from the collar and chest bones to the temporal bone behind the ear. Its action draws the head to one side or down toward the chest.

Muscles of the thorax

1. Pectoralis major: This muscle covers the chest down to about the sixth rib. Its action rotates the arm and draws it toward the body.

2. Trapezius: This muscle covers the back of the neck and the entire upper region of the back. Its action draws the head backwards or to one side.

3. Latissimus dorsi: This muscle covers the middle region of the back below the trapezius. It draws the arm in and back.

Muscles of the extremities

The muscles of the upper arm affected by massage are:

1. Deltoid: This is a large thick muscle that covers the shoulder. Its action raises and rotates the arm.

2. Biceps: This is the principal muscle on the front of the upper arm. It raises the forearm and rotates the palm outward.

3. Triceps: This is a three-headed muscle which originates in and around the head of the humerus. It covers the entire back of the upper arm. Its action opposes the biceps and extends the forearm.

The muscles of the forearm are arranged in opposing pairs:

1. Pronators: These turn the hand inward so that the palm faces backward.

2. Supinators: These turn the hand outward so that the palm faces frontward.

3. Flexors: These bend the wrist, drawing the hand toward the forearm. They bend the fingers by means of their continuations out into the hand.

4. Extensors: These straighten the wrist and fingers, drawing them up and back toward the forearm.

Muscles of the hand

The hand has many small muscles which give it great flexibility and strength. The two muscles that open and close the hand and fingers are:

1. Abductor muscles: Their action separates the fingers.

2. Adductor muscles: Their action brings the fingers together.

Both muscles are located at the base of the fingers.

Muscles of the leg

The principal muscles of the lower leg affected by massage are:

1. Tibialis anterior: This muscle covers the front of the shin. It bends the foot upward and inward.

2. Extensor digitorum longus: This muscle originates on the side of the tibia and on the upper surface of the fibula. It bends the foot up and extends the toes.

3. Peroneus longus: This muscle covers the outer side of the calf. Its action allows the foot to turn down and out.

4. Peroneus brevis: This muscle originates on the lower surface of the fibula. It bends the foot down and out.

5. Soleus: This muscle originates at the rear of the head and upper portion of the fibula. It bends the foot down.

6. Gastrocnemius: This muscle originates as two heads attached to prominences at the lower end of the thigh bone. It is attached to the lower rear surface of the heel. It pulls the foot down.

The principal tendon at the back of the heel is called the Tendon of Achilles.

The muscles of the foot are well designed and placed to ensure proper support for the delicate bones and adequate padding for good contour. They are connected by tendons in the area going from the region around the tarsus to the toes. Cosmetologists do not have to know the names and functions of these small muscles.

All the tendons are held in place by a strong transverse ligament around the ankle. All the structures of the foot are encased in strong bands.

Table of muscles which are of varying degrees of importance to the cosmetologist

Muscle	Function
Abductor	Draws a part of the body away from the median line
Adductor	Draws a part of the body toward the median line
Agonist	Flexor or prime mover muscle which executes movements such as bending the leg at the knee joint
Anconeus	Extends the elbow joint
Antagonist	Extensor muscle which executes movements opposite to those executed by the agonists
Arrector pilorum	Elevates the hair of the skin
Auricularis	
Anterior auricularis	Draws the ear forward
Posterior auricularis	Draws the ear backward
Superior auricularis	Draws the ear upward
Biceps	Flexes the elbow, lifts the forearm and turns the palm downward
Biceps brachii	Flexes the elbow, lifts the forearm and turns the palm downward
Brachialis	Flexes the elbow joint
Brachioradialis	Prominent muscle of the lower arm which assists the biceps in bending the elbow joint
Buccinator	Compresses the cheeks and retracts the angle of the mouth
Caninus	Lifts the angle of the mouth
Cardiac	Muscle which makes up the heart
Chondroglossus	Depresses the tongue

Muscle	Function
Corrugator supercilli	Draws the eyebrows inward and downward
Deltoid	Raises the arm laterally
Depressor	Presses or draws a part of the body down
Depressor labii inferioris	Draws the lower lip down and sideways
Depressor labii superioris	Depresses the lower lip
Depressor oris	Draws the corners of the mouth down
Dorsiflexor	Turns the foot upward
Epicranius	Elevates the eyebrows and draws the scalp forward
Extensor	Extends the wrist
Extensor carpi radialis	Functions with other muscles to bend the hand backward
Extensor digitorum longus	Extends the toes and bends the foot upward
Flexor	Bends or flexes a part of the body
Flexor carpi ulnaris	Functions along with other muscles in bending the hand backward
Frontalis	Elevates the eyebrows and draws the scalp forward
Gastrocnemius	Flexes the knee and plantarflexes the foot at the ankle
Gluteal	Any of several muscles which make up the buttocks and help to draw the thigh backward and raise the trunk from a stooping position
Gracilis	Flexes the leg and rotates it medially
Hamstring	Muscles comprising the back of the thigh
Hyoglossus	Depresses the tongue
Latissimus dorsi	Draws the arm backward and downward
Levator	Elevates a part of the body
Levator anguli oris	Raises the angle of the mouth and draws it in
Levator labii superioris	Elevates the upper lip and dilates the nostrils
Levator palpebrae	Raises the upper eyelid
Masseter	Closes the mouth and clenches the teeth
Mentalis	Elevates the lower lip and raises and wrinkles the skin of the chin
Nasalis	Widens the nasal opening and depresses the nasal cartilage
Occipitalis	Draws the scalp backward
Occipito-Frontalis	Elevates the eyebrows and draws the scalp forward
Opponens digiti	Deepens the palm
Orbicularis oculi	Closes the eyelids
Orbicularis oris	Closes the lips
Palmaris brevis	Deepens the palm
Pectoralis major	Flexes the shoulder joint and rotates the arm inward
Pectoralis minor	Draws the shoulder forward and rotates the scapula downward

Muscle	Function
Peroneus brevis	Flexes and bends the foot down and outward
Peroneus longus	Allows the foot to turn down and out
Plantarflexors	Turn the foot down
Platysma	Depresses the lower jaw and lip
Procerus	Draws the eyebrows down
Pronators	Turn the forearm so that the palm faces down
Pterygoid	
Medial pterygoid	Clenches the teeth
Quadratus labii inferioris	Draws the lower lip down and sideways
Quadratus labii superioris	Raises and draws the upper lip back
Quadriceps femoris	Comprises the frontal aspect of the thigh and consists of four muscles which function as a powerful extensor group in activities such as walking and kicking
Rectus abdominis	Strap-like muscles that run vertically on each side of the midline of the abdominal wall; flexes the spine
Rectus capitis anterior	Flexes the head
Rectus capitis lateralis	Assists in the lateral movements of the head
Rectus capitis posterior major	Extends the head
Risorius	Draws the corners of the mouth out and back
Sartorius	Assists in adducting and rotating the thigh laterally
Serratus anterior	Assists in breathing and draws the scapula forward
Soleus	Plantarflexes the foot
Sternocleidomastoid	Rotates and bends the head
Supinator	Turns the hand outward so that the palm faces upward
Synergists	Assist the agonists in producing a desired movement or hold a part of the body steady to permit the agonists to produce a more effective movement
Temporalis	Opens and closes the jaw
Tibialis anterior	Bends the foot upward and inward
Transversus abdominis	Supports the viscera and gives firmness to the abdominal wall
Trapezius	Draws the head backward and sideways; rotates the shoulder blades and raises the shoulders
Triangularis	Pulls the corners of the mouth down
Triangularis labii inferioris	Draws the corners of the mouth down
Triangularis labii superioris	Raises the angle of the mouth
Triceps	Extends the forearm forward
Triceps brachii	Extends the forearm forward
Vastus	Extends the knee joint
Zygomaticus	Draws the upper lip upward and outward

Unit 7

The nervous system

General objectives-student goals:
After study, instruction and completion of this unit, you will be able to demonstrate understanding of the nervous system by writing and/or giving a brief overview of the subject.

Neurology is the study of the structure and functions of the nervous system, one of the most important systems of the body. The activity of the nervous system coordinates all other biological activities of the body. This activity makes all the higher functions of human life possible:

1. Thinking and learning

2. Speech

3. Sight and hearing

4. Taste and smell

Knowledge of the structure of the nervous system will help the cosmetologist to understand the effect of massage on the nerves in the skin during facial and scalp treatments. It is especially important to learn the motor points which are stimulated by pressure.

Nervous tissue is composed of individual cells with a distinctive structure and function. A nerve cell, or neuron, may vary greatly in size and shape, but it always consists essentially of a central portion called the cell body and various extensions called processes. Nervous tissue has the characteristic property of excitability or irritability. Once stimulated, it exhibits its property of conductivity. This is its means of conveying impulses and coordinating the body as a whole.

The nervous system includes the:

1. Brain: This organ is a soft pulpy mass which fills the cavity of the cranium. It is made up of gray matter containing nerve cells and white matter composed of nerve fibers.

2. Spinal cord: This is a continuation of the brain. It extends from the skull and goes through the vertebrae of the spinal column.

3. Ganglia: These are small knots of nervous tissue, massed in front of the spinal column and in various other regions of the body.

4. Nerves:

   A. Cerebral nerves: These originate in the brain.

   B. Spinal nerves: These originate in the spinal cord.

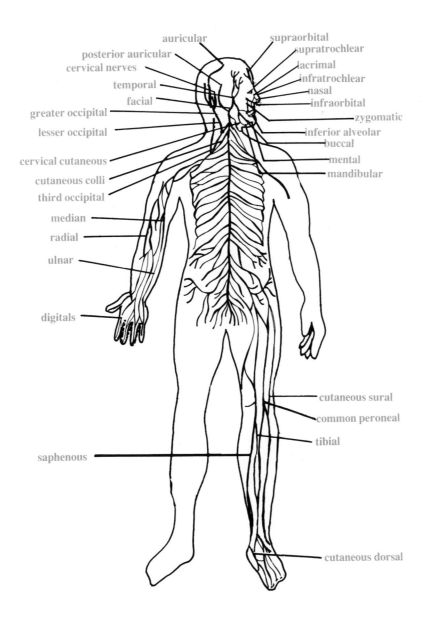

auricular

posterior auricular

cervical nerves

temporal

facial

greater occipital

lesser occipital

cervical cutaneous

cutaneous colli

third occipital

median

radial

ulnar

digitals

saphenous

supraorbital

supratrochlear

lacrimal

infratrochlear

nasal

infraorbital

zygomatic

inferior alveolar

buccal

mental

mandibular

cutaneous sural

common peroneal

tibial

cutaneous dorsal

**Anatomy and physiology
in beauty culture**

AN EXAMPLE OF HOW THE NERVOUS SYSTEM WORKS

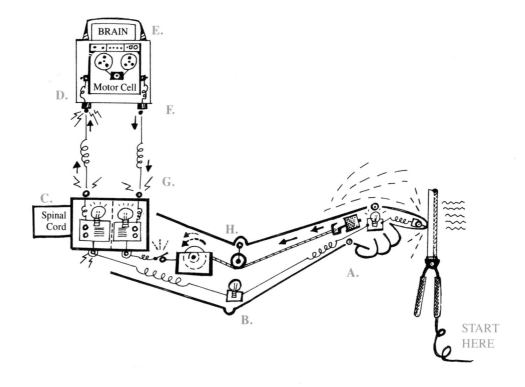

A. Finger touches hot curling iron...
B. Sensory nerve carries impulse to spinal cord which...
C. Sends signals to cell in brain that receives sensation of touch...
D. Activating motor cell...
E. Then the thought cell which relays message along...
F. The motor nerve to...
G. Muscles controlling the hand...
H. Cause it to pull away.

C. **Sympathetic nerves:** These originate in the ganglia.

D. **Autonomic nerves:** These originate in the medulla and lower spinal cord.

The brain, the spinal cord and the nerves that originate in these organs comprise the central nervous system. The spinal cord is composed of nerve cells with fibers. It originates in the brain and extends to the lower trunk. The spinal nerves extend from the spinal cord. They run to the muscles and skin of the trunk and limbs.

A nerve is a long, white cord, composed of fibers. It transmits stimuli between the nervous system and other parts of the body. Nerves are classified as:

1. **Sensory nerves:** These carry impulses from outside the body to nerve centers where they are registered as sensations such as cold, heat, sight, pain, taste, smell and hearing. Sensory nerves are situated near the surface of the skin.

2. **Motor nerves:** These carry impulses from the nerve centers and stimulate muscular contraction in some organs of the body. They are found throughout all muscular tissue.

Nerve stimulation is accomplished:

1. **Mechanically:** By exercise or massage

2. **Chemically:** By changes in nutrition or the use of drugs

3. **Physically:** By the application of electrical current, heat or light

4. **By reflex action:** By an involuntary reaction to a stimulus

Any response to a stimulus is a reflex act. The term reflex action is applied to nervous impulses that operate through the spinal cord instead of through the brain. For instance, if the hand is accidentally placed on a hot iron, the sensation of extreme heat travels to the brain. However, the impulse to move the hand goes back from the spinal cord instantly. Usually, the hand has already been removed from the hot iron by the time the brain receives the sensation of heat.

Nerves of the head and face

The head and face receive their nerve supply from 12 pairs of cerebral nerves. These nerves originate in the brain and pass through openings in the cranium. They are numbered in the order of their apparent origin. They receive their names from the organs they activate. Of the 12 cerebral nerves, only three are of interest to the cosmetologist:

1. Fifth cerebral nerve   2. Seventh cerebral nerve   3. Eleventh cerebral nerve

Anatomy and physiology
in beauty culture

507

The fifth cerebral nerve is called the trigeminal nerve. It is the largest of the cerebral nerves. When it emerges from the brain, it forms a ganglion just forward of the ear and just inside the skull. It splits into three main divisions:

1. Ophthalmic division

2. Maxillary division

3. Mandibular division

The ophthalmic division is a sensory nerve which affects the skin of the forehead, eyelids and nose. Its branches are:

1. Supraorbital: This affects the forehead, scalp, eyebrow and upper eyelid.

2. Supratrochlear: This affects the skin between the eyes, and the upper side of the nose.

3. Infratrochlear: This affects the membrane and skin of the nose.

4. Nasal: This affects the tip and lower side of the nose.

5. Lacrimal: This affects the upper eyelid and the tear glands.

The maxillary division is a sensory nerve which affects the side of the face, the lower eyelid and upper lip. Its branches are:

1. Zygomatic nerve: This affects the temple, the side of the forehead and the skin of the upper cheek.

2. Infraorbital nerve: This affects the skin of the eyelids, the side of the nose, the upper lip, mouth and associated glands.

The mandibular division is the largest of the three divisions of the fifth nerve. It affects the skin of the lower part of the face and the inner and outer muscles. Its branches are:

1. Anterior portion: This splits into several branches which affect the muscles of mastication, the buccinator muscle and the skin of the cheek.

2. The posterior portion is both motor and sensory. It subdivides to form:

   A. Auriculotemporal nerve: This affects the external ear and the skin over the temples and up to the vertex of the skull.

   B. Inferior alveolar nerve: This affects the lower jaw and teeth. One branch, the mental nerve, affects the lower lip and chin.

NERVES

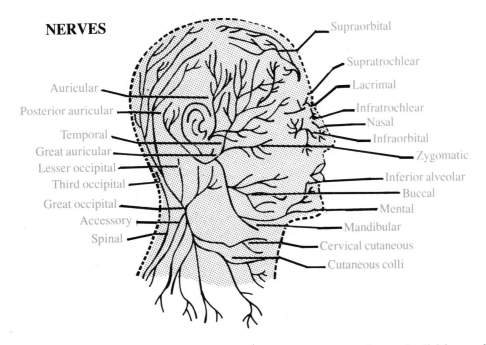

Auricular
Posterior auricular
Temporal
Great auricular
Lesser occipital
Third occipital
Great occipital
Accessory
Spinal

Supraorbital
Supratrochlear
Lacrimal
Infratrochlear
Nasal
Infraorbital
Zygomatic
Inferior alveolar
Buccal
Mental
Mandibular
Cervical cutaneous
Cutaneous colli

The **seventh cerebral (facial) nerve** is the chief motor nerve of the face. It emerges near the ear. Its divisions and branches spread through all the muscles of expression. The most important branches of the facial nerve are:

1. **Posterior auricular nerve:** This affects the muscles behind the ear and at the base of the skull.

2. **Temporal nerve:** This affects the muscles of the forehead, temples, eyelids and upper cheek.

3. **Zygomatic nerve:** This affects the muscles of the upper cheek.

4. **Buccal nerve:** This affects the muscles of the mouth.

5. **Mandibular nerve:** This affects the muscles of the lip and chin.

6. **Cervical nerve:** This affects the side of the neck and platysma.

The **eleventh cerebral (accessory) nerve** is a motor nerve which extends over the neck and upper part of the back. It consists of two branches:

1. **Accessory:** This is the smaller of the two. It affects only internal structures.

2. **Spinal:** This branch affects the sternocleidomastoid and trapezius muscles in the neck and back.

The anterior branches supply impulses to the skin of the face and ear. They connect with the trigeminal nerves and the nerves of the face. The posterior branches affect the skin behind the ear.

The cervical plexus is the interior division of the first four cervical nerves. These nerves are joined together. They originate from the spinal cord and are called spinal nerves. The grouping of these nerves is developed according to the location of their points of origin. A good example of this is the thoracic nerve which originates from the vertebrae between the neck and waist. Another example is the cervical nerve which originates from the vertebrae in the neck.

There are two divisions of the cervical nerves:

1. Anterior

2. Posterior

The many branches of the anterior and posterior nerves are divided into two groups:

1. Superficial

2. Deep

The cosmetologist is concerned only with the superficial nerves of the cervical plexus. These are divided into two groups:

1. Ascending

2. Descending

The ascending nerves of the cervical plexus are the great auricular, the lesser occipital and the cutaneous colli.

1. Great auricular nerve: This affects the external ear and the area in front of and behind the ear.

2. Lesser occipital nerve: This affects the scalp and the muscles at the base of the skull.

3. Cutaneous colli: This affects the front and side of the neck, the platysma and areas as far down as the breastbone.

The descending branches of the cervical plexus arise in the third and fourth cervical nerves. They emerge behind the sternocleidomastoid muscle, and pass downward between that muscle and the trapezius. The external branches are:

1. Supraclavicular anterior: It slants over the clavicle and affects the skin of the upper chest as far down as the breastbone.

2. Supraclavicular posterior: This crosses the clavicle and affects the skin over the pectoral and deltoid muscles. It also slants across the trapezius and affects the skin of the top and back of the shoulder.

The posterior divisions of the cervical nerves pass backwards and subdivide into two groups: internal and external. The latter affect the muscles at the side of the neck. The posterior divisions of a few of the cervical nerves of special interest to cosmetologists are:

1. Great occipital nerve: This is one of the most important of all the nerves affected by massage. It is the internal branch of the posterior division of the second cervical nerve. It slants inward, passing through the trapezius muscle, and emerges at the base of the skull. It affects the skin as far up as the vertex.

2. Third occipital nerve: This is the posterior division of the third cervical nerve. It passes through the trapezius muscle at the median line of the neck. It affects the skin at the base of the skull.

The occipital nerves, originating in different centers, communicate with one another across the back of the head. Branches of some of the lower cervical nerves extend down to the latissimus dorsi.

Nerves of the arm and hand

The most important branches of the nerves which supply impulses to the arm and hand are:

1. Axillary nerve: This nerve originates in the armpit and affects the deltoid muscle.

2. Ulnar nerve: This nerve affects the forearm and hand. It passes over the joint of the elbow at the funny bone.

3. Radial nerve: This nerve affects the thumb side of the arm and the back of the hand.

4. Musculocutaneous nerve: This nerve originates in three of the cervical nerves. It passes among the muscles of the upper arm and spreads out as a sensory nerve along the side of the forearm.

Two groups of superficial nerves, which originate in principal nerves and are always affected during massage, are the:

1. Cutaneous brachii (lateral, medial, posterior): These supply impulses to the skin of the upper arm.

2. Cutaneous antibrachii (lateral, medial, dorsal): These supply impulses to the skin of the forearm.

Nerves of the lower leg and foot

The principal nerves of the lower leg and foot are:

1. Tibial nerve: This is a nerve in the thigh which passes behind the knee. It forms subdivisions and supplies impulses to the knee, the muscles of the calf, the skin of the leg, heel, sole and the underside of the toes.

Anatomy and physiology
in beauty culture

2. Common peroneal nerve: This is another division of the sciatic nerve. It slants down behind the knee to about the head of the tibia where it divides into the:

A. Deep peroneal nerve: This nerve passes down the front of the leg. It subdivides and supplies impulses to various muscles at the top of the foot and toes.

B. Superficial peroneal: This nerve passes downward in front of the fibula. It supplies impulses to the peroneal muscles, the skin of the foot, and the toes.

Important superficial nerves, which are terminations of principal nerves and always affected during massage, are the:

1. Saphenous: This nerve supplies impulses to the skin of the inner side of the leg and foot.

2. Cutaneous sural: This nerve supplies impulses to the outer side and back of the leg and foot.

3. Sural: This nerve supplies impulses to the outer side and back of the leg and foot.

4. Cutaneous dorsal: This nerve supplies impulses to the top of the foot.

Table of nerves which are of varying degrees of importance to the cosmetologist

Nerve	Type	Function
Accessory	Motor	Stimulates the striated muscles of the larynx and the pharynx
Acoustic	Sensory	Receives stimuli from the hearing canal and helps maintain body balance
Aducens	Motor	Stimulates the muscles of the eye
Alveolar		
Inferior alveolar	Sensory	Receives sensation from the teeth, the skin of the lip and the chin
Middle superior alveolar	Sensory	Receives sensation from the upper premolar teeth
Posterior superior alveolar	Sensory	Receives sensation from the upper molar teeth
Auricular		
Anterior auricular	Sensory	Receives stimuli from the skin anterior to the external ear
Great auricular	Sensory	Receives stimuli from the skin to the front and back of the ear
Posterior auricular	Motor	Stimulates the muscles behind the ear at the base of the skull
Auricular temporal	Sensory	Receives stimuli from the skin of the scalp and temple

Nerve	Type	Function
Axillary	Motor	Stimulates the deltoid muscles
Axillary	Sensory	Receives stimuli from the skin of the lateral aspect of the shoulder and arm
Buccal	Sensory	Receives stimuli from the buccinator and the orbicularis oris muscle
Calcaneal	Sensory	Receives stimuli from the skin of the heel
Cardiac	Visceral sensory	Affects the heart
Carotid	Sympathetic	Filaments to the smooth muscle and glands of the head
Cervical		
Fifth to eighth cervical ventri ramus	Motor-sensory	Affects the muscles of the skin and the upper extremities
First cervical dorsal ramus	Motor	Affects the deep muscles of the back of the neck
First cervical ventral ramus	Motor	Stimulates the neck muscles
Fourth cervical ventral ramus	Motor-sensory	Affects the deep muscles of the neck and upper portion of the back
Second and third cervical dorsal ramus	Motor	Stimulates the deep muscles of the back of the neck
Second and third cervical dorsal ramus	Sensory	Receives stimuli from the skin of the back of the neck
Second and third cervical ventral ramus	Motor	Stimulates the neck muscles
Second and third cervical ventral ramus	Sensory	Receives stimuli from the skin of the neck
Cervical cutaneous	Sensory	Receives stimuli from the front and side of the neck
Chorda tympani	Sensory	Receives stimuli from the taste buds of the anterior two-thirds of the tongue
Cutaneous		
Cutaneous of the foot	Sensory	Receives stimuli from the skin of the foot
Lateral cutaneous	Sensory	Receives stimuli from the skin of the lateral aspect of the forearm
Posterior cutaneous	Sensory	Receives stimuli from the skin of the posterior part of the arm
Digital of the fingers	Sensory	Receives stimuli from the fingers

Nerve	Type	Function
Digital of the toes	Sensory	Receives stimuli from the toes
Facial	Motor	Stimulates the muscles of facial expression
Frontal	Sensory	Receives stimuli from the upper eyelid, the forehead and the scalp
Glossopharyngeal	Motor	Stimulates the tongue
Glossopharyngeal	Sensory	Receives stimuli from the tongue
Hypoglossal	Motor	Stimulates the muscles of the tongue
Infraorbital	Sensory	Receives stimuli from the upper teeth, the skin of the face, the lower eyelids, the side of the nose, the mouth and the upper lip
Infratrochlear	Sensory	Receives stimuli from the skin of the eyelids and the root of the nose
Interosseous		
Crucal interosseous	Sensory	Receives stimuli from the ankle joint
Labial		
Inferior labial	Sensory	Receives stimuli from the skin of the lower lip
Superior labial	Sensory	Receives stimuli from the skin of the upper lip
Lacrimal	Sensory	Affects the tear glands and the upper eyelids
Mandibular	Motor	Stimulates the muscles and skin of the lower part of the face and the muscles of mastication
Mandibular	Sensory	Receives stimuli from the buccinator and the skin of the cheek
Masseteric	Motor	Stimulates the masseter
Maxillary	Sensory	Receives stimuli from the skin of the upper part of the face
Median	Motor-sensory	Affects the flexor muscles of the forearm and the small muscles of the thumb
Mental	Sensory	Receives stimuli from the lower lip and chin
Nasal	Sensory	Receives stimuli from the skin on the side of the nose
Occipital		
Greater occipital	Sensory	Receives stimuli from the skin of the posterior portion of the scalp
Lesser occipital	Sensory	Receives stimuli from the skin of the lateral portion of the scalp

Nerve	Type	Function
Third occipital	Sensory	Receives stimuli from the skin of the posterior aspect of the neck and the scalp
Oculomotor	Motor	Stimulates the muscles controlling the eye
Olfactory	Sensory	Conducts impulses from the mucous membranes of the nose to the brain
Ophthalmic	Sensory	Distributed on the skin of the forehead, upper eyelids and anterior part of the scalp
Optic	Sensory	Conducts impulses from the retina to the brain
Palpebral		
Inferior palpebral	Sensory	Receives stimuli from the lower eyelid
Superior palpebral	Sensory	Receives stimuli from the upper eyelid
Pectoral		
Lateral pectoral	Motor	Stimulates the pectoralis major and minor muscles
Peroneal		
Anastomotic peroneal	Sensory	Receives stimuli from the lateral aspect of the leg
Common peroneal	Motor	Stimulates the knee joint
Radial	Motor-sensory	Affects the arm and the hand
Saphenous	Sensory	Receives stimuli from the skin of the leg, foot and knee joint
Suboccipital	Motor	Stimulates the deep muscles of the back of the neck
Supraclavicular		
Intermediate supraclavicular	Sensory	Receives stimuli from the lower anterior aspect of the neck and the chest wall
Lateral supraclavicular	Sensory	Receives stimuli from the lateral aspect of the neck and the shoulder
Supraorbital	Sensory	Receives stimuli from the skin of the upper eyelid and forehead
Supratrochlear	Sensory	Receives stimuli from the forehead, the root of the nose and the upper eyelid
Temporal	Sensory	Receives stimuli from the skin of the temple
Tibial	Motor	Stimulates the muscles of the back of the leg and the sole of the foot
Tibial	Sensory	Receives stimuli from the back of the leg, the sole of the foot, the knee and the foot joints

**Anatomy and physiology
in beauty culture**

Nerve	Type	Function
Transverse	Sensory	Receives stimuli from the skin of the neck
Trifacial	Sensory	Receives stimuli from the scalp and the face
Trigeminal	Motor	Stimulates the face
Trigeminal	Sensory	Receives stimuli from the face
Trochlear	Motor	Stimulates the superior oblique muscle of the eye
Ulnar	Motor-sensory	Affects the little finger side of the forearm and hand
Vagus	Motor	Stimulates the heart, the respiratory and the digestive organs
Vagus	Sensory	Receives stimuli from the respiratory and the digestive organs
Vestibulocochlear	Sensory	Receives stimuli from the hearing canal and helps maintain body balance
Zygomatic	Sensory	Affects the skin of the temple, the side of the forehead and the upper part of the cheek
Zygomaticotemporal	Sensory	Receives stimuli from the skin of the temple

Unit 8

The digestive system

Unit 8

The digestive system

General objectives-student goals:
After study, instruction and completion of this unit, you will be able to demonstrate understanding of the digestive system by writing and/or giving a brief overview of the subject.

The digestive system changes food into a form that can be taken up by the blood and made available to the body tissues.

The process of digestion starts with the cooking of food. Various methods of cooking have different effects on the food substances and the digestive organs themselves.

The digestive system is also referred to as the alimentary canal. It consists of the:

1. Mouth
2. Throat
3. Esophagus
4. Stomach
5. Intestines

For food to have the effect of body building, it must be converted into a liquid. Of all the food substances that enter the body, only water and mineral salts remain unchanged. Digestive juices convert solids into a liquid or semiliquid form. The process in which food substances pass from the alimentary canal into the blood takes place mostly in the small intestine. The blood carries the food materials around the body, where each cell takes what it needs to produce heat, weight or energy.

1. Excitement, fatigue and emotions disturb digestion.

2. Food is digested completely in the small intestine, and the waste is stored in the large intestine until it is eliminated.

3. Absorption is the process by which food substances pass from the alimentary canal into the blood. This process takes place chiefly in the small intestine.

4. Assimilation is the process by which digested food is incorporated into the body tissues. This process takes place in the cells.

5. Metabolism is a combination of processes. It involves all the chemical changes within the body which are related to nourishment or the utilization of food. Metabolism takes place in two phases:

   A. Anabolism: This is the building up process by which the cells take in whatever they need: food, water and oxygen.

   B. Catabolism: This is the tearing down process during which the cells use up whatever they take in.

This double process is going on continuously in every living body from the smallest cell up. In the normal healthy body, the two phases balance each other.

6. A certain amount of oxygen is always needed to consume the food that is taken into the body. The oxygen is obtained from the air during respiration.

One of the most important factors in any health examination is the individual's basal metabolism. This may be defined as the minimum amount of heat production required to keep the body alive and performing its normal functions. The basal rate of metabolism is directly related to the state of the thyroid gland, and through it, to the entire glandular system.

A gland is an organ of the body which absorbs selected materials from the blood and converts them into a new chemical fluid known as a secretion. While all the glands of the body may be called secretory organs, and all the fluids formed by them are properly called secretions, a distinction in name has been made between those body fluids that are useful and those that are not. A secretion is a fluid, produced by a gland, which is useful to some other organ or necessary for some special function of the body. Excretion is the process by which the body rids itself of waste products.

The active agents of the thyroid and other glands of internal secretion are called hormones. In cases of low metabolism and other glandular deficiencies, the missing hormones must be supplied to the body by the daily intake of food.

Unit 9
The excretory system

Excretion is the physiological process by means of which the body rids itself of the waste products of metabolism. Excretion takes place in a variety of ways:

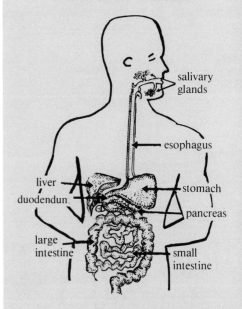

DIGESTIVE SYSTEM

salivary glands

esophagus

liver

duodendun

stomach

pancreas

large intestine

small intestine

Unit 9
The excretory system

General objectives-student goals:
After study, instruction and comple-

Anatomy and physiology in beauty culture

tion of this unit, you will be able to demonstrate understanding of the excretory system by writing and/or giving a brief overview of the subject.

EXCRETORY SYSTEM

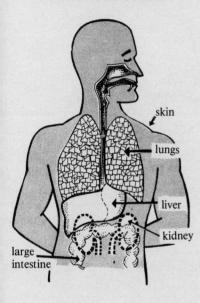

skin

lungs

liver

kidney

large intestine

Unit 10
The respiratory system

General objectives-student goals:
After study, instruction and comple-

1. The skin secretes and excretes perspiration.

2. The lungs exhale carbon dioxide.

3. The kidneys excrete urine.

4. The large intestine eliminates decomposed food.

5. The liver discharges bile.

The best method of assuring the proper excretory functions of the body is regular exercise and drinking plenty of water. Any interference with the normal process of excretion may cause conditions which reduce body efficiency. It may also cause the individual to have an ill feeling and eventually do serious harm.

An excretion is a fluid produced by a gland. This fluid is of no further use to the body. It is, therefore, eliminated as a waste product. The only difference between an excretion and any other kind of secretion is the nature of the product formed from the blood.

Excretion takes place in every individual cell. However, it is controlled by a very efficient system composed of the kidneys, ureter and bladder.

The lungs and skin are only supplementary organs of excretion.

The large intestine is considered an excretory organ because it voids solid waste. However, it is not an excretory organ in the true sense because this waste matter is never a part of the body cells. It is indigestible matter from food that has been consumed.

The disposal of waste matter is just as important as feeding the body. The normal physiological process forms waste matter constantly in every individual cell. The lymph spaces are always filled with both useful and useless products. If the useless products were to remain in the body, they could do serious harm.

The products of metabolism in the cells are carbon dioxide and water vapor from tissue oxidation, soluble salts and rejected solid waste matter. Excretion by the skin is brought about by perspiration. Waste gases are expelled from the lungs with every breath. Salts and the products of all chemical changes in the body pass out through the kidney with the urine. The large intestines store the undigested food for elimination through the rectum. The liver neutralizes toxic substances and discharges bile.

Unit 10
The respiratory system

Respiration is the biological process by which the body takes in oxygen and gives out the waste products of tissue oxidation in the form of carbon dioxide and water vapor.

The respiratory system consists of the:

1. Nose: This is the air passage.

2. Pharynx: This is the upper portion of the digestive tube.

3. Larynx: This is the voice box.

4. Trachea: This is the windpipe.

5. Bronchi: These are the main branches of the windpipe.

6. Lungs: These organs contain the air cells.

Respiration has a double action:

1. Inhalation: This draws air into the lungs.

2. Exhalation: This drives out used air.

The normal rate of respiration is 18 times a minute. Oxygen is of greater importance than either water or food. Man may live for extended periods of time without water and food. However, man would be dead within minutes without air.

About 25 ounces (708.75 g.) of oxygen are required daily. The amounts of pure oxygen and carbon dioxide in the lungs are always in balance. If the air that we breathe consisted of pure oxygen, the oxidation within the body would proceed too quickly for comfort or safety. Air, however, is a mixture of gases which contains a large percentage of nitrogen and other gases in varying proportions. A certain amount of carbon dioxide is also always present because of the constant exhalations from other living bodies. Carbon dioxide is not poisonous in itself. However, if too much carbon dioxide is in the air supply, it may prevent oxygen from entering the lungs. The result would be suffocation.

Rescue breathing

1. Place the victim on his or her back and start at once.

2. Lift the victim's neck and push the head down. Pull the jaw up by holding the chin.

3. Breathe deeply. Put your mouth over the victim's. Pinch the victim's nose and blow into the air passage.

4. Remove your mouth. Let the victim exhale. Inflate the lungs again.

   Note: Repeat 12 times a minute. For a small child, 20 times a minute.

tion of this unit, you will be able to demonstrate understanding of the respiratory system by writing and/or giving a brief overview of the subject.

RESPIRATORY SYSTEM

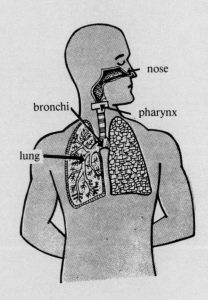

nose

bronchi

pharynx

lung

Anatomy and physiology in beauty culture

1. What is anatomy?

2. Why must the cosmetologist know and understand the anatomy of the region that he or she will treat?

3. What is the study of the bones, their structure and their function called?

4. What is the bony framework of the body called?

5. What are cartilage and ligaments?

6. Is there much difference in structure between the arms and the legs?

7. What is the nutrient fluid of the body?

8. What is the function of the white cells?

9. How many systems of blood circulation are there?

10. Name the systems of blood circulation.

11. Name four of the branches of the external maxillary artery and describe which region of the face they supply.

12. Do muscles react to stimulus?

13. Name the muscle of the mouth that raises the wing of the nose and lip, and draws them back.

14. Name the muscle of the thorax (chest) that draws the head backwards or to one side.

15. Are the muscles in the forearm arranged in a parallel position?

16. Why is it necessary for the cosmetologist to have knowledge of the structure of the nervous system?

17. Are all nerve cells the same size?

18. Describe the effects of the six branches of the seventh cerebral nerve.

19. Describe the effects of the five superficial cervical nerves.

20. Describe the process of respiration.

21. Approximately how many muscles does the body contain?

22. Approximately what percentage of the total body weight do the muscles constitute?

23. Do all muscles have the same size and shape?

24. How many types of muscular tissue are there?

Anatomy and physiology
in beauty culture

Electricity and the cosmetologist

Electricity and the cosmetologist: Electricity is a source of power which a beauty salon needs in order to function.

Overview: This chapter provides you with the information about electricity which is required for the practice of cosmetology.

Behavioral objectives-student goals: After completion of this chapter, and after instruction and study, you will be able to perform and demonstrate competency and knowledge of electricity as it relates to the cosmetologist by identifying, explaining and/or listing: the function of high frequency current, galvanic current, faradic current, sinusoidal current, light rays, and electrical and mechanical devices.

Although a beauty salon could not function without electricity, the cosmetologist is not required to have a full knowledge of electrical wiring and the energy source that supplies electrical power. However, it is of great importance that the cosmetologist have a thorough understanding of the mechanical operation and function of the electrical equipment and appliances which are used in the practice of cosmetology as we know it today.

The amount of knowledge about electricity required by the cosmetologist is so small that a complete study of electricity is generally not considered to be of any great importance. This material is written for the few State Boards which still require a basic knowledge of electricity as related to cosmetology, and to familiarize the cosmetologist with the operation and principal uses of some of the electrical devices that were once very widely used in cosmetology as well as with some of the appliances that are in use today.

Electricity is a source of power. It develops from the existence and interactions of electrical charges. The interactions are caused by the relative position and relative movement of electrons and protons. Static electricity owes its origin to the position of these particles. The accompanying movement of these particles is current electricity.

The basis of electricity is the attraction and repulsion which exists between electrons and protons. These phenomena arise because of the electric charge of the particles. The electron has a negative charge. An equal and opposite charge is the proton's positive charge. Two electrons will repel each other. Two protons will repel each other. However, an electron and a proton will attract each other.

For practical use, electricity may be generated:

1. By mechanical equipment (generator or dynamos) 2. Chemically (cells or batteries)

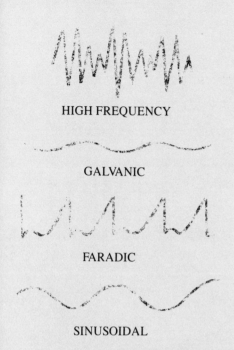

HIGH FREQUENCY

GALVANIC

FARADIC

SINUSOIDAL

Electricity may be classified as:

1. Static electricity (electricity at rest)

2. Magnetic electricity (produced by magnets)

There are two types of electrical currents:

1. A.C.: Alternating current

2. D.C.: Direct current

Alternating current is electric current generated by magnetos. It reverses its flow at regular intervals and is transmitted in cycles. Direct current may be generated mechanically by dynamos or chemically by cells. The flow of the current is always in one direction.

Equipment or appliances that are labeled A.C. or D.C. may be used only for the current for which they are designed. Some equipment is manufactured for use with both A.C. or D.C. current. There are several forms of current which are obtained from A.C. and D.C. Those of interest to the cosmetologist are:

1. High frequency current

2. Galvanic current

3. Faradic current

4. Sinusoidal current

Sanitary and safety precautions for electricity and the cosmetologist

1. Keep all electric appliances dry.

2. Disconnect electric appliances when they are not in use.

3. Discard worn or frayed appliance cords.

4. Never overload electric outlets. To do so could cause loss of electricity and an electrical fire.

5. Never disconnect an appliance by pulling the wire (cord). Disconnect it by pulling the plug.

6. Never leave patrons unattended while they are receiving a service with an electric appliance.

7. Always follow the manufacturer's instructions when operating electric appliances.

Electricity and the cosmetologist

8. Keep appliance and equipment cords from coming in contact with the patron.

9. Do not touch the metal parts of an appliance while it is in operation.

10. Do not plug an appliance into an outlet or disconnect it while your hands are wet.

Unit 1
High frequency electric current

There are three types of high frequency current:

   1. Tesla   2. d'Arsonval   3. Oudin

The high frequency current used by the cosmetologist is Tesla. It is of medium voltage and medium amperage. However, some authorities define it as high voltage and low amperage.

The applicators for high frequency current are made of glass tubes from which the air has been removed. When the current passes through the tube, it causes it to light up with a violet colored discharge. It produces a buzzing sound. These tubes come in different shapes for treating the scalp, hair, face and various parts of the body.

The Tesla high frequency current may be applied directly to the patron or indirectly by having the patron hold the electrode. Indirect applications given with the cosmetologist's fingertips are recommended for dry conditions. Direct applications, given with the use of a glass electrode, are very effective for oily conditions.

Caution should be taken never to use a flammable lotion, oil or tonic in combination with high frequency current. It is possible for the violet ray spark or friction of the current to cause combustion. It is always best to know whether the materials used are flammable. Use the simple test of saturating a piece of absorbent cotton with the substance and applying the high frequency current close to the cotton. If the substance is flammable, the cotton will burst into flame almost immediately.

Ultraviolet rays have proven to be very effective for treating skin conditions. Results are excellent when acne vulgaris is treated with violet rays. These rays are also excellent for treating oily skin.

Violet ray causes a germicidal effect by liberating pure ozone. The spark discharged by the glass electrode generates nitrous oxide gas. The pure ozone and the nitrous oxide break up the tiny air particles and free the air of impurities. It leaves only pure oxygen in the area being treated.

In addition, the violet ray can be used to remove and destroy warts and some growths. This technique is called fulguration. The procedure involves directing a violet ray spark which is held a short distance from the growth and kept moving in a circular motion, thus distributing the spark evenly around and over the growth.

General objectives-student goals: After study, instruction and completion of this unit, you will be able to demonstrate understanding of high frequency electric current by writing and/or giving a brief overview of the subject.

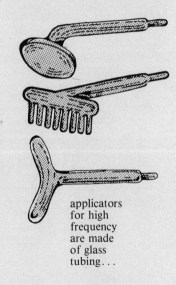

applicators for high frequency are made of glass tubing...

Electricity and the cosmetologist

The d'Arsonval current is of low voltage and high amperage. It is used by the medical profession for diathermy treatments, removal of warts (coagulation) and removal of superfluous hair (thermolysis).

The Oudin current is of high voltage and low amperage. It produces very little heat. This too is used by the medical profession for the removal of growths. Removal is accomplished by desiccation (drying) of the growth rather than burning it off.

Unit 2
Galvanic current and the wall plate

Galvanic current is a direct current (D.C.) of low voltage and high amperage. The current available in the salon is alternating current. Your wall plate must have a rectifier. A typical wall plate also includes an electric outlet, a faradic coil, a rheostat, a selector switch, a milliamperemeter and two wire terminals.

A good wall plate should supply galvanic, faradic and sinusoidal currents. It should also be capable of supplying high frequency current. Galvanic current is entirely chemical. Faradic and sinusoidal currents are mechanical with a slight chemical action. High frequency current is a heat producing current. It has no chemical reaction.

The rectifier changes alternating current (A.C.) to direct current (D.C.). The outlet is used to connect appliances, machines or equipment to the electric current. The faradic coil produces faradic current. The rheostat controls the amount of current applied. The selector switch allows you to turn on the type of current you need. A milliamperemeter registers the amount of current used to overcome the resistance that the skin offers the current. This is important when using galvanic current for electrolysis. The two wire terminals are designed for connecting the conducting wires which carry the current to the patron. The action of the current as it leaves the machine by means of one terminal and reenters it by means of the other terminal is known as polarity. Polarity is a reaction necessary in order to complete an electric circuit.

There are many accessories which operate from the wall plate. Some of the more important ones are:

1. A wrist electrode for the cosmetologist

2. A carbon electrode for the patron

3. A massage roller electrode

4. A metal rake electrode for the scalp

5. A comb electrode

6. Two conducting cords and an extension wire

An electrode, regardless of type, is the only medium by means of which contact is made between the current and the person who is to receive or apply the current. Faradic and sinusoidal currents are transmitted to the patron through the operator. Galvanic current is transmitted through the patron only. The cosmetologist is never connected to galvanic current.

General objectives-student goals:
After study, instruction and completion of this unit, you will be able to demonstrate understanding of galvanic current and the wall plate by writing and/or giving a brief overview of the subject.

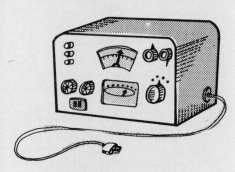

supplies galvanic, faradic and sinusoidal currents

Electricity and the cosmetologist

526

Unit 3
Faradic current

Faradic current is an induced current produced by the making and breaking of the galvanic current. It is of high voltage and low amperage. It is classified as a mechanical current.

The buzzing sound heard when the faradic current is turned on is caused by the making and breaking (interruption) of the current and by the very rapid movement of the adjustable vibrator spring. It is the magnetic force that attracts the vibrator spring and starts it vibrating as it is pulled away from the adjustable screw, breaking the contact. The vibrator spring is then released. It makes contact with the adjustable screw. This causes the flow of current for producing faradic current.

There are two forms of faradic current:

1. Primary which is positive and gives off more current and less force. It causes a definite action at the terminals.

2. Secondary which is negative and gives off more force and less current. It causes the action at the terminals to be practically eliminated.

During application, the current is controlled by the rheostat according to the patron's tolerance.

There are a few methods of applying faradic current. The most effective method is using the cosmetologist's fingertips. The metal comb and brush electrodes are used for oily hair and scalp conditions. Special electrodes are used for the face. Faradic current is also applied either by means of a wrist electrode or a combination of two electrodes, both of which are applied to the patron.

Faradic current causes muscular contraction and nerve tonicity. It increases blood and nerve stimulation, exercises the muscles and increases glandular activity. It is also used to release tension and prevent an aging appearance of the skin. Both capillary and lymphatic circulation are improved. Strained and tense muscles are relaxed.

Unit 4
Sinusoidal current

Sinusoidal current is the least important of the currents which are available to the cosmetologist. Most wall plates do not produce this type of current. There are two types of sinusoidal current:

1. Rapid   2. Slow

The rapid current is alternating current. It has 120 cycles per second instead of the ordinary 60 cycles per second. It has no definite polarity.

Unit 3
Faradic current

General objectives-student goals:
After study, instruction and completion of this unit, you will be able to demonstrate understanding of faradic current by writing and/or giving a brief overview of the subject.

two electrodes applied to patron...

Unit 4
Sinusoidal current

General objectives-student goals:
After study, instruction and completion of this unit, you will be able to demonstrate understanding of sinusoidal current by writing and/or giving a brief overview of the subject.

Electricity and the cosmetologist

General objectives-student goals: After study, instruction and completion of this unit, you will be able to demonstrate understanding of light rays by writing and/or giving a brief overview of the subject.

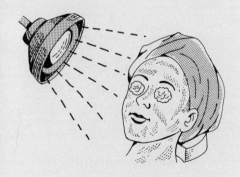

The slow sinusoidal current is a true galvanic current which blends into alternating continuous cycles through a rotor.

Sinusoidal current is a mechanical current, and its stimulation to muscles, glands and organs is deeper and less irritating than faradic current. There is no buzzing sound from sinusoidal current such as is the case with faradic current. Sinusoidal current is applied in the same manner as faradic current. The patron holds a cylindrical electrode while the cosmetologist uses the wrist electrode. Alternatively, both electrodes work through the patron.

The cosmetologist should avoid overstimulation of tissues. This is a possibility when using sinusoidal current. It is wise never to use any form of current long enough to overstimulate tissues. A maximum of ten minutes is considered normal for any form of current treatment employed by the cosmetologist.

Unit 5
Light rays

Basically, there are three types of light rays which are important to the cosmetologist:

1. Infrared

2. Visible light

3. Ultraviolet

The infrared rays (heat rays) assist the cosmetologist because they dry facial packs and bleaches. Their use promotes the absorption of cream, oil, tonic and ointments used during treatments. These heat rays also stimulate circulation, activate the glands and open the pores. Infrared rays can pass through the body without raising the normal body temperature. They should be applied at a distance of 30 inches (76.20 cm.). They may be used with satisfactory results for an indefinite length of time. Infrared rays are excellent for dry, wrinkled and scaly skin.

Visible light rays are produced in various colors:

1. White: These contain elements of heat and light.

2. Blue: These are antiseptic. They are used for treating dermatitis.

3. Red: These produce heat but no chemical or germicidal action. They have the deepest penetrating action and are excellent for oily conditions.

4. Green: These have a slight influence on metabolism. Their effects are sedative.

Ultraviolet rays have a germicidal action. They can cause a sunburn or tanning of the skin. An overdose may cause a severe burn and blistering of the skin. When using a lamp of this type, the patron's eyes must be protected. The lamp must be placed 12 inches (30.48 cm.) from the skin for three minutes during the first treatment. The time may be increased by one minute with each successive treatment up to nine minutes. It is advisable to use a special tanning lotion before using an ultraviolet ray lamp. A good tanning lotion will keep the burning rays out and allow only the tanning rays to be effective.

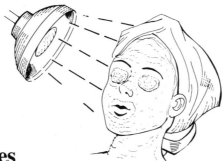

Unit 6
Electrical and mechanical devices

1. The **vibrator**, which is used for scalp, facial and body massage, is one of the many mechanical devices available to the cosmetologist. The vibrator is recommended for the treatment of dry skin and scalp conditions.

2. The **thermostatically controlled thermal curling iron**, which is used to set hair that is not wet, is available in **Teflon**. It can create protective oil vapors to prevent dryness during the curling process.

3. The **hot air comb** is an electric hair dryer designed to comb the hair into style during the drying process. This comb is available with many special attachments.

4. The **thermostatically controlled hair pressing comb** is available in two sizes. It is used in order to obtain uniform hair pressing.

5. The **blow dryer** has power ratings that vary from 250 to 1650 watts. The higher the rating, the hotter the flow of air. The electrical code requires manufacturers of this type of appliance to record the power rating on each blower.

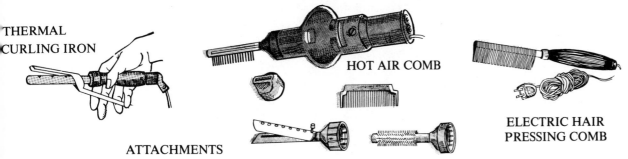

THERMAL CURLING IRON

HOT AIR COMB

ELECTRIC HAIR PRESSING COMB

ATTACHMENTS

General objectives-student goals: After study, instruction and completion of this unit, you will be able to demonstrate understanding of some of the electrical and mechanical devices used in the practice of cosmetology by writing and/or giving a brief overview of the subject.

BLOW DRYER

PRESSURE SPRAY

Electricity and the cosmetologist

INSTANT
HAIR ROLLERS

accelerating
machines
shorten processing
time up to
80%

Unit 7

Important points
about electricity

General objectives-student goals:
After study, instruction and completion of this unit, you will be able to demonstrate understanding of five important points about electricity that every cosmetologist should know by writing and/or giving a brief overview of the subject.

Electricity and
the cosmetologist

530

6. Instant hair rollers are thermal rollers designed to hold heat long enough to set hair within a few minutes. This is a preheat method of setting hair that is not wet.

7. The accelerating machine, which is used during hair coloring treatments to shorten the processing time up to 80%, utilizes photon units of energy. The use of this machine during the neutralization of a permanent wave greatly reduces the relaxation of a cold wave.

8. The special modern electrical devices for facial work performed by the cosmetologist and the esthetician are also very popular today. Some of these attachments are a suction tube used to remove blackheads and a liquid pressure spray for stimulation.

Electricity can produce mechanical, heat and chemical effects depending on the device used.

1. Mechanical effects: Vibrators, electric hair clippers, motor driven hair spray units and electric manicure implements.

2. Heat effects: Curling irons, heating caps, hair dryers, heat lamps (infrared), light bulbs, manicure oil heaters and depilatory wax heaters.

3. Chemical effects: Electrolysis destroys the hair follicles by means of the breakup of a chemical compound.

Note: Hair dryers produce both mechanical and heat effects.

Unit 7
Important points about electricity

Here are five important points about electricity and the electrical equipment and appliances used in the practice of cosmetology.

1. Electric shock: Electric shock can be mild, severe or fatal. Mild shocks cause discomfort. Severe shocks may cause burns and convulsions. Death is the result when an electric current passes through the central nervous system beyond the point that the body can tolerate. For your protection against shock, all equipment should be of the three wire system. Your wall outlet must have three holes, and your equipment must have plugs with three prongs. Two of the prongs are the feed and return of the electric circuit. The third is the ground. The third wire of the three wire system carries the safety ground wire all the way from the outlet to the case of the appliance. The earth can absorb large amounts of unwanted electric charge without being affected. When a conducting path is provided from an electrically charged appliance to the earth, the charge will run off to the ground. This grounds the appliance. This action protects the cosmetologist and patron from shock. If the patron or operator becomes a victim of electric shock, remove the source of electricity from the person by using an insulator. For example, push the appliance away with a stick, rubber comb or hair brush. Never use an object that conducts electricity (any metal or water). Disconnect the appliance carefully. Tend to the injured person. Check for burns. If the shock was mild and burns are present, treat them like normal heat burns. Seek medical treatment for cases of severe shock.

3 WIRE
OUTLET

outlet and plug
with ground

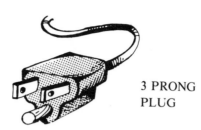

3 PRONG
PLUG

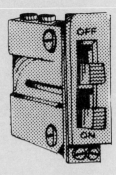

FUSE
OR
CIRCUIT
BREAKER

2. **Circuit breakers and fuses:** Circuit breakers and fuses are part of the permanent wiring. Their function is to cut off the flow of excess current before a fire can start. This dangerous situation is created by drawing more current through a circuit than it was designed for. Overloading and short circuits are the prime offenders. Overloading means the use of too many lights and/or appliances on one circuit. A short circuit is a breakdown in a normal operating circuit. A short circuited or a shorted appliance can be very dangerous because it produces a tremendous amount of heat. The heat is so great that it can cause something to burn or melt. A disconnected, broken, poorly insulated or cracked wire is the most common cause of a short circuit. When any of these conditions occur, the return wire becomes connected directly to the feed wire, thus bypassing the load impedance (the appliance). The result is a breakdown of the normal operating circuit. This causes an overloading short circuit. When a circuit breaker cuts off or a fuse blows:

overloading
causes a
short circuit...

A. Disconnect all appliances connected to the circuit that is without electricity.

B. Go to the junction box and locate the popped breaker or blown fuse. If there is a circuit breaker, push the reset lever back to the on position. If a fuse was blown, unscrew the fuse and screw in a new one. The new fuse must have the proper rating.

Always keep a flashlight in a place to which you can get easily in the dark. If your junction box requires fuses, keep a supply of each size in the same area as the junction box.

3. **Conductors and insulators:** All metals are conductors of electric current. Wood, rubber, plastic, glass and brick are good insulators. Extreme caution should be taken while working with conductors around electricity because all conductors carry electric current. Insulators are protective because they prevent the passage of electric current. When working with electricity, especially when standing on the ground, always stand on a wooden board or a wooden ladder in order to avoid being part of the ground in case of an accident.

**Electricity and
the cosmetologist**

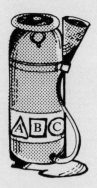

 RUBBISH

B LIQUID FIRES

C ELECTRICAL

4. **Electrical fires:** Electrical fires should be smothered or put out with a fire extinguisher specifically made for use with electrical fires. Never use water or wet materials. All fire extinguishers are coded A, B and/or C:

A   extinguishes rubbish, paper and wood fires.

B   extinguishes liquid fires (gasoline and oil).

C   extinguishes electrical fires.

Check the name plate to determine for which fires the extinguisher can be used. It is recommended that all beauty salons have A-B-C fire extinguishers. These may be used on all three types of fires.

5. **U.L. Approval:** Most of the apparatus, equipment and appliances used by the cosmetologist are operated by electricity. A fair amount of this equipment also comes in direct contact with the patron. Therefore, to ensure safety for yourself and your patron, all apparatus, equipment and appliances used by the cosmetologist should carry a U.L. approved label or any seal of approval used by your state. The seal of approval is used to identify electrical apparatus, equipment and appliances as having been tested in order to determine whether they were manufactured to comply with a set of standards that allows them to be judged safe for use by any individual.

Review questions

1. Can a beauty salon function without electricity?

2. Why do most schools teach basic electricity as it relates to cosmetology?

3. Name the two methods of generating electricity for practical use.

4. There are two types of electrical current. Name them.

5. Can A.C. equipment be used with direct current?

6. Which is the high frequency current used by the cosmetologist?

7. Ultraviolet rays have proven to be very effective for treating skin conditions. Name two conditions for which the results have been excellent.

8. How can a lotion, oil or tonic be checked for combustion possibilities when used in combination with high frequency current?

9. Can violet ray be used to remove or destroy warts and growths?

10. Is galvanic current A.C. or D.C.?

11. Does high frequency current have a chemical reaction?

12. What are the three types of light rays which are important to the cosmetologist?

13. What is the correct distance between the skin and lamp for the application of infrared rays?

14. Are ultraviolet rays germicidal?

15. Do ultraviolet rays have a tanning effect on the skin?

16. What are the effects of an overdose of ultraviolet rays?

17. When giving an ultraviolet ray treatment, what is considered the correct distance between the skin and lamp?

18. Is the vibrator recommended for treating dry or oily skin and scalp conditions?

19. What is the wattage range of blow dryers?

20. What causes a circuit breaker or fuse to cut off the electric current?

21. What is meant by overloading?

22. What are conductors of electricity?

23. Which materials are considered conductors of electric current?

24. What is the function of insulators of electric current?

25. Name a few materials which are good electric insulators.

Electricity and the cosmetologist

Electricity and
the cosmetologist

Job interviews

Job interviews: Preparing for your first job in the field of cosmetology.

Overview: This chapter provides you with suggestions and information which will prepare you for securing a job. They will increase your chances of getting your first job.

Behavioral objectives-student goals: After completion of this chapter, and after instruction and study, you will be able to perform and demonstrate competency as an applicant for a job by identifying, explaining and/or listing: the required preparation for a job interview, points to emphasize during an interview, the resume, ten do's and don'ts and the interview acknowledgement letter.

Upon graduation, job seeking becomes the true test of all that you have learned. Although most beauty culture and cosmetology schools have a job placement service, the responsibility for getting the job rests with you at the time of the interview.

The interview is an interpersonal situation. The employer needs a qualified individual to fill an open position, and you are interested in the position. Your interview begins the moment you walk through the door. Your appearance has already said something about you. Your voice and your manner of speaking will make the next most important impact during the interview. You should, therefore, speak first and say something like "Good morning, my name is John Brown. Harper Method Beauty School sent me to apply for the hairdresser's job that is open." At this point, you will be asked to have a seat, and the interview will begin.

Unit 1
Preparing for the interview

Preparation is the key word. A few moments spent preparing for the interview will enhance your chances of landing the job. It will make you appear confident, natural and place you at ease. You should:

1. Have some general information about the salon

2. Know what the employer expects from his staff of cosmetologists

3. Spend some time learning the type work the clientele in that particular salon expect

Unit 1
Preparing for the interview

General objectives-student goals: After study, instruction and completion of this unit, you will be able to demonstrate understanding of the importance of preparing for the interview by writing and/or giving a brief overview of the subject.

Job interviews

The first few minutes of the interview afford you the opportunity to put your best foot forward. Every interview works two ways. The employer is seeking someone qualified for the job opening, and you are interested in securing a position. Know your qualifications and measure them against what the employer is looking for.

The easier you make it for the interviewer to evaluate your ability to handle the job, the more successful the interview will be. Talk about and emphasize only what is relevant to the job:

1. Education

2. Interests

3. Experience

Let the interviewer know that you are aware of the standards that will have to be met.

Unit 2
The resume

The resume represents your life's experience condensed into one or two pages. The resume should be prepared with much thought because it may serve as the outline that will be followed during the interview. All details should be factual and to the point. This will enhance your opportunity for getting the job.

Prepare a resume that includes your name, address, phone number and:

1. Education

2. Age

3. Work experience

4. Occupational goals

5. Hobbies and interests

6. References

Unit 2
The resume

General objectives-student goals:
After study, instruction and completion of this unit, you will be able to demonstrate understanding of a resume by giving a brief overview of the subject and by writing a resume.

Job interviews

536

A resume saves time during the interview. It works in your favor when there are others who will be interviewed after you.

Do not bring letters of reference to an interview. Supply them only upon request.

Sample resume

Name: Mary Brown   Marital Status: Single
Address: 70 Bay Street, Springfield, Illinois 10301
Telephone: 481-3700   Age: 20

Education: Harper Method Beauty School
                  Graduate of Midway High School

Work
Experience: Part time receptionist, Franklin Insurance Company
                  Evening cashier, Lowe's Theatre
                  Part time sales clerk, Broad's Department Store

Occupational
Goals: It is my ultimate desire to specialize in professional hair tinting. During the time I spent at Harper Method Beauty School, my greatest interest and achievement was in the area of hair coloring. I was awarded first prize in the student hair coloring competition at the school. This gave me the opportunity to represent my school in the National student competition where I won first prize. One of my main interests in high school was public speaking. I have no plans for marriage at the present time. I would like to be employed by you because you operate a modern unisex salon to which I can contribute.

References: Ms. Mary Anthony, Franklin Insurance Company
                  Mr. John Philips, Personnel Manager, Broad's Department Store
                  Mr. Robert Bernard, Manager, Lowe's Theatre

First impressions are important. An employer's quick judgment will be based on those first impressions. A neat well-groomed appearance is most important. You will not get a second chance to make a first impression.

The female cosmetologist should:

1. Wear a simple style dress with sleeves and a reasonable neckline. The length of the dress should also be reasonable.

2. Wear conservative colors.

3. Wear hosiery.

4. Carry a hand bag.

5. Have manicured nails.

6. Wear an attractive make-up application and hairdo.

Job interviews

The male cosmetologist should:

1. Wear a suit or sport jacket.

2. Be well-groomed with:

   A. Hair trimmed   C. Beard and/or mustache trimmed

   B. Face shaved   D. Nails manicured

3. Wear conservative shoes and socks that blend with your outfit.

Unit 3
Do's and don'ts

At the time of the interview, both male and female job applicants should:

1. Not smoke unless invited to.

2. Not carry packages to the interview.

3. Have your social security card with you.

4. Have copies of your resume with you.

5. Not sit until you are invited to.

6. Discuss salary only after you and the employer have agreed you are qualified for the job.

7. Sit correctly and not fidget.

8. Not chew gum.

9. Allow the interviewer to speak when he or she interrupts.

10. Not speak for longer than two minutes. Everything you talk about must be related to your qualifications for the job. When the employer says "Tell me something about yourself," be prepared to respond without hesitation. Tell him or her:

    A. Why you qualify for this job   C. The things you do best

    B. Why you think you would be   D. Some of the other qualifications you may have
       happy working for him or her   that have not as yet been talked about

Unit 3
Do's and don'ts

General objectives-student goals: After study, instruction and completion of this unit, you will be able to demonstrate understanding of ten important do's and don'ts as they apply to the job interview by listing all ten.

Job interviews

Unit 4
Acknowledgement letter

A short note acknowledging the interview and thanking the employer for seeing you helps to create a favorable impression in the employer's mind. The note should:

1. Be sent within 24 hours after the interview

2. Express your appreciation for the interview

3. Indicate that you are hoping for a favorable response

4. Say that you are looking forward to starting work if you have already been hired

Sample acknowledgement if waiting for a response

Dear Mr. Salon Owner,

Just a note to express my appreciation for having had the opportunity of a personal interview on Thursday, February 2nd. I enjoyed speaking with you.

I am ready to supply any additional information you may need and look forward to the opportunity of joining your staff.

If hired, change the second paragraph as follows:

I thank you for your kind consideration and look forward to starting work on Monday.

Cordially yours,

Jennifer Jeannine

Review questions

1. Do most beauty culture schools have a job placement service?

2. Why is it important to prepare for a job interview?

3. Is a job interview for the benefit of the employer?

4. How can the applicant let the interviewer know that he or she is qualified for the job?

General objectives-student goals: After study, instruction and completion of this unit, you will be able to demonstrate understanding of the importance of an acknowledgement letter by writing a sample letter and by giving a brief overview of the subject.

Job interviews

539

5. Why is a resume important?

6. What information should a good resume include?

7. Should an applicant smoke during a personal interview?

8. Name two items that are important to have with you during your interview.

9. Is it appropriate to sit as soon as you enter the office for a job interview?

10. When should salary be discussed during a job interview?

11. What should an acknowledgement note, sent to the interviewer after the personal interview, contain?

12. Is it advisable to send an acknowledgement note to the interviewer after a personal interview?

13. Is it an accepted practice to chew gum during a job interview?

14. Is posture important during a job interview?

15. Is it acceptable to carry packages when going for a job interview?

16. Why are first impressions important during a job interview?

17. Why are the first few minutes of a job interview important?

18. How can you prepare for a job interview?

19. What are the three most important items to talk about and emphasize during a job interview?

20. Is a well-groomed appearance important at the time of a personal interview?

21. At the time of a job interview, why is it necessary to know your qualifications?

22. Why is it important for you to make it easy for the interviewer to evaluate your ability to handle the job for which you have applied?

Beauty salon management

Beauty salon management: As a cosmetologist, you have the opportunity to own and operate your own business. The key to developing a successful salon is careful planning.

Overview: This chapter provides you with a knowledge of business principles and management as they relate to the operation of a full service salon as well as a specialized service salon, e.g., unisex haircutting, esthetics, hair coloring.

Behavioral objectives-student goals: After completion of this chapter, and after instruction and study, you will be able to perform and demonstrate competency, knowledge and understanding of beauty salon management by describing and/or listing a brief description of the six area type salons, the importance of a lease, the physical layout of a salon, color scheme, business insurance, business laws, customer reception, management-operator relations, financial control and record keeping, salesmanship and merchandising, advertising, budget and average expenses, professional ethics, telephone techniques, contemporary salons, in-salon training and operational policy.

Each year, many cosmetologists enter the business world as salon owners with little or no experience as business administrators. As a result, many of these individuals face failure.

Although the key to successful beauty salon management is the owner-manager being a thoroughly trained and experienced cosmetologist, many salons fail because the owners and/or managers are ill equipped to deal with the daily problems of the salon.

Successful salon ownership is based on careful planning. Operating a beauty salon is a considerable responsibility, and only those who are adequately prepared to manage a business will be able to realize their ambition: a successful operation.

This chapter provides basic information and data which will serve as a guide for the cosmetologist who undertakes the responsibility for operating a beauty salon as a manager or owner. You will learn and understand the important principles to follow when planning and operating a salon. These include types of ownership, selecting a salon, the lease, the physical layout of the salon, structural limitations, lighting and decor, color scheme, insurance, business laws, health regulations, patron reception, management-operator relations, financial control and record keeping, time allotted for services, merchandising, salesmanship, advertising, operating expenses, rules of good professional ethics, telephone techniques, gratuities, the new concept of contemporary salons, selecting a name and logo, staffing, in-salon training, school training and operational policy.

General objectives-student goals:
After study, instruction and completion of this unit, you will be able to demonstrate understanding of four kinds of beauty salon ownership by writing and/or giving a brief overview of the subject.

General objectives-student goals:
After study, instruction and completion of this unit, you will be able to demonstrate understanding of the different types of salon locations by writing and/or giving a brief overview of the subject.

Beauty salon management

542

Unit 1
Salon ownership

There are four types of salon ownership:

1. Individual ownership
   A. Sole owner
   B. Individual owner with a franchise
2. Partnership
3. Cooperative
4. Corporation

1A. **Individual ownership as a sole owner** is when one person provides all the money for starting and operating the business, sets the standards, makes all decisions and receives all the profits. As a sole owner, however, he or she is personally responsible and liable for all debts incurred by the business.

1B. **Individual ownership with a franchise** is the same as 1A except that the franchised salon is operated under a given name in accordance with the systems and methods established, regulated and mandated by the franchiser. The individual owner pays the franchiser a certain percentage of the salon income in return for the use of their name, logo and system.

2. A **partnership** is when two or more persons provide the necessary funds to start and operate a business. A partnership can be made up of cosmetologists who work and manage the salon on a daily basis or with a silent partner(s) who provides capital and shares in the profit but is not active in the operation of the salon. Working partners receive a salary plus profits while the silent partner(s) receives income only from the profits.

3. A **cooperative** is a beauty salon that is owned by and operated for the benefit of all the cosmetologists working in the salon. Each of the cosmetologists has an equal share in the corporation and an equal say in its policy and operation. They share the profits equally.

4. A **corporation** has an elected Board of Directors. The Board conducts the business. The stockholders in the corporation have a limited liability for business debts. They cannot lose more than their investment. A corporation charter has to be obtained from the state in order to form a corporation. It is subject to regulations and corporate taxation by the state.

Unit 2
Selecting a salon location

Choosing the proper location for your beauty salon is one of the most important decisions you will make. Generally, the fee you wish to charge for your services will determine where you locate the salon. It stands to reason that if you wish to charge more for your services than the average salon does, locate it in an exclusive neighborhood. Once you have chosen the general area, make the following observations:

1. Is there too much competition?

2. Is the trading area large enough to support your salon?

3. Are you close enough to a supermarket, department store, theater or any group of stores which will attract women shoppers?

4. A new and rapidly developing neighborhood usually offers more opportunities.

5. Check the location by clocking the number of women passing by at various hours on both sunny and rainy days.

6. Avoid the sunny side of the street. People would rather walk in the shade.

7. A ground floor location is usually better than a loft. However, there are times when, dollar for dollar, renting a loft offers worthwhile advantages.

The type of salon you operate will have a great influence on the charges for your services and the clientele you will attract. There are six major groups of beauty salons from which one can operate. They are:

1. Neighborhood
2. Shopping strip (main street)
3. Office buildings (business areas)
4. Shopping centers
5. Department stores
6. Hotels and motels

The **neighborhood salon** is the oldest type of salon. It is the most popular of the six types. Neighborhood salons are usually of moderate or small size. The cost of opening a neighborhood salon is quite low, and the inventory can be purchased as needed. The owner is usually an operator who doubles as a receptionist, bookkeeper, cashier and repairman. The percentage of profit shown by a successful neighborhood operation is the highest of the six salon categories. Most of the patrons live in the same neighborhood, and the prices for services are usually low.

The beauty salon located in one of the **shopping strips** on one of the main streets in town is an expanded version of the neighborhood salon. Most of the patrons are from within the town or a neighboring town. The prices for services are a little higher than those of a neighborhood salon.

Salons in **office buildings** cater to the employees in the building as well as in neighboring office buildings. In addition, they can be recommended to people who live and/or work outside the area by those who work in the office building. The prices for services in this type of salon are moderately higher than those of a neighborhood salon. Some office buildings provide all or some of the partitioning of the booths, electrical work, plumbing work, air conditioning and flooring. The availability of the services should be investigated. The working hours in an office building beauty salon are usually shorter than all other types of salons. Many of these salons do not open on Saturday since most offices are closed. Cleaning and maintenance are usually included in the rent.

Beauty salon
management

543

Shopping center beauty salons are the newest additions to the beauty industry. Their success is attributed to the big name stores that attract people to the area and the convenience of ample parking for patrons. The size of the beauty salons varies from small to large depending on the size of the shopping center. This type of operation usually requires a receptionist-cashier. In most shopping centers, the rent is a guaranteed amount plus a percentage of the gross income after a certain amount of gross income. Doing business in a shopping center involves extra charges for: parking lot lighting, snow removal, trash collection, liability insurance and Christmas decorations. Patrons come from all neighboring towns. The prices for services are higher than in neighborhood salons. In order to maintain the same hours as all other shops in the shopping center, most salons have two shifts of working hours for their employees. The hours are scheduled so that both shifts are working during the busiest hours.

Department store salons are usually a concession operation. The major department stores usually give the concession to one of the nationwide chains of beauty salons. Most department store beauty salons are required to maintain the same policy as the department store including their charge system and refund policy. The salon also becomes part of the store's accounting and auditing system. The renting terms are very similar to those for a shopping center salon. The higher prices for services in the department store salon automatically attract a clientele that is willing to pay more for their beauty services. Most department store operations require a double shift of operators in order to maintain the same working hours as the department store. The special benefit of working in a department store salon is discount shopping. The discount is the same as that offered to all the other employees. Cleaning and maintenance work are usually included in the rent.

Hotel and motel beauty salons are usually as small as a neighborhood salon. Although the majority of the patrons are hotel guests (transient), these salons have many regular patrons. Charges for services are usually much higher than in most salons. Most hotels allow the guests to charge beauty salon services to their hotel invoice. Adjustments are made with the salon on a regular basis in the form of a rent credit or cash refund. Depending on your lease, special provisions should be made for the opening and closing hours of the salon, the responsibility for cleaning and maintenance, and for advertising signs in strategic areas.

Unit 3
The lease

A lease for a store or loft should be drawn especially for you. It should guard against unwarranted increases in rent. It should carefully spell out all the special concessions and options to which you are entitled.

Before signing a lease, a contract should be drawn which will cancel the agreement, without cost, if the space cannot pass zoning regulations or state approval. The agreement should not be valid if you cannot get a Certificate of Occupancy, a permit for signs, redecorating, and electrical and plumbing work. Most important, if the building lacks the required amount of electrical power needed to meet your requirements, the agreement should be void.

The owner of the building is called the lessor and the renter is known as the lessee. The lease guarantees you, the lessee, the use of the negotiated space for a specified period of time at a set annual price to be paid monthly. The length of a lease can be for one or more years. A lease usually provides an option for renewal, the right to assign the lease to another individual or corporation and a sublease clause.

Unit 3

The lease

General objectives-student goals:
After study, instruction and completion of this unit, you will be able to demonstrate understanding of the value of a lease by writing and/or giving a brief overview of the subject.

Beauty salon management

The lease should indicate who is responsible for alterations and maintaining the interior and/or exterior of the building as well as the hallways and public portions of the building.

A lease usually protects you, the lessee, but it is of utmost importance that you and your attorney read the lease with extreme care and understand exactly what your responsibilities are.

Unit 4
Physical layout of the salon

Analyze the flow of operations to make it comfortable for your patrons and efficient for your operators. Generally, the flow is as follows:

1. Reception desk

2. Patron dressing room, checkroom or lounge

3. Shampoo area

4. Hair coloring and permanent wave section

5. Styling section

6. Drying and manicuring area

7. Cashier and appointment desk

A layout that directs the patron in a circular flow is generally the most efficient.

Check list for structural limitations

Look for:

1. Immovable walls, pillars and partitions.

2. Sufficient plumbing and heating.

3. Sources of natural light (excellent for the hair coloring section).

4. Adequate aisle space.

5. Large drain pipes. Chemicals and hair tend to clog the drain.

6. Strong water pressure and plenty of hot water.

7. Adequate electric power and outlets for your needs. Overloaded power lines spell trouble.

The plan for the layout of a salon is usually provided by the manufacturer of the equipment and fixtures which you purchase for your salon. The furniture fixtures and equipment are selected on the basis of appearance, durability and cost.

The layout can be a(n):

1. Closed booth operation

2. Open section operation

3. Combination closed booth and open section operation

Unit 4
Physical layout of the salon

General objectives-student goals: After study, instruction and completion of this unit, you will be able to demonstrate understanding of the importance of the physical layout of a salon and its structural limitations by writing and/or giving a brief overview of the subject.

Beauty salon management

545

1. The closed booth operation: Each work station is partitioned so that the patrons and operators in each work area are not within the view of each other. Only drying and manicuring services are given in open sections.

2. The open section operation: All work stations are in line with each other. There are either no partitions or only low partitions between the hairstyling, hair coloring, hair drying and manicuring sections.

3. The combination closed booth and open section operation provides individual booths for facials, superfluous hair removal, hair coloring and chemical treatments. There are open sections for hairstyling, haircutting, manicuring and hair drying.

Unit 5
Color scheme

A beautiful interior done in a psychologically correct color scheme can help increase your business. The color(s) of paint used in all areas should be coordinated with the fabrics, furniture and fixtures of each area. Wallpaper and wood panels are excellent for decorating walls. Wallpaper should blend with the basic color within the area. Avoid large bold patterns. Do not let the pattern dominate the area. Wood panels should complement the furniture and fixtures.

When painting, the lower portion (4-5 feet [1.22-1.52 m.]) of the walls may be a darker color, and the upper portion of the wall may be a light color. White ceilings make your salon appear clean and light. Light colors make the salon appear larger and provide a better work atmosphere.

Whether you use paint, wallpaper or paneling, be certain that they are of a good washable grade. Use this guide when selecting colors:

White is too glaring.

Off-white or ivory are next in reflective value and should be used predominantly. Light colors add life to the salon.

Yellow, red and orange are advancing colors. They make an area look smaller.

Light blue, green and gray are cool and receding. They can be used in small sunny areas.

Deep blue can be depressing and should be used carefully. Dark colors create an effect which can make people lazy and sleepy.

Unit 6
Insurance, business laws and health regulations

Insurance is of major importance in the operation of a beauty salon. It protects the salon owner from unforeseen or unpredictable problems that can arise during the normal course of a salon operation.

Unit 5
Color scheme

General objectives-student goals:
After study, instruction and completion of this unit, you will be able to demonstrate understanding of the importance of color when decorating a salon by writing and/or giving a brief overview of the subject.

Unit 6
Insurance, business laws and health regulations

General objectives-student goals:
After study, instruction and comple-

Beauty salon management

546

Buying the right kind of insurance will eliminate risks and give you peace of mind. The cost of proper insurance amounts to no more than an attorney's fee for one suit. Adequate insurance should include at least the following:

1. Malpractice
2. Premise liability
3. Fire
4. Property damage
5. Burglary and theft
6. Compensation
7. Business interruption
8. Product liability

tion of this unit, you will be able to demonstrate understanding of insurance, business laws and health regulations by writing and/or giving a brief overview of the subject.

1. Malpractice insurance protects you from claims made for any injury received in your salon as a result of carelessness or negligence during the performance of any service by you or your operators. The injury could also owe its origin to the improper application of a product and the improper operation of equipment. Without this insurance, it is possible for a salon to suffer complete financial ruin.

2. Premise liability insurance protects you from claims made for accidents that occur in or around your salon, e.g., the patron receives an injury while stepping up or down a step or stairs, slips on a wet floor near the shampoo area, styling station or toilet, or falls on the sidewalk in front of your salon.

3. Fire insurance protects your investment in your building, furniture, fixtures and equipment. Without fire insurance, the cost of rebuilding your salon could leave you without a profit for years to come. Fire insurance is based on the value of your property. It is important, therefore, to increase the dollar value of your protection whenever you add new equipment or furnishings to the salon.

4. Property damage insurance protects you when your property is damaged by anyone or anything other than from your normal operation, e.g., a car accidently backing into your storefront.

5. Burglary and theft insurance protects you against loss and/or damage resulting from or following the unlawful breaking and entering of your premises. This type of insurance covers the loss of money, supplies and equipment.

6. Compensation insurance protects the employees from financial loss and medical costs when an injury or disease is caused by the work which they performed. State regulations require employees to have this type of insurance coverage.

7. Business interruption insurance protects the salon owner's income in the event the salon cannot open for business because of fire or any other catastrophe. The amount of income protected should be sufficient to meet all normal expenses and employee wages until the salon returns to its normal operation.

8. Product liability insurance is available to you at no extra charge from all dependable manufacturers. The insurance protects the manufacturer and salon owner against claims for damage or injuries resulting from the use of their product. This insurance protects you only when the product is used according to manufacturer's instructions, and the damage or injury was caused by the product. Product liability insurance does not take the place of malpractice insurance. Request product liability certificates of insurance from the manufacturers of all the products you use. Keep them on file.

Beauty salon management

547

Business laws vary from community to community. Generally, they cover the employer's obligation regarding taxes and insurance for the employees. The employer must withhold Social Security taxes and federal taxes. He must maintain the proper wages, hours and working conditions for all employees. He must keep records of the employees' tips.

Town regulations, state laws, federal laws, income tax laws and insurance regulations must be complied with in order to conduct a business.

Health regulations usually cover the number of toilets required and salon sanitation practices. In some areas, these regulations are part of the local building code.

Unit 7
Customer reception

The reception desk is the first thing the patron sees upon entering the salon. The impression he or she gets of your salon at this point is swift and lasting. Their satisfaction must begin here. The reception desk controls all the salon's activities. A poorly organized receptionist is very costly to the operation. The desk must be clean and orderly at all times. Appointment records should be kept in privacy and should not be visible to patrons on the other side of the desk. Each appointment should be recorded in every detail.

The appointment system should include abbreviations and marks which indicate different situations. Some suggested symbols are:

√ Requested the operator of her choice. Do not make a change.

X Transient patron. The appointment may be assigned to any operator free at that time.

CPT Complaint on service.

PAS Possible additional services may be required.

Avoid playing favorites. Partiality in the distribution of patrons can create serious problems.

Unit 8
Management-operator relations

The relationship between the operator and management is affected by the supervision of the salon personnel. Good supervision includes:

1. Careful selection of personnel

2. The owner's high standards for operators

Unit 7
Customer reception

General objectives-student goals:
After study, instruction and completion of this unit, you will be able to demonstrate understanding of the reception desk by writing and/or giving a brief overview of the subject.

Unit 8

Management-operator relations

General objectives-student goals:
After study, instruction and comple-

Beauty salon management

548

3. Continuous in-service training of the operators

4. Adequate operator's compensation (salary, commission and employee benefits)

5. Regular monthly staff meetings

The success or failure of a beauty salon will depend in a large measure on operator loyalty. Operator loyalty is a direct reflection of the relationship between owner and operator.

1. **Careful selection of personnel** includes writing and placing good help wanted ads in your local newspaper, interviewing prospective employees and evaluating their appearance, facial expressions, speech, voice volume, attitude, and the results of a trial operation.

2. **The owner's high standards for operators** include appearance, their ability to answer the phone, make appointments, sell services, sell beauty products, handle complaints, resolve most problems as they arise and build a solid clientele.

3. **Continuous in-service training of the operators** results in the staff using the same methods, procedures, techniques and jargon to create the image you want. Each training session should include a demonstration, workshop and an exchange of ideas. Each stylist should provide a model for the workshop portion of the session. These in-salon training sessions should be scheduled on a regular routine basis. It may be wise to bring someone from the outside to do the teaching.

4. **Adequate operator's compensation** (salary, commission and employee benefits) may consist of any one or more of the following:

   A. Straight salary

   B. Straight percentage

   C. Salary and percentage

   D. Sliding percentage (increases or decreases after reaching a certain level)

   E. Dual percentage (a different percentage is paid for chemical or corrective services as compared to conventional work)

   F. Paid vacation

   G. Paid holidays

   H. Sick pay

   I. Medical plan

   J. Life insurance plan

   K. Annual performance increase

   L. Annual bonus

   M. Pension plan

   N. Profit sharing

tion of this unit, you will be able to demonstrate understanding of management-operator relations by writing and/or giving a brief overview of the subject.

Beauty salon
management

5. Regular monthly meetings are held during off-hours or after hours. Meetings last from one to three hours. Attendance must be mandatory for all employees. Meetings should be well planned and are used for:

A. Exchanging ideas and working techniques

B. Reviewing product instructions

C. Introducing new products

D. Developing telephone techniques

E. Performance reviews

F. Reviewing individual patron problems

G. Developing ideas for improving operations

H. Developing ideas for creating an improved work atmosphere in the salon

Unit 9
Financial control and record keeping

It is necessary to maintain adequate financial control and record keeping in order to conduct a successful beauty salon operation. Records of all money withheld from employees' wages are required by law. The true value of record keeping is that it lets you know—not guess—the exact condition of all factors affecting your profits and losses. A good record keeping system includes:

1. A simple bookkeeping system	5. Chemical hair straightening records
2. A cash register system (service records and pay-outs)	6. Scalp, facial and make-up service records
3. Cold wave records	7. A stock inventory record
4. Hair coloring records	8. A record of merchandise sold

Bookkeeping in a salon is the only means of maintaining accurate business control. Good records provide the accurate, day-by-day results of the salon's operation. They also indicate the business' strengths, weaknesses and problem areas.

A complete record system will identify which of the operators are business builders, attract new patrons, sell services other than those requested and other factors.

The balance sheet compares the assets (what you own) and the liabilities (what you owe). The difference between assets and liabilities is your net worth. It is the net worth that determines the value of your business.

Unit 9
Financial control and record keeping

General objectives-student goals:
After study, instruction and completion of this unit, you will be able to demonstrate understanding of financial control and record keeping as it relates to a beauty salon operation by writing and/or giving a brief overview of the subject.

Beauty salon management

550

Appointment records provide the owner with information concerning which operators are most productive and which patrons are repeat customers.

Service record cards provide the cosmetologist with a record of all services, treatments and merchandise sold to each patron. All service record cards should also contain a note concerning the patron's taste and preferences. Service records help you prevent problems and the repetition of errors.

Unit 10
Salesmanship and merchandising

Any business that sells service, sells time. Because there are only a limited number of hours in the day, you can sell only a limited amount of personal services. To avoid having a limited income, the cosmetologist must sell added services. This can be done within the allotted time of the appointment if extra time is not available. For example, a patron may be booked for a shampoo and set, and the operator has allocated 30 minutes for this service. Income from this patron can be increased easily by selling an additional service. It could be a temporary color rinse, a creme rinse, a conditioning rinse, a special shampoo, an eyebrow arch or hair trim, all of which can be given without going over the allotted time.

Merchandising is the cosmetologist's best source of income because it requires a minimum amount of time, and the profit is determined by the type and amount of merchandise you sell. Percentage of profit and volume are the principal elements in merchandising. To be successful in merchandising, you must carry items that will sell in your area and to your type of clientele. You must also have the right source of supply so that you buy at the correct price.

Hair, skin and nail cosmetics are easy to sell in the beauty salon. A cosmetologist's recommendation is usually accepted because it is based on the stylist's knowledge of the patron's needs. The in-salon use of the products demonstrates the effectiveness of them. The patron's trust and confidence in the cosmetologist who serves him or her also helps sell products.

Salon patrons find it convenient to buy and repurchase cosmetics while visiting the salon for their services. The quality of the products is recognized as high and professional. The formulation, concentration, size and price charged for cosmetics sold in the beauty salon guarantee repeat sales. When you sell the items you use in professional sizes, you eliminate the competition from food and discount stores.

Establish your retail business as a separate operation in a specific area of your salon and state your retail objectives clearly to your employees.

Salesmanship

You must have knowledge of the service you expect to sell and you must be sold yourself before you can sell to others.

You must recognize a patron's standards of merchandise and services.

You must evaluate a patron's buying habits, tendencies, personal appearance and conversation.

Unit 10
Salesmanship and merchandising

General objectives-student goals: After study, instruction and completion of this unit, you will be able to demonstrate understanding of the importance of salesmanship and merchandising to a beauty salon operation by writing and/or giving a brief overview of the subject.

Beauty salon
management

551

Your sales approach must be influenced by the patron's actions and expression.

You must be capable of attracting attention, arousing interest, creating a desire and stimulating action.

Your facial expression and tone of voice reflect the sincerity of your sales talk.

Unit 11
Advertising

Unit 11
Advertising

General objectives-student goals:
After study, instruction and completion of this unit, you will be able to demonstrate understanding of advertising as it relates to a beauty salon operation by writing and/or giving a brief overview of the subject.

Advertising does not consist exclusively of the printed word or picture. It consists of all those activities which attract attention to your salon and create a favorable impression of it.

Natural advertising consists of:

1. Your personality
2. The attitude of your cosmetologists and staff
3. The quality of work that leaves your salon
4. Your merchandise
5. The attractiveness of your salon's interior and exterior

The best form of advertising is word of mouth. This happens when pleased patrons speak well of your salon.

The types of printed advertising you choose should be determined by your area and the clientele you want to attract. Those to consider are:

1. Newspaper
2. Window trim and signs
3. Formal letters
4. Post cards
5. Handbills
6. The yellow pages of the phone book

A properly used telephone is also an excellent advertising medium.

Your advertising should concentrate on big ideas, have only one thought, be brief and never exaggerate.

Window display advertising is second best for the neighborhood beauty salon. It is your silent advertising program. Your window reflects who and what you are, and what can be expected from you. It should be well lighted, colorful and changed frequently. It is suggested that you advertise the price of one of your services in the window so that people will have an approximate idea of the price range for other services. Make your windows attractive and beautiful. Avoid the impression that your prices are unnecessarily higher than other salons in the same area.

Unit 12
Budget and average expenses

As part of your operation, you are required to know where your money is being spent. There are many hidden costs that go into operating a salon. Approximately 90% of the gross income is used to cover operating expenses and slightly more than 50% of the 90% is used for wages, salaries and commissions.

The following figures will vary in different localities. They are also affected by an individual's management policy. Reducing expenses will increase profits. The amounts indicated for each expense represent an average paid out on a nationwide basis.

Budget and average expenses

Expenses	Percent of income
Salaries, commissions and taxes	57.23
Rent	4.70
Supplies	6.39
Advertising	3.19
Depreciation of equipment, furniture and fixtures	2.29
Laundry	.99
Cleaning	1.00
Electricity, heat and water	2.06
Repairs and maintenance	1.56
Fees, taxes and legal services	4.22
Insurance	1.80
Fringe benefits	1.17
Telephone	1.01
Interest and carrying charges	.93
Miscellaneous (dues, subscriptions and education)	2.19
Total expenses	90.73
Net profit	9.27

The percentage of profit rises sharply once the break-even point is reached

General objectives-student goals: After study, instruction and completion of this unit, you will be able to demonstrate understanding of budgeting and determining operating expenses by writing and/or giving a brief overview of the subject.

Beauty salon management

553

Salaries	57.23%
Net profit	9.27%
Rent	4.70%
Supplies	6.39%
Advertising	3.19%
Depreciation	2.29%
Laundry	.99%
Cleaning	1%
Miscellaneous	2.19%
Interest and carrying charges	.93%
Telephone	1.01%
Fringe benefits	1.17%
Insurance	1.80%
Fees	4.22%
Repairs	1.56%
Electric	2.06%

The figures noted above are approximate. Some salons will go over in the areas of salaries, wages and rent and cut back in other areas. A salon owner who repeatedly fails to operate within these percentages will operate a money-losing salon.

Unit 13
Professional ethics

Ethics in cosmetology deal with the conduct of the cosmetologists toward their patrons, business associates and other cosmetologists. Good ethics reflect the integrity of the entire profession. Remember, the cosmetologist sells a personal service. High standards of ethics build confidence in the cosmetologist.

Poor ethics such as unrealistic claims, misleading advertising and questionable practices are in direct violation of the basic rules of good business practice.

Unit 13

Professional ethics

General objectives-student goals:
After study, instruction and completion of this unit, you will be able to demonstrate understanding of professional ethics by writing and/or giving a brief overview of the subject.

Beauty salon
management

554

Rules of good ethics

1. Follow all the provisions of the state cosmetology law.

2. Keep your hairdressing skills up-to-date.

3. Comply with the rules and regulations of your establishment.

4. Be loyal to your employees, employer or associates.

5. Give courteous service.

6. Do not show favoritism among patrons.

7. Maintain a high standard of sanitation and sterilization.

8. A good reputation should include reference to your ethics.

9. Be fair and firm. Respect the rights of others.

10. Fulfill your obligations.

Unit 14
Beauty salon telephone techniques

An integral part of the beauty salon operation is answering the telephone. Although the telephone serves many useful purposes, the two prime purposes of it are making, changing or breaking appointments and reminding patrons of needed services.

Success in using the phone depends, to a large extent, on observation and the practice of certain fundamental principles. A cosmetologist's telephone manner reflects not only the professionalism of the salon but also his or her own professionalism.

Develop and practice the following telephone techniques and habits:

1. Answer promptly. If at all possible, answer on the first or second ring.

2. Speak directly into the mouthpiece. The telephone mouthpiece should be held directly in line with the lips and about 2 inches (5.08 cm.) away.

3. Identify your salon and yourself.

Unit 14
Beauty salon telephone techniques

General objectives-student goals: After study, instruction and completion of this unit, you will be able to demonstrate understanding of beauty salon telephone techniques by writing and/or giving a brief overview of the subject.

Beauty salon management

4. Identify yourself if you come on the line after the telephone has been answered by someone else.

5. Be friendly. Listen carefully to what the caller is saying. Try to help him or her. Be a good representative of your salon. Suggest additional beauty services which the patron may have overlooked. If you delay your conversation, excuse yourself before leaving the line and always say "Thank you for waiting" when you return. If you think the delay may be lengthy, offer to call back.

6. When you place an outgoing call, identify your salon and yourself immediately.

7. Put a smile in your voice. This can be accomplished by saying "please," "thank you," "you're welcome," "sorry."

Booking appointments over the telephone must be done more carefully than when done in person.

1. It requires tact and a pleasant voice. The patrons cannot see the receptionist. Therefore, the patron must respond to the sound of the receptionist's voice, what she says and how she says it.

2. It requires attentive hearing to get the patron's name, desired services and appointment time. Names must be spelled correctly.

3. The receptionist must think quickly. If the time requested is not available, tact and quick thinking can sell another time. The receptionist should have a good memory for names and faces.

4. The receptionist must always place the receiver back on the phone carefully because she knows that she must never make a slamming sound in anyone's ear.

5. Extra services can be sold frequently by suggesting them at the time the patron makes her appointment. Often, patrons do not think of services in addition to the ones they usually get. Many patrons do not know all the services that are available to them in a beauty salon. Once patrons try other services, they may like them and have them more often.

It has been firmly established that salon patrons are becoming increasingly selective in their choice of establishments. They are seeking out those salons which offer the best hair services and the most pleasant environment. Telephone conversations are an integral part of the environment of any business including the beauty salon.

Unit 15
Gratuities

Gratuities are, and always were, an important part of a cosmetologist's income. The word tips originated many years ago from a sign that was posted over a coin bank by waiters in many of the better restaurants. The sign read:

T o
I nsure
P rompt
S ervice

Unit 15

Gratuities

General objectives-student goals:
After study, instruction and completion of this unit, you will be able to demonstrate understanding of gratuities by writing and/or giving a brief overview of the subject.

Beauty salon management

556

Employees who receive cash tips of $20.00 or more in any calendar month, while working for one employer, are subject to withholding and Social Security taxes. Tips count toward Social Security benefits. Daily records should be kept, and monthly totals must be reported to the employer. Special forms are available for record keeping and reporting.

Unit 16
Contemporary salons

An exciting new concept has developed around the structure and layout of contemporary beauty salons. These salons represent a new concept, not a passing fad. They are here to stay. A new kind of hairstyling for both men and women (unisex) has created this new image for the cosmetologist and salon. In turn, it has created new salon patrons.

The **hairstyling trend** which is responsible for this change is characterized by total freedom from conventional hairstyling practices. The hair is left free to move with the motions of the wearer and the wind. It is not restricted by back combing, teasing or any form of rigidity.

The single most important ingredient responsible for the success of this new concept in hairstyling is the technique of **precision haircutting**. The free-flowing hairstyles were born when the hair was cut and shaped perfectly, in a direction which let it fall naturally in the most becoming silhouette. With the touch of a hair brush, comb or just the fingers, the hair falls into the style line and maintains a professional salon look from one haircut to the next. This contemporary styling is flattering to almost everyone. It can be achieved with long or short hair cut in a one length cut or in a blended layer cut.

General objectives-student goals: After study, instruction and completion of this unit, you will be able to demonstrate understanding of contemporary salons by writing and/or giving a brief overview of the subject.

Beauty salon management

557

The three most important implements which help make precision results possible are the mini-scissors, the hand-held dryer (blower) and the thermal curling iron. The use of these implements can result in hairstyling that takes care of itself.

This new concept has created new salon patrons for the new contemporary salons. The generation of young do-it-yourselfers and the fashion conscious youths who let their hair grow longer were the greatest contributors to the success of this new hairstyling concept. Now, men and women of all ages who want hairstyling that is the "in" thing, and which is being shown in leading fashion and trade publications, represent a large percentage of the clientele who patronize the new contemporary salons.

Conventional beauty salons are also participating in the contemporary hairstyling concept. Although it is ideal to have an independent contemporary salon next to the conventional salon, it is not necessary. It could be just one corner or section of the conventional beauty salon. That section or corner, however, must be decorated, equipped and distinguished in the same manner as the contemporary salon.

Planning a contemporary hairstyling salon or converting a section in the existing salon necessitates thinking that is tuned in to meet the necessary requirements. The main objective is to create a non-salon appearance and atmosphere distinguished by a staff of chic stylists, current music background, dramatic color and decor, and special lighting fixtures as well as special styling stations and chairs. A contemporary salon may require less money to start than a conventional salon, but it will require a great deal of display and decorating talent. Plan as follows:

1. Select a name and logo: The name should be short, meaningful, easy to remember and related to the type of operation you are planning. Some names currently used are: Imagination Plus, Hair Creations, New Look Hair Designs, Hair Trimmers, Great Hair Expectations, Golden Touch Haircutters, Numero Uno Hair Salon, Unisex Haircutters, Snipper's Hair Place, Haircutters and Style Portfolio, The Cutting Stones, Hair Factory, Hair Designer's Studio, Sunshine Scissors, and Guys and Gals Haircutting and Styling. Avoid using your own name unless you want to be a one person operation. Salon owners have learned that when the salon owner's name is part of the salon name, the owner will be doing most of the work while the staff sits and watches. Care should be exercised when selecting a logo because your logo will help establish your identity and recognition.

2. Staffing: Each stylist should look the part. Their clothing and hairstyles should be natural and have the "now" look. The best qualified must know how to use the blow dryer, mini-scissors and thermal irons. They must know how to do the no-set, no-tease concept of hairstyling.

3. The physical setup: The salon should have more working stations than stylists. The stylists on the staff who have all the expertise, i.e., lamp cutting, perming to curve the hair (not curling it), illuminizing, nuancing and other techniques work with a minimum of two stations. To get the maximum use of the available space, plan on a minimum of 90 square feet (8.36 m.) per working station. This figure takes into account a prorated share per station of the space needed for a dispensary, reception room, storage, rest rooms, coatroom, working aisles and all other essentials necessary in a modern functional salon. When space is no problem, 105 square feet (9.75 m.) per station is most desirable. When using a corner or a side wall of a conventional beauty salon for the contemporary styling area, allow approximately 39 square feet (3.62 m.) for one stylist or 67 square feet (6.22 m.) for two stations. If a corner is used for two stylists, 90 square feet (8.36 m.) will be required. Select the best existing area as close to the front of the salon as possible. If there is a storefront, the front street window area is always the best because this area creates outside excitement.

Beauty salon
management

4. **A non-salon look is essential:** Avoid conventional styling stations and styling chairs. The color scheme is very important. Use vibrant colors.

Use see-through items to separate areas. Hanging beads, ropes and tension poles are excellent dividers.

Use bold hanging signs from the ceiling to feature the specialties, identify areas and get the message across to the patrons.

Use molded plastic, wicker or director's chairs.

Use unusual lighting effects, spotlights at each station, small frosted lights around the mirrors and flashing frosted lights around the store windows.

Use mirrors all the way down to the floor or in interesting octagon-shaped frames. Try to use all mirrors in an unusual way.

Use all kinds of props: cutouts, flowers and posters.

Use current music backgrounds from an FM radio, records or tapes.

Train the staff to use the same methods, procedures, techniques and jargon. This will create the image you want. Each training session should include a demonstration, workshop and an exchange of ideas. Each stylist should provide a model for the workshop portion of the session. These in-salon training sessions should be scheduled on a regular basis. It may be wise to bring someone from the outside to do the teaching.

It is recommended that employers send their stylists to a school for advanced training once a year for a period of not less than one week (35 hours). At this session, stylists will learn the latest methods, techniques and styles. As part of the training, stylists should be given time to attend trade shows. Several trade publications should be made available to the stylists.

Depending on your area, location, clientele and the price range for your services, you should consider the following when forming your operational policy:

1. Operate by appointment only.

2. Eliminate appointments. A simple drop-in and wait your turn has become a successful method for contemporary salons.

3. Combine no appointments necessary and making appointments for those who desire them.

4. Have one price for all haircuts.

Beauty salon
management

559

5. Charge extra for long hair services.

6. All haircuts should include a shampoo, conditioner and blow dry or thermal curl styling.

7. Have three separate charges for the haircut and blow dry, shampoo and conditioner.

8. No tipping. This is possible by including the stylist's percentage in the charge for the service rendered. For example, an $11.50 haircut would break down as $10.00 for the haircut and $1.50 for the stylist.

9. Retailing. Sales of merchandise can produce profits faster than services. You may consider retailing costume jewelry, cosmetics, travel items and fashion accessories as well as hair care and skin care items.

All this adds up to an unparalleled opportunity for the cosmetologist and the beauty salon business. The full service salon still has and always will have a large market for conventional beauty salon services and styling.

Unit 17
Purchasing an existing salon

There are many advantages to purchasing an existing salon. An existing salon provides you with instant clientele and income. The clientele that is there at the time of the purchase will usually continue to patronize the salon. In addition, some of the patrons who have discontinued coming return when the salon goes under new management.

The disadvantages include purchasing the problems of the former owner, his or her poor reputation if it is poor and a staff of operators who may not meet your standards.

The following items should be considered seriously before purchasing an existing salon:

1. The time remaining on the existing lease and the factors which affect your obligations.

2. The condition of the equipment, furniture and fixtures. Determine how long it will be before they have to be replaced.

3. Evaluate the operators' methods and techniques.

4. Question the operators concerning whether they plan to remain with the new management.

5. Determine the period of time during which the seller will agree not to compete with you.

6. Determine the obligations you will assume along with the purchase.

Unit 17
Purchasing an existing salon

General objectives-student goals:
After study, instruction and completion of this unit, you will be able to demonstrate understanding of the advantages and disadvantages of purchasing an existing salon by writing and/or giving a brief overview of the subject.

Beauty salon
management

560

Do's and don'ts of beauty salon management

1. **Don't** rent a location on a month to month basis.

2. **Do** include an option to renew your lease at the time you sign your lease.

3. **Do** keep accurate records.

4. **Don't** operate your salon without the proper insurance coverage.

5. **Do** require your operators to record their tips for tax purposes.

6. **Do** sell merchandise related to the hair, skin and nails.

7. **Do** secure and renew all licenses and permits in order to operate legally.

8. **Do** repair and maintain equipment in order to avoid accidents.

9. **Don't** neglect your storefront windows because they indicate what can be expected inside.

10. **Don't** neglect your reception desk.

Review questions

1. The contemporary beauty salon has attracted new beauty salon patrons. Who are they?

2. There are four types of salon ownership. Name them.

3. Name three of the six major groups of beauty salons from which one can operate.

4. Start with the reception desk and describe the physical layout of a beauty salon which has an efficient flow of operations.

Beauty salon
management

5. Adequate beauty salon insurance coverage includes eight areas of protection. Name them.

6. Name the eight areas of record keeping required for an efficient beauty salon operation.

7. What are the six kinds of printed advertising available to a salon owner?

8. Name five expense items incurred by all beauty salons.

9. Professional ethics are an important part of a beauty salon operation. Name five rules of good ethics.

10. Give three reasons why booking appointments over the telephone must be done more carefully than when made in person.

11. Name five items which should be considered seriously before purchasing an existing beauty salon.

Beauty salon
management

CHARTS AND TABLES

WEIGHTS AND MEASURES

APOTHECARIES' WEIGHT

20 grains..............................1 scruple
3 scruples.............................1 dram
8 drams................................1 ounce
12 ounces..............................1 pound

AVOIRDUPOIS WEIGHT

27 11/32 grains........................1 dram
16 drams...............................1 ounce
16 ounces..............................1 pound
25 pounds..............................1 quarter
4 quarters...........1 hundredweight (cwt)

DRY MEASURE

2 pints................................1 quart
8 quarts...............................1 peck
4 pecks................................1 bushel
36 bushels.............................1 chaldron

LIQUID MEASURE

4 ounces...............................1 gill
4 gills................................1 pint
2 pints................................1 quart
4 quarts...............................1 gallon
31½ gallons............................1 barrel

LONG MEASURE

12 inches..............................1 foot
3 feet.................................1 yard
5½ yards...............................1 rod
1760 yards.....................1 statute mile

SQUARE MEASURE

144 sq. inches.........................1 sq. foot
9 sq. feet.............................1 sq. yard
30¼ sq. yards..........................1 sq. rod
40 sq. rods............................1 rood
4 roods................................1 acre
640 acres..............................1 sq. mile

TIME MEASURE

60 seconds.............................1 minute
60 minutes.............................1 hour
24 hours...............................1 day
7 days.................................1 week
365 days...............................1 year
366 days...............................1 leap year
52 weeks...............................1 year

TROY WEIGHT

24 grains...............1 pennyweight (pwt)
20 pwt.................................1 ounce
12 ounces..............................1 pound

Metric tables

United States Equivalents of Metric Units

METRIC LENGTH (METERS)

UNIT	NUMBER OF METERS	UNITED STATES EQUIVALENT
myriameter (mym)	10,000	6.2 miles
kilometer (km)	1,000	0.62 mile
hectometer (hm)	100	109.36 yards
dekameter (dam)	10	32.81 feet
meter (m)	1	39.37 inches
decimeter (dm)	0.1	3.94 inches
centimeter (cm)	0.01	0.39 inch
millimeter (mm)	0.001	0.04 inch

METRIC VOLUME (CUBIC METERS)

UNIT	NUMBER OF CUBIC METERS	UNITED STATES EQUIVALENT
dekastere (das)	10	13.10 cubic yards
stere (s)	1	1.31 cubic yards
decistere (ds)	0.10	3.53 cubic feet
cubic centimeter (cc)	0.000001	0.061 cubic inch

METRIC AREA (SQUARE METERS)

UNIT	NUMBER OF SQUARE METERS	UNITED STATES EQUIVALENT
square kilometer (sq km)	1,000,000	1.3861 square mile
hectare (ha)	10,000	2.47 acres
are (a)	100	1119.60 square yards
centare (ca)	1	10.76 square feet
square centimeter (sq cm)	0.0001	0.155 square inch

METRIC WEIGHT (GRAMS)

UNIT	NUMBER OF GRAMS	UNITED STATES EQUIVALENT
metric ton (MT)	1,000,000	1.1 tons
quintal (q)	100,000	220.46 pounds
kilogram (kg)	1,000	2.2046 pounds
hectogram (hg)	100	3.527 ounces
dekagram (dag)	10	0.353 ounce
gram (gm)	1	0.035 ounce
decigram (dg)	0.10	1.543 grains
centigram (cg)	0.01	0.154 grain
milligram (mg)	0.001	0.015 grain

METRIC CAPACITY (LITERS)

UNIT	NUMBER OF LITERS	UNITED STATES EQUIVALENT		
		DRY MEASURE	LIQUID MEASURE	CUBIC MEASURE
kiloliter (kl)	1,000	.788 chaldrons	4.19 hogsheads	1.31 cubic yards
hectoliter (hl)	100	2.84 bushels	0.838 barrels	3.53 cubic feet
dekaliter (dal)	10	1.14 pecks	2.64 gallons	0.35 cubic foot
liter (l)	1	0.908 quart	1.057 quarts	61.02 cubic inches
deciliter (dl)	0.10	0.18 pint	0.21 pint	6.1 cubic inches
centiliter (cl)	0.01	0.018 pint	0.338 fluidounce	0.6 cubic inch
milliliter (ml)	0.001	0.0018 pint	0.27 fluidram	0.06 cubic inch

Metric tables

Metric Equivalents of United States Units

LENGTH (METERS)

UNIT	LENGTH	METRIC EQUIVALENT
1 inch (in)	0.083 feet	2.54 centimeters
1 foot (ft)	12 inches	30.480 centimeters
1 yard (yd)	36 inches (3 feet)	.914401 meters
1 mile (mi)	5280 feet (1760 yards)	1.609347 kilometers

VOLUME (CUBIC METERS)

UNIT	VOLUME	METRIC EQUIVALENT
1 cubic inch (cu in)	0.00058 cubic feet	16.372 cubic centimeters
1 cubic foot (cu ft)	1728 cubic inches	.028317 cubic meters
1 cubic yard (cu yd)	27 cubic feet	.7646 cubic meters

AREA (SQUARE METERS)

UNIT	AREA	METRIC EQUIVALENT
1 square inch (sq in)	0.007 square feet	6.45165 square centimeters
1 square foot (sq ft)	144 square inches	9.290034 square decimeters
1 square yard (sq yd)	9 square feet	.836161 square meters
1 acre (a)	4840 square yards	.40469 hectares
1 square mile (sq mi)	640 acres	2.59 square kilometers = 259 hectares

WEIGHT (GRAMS)

UNIT	WEIGHT	METRIC EQUIVALENT
1 dram (dr)	0.0625 ounces	1.771 grams
1 avoirdupois ounce (oz)	16 drams	28.349 grams
1 avoirdupois pound (lb)	16 ounces	0.453 kilograms
1 short ton (tn)	2000 pounds	0.907 metric tons
1 long ton (tn)	2240 pounds	1.016 metric tons

CAPACITY (LITERS)

UNIT	CAPACITY	METRIC EQUIVALENT
1 gill (gi)	4 fluidounces	118.291 milliliters
1 pint (liquid) (pt)	4 gills	.473167 liters
1 pint (dry) (pt)	$^1\!/_2$ quart	.550599 liters
1 quart (liquid) (qt)	2 pints	.9463 liters
1 quart (dry) (qt)	2 pints	1.101198 liters
1 peck (pk)	8 quarts	8.80958 liters
1 gallon (gal)	4 quarts	3.7853 liters
1 bushel (bu)	4 pecks	.35238 hectoliters

Metric tables

Approximate Conversion Factors

TO METRIC MEASURES

MEASUREMENT	KNOWN FACTOR	MULTIPLY BY	EQUALS	SYMBOL
Length	inches	2.5	centimeters	cm
	feet	30	centimeters	cm
	yards	0.9	meters	m
	miles	1.6	kilometers	km
Area	square inches	6.5	square centimeters	cm
	square feet	0.09	square meters	m
	square yards	0.8	square meters	m
	square miles	2.6	square kilometers	km
	acres	0.4	hectares	ha
Mass (Weight)	ounces	28	grams	g
	pounds	.045	kilograms	kg
	short tons (2000 lb)	0.9	metric tons	t
Volume	teaspoons	5	milliliters	ml
	tablespoons	15	milliliters	ml
	fluid ounces	30	milliliters	ml
	cups	0.25	liters	l
	pints	0.47	liters	l
	quarts	0.95	liters	l
	gallons	3.8	liters	l
	cubic feet	0.03	cubic meters	m
	cubic yards	0.76	cubic meters	m
Temperature	Fahrenheit	5/9 (after subtracting 32)	Celsius temperature	°C

FROM METRIC MEASURES

MEASUREMENT	KNOWN FACTOR	MULTIPLY BY	EQUALS	SYMBOL
Length	millimeters	0.04	inches	in
	centimeters	0.4	inches	in
	meters	3.3	feet	ft
	meters	1.1	yards	yd
	kilometers	0.6	miles	mi
Area	square centimeters	0.16	square inches	in
	square meters	1.2	square yards	yd
	square kilometers	0.4	square miles	mi
	hectares (10,000 m)	2.5	acres	a
Mass (Weight)	grams	0.035	ounces	oz
	kilograms	2.2	pounds	lb
	metric tons (1000 kg)	1.1	short tons	tn
Volume	milliliters	0.03	fluidounces	fl oz
	liters	2.1	pints	pt
	liters	1.06	quarts	qt
	liters	0.26	gallons	gal
	cubic meters	35	cubic feet	ft
	cubic meters	1.3	cubic yards	yd
Temperature	Celsuis temperature	9 5 (then add 32)	Fahrenheit temperature	F

Table of word-forming elements

Many of the prefixes and suffixes found in words used in this book and other cosmetology books originate from the anatomical terms of ancient times. These prefixes and suffixes are also known as word-forming elements and when used in combination with other elements, create words commonly found in usage today. Examples are the terms postnasal meaning behind the nose and supracostal meaning above the ribs. Such terms, therefore, are not unusual English, but rather terms stemming from classical Greek and Latin.

Set out below is a list of plain English words followed by the prefixes, suffixes and stems which contribute to their meaning. Prefixes are identified by a hyphen at the end. Suffixes are identified by a hyphen at the beginning. Stems which occur in various positions in words are identified by a hyphen both at the beginning and the end.

Word or term	Word-forming element	Word or term	Word-forming element
Abdomen	-coel-, -cel- [L]	End, extremity	-acr-, -tel- [Gk], -dist- [L]
After	post- [L]	Excess(ive)	-poly-, hyper- [Gk], super- [L]
Against	anti- [Gk], contra- [L]	Extremity	-acr- [Gk]
Ankle	-tars- [L]	Eye	-ocul- [L], -op(t)-, -opthalm- [Gk]
Arm	-brachi- [L]	Eyelid	-palpebr- [L], -blephar- [Gk]
Armpit	-axill- [L]	Face	-prosop- [Gk]
Artery	-arteri- [L]	Far, end	-dist- [L], -tel- [Gk]
Back (body)	-dors- [L], not (o)- [Gk]	Fat (tissue)	-adip [L]
Back, hind, rear	-poster(i)- [L]	Finger (and toe)	-digit- [L], -dactyl- [Gk]
Before	pre- [L], ante- [L], pro- [Gk]	Fingernail (and toenail)	-ungu(i) [L], -onych- [Gk]
Behind	post [L]	Flesh	-sarc-, -cre(at)- [L]
Below	infra-, sub- [L], hyp(o)- [Gk]	Foot	-ped- [L], -pod- [Gk]
Between, among	inter- [L]	Fore	-anter(i)-, ante- [L], pro- [Gk]
Beyond	ultr(a)- [L], met(a)- [Gk]	Forehead	-front- [L]
Blood	-hemat-, -hem-, -em- [Gk], -sangu- [L]	Forward	pro- [Gk], ante-, -anter(i)- [L]
		Front	-anter(i) [L]
Body	-corpor- [L], som(at)- [Gk]	Gland	-aden- [Gk]
Brain	-encephal- [Gk], -cerebr- [L]	Hair	-pil- [L], -trich- [Gk]
Calf	-sur- [L], -cnem [Gk]	Hand	-man(u)- [L], -cheir- [Gk]
Cartilage	-chondr- [Gk]	Head	-cephal- [Gk], -capit- [L]
Cell	-cyt- [Gk]	Hear, hearing	-aud(i)- [L], -ac(o)u- [Gk]
Cheek	-bucc- [L]	Heart	-cardi- [Gk], -cord- [L]
Cheek bone	-mal- [L], -zygom(at)- [Gk]	Heel	-calc- [L]
Chest	-pect- [L], -steth-, -thorac- [Gk]	High	hyper- [Gk], super- [L]
Collarbone	-cleid- [Gk], clavicul- [L]	Hind, behind	-poster(i)- [L]
Ear	-aur(i) [L], -ot- [Gk]	Hip, hipbone	-cox- [L], -isch- [Gk]
Elbow	-cubit- [L]	Hollow	-cav- [L], -coel-, -cel- [Gk]

Word or term	Word-forming element	Word or term	Word-forming element
Inflammation	-itis [Gk]	Nose	-rhin- [Gk], -nas- [L]
Injury	-trauma(t)- [Gk], -noci- [L]	Repair	-plasty [Gk]
Inside, within	intra- [L], en- [Gk]	Rib	-cost- [L]
Jaw	-gnath- [Gk]	Short	-brev- [L], -brach(y)-, -micr- [Gk]
Jaw, upper	-maxill- [L]	Shoulder	-om- [Gk], -humer- [L]
Jaw, lower	-mandibul- [L]	Shoulder blade	-scapul- [L]
Joint	-arthr- [Gk], -articul- [L]	Skin	-cut(i)- [L], -derm- [Gk]
Knee	-gen(u)- [L], -gon(y)- [Gk]	Spine, spinal column	-rhachi(d)- [L]
Leg	-crur- [L], -skel-, -scel- [Gk]	Stomach	-gastr- [Gk]
Less, below	infra-, sub- [L], hyp(o)- [Gk]	Sweat	-hidr- [Gk]
Ligament	-desm- [Gk]	Swell (ing)	-ede-, -oede-, -cele [Gk], -tum- [L]
Limb	-mel(o)- [Gk], -membr- [L]	Tears	-lacrim- [L], -dacry- [Gk]
Lip	lab(i)- [L], -cheil- [Gk]	Thigh	-femor- [L], -mer- [Gk]
Low	sub- [L], hyp(o)- [Gk]	Throat	-jugul-, -guttur- [L]
Lower	-infer(i) [L]	Tip, extremity	-acr(o) [Gk]
Lung	-pneumon- [Gk], -pulmon- [L]	Tissue	-hist [Gk]
Man, human	-anthrop- [Gk], -humin- [L]	Toe (and finger)	-dactyl- [Gk], -digit- [L]
Mouth	-or- [L], -stom(at)- [Gk]	Tongue	-lingu- [L], -gloss- [Gk]
Muscle	-my(o)- [Gk]	Under, below	sub- [L], hyp(o)- [Gk]
Nail (finger-toe)	-ungu(i)- [L], -onych- [Gk]	Up, upward	-sursum-, -superi- [L], -ana- [Gk]
Nape	-nuch- [L]	Upon, on	supra- [L]
Neck	-cervic-, -coll- [L], -trachel- [Gk]	Upper	-super(i)- [L], hyper- [Gk]
Nerve	-neur- [Gk]	Vein	-phleb- [Gk], -ven- [L]
		Vertebra	-spondyl- [Gk]

I. Table of thermometric equivalents
(fahrenheit to celsius scales)

CONVERSION FORMULA: (FAHRENHEIT DEGREES − 32) x 5/9 = CELSIUS DEGREES

F°	C°	F°	C°	F°	C°	F°	C°	F°	C°
0	− 17.78	21	− 6.11	42	5.56	63	17.22	84	28.89
1	− 17.22	22	− 5.56	43	6.11	64	17.78	85	29.44
2	− 16.67	23	− 5.00	44	6.67	65	18.33	86	30.00
3	− 16.11	24	− 4.44	45	7.22	66	18.89	87	30.56
4	− 15.56	25	− 3.89	46	7.78	67	19.44	88	31.11
5	− 15.00	26	− 3.33	47	8.33	68	20.00	89	31.67
6	− 14.44	27	− 2.78	48	8.89	69	20.56	90	32.22
7	− 13.89	28	− 2.22	49	9.44	70	21.11	91	32.78
8	− 13.33	29	− 1.67	50	10.00	71	21.67	92	33.33
9	− 12.78	30	− 1.11	51	10.56	72	22.22	93	33.89
10	− 12.22	31	− 0.56	52	11.11	73	22.78	94	34.44
11	− 11.67	32	0.00	53	11.67	74	23.33	95	35.00
12	− 11.11	33	0.56	54	12.22	75	23.89	96	35.56
13	− 10.56	34	1.11	55	12.78	76	24.44	97	36.11
14	− 10.00	35	1.67	56	13.33	77	25.00	98	36.67
15	− 9.44	36	2.22	57	13.89	78	25.56	99	37.22
16	− 8.89	37	2.78	58	14.44	79	26.11	100	37.78
17	− 8.33	38	3.33	59	15.00	80	26.67	101	38.33
18	− 7.78	39	3.89	60	15.56	81	27.22	102	38.89
19	− 7.22	40	4.44	61	16.11	82	27.78	103	39.44
20	− 6.67	41	5.00	62	16.67	83	28.33	104	40.00

CONVERSION FORMULA: (FAHRENHEIT DEGREES − 32) x 5/9 = CELSIUS DEGREES

F°	C°	F°	C°	F°	C°	F°	C°	F°	C°
105	40.56	134	56.67	163	72.78	192	88.89	221	105.00
106	41.11	135	57.22	164	73.33	193	89.44	222	105.56
107	41.67	136	57.78	165	73.89	194	90.00	223	106.11
108	42.22	137	58.38	166	74.44	195	90.56	224	106.67
109	42.78	138	58.89	167	75.00	196	91.11	225	107.22
110	43.33	139	59.44	168	75.56	197	91.67	226	107.78
111	43.89	140	60.00	169	76.11	198	92.22	227	108.33
112	44.44	141	60.56	170	76.67	199	92.78	228	108.89
113	45.00	142	61.11	171	77.22	200	93.33	229	109.44
114	45.56	143	61.67	172	77.78	201	93.89	230	110.00
115	46.11	144	62.22	173	78.33	202	94.44	231	110.56
116	46.67	145	62.78	174	78.89	203	95.00	232	111.11
117	47.22	146	63.33	175	79.44	204	95.56	233	111.67
118	47.78	147	63.89	176	80.00	205	96.11	234	112.22
119	48.33	148	64.44	177	80.56	206	96.67	235	112.78
120	48.89	149	65.00	178	81.11	207	97.22	236	113.33
121	49.44	150	65.56	179	81.67	208	97.78	237	113.89
122	50.00	151	66.11	180	82.22	209	98.33	238	114.44
123	50.56	152	66.67	181	82.78	210	98.89	239	115.00
124	51.11	153	67.22	182	83.33	211	99.44	240	115.56
125	51.67	154	67.78	183	83.89	212	100.00	241	116.11
126	52.22	155	68.33	184	84.44	213	100.56	242	116.67
127	52.78	156	68.89	185	85.00	214	101.11	243	117.22
128	53.33	157	69.44	186	85.56	215	101.67	244	117.78
129	53.89	158	70.00	187	86.11	216	102.22	245	118.33
130	54.44	159	70.56	188	86.67	217	102.78	246	118.89
131	55.00	160	71.11	189	87.22	218	103.33	247	119.44
132	55.56	161	71.67	190	87.78	219	103.89	248	120.00
133	56.11	162	72.22	191	88.33	220	104.44	249	120.56
								250	121.11

II. Table of thermometric equivalents:
(celsius to fahrenheit scales)

CONVERSION FORMULA: 9/5 CELSIUS DEGREES + 32 = FAHRENHEIT DEGREES

C°	F°	C°	F°	C°	F°	C°	F°	C°	F°
−20	−4.0	− 4	24.8	12	53.6	28	82.4	44	111.2
−19	−2.2	− 3	26.6	13	55.4	29	84.2	45	113.0
−18	−0.4	− 2	28.4	14	57.2	30	86.0	46	114.8
−17	1.4	− 1	30.2	15	59.0	31	87.8	47	116.6
−16	3.2	0	32.0	16	60.8	32	89.6	48	118.4
−15	5.0	1	33.8	17	62.6	33	91.4	49	120.2
−14	6.8	2	35.6	18	64.4	34	93.2	50	122.0
−13	8.6	3	37.4	19	66.2	35	95.0	51	123.8
−12	10.4	4	39.2	20	68.0	36	96.8	52	125.6
−11	12.2	5	41.0	21	69.8	37	98.6	53	127.4
−10	14.0	6	42.8	22	71.6	38	100.4	54	129.2
− 9	15.8	7	44.6	23	73.4	39	102.2	55	131.0
− 8	17.6	8	46.4	24	75.2	40	104.0	56	132.8
− 7	19.4	9	48.2	25	77.0	41	105.8	57	134.6
− 6	21.2	10	50.0	26	78.8	42	107.6	58	136.4
− 5	23.0	11	51.8	27	80.6	43	109.4	59	138.2

CONVERSION FORMULA: 9/5 CELSIUS DEGREES + 32 = FAHRENHEIT DEGREES

C°	F°	C°	F°	C°	F°	C°	F°	C°	F°
60	140.0	84	183.2	108	226.4	132	269.6	156	312.8
61	141.8	85	185.0	109	228.2	133	271.4	157	314.6
62	143.6	86	186.8	110	230.0	134	273.2	158	316.4
63	145.4	87	188.6	111	231.8	135	275.0	159	318.2
64	147.2	88	190.4	112	233.6	136	276.8	160	320.0
65	149.0	89	192.2	113	235.4	137	278.6	161	321.8
66	150.8	90	194.0	114	237.2	138	280.4	162	323.6
67	152.6	91	195.8	115	239.0	139	282.2	163	325.4
68	154.4	92	197.6	116	240.8	140	284.0	164	327.2
69	156.2	93	199.4	117	242.6	141	285.8	165	329.0
70	158.0	94	201.2	118	244.4	142	287.6	166	330.8
71	159.8	95	203.0	119	246.2	143	289.4	167	332.6
72	161.6	96	204.8	120	248.0	144	291.2	168	334.4
73	163.4	97	206.6	121	249.8	145	293.0	169	336.2
74	165.2	98	208.4	122	251.6	146	294.8	170	338.0
75	167.0	99	210.2	123	253.4	147	296.6	171	339.8
76	168.8	100	212.0	124	255.2	148	298.4	172	341.6
77	170.6	101	213.8	125	257.0	149	300.2	173	343.4
78	172.4	102	215.6	126	258.8	150	302.0	174	345.2
79	174.2	103	217.4	127	260.6	151	303.8	175	347.0
80	176.0	104	219.2	128	262.4	152	305.6	176	348.8
81	177.8	105	221.0	129	264.2	153	307.4	177	350.6
82	179.6	106	222.8	130	266.0	154	309.2	178	352.4
83	181.4	107	224.6	131	267.8	155	311.0	179	354.2
								180	356.0

GLOSSARY

OF

COSMETOLOGY TERMS

This Glossary lists words and terms used in practical cosmetology. In almost every instance the definitions refer to how the word is used in the field of cosmetology.

A

abarticulation—in anatomy, that species of articulation or structure of joints which admits manifest motion.

abbreviated—A shortened, reduced or briefer form.

abdomen—the belly; between the thorax and the pelvis.

abducent nerve—a motor nerve supplying the small muscles of the eye.

abductor—a muscle that draws a part of the body away from the axis line.

ability—quota or state of being able to perform.

abnormal—unusual; contrary to natural law or normal order.

abrasion—a scraping injury to the skin.

abscess—a hollow space containing pus.

absorb—to engulf, suck up or take in.

absorption—taking up or assimilation of one substance by another.

acceleration—an increase in rapidity.

accelerator—any agent or machine which increases rapidity of action.

accent—in hair tinting: color used to highlight or add to color tone.

accessory nerve—eleventh cranial nerve; affects the mastoid and muscles of the neck.

acetic acid—a colorless solution that is the chief acid of vinegar.

acetone—a colorless, inflammable volatile liquid, used as a nail enamel remover.

acid—chemical compound containing hydrogen ions that reacts with a base to form a salt; having a pH of less than 7.

acid rinse—a mixture of water and lemon juice or vinegar.

acne—inflammation of the sebaceous gland causing skin pustules.

acne albida—whitehead.

acne cream—a facial cream containing medicaments such as benzoin, boric acid, zinc oxide and calamine.

acne hypertrophica—pimples in which the lesions leave scars after healing.

acne keratosa—an eruption of papules consisting of horny plugs projecting from the hair follicles.

acne punctata—acne appearing as red papules in which are usually found blackheads.

acne pustulosa—acne in which the pustular lesions predominate.

acne rosacea—a form of acne due to congestion, in which the capillaries become dilated and sometimes broken.

acoustic nerve—eighth cranial nerve controlling the sense of hearing.

acrolein—a light volatile oily liquid giving off irritation vapor.

actinic—relating to the radiant energy of the chemically active rays of the spectrum.

activator—any agent, instrument, chemical, or device which induces action in an otherwise dormant substance.

activator machine (facials)—cleanses, stimulates, and helps firm the skin.

acute—severe symptoms; having a short course; not chronic.

adenoma sebaceum—small tumor originating in the sebaceous glands.

adhere—to remain in contact; to unite.

adhesive—a sticky substance that tends to adhere to others.

adipose tissue—fatty tissue.

adjust—to make exact; to fit.

adolescence—state or process of growing from childhood to manhood or womanhood.

adrenal—an endocrine gland situated on the top of the kidneys.

adult—grown up to full age or size.

adulterate—to alter, or to make impure by the addition of a foreign substance.

aeration—airing; saturating a fluid with air, carbon dioxide or other gas.

afferent nerves—convey stimulus from the external organs to the brain.

affinity—the force which impels certain atoms to unite with certain others to form compounds.

Afro styling—cutting and styling extremely curly (kinky) hair following its natural tendencies and according to its condition, so as to fit the head contour, facial structure and features.

afterrinse—a product used after a hair treatment for special purposes such as making hair easy to comb.

agent—an active power which can produce a physical or chemical effect.

agnail—hangnail.

alae nasi—the wing cartilage of the nose.

albinism—absence of pigment in the skin and its appendages.

albino—a person with very little or no pigment in the skin or hair.

alcohol—a readily evaporating colorless liquid, powerful stimulant, and antiseptic.

alimentary—the alimentary canal extends from the mouth to the anus.

alkali—the hydroxide of a metal; a substance having marked properties of a base (see **base**); opposite to acid.

alkaline—having the properties of an alkali; having a pH of more than 7.

allergic—sensitive to certain substances so as to cause an unpleasant reaction.

allergy—a disorder due to extreme sensitivity to certain foods or chemicals.

allergy test—a test to determine the existence or non-existence of extreme sensitivity to certain things, foods, or chemicals, etc., which do not adversely affect most individuals. Sometimes referred to as predisposition test, patch test, or skin test.

alopecia—baldness.

alopecia adnata—baldness at birth.

alopecia areata—baldness in spots.

alopecia dynamica—loss of hair due to destruction of the hair follicle.

alopecia follicularis—loss of hair due to inflamed hair follicles.

alopecia localis—loss of hair occurring at the site of an injury.

alopecia maligna—any form of alopecia that is severe and persistent.

alopecia prematura—baldness beginning before middle age.

alopecia seborrheica—baldness caused by diseased sebaceous glands.

alopecia senilis—baldness occurring in old age.

alum—sulphate of potassium and aluminum; used as a styptic.

alveola—a small hollow; branch of the internal maxillary artery.

amino acid—an organic acid, molecules of which combine into long chains to form proteins.

amino dye—a synthetic organic chemical dye; also called aniline dye, or coal-tar dye.

ammonia—a colorless gas with a pungent odor; soluble in water to form ammonium hydroxide (ammonia water).

ammonium hydroxide—a chemical formed from ammonia which is used to make ammonium thioglycolate.

ammonium sulfite—a chemical sometimes employed in a technique of chemical hair straightening.

ammonium thioglycolate—a chemical used in cold permanent waving and hair relaxing, sometimes referred to simply as "thio."

amyl acetate—a colorless, aromatic liquid employed in making nail polishes.

analysis—a process by which a substance is recognized and its chemical composition determined.

analysis, hair—an examination to determine the condition of the hair.

anatomy—the science of the organic structure of the body.

anemia—the condition in which the blood is lacking in red corpuscles or hemoglobin or both.

anesthetic—a substance to make the body incapable of feeling pain.

angiology—the study of blood vessels and lymphatics.

angle—the figure formed by the intersection of two straight lines at a given point. The size of the angle is expressed in degrees based on 360 degrees in a complete circle. An angle whose sides are perpendicular is a right angle and contains 90 degrees.

angular artery—supplies the lacrimal sac and the eye muscle.

aniline derivative hair tint—a synthetic organic hair dye or tint produced from aniline which in turn can be produced from coal tar; also known as coal-tar dyes or coal-tar derivative tints, amino dyes, etc.

aniline dye—see **aniline derivative hair tint**.

annular finger—ring finger.

anterior—situated before or in front of.

anthrax—malignant pustule; gangrenous carbuncle-like lesion.

antibody—a substance in the blood which builds resistance to disease.

antidote—an agent preventing or counteracting the action of a poison.

anti-perspirant—a strong astringent liquid or cream used to stop the flow of perspiration in the region of the armpits.

antiseptic—a chemical that prevents the growth of bacteria, temporary in action and milder than a disinfectant.

antitoxin—a substance in serum which binds and neutralizes poison.

aorta—the main arterial trunk leaving the heart and carrying blood to the various arteries throughout the body.

apex—the summit or extremity; the bottom end of the heart.

appendage—that which is attached to something else, and is a part of it.

appendix—a small intestinal organ.

applicator—an implement used for applying substances.

aqueous—pertaining to water.

aromatic—pertaining to or containing aroma.

arrector pili—the involuntary muscles originating in the papillary layer of the skin and connecting bases of the hair follicles, the contraction of which causes "goose pimples."

art—an especial facility in performing any operation, intellectual or physical.

arterial—pertaining to an artery.

arteriole—a terminal artery continuous with the capillary network.

arteriosclerosis—abnormal hardness and dryness of the arterial coats resulting from chronic inflammation.

artery—a vessel that conveys blood from the heart.

articulation—a connection between two or more bones.

artificial nails—plastic pre-manufactured nails, or plastic nails formed and hardened right on the customer.

asepsis—a condition in which bacteria are absent.

aseptic—free from bacteria.

ash—in hair tinting: a shade containing no red or gold tones (drab).

ash blonde—hair that is not brassy.

assimilation—the incorporation of materials prepared by digestion from food into the tissues of the body.

asteotosis—a deficiency of the sebaceous secretions.

astringent—a lotion or medicine that causes contraction of the tissues.

asymmetrical—lack of symmetry or balance - hair styled to one side – without equal proportion.

athlete's foot—a fungus foot infection.

atom—the smallest particle of an element which still retains all of the properties of that element.

atrichia—absence of hair.

atrium—the auricle of the heart.

atrophy—a wasting away of the tissues from lack of nutrition.

auditory nerve—eighth cranial nerve, controlling the sense of hearing.

auriculotemporal—sensory nerve affecting the temple, just in front of the ear.

autonomic nervous system—the sympathetic nervous system; controls the involuntary muscles.

B

baby fine hair—a hair fiber that is fine to an extreme degree, due to its particularly small diameter and delicate construction.

bacillus—rod-like shaped bacterium.

back combing—combing the short hair toward the scalp, starting at the scalp and working toward the ends, while the hair strand is held in a vertical position.

backward curl—curls wound in a counterclockwise direction on the left side of the head; on the right side of the head, such curls will be wound in a clockwise direction.

bacteria—(singular: **bacterium**)—microscopic vegetable growths having single celled or non-cellular bodies of various shapes living in soil, water and organic matter; microbes or germs.

bactericide—an agent that destroys bacteria.

bacteriology—the science which deals with bacteria.

balance—(hairstyling) the harmony with the degree of height and proper width designed in a hairstyle.

baldness—a deficiency of hair.

bandeau—hairpiece: one which is sewn to a headband covering the hairline.

band wig—hairpiece: one which is sewn to a headband covering hairline.

bang—the front hair cut so as to fall over the forehead.

barrel curl—a strand of hair held directly up from the scalp and wound, with a large center opening, in a croquignole fashion and fastened to the scalp in a standing position.

basal layer—the layer of cells at base of epidermis closest to the dermis.

base—the lower part or bottom; (i.e., the area on which a curl is placed); chemically: the hydroxide of a metal—a bitter tasting corrosive compound having a pH of over 7 (opposite of an acid); hair straightening: a preparation used to protect the scalp which is applied before application of chemical straightener.

base direction—line of motion created in base area.

basic hair shaping—a haircut that is sufficiently versatile to accept a variety of contemporary hair fashions of equal facility.

beautician—one trained in the art of beautifying the personal appearance: a cosmetologist.

beauty culture—the study and practice of the improvement of personal appearance.

beeswax—the prepared secretion of the bee, used in hairdressing for unruly ends and strengthening sewing in making hairpieces.

benign—mild in character; inactive.

benzine—an inflammable solvent used as a cleansing fluid.

benzoin—a balsamic resin used as a stimulant.

bevel—to slope the edge of a surface.

bicarbonate of soda—baking soda; relieves burns, itching, urticarial lesions and insect bites.

biceps—a muscle producing the contour of the front and inner side of the upper arm.

bichloride—a compound having two parts or equivalents of chlorine to one of the other elements.

bigoudi—a small wooden curler on which the hair is wound for curling in wig work.

bile—a yellowish or greenish viscid fluid secreted by the liver to aid digestion.

bind—(in wiggery) a piece of ribbon which is attached to the underside of the wig, encircling the head.

biochemistry—study of the chemical compounds and processes occurring in living organisms; a combination of biology and chemistry.

biology—the science of life and living things.

birthmark—any mark which is present at birth, usually lasting.

blackhead—a comedone; a plug of sebaceous matter.

bleach—see **hair lightening**.

bleached hair—hair from which the color has been wholly or partially removed by means of a bleaching or lightening solution.

bleaching solution—used to remove color, usually hydrogen peroxide with addition of ammonia or other agents.

bleach pack—a bleach solution prepared in a thick consistency.

blemish—a mark, spot or defect marring the appearance.

blend—(hair shaping) to cut layers of hair so that they merge into each other smoothly with little variation in length apparent.

blending—(hair coloring) a merging of one tint with another.

blister—a collection of serous fluid causing a raised elevation of the skin.

block—a head-shaped form upon which a wig is placed for a specific purpose.

blocking—the division of the hair into practical working areas. (See **sectioning** and **scale**.)

blond, blonde—a person of fair complexion, with light hair; a color of hair.

blonde on blonde—two blonde colors used on separate areas of the head, to achieve a blending of light and dark shades of blonde.

blonding—to lighten hair, preparing it for a toner.

blood—the nutritive fluid circulating through the arteries and veins.

blood poison—an infection which gets into the blood stream.

blood vascular system—comprised of the heart, arteries, veins, and capillaries, which distribute blood throughout the body.

blood vessel—an artery, vein or capillary.

blue light—a therapeutic lamp used to soothe the nerves and ease pain.

bluing rinse—a solution used to neutralize the unbecoming yellowish tinge on gray or white hair.

blunt—having an edge or point that is not sharp.

blunt cutting—cutting straight across a strand of hair held between the index and middle fingers, resulting in a slight tapered effect. (See **club cutting**.)

blusher (make-up)—a rouge of subtle color used for highlighting.

bob—a short haircut for women.

bobby pin—a "U" shaped clamp type pin with ends pressed close together.

body—consistency; solidity of texture.

body permanent—a permanent given to impart body, rather than a curl or visible wave to the hair.

boil—a subcutaneous abscess which drains out onto the surface of the skin.

boiling point—the temperature at which a liquid begins to boil.

bond—a linkage between two atoms forming a molecule.

bone—the hard tissue forming the framework of the body.

boom-boom iron—a curling iron with oversized rod and groove.

booster—a trade name for an agent which raises the potency of an activated substance; a bleach and peroxide accelerator.

bop iron—a curling iron with oversized rod and groove. (See **boom-boom iron** and **directional iron**.)

boric acid—used as an antiseptic.

bouffant—extreme height and fullness in a finished hairstyle.

braid—to weave or interlace together.

brain—that part of the central nervous system contained in the cranial cavity, and consisting of the cerebrum, the cerebellum, the pons, and the medulla oblongata.

brassy tone—a harsh brassy-like color quality. Red and/or gold highlights.

breakage—a condition in which hair splits and breaks off.

brightening—highlighting the appearance of hair by slightly lightening or toning the natural shade.

brilliantine—an oily composition that imparts luster to the hair.

bristle—short, stiff hairs found on brushes.

brittle—easily broken; fragile.

brittle hair—dry, fragile hair that is easily broken.

brow—the forehead.

bruise—to injure without laceration.

brunette—a person having dark brown or black hair.

brush-combing—back combing with a brush.

brush curl—to turn, blend, or form the hair into curls with the use of hair brush, fingers, and/or comb.

brushing—(facials) a machine with a facial brush attachment which rotates at high speed. Used for oily skin and back or shoulder treatments.

brush out—the opening and blending of the hair setting, curls, waves, etc., into the finished style, using a hair brush and/or a comb.

buccal nerve—a motor nerve affecting the buccinator and the orbicularis oris muscle.

buccinator—a thin, flat muscle of the cheek.

buckles—(hairstyling) distortion of, or a bend in a curl.

buffer—a manicuring instrument which is used with powdered polish to add lustre on the nails.

bulb—the lowest extremity of the hair.

bulbous—pertaining to, or like a bulb in shape.

bulky—a great thickness.

C

cache peigne—a covered comb used for attaching a chignon to the hair.

calamine lotion—zinc carbonate in alcohol used for dermatitis.

calcium—enters into the composition of bone.

callus—skin which has become hardened.

camomile—an herb used as a brightening rinse for blond hair.

camphor—a mild cutaneous stimulant; has a slightly anaesthetic and cooling effect.

cancellous—having a porous or spongy structure.

candlelighting—a light-tone blond with dark overtones.

caninus—the levator anguli oris muscle which lifts the angle of the mouth.

canities—the science which treats canities. (White

hair).

canities—grayness or whiteness of the hair.

canities, congenital—a type of gray hair transmitted by heredity as in albinism.

canities, premature—grayness of hair at an early age.

canities, senile—grayness of hair in old age.

cap—(wiggery) the netting and binding of a wig which together form the base to which the hair is attached.

cape—a waterproof garment used to protect the patron's clothing during beauty treatment.

capillary—any one of the minute blood vessels which connect the arteries and veins.

caput—pertaining to the head.

carbohydrate—a substance containing carbon, hydrogen, and oxygen.

carbolic acid—phenol made from coal tar; used in dilute solution as an antiseptic.

carbon—coal; an elementary substance in nature which predominates in all organic compounds.

carbon-arc lamp—an instrument which produces ultraviolet rays.

carbon dioxide—carbonic acid gas; product of the combustion of carbon with a free supply of air.

carbuncle—a large circumscribed inflammation of the subcutaneous tissue.

cardiac—pertaining to the heart.

carotid—the principal artery of the neck.

cartilage—gristle; a nonvascular connective tissue softer than bone.

carved curl—a section of hair, sliced with a comb from a shaping and formed into a curl without lifting the stem from the shaping.

cascade—a hairpiece with an oblong-shaped base primarily worn on the back of the head.

cascade curl—a pin curl with a large open center and fastened to the scalp in a standing position.

castile soap—soap made from olive oil and other oils as opposed to synthetic detergents.

catabolism—chemical changes which involve the breaking down process within the cells.

catalyst—an agent that causes an increased rate of chemical change; or converts the relatively inactive molecules of an element into active atoms of that element; hastens a chemical reaction.

caustic—a strong alkali capable of eating away other substances by chemical action.

caustic soda—common name for sodium hydroxide.

cell—a small mass of protoplasm containing one or more nuclei capable alone or with other cells of performing functions of life; the smallest form of living matter capable of functioning as an independent unit.

cellular—consisting of, or pertaining to cells.

centigrade—consisting of 100 degrees; the centigrade thermometer assigns zero to the freezing point of water and 100 to the boiling point.

cerebellum—the posterior and lower part of the brain.

cerebral—pertaining to the cerebrum.

cerebrospinal system—consists of the brain, spinal cord, spinal nerves and the cranial nerves.

cerebrum—the superior and larger part of the brain.

certified color—a pure commercial coloring product usually temporary in effect.

chemical—relating to chemistry.

chemical change—a reaction resulting in the formation of one or more new substances, each having its own properties.

chemical compound—a combination of elements chemically united in definite proportions.

chemical hair relaxer—a chemical agent which is employed to partially straighten curly hair.

chemical hair relaxing—the process of partially straightening curly hair by the use of chemical agents.

chemical hair straightener—a chemical product used to completely straighten kinky hair.

chemistry—the science dealing with the composition of substances and the many ways they change or react with others.

chignon—a pattern of hair worn at the crown or nape, created from hair, or from a hairpiece.

chiropody—the art of treating minor conditions of the feet.

chloasma—large brown irregular patches on the skin, such as liver spots.

chlorazene—a trade term for the chemical chloramine T used as an antiseptic or disinfectant.

chlorine—a greenish yellow gas used in combined form, such as sodium hypochlorite (clorox) and chloramine T, as a disinfectant and bleaching agent.

chloro-zol—a trade name for a special tablet of chloramine T used for preparing a germicide.

cholesterol—a waxy substance, called a lipid, found in animal tissues and the bloodstream; it is present in lanolin, and is used to prevent dryness of the hair and scalp.

chromosomes—tiny dark-stained bodies found in the nucleus of the cell; transmit hereditary characteristics in cell division.

chronic—long-continued; the opposite of acute.

chrysarobin—a powerful parasiticide powder used in the treatment of skin diseases.

chuck—to strike vigorously; a term used in massage.

cicatrix—the skin or film which gradually forms a scar over a wound.

cilia—the eyelashes.

circle—a geometric shape formed by a curved line every point of which is equal distance from a center point.

circle design—equal distribution of straight or curved lines from a center point; a rotary flow.

circulation—orderly flow, such as the passage of blood throughout the body.

circulation, pulmonary—blood circulation from the heart to the lungs and back to the heart.

circumscribed—surrounded by a line or boundary.

citric acid—an acid obtained from lemon and lime juices or fermentation used for making rinses.

clamp—a device for compressing or holding something, such as a mannequin on a shelf or hair within a wave-clamp or in heat waving.

clavicle—collar bone, linking the sternum and scapula.

clay—an earthy silicate and mineral material, which hardens when dried, used for facial packs.

clay pack—a colloidal clay preparation used in facial treatments to stimulate the circulation and temporarily contract the pores. Recommended for oily skin.

cleansing cream—a water-in-oil emulsion used to remove make-up and impurities.

clip—a small, clamp-like device used to secure pin curls, hair rollers, or waves.

clipping—(haircutting) the act of cutting split hair ends with the scissors; the operation of removing the hair by the use of hair clippers.

clockwise—(hairstyling) the movement of hair, in shapings or curls, in the same direction as the hands of a clock.

clot—a mass or lump of coagulated blood.

club cutting—cutting the hair straight off, while being held flat to the contour of the head, which results in a straight line without a tapered effect.

coagulate—to clot.

coal tar dye—another term for aniline dye. (See **aniline derivative hair tint**.)

coarse hair—a hair fiber that is relatively large in diameter or circumference.

coating—residue left on the hair shaft which retards the action of chemicals upon the hair fiber.

coccus—spherical cell bacterium.

cocktail shampoo—the process of diluting tint with shampoo or water, and working it through the head like a shampoo without developing time.

coiffeur—a male hairdresser.

coiffeuse—a female hairdresser.

coiffure—a hairstyle.

coil—to twist or wind spirally.

cold waving—a system of permanent waving involving the use of chemicals rather than heat.

cold waving lotion—often ammonium thioglycolate, a chemical solution, used to break the bonds in the polypeptide chains in the hair molecules so they can be re-formed on a rod.

collodion—a thick liquid used to form an adhesive covering.

colloid—a suspension of fine particles of a solid, or another liquid, in liquid to form a translucent solution.

color—any tint or hue as distinguished from white.

color blender—(hair coloring) a product which cleanses, highlights, blends in gray and streaked hair to the natural color.

color builder—(hair coloring) a filler to build color on over-porous hair so it can take and hold color evenly.

color-fast shampoo—a mild shampoo especially formulated for cleansing and protecting the color stability of hair that has been tinted or lightened.

color filler—(hair coloring) a preparation used to provide fill for porous spots in the hair during tinting, lightening, and after permanent waving.

colorist—a qualified hairdresser specializing in the application of hair colors.

color lifter—a dye remover; a chemical to remove artificial color from the hair.

color mixing—mixing two shades together for an in-between color.

color remover—a prepared commercial product which removes tint from the hair.

color rinse—a rinse which gives a temporary tint to the hair.

color shampoo—a preparation which colors and cleanses the hair permanently without requiring sectioning and subsectioning.

color test—a test performed prior to coloring, from which a strand of hair is treated with the precise formula in order to determine timing and the correctness of formula.

comb—an instrument used to dress, part and arrange the hair.

combout—(hairstyling) the opening and blending of the hair setting, curls, waves, etc., into the finished style, using a hair brush and/or a comb.

combustion—the rapid oxidation of any substance, accompanied by the production of heat and light.

comedone extractor—an instrument used for the removal of blackheads.

comedones—blackheads; tiny facial spots caused by obstructed pores.

communicable—able to be communicated; transferable.

complexion—hue or general appearance of the skin, and the face.

component—an ingredient, a part of the whole.

composition—the quality of being put together.

compound—a combination of elements chemically united in definite proportions to the original ingredients.

compound henna—Egyptian henna to which has been added other dye preparations.

compressor—a muscle that compresses a part of the body.

concave—hollow or incurved.

concentrated—condensed; increasing the strength by diminishing the bulk.

concentric—having a common center such as hair movements and growths radiating from a common point.

condensation—a physical change of a gas into a liquid.

conditioner—any product applied to the hair to improve its condition.

conditioning—the application of special chemical agents to the hair to help restore its strength and body.

condyle—a rounded articular surface at the extremity of bone.

congeal—to change from a fluid to a solid state.

congenital—existing at birth; born with.

congestion—overfullness of the capillary and other blood vessels in any locality or organ.

connecting—(fingerwaving) the meeting of a ridge from one side of the head with a ridge from the opposite side of the head.

connecting line—connection between two circular shapes of clockwise and counterclockwise forces. Also referred to as dividing.

conoid—cone shaped.

consistency—a degree of density or firmness of either a solid or a liquid.

contact—bringing together so as to touch.

contagion—transmission of specific diseases by contact.

contagious—transmittable by contact.

contamination—pollution; soiling with infectious matter.

contour—the outline of a figure or body.

contractility—the property of contracting or shortening, as in muscular stimulation.

contraction—having power to become shorter; the act of shrinking.

contrast—exhibiting notable difference by comparison.

convex—curving outward like the segment of a circle, rising or swelling on the exterior surface into a round form; arched; opposite of concave.

corium—the derma or true skin.

cornification—the process of becoming a horny substance or tissue; a callosity.

coronary—resembling a crown; encircling another body part; relating to the heart.

corpuscles, red—cells in blood whose function is to carry oxygen to the body tissue.

corpuscles, white—cells in the blood whose function is to destroy disease germs.

corrode—to destroy gradually by chemical action.

corrugations—alternate ridges and furrows.

corrugator supercilli—draws eyebrows inward and downward, thus causing vertical wrinkles at the root of the nose.

cortex—the second layer of the hair.

cosmetic dermatology—a branch of dermatology devoted to improving the health and beauty of the skin and its appendages.

cosmeticians—those professionally engaged in improving the complexion, skin, and hair.

cosmetics—any substances used externally to cleanse, alter or improve the appearance of a person.

cosmetic therapy—improving a person's appearance and mental attitude through cosmetology.

cosmetologist—one skilled in the professional practice of improving beauty.

cosmetology—the science of beautifying and improving the complexion, skin, hair or nails.

counterclockwise—the movement of hair in the opposite direction to the hands of a clock.

coverage—(hair coloring) the degree to which gray and white hair has been colored.

cowlick—a tuft of hair forming a spiral turn, growing contrary to the usual growth pattern of the hair.

cranial—pertaining to the cranium.

cranium—the bones of the head that enclose the brain.

crayon—(hair coloring) a stick of temporary coloring material.

cream—a semisolid cosmetic usually in a jar.

creme—a thick liquid usually in a bottle.

creme rinse—a hair rinse containing surface-active agents which deposit a light film on the hair making it feel silky and easier to comb.

crepe wool—wool strands sometimes used to confine hair ends in winding.

cresol—a colorless, oily liquid or solid derived from coal tar and used as a disinfectant.

crest—a ridge, line or thin mark made by folding or doubling, as a crest between two waves, where one begins and the other ends.

croquignole—winding of the hair from ends to the scalp.

croquignole curling (thermal waving)—curling a strand of hair with hot curling iron, developing the entire curl at about 1 inch from the scalp.

crown of the head—the top back part of the head.

curd—soap residue found on the hair after an unsatisfactory shampoo.

curl—a circle, or circles, within a circle.

curl, barrel—a strand of hair held directly up from the scalp and wound, with a large center opening, in a croquignole fashion and fastened to the scalp in a standing position.

curl, base—foundation of the curl, at the scalp.

curl, cascade—a pin curl with a large open center and fastened to the scalp in a standing position.

curl, directional—a pin curl made in the opposite direction of the front line curl.

curl direction—the movement of hair in order to form a particular pattern or style (i.e., forward, toward the face; backward, away from the face, clockwise, counterclockwise).

curl, maypole—overlapping around finger with ends on outside.

curl, overlapping—a pin curl which partially rests on a previously made pin curl.

curl, pin—a strand of hair which is combed smooth and ribbon-like and wound into a circle with the ends on the inside.

curl, ridge—a curl placed behind and close to the ridge of a fingerwave.

curl, roller—a section of wet hair wrapped around a roller.

curl, sculpture—same as pin curl.

curl, stand-up—a pin curl with a large open center and fastened to the scalp in a standing position.

curl, supporting—a pin curl made in the same direction of the front line curl.

curl stem—that part of the pin curl between the base and the first arc of the circle.

curler—that which curls hair, either using water or heat.

curling—a process of hair curling and waving.

curling paper—used in a technique of making a pin curl with a folded piece of paper to help control short, wiry hair. Also used with a paper-curling iron.

curling, round—a process of rolling the hair tightly and evenly around a heated curling iron, starting at the ends.

curly—tending to curl; full of curls.

curriculum—the course outline of study in a school.

curvature lines—moldings; shapings; combing out into a combined concave and convex flow.

curved line—a half circle or a shaping started from a given point.

cutaneous—pertaining to the skin.

cuticle—the outer layer of the skin (epidermis) or hair; also refers to the fold of epidermis around the fingernail.

cuticle remover—a solution of alkali, glycerine and water used to soften and remove dead cuticle around the nail.

cutis—the derma or deeper layer of the skin.

cylindrical—having the form of a cylinder—the surface formed by a straight line moving in a circle around a parallel straight line.

cyst—a closed abnormally developed sac containing fluid.

cysteine—an amino acid containing sulfur which is easily oxidized to cystine.

cystine—a crystalline amino acid containing two sulfur atoms found in proteins (as keratins).

D

damaged hair—a hair condition characterized by one or more of the following: high porosity, brittleness, split ends, lightened ends, dryness, lack of gloss and elasticity.

dandruff—pityriasis: scales formed upon the scalp.

dandruff shampoo—a commercially prepared product to aid in the control and elimination of dandruff when used as directed.

decalvant—removing the hair, making bald.

decomposition—breaking down into constituent parts by chemical action or delay.

deficiency—a lacking.

deltoid—a muscle of the shoulder.

demarcation—a line setting bounds.

dendrite—a treelike branching of nerve fibers extending from a nerve cell.

dense—thick, heavy.

density—the number of hairs per square inch at the scalp.

deodorant—a substance that conceals offensive odors, or stops perspiration.

deodorize—to free from odor.

depilation—removal of hair above the skin.

depilatory—a caustic alkali, used to remove hair.

deportment—manner of conduct or behavior.

depression—a hollow or sunken area.

depressor—that which presses or draws down; a muscle that depresses.

depressor alae nasi—a muscle which contracts the nostril.

depressor anguli oris—a muscle that depresses the angle of the mouth.

depressor labii inferioris—a muscle that depresses the lower lip.

derivative—that which is derived or deduced from another.

derma—the true skin; the sensitive layer of the skin below the epidermis.

dermal—pertaining to the skin.

dermatitis—inflammation of the skin.

dermatitis seborrheica—dermatitis found with overactive sebaceous glands.

dermatitis venenata—technical term for hair dye poisoning; inflammation of skin caused by hair dye.

dermatologist—a professional specialist in the science of treating the skin and its diseases.

dermatology—the science which treats the skin and its diseases.

dermatosis—any disease of the skin.

dermis—the layer of the skin below the epidermis.

design—arrangement of shapes, lines, and ornamental effects which create an artistic unit.

design (two dimensional)—a pattern effect on a flat surface.

design (three dimensional)—a sculpturing effect with hair, creating volume and/or indentation into a shape.

detergent—an agent that cleanses; a synthetic soap.

develop—the action of a hair tint or bleach taking effect.

developer—a chemical agent which is mixed with tints, dyes, and bleaches; usually a peroxide.

developing time—(tinting and bleaching) the period required for the hair bleach or tint solutions to act upon the hair. Timing begins at completion of application.

dexterity—skill, expertness in manual acts.

diagnosis—the recognition of a disease or problem from its symptoms.

diagram—a drawing that explains rather than represents.

dialysis—the separation of different substances in solution by their unequal diffusion through membranes.

diamond mesh—(wig making) a method of sewing weft into diamond-shaped meshes. The weaving incorporates one strand of wire.

diaphragm—a muscular wall which separates the thorax from the abdomen.

diet—a course of food selected with reference to a particular health condition.

differentiate—to indicate specific differences.

diffusion—a spreading out.

digestion—the process of converting food into a form which can be readily absorbed by the body.

digits—fingers or toes.

dilator naris anterior—a muscle which dilates the nostril.

dilute—to make thinner by mixing.

dimension—measure as to length, with height, thickness or circumference.

dimensional coloring—(two or three dimensional)—two or three shades of the same color cast on one head of hair.

dimensional design or form—(hairstyling) three dimensional sculpturing effect with hair, creating volume or volume indentation into a shape and silhouette. (See **design**.)

diplococcus—bacteria exhibiting pairs.

direct point—parting of straight or curved lines from a point to the outline of a circular shape.

directional curl—a pin curl made in the opposite direction of the front line curl.

directional iron—a curling iron with oversized rod and groove used for straight, smooth lines in styling.

discoloration—the development of an undesired color.

disease—a pathologic condition of any part or organ of the body.

disease carrier—a healthy person capable of transmitting germs to another person.

disinfectant—a substance that completely destroys bacteria.

dispensary—a place where supplies are prepared and dispensed.

dissolve—to make a solution of; to break up.

distill—to concentrate or extract the essence of a substance.

distinctive—characteristic, making a difference.

disulfide links—bonds or cross-linkages in the polypeptide chains of hair molecules which are broken by the action of cold waving lotions or hair straighteners so the hair can be reformed.

dormant—inactive.

dorsal—pertaining to the back.

double knotting—the means of attaching hair to the netting of hairpieces.

downward—(hairstyling) toward the shoulder—usually away from the part.

drab—(hair coloring) a yellowish gray color. No red or gold.

dropping a wave—to discontinue a wave instead of carrying it around the entire head.

dry hair—hair that is devoid of sufficient or normal natural oils.

dry shampoo—a substance used to cleanse the hair without the use of soap and water. (Powder or liquid.)

duct—a passage or canal for fluids.

dye—(haircoloring) a chemical that adds color to hair.

dye remover—a substance that removes dye from hair.

dye solvent—a chemical compound used to remove artificial color from the hair.

dynel—a synthetic hair-like fiber used in making ready-to-wear wigs and hairpieces.

E

eczema—an inflammatory condition of the skin, characterized by redness, itching and lesions.

efferent nerves—nerves conveying impulses away from the central nervous system.

effilate—to cut the hair strand by a sliding movement of the scissors in an opened position.

effileing—(haircutting) slithering; the tapering of hair to graduated lengths. From the French term "effile".

effleurage—a light, stroking movement in massage.

Egyptian henna—a pure vegetable hair dye.

elasticity—the ability of hair to be stretched and return to its original length.

electricity—a form of energy, exhibiting magnetic, illuminating or thermal effects usually utilized in the form of electric current.

electrification—the application of electricity to the body by holding an electrode in the hand and charging the body with electricity.

electrocoagulation—short wave, single needle method of electrolysis.

electrode—an applicator for directing the use of electricity on a patron.

electrologist—skilled in applying the science of electrolysis.

electrology—science in relation to electricity.

electrolysis—destruction of body tissues and hair roots by means of an electric current.

electrolytic cup—an appliance used to cleanse the skin, before giving a massage.

element—a simple substance which cannot be decomposed or separated into any other substance.

embryo—in the first stages of development.

emery board—a disposable instrument having cutting ridges, used to remove a portion of the free edge of the nail.

emollient—an agent that softens or soothes the surface of the skin.

emotion—mental excitement.

emulsified—a binder or surface active agent added to a mixture of two liquids to keep the particles of each in suspension.

emulsion—a mixture of two liquids shaken together until they break up into minute globules held in suspension by an emulsifier.

enamel—gloss; polish.

endocrine—internal secretion or hormone.

endosteum—the membrane covering the inner surface of bone in the medullary cavity.

end papers—special papers used to control the ends of hair in wrapping. (i.e., in winding hair on rods or rollers).

ends, hair—last inch of a strand of hair furthest from the scalp.

environment—surrounding conditions.

enzyme—a substance which induces a chemical change in other substances, without undergoing any change itself.

epicranium—the structure covering the cranium.

epicranius—the scalp muscle.

epidemic—affecting many people; a prevailing disease.

epidermis—the outer epithelial portion of the skin.

epilation—the removal of hair from beneath the surface of the skin.

epithelial tissue—a term applied to cells that form the epidermis.

epithelium—a cellular tissue or membrane, with little intercellular substance, lining a cavity.

eponychium—the extension of cuticle at base of nail and the continuous fold of epidermis at the sides.

equation—a shorthand method of expressing a chemical reaction.

eruption—a visible lesion of the skin marked by redness.

erysipelas—an acute infectious disease accompanied by inflammation of the skin.

erythema—a superficial blush or redness of the skin.

erythrocyte—a red blood cell; red corpuscle.

esophagus—the canal leading from the pharynx to the stomach.

esthetic—relating to the nature and principles of beauty. (Also spelled aesthetic.)

ether—obtained from distilling alcohol with sulphuric acid; used as an anesthetic.

ethics—principles of good character and proper conduct.

ethmoid—a bone forming part of the walls of the nasal cavity.

etiology—the science of the causes of disease.

European hair—human hair found in Europe and considered to be the finest hair available; used in constructing wigs and hairpieces.

evaporation—change from liquid to vapor.

excitation—the act of stimulating.

excoriation—act of stripping or wearing off the skin.

excretion—that which is eliminated from the body.

exfoliation—throwing off scales from the skin as in dandruff.

exhalation—breathing outward.

exhaustion—loss of vital power from fatigue, nerves, or disease.

expansion—dilation or swelling.

expert—one who has special knowledge or skill in a particular subject.

extensibility—capable of being extended or stretched.

extensor—a muscle which extends or straightens out a limb or part.

externus—external; the outside.

extremity—the distant end or part of any organ; a hand or foot.

exudation—act of discharging from a body through pores, as sweat or moisture; oozing out.

eyeball—the globe of the eye.

eyebrow—the hair and tissue above the eye.

eyelashes—the hair of the eyelids.

eyelid—the protective covering of the eyeball.

eye-shadow—a cosmetic applied on the eyelids, consisting of waxes, oils and coloring matter in various forms.

F

face framing—(hair coloring) a narrow section of hair around the face (1" to 1¹/₂") lightened one or two shades.

facial—pertaining to the face, also a short term for facial treatment.

fade—to become indistinct; to gradually disappear.

Fahrenheit—pertaining to the Fahrenheit thermometer. Water freezes at 32° F. and boils at 212° F.

fall—a long artificial section of hair worn at the top back of the head.

faradism—electrical treatment used for stimulating activity of the tissues.

fascia—a sheet of connective tissue covering internal parts of the body.

fat—soft-solid material found in animal tissue.

fatigue—bodily or mental exhaustion.

favus—a contagious disease of the skin, with crusts.

feathercut—a basic hair shaping consisting of a smooth crown, surrounded by tapered ends.

featheredge—shortening the hair in a graduated effect to a fine edge.

felon—paronychia of the nail.

fermentation—a chemical decomposition of organic compounds into more simple compounds, by the action of an enzyme.

fetid—having a foul smell.

fever—rise of body temperature.

fever blister—the presence of vesicles over an inflammatory base; herpes simplex.

fiber—a slender thread or filament.

fibrin—the agent in coagulation of the blood.

fibrinogen—a substance producing fibrin.

fibrous—consisting of or like fibers.

file—a hardened steel instrument having cutting edges used to remove a portion of the free edge of the nail.

filler—a preparation used to provide fill for porous spots in the hair during tinting, lightening and permanent waving.

filter—anything through which a gas or a liquid is passed to cleanse or strain it.

fine—(texture) being of a small diameter, not coarse or thick.

fine hair—a hair fiber that is relatively small in diameter or circumference.

finesse—delicate skill.

fingerwave—the process of setting the hair in a pattern of waves through the use of fingers, comb and a waving lotion.

finishing cream—an emulsion of stearic acid in water, such as powder base and foundation cream, used before make-up is applied.

finishing knot—the manner of weaving the final strand of hair, on a hairpiece, to prevent the work from becoming loose.

fishhook—a flaw in the curling of hair which results in the tip ends of hair bending in a direction other than that of the rest of the curl.

fission—(biology) reproduction of bacteria by cellular division.

fissure—a narrow opening made by separation of parts; a slit.

fixative—(in hairstyling) a hairdressing used to

keep hair in place; (in cold waving) a chemical agent stopping the chemical action of the waving solution; (in hair straightening) a chemical agent stopping the processing of the chemical hair relaxer.

flabby—lacking firmness.

flat weft—once-in weaving; in hairstyling used to practice fingerwaving.

flexor—a muscle that bends or flexes a part or a joint.

florid—flushed with red.

fluff—hair that is combed so that it has a soft, airy effect.

fluid—a non-solid substance (liquid, cream, or gas).

fly weft—fine weaving used for the top row of a hairpiece made of a weft.

foil—a thin sheet of metal such as aluminum or tin.

follicle—the depression in the skin containing the hair root.

folliculitis—an inflammation of any follicle.

foramen—a passage through a bone or membrane.

forces—causes of motion or change, also in hairstyling, the direction of motion from a point in straight or curved degrees.

formaldehyde—a poisonous gas with powerful disinfectant properties, formerly used in sterilizing cabinets.

formalin—a 40% solution of formaldehyde in water.

formula—abbreviation for a chemical compound giving the symbols of the elements that compose it and the proportions in which they are combined.

forward curl—curls wound toward the face, in a clockwise direction on the left side of the head and a counterclockwise direction on the right side.

forward wave—a wave shaped toward the face.

foundation—(wig making) the base of a hairpiece, made of net, to which the hair is attached.

foundation cream—an emulsion used as a base for make-up. (See finishing cream.)

fragile hair—hair which is lacking in normal flexibility, tensile strength, and resilience; usually brittle and easily broken.

fragilitas crinium—brittleness of the hair.

frayed—worn away by friction.

freckle—a brown spot on the skin, caused by uneven development of pigment.

free edge—the part of the nail body extending over the fingertip.

French flow technique—using a double row of rollers or pin curls in an oblong shape.

French fluff (soap cap)—the process of diluting a bleaching or tint with shampoo or water, and working it through the head like a shampoo.

French lacing—same as teasing.

French twist—a vertical seam-like arrangement of hair at the back of the head.

friction—resistance when one body is rubbed against another.

fringe—a wispy type bang.

frizz—hair having too much curl.

frontal—in front; relating to the forehead.

frontalis—muscle of the scalp.

frosting—(haircoloring) to lighten or darken small selected strands of hair over the entire head.

fuller's earth—a soapy clay used as a foundation for packs and masks.

fulling—a massage movement.

fumigant—a gaseous substance capable of destroying bacteria.

fumigation—destruction of germs by a fumigant.

function—a normal action of a part.

fungus—a spongy growth of diseased tissue on the body.

funny bone—the bone on the inner side of the forearm; a tingling sensation is felt when the nerve is struck.

furrow—a groove.

furuncle—a boil.

G

ganglion—a subcutaneous tumor or cystic swelling connected with tendon sheaths.

gangrene—the dying of tissue.

gastric juice—the digestive fluid secreted by the glands of the stomach.

gauze—a thin open-meshed cloth used for dressings.

gel, styling—a jelly-like hair setting preparation; in chemistry, a word for the semisolid mass formed by some colloidal materials in water.

gentian violet—an antiseptic used in the first aid treatment of a burn.

germ—a bacillus; a microbe.

germicide—a solution that will destroy germs.

germinative layer—the deepest layer of the epidermis resting on the corium.

glamour—alluring and often illusory charm.

gland—a secretory organ of the body.

glimmer—a rouge which imparts a gloss.

glint—luster; shine.

glycerine—a syrupy, alcoholic compound which is soluble in water. Used in many cosmetic creams.

goiter—enlargement of the thyroid gland.

granular layer—the stratum granulosum of the skin.

granules—small grains.

granulosum—granular layer of the epidermis.

great auricular—a nerve affecting the face, ears, neck and parotid gland.

greater occipital—sensory and motor nerve affecting the splenius, complexus and scalp.

gristle—cartilage.

groom—to make neat.

groove—(hairstyling) the valley between two ridges; (in thermal irons) the shell part of the iron into which the rod fits.

Guiche curl—a short flat "C" shaped curl placed on the skin near the cheek bone.

H

hacking—a chopping stroke made with the edge of the hand in massage.

hackling—(wig making)—a process by which tangled hair may be disentangled.

hair—slender thread-like outgrowth on the body.

hair bleaching—removing the natural pigment from the hair.

hair bobbing—the cutting of women's hair in a short fashion.

hair bulb—the lowest extremity of the hair.

hair clipping—removing split ends with the scissors.

hair color lotion—a semipermanent hair coloring which does not need a developer.

haircutting—shortening and thinning of the hair.

hairdressing—the art of arranging the hair into styles.

hair dyeing—the process of giving the hair new and permanent color.

hair follicle—the depression in the skin containing the root of the hair.

hair lace—(wig making) a form of net foundation made of stiffened human hair.

hair lift—an implement used to lift hair into balance while combing.

hair lightening—removing color pigment from hair; bleaching.

hairline—the edge of the scalp where the hair begins.

hair papilla—a small cone-shaped elevation at the bottom of the hair follicle.

hairpiece—wiglet; fall; cascade.

hair pressing—straightening curly or kinky hair with heated iron or comb.

hair pressing cream—a cream used in hair pressing as a protective lubricant for normal hair.

hair pressing oil—an oil used in hair pressing as a protective lubricant for dry hair.

hair restorer—a metallic, progressive dye.

hair root—that part of the hair within the follicle.

hair set tape—a tape which sticks to wet hair when setting bangs, side curls, and back of neck hair when designing straight lines or when the hair is too short to set on rollers or in pin curls.

hair shaft—the hair which projects beyond the skin.

hair shaping—the art of haircutting.

hair softener—(in hairstyling) a hair pomade, cream or creme rinse; (in hair tinting) a peroxide and ammonia mixture applied before tinting.

hair spray—a cosmetic applied in the form of a mist to hold the hairstyle in place.

hair straightener—a chemical agent used in straightening kinky or curly hair.

hair test—a sampling of how the hair will react.

hair tinting—the act of adding color pigment to hair.

hair trim—the act of cutting the hair lightly.

hair weaving—the process of sewing a base of nylon thread into the remaining natural hair and tying wefted hairs to that base to eliminate the appearance of baldness.

half wig—a front or back hairpiece made on half of a wig base to blend with the wearer's natural hair.

halitosis—foul breath.

halo lightening—(hair coloring) only the crown hair is lightened one or two shades.

handmade—describes a wig or hairpiece made by hand.

hand tied—(wig making) a process in which individual hairs are inserted with a needle into a mesh in designing a hairpiece; also referred to as a ventilated hairpiece.

hangnail—a strip of epidermis at the side of the nail.

hard water—water containing certain salts of calcium and magnesium which do not lather easily with soap.

harmony—relationship of shapes and lines.

heart—a hollow muscular organ which keeps up the circulation of the blood.

heating cap—an insulated cap, containing interwoven electrical wires, which is used for heating the hair and scalp in corrective treatments.

heat waving—a system of permanent waving employing either machines or chemicals to generate heat.

heavy side of the head—the side of the head to which most of the hair is directed.

hematocyte—a blood corpuscle.

hemoglobin—the iron-containing protein pigment in the red blood cells.

hemorrhage—bleeding.

henna—used as a dye, imparting a reddish tint only.

henna, compound—pure henna to which has been added one or more metallic preparations.

henna, white—magnesium carbonate; mixed with peroxide and ammonia, it is used to bleach hair. Excellent for bleaching hair on arms, legs and face.

heredity—transmission of qualities from parents to their children genetically.

herpes—an inflammation of the skin having small vesicles in clusters.

herpes simplex—fever blister; cold sore.

hidrosis—abnormal sweating.

high fashion—the accentuated design of the day's fashion trends, either in hairstyling or hair coloring.

high fashion blonding—a double process coloring where the hair is lightened and then toned.

high frequency—violet ray machine used for stimulation.

highlighting—the introduction of color to increase the brightness of the hair.

hirsute—hairy; often used to refer to overgrown or pubescent hair.

hirsuties—growth of hair in unusual locations, as on the faces of women.

histology—the science of the structure of organic tissues.

hives—a skin eruption.

horizontal—parallel to the ground; usually

described in terms of left and right as opposed to up and down.

hormone—substance formed in one organ and carried in the blood to another organ, which it stimulates to functional activity.

horny—hard.

humidity—moisture in the air.

hydro—a prefix denoting water.

hydrocystoma—a variety of sudamen appearing on the face.

hydrogen—a colorless, odorless and tasteless gas which readily combines with other elements to form millions of chemical compounds.

hydrogenate—to add hydrogen to the molecules of an unsaturated organic compound usually for the purpose of changing it to a cream consistency.

hydrogen peroxide—an oxidizing agent used in cosmetology for bleaching, developing aniline dyes, and as a fixative for thio cold waving lotions.

hydroxy cellulose—a chemical thickening agent; makes watery liquids thick.

hygiene—the science of preserving health.

hygroscopic—absorbing and retaining moisture.

hyperhydrosis—excessive sweating.

hypersecretion—excessive secretion.

hypersensitivity—usually affected by external agencies or influences to which a normal individual does not react.

hypertrophy—abnormal increase in the size of an organ; overgrowth.

hypodermic—beneath the skin.

hypoglossal—under the tongue.

hyponychium—the extension of the skin underneath the free edge of the nail.

I

icing—(hair coloring) a half frosting (front half or back half).

idiosyncrasy—an individual characteristic or peculiarity due to the action of certain drugs, articles of diet, etc.

illuminating—(hair coloring) a process in which one specific area, usually bangs, is lightened two or three shades.

imbrications of hair—tiny overlapping scales on the hair cuticle.

immerse—to dip, submerge in a liquid.

immiscible—a liquid that will not mix with another liquid.

immunity—freedom from or resistance to.

impetigo contagiosa—a contagious disease, characterized by an eruption which develops into pustules.

implement—an instrument used to accomplish a given work.

incandescent—giving light and heat.

incubation—the period between the implanting of the contagion and the development of the symptoms.

indentation—a curved, hollow or spaced form.

index—the forefinger.

indigo—a blue dyestuff (rinse).

indirect point—partings of an oval shape, using straight or curved lines, first parting out of the circumference, then inner section all from one point.

inelasticity—the ability of hair to stretch but not return to its former shape.

inert—inactive.

infect—to cause infection.

infection—contamination of the body tissues by germs.

infection, general—the result of germs gaining entrance into the blood stream.

infection, local—confined to only certain portions of the body.

infectious—capable of causing infection.

inferioris—below; lower.

inflammation—the reaction of the body to irritation.

infraorbital—below the orbit; a sensory and motor nerve affecting the cheek muscles, nose, and upper lip.

infrared—thermal radiation of wavelengths lying outside of the visible spectrum.

infratrochlear—sensory nerve affecting the skin of the nose and the inner muscle of the eye.

ingrown hair—a hair that has grown underneath the skin.

ingrown nail—the growth of the nail into the flesh instead of the tip of the finger or toe.

inhalation—the inbreathing of air.

inner and outer circle—(hair sectioning) inner has a pie-shape base section; outer has an oblique base.

innominate veins—veins of the neck.

inoculation—the means by which protective agents are introduced into the body.

inorganic—matter not relating to living organisms.

insanitary—so unclean as to endanger health.

insoluble—incapable of being dissolved.

insulin—a protein hormone essential to carbohydrate metabolism, used in treatment of diabetes.

insurance—protection against loss, damage or injury.

integument—a covering of the skin.

internus—pertaining to the inside.

interosseous—lying between or connecting bones.

interstice—a small hole in a tissue; pore.

intestine—the digestive tube from the stomach to the anus.

inversion—turning inward.

involuntary muscles—muscles that function without the action of the will.

iodine—an antiseptic for cuts, bruises, etc.

ion—an atom carrying an electric charge.

iris—the colored, muscular diaphragm of the eye which regulates the pupil.

irradiation—the process of exposing to sunlight rays.

irritant—an irritating agent, a stimulus.

J

J.L. (International Hairgoods Color Ring)—original color ring developed by Jacques Leclebart and accepted by the industry.

joining—(hairstyling) the process whereby a fingerwave is lengthened; connecting.

joint—a connection between bones.

jowl—the hanging part of the chin.

jugular—the large vein in the neck.

K

kaolin—fuller's earth; used in a poultice with glycerine (mud pack).

karaya gum—a gum obtained in India and Africa; used to make wave set preparations.

keratin—the basic constituent molecule of hair and nails.

keratoma—an acquired thickened patch of the epidermis.

keratosis—the presence of circumscribed overgrowths of the horny layer.

kidney—the organ which excretes urine.

kinky—very curly hair.

knead—to work and press with the hands as in massage.

knotting—(wig making) a process in which individual hairs are inserted with a needle into a mesh or net base and locked in place by a hand-twisting or hooking action.

L

labium—lip.

laboratory—a space containing apparatus for conducting experiments and analysis.

laceration—a tear of the skin.

lacrimal—bone at the front of the orbits.

lacing—(hairstyling) a delicate teasing along the entire strand of hair giving the hair a lacy quality.

lacquer, nail—a thick liquid which forms a glossy film on the nail—colored and colorless.

lacteals—the lymphatics of the small intestines that take up the chyle.

lanolin—purified wool fat.

lanugo—the fine hair which covers most of the body.

larynx—the upper part of the trachea or wind pipe; voice box.

latissimus dorsi—a broad, flat muscle of the back.

layer—(hairstyling) a single horizontal thickness or line of hair.

lemon rinse—lemon juice or citric acid diluted; used to lighten the color of the hair.

lentigo—a freckle; pigmentation in the skin.

lesion—an abnormal change caused by injury or disease.

lesser occipital—the nerve supplying muscles at the back of the ear.

leucocyte—a white corpuscle.

leucoderma—white patches on the skin.

leuconychia—a whitish discoloration of nails.

levator—a muscle that elevates a part.

levator anguli oris—muscle that raises the angle of the mouth and draws it in.

levator labii superioris—muscle that elevates upper lip and dilates the nostrils.

levator palpebrae—muscle that raises upper eyelid.

lift—(hair coloring) to lighten by a barely perceptible amount, without definite color change.

lift, hair—an implement used to lift hair into balance while combing.

ligament—band of fibrous tissue that connects bones or holds an organ in place.

light—(hairstyling) the high area of a convex effect in a hairstyle; volume.

lighten—to partially remove color.

lightener—a chemical agent used to lighten or remove the color from hair.

light therapy—the application of light rays for treatment.

limp—lacking firmness or strength.

line of demarcation—a line in the hair which distorts the evenness of the hair either in form or color.

liquefy—to reduce to the liquid state.

litmus paper—paper strips that are reddened by acids and turned blue by alkalies.

liver—an internal organ which secretes bile for digestion.

lobe—a curved or rounded projection (i.e., ear lobe).

lockjaw—a firm closing of the jaw due to tonic spasm of the muscles of mastication.

long lasting rinse—a semipermanent color.

loose scalp—a scalp that can be moved easily with finger manipulations.

lotion—a liquid preparation for cosmetic and external medicinal use.

louse—(plural: lice)—pediculous; an animal parasite infesting the hairs of the head.

lubricant—an agent that makes things smooth and slippery; eliminates friction.

lucidum—the clear layer of the epidermis.

lung—an organ of respiration.

lunula—the half-moon shape at the base of the nail.

lustre—glass; gleam; radiance.

lustreless—without shine or gloss; dull.

luxuriant—abundant.

lymph—a pale yellow coagulable fluid, produced by the filtration of the blood through the walls of the capillaries, which circulates in the lymphatics of the body.

lymphatic system—lymph flowing through lymph spaces, lymph vessels, and lymph nodes (an accessory to the blood vascular system).

machineless—without a machine; permanent waving by heat from a chemical reaction.

machine made—describes a wig or hairpiece made by machine, rather than by hand.

macula—a spot or discoloration level with the skin; a freckle.

magnet—having the power to attract iron bodies.

magnify—to increase the size of.

magnum—largest bone of the wrist.

make-up—skin cosmetics; and application thereof.

malar—the cheek bone.

malformation—an abnormal shape or structure.

malignant—resistant to treatment; a tumor occurring in severe form.

malpighian—the deeper portion of the epidermis.

management—directing; carrying on; control; administrating.

mandible—the lower jawbone.

mandibular nerve—the fifth cranial nerve which supplies the muscles and skin of the lower part of the face.

manicure—the care of the hands and nails.

manicurist—one who specializes in the care of the hands and nails.

manipulation—working or operating with the hands or by mechanical means.

mantle—the fold of the skin into which the nail root is lodged.

manus—the hand.

marbleizing—(hair coloring) interlacing light and dark sections or shades of hair within one head of hair.

marcel waving—a technique of forming waves in the hair by means of thermal irons.

marrow—a soft fatty substance filling the cavities of bone.

mascara—a cosmetic containing synthetic waxes plus lampblack or synthetic dyes, used to darken the eyelashes.

masque—(facials) a jellied, vegetal product, aids the skin in moisture retention.

massage—manipulation of the face or body by rubbing, kneading, tapping, etc., to increase circulation, promote absorption.

massage cream—an emollient cream intended for lubrication of the skin, also called tissue creams or nourishing creams.

masseter—a muscle of the jaw used in mastication (chewing).

masseur—a man who practices massage.

masseuse—a woman who practices massage.

mastication—the act of chewing.

mastoid—a process of the temporal bone behind ear.

matching—(hairstyling) the meeting of a ridge from one side of the head with a ridge from the opposite side of the head.

matrix—the formative portion of a nail.

matter—a substance that occupies space and has weight.

matting—the packing of hair at the scalp area as a result of teasing or back combing hair.

maxilla, inferior—lower jawbone.

maxilla, superior—upper jawbone.

maypole curl—a curl made by overlapping a hair strand around the finger with the ends on the outside.

meatus—passage or channel of the ear.

medial—pertaining to the middle.

medium hair—a hair fiber neither especially large nor small in circumference, but a thickness about halfway between fine and coarse.

medulla—innermost portion or pith of hair fiber.

medulla oblongata—the posterior part of the brain, continuous with the spinal cord.

medullary—pertaining to the innermost portion or medulla.

melanin—the tiny grains of pigment in the hair cortex which causes natural hair color.

membrane—a thin layer of pliable tissue, serving as a covering.

mentalis—the muscle that elevates the lower lip, and the skin of the chin.

mental nerve—a nerve which supplies the skin of the lower lip and chin.

mesh—(foundation) a wig base made of net.

metabolism—the life process of the cell.

metacarpus—the bones of the palm of the hand.

metatarsus—the bones which comprise the instep of the foot.

metallic—relating to metal.

metallic dye—a progressive hair dye which is composed of a mixture of metallic salts from copper, or lead, or silver, and vegetable dyes.

meter—an instrument used for measuring; the basis of the metric system (equivalent to approximately 39.37 inches).

method—an established procedure or order of doing something.

metric—pertaining to the meter as a measurement.

micro—very small; slight; millionth part of.

microbe—a microorganism; a minute one-celled bacterium.

micrococcus—a minute bacterial cell having a spherical shape.

micron—particle visible under the microscope; one millionth of a meter.

microorganism—microscopic plant or animal cell.

microscope—an instrument for making enlarged views of minute objects.

microspira—pathogenic bacteria which cause cholera.

miliaria—an eruption of minute vesicles due to retention of fluid.

miliaria rubra—prickly heat; burning and itching.

milium—a small whitish pimple due to a retention of sebum; a whitehead.

milliamperemeter—an instrument measuring a small flow of electric current.

mineral—any inorganic material found in the earth's crust.

mineral salts—salts derived from an inorganic chemical compound.

mini-braid—a very narrow, sometimes pencil slim, strands of hair worn in loops, bands, or wired into fantasy shapes.

mini-fall—a loose-hanging hairpiece, above shoulder length, attached at the crown; shorter than a fall.

mini-wig—a very short wig with short ends over the entire hairpiece.

minking—(hair coloring) reverse frosting.

mitosis—the usual process of cell reproduction of the human tissues.

mixing—(hair coloring) mixing two shades together for an in-between color; (wig making) the intermingling of hair of various shades and/or lengths.

mixture—a combination of substances in which the ingredients are mechanically mixed, but not chemically changed.

mobility—being easily moved.

mode—fashion; style.

mold—a directional movement which will not maintain its shape, when combed freely, unless it is combed back into its molded line.

mold—(hairstyling) curved or straight lines in a shape creating a pattern.

molded curl—a pin curl, sliced with a comb from a shaping and formed into a curl without lifting the stem from shaping.

molded shape—outline of a straight or curved line, on the head form, scaled to a certain size.

mole—a small spot on the skin.

molecule—the smallest particle of an element or compound that can exist independently.

monilethrix—beaded hair; a condition of constrictions, giving the appearance of a string of beads.

moonlighting—(hair coloring) lightening and interlacing sections of light and dark hair within one head of hair.

moons—(manicuring) a crescent-shaped area exposed at the base of the nail created with the application of nail enamel.

motor nerves—nerves that carry impulses from nerve centers to muscles.

mount—(wig making) the intermingling of hair of various shades and/or lengths.

movement—a position of a hair motion; a change of place, condition or posture; a rhythmic quality.

mucous membrane—a membrane, secreting mucus, which lines the passages which lead to the exterior.

mucus—a clear slippery secretion of the mucous membranes produced to moisten and protect those passages.

muscle—the contractile tissue by which movement is accomplished.

muscle strapping—a massage treatment used to reduce fatty deposits.

muscle tone—the normal degree of tension in a muscle.

mutation blonding—(hair coloring) blending of light and darker blonde shades; also known as blonde on blonde.

myocardium—the muscular substance of the heart.

myology—a scientific study of muscles.

naevus—a congenital skin blemish.

nail—the horny plate located toward the end of the finger or toe.

nail bed—where the body of the nail rests.

nail body—where the horny nail blade is upon the nail bed.

nail fold—nail wall.

nail grooves—grooves between the nail walls and the nail bed.

nail lacquer—a liquid which forms a glossy film on the nail, colored or colorless; nail enamel.

nail matrix—the portion of the nail bed extending beneath the nail root.

nail mold—a form fitting the natural nail into which is placed a plastic compound plus a conversion liquid so that it can be inverted on the nail, thus forming an artificial nail.

nail root—located at the base of the nail.

nail rouge—a dry or paste polish.

nail wall—cuticle covering the sides and base of the nail body.

nail white—a nail cosmetic used to whiten the free edge of the nail; in pencil, paste, or string form.

nape—the back part of the neck.

naris—a nostril.

nasalis—a muscle and nerve on the side of the nose, just above the top.

nasocilliary—a nerve affecting the mucous membrane of the nose.

natural growth pattern—the direction (grain) in which the hair grows naturally.

neckline—where the hair growth of the head ends and the neck begins.

negative skin test—direct proof that the substance involved is compatible with the body.

nerve—a cord, made up of bundles of nerve fibers, through which impulses are transmitted.

nervous system—made up of the brain, spinal cord, nerves, ganglia and parts of the receptor.

net foundation—a wig base made of silk, cotton, linen, or nylon net.

network—any interconnected chain, group, or system of lines.

neuritis—inflammation of nerves.

neurology—the science of the structure of the nervous system.

neuron—the unit of the nervous system.

neutral—indifferent; (in chemistry) neither acid nor alkaline, having a pH of 7.

neutral blonde—a color neither ash nor gold, but rather a beige blonde.

neutralization—(in cosmetology) stopping any action or process.

neutralizer—(in cosmetology) refers to the oxidizing agent which stops the action of cold wave lotion, dyes, etc.

nit—the egg of a louse attached to a hair.

nitrogen—a gaseous element, found in air and living tissue.

no-base—(hair straightening) a milder chemical straightener usually having the base included in the product.

node—a knot or knob; a knuckle.

nodosa—having knot-like swellings.

nodule—a small node.

nonpathogenic—non-disease producing.

nonresistant—the condition of the hair which does not repel or offer opposition to penetration or softening.

nonstriated—involuntary muscle function without the action of the will.

nonvascular—not supplied with blood vessels.

nostril—an external opening of the nose.

noxious—poisonous.

nozzle—the projecting end of a hose or container.

nucleus—nuclei (plural)—the active center of cells.

numectron pads—(facial) used when oil is applied to penetrate the skin by means of electronic movements.

O

obese—fat.

oblique—slanting.

oblong—an elongated oval shape.

oblong design—concentric oval curves from a given point.

obnoxious—offensive.

obsolete—out of date.

occipital—the bone which forms the posterior part of the skull.

occipito-frontalis—the scalp muscle.

occiput—the back of the head.

occupational disease—disease due to certain kinds of employment, often due to contact with chemicals.

oculist—a specialist in diseases of the eyes.

oculomotor—third cranial nerve; controlling the eye.

oculus—the eye.

oil bleach—a combination of sulphonated oil, with or without coloring, usually activated just before use by the addition of hydrogen peroxide.

oiled silk—(wig making) used to protect those areas of a man's hairpiece where an adhesive is placed.

oily hair—hair with an above normal secretion of natural scalp oil.

oily skin—skin that is excessively oily due primarily to overactive sebaceous glands.

ointment—a fatty mixture used externally.

olfactory—first cranial nerve, the special nerve of smell.

one application, one process, or one step coloring—a process that decolorizes (bleaches) and colors in one application.

onychatrophia—atrophy of the nails.

onychauxis—enlargement of the nails.

onychia—inflammation of the matrix of the nail.

onychoclasis—breaking of the nail.

onychocryptosis—ingrowing nail.

onychogryposis—denotes enlargement with increased curvature of the nail.

onycholysis—loosening of the nail without shedding.

onychophagy—biting the nails.

onychophosis—growth of epithelium in the nail bed.

onychophyma—degeneration of the nail.

onychoptosis—falling off of the nails.

onychorrhexis—abnormal brittleness of the nails and splitting of the free edge.

onychosis—any disease of the nails.

onyx—a nail of the fingers or toes.

opaque—not transparent to light.

operator—(beauty salon) one who is able to perform correctly any service rendered professionally in the care of the face, hair. A cosmetologist.

ophthalmic—pertaining to the eye.

optik—second cranial nerve; the nerve of sight.

optimistic—hoping for the best.

orangewood stick—a stick made of orangewood used in manicuring.

orbicularis oculi—the ring muscle of the eye.

orbicularis oris—a muscle of the mouth.

orbit—the bony cavity of the eyeball; the eye-socket.

organ—a part of the body exercising a function.

organic—pertaining to substances derived from living organisms.

organism—any living being, animal or vegetable.

orifice—a mouth; an opening.

origin—the starting point of a nerve; the place of attachment of a muscle to a bone.

osmidrosis—foul smelling perspiration.

osmosis—the passage of fluids and solutions through a membrane.

osseous—bony.

osteology—science of the anatomy.

ottoman—a footstool.

outline—a line that defines a shape.

oval—an enclosed curved line with unequal distance from a given central point.

oval design—unequal curvature lines from a given central point.

ovary—one of the two reproductive glands in the female, containing the ova.

overlap—when tint or lightener is allowed to run on to the previously tinted or lightened hair during applications.

overlapping curl—a pin curl which partially covers its adjacent curl.

over porosity—a condition where hair reaches an undesirable stage of porosity requiring correction; difficult to color or permanent wave.

over processing—overexposure of hair to the action of chemicals or materials used.

oxidation—the addition of oxygen to another substance, or chemical process.

oxidation dye—another term for aniline derivative hair tint.

oxidize—to combine oxygen with another substance.

oxidizing agent—a substance which releases oxygen in a chemical reaction.

oxygen—an element found free in the atmosphere as a colorless, tasteless, odorless gas, also capable of combining with all other elements except inert gases.

P

pack—a special cosmetic formula used to beautify the face, and treat oily conditions.

packing—severe back combing, teasing, etc.; emphasis at the scalp, giving the strand of hair almost a rigid quality.

palate—the roof of the mouth.

palatine bones—the bones at the back part of the nasal fossae.

palmar—referring to the palm of the hand.

palpebra—eyelid.

palpebrarum—pertaining to the eyelids.

pancreas—a gland connected with the digestive tract.

panel—an area between two partings.

paper curling—a method of curling hair, using a triangular piece of paper and a heated pinching iron.

papilla, hair—a small elevation at the bottom of the hair follicle.

papillary layer—the outer layer of the dermis.

papular—characterized by papules.

papule—a pimple; a small elevation on the skin.

paraffin—a white mineral wax consisting of hydrocarbons.

para dye—an aniline derivative hair tint.

parasite—an organism living on or in another organism, and drawing its existence therefrom.

parasiticide—a substance that destroys parasites.

paronychia—felon; an inflammation of the tissues surrounding the nail.

paratoid—a gland near the ear.

paraphenylene-diamine—an aniline derivative used in hair coloring products.

parting—a dividing line separating hair.

parting silk—(wig making) fine, strong silk used for making partings on wigs.

patch test—a skin test designed to determine an individual's sensitivity to chemicals.

pate—top of the head.

pathogenic—disease producing.

pathology—the study of modifications of the functions and changes in structure caused by disease, something abnormal.

pattern forms—(hairstyling) an outline of head shapes into which the diagram of a style is recorded.

pectoralis—a muscle of the breast.

pedicare—the care of the feet and toenails; pedicure.

pediculosis capitis—infestation of lice in the hair (on the head).

pedicure—the care of the feet and toenails; pedicare.

pencil—(hair coloring) a temporary hair color (in the shape of a lipstick).

penetrating color—color that enters the hair cortex to effect a change in pigmentation.

pep bags—a trade name for a bleach and peroxide accelerator.

pepper and salt—a term used for a mixture of gray and white hair.

pepsin—an enzyme which digests protein.

percussion—a form of massage consisting of repeated taps of varying force.

perfume—a preparation having an essence, used for scenting.

pericardium—the membranous sac around the heart.

periosteum—the fibrous membrane covering the surface of the bones.

peripheral system—the nerve endings in the skin and sense organs.

peristalsis—muscular movements of the digestive tract.

permanent color—color that never shampoos out, nor diminishes over a period of time, but remains until hair grows out.

permanent wave, cold—a wave produced by breaking the cross-linkages in the hair molecule by use of a chemical solution (cold wave lotion) and reforming the hair structure on a rod.

permanent wave, heat—a system of permanent waving employing heat rather than chemicals.

permanent wave, pin curl—a cold permanent in which the hair is set in pin curls and/or rollers instead of being wound on rods.

permanent waving—the alteration of the hair structure by a process of softening, re-shaping, and then hardening into its new form.

permeable—capable of passing fluids through its pores.

peroxide—short term for hydrogen peroxide.

peroxide rinse—a rinse used to lighten the color of the hair slightly.

peroxometer—(hydrometer)—a device which measures the strength of hydrogen peroxide.

personality—the physical and mental qualities in a person.

perspiration—sweat; the fluid excreted from the sweat glands.

petrissage—the kneading movements in massage.

petrolatum—vaseline; a yellow mixture of semisolid hydrocarbons obtained from petroleum.

peruke—an old fashioned name for a wig.

pharynx—the upper portion of the digestive tube, behind the nose and mouth.

pH (potential of hydrogen)—the symbol for hydrogen ion concentration; the pH scale expresses the relative degree of acidity or alkalinity in numbers from 0 to 14 (these numbers are actually the negative logarithm of the number of hydrogen gram-ions per liter).

pH papers—indicators of pH by change of color.

phenol—carbolic acid; dilute solution is used as an antiseptic and disinfectant.

phosphorus—an element found in the bones, muscles and nerves.

phyma—a swelling on the skin larger than a tubercle.

physical—relating to the body.

physical change—altering a substance in form or state without changing chemical composition.

physics—science that deals with matter and motion.

physiognomical haircutting—cutting hair into a particular hairstyle and adapting it to an individual, with relation to facial features.

physiology—the science of the functions of living things.

physiotherapy—the use of natural forces such as light, heat, air, water, and exercise in the treatment of disease.

pigment—any organic coloring matter.

pigmentation—the deposition of pigment in the skin.

pilose—covered with hair.

pilus—hair.

pimple—any small elevation of the skin.

pin curl—a strand of hairs organized into a flat ribbon form, and wound into a series of continuous untwisted circles within circles.

pit—a surface depression.

pith—the innermost portion of the hair shaft.

pituitary—a ductless gland located at the base of the brain which produces various secretions essential to basic body functions.

pityriasis—dandruff.

pityriasis capitis simplex—a scalp inflammation marked by dry dandruff.

pityriasis pilaris—a scalp inflammation characterized by an eruption of papules surrounding the hair follicles.

pityriasis steatoides—a scalp inflammation marked by oily type of dandruff.

pivot—the exact point from which the hair is directed in forming a curvature shaping.

pivot point—a given point; origin or beginning of design.

planned pattern—a circular formation or design to be followed in order to achieve definite effects.

plasma—the fluid part of the blood and lymph.

plastic applicator—a squeeze bottle used for applying tints, lightener, and permanent waving lotion.

plastic cap—a cap made of plastic used as a head covering to help hold in the body heat when coloring and/or permanent waving: (also protects against the effects of air conditioning during the processing or developing time.)

platelets—blood cells which aid in the formation of clots.

platysma—a broad thin muscle in the neck area.

pledget—absorbent cotton wrapped in gauze (about the size of a twenty-five cent piece).

plexus—a network of nerves or vines.

pluck—a firm sudden pull.

pneumogastric nerve—tenth cranial nerve relating to the lungs and the stomach.

podiatrist—one who treats diseases of the feet.

point knotting—(wig making)—a method of knotting which ensures that only the points of the hair remain as part of the finished work.

pomade—a lubricant for the hair which imparts sheen.

pompadour—horizontal waves set and combed without a part, with or without height.

pomphus—a whitish elevation of the skin.

pore—a small opening of the sweat glands of the skin.

porosity—ability of the hair to absorb liquids.

porous—full of pores; permeable to liquids.

porous hair—a hair condition which is characterized by pore-like spaces between the overlapping scales of the cuticle layer.

portable—carried easily.

position—location of special line of effect; location of scale relating to the head form.

posterior—situated behind.

posterior auricular—a nerve which regulates muscles in the posterior surface of the ear.

postiche—an artificial hairpiece; curls, braids, wiglets, falls, cascades, or other extra hairpieces used in creating coiffures.

posture—the position of the body.

potassium hydroxide—an alkali used in the manufacture of soft soaps.

pour-it-on tints—hair coloring preparations which are applied in the same manner as shampooing hair. Require no partings, sectioning, or subsectioning.

powder base—a finishing cream used before applying make-up.

powder bleach—a fast acting oxygen-releasing agent such as sodium perborate usually mixed with peroxide to form a strong bleaching paste.

powder dry shampoo—a substance used to cleanse the hair, employing a mixture of oris root, borax, whitemeal, etc. (No soap or water.)

prebleaching—a decolorizing process, preliminary to the application of the desired color.

precipitation—the formation of an insoluble substance.

predisposition—susceptibility to disease; allergy.

predisposition test—a skin test designed to determine an individual's sensitivity to chemicals.

prelighten—to lighten in preparation for a second coloring procedure.

pressing—a method of straightening kinky hair with a heated comb or iron.

presoftener—a mixture of peroxide and ammonia applied to the hair in order to make easier the penetration of tint into the hair. Insures complete coverage.

preventive—warding off.

primary—first.

problem hair—hair that is difficult to color, permanent wave or straighten.

procerus—pyramidalis nasi muscle of the nose.

processing time—the period of time required for a

chemical action upon the hair to achieve the desired results.

profession—vocation; work which requires special knowledge and training.

profuse—abundant.

prognosis—the foretelling of the probable course of a disease.

progressive dyes—hair color restorers; color develops with continued applications.

pronate—to bend forward.

prong—the round rod of the thermal iron.

prophylactic—preventing disease.

prophylaxis—the prevention of disease.

proportion—a harmonious relationship or balance; scale or size.

prostration—the state of being weak.

protective base—a petroleum base, applied to the hair and scalp as necessary in order to protect them from the active agents contained in the chemical hair straightener.

protectors—articles or equipment which protect a patron of a beauty salon. (Neck strips, shampoo cape, ear pads, etc.)

protein—a complex organic substance, present in all living tissues, necessary in the diet.

protinator—a trade name for an agent which accelerates the release of oxygen in bleaching.

protrude—to project forward or outward.

psoriasis—a skin disease with red patches, covered with adherent white scales.

psychic—relating to the mind.

psychology—the science of the mind and its functions.

pterygium—a forward growth of the eponychium with adherence to the surface of the nail.

pterygoideus—the internus and externus muscle between mandible and cheek bone.

ptomaine—a poison produced during the decomposition of vegetable matter.

puberty—the period of life in which the organs of reproduction are developed.

pull test—a test to determine the degree of elasticity of the hair.

pulmonary—relating to the lungs.

pumice—a light, rough volcanic glass used in manicuring (available as stone or powder).

pungent—acrid; caustic; stinging.

pupil—a small opening in the iris of the eye through which light enters.

purification—freeing from foreign matter.

pus—a fluid consisting of a liquid containing leucocytes and the debris of dead cells and tissue elements.

pusher—a steel instrument used to loosen the cuticle from the nail.

pustule—an inflamed pimple containing pus.

PVP (polyvinylpyrrolidone)—a protein like compound to repair damaged hair.

pylorus—an opening found between the stomach and the small intestine.

pyloric—relating to the pylorus.

pyogenic—pus forming.

pyramidalis nasi—muscle of the nose.

Q

quadrant—any of the four parts into which something is divided by two real or imaginary lines that intersect each other at right angles.

quadratus labii superioris—a muscle of the upper lip.

qualitative scale—a substance in the quantity necessary for compatibility to other substances; the amount needed to arrive at 100% of a formula.

quarantine—a state of enforced isolation to prevent disease.

quaternary ammonium compounds—organic salts of ammonia which are powerful germicides, sold under trade names such as Barbicide, Nutrisept, etc.

R

radial nerve—a nerve which affects the arm and hand.

radiation—giving off light or heat rays.

radius—the outer and smaller bone of the forearm; an imaginary line from the center of a circle to the outside curve.

raking action—continuous short strokes, with a comb, or brush, on the surface of the hair, used during the combout of a hairstyle.

ramus—a branch of an artery, vein or nerve.

rash—a skin eruption having little or no elevation.

ratting—same as teasing.

reconditioning—the application of a special chemical to the hair in order to improve its condition.

rectum—the terminal portion of the digestive tube.

rectus—the name of small muscles of the eye.

reddish cast—a tinge of red.

reduction—(chemistry) the opposite of oxidation, i.e., the process of adding hydrogen to a substance or chemical process.

refined hair—(wig making) hair that has been treated with acid to make it more pliable for use in wigs and hair pieces.

reflex—an involuntary nerve reaction.

rejuvenate—to make young again.

relapse—slipping back to a former condition.

relaxation—the act of being loose and less tense.

relaxer—a chemical applied to the hair to remove the natural curl.

Rembrandt look—(hair coloring) three color tones in same cast are used to lighten hair for a graduation of color. Also called three-dimensional shading.

remover—(dye stain) a preparation used to remove dye stains from skin; (hair coloring) a dye solvent, a chemical compound used to remove artificial color from the hair; (manicuring) acetone, a chemical compound used to remove nail enamel from nails.

renal—relating to a kidney.

reprocess—to repeat a related series of changes to produce a definite result.

research—investigation of experimentation aimed at the discovery of products, facts or principles.

residue—that which remains after a part is taken.

resilient—elastic.

resistance—the difficulty of chemical solutions in penetrating the hair shaft.

respiration—breathing; inhaling air into the lungs and expelling it.

respiratory system—consists of the nose, pharynx, larynx, trachea, bronchi, and lungs.

rete—interlacing of either blood vessels or nerves.

retention papers—an end paper used in permanent waving and hair setting.

reticular layer—the inner layer of the corium.

retina—the sensitive membrane of the eye which receives the image formed by the lens.

retouch—application of hair tint or hair straightener to new growth of hair.

retrahens aurem—a muscle behind the ear.

reverse curl—a curl which is placed on the head in the opposite direction to which it was formed; also used in some localities to refer to a backward curl.

revert—to return to a former condition (kinky, curly or straight).

rewave—a permanent wave given to hair which still retains some of the former permanent, which is not effective.

rhagades—chaps on the skin.

rhythm—speed and motion of a movement; also the arrangement of a variety of movements.

rickettsia—a type of pathogenic microorganism.

ridge—(fingernails) an elevation in the structure of the nail body; (hairstyling) an elevation or crest of a wave.

ridge curl—a pin curl placed immediately behind or below a ridge to form a wave.

ridge end curl—a ridge following a shaping against which is placed a series of overlapping pin curls.

right angle—an angle whose sides are perpendicular to each other; a 90 degree angle.

ringed hair—a variety of canities in which the hair appears white or colored in rings.

ringlet—similar to a pin curl; a small curl.

ringworm—a disease of the skin which appears in circular lesions and is contagious.

rinse—the act of cleansing hair with water after shampooing, processing, or developing; also the liquid used in treating hair; a temporary color applied in liquid form.

risorius—a muscle at the side of the mouth.

rod—(permanent waving) a cylindrical form of various diameters and lengths, around which the softened hair is wound so it can be reformed in the desired structure; (thermal waving) the round solid prong of a curling iron.

roller—a cylindrical object, around which hair may be wound, used in setting hair.

roller clip—a metal pin about three inches in length used to secure a hair roller.

roller curl—a wet strand of hair wound around a cylindrical object in a croquignole fashion (a variation of a stand-up curl).

roller pin—a plastic pin about three inches in length, used to secure a hair roller.

root—the foundation or beginning of any part.

roots—(hair coloring) the new growth showing the natural color.

rotary—circular motion of the fingers as in massage.

rouge—any of various cosmetics for coloring cheeks or lips including cream, liquid, powder and cake rouge, lipstick, etc.

round curling—a process of rolling the hair tightly and evenly around a heated curling iron, starting at the ends.

ruffing—back combing with a brush; (haircutting) a technique of separating hairs with the fingers before cutting split ends.

S

saliva—the secretion of the salivary glands.

salivary gland—the gland in the mouth secreting spittle.

sallow—having a yellowish color.

salt—a compound formed by the union of a base with an acid; also table salt which is sodium chloride.

sanitary—maintaining cleanliness in relation to health.

sanitation—methods to prevent disease by maintaining sanitary conditions.

sanitize—to make sanitary.

saponify—to make into soap.

saprophyte—a microorganism which grows on dead matter.

scab—a crust formed on the surface of a sore.

scabies—a skin disease caused by an animal parasite.

scale—(hairstyling) to section and subsection hair prior to setting; size of shaping.

scales—small thin plates of horny epidermis, forming the outer surface of hair, skin, etc.

scalp—the skin covering of the cranium.

scalp cream—a special cream designed to help restore some of the natural oils; also called pomade; may include sulfur or other dandruff combatants.

scalp lotion—a solution containing products to prevent dryness, combat dandruff, etc.

scaphoid bone—bone of the tarsus and the carpus.

scar—a mark remaining after a wound has healed.

scarf skin—the outermost protective layer of the skin; also called the cuticle.

scissors—two-bladed instruments used for cutting, typically smaller than shears.

scrum-pox—impetigo contagiosa.

sculpture curl (pin curl)—a strand of hairs organized into a flat ribbon form and wound, with its end on the inside, into a series of continuous untwisted circles within circles and secured in place with a curl clip.

scurf—thin dry scales or scabs on the scalp.

sebaceous—oily; fatty.

sebaceous cyst—a distended oily or fatty sac.

sebaceous glands—oil glands of the skin.

seborrhea—over-action of the sebaceous glands.

seborrhea capitis—seborrhea of the scalp; dandruff; pityriasis.

seborrhea oleosa—excessive oiliness of the skin.

seborrhea sicca—greasy scales or crusts, due to over-action of the sebaceous glands; pityriasis.

sebum—oily secretions of the sebaceous glands.

secretion—a product developed by a gland for a bodily function.

sectioning—dividing the hair into separate parts.

segment—a section or separate portion cut out by a dividing line.

semipermanent hair coloring—hair coloring that lasts through several shampoos but diminishes gradually over a number of weeks.

semiwave—a wave formed at a 45° angle to the part.

senility—state of being old.

sensation—a feeling arising as the result of the stimulation of an afferent nerve.

sensitivity—the state of being easily affected by chemicals or conditions.

sensory nerve—a nerve carrying sensations.

sepsis—the presence of various pus-forming organisms in the blood or tissues.

septum—a dividing wall; a partition.

serratus anterior—a muscle of the chest assisting in breathing and in raising the arm.

set—(hairstyling) to form hair into a pattern of curls or waves to produce a style.

shadow—(hairstyling) the low area of a concave effect in a hairstyle; indentation.

shadow wave—a shaping which resembles the outline of a fingerwave but does not have a definite ridge and formation.

shaft—the long slender part of the hair above the scalp.

shampoo—to wash the scalp and hair with soap and water.

shampoo bleach—a hair lightener without pigment; contains peroxide and shampoo.

shampoo tint—a product that both cleans the hair and imparts color at the same time. Also known as color shampoo.

shaper—a razor-like device used for shaping or cutting the hair.

shaping—(haircutting) shortening and thinning the hair to style or to the contour of the head; (hairstyling) the formation of uniform arcs or curves, providing a base for fingerwaves, pin curls and rollers.

shaping—(hair set) a directional movement which will maintain and hold its original line after combing freely.

shears—an instrument used for cutting cloth and other substances; larger than a scissors.

sheath—a covering surrounding some organ.

sheen—gloss; brightness; shine.

shingling—cutting the hair close to the nape and gradually longer toward the crown.

shortwave—a form of high frequency current used in permanent hair removal; electrolysis.

singeing—process of lightly burning hair ends with a lighted wax taper; treatment for split ends.

single application coloring—a process that lightens and colors hair in one application.

sinus—a cavity or a hollow in bone.

skeletal muscles—muscles connected to the skeleton.

skeleton—the bony framework of the body.

skin—the external covering of the body.

skip wave—a ridge following a shaping, against which is placed a series of overlapping pin curls, then repeat the shaping, ridge and curls placed in the same manner.

skull—the framework of the head.

sleek—to render smooth, soft, and glossy.

slicing—(hairstyling) carefully lifting a section of hair from a shaping, with a comb, in preparation for making a pin curl.

slithering—tapering the hair to graduated lengths with scissors or razor.

smaller occipital—sensory nerve affecting skin behind the ear.

snarls—tangles, as of hair.

snowflaking—(hair coloring) the use of platinum or silver tones on selected strands of hair to highlight darker natural shade.

soap—compound of fatty acid or oil with an alkaline base as contrasted with a synthetic detergent.

soap cap—a combination of prepared tint and shampoo which is applied to the hair like a regular shampoo. Adds color and brightness to faded hair. Used as a final step in hair coloring.

soapless shampoo—a synthetic shampoo made with sulfonated oil, alcohol, mineral oil and water.

sodium—a metallic element of the alkaline group.

sodium bicarbonate—baking soda; an antacid which also relieves burns, bites, etc.

sodium carbonate—washing soda; used to prevent corrosion of metallic instruments when added to boiling water.

sodium hydroxide—a caustic used in some chemical hair relaxers; caustic soda.

soft water—water which readily lathers with soap because the dissolved minerals have been removed.

softening—the application of a chemical to hair to make it more receptive to hair coloring, permanent waving or hair straightening.

solid—any substance which does not flow.

soluble—capable of being dissolved.

solute—the dissolved substance in a solution.

solution—a homogeneous mixture of one or more substances dissolved in another.

solvent—the substance in which the solute is dissolved.

space base—an elongated stem creating a wider area between two rows of pin curls.

spatula—a flexible implement for handling creams.

specialist—one who devotes himself to some special branch of learning, art or practice.

spinal accessory—eleventh cranial nerve.

spinal column—the backbone or vertebral column.

spinal cord—the portion of the central nervous system contained within the spinal or vertebral canal.

spinal nerves—the nerves arising from the spinal cord.

spine—the backbone.

spiral—coil; winding around a center.

spiral rod—a rod with which the hair is wound in a spiral manner for a permanent wave.

spiral winding—winding the hair on a rod from the scalp to the ends.

spirillum—curved bacterium.

spleen—a large vascular ductless gland between the stomach and the diaphragm.

split ends—a condition of splitting of the hair ends giving a damaged and abused feathery appearance. Trichoptilosis.

spongy—porous.

spore—a tiny bacterial body which can withstand unfavorable conditions.

spot bleaching—applying bleach to correct areas insufficiently lightened in order to produce even results.

spot tinting—corrective work in hair coloring; applying tint to areas insufficiently colored in order to produce even results.

spray machine—(facials) used to apply a very fine mist of astringent, which massages the nerve ends as it hits the skin.

squama—an epidermic scale made of thin, flat cells.

stabilized—not readily changeable (i.e., hydrogen peroxide treated to prevent decomposition).

stand-up curls—(cascade) a strand of hair held directly up from the scalp and wound with a large center opening in a croquignole fashion and secured in a standing position.

steam—part of a procedure to open pores during a facial treatment. Vapor; mist.

steamer, facial—an apparatus used for steaming the face.

steamer, scalp—an apparatus used for steaming the scalp. Hair and scalp treatments.

steatoma—a sebaceous cyst; a fatty tumor.

stem direction—the direction in which the stem moves from the base to the first arc.

stem, pin curl—that part of the pin curl between the base and the first arc of the circle.

step-up—to use an accelerator to quicken action.

sterile—free from all living organisms.

sterilization—the process of making sterile; the destruction of germs.

sterilizer—an agent or receptacle for sterilization.

sterilizer, cabinet (dry)—a closed receptacle containing chemical vapors to keep sterilized objects ready for use.

sterilizer, wet—a receptacle containing a disinfectant for the purpose of sterilizing implements by immersing.

sterno-cleido-mastoideus—a muscle of the neck which depresses and rotates the head.

sternomastoid—pertaining to the mastoid process.

stimulant—arouses organic activity.

stimulation—increased functional activity.

stomach—the dilated portion of the alimentary canal, in which the first process of digestion takes place.

straight wave—a wave running parallel to the part.

strand—a group of hairs held parallel or twisted to form a unit.

strand test—a preliminary test on a strand of hairs before or during a treatment to determine the required development time and the ability of the hair to withstand the effects of chemicals.

stratum—layer of tissue.

stratum corneum—horny layer of the skin.

stratum germinativum—the deepest layer of the epidermis resting on the corneum.

stratum granulosum—granular layer of the skin.

stratum lucidum—clear layer of the skin.

stratum mucosum—malpighian layer of the skin.

streak—(hair goods) a short length of hair in an obviously lighter, darker, or contrasting color than the wearer's, attached to a bobby pin or comb for securing in the hair to give the appearance of streaking.

streaking—lightening broad sections of hair attractively placed around the face and head.

streptococcus—pus-forming bacteria; blood poisoning.

stress—pressure; tension.

stretch base—see **space base**.

stretch wig—a wig with a completely elasticized foundation that will expand to fit a wide range of head sizes.

striated—striped; voluntary muscle.

stripping—the removal of color from the hair shaft; bleaching.

stroking—a gliding movement over a surface; effleurage.

structure—construction; manner of building.

sty—inflammation of one of the sebaceous glands of the eyelid.

styptic—an agent causing contraction of tissue; used to stop bleeding.

subcutaneous—under the skin.

subcutis—subcutaneous tissue; under the dermis.

subdermis—subcutaneous tissue of skin.

sublingual—under the tongue.

submental artery—supplies blood to the chin and lower lip.

subsection—making sections within a section; scale.

subsidiary—supplementary.

suction—(facials) a machine which "vacuum cleans" the skin. A small suction cup glides along the skin to remove blackheads and other waste materials from open pores.

sudamen—a disorder of the sweat glands with obstruction of their ducts.

sudor—sweat; perspiration.

sudoriferous glands—sweat glands of the skin.

sulfonated oil—an organic substance prepared with sulfuric acid used as a base in soapless shampoos.

sunburn—excessive exposure to the sun.

sunburst—(hair bleaching) a heavy frosting.

sunshining—(sun streaking) lightening and interlacing sections of hair in more than one shade from the root out.

superior maxillary—the upper jawbone.

supporting curl—a pin curl made in the same direction of the front line curl.

suppuration—the formation of pus.

supraorbital—above the orbit or eye.

supratrochlear nerve—above the trochlea of the superior oblique muscle (between the eyes on both sides of the upper nose).

susceptible—capable of being easily acted on.

suspension—a solution of coarse particles which settle out on standing.

swab—absorbent cotton wrapped about the end of a stick; used primarily for the application of solutions.

swathe—(wig making) a knotted hairpiece usually worn at the nape.

swirl—a hairstyle moving diagonally across the back of the head.

switch—long wefts of hair; tail-like in formation, mounted with a loop at the end; braid.

sycosis—chronic pustular inflammation of the hair follicles.

sycosis vulgaris—chronic pustular inflammation of the hair follicles of the beard.

sympathetic nervous system—controls the involuntary muscles which affect respiration, circulation, and digestion.

symptom—evidence of disease or physical disturbance.

synovia—lubricating fluid secreted by the lining membranes of joints.

synthetic—compounded artificially from other substances by a chemical process.

synthetic hair—any manmade, hair-like fiber, with trade names such as nylon, dynel, kanekalon, modacrylic, myerlon, etc.

system—a group of body organs that together perform one or more vital functions; also, an organized set of principles for learning or applying procedures.

systematic—proceeding according to regular method.

T

tactile corpuscle—nerve endings, affecting touch, found within the skin.

tail comb—a comb, half of which is shaped into a slender, tail-like end.

taper—to diminish gradually toward a point.

tapering—(hair cutting) cutting a head of hair so that individual hairs of varying lengths are uniformly blended and the bulk of the hair is greatly reduced at the hair ends.

tapotement—a massage movement using a short,

quick slapping or tapping movement.

tapping—a massage movement; striking lightly with the partly flexed fingers.

taut—tensely stretched.

teasing—combing small sections of hair from the ends toward the scalp, causing the shorter hair to mat at the scalp, forming a base. Also known as ratting or French lacing.

technique—a method of accomplishing a desired aim.

technical—relating to a practical technique.

temple—the flattened space on the side of the forehead.

temporal bone—the bone at the side and base of the skull.

temporalis—the temporal muscle.

temporary color—any nonpermanent color that may be removed by simple shampooing, such as color rinses, color shampoos, crayons, etc.

tendon—fibrous cord connecting muscle with bone.

tension—stress caused by stretching; firmness in winding.

tepid—neither hot nor cold.

terminal—pertaining to the end or extremity.

test curl—used in permanent waving to determine the correct processing time.

test, hair dye—a test made behind the ear, or in the bend of the arm, for predisposition to the dye used; to determine the reaction of the dye upon the sample strand regarding color, timing, and breakage.

tetanus—continuous contraction of the muscles; lockjaw.

textometer—a device used to measure the elasticity and reaction of the hair to alkali solutions.

texture of hair—the general quality as to coarse, medium, or fine.

thenar—the fleshy prominence of the palm corresponding to the base of the thumb.

theory—a reasoned and probable explanation.

therapeutic lamp—an electrical apparatus producing any of the various rays used for skin and scalp treatments. Heat lamp.

therapy—the science of healing.

thermal—pertaining to heat.

thermal irons—marcel irons; curling irons.

thermometer—any device for measuring temperature.

thermostat—an automatic device for controlling temperature.

thickening agent—a substance which thickens watery liquids.

thin hair—sparse hair growth in number of hairs per square inch.

thinning, hair—decreasing the thickness of the hair by use of razor, scissors (effileing) or thinning scissors.

thinsors—a brand name for a scissors specially designed to remove bulk from hair by blunt cutting while leaving tapered ends.

thio (ammonium thioglycolate)—a short term for the chemical employed in breaking the cross-linkages of the hair in chemical straightening and cold waving.

thorax—the part of the body between the neck and the abdomen; the chest.

thrombocyte—a blood platelet which aids in clotting.

thyroid gland—a large ductless gland in the neck affecting growth and metabolic rate.

tincture—an alcoholic solution of a medicinal substance.

tinea—ringworm.

tinea capitis—ringworm of the scalp.

tinea sycosis—barber's itch.

tinea unguium—ringworm of the nail.

tinge—a slight shade or touch of color.

tint—to give a coloring to; pertaining to hair dyeing; to color the hair by means of a hair dye.

tipping—hair coloring wherein the darkening or lightening is confined to the very ends of small strands of hair.

tissue—an aggregate of cells of a particular kind, together with their intercellular substance, forming one of the structural materials of the body.

tissue, connective—binding and supporting tissue.

tissue, facial—a soft textured paper used for removing creams during the facial procedure.

tone—(anatomy) healthy functioning of the body; (coloring) hue; color; shade.

tone on tone—(hair coloring) hair is divided into two sections that are lightened and toned to be two shades of the same color cast.

toner—pastel or diluted form of any tint color; to be applied to prelightened hair.

topette—wig; wiglet; cascade; fall.

tortoise shelling—(hair coloring) use of varying shades of golden blonde and platinum on dark and medium dark hair for contrast.

touch up—the process of coloring the new growth on tinted or lightened hair; or to straighten the new growth of curly hair.

toupee—a small wig used to cover the top or crown of the head.

toxemia—blood poisoning.

toxic—poisonous.

trachea—windpipe.

trachoma—a contagious disease of the eyelids characterized by small granular elevations.

transformation—(wiggery) artificial band of hair worn over a person's own hair.

transparent—admitting the passage of light.

transverse—(facial) an artery supplying the skin, the parotid gland and the masseter muscle.

trapezium—the first bone of the second row of the carpus.

trapezius—muscle that draws the head backward and sideways.

triangularis—depressor anguli oris; a muscle that pulls down corners of the mouth.

triceps—a muscle having three heads.

trichology—the science of the hair and its diseases.

trichonosus—any disease of the hair.

trichophyton—a fungus parasite responsible for ringworm.

trichophytosis—ringworm of the skin and scalp, due to growth of a fungus parasite.

trichoptilosis—a splitting of the hair ends, giving them a feathery appearance.

trichosis—abnormal growth of hair.

trifacial—the fifth cranial nerve.

trim—cutting the hair slightly without altering the shape of the existing lines.

true skin—the corium.

tubercle—a rounded, solid elevation on the skin or membrane.

tumor—swelling; an abnormal enlargement.

turbinal—a bone in the nose.

turning—(wig making) the process by which hair cuttings or combings are arranged so that the root ends are together.

tweezers—a pair of small forceps to remove hair from skin.

tweezing—removing hair with use of a tweezer.

twice-in-weft—a more widely spaced method of weaving than once-in weaving.

two-dimensional shading—hair is divided into two sections that are lightened and toned to be two shades of the same color cast.

U

ulcer—an open sore not caused by a wound.

ultra violet—invisible rays of the spectrum, beyond the violet rays, used for treatment of skin conditions, artificial sun tan, etc.

unadulterated—pure.

underprocessing—insufficient exposure of the hair to the chemical action of the permanent waving solution, resulting in little or no change in the structure and condition of the hair.

undulation—a wave-like movement or shape.

unguis—the nail of a finger or toe.

unguium, tinea—ringworm of the nails.

unipolar—a treatment in which one electrode of a direct current is applied to the body.

unit—a single thing or value.

United States Pharmacopeia—an official book of drug and medicinal standards.

unsanitary—unclean enough to endanger health; contaminated.

upsweep—a hairstyle combed up from the nape toward the crown.

upwards—towards the top of the head.

uric acid—a crystalline acid contained in the urine.

uridrosis—the presence of urea in sweat.

urine—the fluid secreted by the kidneys.

U.S.P.—see **United States Pharmacopeia.**

V

vaccine—any substance used for preventive inoculation.

vagus—pneumogastric nerve.

valve—a structure which temporarily closes a passage or permits flow in one direction only.

vapor—the gaseous state of a liquid or solid.

variable—changeable; completely alterable.

variation—changes or differences in procedures or styles.

varicose veins—swollen or knotted veins.

variegating—(hair coloring) lightening small strands or sections of hair throughout the head from the root out (frosting).

vascular—pertaining to a vessel for the conveyance of blood.

vaseline—a trade mark for petrolatum (a neutral, odorless, tasteless substance obtained from petroleum and used in ointments and dressings).

vasoconstrictor—a nerve which causes narrowing of blood vessels.

vasodilator—a nerve which causes expansion of the blood vessels.

vegetable tints—hair dyes or hair rinses comprised of Egyptian henna, indigo and other vegetable derivatives.

vein—a canal or tube in the circulatory system carrying blood toward the heart.

vena cava—one of the large veins which carry the blood to the right auricle of the heart.

ventilate—to expose to fresh air for purifying, curing or refreshing.

ventilated—(wig making) describes a method of construction of a handmade wig or hairpiece.

ventricle—a small cavity in the brain or heart.

vermin—parasitic insects (e.g., lice and bedbugs).

verruca—a wart.

vertebra—a bony segment of the spinal column.

vertex—the crown of the head.

vertical—in an upright position, usually described in terms of up and down as opposed to left and right.

vesicle—a small blister or sac.

vessel—tube or canal in which blood is contained or circulated.

vibration—shaking; periodic motion in alternately opposite directions as in a massage movement.

vibrator—an electric massage apparatus causing a shaking sensation on the body, producing stimulation.

vibrissae—stiff hairs in the nostrils.

vibroid—a vibratory movement in massage.

vinegar—a liquid containing acetic acid; used as a rinse to remove soap curds from the hair and to disentangle hair.

violet ray—the pinkish violet discharge from high frequency apparatus used for scalp and facial stimulations.

virgin hair—normal hair which has had no previous chemical treatments.

virulent—poisonous, disease-producing microorganisms.

virus—the causative agent of an infectious disease.

viscid—sticky or adhesive.

viscosity—the degree of density, thickness, stickiness, and adhesiveness of a substance.

vitality—the power of enduring or continuing.

vitamin—organic substances present in a very small quantity in natural foodstuffs, which are essential to normal metabolism.

vitiligo—milky-white spots of the skin.

vogue—fashion; custom; style.

vola—the palm of the hand or the sole of the foot.

volatile—easily evaporating; not permanent.

volume—(chemistry) space occupied, as measured in cubic units; also the strength of solutions like hydrogen peroxide measured in the gas released per volume of solution; (hairstyling) a raised quantity or mass of hair creating a silhouette.

voluntary—under the control of the will.

vomer—the thin bone between the nostrils.

vulgaris, acne—common pimple.

W

warm—(hair coloring) containing red or gold tones.

wart—a circumscribed hypertrophy of the papillae of the corium, covered by thickened epidermis.

water softener—a chemical or a zeolite tank that removes the salts which cause hard water.

wave—the design formed by arranging the hair in a semicircle between two ridges going in opposite directions.

wave bang—a bang which has a wave formation in it.

wave, cold—a method of permanent waving requiring the use of chemicals rather than heat.

wave, croquignole marcel—a wave produced with a thermal iron.

wave, finger—producing a wave pattern in wet hair through the use of fingers, comb and waving lotions.

wave, permanent—a wave produced by breaking down the hair structure by chemicals or heat and reforming into a wave pattern.

wave, pin curl—a method in which the direction of rows of pin curls are alternated in order to form a wave pattern.

waves—hair formations resulting in a side-by-side series of ess (s)-like movements; or semicircles going in opposite directions.

wave, semi—a wave formed at a 45 degree angle to the part.

wave, skip—a pattern formed by a combination of alternating ridges and pin curls.

wave, straight—a hair wave running parallel to the part.

weaving, hair—a process of sewing a base of nylon thread into the remaining natural hair and tying wefted hairs to that base to eliminate the appearance of baldness.

weft—an artificial section of woven hair used for practice work or as a substitute for natural hair.

weft wig—a wig made of hair first stitched into a weft, then sewn to the wig base; a machine made wig.

wen—a sebaceous cyst, usually on the scalp.

wheal—a raised ridge on the skin, caused by a blow or a bite of an insect.

whitehead—milium (a small whitish lump on the skin due to the retention of secretion in an oil gland duct).

white henna—a powdered magnesium carbonate having no bleaching qualities used as a binder in bleaching paste, etc.

whorl—a cowlick; a spiral turn causing a tuft of hair which goes contrary to the usual growth of the hair.

widow's peak—a hairline having a V-shaped point at the middle of the forehead.

wig—an artificial covering for the head consisting of a network of interwoven hair on a netting.

wig bar—a counter where ready-to-wear wigs and hairpieces are tried on and purchased.

wig block—a head-shaped block of styrofoam, plastic, or cork-filled cloth.

wig cleaner—a dry cleaning fluid for cleaning wigs.

wiglet—a hairpiece with a flat base which is used in special areas of the head for hairstyling.

wig net—a narrow-meshed, soft net of silk, cotton, linen, or nylon used as part of the base of a wig or hairpiece.

winding, croquignole—winding the hair under from the hair ends towards the scalp.

winding, spiral—winding the hair from the scalp to the ends in a coil-like fashion.

windpipe—trachea (the breath passage from the larynx to the lungs).

wiry hair—a hair fiber that is strong and resilient; difficult to form into a wave formation; having a smooth, hard, glossy surface.

wool crepe—a substance used in place of end papers to control hair when winding in permanent waving, pin curling, and roller setting.

wrapping—synonymous with winding; more generally identified with permanent waving.

wrinkle—a small ridge or a furrow.

X

xanthoma—a skin disease characterized by the presence of yellow nodules around the eyelids.

Y

yak hair—hair from a long-haired ox of Tibet sometimes used in making wigs and hairpieces.

Z

zeolite—a chemical of natural or synthesized silicates used in water softening.

zinc sulphate—a salt employed as an astringent in lotions and creams.

zinc sulphocarbonate—a fine white powder used as an antiseptic and astringent in deodorant preparations.

zygoma—a bone of the skull which extends along the front or side of the face, below the eye.

zygomaticus—a muscle that draws the upper lip upward and outward.

INDICES

Task index

The Task Index covers every unit of the 25 chapters in this book and provides one or more activities that the student must perform after completing each unit. Organized by chapters and units, the index includes the page number in the text where the behavioral objectives and tasks are discussed in greater detail.